Casio Moonlander

Smoke

An Android Echo Software Application

Personal Chat Messenger

Open Source Technical Website Reference
Documentation 2020-11-15

Volume I: Smoke

[Volume II: SmokeStack]

Impressum

Moonlander, Casio: Smoke
- An Android Echo Software Application:
Personal Chat Messenger /
Open Source Technical Website Reference Documentation 2020-11-15,
Volume I: Smoke,
Norderstedt 2020, ISBN 9783752691993.

[Volume II: SmokeStack – ISBN 9783752692006],

© 2020 Moonlander, Casio

Manufacturing & Publisher:
BoD - Books on Demand, Norderstedt.
Further bibliographic Information under: https://portal.dnb.de

This book is also available as ePDF.

Welcome to Smoke!

Smoke is an open source communications project. The purpose of Smoke is to introduce and investigate the Echo protocol on mobile technologies.

Some of the characteristics of Smoke are summarized below.

- Aliases. Preserve your contacts.
- Almost zero-dependency software.
- Argon2id key-derivation function.
- Automatic, oscillatory public-key exchange protocol, EPKS, via SipHash.
- BSD 3-clause license.
- Decentralized. TCP, and UDP multicast and unicast.
- Does not require Internet connectivity.
- Does not require registration. Telephone numbers are not required.
- Fiasco forward secrecy.
- Introduces Cryptographic Discovery. Cryptographic Discovery is a practical protocol which creates coordinated data paths.
- Juggling Juggernaut Protocol!
- McEliece Fujisaka and Pointcheval.
- Message structures do not explicitly expose contents. Header-less protocols!
- Mobile servers via SmokeStack.
- Optional foreground services.
- Post offices for messages of the past.
- Private servers.
- Public and private public-key servers.
- SSL/TLS through SmokeStack.
- Semi-compatible with Spot-On via Fire.
- Share files with TCP utilities such as Netcat.
- Software congestion control.
- Steam file sharing.

This Open Source Technical Website Reference Documentation on paper addresses to students, teachers, and developers to create a Personal Communication Software based on Java for learning and teaching purposes.

Casio Moonlander, 2020-11-15.

Content

About

Smoke is an Android communications project. The software is composed of a single multitasking application. A companion application, SmokeStack, provides mobile server services.

Application descriptions and the references to the content of this book are available at https://github.com/textbrowser/smoke and https://github.com/textbrowser/smokestack.

https://textbrowser.github.io/smoke/

Activity Authenticate

After launching a prepared Smoke instance, the Authenticate activity is displayed. The original password must be provided. If the correct password is provided, essential containers are populated and the kernel is activated. The previously-accessed activity is also activated.

Smoke may be reset within the Authenticate activity.

Activity Chat

The Chat activity is one of three messaging activities. From this activity, one may message one or more defined participants. The Send button is enabled if at least one participant is selected and a writable neighbor (not necessarily network-ready) is available.

Before a messaging session may begin between two participants, the participants must exchange private key material. Exchanging private key material may be achieved via the Call and Custom Session mechanisms.

A context menu may be activated by pressing and holding on the right-hand Participants widget. Context-menu items are described below.

Custom Session

> Private key material may be generated per the selected participant. The generated material is not transferred over the network. Please note the following conversion of the input string: if the input string's length is less than or equal to 64, the input string is converted to Base64(SHA512(string)).

New Window

> Display a new Member Chat activity with the selected participant.

Optional Signatures

> Messaging and status messages are digitally signed. Signatures may be disabled per participant. Please note that if one party requires digital signatures and digital signatures are not provided by the other party, messages will be ignored by the receiving party. Juggernaut messages and read-acknowledgments are always signed.

Purge Session

> Discard the session's private key material for the specified participant.

Refresh Participants Table

> Refresh the Participants widget.

Retrieve Messages

> Retrieve messages from SmokeStack instances. An Ozone and an active network must be present for this option to be enabled.

Show Details

Disable or enable various Participants details.

Show Icons

Disable or enable Participants status icons.

Activity Fire

The Fire activity is one of three messaging activities. From this activity, one may communicate with one or more groups of anonymous participants. Fire is compatible with Spot-On's Buzz. 256-bit AES-CBC along with SHA-384 HMAC provide encryption and authentication.

The Send button is enabled if at least one network-ready neighbor is available.

Activity Member Chat

The Member Chat activity is one of three messaging activities. From this activity, one may message one participant.

Before a messaging session may begin between two participants, the parties must exchange private key material. Exchanging private key material may be achieved via the Call and Custom Session mechanisms. The Send button is enabled if a session is established and if a writable neighbor (not necessarily network-ready) is available.

Context menus may be activated by pressing and holding various widgets. Context-menu items are described below.

Call via McEliece

Exchange private key material via an ephemeral McEliece ($m = 11$, $t = 50$) public-key pair.

Call via RSA

Exchange private key material via an ephemeral RSA (2048-bit) public-key pair.

Copy Text

Place the selected message's text into the clipboard buffer.

Custom Session

Private key material may be generated. The generated material is not transferred over the network.

Delete All Messages

If confirmed, all messages associated with the specified participant are deleted.

Delete Message

If confirmed, the selected message is deleted.

JuggerKnot Credentials

Display an input dialog. If the dialog is confirmed, the Juggernaut Protocol is initiated with the specified participant. If the protocol completes successfully, authentication and encryption credentials are created.

Juggernaut

Display an input dialog. If the dialog is confirmed, the Juggernaut Protocol is initiated with the specified participant.

Optional Signatures

Messaging and status messages are digitally signed. Signatures may be disabled per participant. Please note that if one party requires digital signatures and digital signatures are not provided by the other party, messages will be ignored by the receiving party. Juggernaut messages and read-acknowledgments are always signed.

Retrieve Messages

Retrieve messages from SmokeStack instances. An Ozone and an active network must be present for this option to be enabled.

Save Attachment

If the selected message contains an image, this option is enabled. Once activated, the attached bitmap is saved.

Activity Settings

The Settings activity contains various configuration items. Smoke may also be reset from this activity. This page will describe miscellaneous portions.

About

Describes software information, including the Android version of the device. Log clearing may also be performed in this section. The Foreground Service option disables or enables a Smoke foreground service. The Prefer Active CPU option, if enabled, ensures that the CPU remains active if the screen is turned off.

Ozone

One Ozone address may be defined in this section. Please refer to the Ozone page for more details.

Participants

A list of participants. A context menu is available.

Password

Generate new local authentication and encryption keys. If confirmed, all existing data will be purged. A new public and private key pair may also be generated.

Public Data

Contains the Smoke Alias and Smoke Chat ID. A Smoke Alias is synonymous to an e-mail address. The Smoke Alias is optional. If provided, it must contain at least eight characters. Preferably, it should be a unique value. A Smoke Identity is synonymous to a telephone number. Basic public-key data are also displayed in this section.

Share Smoke ID

Share the Smoke ID with a SmokeStack instance via the defined Ozone. Please note that the Smoke Alias, if one is defined, is transformed into a Smoke ID.

Activity Smokescreen

Lock or unlock the Smoke application.

Activity Steam

The Steam activity allows for the transferring of files to Steam participants and/or anonymous destinations. Received files are stored in the Downloads folder.

Please note that Simple Steams (files transferred to anonymous destinations) will be streamed sequentially in the order in which they were registered for transfer.

Android

Smoke has been successfully tested on Android versions 7.x, 8.x, and 9.x. Versions older than 7.x are not supported.

Congestion Control

Smoke implements a software-based congestion control mechanism. The SipHash algorithm is used for computing digests. Computed digests are stored in an SQLite database table.

Congestion-control items are inspected every 5 seconds. Items older than 60 seconds are discarded.

Corrupted Database Values

Encrypted database values pose an interesting design problem. How should an application depict a faulty database value to the user if the application is unable to properly decipher an encrypted value? Some software packages ignore the potential problem altogether. Others delete or hide the corrupted entries; logging the failures in squandered logs. Smoke offers an exceptionally-transparent solution. Damaged database entries are depicted in various widgets. These depictions offer insight into potential system failures.

Custom Session Credentials

Credentials are generated as follows (stretch the first key stream):

```
keystream1 := pbkdf2(sha512(string), // Salt
                     string,
                     4096,          // Iteration Count
                     160)           // Bits (20 Bytes)
keystream2 := pbkdf2(sha512(string), // Salt
                     base64(keystream1),
                     1,             // Iteration Count
                     768)           // Bits (96 Bytes)
```

Database Containers

Most of the database fields contain authentically-encrypted values. Some fields contain keyed digests, including keyed digests of binary (false / true) values. Values are stored as $E(Data, K_e) \parallel HMAC(E(Data, K_e), K_a)$ and $HMAC(Data, K_a)$. 256-bit AES-CBC is used for encrypting data. SHA-512 HMAC is used for data authentication.

Developers

Android Studio is required for development. Please download the application from https://developer.android.com/studio/index.html. Building Smoke may be performed via Studio or a terminal. Please refer to the included Makefile and Makefile.linux files for guidance.

Discovery via Cryptography

Cryptographic Discovery is a novel mechanism which allows servers to lighten the computational and data responsibilities of mobile devices.

Shortly after a Smoke instance connects to a SmokeStack service, the Smoke instance shares some non-private material. The material allows a SmokeStack server to transfer messages to their correct destinations.

To mitigate replay attacks, Smoke instances offer SmokeStack instances random identity streams during message-retrieval requests. The identity streams self-expire.

Exchanging Private Credentials

The Calling feature allows two parties to exchange private key material. The process of exchanging private credentials is as follows:

1. A participant issues a Call via a selected participant. A new ephemeral McEliece or RSA public-key pair is generated. A signature binding the two participants is computed. The bundle is then transferred to the recipient.

2. A participant receives the bundle, verifies the included signature, and generates private authentication and encryption keys. The private key material is bundled via the included public McEliece or RSA key. The participant transfers the signed private key material bundle to the initial participant.

3. The initiating participant receives the private key material, verifies the included signature, and unpacks the private key material via the ephemeral private key. The two participants are now paired.

Exporting / Importing Participant Personalities

Smoke provides an elegant, yet tedious, process for exporting and importing participant credentials. Available in the Settings activity, participant credentials may be shared with SmokeStack instances. Simply select individual participants and share the identifiers followed by the public-key personalities. The important process is similarly simple. After participant identifiers have been recorded, request public-key personalities via selected identifiers.

Fiasco Keys

Authentication and encryption key data which are established via the so-called calling mechanism are recorded within the participants_keys database table. Whenever a message from a SmokeStack instance is received, the message's digest is verified using each of the recorded authentication keys. Smoke iterates through the set of Fiasco authentication keys until a correct authentication key is discovered or the search is exhausted. If an authentication key is recovered, the message is deciphered and delivered locally. Newer authentication keys are tested first.

A key pair has a lifetime of 864,000 seconds.

Fire

Fire introduces communication channels between Smoke and Spot-On. Key generation is described below.

```
authentication_key = pbkdf2(sha512(Digest || "sha384"), // Salt
```

```
                    Digest,
                    10000,
                    896)                              // Bits (112 Bytes)
authentication_key, destination_key := authentication_key[0 … 48],
authentication_key[48 … ]
encryption_key := pbkdf2(Salt,
                    Channel || "aes256" || "sha384",
                    10000,          // Iteration Count
                    2304)           // Bits (288 Bytes)
encryption_key := encryption_key[0 … 31]
```

Forward Secrecy and SmokeStack

Smoke includes a mechanism for establishing session-based authentication and encryption keys. The key material is exchanged via ephemeral and permanent public keys. Forward secrecy is constituted by the use of ephemeral public keys.

The Forward Fiasco release provides a mechanism for storing secret key pairs for some period of time. After a message-retrieval request has been initiated, a Smoke instance will attempt to uncover the received content using previously-established secret keys.

Inflate

Smoke expands text-messaging data to 8192 bytes. If the provided data exceeds 8192 bytes, Smoke expands the provided data by 1024 + mod(data length, 2) bytes. Inflation does not apply to Fire as Fire must remain compatible with Spot-On.

Juggernaut Protocol

Smoke implements the Password Authenticated Key Exchange by Juggling protocol. The data are exchanged within a messaging session. Please note the following conversion of the input string: if the input string's length is less than or equal to 64, the input string is converted to Base64(SHA512(string)). JuggerKnot credentials are generated as follows (stretch the first key stream):

```
keystream1 := pbkdf2(sha512(key material), // Salt
                base64(key material),
                4096,          // Iteration Count
                160)           // Bits (20 Bytes)
keystream2 := pbkdf2(sha512(key material), // Salt
                base64(keystream1),
                1,             // Iteration Count
                768)           // Bits (96 Bytes)
```

Please read https://en.wikipedia.org/wiki/Password_Authenticated_Key_Exchange_by_Juggling for more information.

Local Broadcast Manager

Communications between the Kernel and the user interface utilize a Local Broadcast Manager instance.

McEliece CCA2

Smoke supports McEliece-Fujisaki and McEliece-Pointcheval via BouncyCastle. Parameters are SHA-256, m = 11, m = 12 (Fujisaki only), t = 50, t = 68 (Fujisaki only). Some discussions:

- Authentication process may require several minutes to complete.

- Communications between McEliece and RSA are fully functional.

- Degraded performance is expected during key sharing.

- During the key-sharing process, McEliece signatures are not provided and therefore are not verified.

- Initialization processes may require several minutes to complete.

Message Structures

This section will detail the various message structures.

```
AUTHENTICATE
[PK Signature] (1)
{
      Random Bytes (1)                                          Variable
}


CALL-HALF-AND-HALF-A
[PK] (1)
{
      AES-256 Key (1)
      SHA-512 Key (2)
}


[AES-256] (2)
{
      0x00 (1)                                                  1 Byte
      A Timestamp (2)                                           8 Bytes (Base-64)
      \n
      Ephemeral Public Key (3)                                 Variable (Base-64)
      \n
      Ephemeral Public Key Type (4)                            1 Byte (Base-64)
      \n
      Sender's Identity (5)                                    8 Bytes (Base-64)
      \n
      Sender's Public Encryption Key SHA-512 Digest (6)    64 Bytes (Base-64)
      \n
      [PK Signature] (7)                                       Variable (Base-64)
      {
            [PK] (1 ... 2) || [AES-256] (1 ... 6) ||
            Recipient's Public Encryption Key SHA-512 Digest (1)
      }
}


[SHA-512 HMAC] (3)                                           64 Bytes
{
      [PK] || [AES-256] (1)
}


/*
** The destination is created via the recipient's Smoke Identity.
*/

[Destination SHA-512 HMAC] (4)                              64 Bytes
{
      [PK] || [AES-256] || [SHA-512] (1)
}
```

CALL-HALF-AND-HALF-B

```
[PK] (1)
{
      AES-256 Key (1)
      SHA-512 Key (2)
}

[AES-256] (2)
{
      0x01 (1)                                          1 Byte
      A Timestamp (2)                                   8 Bytes (Base-64)
      \n
      Ephemeral Public Key (3)                          Variable (Base-64)
      {
            AES-256 Key (1)
            SHA-512 Key (2)
      }
      \n
      Ephemeral Public Key Type (Ignored) (4)           1 Byte (Base-64)
      \n
      Sender's Identity (5)                             8 Bytes (Base-64)
      \n
      Sender's Public Encryption Key SHA-512 Digest (6)   64 Bytes (Base-64)
      \n
      [PK Signature] (7)                                Variable (Base-64)
      {
            [PK] (1 ... 2) || [AES-256] (1 ... 6) ||
            Recipient's Public Encryption Key SHA-512 Digest (1)
      }
}

[SHA-512 HMAC] (3)                                      64 Bytes
{
      [PK] || [AES-256] (1)
}

/*
** The destination is created via the recipient's Smoke Identity.
*/

[Destination SHA-512 HMAC] (4)                          64 Bytes
{
      [PK] || [AES-256] || [SHA-512] (1)
}
```

CHAT

```
[PK] (1)
{
      Sender's Public Encryption Key SHA-512 Digest (1)   64 Bytes
}

[AES-256] (2)
{
      0x00 (1)                                          1 Byte
      A Timestamp (2)                                   8 Bytes (Base-64)
      \n
      Message (3)                                       Variable (Base-64)
      \n
      Sequence (4)                                      8 Bytes (Base-64)
      \n
      Attachment (5)                                    Variable (Base-64)
      \n
      Message Identity (6)                              64 Bytes (Base-64)
      \n
      [PK Signature] (7)                                Variable (Base-64)
      {
```

```
                  [PK] (1) || [AES-256] (1 ... 6) ||
                  Recipient's Public Encryption Key SHA-512 Digest (1)
        }
}


[SHA-512 HMAC] (3)                                        64 Bytes
{
     [PK] || [AES-256] (1)
}


/*
** The destination is created via the recipient's Smoke Identity.
*/

[Destination SHA-512 HMAC] (4)                            64 Bytes
{
     [PK] || [AES-256] || [SHA-512 HMAC] (1)
}
```

CHAT-RETRIEVAL (Via Ozone)

```
[AES-256] (1)
{
     0x00 (1)                                         1 Byte
     A Timestamp (2)                                  8 Bytes
     An Identity (3)                                  64 Bytes
     Sender's Public Encryption Key SHA-512 Digest (4)   64 Bytes
     [PK Signature] (5)                               Variable
     {
          [AES-256] (1 ... 4) (1)
     }
}


[SHA-512 HMAC] (2)                                        64 Bytes
{
     [AES-256] (1)
}
```

CHAT-STATUS

```
[PK] (1)
{
     Sender's Public Encryption Key SHA-512 Digest (1)    64 Bytes
}


[AES-256] (2)
{
     0x01 (1)                                         1 Byte
     A Timestamp (2)                                  8 Bytes
     Status (3)                                       1 Byte (Ignored)
     [PK Signature] (4)                               Variable
     {
          [PK] (1) || [AES-256] (1 ... 3) ||
          Recipient's Public Encryption Key SHA-512 Digest (1)
     }
}


[SHA-512 HMAC] (3)                                        64 Bytes
{
     [PK] || [AES-256] (1)
}


/*
** The destination is created via the recipient's Smoke Identity.
*/

[Destination SHA-512 HMAC] (4)                            64 Bytes
```

```
{
    [PK] || [AES-256] || [SHA-512 HMAC] (1)
}
```

EPKS

```
[AES-256] (1)
{
    A Timestamp (1)                                  8 Bytes (Base-64)
    \n
    Key Type (2)                                     1 Byte (Base-64)
    \n
    Sender's Smoke Identity (3)                      Variable (Base-64)
    \n
    Public Key (4)                                   Variable (Base-64)
    \n
    Public Key Signature ((3) || (4) || (6)) (5)     Variable (Base-64)
    \n
    Signature Public Key (6)                         Variable (Base-64)
    \n
    Signature Public Key Signature ((3) || (4) || (6)) (7)
                                                     Variable (Base-64)
}

[SHA-512 HMAC] (2)                                   64 Bytes
{
    [AES-256] (1)
}

/*
** The destination is created via the recipient's Smoke Identity.
*/

[Destination SHA-512 HMAC] (3)                       64 Bytes
{
    [AES-256] || [SHA-512 HMAC] (1)
}
```

FIRE-CHAT

```
[AES-256] (1)
{
    0040b (1)                                        Base-64
    \n
    Name (2)                                         Base-64
    \n
    ID (3)                                           Base-64
    \n
    Message (4)                                      Base-64
    \n
    UTC Date (5)                                     Base-64
}

[SHA-384 HMAC] (2)                                   Base-64
{
    [AES-256] (1)
}

[Destination SHA-512 HMAC] (3)                       Base-64
{
    [AES-256] || [SHA-384 HMAC] (1)
}
```

FIRE-STATUS

```
[AES-256] (1)
{
    0040a (1)                                        Base-64
```

        \n
        Name (2)   Base-64
        \n
        ID (3)   Base-64
        \n
        UTC Date (4)   Base-64
}

[SHA-384 HMAC] (2)   Base-64
{
        [AES-256] (1)
}

[Destination SHA-512 HMAC] (3)   Base-64
{
        [AES-256] || [SHA-384 HMAC] (1)
}

JUGGERNAUT

[PK] (1)
{
        Sender's Public Encryption Key SHA-512 Digest (1)   64 Bytes
}

[AES-256] (2)
{
        0x03 (1)   1 Byte
        A Timestamp (2)   8 Bytes (Base-64)
        \n
        Payload (3)   Variable (Base-64)
        \n
        [PK Signature] (4)   Variable (Base-64)
        {
                [PK] (1) || [AES-256] (1 ... 3) ||
                Recipient's Public Encryption Key SHA-512 Digest (1)
        }
}

[SHA-512 HMAC] (3)   64 Bytes
{
        [PK] || [AES-256] (1)
}

/*
** The destination is created via the recipient's Smoke Identity.
*/

[Destination SHA-512 HMAC] (4)   64 Bytes
{
        [PK] || [AES-256] || [SHA-512 HMAC] (1)
}

MESSAGE-READ

[PK] (1)
{
        Sender's Public Encryption Key SHA-512 Digest (1)   64 Bytes
}

[AES-256] (2)
{
        0x02 (1)   1 Byte
        Message Identity (2)   64 Bytes
        [PK Signature] (3)   Variable
        {
                [PK] (1) || [AES-256] (1 ... 2) ||

```
                Recipient's Public Encryption Key SHA-512 Digest (1)
        }
}


[SHA-512 HMAC] (3)                                           64 Bytes
{
        [PK] || [AES-256] (1)
}


/*
** The destination is created via the recipient's Smoke Identity.
*/

[Destination SHA-512 HMAC] (4)                               64 Bytes
{
        [PK] || [AES-256] || [SHA-512] (1)
}
```

MESSAGE-READ (Via Ozone)

```
[AES-256] (1)
{
        0x04 (1)                                             1 Byte
        A Timestamp (2)                                      8 Bytes
        Message Identity SHA-512 Digest (3)                  64 Bytes
        Sender's Public Encryption Key SHA-512 Digest (4)    64 Bytes
        [PK Signature] (5)                                   Variable
        {
                [AES-256] (1 ... 4) (1)
        }
}


[SHA-512 HMAC] (2)                                           64 Bytes
{
        [AES-256] (1)
}
```

PKP-REQUEST (Via Ozone)

```
[AES-256] (1)
{
        0x01 (1)                                             1 Byte
        A Timestamp (2)                                      8 Bytes
        Destination Smoke Identity (3)                       Variable
        Requested Smoke Identity (4)                         Variable
}


[SHA-512 HMAC] (2)                                           64 Bytes
{
        [AES-256] (1)
}
```

SHARE-SMOKE-ID (Via Ozone)

```
[AES-256] (1)
{
        0x02 (1)                                             1 Byte
        A Timestamp (2)                                      8 Bytes
        Smoke Identity (3)                                   Variable
        Temporary Identity (4)                               8 Bytes
}


[SHA-512 HMAC] (2)                                           64 Bytes
{
        [AES-256] (1)
}
```

SHARE-SMOKE-ID-CONFIRMATION (Via Ozone)

```
[AES-256] (1)
{
    0x03 (1)                                        1 Byte
    A Timestamp (2)                                 8 Bytes
    Smoke Identity (3)                              Variable
    Temporary Identity (4)                          8 Bytes
}

[SHA-512 HMAC] (2)                                  64 Bytes
{
    [AES-256] (1)
}


/*
** The destination is created via the recipient's Smoke Identity.
*/

[Destination SHA-512 HMAC] (3)                      64 Bytes
{
    [AES-256] || [SHA-512] (1)
}
```

STEAM-KEY-EXCHANGE-A

```
[PK] (1)
{
    AES-256 Key (1)
    SHA-512 Key (2)
}

[AES-256] (2)
{
    0x04 (1)                                        1 Byte
    A Timestamp (2)                                 8 Bytes (Base-64)
    \n
    Ephemeral Public Key (3)                        Variable (Base-64)
    \n
    Ephemeral Public Key Type (4)                   1 Byte (Base-64)
    \n
    File Digest (5)                                 32 Bytes (Base-64)
    \n
    File Identity (6)                               48 Bytes (Base-64)
    \n
    File Name (7)                                   Variable (Base-64)
    \n
    File Size (8)                                   8 Bytes (Base-64)
    \n
    Sender's Public Encryption Key SHA-512 Digest (9)   64 Bytes (Base-64)
    \n
    [PK Signature] (10)                             Variable (Base-64)
    {
        [PK] (1 ... 2) || [AES-256] (1 ... 9) ||
        Recipient's Public Encryption Key SHA-512 Digest (1)
    }
}

[SHA-512 HMAC] (3)                                  64 Bytes
{
    [PK] || [AES-256] (1)
}


/*
** The destination is created via the recipient's Smoke Identity.
*/

[Destination SHA-512 HMAC] (4)                      64 Bytes
{
```

```
        [PK] || [AES-256] || [SHA-512] (1)
}


STEAM-KEY-EXCHANGE-B
[PK] (1)
{
      AES-256 Key (1)
      SHA-512 Key (2)
}


[AES-256] (2)
{
      0x05 (1)                                          1 Byte
      A Timestamp (2)                                   8 Bytes (Base-64)
      \n
      Ephemeral Public Key (3)                          Variable (Base-64)
      {
           AES-256 Key (1)
           SHA-512 Key (2)
      }
      \n
      Ephemeral Public Key Type (4)                     1 Byte (Base-64)
      \n
      File Digest (5)                                   32 Bytes (Base-64)
      \n
      File Identity (6)                                 48 Bytes (Base-64)
      \n
      File Name (Empty) (7)                             Variable (Base-64)
      \n
      File Size (8)                                     8 Bytes (Base-64)
      \n
      Sender's Public Encryption Key SHA-512 Digest (9)   64 Bytes (Base-64)
      \n
      [PK Signature] (10)                               Variable (Base-64)
      {
           [PK] (1 ... 2) || [AES-256] (1 ... 9) ||
           Recipient's Public Encryption Key SHA-512 Digest (1)
      }
}


[SHA-512 HMAC] (3)                                      64 Bytes
{
      [PK] || [AES-256] (1)
}


/*
** The destination is created via the recipient's Smoke Identity.
*/

[Destination SHA-512 HMAC] (4)                          64 Bytes
{
      [PK] || [AES-256] || [SHA-512] (1)
}


STEAM-SHARE-A
[PK] (1)
{
      File Identity (1)                                 48 Bytes
}


[AES-256] (2)
{
      0x06 (1)                                          1 Byte
      A Timestamp (2)                                   8 Bytes
      File Offset (3)                                   8 Bytes
```

```
        File Packet (4)                                              Variable
}

[SHA-512 HMAC] (3)                                                   64 Bytes
{
        [PK] || [AES-256] (1)
}


/*
** The destination is created via the recipient's Smoke Identity.
*/

[Destination SHA-512 HMAC] (4)                                       64 Bytes
{
        [PK] || [AES-256] || [SHA-512] (1)
}
```

STEAM-SHARE-B

```
[PK] (1)
{
        File Identity (1)                                            48 Bytes
}

[AES-256] (2)
{
        0x07 (1)                                                     1 Byte
        A Timestamp (2)                                              8 Bytes
        File Offset (3)                                              8 Bytes
}

[SHA-512 HMAC] (3)                                                   64 Bytes
{
        [PK] || [AES-256] (1)
}

/*
** The destination is created via the recipient's Smoke Identity.
*/

[Destination SHA-512 HMAC] (4)                                       64 Bytes
{
        [PK] || [AES-256] || [SHA-512] (1)
}
```

Neighbors

Neighbors may be defined via the Settings activity. This page will describe the various nuances of network peers.

Smoke offers infinitely-many IPv4 and IPv6 TCP and UDP client definitions. Each network peer includes dedicated and independent data-parsing, socket-reading, and socket-writing tasks. TCP neighbors support HTTP and SOCKS proxies. Please note that host translations are not performed via assigned proxies.

Initialize Ozone

If enabled, the Ozone credentials will be generated from the specified neighbor values. For example, let's suppose that a SmokeStack is attached to the service bee.service.org:4710. When preparing the neighbor information in Smoke using the aforementioned SmokeStack destination, the Ozone will be initialized to bee.service.org:4710:TCP. In SmokeStack, the Ozone bee.service.org:4710:TCP should also be defined. When completed, the Smoke and SmokeStack instances are artificially paired.

Non-TLS

Allows the neighbor to observe traditional socket operations.

Passthrough

Passthrough neighbors are special full-duplex connections which Smoke utilizes for distributing data to non-Smoke destinations. Data which is received on passthrough connections is echoed directly to other non-passthrough neighbors if echoing is enabled.

A menu accompanies each defined neighbor.

Connect

> Instruct Smoke to place the specified neighbor in a connect status. Connection attempts are performed every 2.5 seconds. A TCP socket is required to connect within 10 seconds. After a connection is established, the SSL/TLS handshake must complete within 10 seconds.

Delete

> Display a confirmation prompt. If confirmed, the specified neighbor is scheduled for deletion.

Disconnect

> Instruct Smoke to place the specified neighbor in a disconnected status.

Purge Queue

> Purge the outbound queue of the specified neighbor.

Reset SSL/TLS Credentials

> Reset the locally-stored SSL/TLS credentials of a TCP neighbor.

A connected neighbor attempts to read 1 MiB of data from its socket every 100 milliseconds. The read request blocks indefinitely. Data are appended to an internal buffer. The internal buffer may accumulate at most 8 MiB of data, with the potential of overflow. Parsing of data occurs every 100 milliseconds. Because the parsing and read tasks are independent, it's possible that the internal buffer may temporarily overflow by $1024^2 - 1$ bytes.

Each neighbor object includes two internal queues, Echo and real-time queues. Echo queues allow Smoke to echo internal data from local neighbor to local neighbor. This mechanism must be enabled via the Echo option. Each Echo queue may contain at most 256 messages. Please note that the Echo mechanism may burden a device. A neighbor will echo data if it discovers that the data are not intended for it. Calling, Chat statuses, Fire statuses, and SmokeStack message-retrieval requests utilize real-time queues. Real-time queues are not limited.

Various per-neighbor statistics are included in the Settings activity. Also included are per-neighbor descriptive errors.

New Installation

After launching a new installation of Smoke, some initial settings are required.

Encryption

> Public-key algorithm. McEliece-Fujisaki, McEliece-Pointcheval, and 3072-bit RSA are supported.

Iteration Count

> Local authentication and encryption keys are generated via Argon2id or PBKDF2. The functions require an iteration count. If the selected value exceeds 10 for Argon2id or 7500 for PBKDF2, a confirmation prompt is displayed.

Password

> At least one character is required.

Signature

>Public-key digital signatures. 384-bit ECDSA and 3072-bit RSA are supported.

Outbound Queues

Smoke offers near-real-time communications. As network services may be unreliable, certain outbound messages are enqueued in an SQLite database table. Each network peer is assigned a separate queue. Messages are dequeued in a timely manner and placed onto the network. Calling messages, retrieval of offline messages, and status messages are considered disposable and are therefore written to network sockets regardless of network availability.

Please note that peers which are in disconnected status-control states are ignored during the enqueue processes.

Ozone Address

An Ozone address may be assigned via the Settings activity. An Ozone address is a pseudo-private string which identifies a virtual entity. Smoke and SmokeStack utilize Ozones as a means of retrieving and storing offline messages and public-key pairs. Smoke supports one Ozone while SmokeStack supports infinitely many. Ozone addresses must be exchanged separately. It is possible for multiple Smoke parties to house distinct Ozones if common SmokeStack instances are aware of the distinct Ozone addresses.

If an Ozone address is defined and the network is available, Smoke will request external messages once per minute.

Please note that public Ozone addresses will introduce denial of service vulnerabilities.

Participants

Smoke Identities may be defined within the Participants section of the Settings activity. After defining a participant, local public-key pairs may be shared manually. An automatic process distributes key pairs to participants which have not been paired. A context menu may be activated by pressing and holding on the Participants widget. The contents of the context menu are described below.

Delete (Smoke Identity)

>Delete the selected participant. A confirmation dialog is displayed.

Delete Fiasco Keys (Smoke Identity)

>Delete all of the recorded Fiasco keys. The current session keys of the selected participant are not deleted. A confirmation dialog is displayed.

Delete Public Keys (Smoke Identity)

>Delete the Fiasco and public keys of the specified participant. A confirmation dialog is displayed.

New Name (Smoke Identity)

>Assign a new name to the selected participant.

Request Keys via Ozone (Smoke Identity)

>Submit a public-key request to SmokeStack instances via the selected Smoke Identity. An Ozone address must be defined for this option to be enabled.

Share Keys Of (Smoke Identity)

The selected participant's public-key pair is distributed using the specified Smoke Identity. If a public-key pair does not exist for the specified participant, the option is disabled.

Share Smoke ID Of (Smoke Identity)

The selected participant's Smoke Identity is distributed using the defined Ozone address. An Ozone address must be defined for this option to be enabled.

View Details (Smoke Identity)

View details of the selected participant.

Performance Considerations

Smoke is a multi-tasking process and several of its internal operations are performed in separate tasks, thus allowing the main thread to remain as responsive as possible.

- A single Steam writer records packets to respective files. The writer contains a separate task for storing status information.
- A special database cursor is maintained for rapid access to data for the Member Chat activity. The cursor is synchronized in various logical regions.
- Automatic requesting of SmokeStack messages is performed in a separate task.
- Neighbor data are written in a separate task.
- Neighbor objects are prepared in a separate task.
- Neighbor statistics and statuses are prepared in a separate task.
- Network data are read in a separate task. Accumulated data are also parsed in a separate task.
- Network status information is gathered in a separate task and reported to the main thread.
- Outbound messages (Chat, Fire, Juggernaut, Message Retrieval Request, Share Smoke Identity) are prepared in a separate task.
- Participant calling keys are generated in a separate task.
- Participant elements for various interface widgets are gathered in a separate task.
- Public-key publications are performed in a separate task.
- Purging of expired Juggernaut credentials, congestion control data, and participant key streams is performed in a separate task.
- Purging of expired temporary identifiers is performed in a separate task.
- Purging of malformed outbound data and participants is performed in a separate task.
- Purging of neighbor queues is performed in a separate task.
- Status message broadcasting is performed in a separate task.
- Steam files are distributed on separate tasks. A separate task prepares Steam tasks.
- Steam files are read in separate tasks.

Private Public-Key Server

In addition to housing messages, SmokeStack also serves as a private public-key server. A SmokeStack administrator is responsible for coordinating the storage of public-key pairs of participants. Participants may request public-key pairs of specific participants via Ozone addresses.

Private Servers

SmokeStack supports the concept of private servers for TCP clients. A private server will disregard non-authentication data until a remote peer has been authenticated. The authentication process is as follows:

1. A private server generates a 64-byte stream of random data and concatenates the data with the current system time.

2. The server submits the SHA-512 hash of the information generated in the previous step to the remote peer after the SSL/TLS handshake has been completed. The server will repeatedly submit unique information every 10 seconds until the peer has authenticated itself.

3. The remote peer retrieves a stream of 64 random bytes as well as its signature key digest. It digitally signs the 64 random bytes, the signature key digest, and the original stream of random data and submits the 64 random bytes, the signature key digest, and the digital signature to the remote server. Please note that SmokeStack servers are conceptually indistinguishable from one another. Therefore, remote peers do not provide SmokeStack identifiers during this step.

4. The server reviews the two random-byte streams for uniqueness. If the two byte streams are dissimilar, it validates the digital signature. If the digital signature is valid and the two random-byte streams are dissimilar, the remote peer is authenticated.

Please define private servers after the desired participants have been completely defined in SmokeStack. This is required because SmokeStack instances must be in possession of public-key pairs.

Please note that multiple devices may contain identical Smoke instances. Thus, several identical Smoke instances may authenticate themselves with a given SmokeStack instance.

Smoke Aliases

A Smoke Alias is a unique stream of characters. The minimum length of a Smoke Alias is eight. Similar to e-mail addresses and telephone numbers, Smoke Aliases allow simple pairing of participants. Internally, a Smoke Alias is transformed into a Smoke Identity via the SipHash algorithm. Let's consider a simple pairing scenario:

1. Participant vanya@nasa.gov assigns the Smoke Alias in the Public Data section of the Settings activity. Once assigned, the participant notifies other participants via e-mail or another form of communication.
2. Notified participants define vanya@nasa.gov within the Participants section of the Settings activity. The Smoke Alias option must be enabled.
3. Participants notify vanya@nasa.gov of their aliases.
4. Within new instances, the pairing process is automatically initiated once the participants are online. Pairing may also be performed via the Share Keys mechanism.

Please note that a Smoke instance must synchronize itself with a remote server after a new Smoke Alias is assigned within Public Data. Synchronization generally completes in approximately 15 seconds.

A Smoke identity is generated as follows:

```
id := siphash(alias,
            pbkdf2(sha512(alias), // Salt
                   alias,
                   4096, // Iteration Count
                   128)) // Bits (16 Bytes)
```

Smoke Identities

Exchanging public-key pairs is often an involved process. Smoke implements the pseudo-random function SipHash to simplify the process. The SipHash function generates outputs of 128 bits (16 bytes). A Smoke identity is generated as follows:

```
id := siphash(public-encryption-key || public-signature-key,
          pbkdf2(sha512(public-encryption-key || public-signature-key), // Salt
                 public-encryption-key || public-signature-key,
                 4096, // Iteration Count
                 128)) // Bits (16 Bytes)
```

Non-confidential authentication and encryption key streams from a Smoke identity are generated as follows (elongate the first key stream):

```
keystream1 := pbkdf2(sha512(id), // Salt
                     id,
                     4096,        // Iteration Count
                     160)         // Bits (20 Bytes)
keystream2 := pbkdf2(sha512(id), // Salt
                     base64(keystream1),
                     1,           // Iteration Count
                     768)         // Bits (96 Bytes)
```

The transport keys which are generated from Smoke identities may be used for exchanging public-key data via the Echo Public-Key Share (EPKS) protocol.

It is impossible to avoid SipHash collisions as there are infinitely-many inputs and a limited number of outputs.

Smoke Pipes (Simple Steams)

Piping through Smoke allows for the transfer of data from Smoke devices to network-capable, non-Smoke devices. The process is as follows:

1. Define a passthrough network interface in the Settings activity. Optionally, disable or enable TLS. If TLS is enabled, it is expected that the defined endpoint supports TLS.

2. Prepare the endpoint service on the destination device. In this example: nc -l 192.168.178.15 4710 > output.

3. In the Steam activity, select a single file and specify the destination as Other (Non-Smoke). Tag the file for transfer. Repeat as often as desired.

4. Resume each file.

5. The first file to be tagged is the first file to be transferred.

Using commands such as head and tail, it's possible to partition the output file into separate files. Data may also be piped to multiple endpoints.

A concrete example follows.

1. In a console: "nc -k -l 192.168.178.15 4710 > output". If necessary, disable the firewall or prepare specific firewall rules on the destination device.

2. Define the non-TLS passthrough 192.168.178.15:4710 in Smoke's Settings activity.

3. Prepare 3 image files for distribution in Smoke.

4. Activate the Rewind & Resume All Steams context-menu option in the Steam activity.

5. Once the 3 files have been transferred, observe the file sizes of each Steam.

6. In a console: "head -c sizeof(file a) output > file1".

7. In a console: "sha256 file1". The digest must match the digest provided by Smoke.

8. In a console: "tail -c "$((sizeof(file a) + sizeof(file b)))" output | head -c sizeof(file a) > file2".

9. In a console: "sha256 file2". The digest must match the digest provided by Smoke.

10. In a console: "tail -c sizeof(file c) output > file3".

11. Finally: "sha256 file3". The digest must match the digest provided by Smoke.

The Scripts directory contains a program for partitioning a received aggregate into individual components.

Software Distribution

Smoke is distributed in debug (smoke-debug.apk) form. Sometimes, a release (smoke.apk) form is also distributed. The release bundle is signed and may include the source.

Steam Ephemeral Key Exchange

Please note that this protocol is a partial forward secrecy key exchange as the generator of the ephemeral public-key pair temporarily records the pair in an SQLite database. The ephemeral key-pair is removed from the database after a response is received from the destination participant. The destination participant removes the ephemeral public key after the first packet is recorded.

1. Generate an ephemeral public-key pair. A public-key pair is generated per file. Do not generate a public-key pair if one already exists or if private keys (4) have been recorded.

2. Locally record the ephemeral public-key pair.

3. Transfer the ephemeral public key to the destination participant.

4. Destination receives the ephemeral public key and generates private keys. Do not generate private keys if private keys already exist.

5. Locally record the private keys, unless the private keys exist.

6. Destination encrypts the private keys via the ephemeral public key and submits the results to the source participant.

7. Source participant receives the bundle and deciphers the private keys via the ephemeral private key.

8. Source participant records the private keys (4).

9. Source participant deletes the ephemeral public-key pair from the local SQLite database.

10. Destination participant the deletes ephemeral public key after the first packet of the Steam is recorded.

TCP, UDP Protocols

Smoke supports both the TCP and UDP network protocols. Multicast and unicast UDP varieties are provided. Multiple clients may be defined via the Settings activity. A limit on the number of clients is not imposed. When defining neighbors, one may define SmokeStack and/or Spot-On neighbors. SmokeStack, the companion application of Smoke, offers mobile server services as well as message and public-key storage.

Example UDP multicast address: 239.255.43.21.

Task Utilization

Smoke is an extremely task-oriented application. For example, the Kernel object utilizes 10 tasks while a single Neighbor object spawns 4 tasks. Various tasks are also defined in the activities.

Time

Time references are included in various message structures. Therefore, it is important that a device's local clock is correct. Smoke also performs numerous internal processes which are time-sensitive.

Smoke shall notify the operator if the device's Unix time differs from the Unix time of an external source by approximately five seconds. Notifications, if enabled, will occur every thirty seconds.

UDP Datagrams

Outbound UDP messages are partitioned into 576-byte datagrams. For example, a 15000-byte message will be partitioned into 27 datagrams.

Verifying Public-Key Ownership

Before initiating an exchange of public-key pairs, Smoke generates digital signatures using the private keys of the encryption and signature public keys. The digital signatures are composed of the concatenation of the public encryption and signature keys. The signatures are included in the EPKS bundle. A recipient verifies the signatures and accepts the public-key pairs if the signatures are valid. McEliece signatures are not included and are therefore not verified. Summary:

1. Concatenate the encoded forms of the encryption and the signature public keys.
2. Digitally sign the concatenated product using the private encryption key.
3. Digitally sign the concatenated product using the private signature key.
4. Bundle the two digital signatures.

dir /s >directory.txt

```
Volume in Laufwerk C: hat keine Bezeichnung.

 Directory of C:\smoke-2020.11.15

15.11.2020  23:01    <DIR>          .
15.11.2020  23:01    <DIR>          ..
15.11.2020  23:01               125 Android
15.11.2020  23:01    <DIR>          Documentation
15.11.2020  23:01    <DIR>          Images
15.11.2020  23:01             1.071 Makefile
15.11.2020  23:01             3.193 Makefile.linux
15.11.2020  23:01             1.568 README.md
15.11.2020  23:01    <DIR>          Scripts
15.11.2020  23:01    <DIR>          Smoke
15.11.2020  23:01            12.402 TO-DO
15.11.2020  23:01               203 adb.bash
15.11.2020  23:01               652 smoke-download-dependencies.bash
               7 File(s),         19.214 Bytes

 Directory of C:\smoke-2020.11.15\Documentation

15.11.2020  23:01    <DIR>          .
15.11.2020  23:01    <DIR>          ..
15.11.2020  23:01           423.594 Argon2.pdf
15.11.2020  23:01               114 BouncyCastle
15.11.2020  23:01               214 DESTINATION-ORIGIN-IDENTITY
15.11.2020  23:01                78 ICONS
15.11.2020  23:01            16.017 Juggernaut.odg
15.11.2020  23:01            12.666 Juggernaut.pdf
15.11.2020  23:01                62 LINKS
15.11.2020  23:01               110 MESSAGES-SIGNATURES
15.11.2020  23:01         1.463.926 Momedo.pdf
15.11.2020  23:01               338 OpenSSL
15.11.2020  23:01            10.621 RELEASE-NOTES.html
15.11.2020  23:01           365.541 SipHash.pdf
15.11.2020  23:01            41.025 Smoke.odt
15.11.2020  23:01           139.906 Smoke.pdf
              14 File(s),      2.474.212 Bytes

 Directory of C:\smoke-2020.11.15\Images

15.11.2020  23:01    <DIR>          .
15.11.2020  23:01    <DIR>          ..
15.11.2020  23:01            36.107 smoke_1.png
15.11.2020  23:01           991.988 smoke_2.png
15.11.2020  23:01           105.782 smoke_3.png
15.11.2020  23:01           134.625 smoke_4.png
15.11.2020  23:01           314.766 smoke_5.png
15.11.2020  23:01           111.352 smoke_6.png
               6 File(s),      1.694.620 Bytes

 Directory of C:\smoke-2020.11.15\Scripts

15.11.2020  23:01    <DIR>          .
15.11.2020  23:01    <DIR>          ..
15.11.2020  15:41               394 split.bash
               1 File(s),          X.193 Bytes
```

```
 Directory of C:\smoke-2020.11.15\Smoke

15.11.2020  23:01    <DIR>          .
15.11.2020  23:01    <DIR>          ..
15.11.2020  23:01               118 .gitignore
15.11.2020  23:01    <DIR>          app
15.11.2020  23:01               533 build.gradle
15.11.2020  23:01               702 gradle.properties
15.11.2020  23:01    <DIR>          gradle
15.11.2020  23:01             4.971 gradlew
15.11.2020  23:01             2.404 gradlew.bat
15.11.2020  23:01                15 settings.gradle
               6 File(s),          8.743 Bytes

 Directory of C:\smoke-2020.11.15\Smoke\app

15.11.2020  23:01    <DIR>          .
15.11.2020  23:01    <DIR>          ..
15.11.2020  23:01                 7 .gitignore
15.11.2020  23:01             1.710 build.gradle
15.11.2020  23:01    <DIR>          libs
15.11.2020  23:01               656 proguard-rules.pro
15.11.2020  23:01    <DIR>          src
               3 File(s),          2.373 Bytes

 Directory of C:\smoke-2020.11.15\Smoke\app\libs

15.11.2020  23:01    <DIR>          .
15.11.2020  23:01    <DIR>          ..
15.11.2020  23:01         6.031.520 bcprov-ext-jdk15on-167.jar
15.11.2020  23:01         9.715.254 bcprov-jdk15on-167.tar.gz
               2 File(s),      15.746.774 Bytes

 Directory of C:\smoke-2020.11.15\Smoke\app\src

15.11.2020  23:01    <DIR>          .
15.11.2020  23:01    <DIR>          ..
15.11.2020  23:01    <DIR>          main
               0 File(s),              0 Bytes

 Directory of C:\smoke-2020.11.15\Smoke\app\src\main

15.11.2020  23:01    <DIR>          .
15.11.2020  23:01    <DIR>          ..
15.11.2020  23:01             1.897 AndroidManifest.xml
15.11.2020  23:01    <DIR>          java
15.11.2020  23:01    <DIR>          res
               1 File(s),         50.506 Bytes

 Directory of C:\smoke-2020.11.15\Smoke\app\src\main\java

15.11.2020  23:01    <DIR>          .
15.11.2020  23:01    <DIR>          ..
15.11.2020  23:01    <DIR>          org
               0 File(s),              0 Bytes

 Directory of C:\smoke-2020.11.15\Smoke\app\src\main\java\org

15.11.2020  23:01    <DIR>          .
15.11.2020  23:01    <DIR>          ..
15.11.2020  23:01    <DIR>          purple
               0 File(s),              0 Bytes
```

```
 Directory of C:\smoke-2020.11.15\Smoke\app\src\main\java\org\purple

15.11.2020  23:01    <DIR>          .
15.11.2020  23:01    <DIR>          ..
15.11.2020  23:01    <DIR>          smoke
               0 File(s),              0 Bytes

 Directory of C:\smoke-2020.11.15\Smoke\app\src\main\java\org\purple\smoke

15.11.2020  23:01    <DIR>          .
15.11.2020  23:01    <DIR>          ..
15.11.2020  15:46             2.711 About.java
15.11.2020  15:48            17.837 Authenticate.java
15.11.2020  15:49            41.530 Chat.java
15.11.2020  15:51            12.355 ChatBubble.java
15.11.2020  15:52            56.262 Cryptography.java
15.11.2020  15:54           129.038 Database.java
15.11.2020  15:55            22.030 Fire.java
15.11.2020  15:56            15.904 FireChannel.java
15.11.2020  15:57             1.609 FireElement.java
15.11.2020  15:58            16.023 Juggernaut.java
15.11.2020  15:59            85.137 Kernel.java
15.11.2020  15:59            40.073 MemberChat.java
15.11.2020  16:00             7.373 MemberChatAdapter.java
15.11.2020  16:18             1.829 MemberChatElement.java
15.11.2020  16:02             2.446 MessageElement.java
15.11.2020  16:03            46.227 Messages.java
15.11.2020  16:03            23.456 Miscellaneous.java
15.11.2020  16:04            17.784 Neighbor.java
15.11.2020  16:05             2.420 NeighborElement.java
15.11.2020  16:05             2.462 ParticipantCall.java
15.11.2020  16:06             1.749 ParticipantElement.java
15.11.2020  16:06           100.442 Settings.java
15.11.2020  16:07             7.557 SipHash.java
15.11.2020  16:08             1.954 SipHashIdElement.java
15.11.2020  16:08             3.151 Smoke.java
15.11.2020  16:09             3.532 SmokeService.java
15.11.2020  16:09             8.668 Smokescreen.java
15.11.2020  16:10            13.521 State.java
15.11.2020  16:10            18.465 Steam.java
15.11.2020  16:11             4.594 SteamAdapter.java
15.11.2020  16:12            13.797 SteamBubble.java
15.11.2020  16:12             2.579 SteamElement.java
15.11.2020  16:13            14.280 SteamKeyExchange.java
15.11.2020  16:13             4.472 SteamReader.java
15.11.2020  16:14             8.115 SteamReaderFull.java
15.11.2020  16:14             5.494 SteamReaderSimple.java
15.11.2020  16:15             7.652 SteamWriter.java
15.11.2020  16:15             8.130 TcpNeighbor.java
15.11.2020  16:16            12.543 TcpTlsNeighbor.java
15.11.2020  16:16             3.702 Time.java
15.11.2020  16:17             7.209 UdpMulticastNeighbor.java
15.11.2020  16:17             7.250 UdpNeighbor.java
15.11.2020  16:18             2.468 Windows.java

 Directory of C:\smoke-2020.11.15\Smoke\app\src\main\res

15.11.2020  23:01    <DIR>          .
15.11.2020  23:01    <DIR>          ..
15.11.2020  23:01    <DIR>          drawable
15.11.2020  23:01    <DIR>          layout
15.11.2020  23:01    <DIR>          menu
15.11.2020  23:01    <DIR>          values-de
```

```
15.11.2020  23:01    <DIR>          values
                0 File(s),              0 Bytes

Directory of C:\smoke-2020.11.15\Smoke\app\src\main\res\drawable

15.11.2020  23:01    <DIR>          .
15.11.2020  23:01    <DIR>          ..
15.11.2020  23:01               344 bubble_error.xml
15.11.2020  23:01               344 bubble_left_text.xml
15.11.2020  23:01               205 bubble_name.xml
15.11.2020  23:01               344 bubble_ozone_text.xml
15.11.2020  23:01               344 bubble_right_text.xml
15.11.2020  23:01               807 chat_faulty_session.png
15.11.2020  23:01             1.041 chat_status_offline.png
15.11.2020  23:01             1.134 chat_status_online.png
15.11.2020  23:01               508 download.png
15.11.2020  23:01               873 file.png
15.11.2020  23:01               607 file_select.png
15.11.2020  23:01               736 file_send.png
15.11.2020  23:01             1.100 help.png
15.11.2020  23:01               832 keys_not_signed.png
15.11.2020  23:01               933 keys_signed.png
15.11.2020  23:01             1.345 lock.png
15.11.2020  23:01               400 menu.png
15.11.2020  23:01               870 message_read.png
15.11.2020  23:01               847 message_sent.png
15.11.2020  23:01             1.142 minus.png
15.11.2020  23:01               284 sectiongradient.xml
15.11.2020  23:01             1.096 send.png
15.11.2020  23:01             1.141 send_disabled.png
15.11.2020  23:01               960 share.png
15.11.2020  23:01           546.059 smoke.png
15.11.2020  23:01             1.345 smokescreen_lock.png
15.11.2020  23:01             1.329 smokescreen_unlock.png
15.11.2020  23:01             1.329 unlock.png
15.11.2020  23:01               521 upload.png
15.11.2020  23:01             1.032 verified.png
15.11.2020  23:01               937 warning.png
               31 File(s),        570.789 Bytes

Directory of C:\smoke-2020.11.15\Smoke\app\src\main\res\layout

15.11.2020  23:01    <DIR>          .
15.11.2020  23:01    <DIR>          ..
15.11.2020  16:44             2.619 activity_authenticate.xml
15.11.2020  23:01             1.057 activity_chat.xml
15.11.2020  23:01            10.019 activity_fire.xml
15.11.2020  23:01             1.070 activity_member_chat.xml
15.11.2020  23:01            32.906 activity_settings.xml
15.11.2020  23:01             2.516 activity_smokescreen.xml
15.11.2020  23:01               516 activity_steam.xml
15.11.2020  23:01             3.001 chat_bubble.xml
15.11.2020  23:01             3.623 content_chat.xml
15.11.2020  23:01             4.698 content_member_chat.xml
15.11.2020  23:01             3.070 content_steam.xml
15.11.2020  23:01             4.046 fire_channel.xml
15.11.2020  23:01             1.380 progress.xml
15.11.2020  23:01             6.464 steam_bubble.xml
               14 File(s),        111.930 Bytes
```

```
 Directory of C:\smoke-2020.11.15\Smoke\app\src\main\res\menu

15.11.2020  23:01    <DIR>          .
15.11.2020  23:01    <DIR>          ..
15.11.2020  23:01               861 authenticate_menu.xml
15.11.2020  23:01             1.018 chat_menu.xml
15.11.2020  23:01               877 fire_menu.xml
15.11.2020  23:01             1.158 member_chat_menu.xml
15.11.2020  23:01               854 settings_menu.xml
15.11.2020  23:01               863 smokescreen_menu.xml
15.11.2020  23:01               867 steam_menu.xml
               7 File(s),          6.498 Bytes

 Directory of C:\smoke-2020.11.15\Smoke\app\src\main\res\values-de

15.11.2020  23:01    <DIR>          .
15.11.2020  23:01    <DIR>          ..
15.11.2020  23:01             4.158 strings.xml
               1 File(s),          4.158 Bytes

 Directory of C:\smoke-2020.11.15\Smoke\app\src\main\res\values

15.11.2020  23:01    <DIR>          .
15.11.2020  23:01    <DIR>          ..
15.11.2020  23:01                94 attrs_fire_channel.xml
15.11.2020  23:01               201 colors.xml
15.11.2020  23:01                97 dimens.xml
15.11.2020  23:01             3.923 strings.xml
15.11.2020  23:01               701 styles.xml
               5 File(s),          5.016 Bytes

 Directory of C:\smoke-2020.11.15\Smoke\gradle

15.11.2020  23:01    <DIR>          .
15.11.2020  23:01    <DIR>          ..
15.11.2020  23:01    <DIR>          wrapper
               0 File(s),              0 Bytes

 Directory of C:\smoke-2020.11.15\Smoke\gradle\wrapper

15.11.2020  23:01    <DIR>          .
15.11.2020  23:01    <DIR>          ..
15.11.2020  23:01            53.636 gradle-wrapper.jar
15.11.2020  23:01               230 gradle-wrapper.properties
               2 File(s),         53.866 Bytes
```

Android

https://github.com/textbrowser/smoke/blob/master/Android
```
Smoke has been successfully tested on Android versions 7.x, 8.x, and 9.x.
Android versions older than 7.x may be functional.
```

Makefile

https://github.com/textbrowser/smoke/blob/master/Makefile
```
UNAME := $(shell uname)

ifeq ($(UNAME), Linux)
    MAKEFILE=Makefile.linux
else
    MAKEFILE=Makefile.windows
endif

all:
    $(MAKE) -f $(MAKEFILE)

clean:
    $(MAKE) -f $(MAKEFILE) clean

clear-smoke:
    $(MAKE) -f $(MAKEFILE) clear-smoke

copy-apk:
    $(MAKE) -f $(MAKEFILE) copy-apk

debug-with-source:
    $(MAKE) -f $(MAKEFILE) debug-with-source

distclean:
    $(MAKE) -f $(MAKEFILE) distclean

kill-adb-server:
    $(MAKE) -f $(MAKEFILE) kill-adb-server

kill-gradle-daemon:
    $(MAKE) -f $(MAKEFILE) kill-gradle-daemon

launch-emulator-1:
    $(MAKE) -f $(MAKEFILE) launch-emulator-1

launch-emulator-2:
    $(MAKE) -f $(MAKEFILE) launch-emulator-2

list-devices:
    $(MAKE) -f $(MAKEFILE) list-devices

list-files:
    $(MAKE) -f $(MAKEFILE) list-files

load-apk:
    $(MAKE) -f $(MAKEFILE) load-apk

load-apk-release:
    $(MAKE) -f $(MAKEFILE) load-apk-release

pull-database:
    $(MAKE) -f $(MAKEFILE) pull-database
```

```makefile
purge:
	$(MAKE) -f $(MAKEFILE) purge

release:
	$(MAKE) -f $(MAKEFILE) release

remove-database:
	$(MAKE) -f $(MAKEFILE) remove-database
```


Makefile.linux

https://github.com/textbrowser/smoke/blob/master/Makefile.linux

```makefile
# You must have at least one AVD defined.

ADB = ~/Android/Sdk/platform-tools/adb
EMULATOR = ~/Android/Sdk/tools/emulator
GRADLEW = ./Smoke/gradlew
JARSIGNER = "/snap/android-studio/current/android-studio/jre/bin/jarsigner"
JDK = "/snap/android-studio/current/android-studio/jre"
export JAVA_HOME = /snap/android-studio/current/android-studio/jre

all:
	$(GRADLEW) -Dorg.gradle.java.home=$(JDK) \
	-Dorg.gradle.warning.mode=all \
	--build-file Smoke/build.gradle assembleDebug \
	--configure-on-demand --daemon --parallel

clean:
	rm -f Smoke/app/src/main/assets/smoke.src.d.zip
	rm -f smoke.src.d.zip
	$(GRADLEW) --build-file Smoke/build.gradle clean

clear-smoke:
	./adb.bash shell pm clear org.purple.smoke

copy-apk: all
	cp ./Smoke/app/build/outputs/apk/debug/apk/smoke.apk ~/Desktop/.

debug-with-source: all
	rm -rf Smoke/build Smoke/captures
	mkdir -p Smoke/app/src/main/assets
	zip -r smoke.src.d.zip \
	Android \
	Documentation \
	Makefile \
	Makefile.linux \
	Smoke \
	TO-DO \
	adb.bash \
	-x *.git* -x *.gradle* -x *.idea* \
	&& mv smoke.src.d.zip Smoke/app/src/main/assets/.
	$(GRADLEW) -Dorg.gradle.java.home=$(JDK) \
	--build-file Smoke/build.gradle assembleDebug \
	--configure-on-demand --daemon --parallel
	rm -f Smoke/app/src/main/assets/smoke.src.d.zip

distclean: clean kill-adb-server kill-gradle-daemon
	rm -f smoke.db

kill-adb-server:
	$(ADB) kill-server
```

```makefile
kill-gradle-daemon:
	$(GRADLEW) --stop

launch-emulator-1:
	$(EMULATOR) -netdelay none -netspeed full -avd \
	`$(EMULATOR) -list-avds | sort | sed "1q;d"` &

launch-emulator-2:
	$(EMULATOR) -netdelay none -netspeed full -avd \
	`$(EMULATOR) -list-avds | sort | sed "2q;d"` &

list-devices:
	$(ADB) devices -l

list-files:
	./adb.bash shell run-as org.purple.smoke \
	ls -l /data/data/org.purple.smoke/databases

load-apk: all
	./adb.bash install -r \
	./Smoke/app/build/outputs/apk/debug/apk/smoke.apk
	./adb.bash shell am start -S -W \
	-n org.purple.smoke/org.purple.smoke.Settings \
	-a android.intent.action.MAIN -c android.intent.category.LAUNCHER

load-apk-release: release
	$(JARSIGNER) -verbose -keystore ~/Android-Keys/smoke-release.keystore \
	./Smoke/app/build/outputs/apk/release/apk/smoke.apk smoke
	$(JARSIGNER) -verify \
	./Smoke/app/build/outputs/apk/release/apk/smoke.apk
	./adb.bash install -r \
	./Smoke/app/build/outputs/apk/release/apk/smoke.apk
	./adb.bash shell am start -S -W \
	-n org.purple.smoke/org.purple.smoke.Settings \
	-a android.intent.action.MAIN -c android.intent.category.LAUNCHER

pull-database:
	./adb.bash exec-out run-as org.purple.smoke \
	cat /data/data/org.purple.smoke/databases/smoke.db > smoke.db

purge:
	find . -name '*~*' -exec rm -f {} \;

release: clean
	rm -rf Smoke/build Smoke/captures
	$(GRADLEW) -Dorg.gradle.java.home=$(JDK) \
	--build-file Smoke/build.gradle assembleRelease \
	--configure-on-demand --daemon --parallel
	rm -f Smoke/app/src/main/assets/smoke.src.d.zip

remove-database:
	./adb.bash shell run-as org.purple.smoke \
	rm -f /data/data/org.purple.smoke/databases/smoke.db
	./adb.bash shell run-as org.purple.smoke \
	rm -f /data/data/org.purple.smoke/databases/smoke.db-journal

stop-smoke:
	./adb.bash shell am force-stop org.purple.smoke
```

README.md

Summary of Smoke

```
<ul>
<li>Aliases. Preserve your contacts.</li>
<li>Almost zero-dependency software.</li>
<li>Argon2id key-derivation function.</li>
<li>Automatic, oscillatory public-key exchange protocol, via SipHash.</li>
<li>BSD 3-clause license.</li>
<li>Content is recorded via authenticated encryption.</li>
<li>Decentralized. TCP, and UDP multicast and unicast.</li>
<li>Does not require Internet connectivity.</li>
<li>Does not require registration. Telephone numbers are not required.</li>
<li>Fiasco forward secrecy.</li>
<li>Introduces Cryptographic Discovery. Cryptographic Discovery is a practical
protocol which creates coordinated data paths.</li>
<li>Juggling Juggernaut Protocol!</li>
<li>McEliece Fujisaka and Pointcheval.</li>
<li>Message structures do not explicitly expose contents. Header-less
protocols!</li>
<li>Mobile servers via <a
href="https://github.com/textbrowser/smokestack">SmokeStack</a>.</li>
<li>Optional foreground services.</li>
<li>Original implementation of SipHash.</li>
<li>Ozone destinations: private and public repositories.</li>
<li>Post offices for messages of the past.</li>
<li>Private servers.</li>
<li>Public and private public-key servers.</li>
<li>Reliable distribution of archived messages.</li>
<li>SSL/TLS through SmokeStack.</li>
<li>Semi-compatible with <a href="https://github.com/textbrowser/spot-
on">Spot-On</a> via Fire.</li>
<li>Share files with TCP utilities such as Netcat.</li>
<li>SipHash-128.</li>
<li>Software congestion control.</li>
<li>Steam, reliable file sharing. TCP over the Echo!</li>
</ul>
```


TO-DO

Completed Items

- A menu item for terminating the application as well as its service.
- A release target for the make files.
- Aliases.
- Allow for two McEliece parameter sets ((11, 50), (12, 68)):
  Eleven of Sixty-One, Twelve of Eighty.
- Allow log clearing.
- Allow resending of messages.
- Allow resetting of Chat session keys via context menu.
- Allow sharing of participant pairs.
- Append new messages in Member Chat.
- Application icon.
- Application lock: Smokescreen.
- As the half-response does not produce a response, the automatic response's
  result is ignored.
- Asynchronous database writes.

- Authenticate activity and member menu: menu is empty if Smoke was
  recently initialized.
- Automatically set the Fire name if the Alias is changed, unless
  the Fire name is not empty.
- Banner text may shadow member status in Member Chat.
- Bind recipient and sender.
- Brief pause after message-retrieval request. Origins are random. No.
  Stack must pause after receiving a message-retrieval request.
- Broadcast a reminder to the Settings activity if a Chat message has been
  received while the Settings activity is active.
- Calling via multiple neighbors is chaotic.
- Capitalize SipHash input.
- Change case of final-static objects in Neighbor, Settings, SipHash,
- Chat activity state is not retained. States of selected items will not be
  retained as such states are expensive.
- Chat messages will appear blue if they are assembled from the internal log
  and are beyond the specific time window.
- Class access privileges.
- Compare provided encryption and signature public keys.
- Complete Cryptography.pkiEncrypt().
- Compress IPv6 Scope ID field when hidden.
- Confirm application termination.
- Connect the state of the Call button to the number of selected participants
  (Chat).
- Connecting status until in/out data has been received/transmitted.
- Connection mutex (m_mutex).
- Connection status text colors.
- Context menu items in Member Chat: delete all, delete selected.
- Copying of read-only values.
- Create random Steam name on initial write.
- Custom key streams via context menus.
- Database method for retrieving neighbor OIDs.
- Decide if the State class requires cryptographic data.
- Define passthrough devices.
- Deleting a connected neighbor and quickly re-adding it is problematic. If
  the current thread has been interrupted, exit run().
- Deleting a neighbor does not cause an immediate disconnect.
- Depict Android version in About. New About.java file too.
- Depict connection status in the Chat activity.
- Depict location of the Downloads folder in the Steam activity.
- Depict successful Steam key exchanges.
- Deploy new user name to Fire channels.
- Describe the Ozone feature.
- Detect network status changes across neighbors.
- Detect removal of neighbors.
- Detect removal of participants.
- Determine gradle's version in the make files.
- Determine if a remote Steam has been restarted.
- Determine path for any file in Steam.
- Digest of PEM(certificate).
- Disable Delete Fiasco Keys, Delete Public Keys on Participants context menu
  if information is not available. Not necessary.
- Disable echo on low memory. Cannot. Instead, clear queues.
- Disable proxy fields for non-TCP.
- Display count of queued echo packets per neighbor.
- Display date and time of sent message.
- Display destination's name during session initialization.
- Display exchange status in the Participants table. Icons.
- Display information pertaining to the owner's public keys.
- Display message-retrieval action.
- Display neighbors contents.
- Display remote server's certificate information. Public key fingerprint.
- Do not enqueue messages in disconnected neighbors.

- Do not save a key stream unless a response is received.
- Duplicates Cryptography. Removed methods from State.
- Dynamic DNS for home servers. Functional.
- Dynamic textview objects trim text. Append an extra new line.
- ECDSA.
- EPKS description bubble.
- EPKS.
- Elongate messages in Member Chat.
- Empty Steam files.
- Enable Settings widgets after an initial password is accepted.
- Erase ephemeral public key from Steam upon recording of first packet.
- Exit menus.
- Expand messages to multiples of 8 KiB.
- Fire channels must be retained if the Fire activity is dismissed.
- Fire through SmokeStack.
- Fire. ("AES/CTS/NoPadding")
- Foreground service, optional.
- Full Steams, reliable Echo.
- Generate and separate.
- Gently notify MemberChat of written messages. Gentle notifications prevent
  bouncy context menus.
- HTTP proxy.
- Highlight results of Juggernaut, if possible.
- Identity-sharing confirmation from SmokeStack.
- If a SipHash ID is deleted, its corresponding participants entry should also
  be removed. Foreign key constraints.
- Improve PBKDF2 uses. Initially, generate a temporary stream of 20 bytes
  (SHA-1). Afterwards, generate a stream using the temporary stream as
  password material. The length of the second stream varies per application.
- Inadvertent calling may sever an established session.
- Inbound database table.
- Include file extensions in Steams.
- Include network information in neighbors pertaining to errors.
- Include status in Smokescreen activity.
- Increase network buffer sizes for large attachments.
- Individual member pages.
- Initialize database ETAs and rates of Steams.
- Inspect destination tags.
- Inspect length in substring() usage.
- Introduce termination logic on critical TCP read/write errors.
- Java serialization requires safety.
  (https://www.oracle.com/technetwork/java/seccodeguide-139067.html#8)
- Kernel.
- Key-sharing messages should be written to smoke.db.
- JuggerKnot (credentials from protocol).
- Juggernaut.
  (https://en.wikipedia.org/wiki/\
        Password_Authenticated_Key_Exchange_by_Juggling)
  (https://www.borelly.net/cb/docs/javaBC-1.4.8/prov/org/\
        bouncycastle/crypto/agreement/jpake/JPAKEParticipant.html)
- Last activity and Member Chat. Restore.
- Less populateParticipants() in the Chat activity.
- Local congestion control.
- Logging class. See Database::writeLog().
- Long constants.
- Material icons.
- McEliece Pointcheval conversion.
- Member status in Member Chat.
- Member Chat attachment.
- Messages from the past may trigger presence.
- Messages may arrive while the Settings activity is the primary activity.
  Calls are not logged.
- Messages must be temporarily retained if the Chat activity loses focus.

- Modify Settings so that TCP neighbors support SOCKS proxies.
- Names or PINs alongside SipHashes. The extra bits will increase the
  possibilities. SipHash-128.
- Neighbor class.
- Neighbor details should be optional.
- Neighbors periodic refresh.
- Network status in Member Chat.
- Network status information is too complex.
- New class for establishing Steam keys.
- New date format: YYYY-MM-DD. ISO-8601.
- New messages should be at the top of the view; Member Chat.
- Next (Tab) order; Settings.
- Non-TLS connections.
- Non-exclusive database transactions.
- Notification causes abnormal exit on Android 7.
- Notify of other member messages in Member Chat.
- Notify operator of incorrect time.
- Notify the Chat activity of new participants.
- Optimize loops.
- Optional per-participant signatures.
- Optional time notification.
- Orderly delivery of chaotic Steams. First-in-first-Steam.
- Organic half-and-half: resolve collisions. As Smoke is not ordered, order is
  impossible to predict.
- Outbound database table.
- Outbound queues must be purged on parent neighbor removal.
- Participant list may be large. Create a special State container and thread
  for retrieval.
- Participant status icon should not be modified if newly-received message is
  from an Ozone.
- Passthrough devices.
- Per request, include the source in the application bundle.
- Periodic key publishing requires more intelligence.
- Populate Chat member list without accessing the database.
- Populate Settings neighbors during new installation. Start timers.
- Potential database locking problem with repeated replacement of neighbor
  objects. Replaced replace() with intelligent insert().
- Prepare for Chat, E-Mail, etc. public key pairs.
- Prevent-sleep option in Settings.
- Preview attachment.
- Prompt for neighbor removal.
- Purging of neighbor queues should occur off of the main thread.
- Push sent messages from Member Chat to Chat.
- Receiving requested keys which do not include signatures should be
functional.
- Record received messages in Chat from Member Chat.
- Refresh context menu on Chat table.
- Remote storage of messages. SmokeStack.
- Remove UI-related references in Settings::prepareListeners()::...::run().
- Remove expired private keystreams.
- Replace 96 with Cryptographic.CIPHER_HASH_KEYS_LENGTH.
- Replace Date object with AtomicLong objects.
- Replace INTEGER_BYTES with Integer.BYTES and LONG_BYTES with Long.BYTES.
- Replace the (final) iterations variable in
- Requesting offline messages stalls if there are several active neighbors.
  https://developer.android.com/reference/android/net/wifi/
  WifiManager.WifiLock.html
- Reset option in Authenticate activity.
- Reset option. Remove smoke.db. Reset widget states.
- Reset spinners after credentials are initialized.
- Resize Member Chat bubbles according to contents.
- Retain Chat participant states on refresh.
- Retain Chat widget selection states. Remove State objects if participants

are removed via the Settings activity.
- Retain first-contact server certificate. Inspect stored bytes with received
  bytes.
- Retrieve a subset of message data in Member Chat. New data via scroll.
- Retrieve/store user name.
- Return message-read status in status messages.
- Rich context menu containing other members.
- SQLite secure delete (onConfigure()).
- Save attachment.
- Save files and images to Downloads folder.
- Schedulers may silently fail. try-catch blocks!
- Scroll on sending of local messages; Member Chat.
- Scroll within scroll in Fire channels.
- Send messages in Member Chat.
- Settings::prepareListeners()::...::run().
- Sign encryption and signature keys as a pair.
- Signed release.
- Simple Steam through UDP.
- Simple binary status in Chat. Kernel scheduler.
- SipHash (https://en.wikipedia.org/wiki/SipHash).
- SipHash description bubble.
- Smoke echo? Expensive. Optional.
- Smokescreen, remove sub-menus on lock.
- Sort table contents.
- Spinner objects in the neighbors table bleed. The table will expand as
  necessary.
- Stack message confirmations. New message type required.
- Status messages.
- Steam context menu items and Steam types.
- Steam context menu.
- Steam rates.
- Steam separators.
- Store a digest of the secret string (Miscellaneous.showTextInputDialog()) if
  the secret is brief.
- Synchronized methods or containers? Both.
- TCP socket setPerformancePreferences().
- TLS 1.3 in Android 10.
- TcpNeighbor classes.
- The Bundle object is not saved.
- The Socket class supports the Proxy class.
- The initial call (1/2-1/2) should store the generated stream in a map
  (or hash).
- The timestamp in participants_messages must be used for sorting.
- UDP multicast.
- UDP sockets.
- Upon receiving a timely response, the total key stream should be saved to
  smoke.db. If a timely response is not received, the partial data should be
  purged.
- Vacuum databases.
- Validate the SipHash implementation. Please see SipHash::test1().
- Verify hexadecimal characters of SipHash identities.
- View Details vanishes on Android 9. Disable Miscellaneous.enableChildren()
  for Android version greater than N (Nougat). Android is garbage.
- When verifying signatures, recipients should retrieve appropriate personal
  identity digests.
- Wrap neighbor text.
- Zero ports are valid. If a system is allowing connections on port
  zero, Smoke will be able to connect to it.

Future Items

- (130 / 16 + 1) * 16 + 8 <= 154.
- Bubbles are too narrow on wide devices.

- Java does not include methods for destroying private containers.
- NTRU via BouncyCastle.
- Option for computing Steam digest.
- Optional cryptographic discovery.
- Resolve DNS through a proxy if a proxy is defined.
- Stronger surreptitious forwarding. Larger RSA keys.

Remaining Items

- As Name option in Alias mode (set alias to name).
- Brands (profiles).
- Clickable preview messages.
- Document available tasks.
- New images for Web page.

adb.bash

https://github.com/textbrowser/smoke/blob/master/adb.bash

```bash
#!/bin/bash

adb="${HOME}/Android/Sdk/platform-tools/adb"

$adb devices | sort -u | grep 'device$' | while read line
do
    device=$(echo $line | awk '{print $1}')
    $adb -s $device $@ &
    wait
done
```

smoke-download-dependencies.bash

https://github.com/textbrowser/smoke/blob/master/smoke-download-dependencies.bash

```bash
#!/bin/bash

# Must be executed in the top-level source directory.

# Bouncy Castle

bouncycastle1=bcprov-ext-jdk15on-167.jar
bouncycastle2=bcprov-jdk15on-167.tar.gz

rm -f $bouncycastle1
rm -f $bouncycastle2
wget --progress=bar https://bouncycastle.org/download/$bouncycastle1
wget --progress=bar https://bouncycastle.org/download/$bouncycastle2

if [ -r "$bouncycastle1" ]; then
    mv $bouncycastle1 Smoke/app/libs/.
else
    echo "Cannot read $bouncycastle1."
fi

if [ -r "$bouncycastle2" ]; then
    mv $bouncycastle2 Smoke/app/libs/.
else
    echo "Cannot read $bouncycastle2."
fi

echo "Please review Smoke/app/build.gradle and Smoke/app/libs!"
```

BouncyCastle

https://github.com/textbrowser/smoke/blob/master/Documentation/BouncyCastle
Please keep Smoke/app/build.gradle and Smoke/app/libs current.

https://www.bouncycastle.org/latest_releases.html

RELEASE-NOTES.html

https://github.com/textbrowser/smoke/blob/master/Documentation/RELEASE-NOTES.html
2020.11.15

<ol>
  <li>Bouncy Castle 1.67.</li>
  <li>Disable Chat:Send if there is at least one selected participant without a session key pair.</li>
  <li>Efficient ArrayList::remove(). Remove from the end of the array.</li>
  <li>Full, reliable, Steam! File sharing.</li>
  <li>Improved TLS handshake-completed state.</li>
  <li>Issue Settings::prepareListeners() shortly after the Settings activity has been instantiated.</li>
  <li>Monitor connection activity; decreased polling.</li>
  <li>Notify the user of incorrect device time via https://worldtimeapi.org/api/timezone/Etc/UTC.txt. Optional.</li>
  <li>Prepare initial private keys during a public-key exchange.</li>
  <li>Provide message-read responses to SmokeStack instances.</li>
  <li>Random identities need not be recorded to databases.</li>
  <li>Removed SecureRandom.getInstance("SHA1PRNG").</li>
  <li>Removed verbose threads and replaced with events.</li>
  <li>Request Ozone messages shortly after a TCP connection has been established or a TLS session has been established.</li>
  <li>SipHash-128.</li>
  <li>Write local identity immediately upon completion of TLS handshake.</li>
</ol>
2020.04.07

<ol>
  <li>Artificial random-access Steam files.</li>
  <li>New Scripts directory.</li>
  <li>Retain Steam rates.</li>
</ol>
2020.04.05

<ol>
  <li>Clear Smokescreen password.</li>
  <li>Static variables.</li>
</ol>
2020.04.04

<ol>
  <li>Bouncy Castle 1.65!</li>
  <li>Denote Juggernaut protocol failures and successes.</li>
  <li>Kernel broadcast receiver for immediate delivery of internal instructions.</li>
  <li>McEliece Pointcheval conversion. Smoke must be reinstalled!</li>
  <li>Non-TLS devices.</li>
  <li>Partial Steam.</li>
  <li>Passthrough devices.</li>
  <li>Smokescreen, or, application lock.</li>
</ol>

```
2020.01.01
<br>
<ol>
 <li>Happy New Year!</li>
 <li>New Argon2id parameters.</li>
</ol>
2019.12.30
<br>
<ol>
 <li>Argon2id key-derivation function.</li>
</ol>
2019.12.10
<br>
<ol>
 <li>Allow Android to recycle bitmaps.</li>
 <li>Corrected the private server authentication protocol.</li>
</ol>
2019.11.30
<br>
<ol>
 <li>Support various McEliece parameters.</li>
</ol>
2019.11.25
<br>
<ol>
 <li>Bouncy Castle version 1.64.</li>
 <li>Corrected primary key in participants table. Please reinstall
Smoke.</li>
 <li>Corrected widget states during initialization.</li>
</ol>
2019.09.30
<br>
<ol>
 <li>Bouncy Castle version 1.63.</li>
 <li>Exit option. May be incomplete on some devices.</li>
 <li>Guard socket buffers.</li>
 <li>New icons.</li>
 <li>Save attachments to Downloads (Internal Storage -> Download).</li>
 <li>Settings -> View Details functional on Android 9.</li>
</ol>
2019.04.14
<br>
<ol>
 <li>JuggerKnot.</li>
 <li>Properly create strings from bytes. Ozones and participants must be
redefined.</li>
</ol>
2019.04.04
<br>
<ol>
 <li>Allow removal of participant public keys.</li>
 <li>Close Java streams.</li>
 <li>Default socket buffer sizes.</li>
 <li>Juggernaut Protocol.</li>
 <li>Minor Fire layout changes.</li>
 <li>Release resources on onPause(), onStop().</li>
 <li>Removed deepCopy().</li>
 <li>Smoke Alias. Change your credentials while preserving your
relationships.</li>
</ol>
2019.03.03
<br>
<ol>
```

  <li>Allow removal of specific messages in MemberChat.</li>
  <li>Decreased maximum buffer size from 32 MiB to 8 MiB.</li>
  <li>Prefer delete() over setLength(0) on buffers.</li>
  <li>Recycle bitmaps.</li>
</ol>
2019.02.25

<ol>
  <li>Bouncy Castle version 1.61.</li>
  <li>Material icons.</li>
  <li>Optional foreground service.</li>
</ol>
2019.02.02

<ol>
  <li>Array lengths may not be negative.</li>
  <li>Automatic removal of incorrect network data. Smoke and SmokeStack.</li>
  <li>Corrected conditional in UdpMulticastNeighbor::send(). SmokeStack.</li>
  <li>Disable Nagle's algorithm.</li>
  <li>Energy and iterations.</li>
  <li>Optional initialization of Ozone during neighbor definition.</li>
  <li>Orderly shutdown of schedules.</li>
  <li>Pause schedules, notify if necessary.
  <li>Replaced Spongy Castle with Bouncy Castle. Please replace existing
listeners. SmokeStack.</li>
  <li>SNAP!</li>
  <li>Smaller lock regions.</li>
  <li>SmokeStack confirmation for identity sharing of personal identity.</li>
  <li>StringBuilder over StringBuffer if possible.</li>
</ol>
2018.10.10

<ol>
  <li>Compute SHA-512 display digest of PEM(certificate).</li>
  <li>Inspect length in String::substring().</li>
  <li>New server (tulip-ipv4.tilaa.cloud).</li>
</ol>
2018.09.01

<ol>
  <li>Allow resending of messages.</li>
  <li>Deleting Fiasco keys lacked proper confirmation.</li>
  <li>Denote messages which have been read by the recipient.</li>
  <li>Denote messages which have been sent.</li>
  <li>Depict Smoke failures.</li>
  <li>Lock SipHash::hmac().</li>
  <li>New participants_messages database fields. Requires new
installation.</li>
</ol>
2018.08.19

<ol>
  [illegible]
  <li>Allow new participant names via context menus;
Settings::Participants.</li>
  <li>Automatically set the Ozone to the Smoke ID on new installations.</li>
  <li>Blocking socket reads.</li>
  <li>Bouncy Castle at version 1.60.</li>
  <li>Calling via ephemeral McEliece; MemberChat only.</li>
  <li>Clear internal messaging log on Chat::Clear.</li>
  <li>Corrected faulty widget listeners in Fire.</li>
  <li>Corrected slight time differences between time stamps in messages
destined for SmokeStacks and messages destined for participants.</li>

  <li>Increased key-publishing period from 15 seconds to 45 seconds. Also removed self-publishing.</li>
  <li>Material Design-compliant color selections.</li>
  <li>McEliece parameters m = 12, t = 68. Compatibility with m = 11, t = 50 is preserved.</li>
  <li>Messages in MemberChat will not be duplicated in the Chat activity.</li>
  <li>New Fiasco Keys column in Settings::Participants.</li>
  <li>New chat-message format. Incompatible with previous releases.</li>
  <li>Pause threads when possible.</li>
  <li>Periodically request Ozone messages.</li>
  <li>Private servers through SmokeStack.</li>
  <li>Removed the superfluous name field from the participants database table.</li>
  <li>Replaced complex if-statements with switch statements.</li>
  <li>Several member variables in the Neighbor class were defined as static. Corrected.</li>
  <li>Share capabilities and identities shortly after the SSL/TLS handshake has completed on TCP sockets.</li>
  <li>Shared keys without signatures are now accepted and properly depicted in Settings.</li>
  <li>Sign encryption and signature public keys as pairs.</li>
  <li>Singular member pages. Single image attachments included.</li>
  <li>Uniquely-persistent Fire identities.</li>
  <li>Viewing of member details now available via Settings::Participants context menu.</li>
</ol>
2018.05.05

<ol>
  <li>Forward secrecy from the past.</li>
</ol>
2018.04.04

<ol>
  <li>LocalBroadcastManager instances.</li>
  <li>Single ID per Fire.</li>
</ol>
2018.03.15

<ol>
  <li>Congestion-control improvements.</li>
  <li>Corrected nested locks (isNetworkConnected()).</li>
  <li>Insert-or-throw SQLite database queries.</li>
  <li>The ProgressDialog class has been deprecated. ProgressBars have now been added.</li>
  <li>The replace method may not be available in a hash table; put().</li>
</ol>
2018.03.03

<ol>
  <li>Attempt socket connections regardless of WiFi availability. Insight.</li>
  <li>Automatically import rosemary-ipv4.tilaa.cloud:4710 on new installations.</li>
  <li>Corrected local echo behavior.</li>
  <li>Echo Fire, if possible!</li>
  <li>Fire Digest Key and Salt fields may not be empty. Corrected.</li>
  <li>Host translation must be performed before every socket connection attempt.</li>
  <li>Large-area congestion-control mutex.</li>
  <li>Partition messages over UDP links into 576-byte datagrams.</li>
  <li>Provide the HMAC algorithm during identity distribution.</li>
  <li>The Call widget should only be enabled if a network is present.</li>

    <li>Time-tag SmokeStack-bound messages before departure. Otherwise,
SmokeStack instances will discard expired messages.</li>
    <li>Wonderful documentation.</li>
</ol>
2018.02.20

<ol>
    <li>Abort simultaneous calls.</li>
    <li>Inspect WiFi availability before attempting socket connections.</li>
    <li>New Chat background color.</li>
    <li>Prepare calling public-key pairs without locking calling queue
object.</li>
    <li>Replaced integers with long integers where necessary.</li>
    <li>Set Fire height to 60% of screen height.</li>
</ol>
2018.02.10

<ol>
    <li>Allow empty Fire participant names.</li>
    <li>Allow purging of neighbor queues.</li>
    <li>Automatic, oscillatory EPKS.</li>
    <li>Avoid non-essential operations if network channels are not
available.</li>
    <li>Depict corrupted database entries.</li>
    <li>Enabled Nagle's algorithm.</li>
    <li>Introduced McEliece-Fujisaki via Bouncy Castle. Cross-communications
supported.</li>
    <li>Minimum password length set to one character.</li>
    <li>New Fire key generation. Destination tags are required for
SmokeStack.</li>
    <li>Participant name changes should be reflected in the Chat activity.</li>
    <li>Trim Channel, Digest Key, and Salt values on Fire.</li>
</ol>
2018.01.05

<ol>
    <li>Fire, or, group communications. Compatible with Spot-On.</li>
    <li>Increased lane widths to 8 MiB.</li>
</ol>
2017.08.19

<ol>
    <li>Set a non-zero SO_TIMEOUT as some devices do not unblock socket reads
after sockets are closed.</li>
</ol>
2017.07.20

<ol>
    <li>AndroidManifest.xml was missing WakeLock permissions.</li>
    <li>Do not attempt to send duplicate data.</li>
    <li>Do not specify timeouts in socket reads as separate threads are
responsible for socket reads.</li>
    <li>Removed all Thread.sleep() instances.</li>
    <li>Replaced StringBuilder Neighbor member with StringBuffer. StringBuffer
is thread-safe.</li>
    <li>Signed release.</li>
    <li>WiFi lock.</li>
</ol>
2017.07.16

<ol>
    <li>Less activity on disconnected neighbors.</li>
</ol>

2017.07.09

<ol>
  <li>Detect existing key pairs in writeParticipant().</li>
  <li>Smaller database transaction areas.</li>
</ol>
2017.07.07

<ol>
  <li>Do not automatically purge the temporary identity for offline message
retrieval unless some inactive period has elapsed.</li>
  <li>Issue SQLiteDatabase.update() whenever a participant is added. This will
allow for replacing of participant names without removal of existing
data.</li>
  <li>SmokeStack as a private public key repository.</li>
</ol>

split.bash

https://github.com/textbrowser/smoke/blob/master/Scripts/split.bash

```bash
#split.bash
#!/bin/bash
# Alexis Megas, 2020.
# Replace contents of sizes with relevant values.
declare -a sizes=(4200090
                  4727417
                  4703426
                  4849242
                  4842605)
declare -i j=0
declare -i total=0
for i in ${sizes[@]}
do
    j=$j+1
    dd bs=1 count=$i if=output of=file$j skip=$total status='progress'
    echo "SHA-256: " $(sha256sum file$j 2> /dev/null)
    total=$i+$total
done
```


.gitignore

https://github.com/textbrowser/smoke/blob/master/Smoke/.gitignore

```
*.iml
.gradle
/local.properties
/.idea/workspace.xml
/.idea/libraries
.DS_Store
/build
/captures
.externalNativeBuild
```


build.gradle

https://github.com/textbrowser/smoke/blob/master/Smoke/build.gradle

```
// Top-level build file where you can add configuration options common to all
sub-projects/modules.
```

```
buildscript {
    repositories {
        google()
        jcenter()
    }
    dependencies {
        classpath 'com.android.tools.build:gradle:4.1.0'

        // NOTE: Do not place your application dependencies here; they belong
        // in the individual module build.gradle files.
    }
}

allprojects {
    repositories {
        jcenter()
        google()
    }
}

task clean(type: Delete) {
    delete rootProject.buildDir
}
```

gradle.properties

https://github.com/textbrowser/smoke/blob/master/Smoke/gradle.properties

```
# Project-wide Gradle settings.

# IDE (e.g. Android Studio) users:
# Gradle settings configured through the IDE *will override*
# any settings specified in this file.

# For more details on how to configure your build environment visit
# http://www.gradle.org/docs/current/userguide/build_environment.html

# Specifies the JVM arguments used for the daemon process.
# The setting is particularly useful for tweaking memory settings.


# When configured, Gradle will run in incubating parallel mode.
# This option should only be used with decoupled projects. More details, visit
#
http://www.gradle.org/docs/current/userguide/multi_project_builds.html#sec:dec
oupled_projects
# org.gradle.parallel=true
```

gradlew


```bash
#!/usr/bin/env bash

##############################################################################
##
##  Gradle start up script for UN*X
##
##############################################################################

# Add default JVM options here. You can also use JAVA_OPTS and GRADLE_OPTS to
# pass JVM options to this script.
DEFAULT_JVM_OPTS=""

APP_NAME="Gradle"
APP_BASE_NAME=`basename "$0"`

# Use the maximum available, or set MAX_FD != -1 to use that value.
MAX_FD="maximum"

warn ( ) {
    echo "$*"
}

die ( ) {
    echo
    echo "$*"
    echo
    exit 1
}

# OS specific support (must be 'true' or 'false').
cygwin=false
msys=false
darwin=false
case "`uname`" in
  CYGWIN* )
    cygwin=true
    ;;
  Darwin* )
    darwin=true
    ;;
  MINGW* )
    msys=true
    ;;
esac

# Attempt to set APP_HOME
# Resolve links: $0 may be a link
PRG="$0"
# Need this for relative symlinks.
while [ -h "$PRG" ] ; do
    ls=`ls -ld "$PRG"`
    link=`expr "$ls" : '.*-> \(.*\)$'`
    if expr "$link" : '/.*' > /dev/null; then
        PRG="$link"
    else
        PRG=`dirname "$PRG"`"/$link"
    fi
done
SAVED="`pwd`"
cd "`dirname \"$PRG\"`/" >/dev/null
```

```
APP_HOME="`pwd -P`"
cd "$SAVED" >/dev/null

CLASSPATH=$APP_HOME/gradle/wrapper/gradle-wrapper.jar

# Determine the Java command to use to start the JVM.
if [ -n "$JAVA_HOME" ] ; then
    if [ -x "$JAVA_HOME/jre/sh/java" ] ; then
        # IBM's JDK on AIX uses strange locations for the executables
        JAVACMD="$JAVA_HOME/jre/sh/java"
    else
        JAVACMD="$JAVA_HOME/bin/java"
    fi
    if [ ! -x "$JAVACMD" ] ; then
        die "ERROR: JAVA_HOME is set to an invalid directory: $JAVA_HOME

Please set the JAVA_HOME variable in your environment to match the
location of your Java installation."
    fi
else
    JAVACMD="java"
    which java >/dev/null 2>&1 || die "ERROR: JAVA_HOME is not set and no
'java' command could be found in your PATH.

Please set the JAVA_HOME variable in your environment to match the
location of your Java installation."
fi

# Increase the maximum file descriptors if we can.
if [ "$cygwin" = "false" -a "$darwin" = "false" ] ; then
    MAX_FD_LIMIT=`ulimit -H -n`
    if [ $? -eq 0 ] ; then
        if [ "$MAX_FD" = "maximum" -o "$MAX_FD" = "max" ] ; then
            MAX_FD="$MAX_FD_LIMIT"
        fi
        ulimit -n $MAX_FD
        if [ $? -ne 0 ] ; then
            warn "Could not set maximum file descriptor limit: $MAX_FD"
        fi
    else
        warn "Could not query maximum file descriptor limit: $MAX_FD_LIMIT"
    fi
fi

# For Darwin, add options to specify how the application appears in the dock
if $darwin; then
    GRADLE_OPTS="$GRADLE_OPTS \"-Xdock:name=$APP_NAME\" \"-
Xdock:icon=$APP_HOME/media/gradle.icns\""
fi

# For Cygwin, switch paths to Windows format before running java
if $cygwin ; then
    APP_HOME=`cygpath --path --mixed "$APP_HOME"`
    CLASSPATH=`cygpath --path --mixed "$CLASSPATH"`
    JAVACMD=`cygpath --unix "$JAVACMD"`

    # We build the pattern for arguments to be converted via cygpath
    ROOTDIRSRAW=`find -L / -maxdepth 1 -mindepth 1 -type d 2>/dev/null`
    SEP=""
    for dir in $ROOTDIRSRAW ; do
        ROOTDIRS="$ROOTDIRS$SEP$dir"
        SEP="|"
    done
```

```sh
    OURCYGPATTERN="(^($ROOTDIRS))"
    # Add a user-defined pattern to the cygpath arguments
    if [ "$GRADLE_CYGPATTERN" != "" ] ; then
        OURCYGPATTERN="$OURCYGPATTERN|($GRADLE_CYGPATTERN)"
    fi
    # Now convert the arguments - kludge to limit ourselves to /bin/sh
    i=0
    for arg in "$@" ; do
        CHECK=`echo "$arg"|egrep -c "$OURCYGPATTERN" -`
        CHECK2=`echo "$arg"|egrep -c "^-"`                                  ### Determine if an option

        if [ $CHECK -ne 0 ] && [ $CHECK2 -eq 0 ] ; then                     ### Added a condition
            eval `echo args$i`=`cygpath --path --ignore --mixed "$arg"`
        else
            eval `echo args$i`="\"$arg\""
        fi
        i=$((i+1))
    done
    case $i in
        (0) set -- ;;
        (1) set -- "$args0" ;;
        (2) set -- "$args0" "$args1" ;;
        (3) set -- "$args0" "$args1" "$args2" ;;
        (4) set -- "$args0" "$args1" "$args2" "$args3" ;;
        (5) set -- "$args0" "$args1" "$args2" "$args3" "$args4" ;;
        (6) set -- "$args0" "$args1" "$args2" "$args3" "$args4" "$args5" ;;
        (7) set -- "$args0" "$args1" "$args2" "$args3" "$args4" "$args5" "$args6" ;;
        (8) set -- "$args0" "$args1" "$args2" "$args3" "$args4" "$args5" "$args6" "$args7" ;;
        (9) set -- "$args0" "$args1" "$args2" "$args3" "$args4" "$args5" "$args6" "$args7" "$args8" ;;
    esac
fi

# Split up the JVM_OPTS And GRADLE_OPTS values into an array, following the
# shell quoting and substitution rules
function splitJvmOpts() {
    JVM_OPTS=("$@")
}
eval splitJvmOpts $DEFAULT_JVM_OPTS $JAVA_OPTS $GRADLE_OPTS
JVM_OPTS[${#JVM_OPTS[*]}]="-Dorg.gradle.appname=$APP_BASE_NAME"

exec "$JAVACMD" "${JVM_OPTS[@]}" -classpath "$CLASSPATH" org.gradle.wrapper.GradleWrapperMain "$@"
```

gradlew.bat


```bat
@if "%DEBUG%" == "" @echo off
@rem
##########################################################################
@rem
@rem  Gradle startup script for Windows
@rem
@rem
##########################################################################

@rem Set local scope for the variables with windows NT shell
if "%OS%"=="Windows_NT" setlocal

@rem Add default JVM options here. You can also use JAVA_OPTS and GRADLE_OPTS
to pass JVM options to this script.
set DEFAULT_JVM_OPTS=

set DIRNAME=%~dp0
if "%DIRNAME%" == "" set DIRNAME=.
set APP_BASE_NAME=%~n0
set APP_HOME=%DIRNAME%

@rem Find java.exe
if defined JAVA_HOME goto findJavaFromJavaHome

set JAVA_EXE=java.exe
%JAVA_EXE% -version >NUL 2>&1
if "%ERRORLEVEL%" == "0" goto init

echo.
echo ERROR: JAVA_HOME is not set and no 'java' command could be found in your
PATH.
echo.
echo Please set the JAVA_HOME variable in your environment to match the
echo location of your Java installation.

goto fail

:findJavaFromJavaHome
set JAVA_HOME=%JAVA_HOME:"=%
set JAVA_EXE=%JAVA_HOME%/bin/java.exe

if exist "%JAVA_EXE%" goto init

echo.
echo ERROR: JAVA_HOME is set to an invalid directory: %JAVA_HOME%
echo.
echo Please set the JAVA_HOME variable in your environment to match the
echo location of your Java installation.

goto fail

:init
@rem Get command-line arguments, handling Windowz variants

if not "%OS%" == "Windows_NT" goto win9xME_args
if "%@eval[2+2]" == "4" goto 4NT_args

:win9xME_args
@rem Slurp the command line arguments.
set CMD_LINE_ARGS=
```

```
set _SKIP=2

:win9xME_args_slurp
if "x%~1" == "x" goto execute

set CMD_LINE_ARGS=%*
goto execute

:4NT_args
@rem Get arguments from the 4NT Shell from JP Software
set CMD_LINE_ARGS=%$

:execute
@rem Setup the command line

set CLASSPATH=%APP_HOME%\gradle\wrapper\gradle-wrapper.jar

@rem Execute Gradle
"%JAVA_EXE%" %DEFAULT_JVM_OPTS% %JAVA_OPTS% %GRADLE_OPTS% "-
Dorg.gradle.appname=%APP_BASE_NAME%" -classpath "%CLASSPATH%"
org.gradle.wrapper.GradleWrapperMain %CMD_LINE_ARGS%

:end
@rem End local scope for the variables with windows NT shell
if "%ERRORLEVEL%"=="0" goto mainEnd

:fail
rem Set variable GRADLE_EXIT_CONSOLE if you need the _script_ return code
instead of
rem the _cmd.exe /c_ return code!
if  not "" == "%GRADLE_EXIT_CONSOLE%" exit 1
exit /b 1

:mainEnd
if "%OS%"=="Windows_NT" endlocal

:omega
```

settings.gradle

https://github.com/textbrowser/smoke/blob/master/Smoke/settings.gradle
```
include ':app'
```

.gitignore

https://github.com/textbrowser/smoke/blob/master/Smoke/app/.gitignore
```
/build
```

build.gradle

https://github.com/textbrowser/smoke/blob/master/Smoke/app/build.gradle
```
// Top-level build file where you can add configuration options common to all
sub-projects/modules.

buildscript {
    repositories {
```

```
    google()
    jcenter()
}
dependencies {
    classpath 'com.android.tools.build:gradle:4.1.0'

    // NOTE: Do not place your application dependencies here; they belong
    // in the individual module build.gradle files.
}
}

allprojects {
    repositories {
        jcenter()
        google()
    }
}

task clean(type: Delete) {
    delete rootProject.buildDir
}
```

proguard-rules.pro

https://github.com/textbrowser/smoke/blob/master/Smoke/app/proguard-rules.pro

```
# Add project specific ProGuard rules here.
# By default, the flags in this file are appended to flags specified
# in /home/monster/Android/Sdk/tools/proguard/proguard-android.txt
# You can edit the include path and order by changing the proguardFiles
# directive in build.gradle.
#
# For more details, see
#   http://developer.android.com/guide/developing/tools/proguard.html

# Add any project specific keep options here:

# If your project uses WebView with JS, uncomment the following
# and specify the fully qualified class name to the JavaScript interface
# class:
#-keepclassmembers class fqcn.of.javascript.interface.for.webview {
#   public *;
#}
```

Libs

https://github.com/textbrowser/smoke/tree/master/Smoke/app/libs
```
15.11.2020  23:01           6.031.520 bcprov-ext-jdk15on-167.jar
15.11.2020  23:01           9.715.254 bcprov-jdk15on-167.tar.gz
```

AndroidManifest.xml


```xml
<?xml version="1.0" encoding="utf-8"?>
<manifest xmlns:android="http://schemas.android.com/apk/res/android"
    package="org.purple.smoke">

    <uses-permission android:name="android.permission.ACCESS_NETWORK_STATE" />
    <uses-permission android:name="android.permission.INTERNET" />
    <uses-permission android:name="android.permission.READ_EXTERNAL_STORAGE"
/>
    <uses-permission android:name="android.permission.WAKE_LOCK" />
    <uses-permission android:name="android.permission.WRITE_EXTERNAL_STORAGE"
/>
    <application
        android:allowBackup="true"
        android:icon="@drawable/smoke"
        android:label="@string/app_name"
        android:name=".Smoke"
        android:supportsRtl="true"
        android:theme="@style/AppTheme">
        <activity
            android:name=".Authenticate"
            android:noHistory="true" />
        <activity
            android:name=".Chat"
            android:noHistory="true"
          android:theme="@style/AppTheme.NoActionBar" />
        <activity
            android:name=".Fire"
            android:noHistory="true" />
        <activity
            android:name=".MemberChat"
            android:noHistory="false"
          android:theme="@style/AppTheme.NoActionBar" />
        <activity
            android:name=".Settings"
            android:label="@string/app_name"
            android:noHistory="true">
            <intent-filter>
                <action android:name="android.intent.action.MAIN" />
                <category android:name="android.intent.category.LAUNCHER" />
            </intent-filter>
        </activity>
      <activity
            android:name=".Smokescreen"
            android:noHistory="false" />
      <activity
            android:name=".Steam"
            android:noHistory="false" />
    <service android:enabled="true"
            android:exported="false"
            android:name=".SmokeService" />
    </application>
</manifest>
```

```java
/* About.java -
https://github.com/textbrowser/smoke/blob/master/Smoke/app/src/main/java/org/purple/smoke/About.java
** Copyright (c) Alexis Megas.
** All rights reserved.
**
** Redistribution and use in source and binary forms, with or without
** modification, are permitted provided that the following conditions
** are met:
** 1. Redistributions of source code must retain the above copyright
**    notice, this list of conditions and the following disclaimer.
** 2. Redistributions in binary form must reproduce the above copyright
**    notice, this list of conditions and the following disclaimer in the
**    documentation and/or other materials provided with the distribution.
** 3. The name of the author may not be used to endorse or promote products
**    derived from Smoke without specific prior written permission.
**
** SMOKE IS PROVIDED BY THE AUTHOR ``AS IS'' AND ANY EXPRESS OR
** IMPLIED WARRANTIES, INCLUDING, BUT NOT LIMITED TO, THE IMPLIED WARRANTIES
** OF MERCHANTABILITY AND FITNESS FOR A PARTICULAR PURPOSE ARE DISCLAIMED.
** IN NO EVENT SHALL THE AUTHOR BE LIABLE FOR ANY DIRECT, INDIRECT,
** INCIDENTAL, SPECIAL, EXEMPLARY, OR CONSEQUENTIAL DAMAGES (INCLUDING, BUT
** NOT LIMITED TO, PROCUREMENT OF SUBSTITUTE GOODS OR SERVICES; LOSS OF USE,
** DATA, OR PROFITS; OR BUSINESS INTERRUPTION) HOWEVER CAUSED AND ON ANY
** THEORY OF LIABILITY, WHETHER IN CONTRACT, STRICT LIABILITY, OR TORT
** (INCLUDING NEGLIGENCE OR OTHERWISE) ARISING IN ANY WAY OUT OF THE USE OF
** SMOKE, EVEN IF ADVISED OF THE POSSIBILITY OF SUCH DAMAGE.
*/

package org.purple.smoke;

import android.os.Build;
import java.text.SimpleDateFormat;
import java.util.Date;
import java.util.Locale;
import java.util.TimeZone;
import org.bouncycastle.jce.provider.BouncyCastleProvider;

public class About
{
    private final static SimpleDateFormat s_simpleDateFormat = new
        SimpleDateFormat("yyyy-MM-dd h:mm:ss", Locale.getDefault());
    public static String s_about = "";

    private About()
    {
    }

    public static synchronized String about()
    {
        try
        {
            if(s_about.isEmpty())
            {
                // The version must agree with Smoke/app/build.gradle.

                s_simpleDateFormat.setTimeZone(TimeZone.getTimeZone("UTC"));
                s_about = "Bouncy Castle Version " +
                    new BouncyCastleProvider().getVersion() +
                    "\nSmoke Version 2020.11.15 Solid Smoke " +
                    (BuildConfig.DEBUG ? "(Debug) " : "(Release)") +
                    "\nBuild Date " +
```

```java
                        s_simpleDateFormat.
                        format(new Date(BuildConfig.BUILD_TIME)) +
                        " UTC\nAndroid " + Build.VERSION.RELEASE +
                        (Build.VERSION.SDK_INT < Build.VERSION_CODES.LOLLIPOP ?
                         "\nAndroid version not supported." : "");
                }
        }
        catch(Exception exception)
        {
            if(s_about.isEmpty())
                s_about = "Smoke Version 2020.11.15 Solid Smoke";
        }

        return s_about;
    }
}


/* Authenticate.java –
```



```java
package org.purple.smoke;

import android.Manifest;
import android.content.DialogInterface;
import android.content.Intent;
import android.os.Bundle;
import android.support.v4.app.ActivityCompat;
import android.support.v7.app.AppCompatActivity;
import android.util.Base64;
import android.view.Menu;
import android.view.MenuItem;
import android.view.View;
import android.view.WindowManager;
import android.widget.Button;
```

```java
import android.widget.ProgressBar;
import android.widget.TextView;
import java.util.Arrays;
import javax.crypto.SecretKey;

public class Authenticate extends AppCompatActivity
{
    private Database m_databaseHelper = null;
    private final static Cryptography s_cryptography =
        Cryptography.getInstance();

    private void prepareForegroundService()
    {
        if(m_databaseHelper.
          readSetting(null, "foreground_service").equals("false"))
            SmokeService.stopForegroundTask(getApplicationContext());
        else
            SmokeService.startForegroundTask(getApplicationContext());
    }

    private void prepareListeners()
    {
        final Button button1 = (Button) findViewById(R.id.authenticate);

        button1.setOnClickListener(new View.OnClickListener()
        {
            public void onClick(View view)
            {
                if(Authenticate.this.isFinishing())
                    return;

                byte encryptionSalt[] = Base64.decode
                    (m_databaseHelper.
                     readSetting(null, "encryptionSalt").getBytes(),
                     Base64.DEFAULT);
                final TextView textView1 = (TextView) findViewById
                    (R.id.password);

                textView1.setSelectAllOnFocus(true);

                if(encryptionSalt == null)
                {
                    Miscellaneous.showErrorDialog
                        (Authenticate.this,
                         "The encryption salt value is zero. System failure.");
                    textView1.setText("");
                    textView1.requestFocus();
                    return;
                }

                byte macSalt[] = Base64.decode
                    (m_databaseHelper.readSetting(null, "macSalt").getBytes(),
                     Base64.DEFAULT);

                if(macSalt == null)
                {
                    Miscellaneous.showErrorDialog
                        (Authenticate.this,
                         "The mac salt value is zero. System failure.");
                    textView1.setText("");
                    textView1.requestFocus();
                    return;
                }
```

```java
byte saltedPassword[] = Cryptography.sha512
    (textView1.getText().toString().getBytes(),
     encryptionSalt,
     macSalt);

if(saltedPassword == null)
{
    Miscellaneous.showErrorDialog
        (Authenticate.this,
         "An error occurred with sha512(). System failure.");
    textView1.setText("");
    textView1.requestFocus();
    return;
}

int iterationCount = 1000;

try
{
    iterationCount = Integer.parseInt
        (m_databaseHelper.
         readSetting(null, "iterationCount"));
}
catch(Exception exception)
{
    iterationCount = -1;
}

if(iterationCount == -1)
{
    Miscellaneous.showErrorDialog
        (Authenticate.this,
         "Invalid iteration count. System failure.");
    textView1.setText("");
    textView1.requestFocus();
    return;
}

int keyDerivationFunction = 1; // PBKDF2

try
{
    keyDerivationFunction = Integer.parseInt
        (m_databaseHelper.
         readSetting(null, "keyDerivationFunction"));
}
catch(Exception exception)
{
    keyDerivationFunction = 1;
}

if(!Cryptography.memcmp(m_databaseHelper.
                        readSetting(null, "saltedPassword").
                        getBytes(),
                        Base64.encode(saltedPassword,
                                      Base64.DEFAULT)))
{
    Miscellaneous.showErrorDialog
        (Authenticate.this,
         "Incorrect password. Please try again.");
    textView1.setText("");
    textView1.requestFocus();
```

```java
            return;
        }

        final ProgressBar bar = (ProgressBar) findViewById
            (R.id.progress_bar);

        bar.setIndeterminate(true);
        bar.setVisibility(ProgressBar.VISIBLE);
        getWindow().setFlags
            (WindowManager.LayoutParams.FLAG_NOT_TOUCHABLE,
             WindowManager.LayoutParams.FLAG_NOT_TOUCHABLE);
        Miscellaneous.enableChildren
            (findViewById(R.id.relative_layout), false);

        class SingleShot implements Runnable
        {
            private String m_error = "";
            private String m_password = "";
            private byte m_encryptionSalt[] = null;
            private byte m_macSalt[] = null;
            private int m_iterationCount = 1000;
            private int m_keyDerivationFunction = 1; // PBKDF2

            SingleShot(String password,
                       byte encryptionSalt[],
                       byte macSalt[],
                       int iterationCount,
                       int keyDerivationFunction)
            {
                m_encryptionSalt = encryptionSalt;
                m_iterationCount = iterationCount;
                m_keyDerivationFunction = keyDerivationFunction;
                m_macSalt = macSalt;
                m_password = password;
            }

            @Override
            public void run()
            {
                SecretKey encryptionKey = null;
                SecretKey macKey = null;

                try
                {
                    m_databaseHelper.cleanDanglingOutboundQueued();
                    m_databaseHelper.cleanDanglingParticipants();
                    m_databaseHelper.cleanDanglingSteams();
                    encryptionKey = Cryptography.generateEncryptionKey
                        (m_encryptionSalt,
                         m_password.toCharArray(),
                         m_iterationCount,
                         m_keyDerivationFunction);
                    macKey = Cryptography.generateMacKey
                        (m_macSalt,
                         m_password.toCharArray(),
                         m_iterationCount,
                         m_keyDerivationFunction);

                    if(encryptionKey != null && macKey != null)
                    {
                        s_cryptography.setEncryptionKey(encryptionKey);
                        s_cryptography.setMacKey(macKey);
```

```java
            String algorithm = "";
            byte ozoneKeyStream[] = Base64.decode
                (m_databaseHelper.
                 readSetting(s_cryptography,
                            "ozone_address_stream").
                            getBytes(), Base64.DEFAULT);
            byte privateBytes[] = Base64.decode
                (m_databaseHelper.
                 readSetting(s_cryptography,
                            "pki_chat_encryption_" +
                            "private_key").
                getBytes(), Base64.DEFAULT);
            byte publicBytes[] = Base64.decode
                (m_databaseHelper.
                 readSetting(s_cryptography,
                            "pki_chat_encryption_" +
                            "public_key").
                getBytes(), Base64.DEFAULT);

            algorithm = m_databaseHelper.
                readSetting(s_cryptography,
                            "pki_chat_encryption_" +
                            "algorithm");
            s_cryptography.
                setChatEncryptionPublicKeyAlgorithm
                (algorithm);
            s_cryptography.setChatEncryptionPublicKeyPair
                (algorithm, privateBytes, publicBytes);
            privateBytes = Base64.decode
                (m_databaseHelper.
                 readSetting(s_cryptography,
                            "pki_chat_signature_" +
                            "private_key").
                getBytes(), Base64.DEFAULT);
            publicBytes = Base64.decode
                (m_databaseHelper.
                 readSetting(s_cryptography,
                            "pki_chat_signature_" +
                            "public_key").
                getBytes(), Base64.DEFAULT);
            algorithm = m_databaseHelper.
                readSetting(s_cryptography,
                            "pki_chat_signature_" +
                            "algorithm");
            s_cryptography.setChatSignaturePublicKeyPair
                (algorithm, privateBytes, publicBytes);

            if(ozoneKeyStream != null &&
               ozoneKeyStream.length == Cryptography.
               CIPHER_HASH_KEYS_LENGTH)
            {
                s_cryptography.setOzoneEncryptionKey
                    (Arrays.copyOfRange(ozoneKeyStream,
                                        0,
                                        Cryptography.
                                        CIPHER_KEY_LENGTH));
                s_cryptography.setOzoneMacKey
                    (Arrays.copyOfRange(ozoneKeyStream,
                                        Cryptography.
                                        CIPHER_KEY_LENGTH,
                                        ozoneKeyStream.
                                        length));
            }
```

```java
            else
            {
                s_cryptography.setOzoneEncryptionKey(null);
                s_cryptography.setOzoneMacKey(null);
            }

            boolean e1 = s_cryptography.
                prepareSipHashIds
                (m_databaseHelper.
                  readSetting(s_cryptography, "alias"));
            boolean e2 = s_cryptography.
                prepareSipHashKeys();

            if(!e1 || !e2 ||
               s_cryptography.
               chatEncryptionKeyPair() == null ||
               s_cryptography.
               chatSignatureKeyPair() == null)
            {
               if(!e1)
                  m_error +=
                     "prepareSipHashIds() failure ";

               if(!e2)
                  m_error += "prepareSipHashKeys() " +
                     "failure ";

               if(s_cryptography.
                  chatEncryptionKeyPair() == null)
                  m_error += "chatEncryptionKeyPair() " +
                     "returned zero ";

               if(s_cryptography.
                  chatSignatureKeyPair() == null)
                  m_error += "chatSignatureKeyPair() " +
                     "return zero ";

               m_error = m_error.trim();
               s_cryptography.reset();
            }
          }
          else
          {
             if(encryptionKey == null)
                m_error = "generateEncryptionKey() " +
                   "failure";
             else
                m_error = "generateMacKey() failure";

             s_cryptography.reset();
          }
        }
      catch(Exception exception)
      {
          m_error = exception.getMessage().toLowerCase().
             trim();
          s_cryptography.reset();
      }

      Authenticate.this.runOnUiThread(new Runnable()
      {
          @Override
          public void run()
```

```java
                            {
                try
                {
                    bar.setVisibility(ProgressBar.INVISIBLE);
                    getWindow().clearFlags
                        (WindowManager.LayoutParams.
                         FLAG_NOT_TOUCHABLE);
                    Miscellaneous.enableChildren
                        (findViewById(R.id.relative_layout),
                         true);

                    if(!m_error.isEmpty())
                        Miscellaneous.showErrorDialog
                            (Authenticate.this,
                             "An error (" + m_error +
                             ") occurred while " +
                             "generating the confidential " +
                             "data.");
                    else
                    {
                        m_databaseHelper.cleanNeighborStatistics
                            (s_cryptography);
                        Kernel.getInstance();
                        State.getInstance().
                            populateParticipants();
                        State.getInstance().
                            setAuthenticated(true);

                        /*
                        ** Disable some widgets.
                        */

                        button1.setEnabled(false);
                        textView1.setEnabled(false);
                        textView1.setText("");

                        String str = m_databaseHelper.
                            readSetting(null, "lastActivity");

                        switch(str)
                        {
                        case "Chat":
                            showChatActivity();
                            break;
                        case "Fire":
                            showFireActivity();
                            break;
                        case "MemberChat":
                            String oid =
                                m_databaseHelper.
                                readSetting(s_cryptography,
                                            "member_chat_oid");
                            String sipHashId =
                                m_databaseHelper.
                                readSetting(s_cryptography,
                                            "member_chat_" +
                                            "siphash_id");

                            if(m_databaseHelper.
                               containsParticipant
                               (s_cryptography,
                               sipHashId))
                            {
```

```java
                                    State.getInstance().setString
                                        ("member_chat_oid", oid);
                                    State.getInstance().setString
                                        ("member_chat_siphash_id",
                                         sipHashId);
                                    showMemberChatActivity();
                                }
                                else
                                {
                                    m_databaseHelper.writeSetting
                                        (s_cryptography,
                                         "member_chat_oid",
                                         "");
                                    m_databaseHelper.writeSetting
                                        (s_cryptography,
                                         "member_chat_siphash_id",
                                         "");
                                }

                                break;
                            case "Settings":
                                showSettingsActivity();
                                break;
                            case "Steam":
                                showSteamActivity();
                                break;
                            default:
                                break;
                            }
                        }
                    }
                    catch(Exception exception)
                    {
                    }
                }
            });

                m_password = "";
            }
        }

        Thread thread = new Thread
            (new SingleShot(textView1.getText().toString(),
                            encryptionSalt,
                            macSalt,
                            iterationCount,
                            keyDerivationFunction));

        thread.start();
        }
    });

    final DialogInterface.OnCancelListener listener1 =
        new DialogInterface.OnCancelListener()
        {
            public void onCancel(DialogInterface dialog)
            {
                if(State.getInstance().getString("dialog_accepted").
                    equals("true"))
                {
                    State.getInstance().reset();
                    m_databaseHelper.resetAndDrop();
                    s_cryptography.reset();
```

```java
                    Intent intent = new Intent
                        (Authenticate.this, Settings.class);

                    startActivity(intent);
                    finish();
                }
            }
        };

    Button button2 = (Button) findViewById(R.id.reset);

    button2.setOnClickListener(new View.OnClickListener()
    {
        public void onClick(View view)
        {
            Miscellaneous.showPromptDialog(Authenticate.this,
                                        listener1,
                                        "Are you sure that you " +
                                        "wish to reset Smoke? All " +
                                        "of the data will be removed.");
        }
    });
}

private void showChatActivity()
{
    Intent intent = new Intent(Authenticate.this, Chat.class);

    startActivity(intent);
    finish();
}

private void showFireActivity()
{
    Intent intent = new Intent(Authenticate.this, Fire.class);

    startActivity(intent);
    finish();
}

private void showMemberChatActivity()
{
    Intent intent = new Intent(Authenticate.this, MemberChat.class);

    startActivity(intent);
    finish();
}

private void showSettingsActivity()
{
    Intent intent = new Intent(Authenticate.this, Settings.class);

    startActivity(intent);
    finish();
}

private void showSmokescreenActivity()
{
    Intent intent = new Intent(Authenticate.this, Smokescreen.class);

    startActivity(intent);
    finish();
```

```java
    }

    private void showSteamActivity()
    {
        Intent intent = new Intent(Authenticate.this, Steam.class);

        startActivity(intent);
        finish();
    }

    @Override
    protected void onCreate(Bundle savedInstanceState)
    {
        super.onCreate(savedInstanceState);
        m_databaseHelper = Database.getInstance(getApplicationContext());
        setContentView(R.layout.activity_authenticate);

        try
        {
            getSupportActionBar().setTitle("Smoke | Authenticate");
        }
        catch(Exception exception)
        {
        }

        State.getInstance().setNeighborsEcho
            (m_databaseHelper.readSetting(null,
                                "neighbors_echo").equals("true"));
        prepareForegroundService();
        prepareListeners();

        boolean isAuthenticated = State.getInstance().isAuthenticated();
        Button button1 = (Button) findViewById(R.id.authenticate);

        button1.setEnabled(!isAuthenticated);

        TextView textView1 = (TextView) findViewById(R.id.password);

        textView1.setEnabled(!isAuthenticated);

        if(!isAuthenticated)
            ActivityCompat.requestPermissions(this, new String[]
            {
                Manifest.permission.WRITE_EXTERNAL_STORAGE
            }, 1);
    }

    @Override
    public boolean onCreateOptionsMenu(Menu menu)
    {
        getMenuInflater().inflate(R.menu.authenticate_menu, menu);
        return true;
    }

    @Override
    public boolean onOptionsItemSelected(MenuItem menuItem)
    {
        int groupId = menuItem.getGroupId();
        int itemId = menuItem.getItemId();

        if(groupId == Menu.NONE)
            switch(itemId)
            {
```

```java
                case R.id.action_chat:
                    m_databaseHelper.writeSetting(null, "lastActivity", "Chat");
                    showChatActivity();
                    return true;
                case R.id.action_exit:
                    Smoke.exit(Authenticate.this);
                    return true;
                case R.id.action_fire:
                    m_databaseHelper.writeSetting(null, "lastActivity", "Fire");
                    showFireActivity();
                    return true;
                case R.id.action_settings:
                    m_databaseHelper.writeSetting(null, "lastActivity", "Settings");
                    showSettingsActivity();
                    return true;
                case R.id.action_smokescreen:
                    showSmokescreenActivity();
                    return true;
                case R.id.action_steam:
                    m_databaseHelper.writeSetting(null, "lastActivity", "Steam");
                    showSteamActivity();
                    return true;
                default:
                    break;
            }
        else
        {
            String sipHashId = menuItem.getTitle().toString();
            int indexOf = sipHashId.indexOf("(");

            if(indexOf >= 0)
                sipHashId = sipHashId.substring(indexOf + 1).replace(")", "");

            sipHashId = Miscellaneous.prepareSipHashId(sipHashId);
            State.getInstance().setString
                ("member_chat_oid", String.valueOf(itemId));
            State.getInstance().setString
                ("member_chat_siphash_id", sipHashId);
            m_databaseHelper.writeSetting
                (null, "lastActivity", "MemberChat");
            m_databaseHelper.writeSetting
                (s_cryptography, "member_chat_oid", String.valueOf(itemId));
            m_databaseHelper.writeSetting
                (s_cryptography, "member_chat_siphash_id", sipHashId);
            showMemberChatActivity();
        }

        return super.onOptionsItemSelected(menuItem);
    }


    @Override
    public boolean onPrepareOptionsMenu(Menu menu)
    {
        boolean isAuthenticated = State.getInstance().isAuthenticated();

        if(!m_databaseHelper.accountPrepared())
            /*
            ** The database may have been modified or removed.
            */

            isAuthenticated = true;

        menu.findItem(R.id.action_chat).setEnabled(isAuthenticated);
```

```java
        menu.findItem(R.id.action_fire).setEnabled(isAuthenticated);
        menu.findItem(R.id.action_settings).setEnabled(isAuthenticated);
        menu.findItem(R.id.action_smokescreen).setEnabled(isAuthenticated);
        menu.findItem(R.id.action_steam).setEnabled(isAuthenticated);
        Miscellaneous.addMembersToMenu(menu, 6, 150);
        return true;
    }
}
```

/* Chat.java –

**https://github.com/textbrowser/smoke/blob/master/Smoke/app/src/main/java/org/p
urple/smoke/Chat.java**

```java
** Copyright (c) Alexis Megas.
** All rights reserved.
**
** Redistribution and use in source and binary forms, with or without
** modification, are permitted provided that the following conditions
** are met:
** 1. Redistributions of source code must retain the above copyright
**    notice, this list of conditions and the following disclaimer.
** 2. Redistributions in binary form must reproduce the above copyright
**    notice, this list of conditions and the following disclaimer in the
**    documentation and/or other materials provided with the distribution.
** 3. The name of the author may not be used to endorse or promote products
**    derived from Smoke without specific prior written permission.
**
** SMOKE IS PROVIDED BY THE AUTHOR ``AS IS'' AND ANY EXPRESS OR
** IMPLIED WARRANTIES, INCLUDING, BUT NOT LIMITED TO, THE IMPLIED WARRANTIES
** OF MERCHANTABILITY AND FITNESS FOR A PARTICULAR PURPOSE ARE DISCLAIMED.
** IN NO EVENT SHALL THE AUTHOR BE LIABLE FOR ANY DIRECT, INDIRECT,
** INCIDENTAL, SPECIAL, EXEMPLARY, OR CONSEQUENTIAL DAMAGES (INCLUDING, BUT
** NOT LIMITED TO, PROCUREMENT OF SUBSTITUTE GOODS OR SERVICES; LOSS OF USE,
** DATA, OR PROFITS; OR BUSINESS INTERRUPTION) HOWEVER CAUSED AND ON ANY
** THEORY OF LIABILITY, WHETHER IN CONTRACT, STRICT LIABILITY, OR TORT
** (INCLUDING NEGLIGENCE OR OTHERWISE) ARISING IN ANY WAY OUT OF THE USE OF
** SMOKE, EVEN IF ADVISED OF THE POSSIBILITY OF SUCH DAMAGE.
*/

package org.purple.smoke;

import android.content.BroadcastReceiver;
import android.content.Context;
import android.content.DialogInterface;
import android.content.Intent;
import android.content.IntentFilter;
import android.graphics.Color;
import android.media.Ringtone;
import android.media.RingtoneManager;
import android.net.Uri;
import android.os.Bundle;
import android.support.v4.content.LocalBroadcastManager;
import android.support.v7.app.AppCompatActivity;
import android.support.v7.widget.Toolbar;
import android.text.Spannable;
import android.text.SpannableStringBuilder;
import android.text.style.ForegroundColorSpan;
import android.text.style.StyleSpan;
import android.util.Base64;
import android.view.ContextMenu.ContextMenuInfo;
import android.view.ContextMenu;
```

```java
import android.view.Menu;
import android.view.MenuItem;
import android.view.View;
import android.view.ViewGroup.LayoutParams;
import android.widget.Button;
import android.widget.CheckBox;
import android.widget.CompoundButton;
import android.widget.ScrollView;
import android.widget.TableLayout;
import android.widget.TableRow;
import android.widget.TextView;
import java.nio.charset.StandardCharsets;
import java.text.SimpleDateFormat;
import java.util.ArrayList;
import java.util.Arrays;
import java.util.Date;
import java.util.Locale;
import java.util.concurrent.Executors;
import java.util.concurrent.ScheduledExecutorService;
import java.util.concurrent.TimeUnit;

public class Chat extends AppCompatActivity
{
    private abstract static class ContextMenuEnumerator
    {
        public final static int CUSTOM_SESSION = 0;
        public final static int NEW_WINDOW = 1;
        public final static int OPTIONAL_SIGNATURES = 2;
        public final static int PURGE_SESSION = 3;
        public final static int REFRESH_PARTICIPANTS_TABLE = 4;
        public final static int RETRIEVE_MESSAGES = 5;
        public final static int SHOW_DETAILS = 6;
        public final static int SHOW_ICONS = 7;
    }

    private final SimpleDateFormat m_simpleDateFormat = new
        SimpleDateFormat("yyyy-MM-dd HH:mm:ss", Locale.getDefault());
    private Database m_databaseHelper = null;

    private class ChatBroadcastReceiver extends BroadcastReceiver
    {
        public ChatBroadcastReceiver()
        {
        }

        @Override
        public void onReceive(Context context, Intent intent)
        {
            if(intent == null || intent.getAction() == null)
                return;

            switch(intent.getAction())
            {
            case "org.purple.smoke.busy_call":
                busyCall
                    (intent.getStringExtra("org.purple.smoke.name"),
                     intent.getStringExtra("org.purple.smoke.sipHashId"));
                break;
            case "org.purple.smoke.chat_message":
                appendMessage
                    (intent.getStringExtra("org.purple.smoke.message"),
                     intent.getStringExtra("org.purple.smoke.name"),
                     intent.getStringExtra("org.purple.smoke.sipHashId"),
```

```java
                        intent.getBooleanExtra("org.purple.smoke.purple", false),
                        false,
                        intent.getLongExtra("org.purple.smoke.sequence", 1),
                        intent.getLongExtra("org.purple.smoke.timestamp", 0));
                break;
            case "org.purple.smoke.half_and_half_call":
                halfAndHalfCall
                    (intent.getStringExtra("org.purple.smoke.name"),
                     intent.getStringExtra("org.purple.smoke.sipHashId"),
                     intent.getBooleanExtra("org.purple.smoke.initial", false),
                     intent.getBooleanExtra("org.purple.smoke.refresh", true),
                     intent.getCharExtra("org.purple.smoke.keyType", 'R'));
                break;
            case "org.purple.smoke.neighbor_aborted":
            case "org.purple.smoke.neighbor_disconnected":
            case "org.purple.smoke.network_connected":
            case "org.purple.smoke.network_disconnected":
                networkStatusChanged();
                break;
            case "org.purple.smoke.populate_participants":
            case "org.purple.smoke.state_participants_populated":
                invalidateOptionsMenu();
                populateParticipants();
                break;
            case "org.purple.smoke.time":
                Miscellaneous.showNotification
                    (Chat.this, intent, findViewById(R.id.main_layout));
                break;
            default:
                break;
            }
        }
    }

    private ChatBroadcastReceiver m_receiver = null;
    private ScheduledExecutorService m_scheduler = null;
    private boolean m_receiverRegistered = false;
    private final static Cryptography s_cryptography =
        Cryptography.getInstance();
    private final static SipHash s_siphash = new SipHash
        (new byte[] {(byte) 0x00, (byte) 0x01, (byte) 0x02, (byte) 0x03,
                     (byte) 0x04, (byte) 0x05, (byte) 0x06, (byte) 0x07,
                     (byte) 0x08, (byte) 0x09, (byte) 0x0a, (byte) 0x0b,
                     (byte) 0x0c, (byte) 0x0d, (byte) 0x0e, (byte) 0x0f});
    private final static int CHECKBOX_TEXT_SIZE = 13;
    private final static long STATUS_INTERVAL = 30000L; // 30 seconds.
    public final static int CHAT_MESSAGE_PREFERRED_SIZE = 8 * 1024;
    public final static int CUSTOM_SESSION_ITERATION_COUNT = 4096;
    public final static long CHAT_WINDOW = 60000L; // 1 Minute
    public final static long CONNECTION_STATUS_INTERVAL = 3500L; // 3.5
seconds.
    public final static long STATUS_WINDOW = 30000L; // 30 seconds.

    private String nameFromCheckBoxText(String text)
    {
        /*
        ** Name
        ** SipHash ID
        ** Text
        */

        if(text == null || text.isEmpty())
            return "unknown";
```

```java
        try
        {
            int indexOf = text.indexOf('\n', 1);

            if(indexOf > 0)
                return text.substring(0, indexOf);
            else
                return text;
        }
        catch(Exception exception)
        {
            return "unknown";
        }
    }

    private void appendMessage(String message,
                              String name,
                              String sipHashId,
                              boolean purple,
                              boolean viaChatLog,
                              long sequence,
                              long timestamp)
    {
        if(message == null || name == null || sipHashId == null)
            return;
        else if(message.trim().length() == 0 ||
                name.trim().length() == 0 ||
                sipHashId.trim().length() == 0)
            return;

        TextView textView1 = (TextView) findViewById(R.id.chat_messages);

        if(purple)
        {
            StringBuilder stringBuilder = new StringBuilder();

            stringBuilder.append("[");

            if(timestamp == 0)
                stringBuilder.append(m_simpleDateFormat.format(new Date()));
            else
                stringBuilder.append
                    (m_simpleDateFormat.format(new Date(timestamp)));

            stringBuilder.append("] ");
            stringBuilder.append(name.trim());
            stringBuilder.append(":");

            if(sequence != -1)
            {
                stringBuilder.append(sequence);
                stringBuilder.append(": ");
            }
            else
                stringBuilder.append(" ");

            stringBuilder.append(message.trim());
            stringBuilder.append("\n\n");

            SpannableStringBuilder spannable = new SpannableStringBuilder
                (stringBuilder.toString());
```

```java
        spannable.setSpan
            (new ForegroundColorSpan(Color.rgb(74, 20, 140)),
             0, stringBuilder.length(), Spannable.SPAN_EXCLUSIVE_EXCLUSIVE);
        textView1.append(spannable);
    }
    else
    {
        textView1.append("[");

        if(timestamp == 0)
            textView1.append(m_simpleDateFormat.format(new Date()));
        else
            textView1.append
                (m_simpleDateFormat.format(new Date(timestamp)));

        textView1.append("] ");

        SpannableStringBuilder spannable = new SpannableStringBuilder
            (name.trim());

        spannable.setSpan
            (new StyleSpan(android.graphics.Typeface.BOLD),
             0, name.trim().length(), Spannable.SPAN_EXCLUSIVE_EXCLUSIVE);
        textView1.append(spannable);
        textView1.append(":");

        if(sequence != -1)
        {
            textView1.append(String.valueOf(sequence));
            textView1.append(": ");
        }
        else
            textView1.append(" ");

        textView1.append(message.trim());
        textView1.append("\n\n");

        if(m_databaseHelper.readSetting(null, "show_chat_icons").
            equals("true"))
        {
            CheckBox checkBox1 = (CheckBox) findViewById
                (R.id.participants).findViewWithTag(sipHashId);

            if(checkBox1 != null)
            {
                if(!Kernel.getInstance().isConnected() ||
                   Math.abs(System.currentTimeMillis() - timestamp) >
                   STATUS_WINDOW)
                   checkBox1.setCompoundDrawablesWithIntrinsicBounds
                        (R.drawable.chat_status_offline, 0, 0, 0);
                else
                   checkBox1.setCompoundDrawablesWithIntrinsicBounds
                        (R.drawable.chat_status_online, 0, 0, 0);

                checkBox1.setCompoundDrawablePadding(5);
            }
        }
    }

    scrollMessagesView();

    if(!viaChatLog)
        try
```

```java
                {
                    Ringtone ringtone = null;
                    Uri notification = RingtoneManager.getDefaultUri
                        (RingtoneManager.TYPE_NOTIFICATION);

                    ringtone = RingtoneManager.getRingtone
                        (getApplicationContext(), notification);
                    ringtone.play();
                }
                catch(Exception exception)
                {
                }

        final TextView textView2 = (TextView) findViewById(R.id.chat_message);

        textView2.post(new Runnable()
        {
            @Override
            public void run()
            {
                textView2.requestFocus();
            }
        });
    }

    private void busyCall(String name, String sipHashId)
    {
        if(name == null || sipHashId == null)
            return;
        else if(name.trim().length() == 0 || sipHashId.trim().length() == 0)
            return;

        StringBuilder stringBuilder = new StringBuilder();
        TextView textView1 = (TextView) findViewById(R.id.chat_messages);

        stringBuilder.append("[");
        stringBuilder.append(m_simpleDateFormat.format(new Date()));
        stringBuilder.append("] ");
        stringBuilder.append
            ("Received a simultaneous half-and-half organic call from ");
        stringBuilder.append(name.trim());
        stringBuilder.append(" (");
        stringBuilder.append(Miscellaneous.prepareSipHashId(sipHashId));
        stringBuilder.append("). Aborting.");
        stringBuilder.append("\n\n");
        textView1.append(stringBuilder);
        scrollMessagesView();

        final TextView textView2 = (TextView) findViewById(R.id.chat_message);

        textView2.post(new Runnable()
        {
            @Override
            public void run()
            {
                textView2.requestFocus();
            }
        });
    }

    private void halfAndHalfCall(String name,
                                 String sipHashId,
                                 boolean initial,
```

```java
                            boolean refresh,
                            char keyType)
    {
        if(name == null || sipHashId == null)
            return;
        else if(name.trim().length() == 0 || sipHashId.trim().length() == 0)
            return;

        StringBuilder stringBuilder = new StringBuilder();
        TextView textView1 = (TextView) findViewById(R.id.chat_messages);

        stringBuilder.append("[");
        stringBuilder.append(m_simpleDateFormat.format(new Date()));
        stringBuilder.append("] ");

        if(initial)
            stringBuilder.append("Received a half-and-half call from ");
        else
            stringBuilder.append
                ("Received a half-and-half call-response from ");

        stringBuilder.append(name.trim());
        stringBuilder.append(" (");
        stringBuilder.append(Miscellaneous.prepareSipHashId(sipHashId));
        stringBuilder.append(")");

        if(initial)
        {
            if(keyType == 'M')
                stringBuilder.append(" via McEliece. ");
            else
                stringBuilder.append(" via RSA. ");

            stringBuilder.append("Dispatching a response. Please be patient.");
        }
        else
            stringBuilder.append(".");

        stringBuilder.append("\n\n");
        textView1.append(stringBuilder);
        scrollMessagesView();

        if(refresh)
            refreshCheckBox(sipHashId);

        final TextView textView2 = (TextView) findViewById(R.id.chat_message);

        textView2.post(new Runnable()
        {
            @Override
            public void run()
            {
                textView2.requestFocus();
            }
        });
    }

    private void networkStatusChanged()
    {
        Button button1 = (Button) findViewById(R.id.call);
        Button button2 = (Button) findViewById(R.id.send_chat_message);
        int chatCheckedParticipants = State.getInstance().
            chatCheckedParticipants();
```

```java
        if(Kernel.getInstance().isConnected() && chatCheckedParticipants > 0)
            button1.setEnabled(true);
        else
            button1.setEnabled(false);

        if(Kernel.getInstance().availableNeighbors() > 0 &&
           chatCheckedParticipants > 0)
        {
            button2.setBackgroundResource(R.drawable.send);
            button2.setEnabled(true);
        }
        else
        {
            button2.setBackgroundResource(R.drawable.warning);
            button2.setEnabled(false);
        }

        try
        {
            getSupportActionBar().setSubtitle(Smoke.networkStatusString());
        }
        catch(Exception exception)
        {
        }
    }

    private void populateChat()
    {
        ArrayList<MessageElement> arrayList = State.getInstance().chatLog();

        if(arrayList == null || arrayList.isEmpty())
            return;

        for(MessageElement messageElement : arrayList)
        {
            if(messageElement == null)
                continue;

            appendMessage(messageElement.m_message,
                          messageElement.m_name,
                          messageElement.m_id,
                          messageElement.m_purple,
                          true,
                          messageElement.m_sequence,
                          messageElement.m_timestamp);
        }

        State.getInstance().clearChatLog();
        arrayList.clear();
    }

    private void populateParticipants()
    {
        ArrayList<ParticipantElement> arrayList = State.getInstance().
            participants();
        TableLayout tableLayout = (TableLayout) findViewById
            (R.id.participants);

        if(arrayList == null || arrayList.isEmpty())
        {
            tableLayout.removeAllViews();
            return;
```

```java
        }

        tableLayout.removeAllViews();

        StringBuilder stringBuilder = new StringBuilder();
        boolean showDetails = m_databaseHelper.readSetting
            (null, "show_chat_details").equals("true");
        boolean showIcons = m_databaseHelper.readSetting
            (null, "show_chat_icons").equals("true");
        boolean state = Kernel.getInstance().isConnected();
        int i = 0;

        for(ParticipantElement participantElement : arrayList)
        {
            if(participantElement == null)
                continue;

            CheckBox checkBox1 = new CheckBox(Chat.this);
            final int oid = participantElement.m_oid;

            if(showIcons)
            {
                if(participantElement.m_keyStream == null ||
                    participantElement.m_keyStream.length !=
                    Cryptography.CIPHER_HASH_KEYS_LENGTH)
                     checkBox1.setCompoundDrawablesWithIntrinsicBounds
                         (R.drawable.chat_faulty_session, 0, 0, 0);
                else if(Math.abs(System.currentTimeMillis() -
                                participantElement.m_lastStatusTimestamp) >
                        STATUS_WINDOW ||
                        !state)
                     checkBox1.setCompoundDrawablesWithIntrinsicBounds
                         (R.drawable.chat_status_offline, 0, 0, 0);
                else
                     checkBox1.setCompoundDrawablesWithIntrinsicBounds
                         (R.drawable.chat_status_online, 0, 0, 0);

                checkBox1.setCompoundDrawablePadding(5);
            }

            registerForContextMenu(checkBox1);
            checkBox1.setChecked
                (State.getInstance().chatCheckBoxIsSelected(oid));
            checkBox1.setId(participantElement.m_oid);
            checkBox1.setLayoutParams
                (new TableRow.LayoutParams(0,
                                    LayoutParams.WRAP_CONTENT,
                                    1));
            checkBox1.setOnCheckedChangeListener
                (new CompoundButton.OnCheckedChangeListener()
                {
                    @Override
                    public void onCheckedChanged
                        (CompoundButton buttonView, boolean isChecked)
                    {
                        State.getInstance().setChatCheckBoxSelected
                            (buttonView.getId(), isChecked);

                        Button button1 = (Button) findViewById(R.id.call);
                        Button button2 = (Button) findViewById
                            (R.id.send_chat_message);

                        if(Kernel.getInstance().availableNeighbors() > 0 &&
```

```java
                    State.getInstance().chatCheckedParticipants() > 0)
                {
                    button1.setEnabled
                        (Kernel.getInstance().isConnected());
                    button2.setBackgroundResource(R.drawable.send);
                    button2.setEnabled(true);
                }
                else
                {
                    button1.setEnabled(false);
                    button2.setBackgroundResource(R.drawable.warning);
                    button2.setEnabled(false);
                }
            }
        });
    stringBuilder.delete(0, stringBuilder.length());
    stringBuilder.append(participantElement.m_name.trim());

    if(showDetails)
    {
        stringBuilder.append("\n");
        stringBuilder.append
            (Miscellaneous.
             prepareSipHashId(participantElement.m_sipHashId));
        stringBuilder.append("\n");

        if(participantElement.m_keyStream == null ||
           participantElement.m_keyStream.length == 0)
            stringBuilder.append("Session Closed");
        else if(participantElement.m_keyStream.length == 48)
            stringBuilder.append("Session Incomplete");
        else if(participantElement.m_keyStream.length ==
                Cryptography.CIPHER_HASH_KEYS_LENGTH)
            stringBuilder.append("Session Ready");
        else
            stringBuilder.append("Session Faulty");

        if(participantElement.m_keyStream != null &&
           participantElement.m_keyStream.length ==
           Cryptography.CIPHER_HASH_KEYS_LENGTH)
        {
            stringBuilder.append("\n");

            long value[] = s_siphash.
                hmac(participantElement.m_keyStream,
                     Cryptography.SIPHASH_OUTPUT_LENGTH);

            stringBuilder.append
                (Miscellaneous.
                 byteArrayAsHexStringDelimited
                 (Miscellaneous.
                  longArrayToByteArray(value), '-', 4).toUpperCase());
        }
    }

    checkBox1.setTag(participantElement.m_sipHashId);
    checkBox1.setText(stringBuilder);
    checkBox1.setTextColor(Color.BLACK);
    checkBox1.setTextSize(CHECKBOX_TEXT_SIZE);

    TableRow row = new TableRow(Chat.this);

    row.addView(checkBox1);
```

```java
            tableLayout.addView(row, i);
            i += 1;
        }

    // Do not clear arrayList!
    }

    private void prepareListeners()
    {
        Button button1 = (Button) findViewById(R.id.call);

        button1.setOnClickListener(new View.OnClickListener()
        {
            public void onClick(View view)
            {
                if(Chat.this.isFinishing())
                    return;

                StringBuilder stringBuilder = new StringBuilder();
                TextView textView1 = (TextView) findViewById
                    (R.id.chat_messages);
                TableLayout tableLayout = (TableLayout) findViewById
                    (R.id.participants);
                int count = tableLayout.getChildCount();

                for(int i = 0; i < count; i++)
                {
                    TableRow row = (TableRow) tableLayout.getChildAt(i);

                    if(row == null)
                        continue;

                    CheckBox checkBox1 = (CheckBox) row.getChildAt(0);

                    if(checkBox1 == null)
                        continue;

                    if(checkBox1.getTag() != null && checkBox1.isChecked())
                    {
                        boolean ok = Kernel.getInstance().call
                            (checkBox1.getId(),
                             ParticipantCall.Algorithms.RSA,
                             checkBox1.getTag().toString());

                        stringBuilder.delete(0, stringBuilder.length());
                        stringBuilder.append("[");
                        stringBuilder.append
                            (m_simpleDateFormat.format(new Date()));
                        stringBuilder.append("] ");

                        if(ok)
                            stringBuilder.append("Initiating a session with ");
                        else
                            stringBuilder.append
                                ("Smoke is currently attempting to " +
                                 "establish a session with ");

                        stringBuilder.append
                            (nameFromCheckBoxText(checkBox1.getText().
                                                  toString()));
                        stringBuilder.append(" (");
                        stringBuilder.append
                            (Miscellaneous.
```

```java
                    prepareSipHashId(checkBox1.getTag().toString()));
                stringBuilder.append("). ");

                if(!ok)
                {
                    stringBuilder.append("Please try again in ");
                    stringBuilder.append
                        (Kernel.getInstance().
                         callTimeRemaining(checkBox1.getTag().
                                           toString())));
                    stringBuilder.append(" second(s).\n\n");
                }
                else
                    stringBuilder.append("Please be patient.\n\n");

                textView1.append(stringBuilder);
                }
            }

            if(tableLayout.getChildCount() > 0)
            {
                scrollMessagesView();

                final TextView textView2 = (TextView)
                    findViewById(R.id.chat_message);

                textView2.post(new Runnable()
                {
                    @Override
                    public void run()
                    {
                        textView2.requestFocus();
                    }
                });
            }
        }
    });
}

private void prepareSchedulers()
{
    if(m_scheduler == null)
    {
        m_scheduler = Executors.newSingleThreadScheduledExecutor();
        m_scheduler.scheduleAtFixedRate(new Runnable()
        {
            @Override
            public void run()
            {
                try
                {
                    if(!m_databaseHelper.
                       readSetting(null, "show_chat_icons").equals("true"))
                        return;

                    ArrayList<String> arrayList =
                        m_databaseHelper.readSipHashIdStrings
                        (s_cryptography);

                    if(arrayList == null || arrayList.isEmpty())
                        return;

                    for(final String string : arrayList)
```

```java
                        Chat.this.runOnUiThread(new Runnable()
                        {
                            @Override
                            public void run()
                            {
                                refreshCheckBox(string);
                            }
                        });

                    arrayList.clear();
                }
                catch(Exception exception)
                {
                }
            }
        }, 0, STATUS_INTERVAL, TimeUnit.MILLISECONDS);
    }
}

    private void refreshCheckBox(String sipHashId)
    {
        CheckBox checkBox1 = (CheckBox)
            findViewById(R.id.participants).findViewWithTag(sipHashId);

        if(checkBox1 == null)
            return;

        ArrayList<ParticipantElement> arrayList =
            m_databaseHelper.readParticipants(s_cryptography, sipHashId);

        if(arrayList == null || arrayList.isEmpty())
            return;

        ParticipantElement participantElement = arrayList.get(0);

        if(participantElement == null)
            return;

        if(m_databaseHelper.readSetting(null, "show_chat_details").
            equals("true"))
        {
            StringBuilder stringBuilder = new StringBuilder();

            stringBuilder.append(participantElement.m_name.trim());
            stringBuilder.append("\n");
            stringBuilder.append
                (Miscellaneous.
                  prepareSipHashId(participantElement.m_sipHashId));
            stringBuilder.append("\n");

            if(participantElement.m_keyStream == null ||
               participantElement.m_keyStream.length == 0)
                stringBuilder.append("Session Closed");
            else if(participantElement.m_keyStream.length == 48)
                stringBuilder.append("Session Incomplete");
            else if(participantElement.m_keyStream.length ==
                    Cryptography.CIPHER_HASH_KEYS_LENGTH)
                stringBuilder.append("Session Ready");
            else
                stringBuilder.append("Session Faulty");

            if(participantElement.m_keyStream != null &&
               participantElement.m_keyStream.length ==
```

```java
                    Cryptography.CIPHER_HASH_KEYS_LENGTH)
                {
                    stringBuilder.append("\n");

                    long value[] = s_siphash.hmac
                        (participantElement.m_keyStream,
                         Cryptography.SIPHASH_OUTPUT_LENGTH);

                    stringBuilder.append
                        (Miscellaneous.
                         byteArrayAsHexStringDelimited(Miscellaneous.
                                                longArrayToByteArray(value),
                                                '-', 4).toUpperCase());
                }

                checkBox1.setText(stringBuilder);
            }

            if(m_databaseHelper.readSetting(null,
    "show_chat_icons").equals("true"))
                {
                    if(participantElement.m_keyStream == null ||
                       participantElement.m_keyStream.length !=
                       Cryptography.CIPHER_HASH_KEYS_LENGTH)
                       checkBox1.setCompoundDrawablesWithIntrinsicBounds
                           (R.drawable.chat_faulty_session, 0, 0, 0);
                    else if(!Kernel.getInstance().isConnected() ||
                            Math.abs(System.currentTimeMillis() -
                                     participantElement.m_lastStatusTimestamp) >
                            STATUS_WINDOW)
                       checkBox1.setCompoundDrawablesWithIntrinsicBounds
                           (R.drawable.chat_status_offline, 0, 0, 0);
                    else
                       checkBox1.setCompoundDrawablesWithIntrinsicBounds
                           (R.drawable.chat_status_online, 0, 0, 0);

                    checkBox1.setCompoundDrawablePadding(5);
                }

            arrayList.clear();
        }

    private void releaseResources()
    {
        if(m_scheduler != null)
        {
            try
            {
                m_scheduler.shutdown();
            }
            catch(Exception exception)
            {
            }

            try
            {
                if(!m_scheduler.awaitTermination(60L, TimeUnit.SECONDS))
                    m_scheduler.shutdownNow();
            }
            catch(Exception exception)
            {
            }
            finally
```

```java
            {
                m_scheduler = null;
            }
        }
    }

    private void requestMessages()
    {
        StringBuilder stringBuilder = new StringBuilder();
        TextView textView1 = (TextView) findViewById(R.id.chat_messages);

        stringBuilder.append("[");
        stringBuilder.append(m_simpleDateFormat.format(new Date()));
        stringBuilder.append("] ");
        stringBuilder.append("A request for retrieving offline messages ");
        stringBuilder.append("has been submitted. Offline messages will be ");
        stringBuilder.append("marked by the color ");
        textView1.append(stringBuilder);

        SpannableStringBuilder spannable = new
SpannableStringBuilder("purple");

        spannable.setSpan
            (new ForegroundColorSpan(Color.rgb(74, 20, 140)),
             0, spannable.length(), Spannable.SPAN_EXCLUSIVE_EXCLUSIVE);
        textView1.append(spannable);
        textView1.append(". Please note that recently-received messages ");
        textView1.append("may be discarded because of congestion
control.\n\n");
        scrollMessagesView();

        final TextView textView2 = (TextView) findViewById(R.id.chat_message);

        textView2.post(new Runnable()
        {
            @Override
            public void run()
            {
                textView2.requestFocus();
            }
        });
    }

    private void saveState()
    {
        TextView textView1 = (TextView) findViewById(R.id.chat_message);

        State.getInstance().writeCharSequence
            ("chat.message", textView1.getText());
        textView1 = (TextView) findViewById(R.id.chat_messages);
        State.getInstance().writeCharSequence
            ("chat.messages", textView1.getText());
    }

    private void scrollMessagesView()
    {
        final ScrollView scrollView = (ScrollView)
            findViewById(R.id.chat_scrollview);

        scrollView.post(new Runnable()
        {
            @Override
            public void run()
```

```java
                {
                    scrollView.fullScroll(ScrollView.FOCUS_DOWN);
                }
            });
    }

    private void showMemberChatActivity()
    {
        saveState();

        Intent intent = new Intent(Chat.this, MemberChat.class);

        startActivity(intent);
        finish();
    }

    private void showSmokescreenActivity()
    {
        Intent intent = new Intent(Chat.this, Smokescreen.class);

        startActivity(intent);
        finish();
    }


    @Override
    protected void onCreate(Bundle savedInstanceState)
    {
        super.onCreate(savedInstanceState);
        m_databaseHelper = Database.getInstance(getApplicationContext());
        m_receiver = new ChatBroadcastReceiver();
         setContentView(R.layout.activity_chat);
        setSupportActionBar((Toolbar) findViewById(R.id.toolbar));

        try
        {
            getSupportActionBar().setSubtitle(Smoke.networkStatusString());
            getSupportActionBar().setTitle("Smoke | Chat");
        }
        catch(Exception exception)
        {
        }

        Button button1 = (Button) findViewById(R.id.clear_chat_messages);

        button1.setOnClickListener(new View.OnClickListener()
        {
            public void onClick(View view)
            {
                if(Chat.this.isFinishing())
                    return;

                State.getInstance().clearChatLog();

                TextView textView1 = (TextView) findViewById
                    (R.id.chat_messages);

                textView1.setText("");
            }
        });

        button1 = (Button) findViewById(R.id.send_chat_message);
        button1.setOnClickListener(new View.OnClickListener()
        {
```

```java
public void onClick(View view)
{
    if(Chat.this.isFinishing())
        return;

    final TextView textView1 = (TextView) findViewById
        (R.id.chat_message);

    if(textView1.getText().toString().trim().isEmpty())
        return;

    String str = textView1.getText().toString().trim();
    StringBuilder stringBuilder = new StringBuilder();
    TableLayout tableLayout = (TableLayout) findViewById
        (R.id.participants);
    TextView textView2 = (TextView) findViewById
        (R.id.chat_messages);

    textView2.append("[");
    textView2.append(m_simpleDateFormat.format(new Date()));
    textView2.append("] ");


    {
        SpannableStringBuilder spannable =
            new SpannableStringBuilder("me");

        spannable.setSpan
            (new StyleSpan(android.graphics.Typeface.BOLD),
             0,
             spannable.length(),
             Spannable.SPAN_EXCLUSIVE_EXCLUSIVE);
        textView2.append(spannable);
    }

    stringBuilder.append(": ");
    stringBuilder.append(str);
    stringBuilder.append("\n\n");
    textView2.append(stringBuilder);
    textView1.setText("");

    int size = CHAT_MESSAGE_PREFERRED_SIZE *
        (int) Math.ceil((1.0 * str.length()) /
                        (1.0 * CHAT_MESSAGE_PREFERRED_SIZE));

    if(size > str.length())
    {
        char a[] = new char[size - str.length()];

        Arrays.fill(a, ' ');
        str += new String(a);
    }
    else if(str.length() > 0)
    {
        char a[] = new char[1024 + str.length() % 2];

        Arrays.fill(a, ' ');
        str += new String(a);
    }

    int count = tableLayout.getChildCount();

    for(int i = 0; i < count; i++)
    {
```

```java
            TableRow row = (TableRow) tableLayout.getChildAt(i);

                if(row == null)
                    continue;

                CheckBox checkBox1 = (CheckBox) row.getChildAt(0);

                if(checkBox1 == null ||
                   checkBox1.getTag() == null ||
                   !checkBox1.isChecked())
                    continue;

                String sipHashId = checkBox1.getTag().toString();
                byte keyStream[] = m_databaseHelper.participantKeyStream
                    (s_cryptography, sipHashId);

                if(keyStream == null ||
                   keyStream.length != Cryptography.CIPHER_HASH_KEYS_LENGTH)
                    continue;

                Kernel.getInstance().enqueueChatMessage
                    (str, sipHashId, null, keyStream);
            }

        scrollMessagesView();
        textView1.post(new Runnable()
        {
            @Override
            public void run()
            {
                textView1.requestFocus();
            }
        });
        }
    });

    TextView textView1 = (TextView) findViewById(R.id.chat_message);

    textView1.requestFocus();

    /*
    ** Restore some data.
    */

    try
    {
        textView1 = (TextView) findViewById(R.id.chat_message);
        textView1.setText
            (State.getInstance().getCharSequence("chat.message"));
        textView1 = (TextView) findViewById(R.id.chat_messages);
        textView1.setText
            (State.getInstance().getCharSequence("chat.messages"));

    }
    catch(Exception exception)
    {
    }

    populateChat();

    if(State.getInstance().isAuthenticated())
        populateParticipants();
```

```java
        prepareListeners();
    }

    @Override
    protected void onPause()
    {
        super.onPause();

        if(m_receiverRegistered)
        {
            LocalBroadcastManager.getInstance(getApplicationContext()).
                unregisterReceiver(m_receiver);
            m_receiverRegistered = false;
        }

        releaseResources();
        saveState();
    }

    @Override
    protected void onResume()
    {
        super.onResume();

        if(!m_receiverRegistered)
        {
            IntentFilter intentFilter = new IntentFilter();

            intentFilter.addAction("org.purple.smoke.busy_call");
            intentFilter.addAction("org.purple.smoke.chat_message");
            intentFilter.addAction("org.purple.smoke.half_and_half_call");
            intentFilter.addAction("org.purple.smoke.neighbor_aborted");
            intentFilter.addAction("org.purple.smoke.neighbor_disconnected");
            intentFilter.addAction("org.purple.smoke.network_connected");
            intentFilter.addAction("org.purple.smoke.network_disconnected");
            intentFilter.addAction("org.purple.smoke.populate_participants");
            intentFilter.addAction
                ("org.purple.smoke.state_participants_populated");
            intentFilter.addAction("org.purple.smoke.time");
            LocalBroadcastManager.getInstance(getApplicationContext()).
                registerReceiver(m_receiver, intentFilter);
            m_receiverRegistered = true;
        }

        networkStatusChanged();
        populateChat();
        populateParticipants();
        prepareSchedulers();
    }

    @Override
    protected void onSaveInstanceState(Bundle savedInstanceState)
    {
        /*
        ** Do not issue a super.onSaveInstanceState().
        */
    }

    @Override
    public boolean onContextItemSelected(MenuItem menuItem)
    {
        if(menuItem == null)
            return false;
```

```java
final String sipHashId = Miscellaneous.prepareSipHashId
    (menuItem.getTitle().toString().replace("Custom Session ", "").
     replace("New Window ", "").
     replace("Optional Signatures ", "").
     replace("Purge Session ", "").replace("(", "").replace(")", ""));
final int groupId = menuItem.getGroupId();
final int itemId = menuItem.getItemId();

/*
** Prepare a listener.
*/

DialogInterface.OnCancelListener listener =
    new DialogInterface.OnCancelListener()
    {
        public void onCancel(DialogInterface dialog)
        {
            if(itemId > -1)
                switch(groupId)
                {
                case ContextMenuEnumerator.CUSTOM_SESSION:
                    try
                    {
                        String string = State.getInstance().
                            getString("chat_secret_input").trim();

                        if(!string.isEmpty())
                        {
                            byte bytes[] = Cryptography.pbkdf2
                                (Cryptography.
                                 sha512(string.
                                        getBytes(StandardCharsets.
                                                 UTF_8)),
                                 string.toCharArray(),
                                 CUSTOM_SESSION_ITERATION_COUNT,
                                 160); // SHA-1

                            if(bytes != null)
                                bytes = Cryptography.pbkdf2
                                    (Cryptography.
                                     sha512(string.
                                            getBytes(StandardCharsets.
                                                     UTF_8)),
                                     Base64.
                                     encodeToString(bytes,
                                                    Base64.NO_WRAP).
                                     toCharArray(),
                                     1,
                                     Cryptography.
                                     CIPHER_HASH_KEYS_LENGTH * 8);

                            if(m_databaseHelper.
                               setParticipantKeyStream(s_cryptography,
                                                       bytes,
                                                       itemId))
                                refreshCheckBox(sipHashId);
                        }
                    }
                    catch(Exception exception)
                    {
                    }
```

```java
                            State.getInstance().removeKey("chat_secret_input");
                            break;
                        case ContextMenuEnumerator.PURGE_SESSION:
                            if(State.getInstance().getString("dialog_accepted").
                                equals("true"))
                                if(m_databaseHelper.
                                    setParticipantKeyStream(s_cryptography,
                                                            null,
                                                            itemId))
                                    refreshCheckBox(sipHashId);

                            break;
                        default:
                            break;
                    }
                }
            };

        if(itemId > -1)
            switch(groupId)
            {
            case ContextMenuEnumerator.CUSTOM_SESSION:
                Miscellaneous.showTextInputDialog
                    (Chat.this,
                     listener,
                     "Please provide a secret for " +
                     menuItem.getTitle().toString().
                     replace("Custom Session (", "").
                     replace(")", "") + ".",
                     "",
                     "Secret");
                break;
            case ContextMenuEnumerator.NEW_WINDOW:
                State.getInstance().setString
                    ("member_chat_oid", String.valueOf(itemId));
                State.getInstance().setString
                    ("member_chat_siphash_id", sipHashId);
                m_databaseHelper.writeSetting
                    (null, "lastActivity", "MemberChat");
                m_databaseHelper.writeSetting
                    (s_cryptography, "member_chat_oid", String.valueOf(itemId));
                m_databaseHelper.writeSetting
                    (s_cryptography, "member_chat_siphash_id", sipHashId);
                showMemberChatActivity();
                break;
            case ContextMenuEnumerator.OPTIONAL_SIGNATURES:
                menuItem.setChecked(!menuItem.isChecked());

                String strings[] = null;
                StringBuilder stringBuilder = new StringBuilder
                    (m_databaseHelper.
                     readParticipantOptions(s_cryptography, sipHashId));

                strings = stringBuilder.toString().split(";");

                if(strings == null || strings.length == 0)
                {
                    if(menuItem.isChecked())
                        stringBuilder.append("optional_signatures = true");
                    else
                        stringBuilder.append("optional_signatures = false");
                }
                else
```

```java
            {
                stringBuilder.delete(0, stringBuilder.length());

                int i = 0;
                int length = strings.length;

                for(String string : strings)
                {
                    if(!(string.equals("optional_signatures = false") ||
                         string.equals("optional_signatures = true")))
                    {
                        stringBuilder.append(string);

                        if(i != length - 1)
                            stringBuilder.append(";");
                    }

                    i += 1;
                }

                if(stringBuilder.length() > 0)
                    stringBuilder.append(";");

                stringBuilder.append("optional_signatures = ");
                stringBuilder.append
                    (menuItem.isChecked() ? "true" : "false");
            }

            m_databaseHelper.writeParticipantOptions
                (s_cryptography, stringBuilder.toString(), sipHashId);
            break;
        case ContextMenuEnumerator.PURGE_SESSION:
            Miscellaneous.showPromptDialog
                (Chat.this,
                 listener,
                 "Are you sure that you " +
                 "wish to purge the session key stream for " +
                 menuItem.getTitle().toString().
                 replace("Purge Session (", "").
                 replace(")", "") + "?");
            break;
        default:
            break;
        }
    else
        switch(groupId)
        {
        case ContextMenuEnumerator.REFRESH_PARTICIPANTS_TABLE:
            State.getInstance().populateParticipants();
            populateParticipants();
            break;
        case ContextMenuEnumerator.RETRIEVE_MESSAGES:
            Kernel.getInstance().retrieveChatMessages("");
            requestMessages();
            break;
        case ContextMenuEnumerator.SHOW_DETAILS:
            State.getInstance().populateParticipants();
            menuItem.setChecked(!menuItem.isChecked());
            m_databaseHelper.writeSetting
                (null,
                 "show_chat_details",
                 menuItem.isChecked() ? "true" : "false");
            populateParticipants();
```

```java
                    break;
                case ContextMenuEnumerator.SHOW_ICONS:
                    menuItem.setChecked(!menuItem.isChecked());
                    m_databaseHelper.writeSetting
                        (null,
                         "show_chat_icons",
                         menuItem.isChecked() ? "true" : "false");
                    populateParticipants();
                    break;
                default:
                    break;
                }

        return true;
    }


    @Override
    public boolean onCreateOptionsMenu(Menu menu)
    {
        getMenuInflater().inflate(R.menu.chat_menu, menu);
         return true;
    }


    @Override
    public void onCreateContextMenu(ContextMenu menu,
                                    View view,
                                    ContextMenuInfo menuInfo)
    {
        if(menu == null || view == null)
            return;

        super.onCreateContextMenu(menu, view, menuInfo);

        MenuItem menuItem = null;

        if(view.getTag() != null)
        {
            menu.add
                (ContextMenuEnumerator.CUSTOM_SESSION,
                 view.getId(),
                 0,
                 "Custom Session (" +
                 Miscellaneous.prepareSipHashId(view.getTag().toString()) +
                 ")");
            menu.add
                (ContextMenuEnumerator.NEW_WINDOW,
                 view.getId(),
                 0,
                 "New Window (" +
                 Miscellaneous.prepareSipHashId(view.getTag().toString()) +
                 ")");
            menuItem = menu.add
                (ContextMenuEnumerator.OPTIONAL_SIGNATURES,
                 view.getId(),
                 0,
                 "Optional Signatures (" +
                 Miscellaneous.prepareSipHashId(view.getTag().toString()) +
                 ")").setCheckable(true);
            menuItem.setChecked
                (m_databaseHelper.
                 readParticipantOptions(s_cryptography, view.getTag().
                                        toString()).
                 contains("optional_signatures = true"));
```

```java
            menuItem = menu.add
                (ContextMenuEnumerator.PURGE_SESSION,
                 view.getId(),
                 0,
                 "Purge Session (" +
                 Miscellaneous.prepareSipHashId(view.getTag().toString()) +
                 ")");
            menuItem.setEnabled
                (m_databaseHelper.
                 participantsWithSessionKeys(view.getId()) > 0);
        }


    menu.add(ContextMenuEnumerator.REFRESH_PARTICIPANTS_TABLE,
             -1,
             0,
             "Refresh Participants Table");
    menuItem = menu.add(ContextMenuEnumerator.RETRIEVE_MESSAGES,
                        -1,
                        0,
                        "Retrieve Messages");
    menuItem.setEnabled
        (Kernel.getInstance().isConnected() &&
         !m_databaseHelper.readSetting(s_cryptography, "ozone_address").
         isEmpty());
    menuItem = menu.add(ContextMenuEnumerator.SHOW_DETAILS,
                        -1,
                        0,
                        "Show Details").setCheckable(true);
    menuItem.setChecked
        (m_databaseHelper.
         readSetting(null, "show_chat_details").equals("true"));
    menuItem = menu.add(ContextMenuEnumerator.SHOW_ICONS,
                        -1,
                        0,
                        "Show Icons").setCheckable(true);
    menuItem.setChecked
        (m_databaseHelper.
         readSetting(null, "show_chat_icons").equals("true"));
    }

    @Override
    public boolean onOptionsItemSelected(MenuItem menuItem)
    {
        int groupId = menuItem.getGroupId();
        int itemId = menuItem.getItemId();

        if(groupId == Menu.NONE)
        {
            switch(itemId)
            {
            case R.id.action_exit:
                Smoke.exit(Chat.this);
                return true;
            case R.id.action_fire:
            {
                saveState();
                m_databaseHelper.writeSetting(null, "lastActivity", "Fire");

                Intent intent = new Intent(Chat.this, Fire.class);

                startActivity(intent);
                finish();
                return true;
```

```java
            }
            case R.id.action_settings:
            {
                saveState();
                m_databaseHelper.writeSetting(null, "lastActivity", "Settings");

                Intent intent = new Intent(Chat.this, Settings.class);

                startActivity(intent);
                finish();
                return true;
            }
            case R.id.action_smokescreen:
                saveState();
                showSmokescreenActivity();
                finish();
                return true;
            case R.id.action_steam:
            {
                saveState();
                m_databaseHelper.writeSetting(null, "lastActivity", "Steam");

                Intent intent = new Intent(Chat.this, Steam.class);

                startActivity(intent);
                finish();
                return true;
            }
            default:
                break;
            }
        }
        else
        {
            String sipHashId = menuItem.getTitle().toString();
            int indexOf = sipHashId.indexOf("(");

            if(indexOf >= 0)
                sipHashId = sipHashId.substring(indexOf + 1).replace(")", "");

            sipHashId = Miscellaneous.prepareSipHashId(sipHashId);
            State.getInstance().setString
                ("member_chat_oid", String.valueOf(itemId));
            State.getInstance().setString("member_chat_siphash_id", sipHashId);
            m_databaseHelper.writeSetting(null, "lastActivity", "MemberChat");
            m_databaseHelper.writeSetting
                (s_cryptography, "member_chat_oid", String.valueOf(itemId));
            m_databaseHelper.writeSetting
                (s_cryptography, "member_chat_siphash_id", sipHashId);
            showMemberChatActivity();
        }

        return super.onOptionsItemSelected(menuItem);
    }

    @Override
    public boolean onPrepareOptionsMenu(Menu menu)
    {
        boolean isAuthenticated = State.getInstance().isAuthenticated();

        if(!m_databaseHelper.accountPrepared())
            /*
            ** The database may have been modified or removed.
```

```java
        */

        isAuthenticated = true;

    menu.findItem(R.id.action_authenticate).setEnabled(!isAuthenticated);
    Miscellaneous.addMembersToMenu(menu, 6, 150);
    return true;
    }
}
```

/* ChatBubble.java –


```java
package org.purple.smoke;

import android.content.Context;
import android.graphics.Bitmap;
import android.graphics.BitmapFactory;
import android.graphics.Color;
import android.support.v4.graphics.drawable.RoundedBitmapDrawable;
import android.support.v4.graphics.drawable.RoundedBitmapDrawableFactory;
import android.text.Spannable;
import android.text.SpannableStringBuilder;
import android.text.style.ForegroundColorSpan;
import android.text.style.RelativeSizeSpan;
import android.view.LayoutInflater;
import android.view.View;
import android.view.ViewGroup;
import android.widget.CheckBox;
import android.widget.CompoundButton;
import android.widget.ImageView;
import android.widget.LinearLayout;
import android.widget.TextView;
import java.io.ByteArrayInputStream;
```

```java
import java.text.SimpleDateFormat;
import java.util.Date;
import java.util.Locale;

public class ChatBubble extends View
{
    private CheckBox m_selected = null;
    private CompoundButton.OnCheckedChangeListener m_selected_listener = null;
    private Context m_context = null;
    private Date m_date = new Date(System.currentTimeMillis());
    private MemberChat m_memberChat = null;
    private View m_view = null;
    private boolean m_error = false;
    private boolean m_fromSmokeStack = false;
    private boolean m_local = false;
    private boolean m_messageRead = false;
    private boolean m_messageSent = false;
    private boolean m_selectionState = false;
    private int m_oid = -1;
    private final SimpleDateFormat m_simpleDateFormat = new
        SimpleDateFormat("yyyy-MM-dd h:mm:ss a", Locale.getDefault());
    public enum Locations {LEFT, RIGHT}

    public ChatBubble(Context context,
                      MemberChat memberChat,
                      ViewGroup viewGroup)
    {
        super(context);
        m_context = context;
        m_memberChat = memberChat;

        LayoutInflater inflater = (LayoutInflater) m_context.getSystemService
            (Context.LAYOUT_INFLATER_SERVICE);

        m_view = inflater.inflate(R.layout.chat_bubble, viewGroup, false);
        m_view.findViewById(R.id.image).setVisibility(View.GONE);
        m_view.findViewById(R.id.message_status).setVisibility(View.INVISIBLE);
        m_view.findViewById(R.id.name_left).setVisibility(View.GONE);
        m_view.findViewById(R.id.name_right).setVisibility(View.GONE);
        m_view.findViewById(R.id.selected).setVisibility(View.GONE);
        m_view.setId(-1);

        /*
        ** Prepare widget variables.
        */

        m_selected = (CheckBox) m_view.findViewById(R.id.selected);
        m_selected_listener = new CompoundButton.OnCheckedChangeListener()
        {
            @Override
            public void onCheckedChanged
                (CompoundButton buttonView, final boolean isChecked)
            {
                m_memberChat.setMessageSelected(m_oid, isChecked);
            }
        };
    }

    public View view()
    {
        return m_view;
    }
```

```java
public void setDate(long timestamp)
{
    m_date = new Date(timestamp);
}

public void setError(boolean state)
{
    m_error = state;
}

public void setFromeSmokeStack(boolean state)
{
    m_fromSmokeStack = state;
}

public void setImageAttachment(byte bytes[])
{
    if(bytes == null || bytes.length == 0)
    {
        m_view.findViewById(R.id.image).setVisibility(View.GONE);
        return;
    }

    ByteArrayInputStream byteArrayInputStream = null;

    try
    {
        byteArrayInputStream = new ByteArrayInputStream(bytes);

        BitmapFactory.Options options = new BitmapFactory.Options();

        options.inSampleSize = 2;

        Bitmap bitmap = BitmapFactory.decodeStream
            (byteArrayInputStream, null, options);
        ImageView imageView = (ImageView) m_view.findViewById(R.id.image);

        if(bitmap != null)
        {
            RoundedBitmapDrawable roundedBitmapDrawable =
                RoundedBitmapDrawableFactory.create(getResources(), bitmap);

            roundedBitmapDrawable.setCornerRadius(10.0f);
            roundedBitmapDrawable.setAntiAlias(true);
            imageView.setImageDrawable(roundedBitmapDrawable);
            imageView.setVisibility(View.VISIBLE);
        }
        else
            imageView.setVisibility(View.GONE);
    }
    catch(Exception exception)
    {
        m_view.findViewById(R.id.image).setVisibility(View.GONE);
    }
    finally
    {
        try
        {
            if(byteArrayInputStream != null)
                byteArrayInputStream.close();
        }
        catch(Exception exception)
        {
```

```java
            }
        }
    }

    public void setLocal(boolean state)
    {
        m_local = state;
    }

    public void setMessageSelected(boolean state)
    {
        m_selected.setOnCheckedChangeListener(null);
        m_selected.setChecked(state);
        m_selected.setOnCheckedChangeListener(m_selected_listener);
    }

    public void setMessageSelectionStateEnabled(boolean state)
    {
        m_selectionState = state;
        m_view.findViewById(R.id.name_left).setVisibility
            (state ? View.INVISIBLE : View.VISIBLE);
        m_view.findViewById(R.id.name_right).setVisibility
            (state ? View.INVISIBLE : View.VISIBLE);
        m_view.findViewById(R.id.selected).setVisibility
            (state ? View.VISIBLE : View.GONE);
    }

    public void setName(Locations location, String name)
    {
        m_view.findViewById(R.id.name_left).setVisibility(View.GONE);
        m_view.findViewById(R.id.name_right).setVisibility(View.GONE);

        if(name == null || name.trim().isEmpty())
            return;

        if(location == Locations.LEFT)
        {
            TextView textView = (TextView) m_view.findViewById(R.id.name_left);

            textView.setText(name.substring(0, 1).toUpperCase());

            if(!m_selectionState)
                textView.setVisibility(View.VISIBLE);
        }
        else
        {
            TextView textView = (TextView)
m_view.findViewById(R.id.name_right);

            textView.setText(name.substring(0, 1).toUpperCase());

            if(!m_selectionState)
                textView.setVisibility(View.VISIBLE);
            else
                textView.setVisibility(View.INVISIBLE);
        }
    }

    public void setOid(int oid)
    {
        m_oid = oid;
        m_view.setId(oid);
    }
```

```java
    public void setRead(Locations location, boolean state)
    {
        m_messageRead = state;

        if(m_error)
        {
            m_messageRead = state;
            m_view.findViewById(R.id.message_status).setVisibility
                (View.INVISIBLE);
            return;
        }

        if(location == Locations.LEFT)
            m_view.findViewById(R.id.message_status).setVisibility
                (View.INVISIBLE);
        else
        {
            ((ImageView) m_view.findViewById(R.id.message_status)).
                setImageResource(R.drawable.message_read);
            m_view.findViewById(R.id.message_status).setVisibility
                (m_messageRead ? View.VISIBLE : View.INVISIBLE);

            float density = m_context.getResources().getDisplayMetrics().
                density;

            m_view.findViewById(R.id.text).setPaddingRelative
                ((int) (10 * density),                                 // Start
                 (int) (10 * density),                                 // Top
                 (int) (10 * density),                                 // End
                 (int) ((m_messageRead ? 20 : 10) * density)); // Bottom
        }
    }

    public void setSent(Locations location, boolean state)
    {
        m_messageSent = state;

        if(m_error)
        {
            m_messageSent = state;
            m_view.findViewById(R.id.message_status).setVisibility
                (View.INVISIBLE);
            return;
        }
        else if(m_messageRead)
            return;

        if(location == Locations.LEFT)
            m_view.findViewById(R.id.message_status).setVisibility
                (View.INVISIBLE);
        else
        {
            ((ImageView) m_view.findViewById(R.id.message_status)).
                setImageResource(R.drawable.message_sent);
            m_view.findViewById(R.id.message_status).setVisibility
                (m_messageSent ? View.VISIBLE : View.INVISIBLE);

            float density = m_context.getResources().getDisplayMetrics().
                density;

            m_view.findViewById(R.id.text).setPaddingRelative
                ((int) (10 * density),                                 // Start
```

```java
                    (int) (10 * density),                               // Top
                    (int) (10 * density),                               // End
                    (int) ((m_messageSent ? 20 : 10) * density)); // Bottom
        }
    }

    public void setText(Locations location, String text)
    {
        LinearLayout linearLayout = (LinearLayout)
            m_view.findViewById(R.id.linear_layout);
        TextView textView = (TextView) m_view.findViewById(R.id.text);

        textView.setText("");

        {
            SpannableStringBuilder spannable = new SpannableStringBuilder
                (text == null ? "" : text);

            if(spannable.length() > 0)
            {
                if(location == Locations.LEFT)
                    spannable.setSpan
                        (new ForegroundColorSpan(Color.rgb(255, 255, 255)),
                         0,
                         spannable.length(),
                         Spannable.SPAN_EXCLUSIVE_EXCLUSIVE);
                else
                    spannable.setSpan
                        (new ForegroundColorSpan(Color.rgb(117, 117, 117)),
                         0,
                         spannable.length(),
                         Spannable.SPAN_EXCLUSIVE_EXCLUSIVE);

                textView.append(spannable);
            }
        }

        {
            SpannableStringBuilder spannable = new SpannableStringBuilder
                ((m_fromSmokeStack ? "Ozone " : "") +
                 m_simpleDateFormat.format(m_date));

            if(spannable.length() > 0)
            {
                if(location == Locations.LEFT)
                    spannable.setSpan
                        (new ForegroundColorSpan(Color.rgb(224, 224, 224)),
                         0,
                         spannable.length(),
                         Spannable.SPAN_EXCLUSIVE_EXCLUSIVE);
                else
                    spannable.setSpan
                        (new ForegroundColorSpan(Color.rgb(158, 158, 158)),
                         0,
                         spannable.length(),
                         Spannable.SPAN_EXCLUSIVE_EXCLUSIVE);

                spannable.setSpan
                    (new RelativeSizeSpan(0.90f),
                     0,
                     spannable.length(),
                     Spannable.SPAN_EXCLUSIVE_EXCLUSIVE);
                textView.append(spannable);
```

```java
                }
            }

        float density = m_context.getResources().getDisplayMetrics().density;

        if(location == Locations.LEFT)
        {
            if(m_error)
                linearLayout.setBackgroundResource(R.drawable.bubble_error);
            else if(m_fromSmokeStack)
                linearLayout.setBackgroundResource
                    (R.drawable.bubble_ozone_text);
            else
                linearLayout.setBackgroundResource
                    (R.drawable.bubble_left_text);

            m_view.findViewById(R.id.text).setPaddingRelative
                ((int) (10 * density),   // Start
                 (int) (10 * density),   // Top
                 (int) (10 * density),   // End
                 (int) (10 * density)); // Bottom
        }
        else
        {
            if(m_error)
                linearLayout.setBackgroundResource(R.drawable.bubble_error);
            else
                linearLayout.setBackgroundResource
                    (R.drawable.bubble_right_text);

            m_view.findViewById(R.id.text).setPaddingRelative
                ((int) (10 * density),                          // Start
                 (int) (10 * density),                          // Top
                 (int) (10 * density),                          // End
                 (int) ((m_messageRead ||
                     m_messageSent ? 20 : 10) * density)); // Bottom
        }

        if(m_local && text != null)
        {
            String t = text.trim();

            if(t.equals("Received a half-and-half call-response.") ||
               t.equals("Received a half-and-half call. " +
                     "Dispatching a response. Please be patient.") ||
               t.equals("The Juggernaut Protocol has been verified!"))
            {
                ((ImageView) m_view.findViewById(R.id.message_status)).
                    setImageResource(R.drawable.verified);
                m_view.findViewById(R.id.message_status).setVisibility
                    (View.VISIBLE);
            }
            else if(t.startsWith("Juggernaut Protocol failure"))
            {
                ((ImageView) m_view.findViewById(R.id.message_status)).
                    setImageResource(R.drawable.warning);
                m_view.findViewById(R.id.message_status).setVisibility
                    (View.VISIBLE);
            }
        }
    }
}
```

/* Cryptography.java –

```
https://github.com/textbrowser/smoke/blob/master/Smoke/app/src/main/java/org/p
urple/smoke/Cryptography.java
** Copyright (c) Alexis Megas.
** All rights reserved.
**
** Redistribution and use in source and binary forms, with or without
** modification, are permitted provided that the following conditions
** are met:
** 1. Redistributions of source code must retain the above copyright
**    notice, this list of conditions and the following disclaimer.
** 2. Redistributions in binary form must reproduce the above copyright
**    notice, this list of conditions and the following disclaimer in the
**    documentation and/or other materials provided with the distribution.
** 3. The name of the author may not be used to endorse or promote products
**    derived from Smoke without specific prior written permission.
**
** SMOKE IS PROVIDED BY THE AUTHOR ``AS IS'' AND ANY EXPRESS OR
** IMPLIED WARRANTIES, INCLUDING, BUT NOT LIMITED TO, THE IMPLIED WARRANTIES
** OF MERCHANTABILITY AND FITNESS FOR A PARTICULAR PURPOSE ARE DISCLAIMED.
** IN NO EVENT SHALL THE AUTHOR BE LIABLE FOR ANY DIRECT, INDIRECT,
** INCIDENTAL, SPECIAL, EXEMPLARY, OR CONSEQUENTIAL DAMAGES (INCLUDING, BUT
** NOT LIMITED TO, PROCUREMENT OF SUBSTITUTE GOODS OR SERVICES; LOSS OF USE,
** DATA, OR PROFITS; OR BUSINESS INTERRUPTION) HOWEVER CAUSED AND ON ANY
** THEORY OF LIABILITY, WHETHER IN CONTRACT, STRICT LIABILITY, OR TORT
** (INCLUDING NEGLIGENCE OR OTHERWISE) ARISING IN ANY WAY OUT OF THE USE OF
** SMOKE, EVEN IF ADVISED OF THE POSSIBILITY OF SUCH DAMAGE.
*/

package org.purple.smoke;

import android.content.res.AssetFileDescriptor;
import android.net.Uri;
import android.util.Base64;
import java.io.FileInputStream;
import java.nio.charset.StandardCharsets;
import java.security.KeyFactory;
import java.security.KeyPair;
import java.security.KeyPairGenerator;
import java.security.MessageDigest;
import java.security.PrivateKey;
import java.security.PublicKey;
import java.security.SecureRandom;
import java.security.Security;
import java.security.Signature;
import java.security.interfaces.ECPublicKey;
import java.security.interfaces.RSAPublicKey;
import java.security.spec.EncodedKeySpec;
import java.security.spec.KeySpec;
import java.security.spec.PKCS8EncodedKeySpec;
import java.security.spec.X509EncodedKeySpec;
import java.util.Arrays;
import java.util.concurrent.locks.ReentrantReadWriteLock;
import javax.crypto.Cipher;
import javax.crypto.KeyGenerator;
import javax.crypto.Mac;
import javax.crypto.SecretKey;
import javax.crypto.SecretKeyFactory;
import javax.crypto.spec.IvParameterSpec;
import javax.crypto.spec.PBEKeySpec;
```

```java
import javax.crypto.spec.SecretKeySpec;
import org.bouncycastle.asn1.ASN1ObjectIdentifier;
import org.bouncycastle.asn1.x509.SubjectPublicKeyInfo;
import org.bouncycastle.crypto.generators.Argon2BytesGenerator;
import org.bouncycastle.crypto.params.Argon2Parameters;
import org.bouncycastle.pqc.asn1.PQCObjectIdentifiers;
import org.bouncycastle.pqc.jcajce.provider.BouncyCastlePQCProvider;
import org.bouncycastle.pqc.jcajce.provider.mceliece.BCMcElieceCCA2PublicKey;
import org.bouncycastle.pqc.jcajce.spec.McElieceCCA2KeyGenParameterSpec;
import org.bouncycastle.util.encoders.Hex;

public class Cryptography
{
    static
    {
        Security.addProvider(new BouncyCastlePQCProvider());
    }

    private KeyPair m_chatEncryptionPublicKeyPair = null;
    private KeyPair m_chatSignaturePublicKeyPair = null;
    private SecretKey m_encryptionKey = null;
    private SecretKey m_macKey = null;
    private String m_chatEncryptionPublicKeyAlgorithm = "";
    private String m_sipHashId = "0000-0000-0000-0000-0000-0000-0000-0000";
    private byte m_identity[] = null; // Random identity.
    private byte m_ozoneEncryptionKey[] = null;
    private byte m_ozoneMacKey[] = null;
    private byte m_sipHashEncryptionKey[] = null;
    private byte m_sipHashIdDigest[] = null;
    private byte m_sipHashMacKey[] = null;
    private final ReentrantReadWriteLock m_chatEncryptionPublicKeyPairMutex =
        new ReentrantReadWriteLock();
    private final ReentrantReadWriteLock m_chatSignaturePublicKeyPairMutex =
        new ReentrantReadWriteLock();
    private final ReentrantReadWriteLock m_encryptionKeyMutex =
        new ReentrantReadWriteLock();
    private final ReentrantReadWriteLock m_identityMutex =
        new ReentrantReadWriteLock();
    private final ReentrantReadWriteLock m_macKeyMutex =
        new ReentrantReadWriteLock();
    private final ReentrantReadWriteLock m_ozoneEncryptionKeyMutex =
        new ReentrantReadWriteLock();
    private final ReentrantReadWriteLock m_ozoneMacKeyMutex =
        new ReentrantReadWriteLock();
    private final ReentrantReadWriteLock m_sipHashEncryptionKeyMutex =
        new ReentrantReadWriteLock();
    private final ReentrantReadWriteLock m_sipHashIdDigestMutex =
        new ReentrantReadWriteLock();
    private final ReentrantReadWriteLock m_sipHashIdMutex =
        new ReentrantReadWriteLock();
    private final ReentrantReadWriteLock m_sipHashMacKeyMutex =
        new ReentrantReadWriteLock();
    private final static String FIRE_HASH_ALGORITHM = "SHA-384";
    private final static String FIRE_HMAC_ALGORITHM = "HmacSHA384";
    private final static String FIRE_SYMMETRIC_ALGORITHM = "AES";
    private final static String FIRE_SYMMETRIC_CIPHER_TRANSFORMATION =
        "AES/CTS/NoPadding";
    private final static String HASH_ALGORITHM = "SHA-512";
    private final static String HMAC_ALGORITHM = "HmacSHA512";
    private final static String PKI_ECDSA_SIGNATURE_ALGORITHM =
        "SHA512withECDSA";
    private final static String PKI_RSA_ENCRYPTION_ALGORITHM =
        "RSA/NONE/OAEPwithSHA-512andMGF1Padding";
```

```java
private final static String PKI_RSA_SIGNATURE_ALGORITHM =
    /*
    ** SHA512withRSA/PSS requires API 23+.
    */

    "SHA512withRSA";
private final static String SYMMETRIC_ALGORITHM = "AES";
private final static String SYMMETRIC_CIPHER_TRANSFORMATION =
    "AES/CBC/PKCS7Padding";
private final static int FIRE_STREAM_CREATION_ITERATION_COUNT = 10000;
private final static int MCELIECE_M[] = {11, 12};
private final static int MCELIECE_T[] = {50, 68};
private final static int SIPHASH_STREAM_CREATION_ITERATION_COUNT = 4096;
private static Cryptography s_instance = null;
private static SecureRandom s_secureRandom = null;
public final static String DEFAULT_SIPHASH_ID =
    "0000-0000-0000-0000-0000-0000-0000-0000";
public final static String PARTICIPANT_CALL_MCELIECE_KEY_SIZE =
    "McEliece-Fujisaki (11, 50)";
public final static String TLS_LEGACY_V12[] = new String[]
    {"SSLv3", "TLSv1", "TLSv1.1", "TLSv1.2"};
public final static String TLS_NEW[] = new String[]
    {"TLSv1", "TLSv1.1", "TLSv1.2", "TLSv1.3"};
public final static String TLS_V1_V12[] = new String[]
    {"TLSv1", "TLSv1.1", "TLSv1.2"};
public final static byte MESSAGES_KEY_TYPES[] =
    new byte[] {(byte) 'M', (byte) 'R'};
public final static int CIPHER_HASH_KEYS_LENGTH = 96;
public final static int CIPHER_IV_LENGTH = 16;
public final static int CIPHER_KEY_LENGTH = 32;
public final static int FIRE_CIPHER_IV_LENGTH = 16;
public final static int FIRE_HASH_KEY_LENGTH = 48;
public final static int HASH_KEY_LENGTH = 64;
public final static int IDENTITY_SIZE = 8; // Size of a long.
public final static int KEY_EXCHANGE_INITIAL_PBKDF2_ITERATION = 1000;
public final static int PARTICIPANT_CALL_RSA_KEY_SIZE = 3072;
public final static int PKI_SIGNATURE_KEY_SIZES[] =
    {384, 4096}; // ECDSA, RSA
public final static int PKI_ENCRYPTION_KEY_SIZES[] = {4096}; // RSA
public final static int SHA_1_OUTPUT_SIZE_BITS = 160;
public final static int SIPHASH_OUTPUT_LENGTH = 16; // Bytes (128 bits).
public final static int SIPHASH_IDENTITY_LENGTH =
    DEFAULT_SIPHASH_ID.length();
public final static int STEAM_FILE_IDENTITY_LENGTH = 48;
public final static int STEAM_KEY_EXCHANGE_RSA_KEY_SIZE = 3096;

private Cryptography()
{
    prepareSecureRandom();
}

private static synchronized void prepareSecureRandom()
{
    if(s_secureRandom != null)
        return;

    try
    {
        s_secureRandom = new SecureRandom();
    }
    catch(Exception exception)
    {
    }
```

```java
    }

    public KeyPair chatEncryptionKeyPair()
    {
        m_chatEncryptionPublicKeyPairMutex.readLock().lock();

        try
        {
            return m_chatEncryptionPublicKeyPair;
        }
        finally
        {
            m_chatEncryptionPublicKeyPairMutex.readLock().unlock();
        }
    }

    public KeyPair chatSignatureKeyPair()
    {
        m_chatSignaturePublicKeyPairMutex.readLock().lock();

        try
        {
            return m_chatSignaturePublicKeyPair;
        }
        finally
        {
            m_chatSignaturePublicKeyPairMutex.readLock().unlock();
        }
    }

    public PublicKey chatEncryptionPublicKey()
    {
        m_chatEncryptionPublicKeyPairMutex.readLock().lock();

        try
        {
            if(m_chatEncryptionPublicKeyPair != null)
                return m_chatEncryptionPublicKeyPair.getPublic();
            else
                return null;
        }
        finally
        {
            m_chatEncryptionPublicKeyPairMutex.readLock().unlock();
        }
    }

    public PublicKey chatSignaturePublicKey()
    {
        m_chatSignaturePublicKeyPairMutex.readLock().lock();

        try
        {
            if(m_chatSignaturePublicKeyPair != null)
                return m_chatSignaturePublicKeyPair.getPublic();
            else
                return null;
        }
        finally
        {
            m_chatSignaturePublicKeyPairMutex.readLock().unlock();
        }
    }
```

```java
public String chatEncryptionPublicKeyAlgorithm()
{
    return m_chatEncryptionPublicKeyAlgorithm;
}

public String etmBase64String(String string)
{
    try
    {
        return Base64.encodeToString
            (etm(string.getBytes()), Base64.DEFAULT);
    }
    catch(Exception exception)
    {
    }

    return null;
}

public String etmBase64String(boolean state)
{
    try
    {
        return Base64.encodeToString
            (etm(String.valueOf(state).getBytes()), Base64.DEFAULT);
    }
    catch(Exception exception)
    {
    }

    return null;
}

public String etmBase64String(byte data[])
{
    try
    {
        if(data == null)
            return Base64.encodeToString
                (etm("".getBytes()), Base64.DEFAULT);
        else
            return Base64.encodeToString(etm(data), Base64.DEFAULT);
    }
    catch(Exception exception)
    {
    }

    return null;
}

public String etmBase64String(int value)
{
    try
    {
        return Base64.encodeToString
            (etm(String.valueOf(value).getBytes()), Base64.DEFAULT);
    }
    catch(Exception exception)
    {
    }

    return null;
```

```java
    }

    public String etmBase64String(long value)
    {
        try
        {
            return Base64.encodeToString
                (etm(String.valueOf(value).getBytes()), Base64.DEFAULT);
        }
        catch(Exception exception)
        {
        }

        return null;
    }

    public String sipHashId()
    {
        m_sipHashIdMutex.readLock().lock();

        try
        {
            return m_sipHashId;
        }
        finally
        {
            m_sipHashIdMutex.readLock().unlock();
        }
    }

    public boolean compareChatEncryptionPublicKey(PublicKey key)
    {
        if(key == null)
            return false;

        m_chatEncryptionPublicKeyPairMutex.readLock().lock();

        try
        {
            if(key.equals(m_chatEncryptionPublicKeyPair.getPublic()))
                return true;
            else if(key.hashCode() ==
                    m_chatEncryptionPublicKeyPair.getPublic().hashCode())
                return true;
        }
        catch(Exception exception)
        {
        }
        finally
        {
            m_chatEncryptionPublicKeyPairMutex.readLock().unlock();
        }

        return false;
    }

    public boolean compareChatSignaturePublicKey(PublicKey key)
    {
        if(key == null)
            return false;

        m_chatSignaturePublicKeyPairMutex.readLock().lock();
```

```
       try
       {
           if(key.equals(m_chatSignaturePublicKeyPair.getPublic()))
               return true;
           else if(key.hashCode() ==
                   m_chatSignaturePublicKeyPair.getPublic().hashCode())
               return true;
       }
       catch(Exception exception)
       {
       }
       finally
       {
           m_chatSignaturePublicKeyPairMutex.readLock().unlock();
       }

       return false;
   }

   public boolean hasValidOzoneKeys()
   {
       byte bytes1[] = ozoneEncryptionKey();
       byte bytes2[] = ozoneMacKey();

       return !(bytes1 == null || bytes1.length != CIPHER_KEY_LENGTH ||
                bytes2 == null || bytes2.length != HASH_KEY_LENGTH);
   }

   public boolean hasValidOzoneMacKey()
   {
       byte bytes[] = ozoneMacKey();

       return !(bytes == null || bytes.length != HASH_KEY_LENGTH);
   }

   public boolean isValidSipHashMac(byte data[], byte mac[])
   {
       if(data == null || mac == null)
           return false;

       m_sipHashMacKeyMutex.readLock().lock();

       try
       {
           return memcmp(hmac(data, m_sipHashMacKey), mac);
       }
       finally
       {
           m_sipHashMacKeyMutex.readLock().unlock();
       }
   }

   public boolean iAmTheDestination(byte data[], byte mac[])
   {
       if(data == null || mac == null)
           return false;

       m_sipHashIdDigestMutex.readLock().lock();

       try
       {
           return memcmp(hmac(data, m_sipHashIdDigest), mac);
       }
```

```java
        finally
        {
            m_sipHashIdDigestMutex.readLock().unlock();
        }
    }

    public boolean prepareSipHashKeys()
    {
        try
        {
            byte bytes[] = null;
            byte salt[] = null;
            byte temporary[] = null;

            m_sipHashIdMutex.readLock().lock();

            try
            {
                salt = sha512(m_sipHashId.getBytes(StandardCharsets.UTF_8));
                temporary = pbkdf2(salt,
                                   m_sipHashId.toCharArray(),
                                   SIPHASH_STREAM_CREATION_ITERATION_COUNT,
                                   SHA_1_OUTPUT_SIZE_BITS); // SHA-1
            }
            finally
            {
                m_sipHashIdMutex.readLock().unlock();
            }

            if(temporary != null)
                bytes = pbkdf2
                    (salt,
                     Base64.encodeToString(temporary,
                                           Base64.NO_WRAP).toCharArray(),
                     1,
                     8 * (CIPHER_KEY_LENGTH + HASH_KEY_LENGTH)); // Bits.

            if(bytes != null)
            {
                m_sipHashEncryptionKeyMutex.writeLock().lock();

                try
                {
                    m_sipHashEncryptionKey = Arrays.copyOfRange
                        (bytes, 0, CIPHER_KEY_LENGTH);
                }
                finally
                {
                    m_sipHashEncryptionKeyMutex.writeLock().unlock();
                }

                m_sipHashMacKeyMutex.writeLock().lock();

                try
                {
                    m_sipHashMacKey = Arrays.copyOfRange
                        (bytes,
                         CIPHER_KEY_LENGTH,
                         CIPHER_KEY_LENGTH + HASH_KEY_LENGTH);
                }
                finally
                {
                    m_sipHashMacKeyMutex.writeLock().unlock();
```

```java
                }
            }
        else
            return false;
        }
    catch(Exception exception)
        {
            return false;
        }

    return true;
    }

public byte[] chatEncryptionPublicKeyDigest()
    {
        m_chatEncryptionPublicKeyPairMutex.readLock().lock();

        try
        {
            if(m_chatEncryptionPublicKeyPair == null ||
               m_chatEncryptionPublicKeyPair.getPublic() == null)
                return null;

            return sha512
                (m_chatEncryptionPublicKeyPair.getPublic().getEncoded());
        }
        catch(Exception exception)
        {
        }
        finally
        {
            m_chatEncryptionPublicKeyPairMutex.readLock().unlock();
        }

        return null;
    }

public byte[] chatSignaturePublicKeyDigest()
    {
        m_chatSignaturePublicKeyPairMutex.readLock().lock();

        try
        {
            if(m_chatSignaturePublicKeyPair == null ||
               m_chatSignaturePublicKeyPair.getPublic() == null)
                return null;

            return sha512
                (m_chatSignaturePublicKeyPair.getPublic().getEncoded());
        }
        catch(Exception exception)
        {
        }
        finally
        {
            m_chatSignaturePublicKeyPairMutex.readLock().unlock();
        }

        return null;
    }

public byte[] decryptWithSipHashKey(byte data[])
    {
```

```java
        if(data == null)
            return null;

        byte bytes[] = null;

        try
        {
            m_sipHashEncryptionKeyMutex.readLock().lock();

            try
            {
                if(m_sipHashEncryptionKey == null)
                    return null;

                Cipher cipher = null;
                SecretKey secretKey = new SecretKeySpec
                    (m_sipHashEncryptionKey, SYMMETRIC_ALGORITHM);
                byte iv[] = Arrays.copyOf(data, CIPHER_IV_LENGTH);

                cipher = Cipher.getInstance(SYMMETRIC_CIPHER_TRANSFORMATION);
                cipher.init(Cipher.DECRYPT_MODE,
                            secretKey,
                            new IvParameterSpec(iv));
                bytes = cipher.doFinal
                    (Arrays.copyOfRange(data, CIPHER_IV_LENGTH, data.length));
            }
            catch(Exception exception)
            {
                return null;
            }
            finally
            {
                m_sipHashEncryptionKeyMutex.readLock().unlock();
            }
        }
        catch(Exception exception)
        {
            bytes = null;
        }

        return bytes;
    }

    public byte[] etm(byte data[]) // Encrypt-Then-MAC
    {
        /*
        ** Encrypt-then-MAC.
        */

        if(data == null)
            return null;

        m_encryptionKeyMutex.readLock().lock();

        try
        {
            if(m_encryptionKey == null)
                return null;
        }
        finally
        {
            m_encryptionKeyMutex.readLock().unlock();
        }
```

```java
        m_macKeyMutex.readLock().lock();

        try
        {
            if(m_macKey == null)
                return null;
        }
        finally
        {
            m_macKeyMutex.readLock().unlock();
        }

        byte bytes[] = null;

        try
        {
            m_encryptionKeyMutex.readLock().lock();

            try
            {
                if(m_encryptionKey == null)
                    return null;

                Cipher cipher = null;
                byte iv[] = new byte[CIPHER_IV_LENGTH];

                cipher = Cipher.getInstance(SYMMETRIC_CIPHER_TRANSFORMATION);
                s_secureRandom.nextBytes(iv);
                cipher.init(Cipher.ENCRYPT_MODE,
                            m_encryptionKey,
                            new IvParameterSpec(iv));
                bytes = cipher.doFinal(data);
                bytes = Miscellaneous.joinByteArrays(iv, bytes);
            }
            catch(Exception exception)
            {
                return null;
            }
            finally
            {
                m_encryptionKeyMutex.readLock().unlock();
            }

            m_macKeyMutex.readLock().lock();

            try
            {
                if(m_macKey == null)
                    return null;

                Mac mac = null;

                mac = Mac.getInstance(HMAC_ALGORITHM);
                mac.init(m_macKey);
                bytes = Miscellaneous.joinByteArrays(bytes, mac.doFinal(bytes));
            }
            catch(Exception exception)
            {
                return null;
            }
            finally
            {
```

```java
            m_macKeyMutex.readLock().unlock();
        }
    }
    catch(Exception exception)
    {
        bytes = null;
    }

    return bytes;
}

public byte[] generateFireDigestKeyStream(String digest)
{
    byte salt[] = null;

    try
    {
        salt = sha512
            (Miscellaneous.
             joinByteArrays(digest.getBytes(StandardCharsets.ISO_8859_1),
                        "sha384".getBytes(StandardCharsets.
                                        ISO_8859_1)));
    }
    catch(Exception exception)
    {
        return null;
    }

    /*
    ** Now, a key stream.
    */

    byte stream[] = null;

    try
    {
        stream = pbkdf2
            (salt,
             new String(digest.getBytes(StandardCharsets.UTF_8)).
             toCharArray(),
             FIRE_STREAM_CREATION_ITERATION_COUNT,
             896);
    }
    catch(Exception exception)
    {
        return null;
    }

    return stream;
}

public byte[] generateFireEncryptionKey(String channel, String salt)
{
    byte ciphertext[] = null;

    try
    {
        ciphertext = "aes256".getBytes
            (StandardCharsets.ISO_8859_1); // Latin-1
    }
    catch(Exception exception)
    {
        return null;
```

```java
        }

    byte c[] = null;

    try
    {
        c = channel.getBytes(StandardCharsets.ISO_8859_1); // Latin-1
    }
    catch(Exception exception)
    {
        return null;
    }

    byte s[] = null;

    try
    {
        s = salt.getBytes(StandardCharsets.ISO_8859_1); // Latin-1
    }
    catch(Exception exception)
    {
        return null;
    }

    byte sha384[] = null;

    try
    {
        sha384 = "sha384".getBytes(StandardCharsets.ISO_8859_1); // Latin-1
    }
    catch(Exception exception)
    {
        return null;
    }

    /*
    ** Now, a key.
    */

    byte key[] = null;

    try
    {
        key = pbkdf2
            (s,
             new String(new String(Miscellaneous.
                                    joinByteArrays(c, ciphertext, sha384)).
                        getBytes(StandardCharsets.UTF_8)).toCharArray(),
             FIRE_STREAM_CREATION_ITERATION_COUNT,
             2304);

        if(key != null)
            key = Arrays.copyOfRange(key, 0, CIPHER_KEY_LENGTH);
    }
    catch(Exception exception)
    {
        return null;
    }

    return key;
    }

    public byte[] hmac(byte data[])
```

```java
    {
        if(data == null)
            return null;

        m_macKeyMutex.readLock().lock();

        try
        {
            if(m_macKey == null)
                rcturn null;

            byte bytes[] = null;

            try
            {
                Mac mac = null;

                mac = Mac.getInstance(HMAC_ALGORITHM);
                mac.init(m_macKey);
                bytes = mac.doFinal(data);
            }
            catch(Exception exception)
            {
                bytes = null;
            }

            return bytes;
        }
        finally
        {
            m_macKeyMutex.readLock().unlock();
        }
    }

    public byte[] identity()
    {
        m_identityMutex.writeLock().lock();

        try
        {
            if(m_identity == null)
            {
                m_identity = new byte[IDENTITY_SIZE];
                s_secureRandom.nextBytes(m_identity);
            }

            return m_identity;
        }
        finally
        {
            m_identityMutex.writeLock().unlock();
        }
    }

    public byte[] mtd(byte data[]) // MAC-Then-Decrypt
    {
        /*
        ** MAC-then-decrypt.
        */

        if(data == null)
            return null;
```

```java
    m_encryptionKeyMutex.readLock().lock();

    try
    {
        if(m_encryptionKey == null)
            return null;
    }
    finally
    {
        m_encryptionKeyMutex.readLock().unlock();
    }

    m_macKeyMutex.readLock().lock();

    try
    {
        if(m_macKey == null)
            return null;
    }
    finally
    {
        m_macKeyMutex.readLock().unlock();
    }

    try
    {
        /*
        ** Verify the computed digest with the provided digest.
        */

        byte digest1[] = null; // Provided digest.
        byte digest2[] = null; // Computed digest.

        digest1 = Arrays.copyOfRange
            (data, data.length - HASH_KEY_LENGTH, data.length);
        m_macKeyMutex.readLock().lock();

        try
        {
            if(m_macKey == null)
                return null;

            Mac mac = null;

            mac = Mac.getInstance(HMAC_ALGORITHM);
            mac.init(m_macKey);
            digest2 = mac.doFinal
                (Arrays.copyOf(data, data.length - HASH_KEY_LENGTH));
        }
        catch(Exception exception)
        {
            return null;
        }
        finally
        {
            m_macKeyMutex.readLock().unlock();
        }

        if(!memcmp(digest1, digest2))
            return null;
    }
    catch(Exception exception)
    {
```

```java
            return null;
        }

    byte bytes[] = null;

    try
    {
        m_encryptionKeyMutex.readLock().lock();

        try
        {
            if(m_encryptionKey == null)
                return null;

            Cipher cipher = null;
            byte iv[] = Arrays.copyOf(data, CIPHER_IV_LENGTH);

            cipher = Cipher.getInstance(SYMMETRIC_CIPHER_TRANSFORMATION);
            cipher.init(Cipher.DECRYPT_MODE,
                        m_encryptionKey,
                        new IvParameterSpec(iv));
            bytes = cipher.doFinal
                (Arrays.copyOfRange(data,
                                    CIPHER_IV_LENGTH,
                                    data.length - HASH_KEY_LENGTH));
        }
        catch(Exception exception)
        {
            bytes = null;
        }
        finally
        {
            m_encryptionKeyMutex.readLock().unlock();
        }
    }
    catch(Exception exception)
    {
        bytes = null;
    }

    return bytes;
}

public byte[] ozoneEncryptionKey()
{
    m_ozoneEncryptionKeyMutex.readLock().lock();

    try
    {
        return m_ozoneEncryptionKey;
    }
    finally
    {
        m_ozoneEncryptionKeyMutex.readLock().unlock();
    }
}

public byte[] ozoneMacKey()
{
    m_ozoneMacKeyMutex.readLock().lock();

    try
    {
```

```java
            return m_ozoneMacKey;
        }
        finally
        {
            m_ozoneMacKeyMutex.readLock().unlock();
        }
    }

    public byte[] pkiDecrypt(byte data[])
    {
        if(data == null)
            return null;

        m_chatEncryptionPublicKeyPairMutex.readLock().lock();

        try
        {
            byte bytes[] = null;

            try
            {
                Cipher cipher = null;

                if(m_chatEncryptionPublicKeyPair.getPrivate().getAlgorithm().
                    equals("McEliece-CCA2"))
                {
                    if(m_chatEncryptionPublicKeyAlgorithm.
                        startsWith("McEliece-Fujisaki"))
                        cipher = Cipher.getInstance("McElieceFujisaki");
                    else
                        cipher = Cipher.getInstance("McEliecePointcheval");

                    cipher.init
                        (Cipher.DECRYPT_MODE,
                         m_chatEncryptionPublicKeyPair.getPrivate(),
                         (McElieceCCA2KeyGenParameterSpec) null);
                }
                else
                {
                    cipher = Cipher.getInstance(PKI_RSA_ENCRYPTION_ALGORITHM);
                    cipher.init
                        (Cipher.DECRYPT_MODE,
                         m_chatEncryptionPublicKeyPair.getPrivate());
                }

                bytes = cipher.doFinal(data);
            }
            catch(Exception exception)
            {
                bytes = null;
            }

            return bytes;
        }
        finally
        {
            m_chatEncryptionPublicKeyPairMutex.readLock().unlock();
        }
    }

    public byte[] signViaChatEncryption(byte data[])
    {
        if(data == null)
```

```java
            return null;

        m_chatEncryptionPublicKeyPairMutex.readLock().lock();

        try
        {
            if(m_chatEncryptionPublicKeyPair == null ||
               m_chatEncryptionPublicKeyPair.getPrivate() == null)
                return null;

            Signature signature = null;
            byte bytes[] = null;

            try
            {
                if(m_chatEncryptionPublicKeyPair.getPrivate().getAlgorithm().
                   equals("EC"))
                    signature = Signature.getInstance
                        (PKI_ECDSA_SIGNATURE_ALGORITHM);
                else
                    signature = Signature.getInstance
                        (PKI_RSA_SIGNATURE_ALGORITHM);

                signature.initSign(m_chatEncryptionPublicKeyPair.getPrivate());
                signature.update(data);
                bytes = signature.sign();
            }
            catch(Exception exception)
            {
                bytes = null;
            }

            return bytes;
        }
        finally
        {
            m_chatEncryptionPublicKeyPairMutex.readLock().unlock();
        }
    }

    public byte[] signViaChatSignature(byte data[])
    {
        if(data == null)
            return null;

        m_chatSignaturePublicKeyPairMutex.readLock().lock();

        try
        {
            if(m_chatSignaturePublicKeyPair == null ||
               m_chatSignaturePublicKeyPair.getPrivate() == null)
                return null;

            Signature signature = null;
            byte bytes[] = null;

            try
            {
                if(m_chatSignaturePublicKeyPair.getPrivate().getAlgorithm().
                   equals("EC"))
                    signature = Signature.getInstance
                        (PKI_ECDSA_SIGNATURE_ALGORITHM);
                else
```

```java
                    signature = Signature.getInstance
                        (PKI_RSA_SIGNATURE_ALGORITHM);

                    signature.initSign(m_chatSignaturePublicKeyPair.getPrivate());
                    signature.update(data);
                    bytes = signature.sign();
                }
                catch(Exception exception)
                {
                    bytes = null;
                }

                return bytes;
            }
            finally
            {
                m_chatSignaturePublicKeyPairMutex.readLock().unlock();
            }
        }

    public byte[] sipHashEncryptionKey()
    {
        m_sipHashEncryptionKeyMutex.readLock().lock();

        try
        {
            return m_sipHashEncryptionKey;
        }
        finally
        {
            m_sipHashEncryptionKeyMutex.readLock().unlock();
        }
    }

    public byte[] sipHashMacKey()
    {
        m_sipHashMacKeyMutex.readLock().lock();

        try
        {
            return m_sipHashMacKey;
        }
        finally
        {
            m_sipHashMacKeyMutex.readLock().unlock();
        }
    }

    public int chatEncryptionPublicKeyT()
    {
        m_chatEncryptionPublicKeyPairMutex.readLock().lock();

        try
        {
            if(m_chatEncryptionPublicKeyPair != null)
                return
                    ((BCMcElieceCCA2PublicKey) m_chatEncryptionPublicKeyPair.
                     getPublic()).getT();
            else
                return 0;
        }
        catch(Exception exception)
        {
```

```java
            }
        finally
        {
            m_chatEncryptionPublicKeyPairMutex.readLock().unlock();
        }

        return 0;
    }

    public static KeyPair generatePrivatePublicKeyPair(String algorithm,
                                                       int keySize1,
                                                       int keySize2)
    {
        if(algorithm.startsWith("McEliece-Fujisaki") ||
           algorithm.startsWith("McEliece-Pointcheval"))
        {
            try
            {
                KeyPairGenerator keyPairGenerator = null;

                if(algorithm.startsWith("McEliece-Fujisaki"))
                    keyPairGenerator = KeyPairGenerator.
                        getInstance("McElieceFujisaki");
                else
                    keyPairGenerator = KeyPairGenerator.
                        getInstance("McEliecePointcheval");

                McElieceCCA2KeyGenParameterSpec parameters = null;

                if(keySize2 == 0 || keySize2 == 1)
                    parameters = new McElieceCCA2KeyGenParameterSpec
                        (MCELIECE_M[keySize2],
                         MCELIECE_T[keySize2],
                         McElieceCCA2KeyGenParameterSpec.SHA256);
                else
                    parameters = new McElieceCCA2KeyGenParameterSpec
                        (MCELIECE_M[0],
                         MCELIECE_T[0],
                         McElieceCCA2KeyGenParameterSpec.SHA256);

                keyPairGenerator.initialize(parameters);
                return keyPairGenerator.generateKeyPair();
            }
            catch(Exception exception)
            {
            }

            return null;
        }
        else
        {
            prepareSecureRandom();

            try
            {
                KeyPairGenerator keyPairGenerator = KeyPairGenerator.
                    getInstance(algorithm);

                keyPairGenerator.initialize(keySize1, s_secureRandom);
                return keyPairGenerator.generateKeyPair();
            }
            catch(Exception exception)
            {
```

```java
                }

            return null;
        }
    }

    public static KeyPair generatePrivatePublicKeyPair(String algorithm,
                                           byte privateBytes[],
                                           byte publicBytes[])
    {
        if(privateBytes == null ||
           privateBytes.length == 0 ||
           publicBytes == null ||
           publicBytes.length == 0)
            return null;

        try
        {
            if(algorithm.startsWith("McEliece-Fujisaki") ||
               algorithm.startsWith("McEliece-Pointcheval"))
            {
                EncodedKeySpec privateKeySpec = new PKCS8EncodedKeySpec
                    (privateBytes);
                EncodedKeySpec publicKeySpec = new X509EncodedKeySpec
                    (publicBytes);
                KeyFactory generator = KeyFactory.getInstance
                    (PQCObjectIdentifiers.mcElieceCca2.getId());
                PrivateKey privateKey = generator.generatePrivate
                    (privateKeySpec);
                PublicKey publicKey = generator.generatePublic(publicKeySpec);

                return new KeyPair(publicKey, privateKey);
            }
            else
            {
                EncodedKeySpec privateKeySpec = new PKCS8EncodedKeySpec
                    (privateBytes);
                EncodedKeySpec publicKeySpec = new X509EncodedKeySpec
                    (publicBytes);
                KeyFactory generator = KeyFactory.getInstance(algorithm);
                PrivateKey privateKey = generator.generatePrivate
                    (privateKeySpec);
                PublicKey publicKey = generator.generatePublic(publicKeySpec);

                return new KeyPair(publicKey, privateKey);
            }
        }
        catch(Exception exception)
        {
            Database.getInstance().writeLog
                ("Cryptography::generatePrivatePublicKeyPair(): " +
                 "exception raised (" +
                 exception.getMessage().toLowerCase().trim()
                 + ").");
        }

        return null;
    }

    public static PrivateKey privateKeyFromBytes(byte privateBytes[])
    {
        if(privateBytes == null || privateBytes.length == 0)
            return null;
```

```java
    try
    {
        EncodedKeySpec privateKeySpec = new PKCS8EncodedKeySpec
            (privateBytes);

        for(int i = 0; i < 3; i++)
            try
            {
                KeyFactory generator = null;

                switch(i)
                {
                case 0:
                    generator = KeyFactory.getInstance("EC");
                    break;
                case 1:
                    generator = KeyFactory.getInstance
                        (PQCObjectIdentifiers.mcElieceCca2.getId());
                    break;
                default:
                    generator = KeyFactory.getInstance("RSA");
                    break;
                }

                return generator.generatePrivate(privateKeySpec);
            }
            catch(Exception exception)
            {
            }
    }
    catch(Exception exception)
    {
    }

    return null;
}

public static PublicKey publicKeyFromBytes(byte publicBytes[])
{
    if(publicBytes == null || publicBytes.length == 0)
        return null;

    try
    {
        EncodedKeySpec publicKeySpec = new X509EncodedKeySpec(publicBytes);

        for(int i = 0; i < 3; i++)
            try
            {
                KeyFactory generator = null;

                switch(i)
                {
                case 0:
                    generator = KeyFactory.getInstance("EC");
                    break;
                case 1:
                    generator = KeyFactory.getInstance
                        (PQCObjectIdentifiers.mcElieceCca2.getId());
                    break;
                default:
                    generator = KeyFactory.getInstance("RSA");
```

```java
                        break;
                    }

                    return generator.generatePublic(publicKeySpec);
                }
                catch(Exception exception)
                {
                }
            }
        catch(Exception exception)
        {
        }

        return null;
    }

    public static PublicKey publicRSAKeyFromBytes(byte publicBytes[])
    {
        if(publicBytes == null)
            return null;

        try
        {
            EncodedKeySpec publicKeySpec = new X509EncodedKeySpec(publicBytes);
            KeyFactory generator = KeyFactory.getInstance("RSA");

            return generator.generatePublic(publicKeySpec);
        }
        catch(Exception exception)
        {
        }

        return null;
    }

    public static SecretKey generateEncryptionKey(byte salt[],
                                                  char password[],
                                                  int iterations,
                                                  int keyDerivationFunction)
    {
        if(password == null || salt == null)
            return null;

        if(keyDerivationFunction == 0) // Argon2id
        {
            try
            {
                Argon2BytesGenerator generator = new Argon2BytesGenerator();
                Argon2Parameters.Builder builder = new Argon2Parameters.Builder
                    (Argon2Parameters.ARGON2_id).
                    withVersion(Argon2Parameters.ARGON2_VERSION_13).
                    withIterations(iterations).
                    withMemoryAsKB(CIPHER_KEY_LENGTH).
                    withParallelism(4). /*
                                        ** Should depend upon the
                                        ** number of CPU cores.
                                        */
                    withAdditional
                    (Hex.decode("0102030405060708090000a0b0c0d0e0f" +
                                "0102030405060708090000a0b0c0d0e0f")).
                    withSecret(new String(password).
                               getBytes(StandardCharsets.UTF_8)).
                    withSalt(salt);
```

```java
            byte bytes[] = new byte[CIPHER_KEY_LENGTH];

            generator.init(builder.build());
            generator.generateBytes(password, bytes);
            return new SecretKeySpec(bytes, SYMMETRIC_ALGORITHM);
        }
        catch(Exception exception)
        {
        }
    }
    else // PBKDF2
    {
        int length = 256; // Bits.

        try
        {
            KeySpec keySpec = new PBEKeySpec
                (password, salt, iterations, length);
            SecretKeyFactory secretKeyFactory = SecretKeyFactory.
                getInstance("PBKDF2WithHmacSHA1");

            return secretKeyFactory.generateSecret(keySpec);
        }
        catch(Exception exception)
        {
        }
    }

    return null;
}

public static SecretKey generateMacKey(byte salt[],
                                       char password[],
                                       int iterations,
                                       int keyDerivationFunction)
{
    if(password == null || salt == null)
        return null;

    if(keyDerivationFunction == 0) // Argon2id
    {
        try
        {
            Argon2BytesGenerator generator = new Argon2BytesGenerator();
            Argon2Parameters.Builder builder = new Argon2Parameters.Builder
                (Argon2Parameters.ARGON2_id).
                withVersion(Argon2Parameters.ARGON2_VERSION_13).
                withIterations(iterations).
                withMemoryAsKB(HASH_KEY_LENGTH).
                withParallelism(4). /*
                                    ** Should depend upon the
                                    ** number of CPU cores.
                                    */
                withAdditional
                (Hex.decode("000908070605040302010f0e0d0c0b0a" +
                            "000908070605040302010f0e0d0c0b0a" +
                            "000908070605040302010f0e0d0c0b0a" +
                            "000908070605040302010f0e0d0c0b0a")).
                withSecret(new String(password).
                            getBytes(StandardCharsets.UTF_8)).
                withSalt(salt);
            byte bytes[] = new byte[HASH_KEY_LENGTH];
```

```java
                generator.init(builder.build());
                generator.generateBytes(password, bytes);
                return new SecretKeySpec(bytes, HASH_ALGORITHM);
            }
            catch(Exception exception)
            {
            }
        }
        else // PBKDF2
        {
            int length = 512; // Bits.

            try
            {
                KeySpec keySpec = new PBEKeySpec
                    (password, salt, iterations, length);
                SecretKeyFactory secretKeyFactory = SecretKeyFactory.
                    getInstance("PBKDF2WithHmacSHA1");

                return secretKeyFactory.generateSecret(keySpec);
            }
            catch(Exception exception)
            {
            }
        }

        return null;
    }

    public static String fancyKeyInformationOutput(KeyPair keyPair,
                                        String algorithmIdentifier)
    {
        if(keyPair == null)
            return "";
        else
            return fancyKeyInformationOutput
                (keyPair.getPublic(), algorithmIdentifier);
    }

    public static String fancyKeyInformationOutput(PublicKey publicKey,
                                        String algorithmIdentifier)
    {
        if(publicKey == null)
            return "";

        try
        {
            String algorithm = publicKeyAlgorithm(publicKey);
            StringBuilder stringBuilder = new StringBuilder();

            stringBuilder.append("Algorithm: ");
            stringBuilder.append(algorithm);

            if(!algorithmIdentifier.isEmpty())
            {
                stringBuilder.append(" (");
                stringBuilder.append(algorithmIdentifier);
                stringBuilder.append(")");
            }

            stringBuilder.append("\n");
            stringBuilder.append("Disk Size: ");
            stringBuilder.append(publicKey.getEncoded().length);
```

```java
        stringBuilder.append(" Bytes\n");
        stringBuilder.append("Fingerprint: ");
        stringBuilder.append(publicKeyFingerPrint(publicKey));
        stringBuilder.append("\n");
        stringBuilder.append("Format: ");
        stringBuilder.append(publicKey.getFormat());

        if(algorithm.equals("EC") ||
           algorithm.equals("RSA") ||
           algorithm.startsWith("McEliece"))
            try
            {
                switch(algorithm)
                {
                case "EC":
                    ECPublicKey ecPublicKey = (ECPublicKey) publicKey;

                    if(ecPublicKey != null)
                        stringBuilder.append("\n").append("Size: ").
                            append(ecPublicKey.getW().getAffineX().
                                    bitLength());

                    break;
                case "McEliece-CCA2":
                case "McEliece-Fujisaki":
                case "McEliece-Pointcheval":
                    BCMcElieceCCA2PublicKey mcEliecePublicKey =
                        (BCMcElieceCCA2PublicKey) publicKey;

                    if(mcEliecePublicKey != null)
                        stringBuilder.append("\n").append("m = ").
                            append((int) (Math.log(mcEliecePublicKey.
                                                   getN()) /
                                    Math.log(2))).
                            append(", t = ").
                            append(mcEliecePublicKey.getT());

                    break;
                case "RSA":
                    RSAPublicKey rsaPublicKey = (RSAPublicKey) publicKey;

                    if(rsaPublicKey != null)
                        stringBuilder.append("\n").append("Size: ").
                            append(rsaPublicKey.getModulus().bitLength());

                    break;
                default:
                    break;
                }
            }
            catch(Exception exception)
            {
            }

        return stringBuilder.toString();
    }
    catch(Exception exception)
    {
    }

    return "";
}
```

```java
public static String fingerPrint(byte bytes[])
{
    String fingerprint =
        "cf83e1357eefb8bdf1542850d66d8007d620e4050b5715dc" +
        "83f4a921d36ce9ce47d0d13c5d85f2b0ff8318d2877eec2f63b931bd4" +
        "7417a81a538327af927da3e";
    StringBuilder stringBuilder = new StringBuilder();

    if(bytes != null)
    {
        bytes = sha512(bytes);

        if(bytes != null)
            fingerprint = Miscellaneous.byteArrayAsHexString(bytes);
    }

    try
    {
        int length = fingerprint.length();

        for(int i = 0; i < length; i += 2)
            if(i < length - 2)
                stringBuilder.append(fingerprint, i, i + 2).
                    append(":");
            else
                stringBuilder.append(fingerprint.substring(i));
    }
    catch(Exception exception)
    {
    }

    return stringBuilder.toString();
}

public static String publicKeyAlgorithm(PublicKey publicKey)
{
    if(publicKey == null)
        return "";

    try
    {
        ASN1ObjectIdentifier asn1ObjectIdentifier = null;
        SubjectPublicKeyInfo subjectPublicKeyInfo =
            SubjectPublicKeyInfo.getInstance(publicKey.getEncoded());

        asn1ObjectIdentifier = subjectPublicKeyInfo.getAlgorithm().
            getAlgorithm();

        if(asn1ObjectIdentifier.equals(PQCObjectIdentifiers.mcElieceCca2))
            return "McEliece-CCA2";
        else if(asn1ObjectIdentifier.
            equals(PQCObjectIdentifiers.mcElieceFujisaki))
            return "McEliece-Fujisaki";
        else if(asn1ObjectIdentifier.
                equals(PQCObjectIdentifiers.mcEliecePointcheval))
            return "McEliece-Pointcheval";
        else if(publicKey.getAlgorithm().equals("EC"))
            return "ECDSA";
        else
            return "RSA";
    }
    catch(Exception exception)
    {
```

```java
        }

        return "";
    }

    public static String publicKeyFingerPrint(PublicKey publicKey)
    {
        if(publicKey == null)
            return fingerPrint(null);
        else
            return fingerPrint(publicKey.getEncoded());
    }

    public static String sipHashIdFromString(String string)
    {
        try
        {
            byte bytes[] = string.getBytes(StandardCharsets.UTF_8);

            if(bytes != null)
            {
                byte key[] = keyForSipHash(bytes);

                if(key == null)
                    return "";

                SipHash sipHash = new SipHash();
                long value[] = sipHash.hmac(bytes, key, SIPHASH_OUTPUT_LENGTH);

                if(value == new long[] {0L, 0L})
                    return "";

                bytes = Miscellaneous.longArrayToByteArray(value);

                if(bytes == null)
                    return "";

                return Miscellaneous.
                    byteArrayAsHexStringDelimited(bytes, '-', 4).toUpperCase();
            }
        }
        catch(Exception exception)
        {
        }

        return "";
    }

    public static boolean memcmp(byte a[], byte b[])
    {
        if(a == null || b == null)
            return false;

        int rc = 0;
        int size = java.lang.Math.max(a.length, b.length);

        for(int i = 0; i < size; i++)
            rc |= (a.length > i ? a[i] : 0) ^ (b.length > i ? b[i] : 0);

        return rc == 0;
    }

    public static boolean verifySignature(PublicKey publicKey,
```

```java
                                byte bytes[],
                                byte data[])
    {
        if(bytes == null || data == null || publicKey == null)
            return false;

        Signature signature = null;
        boolean ok = false;

        try
        {
            if(publicKey.getAlgorithm().equals("EC"))
                signature = Signature.getInstance
                    (PKI_ECDSA_SIGNATURE_ALGORITHM);
            else
                signature = Signature.getInstance(PKI_RSA_SIGNATURE_ALGORITHM);

            signature.initVerify(publicKey);
            signature.update(data);
            ok = signature.verify(bytes);
        }
        catch(Exception exception)
        {
            return false;
        }

        return ok;
    }

    public static byte[] aes256KeyBytes()
    {
        try
        {
            KeyGenerator keyGenerator = KeyGenerator.getInstance("AES");

            keyGenerator.init(256);
            return keyGenerator.generateKey().getEncoded();
        }
        catch(Exception exception)
        {
            return null;
        }
    }

    public static byte[] decrypt(byte data[], byte keyBytes[])
    {
        if(data == null || keyBytes == null)
            return null;

        byte bytes[] = null;

        try
        {
            Cipher cipher = null;
            SecretKey secretKey = new SecretKeySpec
                (keyBytes, SYMMETRIC_ALGORITHM);
            byte iv[] = Arrays.copyOf(data, CIPHER_IV_LENGTH);

            cipher = Cipher.getInstance(SYMMETRIC_CIPHER_TRANSFORMATION);
            cipher.init(Cipher.DECRYPT_MODE,
                        secretKey,
                        new IvParameterSpec(iv));
            bytes = cipher.doFinal
```

```java
                (Arrays.copyOfRange(data, CIPHER_IV_LENGTH, data.length));
        }
        catch(Exception exception)
        {
            bytes = null;
        }

        return bytes;
    }

    public static byte[] decryptFire(byte data[], byte keyBytes[])
    {
        if(data == null || keyBytes == null)
            return null;

        byte bytes[] = null;

        try
        {
            Cipher cipher = null;
            SecretKey secretKey = new SecretKeySpec
                (keyBytes, FIRE_SYMMETRIC_ALGORITHM);
            byte iv[] = Arrays.copyOf(data, FIRE_CIPHER_IV_LENGTH);

            cipher = Cipher.getInstance(FIRE_SYMMETRIC_CIPHER_TRANSFORMATION);
            cipher.init(Cipher.DECRYPT_MODE,
                        secretKey,
                        new IvParameterSpec(iv));
            bytes = cipher.doFinal
                (Arrays.copyOfRange(data, FIRE_CIPHER_IV_LENGTH, data.length));
        }
        catch(Exception exception)
        {
            bytes = null;
        }

        return bytes;
    }

    public static byte[] encrypt(byte data[], byte keyBytes[])
    {
        if(data == null || keyBytes == null)
            return null;

        prepareSecureRandom();

        byte bytes[] = null;

        try
        {
            Cipher cipher = null;
            SecretKey secretKey = new SecretKeySpec
                (keyBytes, SYMMETRIC_ALGORITHM);
            byte iv[] = new byte[CIPHER_IV_LENGTH];

            cipher = Cipher.getInstance(SYMMETRIC_CIPHER_TRANSFORMATION);
            s_secureRandom.nextBytes(iv);
            cipher.init(Cipher.ENCRYPT_MODE,
                        secretKey,
                        new IvParameterSpec(iv));
            bytes = cipher.doFinal(data);
            bytes = Miscellaneous.joinByteArrays(iv, bytes);
        }
```

```java
        catch(Exception exception)
        {
            bytes = null;
        }

        return bytes;
    }

    public static byte[] encryptFire(byte data[], byte keyBytes[])
    {
        if(data == null || keyBytes == null)
            return null;

        prepareSecureRandom();

        byte bytes[] = null;

        try
        {
            Cipher cipher = null;
            SecretKey secretKey = new SecretKeySpec
                (keyBytes, FIRE_SYMMETRIC_ALGORITHM);
            byte iv[] = new byte[FIRE_CIPHER_IV_LENGTH];

            cipher = Cipher.getInstance(FIRE_SYMMETRIC_CIPHER_TRANSFORMATION);
            s_secureRandom.nextBytes(iv);
            cipher.init(Cipher.ENCRYPT_MODE,
                        secretKey,
                        new IvParameterSpec(iv));
            bytes = cipher.doFinal
                (Miscellaneous.
                 joinByteArrays(data,

                                /*
                                ** Add the size of the original data.
                                */

                                Miscellaneous.intToByteArray(data.length)));
            bytes = Miscellaneous.joinByteArrays(iv, bytes);
        }
        catch(Exception exception)
        {
            bytes = null;
        }

        return bytes;
    }

    public static byte[] keyForSipHash(byte data[])
    {
        if(data == null)
            return null;

        return pbkdf2(sha512(data),
                      Miscellaneous.byteArrayAsHexString(data).toCharArray(),
                      SIPHASH_STREAM_CREATION_ITERATION_COUNT,
                      8 * SipHash.KEY_LENGTH);
    }

    public static byte[] hmac(byte data[], byte keyBytes[])
    {
        if(data == null || keyBytes == null)
            return null;
```

```java
        byte bytes[] = null;

        try
        {
            Mac mac = null;
            SecretKey key = new SecretKeySpec(keyBytes, HASH_ALGORITHM);

            mac = Mac.getInstance(HMAC_ALGORITHM);
            mac.init(key);
            bytes = mac.doFinal(data);
        }
        catch(Exception exception)
        {
            bytes = null;
        }

        return bytes;
    }

    public static byte[] hmacFire(byte data[], byte keyBytes[])
    {
        if(data == null || keyBytes == null)
            return null;

        byte bytes[] = null;

        try
        {
            Mac mac = null;
            SecretKey key = new SecretKeySpec(keyBytes, FIRE_HASH_ALGORITHM);

            mac = Mac.getInstance(FIRE_HMAC_ALGORITHM);
            mac.init(key);
            bytes = mac.doFinal(data);
        }
        catch(Exception exception)
        {
            bytes = null;
        }

        return bytes;
    }

    public static byte[] pbkdf2(byte salt[],
                                char password[],
                                int iterations,
                                int length)
    {
        if(password == null || salt == null)
            return null;

        try
        {
            KeySpec keySpec = new PBEKeySpec
                (password, salt, iterations, length);
            SecretKeyFactory secretKeyFactory = SecretKeyFactory.getInstance
                ("PBKDF2WithHmacSHA1");

            return secretKeyFactory.generateSecret(keySpec).getEncoded();
        }
        catch(Exception exception)
        {
```

```java
        return null;
    }
}

public static byte[] pkiDecrypt(PrivateKey privateKey, byte data[])
{
    if(data == null || privateKey == null)
        return null;

    byte bytes[] = null;

    try
    {
        Cipher cipher = null;

        if(privateKey.getAlgorithm().equals("McEliece-CCA2"))
            cipher = Cipher.getInstance("McElieceFujisaki");
        else
            cipher = Cipher.getInstance(PKI_RSA_ENCRYPTION_ALGORITHM);

        cipher.init(Cipher.DECRYPT_MODE, privateKey);
        bytes = cipher.doFinal(data);
    }
    catch(Exception exception)
    {
        bytes = null;
    }

    return bytes;
}

public static byte[] pkiEncrypt(PublicKey publicKey,
                                String algorithm,
                                byte data[])
{
    if(data == null || publicKey == null)
        return null;

    prepareSecureRandom();

    byte bytes[] = null;

    try
    {
        Cipher cipher = null;

        if(publicKey.getAlgorithm().equals("McEliece-CCA2"))
        {
            if(algorithm.startsWith("McEliece-Fujisaki"))
                cipher = Cipher.getInstance("McElieceFujisaki");
            else
                cipher = Cipher.getInstance("McEliecePointcheval");

            cipher.init
                (Cipher.ENCRYPT_MODE,
                 publicKey,
                 (McElieceCCA2KeyGenParameterSpec) null,
                 s_secureRandom);
        }
        else
        {
            cipher = Cipher.getInstance(PKI_RSA_ENCRYPTION_ALGORITHM);
            cipher.init(Cipher.ENCRYPT_MODE, publicKey);
```

```java
        }

        bytes = cipher.doFinal(data);
    }
    catch(Exception exception)
    {
        bytes = null;
    }

    return bytes;
}

public static byte[] randomBytes(int length)
{
    if(length <= 0)
        return null;

    prepareSecureRandom();

    byte bytes[] = null;

    try
    {
        bytes = new byte[length];
        s_secureRandom.nextBytes(bytes);
    }
    catch(Exception exception)
    {
        bytes = null;
    }

    return bytes;
}

public static byte[] sha256(byte[] ... data)
{
    byte bytes[] = null;

    try
    {
        MessageDigest messageDigest = MessageDigest.getInstance("SHA-256");

        for(byte b[] : data)
            if(b != null)
                messageDigest.update(b);

        bytes = messageDigest.digest();
    }
    catch(Exception exception)
    {
        bytes = null;
    }

    return bytes;
}

public static byte[] sha256FileDigest(String fileName)
{
    AssetFileDescriptor assetFileDescriptor = null;

    try
    {
        Uri uri = Uri.parse(fileName);
```

```java
            assetFileDescriptor = Smoke.getApplication().getContentResolver().
                openAssetFileDescriptor(uri, "r");

            FileInputStream fileInputStream = assetFileDescriptor.
                createInputStream();
            MessageDigest messageDigest = MessageDigest.getInstance("SHA-256");
            byte buffer[] = new byte[4096];
            int n = 0;

            while(n != -1)
            {
                if(Thread.currentThread().isInterrupted())
                    return null;

                n = fileInputStream.read(buffer);

                if(n > 0)
                    messageDigest.update(buffer, 0, n);
            }

            return messageDigest.digest();
        }
        catch(Exception exception)
        {
        }
        finally
        {
            try
            {
                if(assetFileDescriptor != null)
                    assetFileDescriptor.close();
            }
            catch(Exception exception)
            {
            }
        }

        return null;
    }

    public static byte[] sha512(byte[] ... data)
    {
        byte bytes[] = null;

        try
        {
            MessageDigest messageDigest = MessageDigest.getInstance("SHA-512");

            for(byte b[] : data)
                if(b != null)
                    messageDigest.update(b);

            bytes = messageDigest.digest();
        }
        catch(Exception exception)
        {
            bytes = null;
        }

        return bytes;
    }
```

```java
    public static byte[] sha512KeyBytes()
    {
        try
        {
            KeyGenerator keyGenerator = KeyGenerator.getInstance("HmacSHA512");

            keyGenerator.init(512);
            return keyGenerator.generateKey().getEncoded();
        }
        catch(Exception exception)
        {
            return null;
        }
    }

    public static byte[] xor(byte[] ... data)
    {
        if(data == null)
            return null;

        try
        {
            int length = 0;

            for(byte b[] : data)
                if(b != null)
                {
                    if(length == 0)
                        length = b.length;
                    else
                        length = Math.min(b.length, length);
                }

            if(length == 0)
                return null;

            byte bytes[] = new byte[length];

            Arrays.fill(bytes, (byte) 0);

            for(byte b[] : data)
                if(b != null)
                    for(int i = 0; i < length; i++)
                        bytes[i] = (byte) (b[i] ^ bytes[i]);

            return bytes;
        }
        catch(Exception exception)
        {
        }

        return null;
    }

    public static synchronized Cryptography getInstance()
    {
        if(s_instance == null)
            s_instance = new Cryptography();

        return s_instance;
    }

    public boolean prepareSipHashIds(String alias)
```

```java
        {
          try
          {
              byte bytes[] = null;

              if(alias == null || alias.trim().isEmpty())
                  bytes = Miscellaneous.joinByteArrays
                      (chatEncryptionKeyPair().getPublic().getEncoded(),
                       chatSignatureKeyPair().getPublic().getEncoded());
              else
                  bytes = alias.getBytes(StandardCharsets.UTF_8);

              if(bytes != null)
              {
                  byte key[] = keyForSipHash(bytes);

                  if(key == null)
                      return false;

                  SipHash sipHash = new SipHash();
                  long value[] = sipHash.hmac(bytes, key, SIPHASH_OUTPUT_LENGTH);

                  if(value == new long[] {0L, 0L})
                      return false;

                  bytes = Miscellaneous.longArrayToByteArray(value);

                  if(bytes == null)
                      return false;

                  m_sipHashIdDigestMutex.writeLock().lock();

                  try
                  {
                      m_sipHashIdDigest =
                          sha512(Miscellaneous.
                                  byteArrayAsHexStringDelimited(bytes, '-', 4).
                                  toUpperCase().getBytes());
                  }
                  catch(Exception exception)
                  {
                  }
                  finally
                  {
                      m_sipHashIdDigestMutex.writeLock().unlock();
                  }

                  m_sipHashIdMutex.writeLock().lock();

                  try
                  {
                      m_sipHashId = Miscellaneous.
                          byteArrayAsHexStringDelimited(bytes, '-', 4).
                          toUpperCase();
                  }
                  catch(Exception exception)
                  {
                  }
                  finally
                  {
                      m_sipHashIdMutex.writeLock().unlock();
                  }
              }
```

```java
            else
                return false;
        }
        catch(Exception exception)
        {
            return false;
        }

        return true;
    }

    public void exit()
    {
        reset();
    }

    public void reset()
    {
        m_chatEncryptionPublicKeyPairMutex.writeLock().lock();

        try
        {
            m_chatEncryptionPublicKeyPair = null;
        }
        finally
        {
            m_chatEncryptionPublicKeyPairMutex.writeLock().unlock();
        }

        m_chatSignaturePublicKeyPairMutex.writeLock().lock();

        try
        {
            m_chatSignaturePublicKeyPair = null;
        }
        finally
        {
            m_chatSignaturePublicKeyPairMutex.writeLock().unlock();
        }

        m_encryptionKeyMutex.writeLock().lock();

        try
        {
            byte bytes[] = new byte[CIPHER_KEY_LENGTH];

            Arrays.fill(bytes, (byte) 0);
            m_encryptionKey = new SecretKeySpec(bytes, SYMMETRIC_ALGORITHM);
        }
        finally
        {
            m_encryptionKeyMutex.writeLock().unlock();
        }

        m_identityMutex.writeLock().lock();

        try
        {
            m_identity = null;
        }
        finally
        {
            m_identityMutex.writeLock().unlock();
```

```java
    }

    m_macKeyMutex.writeLock().lock();

    try
    {
        byte bytes[] = new byte[HASH_KEY_LENGTH];

        Arrays.fill(bytes, (byte) 0);
        m_encryptionKey = new SecretKeySpec(bytes, HASH_ALGORITHM);
    }
    finally
    {
        m_macKeyMutex.writeLock().unlock();
    }

    m_ozoneEncryptionKeyMutex.writeLock().lock();

    try
    {
        if(m_ozoneEncryptionKey != null)
            Arrays.fill(m_ozoneEncryptionKey, (byte) 0);

        m_ozoneEncryptionKey = null;
    }
    catch(Exception exception)
    {
    }
    finally
    {
        m_ozoneEncryptionKeyMutex.writeLock().unlock();
    }

    m_ozoneMacKeyMutex.writeLock().lock();

    try
    {
        if(m_ozoneMacKey != null)
            Arrays.fill(m_ozoneMacKey, (byte) 0);

        m_ozoneMacKey = null;
    }
    catch(Exception exception)
    {
    }
    finally
    {
        m_ozoneMacKeyMutex.writeLock().unlock();
    }

    m_sipHashEncryptionKeyMutex.writeLock().lock();

    try
    {
        if(m_sipHashEncryptionKey != null)
            Arrays.fill(m_sipHashEncryptionKey, (byte) 0);

        m_sipHashEncryptionKey = null;
    }
    catch(Exception exception)
    {
    }
    finally
```

```java
        {
            m_sipHashEncryptionKeyMutex.writeLock().unlock();
        }

        m_sipHashIdDigestMutex.writeLock().lock();

        try
        {
            if(m_sipHashIdDigest != null)
                Arrays.fill(m_sipHashIdDigest, (byte) 0);

            m_sipHashIdDigest = null;
        }
        catch(Exception exception)
        {
        }
        finally
        {
            m_sipHashIdDigestMutex.writeLock().unlock();
        }

        m_sipHashIdMutex.writeLock().lock();

        try
        {
            m_sipHashId = DEFAULT_SIPHASH_ID;
        }
        finally
        {
            m_sipHashIdMutex.writeLock().unlock();
        }

        m_sipHashMacKeyMutex.writeLock().lock();

        try
        {
            if(m_sipHashMacKey != null)
                Arrays.fill(m_sipHashMacKey, (byte) 0);

            m_sipHashMacKey = null;
        }
        catch(Exception exception)
        {
        }
        finally
        {
            m_sipHashMacKeyMutex.writeLock().unlock();
        }
    }

    public void resetPKI()
    {
        m_chatEncryptionPublicKeyPairMutex.writeLock().lock();

        try
        {
            m_chatEncryptionPublicKeyPair = null;
        }
        finally
        {
            m_chatEncryptionPublicKeyPairMutex.writeLock().unlock();
        }
```

```java
m_chatSignaturePublicKeyPairMutex.writeLock().lock();

try
{
    m_chatSignaturePublicKeyPair = null;
}
finally
{
    m_chatSignaturePublicKeyPairMutex.writeLock().unlock();
}

m_identityMutex.writeLock().lock();

try
{
    m_identity = null;
}
finally
{
    m_identityMutex.writeLock().unlock();
}

m_ozoneEncryptionKeyMutex.writeLock().lock();

try
{
    if(m_ozoneEncryptionKey != null)
        Arrays.fill(m_ozoneEncryptionKey, (byte) 0);

    m_ozoneEncryptionKey = null;
}
catch(Exception exception)
{
}
finally
{
    m_ozoneEncryptionKeyMutex.writeLock().unlock();
}

m_ozoneMacKeyMutex.writeLock().lock();

try
{
    if(m_ozoneMacKey != null)
        Arrays.fill(m_ozoneMacKey, (byte) 0);

    m_ozoneMacKey = null;
}
catch(Exception exception)
{
}
finally
{
    m_ozoneMacKeyMutex.writeLock().unlock();
}

m_sipHashEncryptionKeyMutex.writeLock().lock();

try
{
    if(m_sipHashEncryptionKey != null)
        Arrays.fill(m_sipHashEncryptionKey, (byte) 0);
```

```java
            m_sipHashEncryptionKey = null;
        }
    catch(Exception exception)
        {
        }
    finally
        {
            m_sipHashEncryptionKeyMutex.writeLock().unlock();
        }

    m_sipHashIdDigestMutex.writeLock().lock();

    try
        {
            if(m_sipHashIdDigest != null)
                Arrays.fill(m_sipHashIdDigest, (byte) 0);

            m_sipHashIdDigest = null;
        }
    catch(Exception exception)
        {
        }
    finally
        {
            m_sipHashIdDigestMutex.writeLock().unlock();
        }

    m_sipHashIdMutex.writeLock().lock();

    try
        {
            m_sipHashId = DEFAULT_SIPHASH_ID;
        }
    finally
        {
            m_sipHashIdMutex.writeLock().unlock();
        }

    m_sipHashMacKeyMutex.writeLock().lock();

    try
        {
            if(m_sipHashMacKey != null)
                Arrays.fill(m_sipHashMacKey, (byte) 0);

            m_sipHashMacKey = null;
        }
    catch(Exception exception)
        {
        }
    finally
        {
            m_sipHashMacKeyMutex.writeLock().unlock();
        }
    }

public void setChatEncryptionPublicKeyAlgorithm(String algorithm)
    {
        m_chatEncryptionPublicKeyAlgorithm = algorithm;
    }

public void setChatEncryptionPublicKeyPair(KeyPair keyPair)
    {
```

```java
        m_chatEncryptionPublicKeyPairMutex.writeLock().lock();

        try
        {
            m_chatEncryptionPublicKeyPair = keyPair;
        }
        finally
        {
            m_chatEncryptionPublicKeyPairMutex.writeLock().unlock();
        }
    }

    public void setChatEncryptionPublicKeyPair(String algorithm,
                                               byte privateBytes[],
                                               byte publicBytes[])
    {
        m_chatEncryptionPublicKeyPairMutex.writeLock().lock();

        try
        {
            m_chatEncryptionPublicKeyPair = generatePrivatePublicKeyPair
                (algorithm, privateBytes, publicBytes);
        }
        catch(Exception exception)
        {
            m_chatEncryptionPublicKeyPair = null;
        }
        finally
        {
            m_chatEncryptionPublicKeyPairMutex.writeLock().unlock();
        }
    }

    public void setChatSignaturePublicKeyPair(KeyPair keyPair)
    {
        m_chatSignaturePublicKeyPairMutex.writeLock().lock();

        try
        {
            m_chatSignaturePublicKeyPair = keyPair;
        }
        finally
        {
            m_chatSignaturePublicKeyPairMutex.writeLock().unlock();
        }
    }

    public void setChatSignaturePublicKeyPair(String algorithm,
                                              byte privateBytes[],
                                              byte publicBytes[])
    {
        m_chatSignaturePublicKeyPairMutex.writeLock().lock();

        try
        {
            m_chatSignaturePublicKeyPair = generatePrivatePublicKeyPair
                (algorithm, privateBytes, publicBytes);
        }
        catch(Exception exception)
        {
            m_chatSignaturePublicKeyPair = null;
        }
        finally
```

```java
    {
        m_chatSignaturePublicKeyPairMutex.writeLock().unlock();
    }
}

public void setEncryptionKey(SecretKey key)
{
    m_encryptionKeyMutex.writeLock().lock();

    try
    {
        m_encryptionKey = key;
    }
    finally
    {
        m_encryptionKeyMutex.writeLock().unlock();
    }
}

public void setMacKey(SecretKey key)
{
    m_macKeyMutex.writeLock().lock();

    try
    {
        m_macKey = key;
    }
    finally
    {
        m_macKeyMutex.writeLock().unlock();
    }
}

public void setOzoneEncryptionKey(byte bytes[])
{
    m_ozoneEncryptionKeyMutex.writeLock().lock();

    try
    {
        if(bytes != null && bytes.length == CIPHER_KEY_LENGTH)
            m_ozoneEncryptionKey = bytes;
        else
        {
            if(m_ozoneEncryptionKey != null)
                Arrays.fill(m_ozoneEncryptionKey, (byte) 0);

            m_ozoneEncryptionKey = null;
        }
    }
    catch(Exception exception)
    {
    }
    finally
    {
        m_ozoneEncryptionKeyMutex.writeLock().unlock();
    }
}

public void setOzoneMacKey(byte bytes[])
{
    m_ozoneMacKeyMutex.writeLock().lock();

    try
```

```java
        {
            if(bytes != null && bytes.length == HASH_KEY_LENGTH)
                m_ozoneMacKey = bytes;
            else
            {
                if(m_ozoneMacKey != null)
                    Arrays.fill(m_ozoneMacKey, (byte) 0);

                m_ozoneMacKey = null;
            }
        }
        catch(Exception exception)
        {
        }
        finally
        {
            m_ozoneMacKeyMutex.writeLock().unlock();
        }
    }
}
```

/* Database.java –

```java
https://github.com/textbrowser/smoke/blob/master/Smoke/app/src/main/java/org/p
urple/smoke/Database.java
** Copyright (c) Alexis Megas.
** All rights reserved.
**
** Redistribution and use in source and binary forms, with or without
** modification, are permitted provided that the following conditions
** are met:
** 1. Redistributions of source code must retain the above copyright
**    notice, this list of conditions and the following disclaimer.
** 2. Redistributions in binary form must reproduce the above copyright
**    notice, this list of conditions and the following disclaimer in the
**    documentation and/or other materials provided with the distribution.
** 3. The name of the author may not be used to endorse or promote products
**    derived from Smoke without specific prior written permission.
**
** SMOKE IS PROVIDED BY THE AUTHOR ``AS IS'' AND ANY EXPRESS OR
** IMPLIED WARRANTIES, INCLUDING, BUT NOT LIMITED TO, THE IMPLIED WARRANTIES
** OF MERCHANTABILITY AND FITNESS FOR A PARTICULAR PURPOSE ARE DISCLAIMED.
** IN NO EVENT SHALL THE AUTHOR BE LIABLE FOR ANY DIRECT, INDIRECT,
** INCIDENTAL, SPECIAL, EXEMPLARY, OR CONSEQUENTIAL DAMAGES (INCLUDING, BUT
** NOT LIMITED TO, PROCUREMENT OF SUBSTITUTE GOODS OR SERVICES; LOSS OF USE,
** DATA, OR PROFITS; OR BUSINESS INTERRUPTION) HOWEVER CAUSED AND ON ANY
** THEORY OF LIABILITY, WHETHER IN CONTRACT, STRICT LIABILITY, OR TORT
** (INCLUDING NEGLIGENCE OR OTHERWISE) ARISING IN ANY WAY OUT OF THE USE OF
** SMOKE, EVEN IF ADVISED OF THE POSSIBILITY OF SUCH DAMAGE.
*/

package org.purple.smoke;

import android.content.ContentValues;
import android.content.Context;
import android.database.Cursor;
import android.database.sqlite.SQLiteConstraintException;
import android.database.sqlite.SQLiteDatabase;
import android.database.sqlite.SQLiteOpenHelper;
import android.util.Base64;
import android.util.Patterns;
```

```java
import android.util.SparseArray;
import java.net.InetAddress;
import java.nio.charset.StandardCharsets;
import java.security.KeyFactory;
import java.security.PublicKey;
import java.security.spec.X509EncodedKeySpec;
import java.util.ArrayList;
import java.util.Arrays;
import java.util.Collections;
import java.util.Comparator;
import java.util.concurrent.Executors;
import java.util.concurrent.TimeUnit;
import java.util.concurrent.locks.ReentrantReadWriteLock;
import java.util.regex.Matcher;
import java.security.KeyPair;

public class Database extends SQLiteOpenHelper
{
    private Cursor m_readMemberChatCursor = null;
    private SQLiteDatabase m_db = null;
    private String m_readMemberChatSipHashId = "";
    private final Object m_readMemberChatCursorMutex = new Object();
    private final static Comparator<FireElement>
        s_readFiresComparator = new Comparator<FireElement> ()
        {
            @Override
            public int compare(FireElement e1, FireElement e2)
            {
                if(e1 == null || e2 == null)
                    return -1;

                return e1.m_name.compareTo(e2.m_name);
            }
        };
    private final static Comparator<NeighborElement>
        s_readNeighborsComparator = new Comparator<NeighborElement> ()
        {
            @Override
            public int compare(NeighborElement e1, NeighborElement e2)
            {
                if(e1 == null || e2 == null)
                    return -1;

                /*
                ** Sort by IP address, port, and transport.
                */

                try
                {
                    byte bytes1[] = InetAddress.getByName(e1.m_remoteIpAddress).
                        getAddress();
                    byte bytes2[] = InetAddress.getByName(e2.m_remoteIpAddress).
                        getAddress();
                    int length = Math.max(bytes1.length, bytes2.length);

                    for(int i = 0; i < length; i++)
                    {
                        byte b1 = (i >= length - bytes1.length) ?
                            bytes1[i - (length - bytes1.length)] : 0;
                        byte b2 = (i >= length - bytes2.length) ?
                            bytes2[i - (length - bytes2.length)] : 0;

                        if(b1 != b2)
```

```java
                        return (0xff & b1) - (0xff & b2);
                    }
                }
                catch(Exception exception)
                {
                }

                int i = e1.m_remotePort.compareTo(e2.m_remotePort);

                if(i != 0)
                    return i;

                return e1.m_transport.compareTo(e2.m_transport);
            }
        };
    private final static Comparator<ParticipantElement>
        s_readParticipantsComparator = new Comparator<ParticipantElement> ()
        {
            @Override
            public int compare(ParticipantElement e1, ParticipantElement e2)
            {
                if(e1 == null || e2 == null)
                    return -1;

                int i = e1.m_name.compareTo(e2.m_name);

                if(i != 0)
                    return i;

                return e1.m_sipHashId.compareTo(e2.m_sipHashId);
            }
        };
    private final static Comparator<SipHashIdElement>
        s_readSipHashIdsComparator = new Comparator<SipHashIdElement> ()
        {
            @Override
            public int compare(SipHashIdElement e1, SipHashIdElement e2)
            {
                if(e1 == null || e2 == null)
                    return -1;

                /*
                ** Sort by name and SipHash identity.
                */

                int i = e1.m_name.compareTo(e2.m_name);

                if(i != 0)
                    return i;

                return e1.m_sipHashId.compareTo(e2.m_sipHashId);
            }
        };
    private final static ReentrantReadWriteLock s_congestionControlMutex =
        new ReentrantReadWriteLock();
    private final static String DATABASE_NAME = "smoke.db";
    private final static int DATABASE_VERSION = 1;
    private final static long WRITE_PARTICIPANT_TIME_DELTA =
        60000L; // 60 seconds.
    private static Database s_instance = null;
    public enum ExceptionLevels
    {
        EXCEPTION_FATAL, EXCEPTION_NONE, EXCEPTION_PERMISSIBLE
```

```java
    }
    public final static int SIPHASH_STREAM_CREATION_ITERATION_COUNT = 4096;

    private Database(Context context)
    {
        super(context, DATABASE_NAME, null, DATABASE_VERSION);

        try
        {
            m_db = getWritableDatabase();
        }
        catch(Exception exception)
        {
            m_db = null;
        }
    }

    public ArrayList<FireElement> readFires(Cryptography cryptography)
    {
        if(cryptography == null || m_db == null)
            return null;

        Cursor cursor = null;
        ArrayList<FireElement> arrayList = null;

        try
        {
            cursor = m_db.rawQuery("SELECT name, oid FROM fire", null);

            if(cursor != null && cursor.moveToFirst())
            {
                arrayList = new ArrayList<> ();

                while(!cursor.isAfterLast())
                {
                    FireElement fireElement = new FireElement();
                    int count = cursor.getColumnCount();
                    int oid = cursor.getInt(count - 1);

                    for(int i = 0; i < count; i++)
                    {
                        if(i == count - 1)
                        {
                            fireElement.m_oid = oid;
                            continue;
                        }

                        byte bytes[] = cryptography.mtd
                            (Base64.decode(cursor.getString(i).getBytes(),
                                    Base64.DEFAULT));

                        if(bytes == null)
                        {
                            StringBuilder stringBuilder = new StringBuilder();

                            stringBuilder.append("Database::readFires(): ");
                            stringBuilder.append("error on column ");
                            stringBuilder.append(cursor.getColumnName(i));
                            stringBuilder.append(".");
                            writeLog(stringBuilder.toString());
                        }

                        switch(i)
```

```java
                    {
                case 0:
                    if(bytes != null)
                        fireElement.m_name = new String
                            (bytes, StandardCharsets.ISO_8859_1).trim();
                    else
                        fireElement.m_name = "error (" + oid + ")";

                    break;
                default:
                    break;
                }
            }

            arrayList.add(fireElement);
            cursor.moveToNext();
        }

        if(arrayList.size() > 1)
            Collections.sort(arrayList, s_readFiresComparator);
    }
}
catch(Exception exception)
{
    if(arrayList != null)
        arrayList.clear();

    arrayList = null;
}
finally
{
    if(cursor != null)
        cursor.close();
}

return arrayList;
}

public ArrayList<NeighborElement> readNeighborOids
    (Cryptography cryptography)
{
    if(cryptography == null || m_db == null)
        return null;

    Cursor cursor = null;
    ArrayList<NeighborElement> arrayList = null;

    try
    {
        cursor = m_db.rawQuery
            ("SELECT passthrough, " +
             "status_control, " +
             "oid FROM neighbors", null);

        if(cursor != null && cursor.moveToFirst())
        {
            arrayList = new ArrayList<> ();

            while(!cursor.isAfterLast())
            {
                NeighborElement neighborElement = new NeighborElement();
                boolean error = false;
                int count = cursor.getColumnCount();
```

```java
                    for(int i = 0; i < count; i++)
                    {
                        if(i == count - 1)
                        {
                            neighborElement.m_oid = cursor.getInt(i);
                            continue;
                        }

                        byte bytes[] = cryptography.mtd
                            (Base64.decode(cursor.getString(i).getBytes(),
                                        Base64.DEFAULT));

                        if(bytes == null)
                        {
                            error = true;

                            StringBuilder stringBuilder = new StringBuilder();

                            stringBuilder.append
                                ("Database::readNeighborOids(): ");
                            stringBuilder.append("error on column ");
                            stringBuilder.append(cursor.getColumnName(i));
                            stringBuilder.append(".");
                            writeLog(stringBuilder.toString());
                            break;
                        }

                        switch(i)
                        {
                        case 0:
                            neighborElement.m_passthrough = new String(bytes);
                            break;
                        case 1:
                            neighborElement.m_statusControl = new String(bytes);
                            break;
                        default:
                            break;
                        }
                    }

                    if(!error)
                        arrayList.add(neighborElement);

                    cursor.moveToNext();
                }
            }
        }
        catch(Exception exception)
        {
            if(arrayList != null)
                arrayList.clear();

            arrayList = null;
        }
        finally
        {
            if(cursor != null)
                cursor.close();
        }

        return arrayList;
    }
```

```java
public ArrayList<NeighborElement> readNeighbors(Cryptography cryptography)
{
    if(!State.getInstance().isAuthenticated())
        return null;

    if(cryptography == null || m_db == null)
        return null;

    Cursor cursor = null;
    ArrayList<NeighborElement> arrayList = null;

    try
    {
        cursor = m_db.rawQuery
            ("SELECT " +
             "(SELECT COUNT(*) FROM outbound_queue o WHERE " +
             "o.neighbor_oid = n.oid), " +
             "n.bytes_read, " +
             "n.bytes_written, " +
             "n.echo_queue_size, " +
             "n.ip_version, " +
             "n.last_error, " +
             "n.local_ip_address, " +
             "n.local_port, " +
             "n.non_tls, " +
             "n.passthrough, " +
             "n.proxy_ip_address, " +
             "n.proxy_port, " +
             "n.proxy_type, " +
             "n.remote_certificate, " +
             "n.remote_ip_address, " +
             "n.remote_port, " +
             "n.remote_scope_id, " +
             "n.session_cipher, " +
             "n.status, " +
             "n.status_control, " +
             "n.transport, " +
             "n.uptime, " +
             "n.oid " +
             "FROM neighbors n ORDER BY n.oid", null);

        if(cursor != null && cursor.moveToFirst())
        {
            arrayList = new ArrayList<> ();

            while(!cursor.isAfterLast())
            {
                NeighborElement neighborElement = new NeighborElement();
                int count = cursor.getColumnCount();
                int oid = cursor.getInt(count - 1);

                for(int i = 0; i < count; i++)
                {
                    if(i == count - 1)
                    {
                        neighborElement.m_oid = oid;
                        continue;
                    }

                    byte bytes[] = null;

                    if(i != 0)
```

```java
            bytes = cryptography.mtd
                (Base64.decode(cursor.getString(i).getBytes(),
                               Base64.DEFAULT));

        if(bytes == null && i != 0)
        {
            StringBuilder stringBuilder = new StringBuilder();

            stringBuilder.append("Database::readNeighbors(): ");
            stringBuilder.append("error on column ");
            stringBuilder.append(cursor.getColumnName(i));
            stringBuilder.append(".");
            writeLog(stringBuilder.toString());
        }

        switch(i)
        {
        case 0:
            neighborElement.m_outboundQueued =
                cursor.getInt(i);
            break;
        case 1:
            if(bytes != null)
                neighborElement.m_bytesRead = new String(bytes);
            else
                neighborElement.m_bytesRead =
                    "error (" + oid + ")";

            break;
        case 2:
            if(bytes != null)
                neighborElement.m_bytesWritten =
                    new String(bytes);
            else
                neighborElement.m_bytesWritten =
                    "error (" + oid + ")";

            break;
        case 3:
            if(bytes != null)
                neighborElement.m_echoQueueSize =
                    new String(bytes);
            else
                neighborElement.m_echoQueueSize =
                    "error (" + oid + ")";

            break;
        case 4:
            if(bytes != null)
                neighborElement.m_ipVersion = new String(bytes);
            else
                neighborElement.m_ipVersion =
                    "error (" + oid + ")";

            break;
        case 5:
            if(bytes != null)
                neighborElement.m_error = new String(bytes);
            else
                neighborElement.m_error =
                    "error (" + oid + ")";

            break;
```

```java
        case 6:
            if(bytes != null)
               neighborElement.m_localIpAddress =
                   new String(bytes);
            else
               neighborElement.m_localIpAddress =
                   "error (" + oid + ")";

           break;
        case 7:
            if(bytes != null)
               neighborElement.m_localPort = new String(bytes);
            else
               neighborElement.m_localPort =
                   "error (" + oid + ")";

           break;
        case 8:
            if(bytes != null)
               neighborElement.m_nonTls = new String(bytes);
            else
               neighborElement.m_nonTls =
                   "error (" + oid + ")";

           break;
        case 9:
            if(bytes != null)
               neighborElement.m_passthrough =
                   new String(bytes);
            else
               neighborElement.m_passthrough =
                   "error (" + oid + ")";

           break;
        case 10:
            if(bytes != null)
               neighborElement.m_proxyIpAddress =
                   new String(bytes);
            else
               neighborElement.m_proxyIpAddress =
                   "error (" + oid + ")";

           break;
        case 11:
            if(bytes != null)
               neighborElement.m_proxyPort = new String(bytes);
            else
               neighborElement.m_proxyPort =
                   "error (" + oid + ")";

           break;
        case 12:
            if(bytes != null)
               neighborElement.m_proxyType = new String(bytes);
            else
               neighborElement.m_proxyType =
                   "error (" + oid + ")";

           break;
        case 13:
            neighborElement.m_remoteCertificate = bytes;
            break;
        case 14:
```

```java
                if(bytes != null)
                    neighborElement.m_remoteIpAddress =
                        new String(bytes);
                else
                    neighborElement.m_remoteIpAddress =
                        "error (" + oid + ")";

                break;
            case 15:
                if(bytes != null)
                    neighborElement.m_remotePort =
                        new String(bytes);
                else
                    neighborElement.m_remotePort =
                        "error (" + oid + ")";

                break;
            case 16:
                if(bytes != null)
                    neighborElement.m_remoteScopeId =
                        new String(bytes);
                else
                    neighborElement.m_remoteScopeId =
                        "error (" + oid + ")";

                break;
            case 17:
                if(bytes != null)
                    neighborElement.m_sessionCipher =
                        new String(bytes);
                else
                    neighborElement.m_sessionCipher =
                        "error (" + oid + ")";

                break;
            case 18:
                if(bytes != null)
                    neighborElement.m_status = new String(bytes);
                else
                    neighborElement.m_status =
                        "error (" + oid + ")";

                break;
            case 19:
                if(bytes != null)
                    neighborElement.m_statusControl =
                        new String(bytes);
                else
                    neighborElement.m_statusControl =
                        "error (" + oid + ")";

                break;
            case 20:
                if(bytes != null)
                    neighborElement.m_transport = new String(bytes);
                else
                    neighborElement.m_transport =
                        "error (" + oid + ")";

                break;
            case 21:
                if(bytes != null)
                    neighborElement.m_uptime = new String(bytes);
```

```java
                        else
                            neighborElement.m_uptime =
                                "error (" + oid + ")";

                        break;
                    default:
                        break;
                    }
                }

                arrayList.add(neighborElement);
                cursor.moveToNext();
            }

            if(arrayList.size() > 1)
                Collections.sort(arrayList, s_readNeighborsComparator);
        }
    }
    catch(Exception exception)
    {
        if(arrayList != null)
            arrayList.clear();

        arrayList = null;
    }
    finally
    {
        if(cursor != null)
            cursor.close();
    }

    return arrayList;
}

public ArrayList<ParticipantElement> readParticipants
    (Cryptography cryptography, String sipHashId)
{
    if(!State.getInstance().isAuthenticated())
        return null;

    if(cryptography == null || m_db == null)
        return null;

    Cursor cursor = null;
    ArrayList<ParticipantElement> arrayList = null;

    try
    {
        if(sipHashId.isEmpty())
            cursor = m_db.rawQuery
                ("SELECT " +
                 "(SELECT s.name FROM siphash_ids s " +
                 "WHERE p.siphash_id_digest = s.siphash_id_digest) " +
                 "AS a, " +
                 "p.keystream, " +
                 "p.last_status_timestamp, " +
                 "p.siphash_id, " +
                 "p.oid " +
                 "FROM participants p", null);
        else
            cursor = m_db.rawQuery
                ("SELECT " +
                 "(SELECT s.name FROM siphash_ids s " +
```

```java
            "WHERE p.siphash_id_digest = s.siphash_id_digest) " +
            "AS a, " +
            "p.keystream, " +
            "p.last_status_timestamp, " +
            "p.siphash_id, " +
            "p.oid " +
            "FROM participants p WHERE p.siphash_id_digest = ?",
            new String[] {Base64.
                        encodeToString
                        (cryptography.
                         hmac(sipHashId.toUpperCase().trim().
                             getBytes(StandardCharsets.UTF_8)),
                         Base64.DEFAULT)});

    if(cursor != null && cursor.moveToFirst())
    {
        arrayList = new ArrayList<> ();

        while(!cursor.isAfterLast())
        {
            ParticipantElement participantElement =
                new ParticipantElement();
            int count = cursor.getColumnCount();
            int oid = cursor.getInt(count - 1);

            for(int i = 0; i < count; i++)
            {
                if(i == count - 1)
                {
                    participantElement.m_oid = oid;
                    continue;
                }

                byte bytes[] = cryptography.mtd
                    (Base64.decode(cursor.getString(i).getBytes(),
                            Base64.DEFAULT));

                if(bytes == null)
                {
                    StringBuilder stringBuilder = new StringBuilder();

                    stringBuilder.append
                        ("Database::readParticipants(): ");
                    stringBuilder.append("error on column ");
                    stringBuilder.append(cursor.getColumnName(i));
                    stringBuilder.append(".");
                    writeLog(stringBuilder.toString());
                }

                switch(i)
                {
                case 0:
                    if(bytes != null)
                        participantElement.m_name = new String(bytes);
                    else
                        participantElement.m_name =
                            "error (" + oid + ")";

                    break;
                case 1:
                    participantElement.m_keyStream = bytes;
                    break;
                case 2:
```

```java
                            if(bytes != null)
                                participantElement.m_lastStatusTimestamp =
                                    Miscellaneous.byteArrayToLong(bytes);

                            break;
                        case 3:
                            if(bytes != null)
                                participantElement.m_sipHashId = new String
                                    (bytes, StandardCharsets.UTF_8);
                            else
                                participantElement.m_sipHashId =
                                    "error (" + oid + ")";

                            break;
                        default:
                            break;
                        }
                    }

                    arrayList.add(participantElement);
                    cursor.moveToNext();
                }

                if(arrayList.size() > 1)
                    Collections.sort(arrayList, s_readParticipantsComparator);
            }
        }
        catch(Exception exception)
        {
            if(arrayList != null)
                arrayList.clear();

            arrayList = null;
        }
        finally
        {
            if(cursor != null)
                cursor.close();
        }

        return arrayList;
    }

    public ArrayList<SipHashIdElement> readNonSharedSipHashIds
        (Cryptography cryptography)
    {
        if(cryptography == null || m_db == null)
            return null;

        ArrayList<SipHashIdElement> arrayList = null;
        Cursor cursor = null;

        try
        {
            cursor = m_db.rawQuery
                ("SELECT siphash_id, stream " +
                 "FROM siphash_ids WHERE siphash_id_digest NOT IN " +
                 "(SELECT siphash_id_digest FROM participants)", null);

            if(cursor != null && cursor.moveToFirst())
            {
                arrayList = new ArrayList<> ();
```

```java
            while(!cursor.isAfterLast())
            {
                SipHashIdElement sipHashIdElement = new SipHashIdElement();
                boolean error = false;
                int count = cursor.getColumnCount();

                for(int i = 0; i < count; i++)
                {
                    byte bytes[] = cryptography.mtd
                        (Base64.decode(cursor.getString(i).getBytes(),
                                    Base64.DEFAULT));

                    if(bytes == null)
                    {
                        error = true;

                        StringBuilder stringBuilder = new StringBuilder();

                        stringBuilder.append
                            ("Database::readNonSharedSipHashIds(): ");
                        stringBuilder.append("error on column ");
                        stringBuilder.append(cursor.getColumnName(i));
                        stringBuilder.append(".");
                        writeLog(stringBuilder.toString());
                        break;
                    }

                    switch(i)
                    {
                    case 0:
                        sipHashIdElement.m_sipHashId = new String
                            (bytes, StandardCharsets.UTF_8);
                        break;
                    case 1:
                        sipHashIdElement.m_stream = bytes;
                        break;
                    default:
                        break;
                    }
                }

                if(!error)
                    arrayList.add(sipHashIdElement);

                cursor.moveToNext();
            }
        }
    catch(Exception exception)
    {
        if(arrayList != null)
            arrayList.clear();

        arrayList = null;
    }
    finally
    {
        if(cursor != null)
            cursor.close();
    }

    return arrayList;
}
```

```java
public ArrayList<SipHashIdElement> readSipHashIds
    (String sipHashId, Cryptography cryptography)
{
    if(cryptography == null || m_db == null)
        return null;

    ArrayList<SipHashIdElement> arrayList = null;
    Cursor cursor = null;

    try
    {
        if(sipHashId.isEmpty())
            cursor = m_db.rawQuery
                ("SELECT " +
                 "(SELECT EXISTS(SELECT 1 FROM participants p WHERE " +
                 "p.siphash_id_digest = s.siphash_id_digest)) AS aa, " +
                 "(SELECT p.encryption_public_key_signed " +
                 "FROM participants p " +
                 "WHERE p.siphash_id_digest = s.siphash_id_digest) AS " +
                 "bb, " +
                 "(SELECT p.signature_public_key_signed " +
                 "FROM participants p " +
                 "WHERE p.siphash_id_digest = s.siphash_id_digest) AS " +
                 "cc, " +
                 "(SELECT COUNT(p.oid) FROM participants_keys p " +
                 "WHERE p.siphash_id_digest = s.siphash_id_digest) AS " +
                 "dd, " +
                 "(SELECT p.encryption_public_key_algorithm FROM " +
                 "participants p WHERE p.siphash_id_digest = " +
                 "s.siphash_id_digest) AS ee, " +
                 "s.name, " +
                 "s.siphash_id, " +
                 "s.stream, " +
                 "s.oid " +
                 "FROM siphash_ids s ORDER BY s.oid", null);
        else
            cursor = m_db.rawQuery
                ("SELECT " +
                 "(SELECT EXISTS(SELECT 1 FROM participants p WHERE " +
                 "p.siphash_id_digest = s.siphash_id_digest)) AS aa, " +
                 "(SELECT p.encryption_public_key_signed " +
                 "FROM participants p " +
                 "WHERE p.siphash_id_digest = s.siphash_id_digest) AS " +
                 "bb, " +
                 "(SELECT p.signature_public_key_signed " +
                 "FROM participants p " +
                 "WHERE p.siphash_id_digest = s.siphash_id_digest) AS " +
                 "cc, " +
                 "(SELECT COUNT(p.oid) FROM participants_keys p " +
                 "WHERE p.siphash_id_digest = s.siphash_id_digest) AS " +
                 "dd, " +
                 "(SELECT p.encryption_public_key_algorithm FROM " +
                 "participants p WHERE p.siphash_id_digest = " +
                 "s.siphash_id_digest) AS ee, " +
                 "s.name, " +
                 "s.siphash_id, " +
                 "s.stream, " +
                 "s.oid " +
                 "FROM siphash_ids s WHERE s.siphash_id_digest = ?",
                 new String[] {Base64.
                               encodeToString
                               (cryptography.
```

```java
                            hmac(sipHashId.toUpperCase().trim().
                                getBytes(StandardCharsets.UTF_8)),
                            Base64.DEFAULT)});

        if(cursor != null && cursor.moveToFirst())
        {
            arrayList = new ArrayList<> ();

            while(!cursor.isAfterLast())
            {
                SipHashIdElement sipHashIdElement = new SipHashIdElement();
                int count = cursor.getColumnCount();
                int oid = cursor.getInt(count - 1);

                for(int i = 0; i < count; i++)
                {
                    if(i == 0)
                    {
                        sipHashIdElement.m_epksCompleted =
                            cursor.getInt(i) > 0;
                        continue;
                    }
                    else if(i == 1 || i == 2)
                    {
                        if(cursor.isNull(i))
                            continue;
                    }
                    else if(i == 3)
                    {
                        sipHashIdElement.m_fiascoKeys = cursor.getInt(i);
                        continue;
                    }
                    else if(i == 4)
                    {
                        if(cursor.isNull(i))
                            continue;
                    }
                    else if(i == count - 1)
                    {
                        sipHashIdElement.m_oid = oid;
                        continue;
                    }

                    byte bytes[] = cryptography.mtd
                        (Base64.decode(cursor.getString(i).getBytes(),
                                    Base64.DEFAULT));

                    if(bytes == null)
                    {
                        StringBuilder stringBuilder = new StringBuilder();

                        stringBuilder.append
                            ("Database::readSipHashIds(): ");
                        stringBuilder.append("error on column ");
                        stringBuilder.append(cursor.getColumnName(i));
                        stringBuilder.append(".");
                        writeLog(stringBuilder.toString());
                    }

                    switch(i)
                    {
                    case 1:
                        if(bytes != null)
```

```java
                        sipHashIdElement.m_keysSigned =
                            Arrays.equals(bytes, "true".getBytes());

                    break;
                case 2:
                    if(bytes != null)
                        sipHashIdElement.m_keysSigned &=
                            Arrays.equals(bytes, "true".getBytes());

                    break;
                case 4:
                    if(bytes != null)
                        sipHashIdElement.m_encryptionAlgorithm =
                            new String(bytes);
                    else
                        sipHashIdElement.m_encryptionAlgorithm =
                            "error (" + oid + ")";

                    break;
                case 5:
                    if(bytes != null)
                        sipHashIdElement.m_name = new String(bytes);
                    else
                        sipHashIdElement.m_name =
                            "error (" + oid + ")";

                    break;
                case 6:
                    if(bytes != null)
                        sipHashIdElement.m_sipHashId = new String
                            (bytes, StandardCharsets.UTF_8);
                    else
                        sipHashIdElement.m_sipHashId =
                            "error (" + oid + ")";

                    break;
                case 7:
                    sipHashIdElement.m_stream = bytes;
                    break;
                default:
                    break;
                }
            }

            arrayList.add(sipHashIdElement);
            cursor.moveToNext();
        }

        if(arrayList.size() > 1)
            Collections.sort(arrayList, s_readSipHashIdsComparator);
        }
    }
    catch(Exception exception)
    {
        if(arrayList != null)
            arrayList.clear();

        arrayList = null;
    }
    finally
    {
        if(cursor != null)
            cursor.close();
```

```java
        }

    return arrayList;
    }

    public ArrayList<SteamElement> readSteams
        (Cryptography cryptography, short direction)
    {
        if(cryptography == null || m_db == null)
            return null;

        ArrayList<SteamElement> arrayList = null;
        Cursor cursor = null;

        try
        {
            cursor = m_db.rawQuery
                ("SELECT absolute_filename, " + // 0
                 "destination, " +              // 1
                 "display_filename, " +         // 2
                 "file_digest, " +              // 3
                 "file_identity, " +            // 4
                 "file_size, " +                // 5
                 "is_download, " +              // 6
                 "read_interval, " +            // 7
                 "read_offset, " +              // 8
                 "status, " +                   // 9
                 "transfer_rate, " +            // 10
                 "oid " +                       // 11
                 "FROM steam_files WHERE is_download = ? " +
                 "ORDER BY someoid",
                 new String[] {String.valueOf(direction)});

            if(cursor != null && cursor.moveToFirst())
            {
                arrayList = new ArrayList<> ();

                while(!cursor.isAfterLast())
                {
                    String status = cursor.getString(8).trim();

                    if(status.equals("deleted"))
                        continue;

                    SteamElement steamElement = new SteamElement();
                    int count = cursor.getColumnCount();
                    int oid = cursor.getInt(count - 1);

                    for(int i = 0; i < count; i++)
                    {
                        if(i == 9)
                        {
                            steamElement.m_status = status;
                            continue;
                        }
                        else if(i == count - 1)
                        {
                            steamElement.m_oid = oid;
                            continue;
                        }

                        byte bytes[] = null;
```

```java
            if(i == 6) // is_download
                bytes = cursor.getString(i).getBytes();
            else
                bytes = cryptography.mtd
                    (Base64.decode(cursor.getString(i).getBytes(),
                              Base64.DEFAULT));

            if(bytes == null)
            {
                StringBuilder stringBuilder = new StringBuilder();

                stringBuilder.append("Database::readSteams(): ");
                stringBuilder.append("error on column ");
                stringBuilder.append(cursor.getColumnName(i));
                stringBuilder.append(".");
                writeLog(stringBuilder.toString());
            }

            switch(i)
             {
            case 0:
                if(bytes != null)
                    steamElement.m_fileName = new String(bytes);
                else
                    steamElement.m_fileName =
                        "error (" + oid + ")";

                break;
            case 1:
                if(bytes != null)
                    steamElement.m_destination = new String
                        (bytes, StandardCharsets.UTF_8);
                else
                    steamElement.m_destination =
                        "error (" + oid + ")";

                break;
            case 2:
                if(bytes != null)
                    steamElement.m_displayFileName = new String
                        (bytes, StandardCharsets.UTF_8);
                else
                    steamElement.m_displayFileName =
                        "error (" + oid + ")";

                break;
            case 3:
                steamElement.m_fileDigest = bytes;
                break;
            case 4:
                steamElement.m_fileIdentity = bytes;
                break;
            case 5:
                if(bytes != null)
                    try
                    {
                        steamElement.m_fileSize = Long.parseLong
                            (new String(bytes));
                    }
                    catch(Exception exception)
                    {
                    }
```

```java
                        break;
                    case 6:
                        if(bytes != null)
                            try
                            {
                                steamElement.m_direction = Short.parseShort
                                    (new String(bytes));
                            }
                            catch(Exception exception)
                            {
                            }

                        break;
                    case 7:
                        if(bytes != null)
                            try
                            {
                                steamElement.m_readInterval =
                                    Long.parseLong(new String(bytes));
                            }
                            catch(Exception exception)
                            {
                            }

                        break;
                    case 8:
                        if(bytes != null)
                            try
                            {
                                steamElement.m_readOffset =
                                    Long.parseLong(new String(bytes));
                            }
                            catch(Exception exception)
                            {
                            }

                        break;
                    case 9:
                        break;
                    case 10:
                        if(bytes != null)
                            steamElement.m_transferRate = new String(bytes);
                        else
                            steamElement.m_transferRate =
                                "error (" + oid + ")";

                        break;
                    default:
                        break;
                    }
                }

                arrayList.add(steamElement);
                cursor.moveToNext();
            }
        }
    }
    catch(Exception exception)
    {
        if(arrayList != null)
            arrayList.clear();

        arrayList = null;
```

```java
        }
        finally
        {
            if(cursor != null)
                cursor.close();
        }

        return arrayList;
    }

    public ArrayList<String> readSipHashIdStrings(Cryptography cryptography)
    {
        if(cryptography == null || m_db == null)
            return null;

        ArrayList<String> arrayList = null;
        Cursor cursor = null;

        try
        {
            cursor = m_db.rawQuery
                ("SELECT siphash_id FROM participants", null);

            if(cursor != null && cursor.moveToFirst())
            {
                arrayList = new ArrayList<> ();

                int count = cursor.getColumnCount();

                while(!cursor.isAfterLast())
                {
                    for(int i = 0; i < count; i++)
                    {
                        byte bytes[] = cryptography.mtd
                            (Base64.decode(cursor.getString(i).getBytes(),
                                    Base64.DEFAULT));

                        if(bytes == null)
                        {
                            StringBuilder stringBuilder = new StringBuilder();

                            stringBuilder.append
                                ("Database::readSipHashIdStrings(): ");
                            stringBuilder.append("error on column ");
                            stringBuilder.append(cursor.getColumnName(i));
                            stringBuilder.append(".");
                            writeLog(stringBuilder.toString());
                            break;
                        }

                        arrayList.add
                            (new String(bytes, StandardCharsets.UTF_8));
                    }

                    cursor.moveToNext();
                }
            }
        }
        catch(Exception exception)
        {
            if(arrayList != null)
                arrayList.clear();
```

```java
            arrayList = null;
        }
    finally
    {
        if(cursor != null)
            cursor.close();
    }

    return arrayList;
}


public ExceptionLevels writeParticipantMessage(Cryptography cryptography,
                                               String fromSmokeStack,
                                               String message,
                                               String sipHashId,
                                               byte attachment[],
                                               byte messageIdentity[],
                                               long timestamp)
{
    if(cryptography == null || m_db == null)
        return ExceptionLevels.EXCEPTION_FATAL;

    m_db.beginTransactionNonExclusive();

    try
    {
        ContentValues values = new ContentValues();

        if(attachment == null || attachment.length <= 1)
            values.put
                ("attachment",
                 Base64.encodeToString(cryptography.etm("".getBytes()),
                                       Base64.DEFAULT));
        else
            values.put
                ("attachment",
                 Base64.encodeToString(cryptography.etm(attachment),
                                       Base64.DEFAULT));

        values.put
            ("from_smokestack",
             Base64.encodeToString(cryptography.etm(fromSmokeStack.
                                                    getBytes()),
                                   Base64.DEFAULT));
        values.put
            ("message",
             Base64.encodeToString(cryptography.etm(message.getBytes()),
                                   Base64.DEFAULT));
        values.put
            ("message_digest",
             Base64.encodeToString(cryptography.
                                   /*
                                   ** It's very possible that a message
                                   ** sent by one device will be identical
                                   ** to the message sent by another
                                   ** device.
                                   */
                                   hmac((message +
                                         sipHashId +
                                         timestamp).getBytes()),
                                   Base64.DEFAULT));

        if(messageIdentity == null)
```

```java
        values.put
            ("message_identity_digest",
             Base64.encodeToString(Cryptography.randomBytes(64),
                                   Base64.DEFAULT));
    else
        values.put
            ("message_identity_digest",
             Base64.encodeToString(cryptography.hmac(messageIdentity),
                                   Base64.DEFAULT));

    values.put
        ("message_read",
         Base64.encodeToString(cryptography.etm("false".getBytes()),
                               Base64.DEFAULT));
    values.put
        ("message_sent",
         Base64.encodeToString(cryptography.etm("false".getBytes()),
                               Base64.DEFAULT));
    values.put
        ("siphash_id_digest",
         Base64.encodeToString(cryptography.
                                   hmac(sipHashId.toUpperCase().trim().
                                       getBytes(StandardCharsets.UTF_8)),
                                   Base64.DEFAULT));

    /*
    ** We want to preserve the order of the time values.
    ** That is, if t_a < t_b, then E(t_a) < E(t_b) must
    ** also be true. Or, H(t_a) < H(t_b). A comment, purely.
    */

    values.put("timestamp", timestamp);

    if(m_db.insertOrThrow("participants_messages", null, values) != -1)
        synchronized(m_readMemberChatCursorMutex)
        {
            if(m_readMemberChatSipHashId.equals(sipHashId))
            {
                if(m_readMemberChatCursor != null)
                    m_readMemberChatCursor.close();

                m_readMemberChatCursor = null;
            }
        }

    m_db.setTransactionSuccessful();
}
catch(SQLiteConstraintException exception)
{
    if(exception.getMessage().toLowerCase().contains("unique"))
        return ExceptionLevels.EXCEPTION_PERMISSIBLE;
    else
        return ExceptionLevels.EXCEPTION_FATAL;
}
catch(Exception exception)
{
    return ExceptionLevels.EXCEPTION_FATAL;
}
finally
{
    m_db.endTransaction();
}
```

```java
        return ExceptionLevels.EXCEPTION_NONE;
    }

    public MemberChatElement readMemberChat
        (Cryptography cryptography, String sipHashId, int position)
    {
        if(cryptography == null || m_db == null)
            return null;

        MemberChatElement memberChatElement = null;

        synchronized(m_readMemberChatCursorMutex)
        {
            try
            {
                if(m_readMemberChatCursor != null)
                    if(!m_readMemberChatSipHashId.equals(sipHashId))
                    {
                        m_readMemberChatCursor.close();
                        m_readMemberChatCursor = null;
                    }

                if(m_readMemberChatCursor == null)
                {
                    m_readMemberChatCursor = m_db.rawQuery
                        ("SELECT attachment, " + // 0
                         "from_smokestack, " +    // 1
                         "message, " +            // 2
                         "message_read, " +       // 3
                         "message_sent, " +       // 4
                         "timestamp, " +          // 5
                         "oid " +                 // 6
                         "FROM participants_messages " +
                         "WHERE siphash_id_digest = ? ORDER BY timestamp",
                         new String[] {Base64.
                                        encodeToString
                                        (cryptography.
                                        hmac(sipHashId.toUpperCase().trim().
                                            getBytes(StandardCharsets.UTF_8)),
                                        Base64.DEFAULT)});
                    m_readMemberChatSipHashId = sipHashId;
                }

                if(m_readMemberChatCursor != null &&
                   m_readMemberChatCursor.moveToPosition(position))
                {
                    memberChatElement = new MemberChatElement();

                    int count = m_readMemberChatCursor.getColumnCount();
                    int oid = m_readMemberChatCursor.getInt(count - 1);

                    for(int i = 0; i < count; i++)
                    {
                        if(i == count - 1)
                        {
                            memberChatElement.m_oid = oid;
                            continue;
                        }
                        else if(i == 5)
                        {
                            memberChatElement.m_timestamp =
                                m_readMemberChatCursor.getLong(i);
                            continue;
```

```java
                }

                byte bytes[] = cryptography.mtd
                    (Base64.decode(m_readMemberChatCursor.
                             getString(i).getBytes(),
                             Base64.DEFAULT));

                if(bytes == null)
                {
                    StringBuilder stringBuilder = new StringBuilder();

                    stringBuilder.append
                        ("Database::readMemberChat(): ");
                    stringBuilder.append("error on column ");
                    stringBuilder.append
                        (m_readMemberChatCursor.getColumnName(i));
                    stringBuilder.append(".");
                    writeLog(stringBuilder.toString());
                }

                switch(i)
                {
                case 0:
                    memberChatElement.m_attachment = bytes;
                    break;
                case 1:
                    if(bytes != null)
                        memberChatElement.m_fromSmokeStack =
                            new String(bytes).trim();
                    else
                        memberChatElement.m_fromSmokeStack =
                            "error (" + oid + ")";

                    break;
                case 2:
                    if(bytes != null)
                        memberChatElement.m_message =
                            new String(bytes);
                    else
                        memberChatElement.m_message =
                            "error (" + oid + ")";

                    break;
                case 3:
                    if(bytes != null)
                        memberChatElement.m_messageRead =
                            (new String(bytes).equals("true"));

                    break;
                case 4:
                    if(bytes != null)
                        memberChatElement.m_messageSent =
                            (new String(bytes).equals("true"));

                    break;
                default:
                    break;
                }
            }
        }
    }
    catch(Exception exception)
    {
```

```java
            memberChatElement = null;

            if(m_readMemberChatCursor != null)
                m_readMemberChatCursor.close();

            m_readMemberChatCursor = null;
            m_readMemberChatSipHashId = "";
        }
    }

    return memberChatElement;
}

public PublicKey publicEncryptionKeyForSipHashId(Cryptography
cryptography,
                                                 String sipHashId)
{
    if(cryptography == null || m_db == null)
        return null;

    Cursor cursor = null;
    PublicKey publicKey = null;

    try
    {
        cursor = m_db.rawQuery
            ("SELECT " +
             "encryption_public_key " +
             "FROM participants WHERE siphash_id_digest = ?",
             new String[] {Base64.
                           encodeToString
                           (cryptography.
                           hmac(sipHashId.toUpperCase().trim().
                               getBytes(StandardCharsets.UTF_8)),
                           Base64.DEFAULT)});

        if(cursor != null && cursor.moveToFirst())
        {
            byte bytes[] = cryptography.mtd
                (Base64.decode(cursor.getString(0).getBytes(),
                            Base64.DEFAULT));

            if(bytes != null)
                publicKey = Cryptography.publicKeyFromBytes(bytes);
        }
    }
    catch(Exception exception)
    {
        publicKey = null;
    }
    finally
    {
        if(cursor != null)
            cursor.close();
    }

    return publicKey;
}

public PublicKey publicSignatureKeyForSipHashId(Cryptography cryptography,
                                                String sipHashId)
{
    if(cryptography == null || m_db == null)
```

```java
            return null;

        Cursor cursor = null;
        PublicKey publicKey = null;

        try
        {
            cursor = m_db.rawQuery
                ("SELECT " +
                 "signature_public_key " +
                 "FROM participants WHERE siphash_id_digest = ?",
                 new String[] {Base64.
                                  encodeToString
                                  (cryptography.
                                  hmac(sipHashId.toUpperCase().trim().
                                       getBytes(StandardCharsets.UTF_8)),
                                  Base64.DEFAULT)});

            if(cursor != null && cursor.moveToFirst())
            {
                byte bytes[] = cryptography.mtd
                    (Base64.decode(cursor.getString(0).getBytes(),
                                   Base64.DEFAULT));

                if(bytes != null)
                    publicKey = Cryptography.publicKeyFromBytes(bytes);
            }
        }
        catch(Exception exception)
        {
            publicKey = null;
        }
        finally
        {
            if(cursor != null)
                cursor.close();
        }

        return publicKey;
    }

    public PublicKey signatureKeyForDigest(Cryptography cryptography,
                                           byte digest[])
    {
        if(cryptography == null || digest == null || m_db == null)
            return null;

        Cursor cursor = null;
        PublicKey publicKey = null;

        try
        {
            cursor = m_db.rawQuery
                ("SELECT " +
                 "signature_public_key " +
                 "FROM participants WHERE encryption_public_key_digest = ?",
                 new String[] {Base64.encodeToString(digest, Base64.DEFAULT)});

            if(cursor != null && cursor.moveToFirst())
            {
                byte bytes[] = cryptography.mtd
                    (Base64.decode(cursor.getString(0).getBytes(),
                                   Base64.DEFAULT));
```

```java
            if(bytes != null)
               for(int i = 0; i < 2; i++)
                   try
                   {
                       if(i == 0)
                           publicKey = KeyFactory.getInstance("EC").
                               generatePublic
                               (new X509EncodedKeySpec(bytes));
                       else
                           publicKey = KeyFactory.getInstance("RSA").
                               generatePublic
                               (new X509EncodedKeySpec(bytes));

                       break;
                   }
                   catch(Exception exception)
                   {
                   }
            }
        }
    catch(Exception exception)
    {
        publicKey = null;
    }
    finally
    {
        if(cursor != null)
            cursor.close();
    }

    return publicKey;
}

public SipHashIdElement readSipHashId(Cryptography cryptography,
                                      String oid)
{
    if(cryptography == null || m_db == null)
        return null;

    SipHashIdElement sipHashIdElement = null;
    Cursor cursor = null;

    try
    {
        cursor = m_db.rawQuery
            ("SELECT " +
            "(SELECT p.encryption_public_key FROM participants p " + // 0
            "WHERE p.siphash_id_digest = s.siphash_id_digest) AS a, " +
            "(SELECT p.signature_public_key FROM participants p " +  // 1
            "WHERE p.siphash_id_digest = s.siphash_id_digest) AS b, " +
            "(SELECT p.encryption_public_key_algorithm FROM " +       // 2
            "participants p WHERE p.siphash_id_digest = " +
            "s.siphash_id_digest) AS c, " +
            "s.siphash_id, " +                                        // 3
            "s.name, " +                                              // 4
            "s.stream, " +                                            // 5
            "s.oid " +
            "FROM siphash_ids s WHERE s.oid = ? ORDER BY s.oid",
            new String[] {oid});

        if(cursor != null && cursor.moveToFirst())
        {
```

```java
        sipHashIdElement = new SipHashIdElement();

    boolean error = false;
    int count = cursor.getColumnCount();

    for(int i = 0; i < count; i++)
    {
        if(i == 2)
        {
            if(cursor.isNull(i))
                continue;
        }
        else if(i == count - 1)
        {
            sipHashIdElement.m_oid = cursor.getInt(i);
            continue;
        }

        byte bytes[] = cryptography.mtd
            (Base64.decode(cursor.getString(i).getBytes(),
                        Base64.DEFAULT));

        if(bytes == null)
        {
            error = true;

            StringBuilder stringBuilder = new StringBuilder();

            stringBuilder.append
                ("Database::readSipHashId(): ");
            stringBuilder.append("error on column ");
            stringBuilder.append(cursor.getColumnName(i));
            stringBuilder.append(".");
            writeLog(stringBuilder.toString());
            break;
        }

        switch(i)
        {
        case 0:
            sipHashIdElement.m_encryptionPublicKey = bytes;
            break;
        case 1:
            sipHashIdElement.m_signaturePublicKey = bytes;
            break;
        case 2:
            sipHashIdElement.m_encryptionAlgorithm =
                new String(bytes);
            break;
        case 3:
            sipHashIdElement.m_sipHashId = new String
                (bytes, StandardCharsets.UTF_8);
            break;
        case 4:
            sipHashIdElement.m_name = new String
                (bytes, StandardCharsets.UTF_8);
            break;
        case 5:
            sipHashIdElement.m_stream = bytes;
            break;
        default:
            break;
        }
```

```java
                }

            if(error)
                sipHashIdElement = null;
        }
    }
    catch(Exception exception)
    {
        sipHashIdElement = null;
    }
    finally
    {
        if(cursor != null)
            cursor.close();
    }

    return sipHashIdElement;
}

public SteamElement readSteam
    (Cryptography cryptography, int position, int someOid)
{
    if(cryptography == null || m_db == null)
        return null;

    Cursor cursor = null;
    SteamElement steamElement = null;

    try
    {
        if(position >= 0)
        {
            cursor = m_db.rawQuery
                ("SELECT absolute_filename, " + // 0
                 "destination, " +              // 1
                 "display_filename, " +         // 2
                 "ephemeral_private_key, " +    // 3
                 "ephemeral_public_key, " +     // 4
                 "file_digest, " +              // 5
                 "file_identity, " +            // 6
                 "file_size, " +                // 7
                 "is_download, " +              // 8
                 "keystream, " +                // 9
                 "read_interval, " +            // 10
                 "read_offset, " +              // 11
                 "someoid, " +                  // 12
                 "status, " +                   // 13
                 "transfer_rate, " +            // 14
                 "oid " +                       // 15
                 "FROM steam_files ORDER BY someoid", null);

            if(cursor == null || !cursor.moveToPosition(position))
                return steamElement;
        }
        else
        {
            cursor = m_db.rawQuery
                ("SELECT absolute_filename, " + // 0
                 "destination, " +              // 1
                 "display_filename, " +         // 2
                 "ephemeral_private_key, " +    // 3
                 "ephemeral_public_key, " +     // 4
                 "file_digest, " +              // 5
```

```java
                    "file_identity, " +                // 6
                    "file_size, " +                    // 7
                    "is_download, " +                  // 8
                    "keystream, " +                    // 9
                    "read_interval, " +                // 10
                    "read_offset, " +                  // 11
                    "someoid, " +                      // 12
                    "status, " +                       // 13
                    "transfer_rate, " +                // 14
                    "oid " +                           // 15
                    "FROM steam_files WHERE someoid > CAST(? AS INTEGER) " +
                    "ORDER BY someoid LIMIT 1",
                    new String[] {String.valueOf(someOid)});

            if(cursor == null || !cursor.moveToFirst())
                return steamElement;
        }

        steamElement = new SteamElement();

        int count = cursor.getColumnCount();
        int oid = cursor.getInt(count - 1);

        for(int i = 0; i < count; i++)
        {
            if(i == 12)
            {
                steamElement.m_someOid = cursor.getInt(i);
                continue;
            }
            else if(i == 13)
            {
                steamElement.m_status = cursor.getString(i).trim();
                continue;
            }
            else if(i == count - 1)
            {
                steamElement.m_oid = oid;
                continue;
            }

            byte bytes[] = null;

            if(i == 8) // is_download
                bytes = cursor.getString(i).getBytes();
            else
                bytes = cryptography.mtd
                    (Base64.decode(cursor.getString(i).getBytes(),
                                Base64.DEFAULT));

            if(bytes == null)
            {
                StringBuilder stringBuilder = new StringBuilder();

                stringBuilder.append("Database::readSteam(): ");
                stringBuilder.append("error on column ");
                stringBuilder.append(cursor.getColumnName(i));
                stringBuilder.append(".");
                writeLog(stringBuilder.toString());
            }

            switch(i)
            {
```

```java
        case 0:
            if(bytes != null)
                steamElement.m_fileName = new String(bytes);
            else
                steamElement.m_fileName = "error (" + oid + ")";

            break;
        case 1:
            if(bytes != null)
                steamElement.m_destination = new String
                    (bytes, StandardCharsets.UTF_8);
            else
                steamElement.m_destination = "error (" + oid + ")";

            break;
        case 2:
            if(bytes != null)
                steamElement.m_displayFileName = new String
                    (bytes, StandardCharsets.UTF_8);
            else
                steamElement.m_displayFileName = "error (" + oid + ")";

            break;
        case 3:
            steamElement.m_ephemeralPrivateKey = bytes;
            break;
        case 4:
            steamElement.m_ephemeralPublicKey = bytes;
            break;
        case 5:
            steamElement.m_fileDigest = bytes;
            break;
        case 6:
            steamElement.m_fileIdentity = bytes;
            break;
        case 7:
            if(bytes != null)
                try
                {
                    steamElement.m_fileSize = Long.parseLong
                        (new String(bytes));
                }
                catch(Exception exception)
                {
                }

            break;
        case 8:
            if(bytes != null)
                try
                {
                    steamElement.m_direction = Short.parseShort
                        (new String(bytes));
                }
                catch(Exception exception)
                {
                }

            break;
        case 9:
            steamElement.m_keyStream = bytes;
            break;
        case 10:
```

```java
                    if(bytes != null)
                        try
                        {
                            steamElement.m_readInterval = Long.parseLong
                                (new String(bytes));
                        }
                        catch(Exception exception)
                        {
                        }

                        break;
                    case 11:
                        if(bytes != null)
                            try
                            {
                                steamElement.m_readOffset = Long.parseLong
                                    (new String(bytes));
                            }
                            catch(Exception exception)
                            {
                            }

                        break;
                    case 12:
                    case 13:
                        break;
                    case 14:
                        if(bytes != null)
                            steamElement.m_transferRate = new String(bytes);
                        else
                            steamElement.m_transferRate = "error (" + oid + ")";

                        break;
                    default:
                        break;
                    }
                }
        }
        catch(Exception exception)
        {
            steamElement = null;
        }
        finally
        {
            if(cursor != null)
                cursor.close();
        }

        return steamElement;
    }

    public String nameFromSipHashId(Cryptography cryptography,
                                    String sipHashId)
    {
        if(cryptography == null || m_db == null)
            return "";

        Cursor cursor = null;
        String name = "";

        try
        {
            cursor = m_db.rawQuery
```

```java
                ("SELECT name FROM siphash_ids WHERE siphash_id_digest = ?",
                new String[] {Base64.
                            encodeToString
                            (cryptography.
                            hmac(sipHashId.toUpperCase().trim().
                                getBytes(StandardCharsets.UTF_8)),
                            Base64.DEFAULT)});

        if(cursor != null && cursor.moveToFirst())
        {
            byte bytes[] = cryptography.mtd
                (Base64.decode(cursor.getString(0).getBytes(),
                            Base64.DEFAULT));

            if(bytes != null)
                name = new String(bytes);
        }
    }
    catch(Exception exception)
    {
    }
    finally
    {
        if(cursor != null)
            cursor.close();
    }

    return name;
}

public String publicKeyEncryptionAlgorithm(Cryptography cryptography,
                                    String sipHashId)
{
    if(cryptography == null || m_db == null)
        return null;

    Cursor cursor = null;

    try
    {
        cursor = m_db.rawQuery
            ("SELECT " +
            "encryption_public_key_algorithm " +
            "FROM participants WHERE siphash_id_digest = ?",
            new String[] {Base64.
                        encodeToString
                        (cryptography.
                        hmac(sipHashId.toUpperCase().trim().
                            getBytes(StandardCharsets.UTF_8)),
                        Base64.DEFAULT)});

        if(cursor != null && cursor.moveToFirst())
        {
            byte bytes[] = cryptography.mtd
                (Base64.decode(cursor.getString(0).getBytes(),
                            Base64.DEFAULT));

            if(bytes != null)
                return new String(bytes);
        }
    }
    catch(Exception exception)
    {
```

```java
        }
        finally
        {
            if(cursor != null)
                cursor.close();
        }

        return "";
    }

    public String readNeighborStatusControl(Cryptography cryptography, int
    oid)
        {
            if(cryptography == null || m_db == null)
                return null;

            Cursor cursor = null;
            String status = "";

            try
            {
                cursor = m_db.rawQuery
                    ("SELECT status_control FROM neighbors WHERE oid = ?",
                     new String[] {String.valueOf(oid)});

                if(cursor != null && cursor.moveToFirst())
                {
                    byte bytes[] = cryptography.mtd
                        (Base64.decode(cursor.getString(0).getBytes(),
                                    Base64.DEFAULT));

                    if(bytes != null)
                        status = new String(bytes);
                }
            }
            catch(Exception exception)
            {
            }
            finally
            {
                if(cursor != null)
                    cursor.close();
            }

            return status;
        }

    public String readParticipantOptions(Cryptography cryptography,
                                     String sipHashId)
        {
            if(cryptography == null || m_db == null)
                return "";

            Cursor cursor = null;
            String string = "";

            try
            {
                cursor = m_db.rawQuery
                    ("SELECT options " +
                     "FROM participants WHERE siphash_id_digest = ?",
                     new String[] {Base64.
                                    encodeToString
```

```java
                                        (cryptography.
                                        hmac(sipHashId.toUpperCase().trim().
                                            getBytes(StandardCharsets.UTF_8)),
                                        Base64.DEFAULT)});

            if(cursor != null && cursor.moveToFirst())
            {
                byte bytes[] = cryptography.mtd
                    (Base64.decode(cursor.getString(0).getBytes(),
                            Base64.DEFAULT));

                if(bytes != null)
                    string = new String(bytes);
            }
        }
        catch(Exception exception)
        {
            string = "";
        }
        finally
        {
            if(cursor != null)
                cursor.close();
        }

        return string;
    }

    public String readSetting(Cryptography cryptography, String name)
    {
        if(m_db == null)
            return "";

        Cursor cursor = null;
        String str = "";

        try
        {
            if(cryptography == null)
                cursor = m_db.rawQuery
                    ("SELECT value FROM settings WHERE name = ?",
                    new String[] {name});
            else
            {
                byte bytes[] = cryptography.hmac(name.getBytes());

                if(bytes != null)
                    cursor = m_db.rawQuery
                        ("SELECT value FROM settings WHERE name_digest = ?",
                        new String[] {Base64.encodeToString(bytes,
                                                Base64.DEFAULT)});
                else
                    str = "An error occurred (hmac() failure).";
            }

            if(cursor != null && cursor.moveToFirst())
                if(cryptography == null)
                    str = cursor.getString(0);
                else
                {
                    byte bytes[] = cryptography.mtd
                        (Base64.decode(cursor.getString(0).getBytes(),
                                Base64.DEFAULT));
```

```java
                    if(bytes != null)
                        str = new String(bytes);
                    else
                        str = "An error occurred (mtd() failure).";
                }
            }
        catch(Exception exception)
            {
                str = "An exception was thrown (" +
                    exception.getMessage().toLowerCase() +
                    ").";
            }
        finally
            {
                if(cursor != null)
                    cursor.close();
            }

        /*
        ** Default values.
        */

        if(name.equals("show_chat_icons") && str.isEmpty())
            return "true";

        return str;
    }

    public String readSipHashIdString(Cryptography cryptography, String oid)
    {
        if(cryptography == null || m_db == null)
            return null;

        Cursor cursor = null;

        try
        {
            cursor = m_db.rawQuery
                ("SELECT siphash_id FROM siphash_ids WHERE oid = ?",
                 new String[] {oid});

            if(cursor != null && cursor.moveToFirst())
            {
                byte bytes[] = cryptography.mtd
                    (Base64.decode(cursor.getString(0).getBytes(),
                            Base64.DEFAULT));

                if(bytes != null)
                    return new String(bytes, StandardCharsets.UTF_8);
            }
        }
        catch(Exception exception)
            {
            }
        finally
            {
                if(cursor != null)
                    cursor.close();
            }

        return "";
    }
```

```java
public String steamSipHashId(Cryptography cryptography,
                             byte fileIdentity[])
{
    if(cryptography == null || fileIdentity == null || m_db == null)
        return "";

    Cursor cursor = null;
    String sipHashId = "";

    try
    {
        cursor = m_db.rawQuery
            ("SELECT destination FROM steam_files " +
             "WHERE file_identity_digest = ?",
             new String[] {Base64.encodeToString(cryptography.
                                         hmac(fileIdentity),
                                         Base64.DEFAULT)});

        if(cursor != null && cursor.moveToFirst())
        {
            sipHashId = new String
                (cryptography.
                 mtd(Base64.decode(cursor.getString(0).getBytes(),
                            Base64.DEFAULT)),
                 StandardCharsets.UTF_8);
            sipHashId = Miscellaneous.sipHashIdFromDestination(sipHashId);
        }
    }
    catch(Exception exception)
    {
        sipHashId = "";
    }
    finally
    {
        if(cursor != null)
            cursor.close();
    }

    return sipHashId;
}

public String steamStatus(int oid)
{
    if(m_db == null)
        return "";

    Cursor cursor = null;
    String status = "";

    try
    {
        cursor = m_db.rawQuery
            ("SELECT status FROM steam_files WHERE oid = ?",
             new String[] {String.valueOf(oid)});

        if(cursor != null && cursor.moveToFirst())
            status = cursor.getString(0).trim();
    }
    catch(Exception exception)
    {
    }
    finally
```

```java
        {
            if(cursor != null)
                cursor.close();
        }

        return status;
    }

    public String writeParticipant(Cryptography cryptography, byte data[])
    {
        if(cryptography == null || data == null || m_db == null)
            return "";

        ContentValues values = null;
        Cursor cursor = null;
        String sipHashId = "";
        boolean exists = false;

        try
        {
            String strings[] = new String(data).split("\\n");

            if(strings.length != Messages.EPKS_GROUP_ONE_ELEMENT_COUNT)
                return "";

            PublicKey encryptionKey = null;
            PublicKey signatureKey = null;
            String encryptionKeyAlgorithm = "";
            boolean encryptionKeySigned = false;
            boolean signatureKeySigned = false;
            byte keyType[] = null;
            byte encryptionKeySignature[] = null;
            byte signatureKeySignature[] = null;
            byte sipHashIdBytes[] = null;
            int ii = 0;

            for(String string : strings)
                switch(ii)
                {
                case 0:
                    long timestamp = Miscellaneous.byteArrayToLong
                        (Base64.decode(string.getBytes(), Base64.NO_WRAP));

                    if(Math.abs(System.currentTimeMillis() - timestamp) >
                       WRITE_PARTICIPANT_TIME_DELTA)
                        return "";

                    ii += 1;
                    break;
                case 1:
                    keyType = Base64.decode
                        (string.getBytes(), Base64.NO_WRAP);

                    if(keyType == null ||
                       keyType.length != 1 ||
                       keyType[0] != Messages.CHAT_KEY_TYPE[0])
                        return "";

                    ii += 1;
                    break;
                case 2:
                    sipHashId = new String
                        (Base64.decode(string.getBytes(), Base64.NO_WRAP),
```

```java
                    StandardCharsets.UTF_8);

            if(sipHashId == null ||
               sipHashId.length() !=
               Cryptography.SIPHASH_IDENTITY_LENGTH)
                return "";
            else
                sipHashIdBytes = sipHashId.getBytes
                    (StandardCharsets.UTF_8);

            ii += 1;
            break;
        case 3:
            cursor = m_db.rawQuery
                ("SELECT EXISTS(SELECT 1 " +
                 "FROM participants WHERE " +
                 "encryption_public_key_digest = ?)",
                 new String[] {Base64.
                                encodeToString(Cryptography.
                                        sha512(Base64.
                                                decode(string.
                                                        getBytes(),
                                                        Base64.
                                                        NO_WRAP)),
                                Base64.DEFAULT)});

            if(cursor != null && cursor.moveToFirst())
                if(cursor.getInt(0) == 1)
                    exists = true;

            if(cursor != null)
            {
                cursor.close();
                cursor = null;
            }

            encryptionKey = Cryptography.publicKeyFromBytes
                (Base64.decode(string.getBytes(), Base64.NO_WRAP));

            if(encryptionKey == null)
                return "";
            else if(cryptography.
                    compareChatEncryptionPublicKey(encryptionKey))
                return "";
            else if(cryptography.
                    compareChatSignaturePublicKey(encryptionKey))
                return "";

            ii += 1;
            break;
        case 4:
            encryptionKeySignature = Base64.decode
                (string.getBytes(), Base64.NO_WRAP);
            ii += 1;
            break;
        case 5:
            cursor = m_db.rawQuery
                ("SELECT EXISTS(SELECT 1 " +
                 "FROM participants WHERE " +
                 "signature_public_key_digest = ?)",
                 new String[] {Base64.
                                encodeToString(Cryptography.
                                        sha512(Base64.
```

```java
                                            decode(string.
                                                getBytes(),
                                                Base64.
                                                NO_WRAP)),
                                    Base64.DEFAULT)});

            if(cursor != null && cursor.moveToFirst())
                if(cursor.getInt(0) == 1)
                    if(exists)
                        return "";

            if(cursor != null)
            {
                cursor.close();
                cursor = null;
            }

            signatureKey = Cryptography.publicKeyFromBytes
                (Base64.decode(string.getBytes(), Base64.NO_WRAP));

            if(signatureKey == null)
                return "";
            else if(cryptography.
                    compareChatEncryptionPublicKey(signatureKey))
                return "";
            else if(cryptography.
                    compareChatSignaturePublicKey(signatureKey))
                return "";

            ii += 1;
            break;
        case 6:
            signatureKeySignature = Base64.decode
                (string.getBytes(), Base64.NO_WRAP);

            if(!encryptionKey.getAlgorithm().equals("McEliece-CCA2"))
            {
                if(Cryptography.
                    verifySignature(encryptionKey,
                                    encryptionKeySignature,
                                    Miscellaneous.
                                    joinByteArrays(sipHashIdBytes,
                                            encryptionKey.
                                            getEncoded(),
                                            signatureKey.
                                            getEncoded())))
                    encryptionKeySigned = true;
            }
            else
            {
                if(encryptionKeySignature[0] ==
                    Messages.MCELIECE_FUJISAKI_11_50)
                        encryptionKeyAlgorithm =
                            "McEliece-Fujisaki (11, 50)";
                else if(encryptionKeySignature[0] ==
                        Messages.MCELIECE_FUJISAKI_12_68)
                        encryptionKeyAlgorithm =
                            "McEliece-Fujisaki (12, 68)";
                else if(encryptionKeySignature[0] ==
                        Messages.MCELIECE_POINTCHEVAL)
                        encryptionKeyAlgorithm =
                            "McEliece-Pointcheval (11, 50)";
            }
```

```java
            if(Cryptography.
               verifySignature(signatureKey,
                               signatureKeySignature,
                               Miscellaneous.
                               joinByteArrays(sipHashIdBytes,
                                              encryptionKey.
                                              getEncoded(),
                                              signatureKey.
                                              getEncoded())))
                signatureKeySigned = true;

            break;
        default:
            break;
        }

    if(nameFromSipHashId(cryptography, sipHashId).isEmpty())
        return "";

    values = new ContentValues();

    SparseArray<String> sparseArray = new SparseArray<> ();

    sparseArray.append(0, "encryption_public_key");
    sparseArray.append(1, "encryption_public_key_algorithm");
    sparseArray.append(2, "encryption_public_key_digest");
    sparseArray.append(3, "encryption_public_key_signed");
    sparseArray.append(4, "identity");
    sparseArray.append(5, "keystream");
    sparseArray.append(6, "last_status_timestamp");
    sparseArray.append(7, "options");
    sparseArray.append(8, "signature_public_key");
    sparseArray.append(9, "signature_public_key_digest");
    sparseArray.append(10, "signature_public_key_signed");
    sparseArray.append(11, "siphash_id");
    sparseArray.append(12, "siphash_id_digest");

    int size = sparseArray.size();

    for(int i = 0; i < size; i++)
    {
        byte bytes[] = null;

        switch(sparseArray.get(i))
        {
        case "encryption_public_key":
            bytes = cryptography.etm(encryptionKey.getEncoded());
            break;
        case "encryption_public_key_algorithm":
            bytes = cryptography.etm
                (encryptionKeyAlgorithm.getBytes());
            break;
        case "encryption_public_key_digest":
            bytes = Cryptography.sha512(encryptionKey.getEncoded());
            break;
        case "encryption_public_key_signed":
            bytes = cryptography.etm
                ((encryptionKeySigned ? "true" : "false").getBytes());
            break;
        case "identity":
            bytes = cryptography.etm("".getBytes());
            break;
```

```java
case "keystream":
    /*
    ** Create an initial pairing.
    */

    try
    {
        byte salt[] = null;

        salt = Cryptography.xor
            (cryptography.chatEncryptionPublicKey().
             getEncoded(),
             cryptography.chatSignaturePublicKey().
             getEncoded(),
             encryptionKey.getEncoded(),
             signatureKey.getEncoded());
        bytes = Cryptography.pbkdf2
            (salt,
             Miscellaneous.
             byteArrayAsHexString(Cryptography.sha512(salt)).
             toCharArray(),
             Cryptography.KEY_EXCHANGE_INITIAL_PBKDF2_ITERATION,
             8 * Cryptography.CIPHER_HASH_KEYS_LENGTH);
        bytes = cryptography.etm(bytes);
    }
    catch(Exception exception)
    {
        bytes = cryptography.etm("".getBytes());
    }

    break;
case "last_status_timestamp":
    bytes = cryptography.etm("".getBytes());
    break;
case "options":
    bytes = cryptography.etm
        ("optional_signatures = false".getBytes());
    break;
case "signature_public_key":
    bytes = cryptography.etm(signatureKey.getEncoded());
    break;
case "signature_public_key_digest":
    bytes = Cryptography.sha512(signatureKey.getEncoded());
    break;
case "signature_public_key_signed":
    bytes = cryptography.etm
        ((signatureKeySigned ? "true" : "false").getBytes());
    break;
case "siphash_id":
    bytes = cryptography.etm
        (sipHashId.getBytes(StandardCharsets.UTF_8));
    break;
case "siphash_id_digest":
    bytes = cryptography.hmac
        (sipHashId.getBytes(StandardCharsets.UTF_8));
    break;
default:
    break;
}

if(bytes == null)
{
    sparseArray.clear();
```

```java
                    return "";
                }

                values.put(sparseArray.get(i),
                        Base64.encodeToString(bytes, Base64.DEFAULT));
            }

            sparseArray.clear();
        }
        catch(Exception exception)
        {
            return "";
        }
        finally
        {
            if(cursor != null)
                cursor.close();
        }

        if(values == null)
            return "";

        m_db.beginTransactionNonExclusive();

        try
        {
            if(m_db.replace("participants", null, values) <= 0)
                sipHashId = "";

            m_db.setTransactionSuccessful();
        }
        catch(Exception exception)
        {
            return "";
        }
        finally
        {
            m_db.endTransaction();
        }

        return sipHashId;
    }

    public String[] keysSigned(Cryptography cryptography, String sipHashId)
    {
        if(cryptography == null || m_db == null)
            return null;

        Cursor cursor = null;
        String strings[] = null;

        try
        {
            cursor = m_db.rawQuery
                ("SELECT encryption_public_key_signed, " +
                 "signature_public_key_signed " +
                 "FROM participants WHERE siphash_id_digest = ?",
                 new String[] {Base64.
                               encodeToString
                               (cryptography.
                               hmac(sipHashId.toUpperCase().trim().
                                   getBytes(StandardCharsets.UTF_8)),
                               Base64.DEFAULT)});
```

```java
            if(cursor != null && cursor.moveToFirst())
            {
                strings = new String[] {"false", "false"};

                for(int i = 0; i < 2; i++)
                {
                    byte bytes[] = cryptography.mtd
                        (Base64.decode(cursor.getString(i).getBytes(),
                                       Base64.DEFAULT));

                    if(bytes == null)
                    {
                        StringBuilder stringBuilder = new StringBuilder();

                        stringBuilder.append("Database::keysSigned(): ");
                        stringBuilder.append("error on column ");
                        stringBuilder.append(cursor.getColumnName(i));
                        stringBuilder.append(".");
                        writeLog(stringBuilder.toString());
                    }
                    else
                        strings[i] = new String(bytes);
                }
            }
        }
        catch(Exception exception)
        {
            strings = null;
        }
        finally
        {
            if(cursor != null)
                cursor.close();
        }

        return strings;
    }

    public String[] nameSipHashIdFromDigest(Cryptography cryptography,
                                            byte digest[])
    {
        if(cryptography == null || digest == null || m_db == null)
            return null;

        Cursor cursor = null;
        String array[] = null;

        try
        {
            cursor = m_db.rawQuery
                ("SELECT name, siphash_id " +
                 "FROM siphash_ids WHERE siphash_id_digest = " +
                 "(SELECT siphash_id_digest FROM participants " +
                 "WHERE encryption_public_key_digest = ?)",
                 new String[] {Base64.encodeToString(digest, Base64.DEFAULT)});

            if(cursor != null && cursor.moveToFirst())
            {
                byte bytes[] = cryptography.mtd
                    (Base64.decode(cursor.getString(0).getBytes(),
                                   Base64.DEFAULT));
```

```java
            if(bytes != null)
            {
                array = new String[2];
                array[0] = new String(bytes);
                bytes = cryptography.mtd
                    (Base64.decode(cursor.getString(1).getBytes(),
                                Base64.DEFAULT));

                if(bytes != null)
                    array[1] = new String(bytes, StandardCharsets.UTF_8);
                else
                    array = null;
            }
        }
        catch(Exception exception)
        {
            array = null;
        }
        finally
        {
            if(cursor != null)
                cursor.close();
        }

        return array;
    }

    public String[] readOutboundMessage(int oid)
    {
        if(m_db == null)
            return null;

        Cursor cursor = null;
        String array[] = null;

        try
        {
            cursor = m_db.rawQuery
                ("SELECT message, message_identity_digest, oid " +
                 "FROM outbound_queue " +
                 "WHERE neighbor_oid = ? ORDER BY oid LIMIT 1",
                 new String[] {String.valueOf(oid)});

            if(cursor != null && cursor.moveToFirst())
            {
                array = new String[3];
                array[0] = cursor.getString(0);
                array[1] = cursor.getString(1);
                array[2] = String.valueOf(cursor.getInt(2));
            }
        }
        catch(Exception exception)
        {
            array = null;
        }
        finally
        {
            if(cursor != null)
                cursor.close();
        }

        return array;
```

```java
    }

    public boolean accountPrepared()
    {
        return !readSetting(null, "encryptionSalt").isEmpty() &&
            !readSetting(null, "macSalt").isEmpty() &&
            !readSetting(null, "saltedPassword").isEmpty();
    }

    public boolean containsCongestionDigest(long value)
    {
        if(m_db == null)
            return false;

        boolean contains = false;

        s_congestionControlMutex.readLock().lock();

        try
        {
            Cursor cursor = null;

            try
            {
                cursor = m_db.rawQuery
                    ("SELECT EXISTS(SELECT 1 FROM " +
                     "congestion_control WHERE digest = ?)",
                     new String[] {Base64.
                                   encodeToString(Miscellaneous.
                                                  longToByteArray(value),
                                                  Base64.DEFAULT)});

                if(cursor != null && cursor.moveToFirst())
                    contains = cursor.getInt(0) == 1;
            }
            catch(Exception exception)
            {
            }
            finally
            {
                if(cursor != null)
                    cursor.close();
            }
        }
        catch(Exception exception)
        {
        }
        finally
        {
            s_congestionControlMutex.readLock().unlock();
        }

        return contains;
    }

    public boolean containsParticipant(Cryptography cryptography,
                                       String sipHashId)
    {
        if(cryptography == null || m_db == null)
            return false;

        Cursor cursor = null;
        boolean contains = false;
```

```java
        try
        {
            cursor = m_db.rawQuery
                ("SELECT EXISTS(SELECT 1 " +
                 "FROM participants WHERE " +
                 "siphash_id_digest = ?)",
                 new String[] {Base64.
                               encodeToString
                               (cryptography.
                               hmac(sipHashId.toUpperCase().trim().
                                   getBytes(StandardCharsets.UTF_8)),
                               Base64.DEFAULT)});

            if(cursor != null && cursor.moveToFirst())
                contains = cursor.getInt(0) == 1;
        }
        catch(Exception exception)
        {
        }
        finally
        {
            if(cursor != null)
                cursor.close();
        }

        return contains;
    }

    public boolean containsSteam(Cryptography cryptography, byte
fileIdentity[])
    {
        if(cryptography == null || fileIdentity == null || m_db == null)
            return false;

        Cursor cursor = null;
        boolean contains = false;

        try
        {
            cursor = m_db.rawQuery
                ("SELECT EXISTS(SELECT 1 " +
                 "FROM steam_files WHERE " +
                 "file_identity_digest = ?)",
                 new String[] {Base64.
                               encodeToString(cryptography.hmac(fileIdentity),
                                   Base64.DEFAULT)});

            if(cursor != null && cursor.moveToFirst())
                contains = cursor.getInt(0) == 1;
        }
        catch(Exception exception)
        {
        }
        finally
        {
            if(cursor != null)
                cursor.close();
        }

        return contains;
    }
```

```java
public boolean deleteEntry(String oid, String table)
{
    if(m_db == null)
        return false;

    boolean ok = false;

    m_db.beginTransactionNonExclusive();

    try
    {
        ok = m_db.delete(table, "oid = ?", new String[] {oid}) > 0;
        m_db.setTransactionSuccessful();
    }
    catch(Exception exception)
    {
        ok = false;
    }
    finally
    {
        m_db.endTransaction();
    }

    return ok;
}

public boolean deleteFiascoKeys(String oid)
{
    if(m_db == null)
        return false;

    m_db.beginTransactionNonExclusive();

    try
    {
        m_db.execSQL
            ("DELETE FROM participants_keys WHERE siphash_id_digest IN " +
             "(SELECT siphash_id_digest FROM siphash_ids WHERE oid = ?)",
             new String[] {oid});
        m_db.setTransactionSuccessful();
    }
    catch(Exception exception)
    {
        return false;
    }
    finally
    {
        m_db.endTransaction();
    }

    return true;
}

public boolean deletePublicKeys(String oid)
{
    if(m_db == null)
        return false;

    m_db.beginTransactionNonExclusive();

    try
    {
        m_db.execSQL
```

```java
                    ("DELETE FROM participants WHERE siphash_id_digest IN " +
                        "(SELECT siphash_id_digest FROM siphash_ids WHERE oid = ?)",
                        new String[] {oid});
                m_db.execSQL
                    ("DELETE FROM participants_keys WHERE siphash_id_digest IN " +
                        "(SELECT siphash_id_digest FROM siphash_ids WHERE oid = ?)",
                        new String[] {oid});
                m_db.setTransactionSuccessful();
            }
        catch(Exception exception)
            {
                return false;
            }
        finally
            {
                m_db.endTransaction();
            }

        return true;
    }

    public boolean setParticipantKeyStream(Cryptography cryptography,
                                           byte keyStream[],
                                           int oid)
    {
        if(cryptography == null || m_db == null)
            return false;

        m_db.beginTransactionNonExclusive();

        try
            {
                ContentValues values = new ContentValues();

                if(keyStream == null)
                    values.put
                        ("keystream",
                         Base64.encodeToString(cryptography.etm("".getBytes()),
                                               Base64.DEFAULT));
                else
                    values.put
                        ("keystream",
                         Base64.encodeToString(cryptography.etm(keyStream),
                                               Base64.DEFAULT));

                m_db.update
                    ("participants",
                     values,
                     "oid = ?",
                     new String[] {String.valueOf(oid)});
                m_db.setTransactionSuccessful();
            }
        catch(Exception exception)
            {
                return false;
            }
        finally
            {
                m_db.endTransaction();
            }

        return true;
    }
```

```java
public boolean writeCongestionDigest(long value)
{
    if(m_db == null)
        return false;

    s_congestionControlMutex.writeLock().lock();

    try
    {
        m_db.beginTransactionNonExclusive();

        try
        {
            ContentValues values = new ContentValues();

            values.put
                ("digest",
                 Base64.encodeToString(Miscellaneous.
                                       longToByteArray(value),
                                       Base64.DEFAULT));
            m_db.insertOrThrow("congestion_control", null, values);
            m_db.setTransactionSuccessful();
        }
        catch(Exception exception)
        {
            if(exception.getMessage().toLowerCase().contains("unique"))
                return true;
        }
        finally
        {
            m_db.endTransaction();
        }
    }
    catch(Exception exception)
    {
    }
    finally
    {
        s_congestionControlMutex.writeLock().unlock();
    }

    return false;
}

public boolean writeEphemeralSteamKeys(Cryptography cryptography,
                                       byte privateKey[],
                                       byte publicKey[],
                                       int oid)
{
    if(cryptography == null || m_db == null)
        return false;

    m_db.beginTransactionNonExclusive();

    try
    {
        ContentValues values = new ContentValues();

        values.put
            ("ephemeral_private_key",
             cryptography.etmBase64String(privateKey));
        values.put
```

```java
                    ("ephemeral_public_key",
                     cryptography.etmBase64String(publicKey));
                m_db.update
                    ("steam_files",
                     values,
                     "oid = ?",
                     new String[] {String.valueOf(oid)});
                m_db.setTransactionSuccessful();
            }
            catch(Exception exception)
            {
                return false;
            }
            finally
            {
                m_db.endTransaction();
            }

            return true;
        }

    public boolean writeMessageStatus(Cryptography cryptography,
                                      String messageIdentityDigest)
    {
        if(cryptography == null || m_db == null)
            return false;

        m_db.beginTransactionNonExclusive();

        try
        {
            ContentValues values = new ContentValues();

            values.put
                ("message_sent",
                 Base64.encodeToString(cryptography.etm("true".getBytes()),
                                Base64.DEFAULT));

            if(m_db.update("participants_messages",
                           values,
                           "message_identity_digest = ?",
                           new String[] {messageIdentityDigest}) > 0)
            {
                Cursor cursor = null;

                try
                {
                    cursor = m_db.rawQuery
                        ("SELECT siphash_id_digest FROM " +
                         "participants_messages " +
                         "WHERE message_identity_digest = ?",
                         new String[] {messageIdentityDigest});

                    if(cursor != null && cursor.moveToFirst())
                    {
                        String sipHashIdDigest1 = cursor.getString(0);

                        synchronized(m_readMemberChatCursorMutex)
                        {
                            String sipHashIdDigest2 = Base64.
                                encodeToString
                                (cryptography.
                                 hmac(m_readMemberChatSipHashId.toUpperCase().
```

```java
                                trim().getBytes(StandardCharsets.UTF_8)),
                            Base64.DEFAULT);

                        if(sipHashIdDigest1.equals(sipHashIdDigest2))
                        {
                            if(m_readMemberChatCursor != null)
                                m_readMemberChatCursor.close();

                            m_readMemberChatCursor = null;
                        }
                    }
                }
            }
            catch(Exception exception)
            {
            }
            finally
            {
                if(cursor != null)
                    cursor.close();
            }
        }

        m_db.setTransactionSuccessful();
    }
    catch(Exception exception)
    {
        return false;
    }
    finally
    {
        m_db.endTransaction();
    }

    return true;
}

public boolean writeMessageStatus(Cryptography cryptography,
                                  String sipHashId,
                                  byte messageIdentity[])
{
    if(cryptography == null || m_db == null || messageIdentity == null)
        return false;

    m_db.beginTransactionNonExclusive();

    try
    {
        ContentValues values = new ContentValues();

        values.put
            ("message_read",
             Base64.encodeToString(cryptography.etm("true".getBytes()),
                        Base64.DEFAULT));

        if(m_db.update
            ("participants_messages",
            values,
            "message_identity_digest = ? AND siphash_id_digest = ?",
            new String[] {Base64.encodeToString(cryptography.
                                        hmac(messageIdentity),
                        Base64.DEFAULT),
                    Base64.encodeToString
```

```java
                            (cryptography.
                             hmac(sipHashId.toUpperCase().trim().
                                 getBytes(StandardCharsets.UTF_8)),
                             Base64.DEFAULT)}) > 0)
                synchronized(m_readMemberChatCursorMutex)
                {
                    if(m_readMemberChatSipHashId.equals(sipHashId))
                    {
                        if(m_readMemberChatCursor != null)
                            m_readMemberChatCursor.close();

                        m_readMemberChatCursor = null;
                    }
                }

            m_db.setTransactionSuccessful();
        }
        catch(Exception exception)
        {
            return false;
        }
        finally
        {
            m_db.endTransaction();
        }

        return true;
    }

    public boolean writeNeighbor(Cryptography cryptography,
                                 String nonTls,
                                 String passthrough,
                                 String proxyIpAddress,
                                 String proxyPort,
                                 String proxyType,
                                 String remoteIpAddress,
                                 String remoteIpPort,
                                 String remoteIpScopeId,
                                 String transport,
                                 String version)
    {
        if(cryptography == null || m_db == null)
            return false;

        ContentValues values = null;
        boolean ok = true;

        try
        {
            values = new ContentValues();
        }
        catch(Exception exception)
        {
            ok = false;
        }

        if(!ok)
            return ok;

        try
        {
            SparseArray<String> sparseArray = new SparseArray<> ();
            byte bytes[] = null;
```

```java
sparseArray.append(0,  "bytes_read");
sparseArray.append(1,  "bytes_written");
sparseArray.append(2,  "echo_queue_size");
sparseArray.append(3,  "ip_version");
sparseArray.append(4,  "last_error");
sparseArray.append(5,  "local_ip_address");
sparseArray.append(6,  "local_ip_address_digest");
sparseArray.append(7,  "local_port");
sparseArray.append(8,  "local_port_digest");
sparseArray.append(9,  "non_tls");
sparseArray.append(10, "passthrough");
sparseArray.append(11, "proxy_ip_address");
sparseArray.append(12, "proxy_port");
sparseArray.append(13, "proxy_type");
sparseArray.append(14, "remote_certificate");
sparseArray.append(15, "remote_ip_address");
sparseArray.append(16, "remote_ip_address_digest");
sparseArray.append(17, "remote_port");
sparseArray.append(18, "remote_port_digest");
sparseArray.append(19, "remote_scope_id");
sparseArray.append(20, "session_cipher");
sparseArray.append(21, "status");
sparseArray.append(22, "status_control");
sparseArray.append(23, "transport");
sparseArray.append(24, "transport_digest");
sparseArray.append(25, "uptime");
sparseArray.append(26, "user_defined_digest");

/*
** Proxy information.
*/

if(!transport.toLowerCase().equals("tcp"))
{
    proxyIpAddress = "";
    proxyPort = "";
    proxyType = "HTTP";
}
else
{
    proxyIpAddress = proxyIpAddress.trim();

    if(proxyIpAddress.isEmpty())
    {
        proxyPort = "";
        proxyType = "HTTP";
    }
}

if(!remoteIpAddress.toLowerCase().trim().matches(".*[a-z].*"))
{
    Matcher matcher = Patterns.IP_ADDRESS.matcher
        (remoteIpAddress.trim());

    if(!matcher.matches())
    {
        if(version.toLowerCase().equals("ipv4"))
            remoteIpAddress = "0.0.0.0";
        else
            remoteIpAddress = "0:0:0:0:0:ffff:0:0";
    }
}
```

```java
        int size = sparseArray.size();

        for(int i = 0; i < size; i++)
        {
            switch(sparseArray.get(i))
            {
            case "echo_queue_size":
                bytes = cryptography.etm("0".getBytes());
                break;
            case "ip_version":
                bytes = cryptography.etm(version.trim().getBytes());
                break;
            case "last_error":
                bytes = cryptography.etm("".getBytes());
                break;
            case "local_ip_address_digest":
                bytes = cryptography.hmac("".getBytes());
                break;
            case "local_port_digest":
                bytes = cryptography.hmac("".getBytes());
                break;
            case "non_tls":
                bytes = cryptography.etm(nonTls.getBytes());
                break;
            case "passthrough":
                bytes = cryptography.etm(passthrough.getBytes());
                break;
            case "proxy_ip_address":
                bytes = cryptography.etm(proxyIpAddress.getBytes());
                break;
            case "proxy_port":
                bytes = cryptography.etm(proxyPort.getBytes());
                break;
            case "proxy_type":
                bytes = cryptography.etm(proxyType.getBytes());
                break;
            case "remote_ip_address":
                bytes = cryptography.etm
                    (remoteIpAddress.trim().getBytes());
                break;
            case "remote_ip_address_digest":
                bytes = cryptography.hmac
                    (remoteIpAddress.trim().getBytes());
                break;
            case "remote_port":
                bytes = cryptography.etm(remoteIpPort.trim().getBytes());
                break;
            case "remote_port_digest":
                bytes = cryptography.hmac(remoteIpPort.trim().getBytes());
                break;
            case "remote_scope_id":
                bytes = cryptography.etm(remoteIpScopeId.trim().getBytes());
                break;
            case "status":
                bytes = cryptography.etm("disconnected".getBytes());
                break;
            case "status_control":
                bytes = cryptography.etm("connect".getBytes());
                break;
            case "transport":
                bytes = cryptography.etm(transport.trim().getBytes());
                break;
```

```java
                case "transport_digest":
                    bytes = cryptography.hmac(transport.trim().getBytes());
                    break;
                case "user_defined_digest":
                    bytes = cryptography.hmac("true".getBytes());
                    break;
                default:
                    bytes = cryptography.etm("".getBytes());
                    break;
                }

                if(bytes == null)
                {
                    sparseArray.clear();

                    StringBuilder stringBuilder = new StringBuilder();

                    stringBuilder.append
                        ("Database::writeNeighbor(): error with ");
                    stringBuilder.append(sparseArray.get(i));
                    stringBuilder.append(" field.");
                    writeLog(stringBuilder.toString());
                    throw new Exception();
                }

                String str = Base64.encodeToString(bytes, Base64.DEFAULT);

                values.put(sparseArray.get(i), str);
            }

        sparseArray.clear();
    }
    catch(Exception exception)
    {
        ok = false;
    }

    m_db.beginTransactionNonExclusive();

    try
    {
        if(ok)
        {
            m_db.insertOrThrow("neighbors", null, values);
            m_db.setTransactionSuccessful();
        }
    }
    catch(SQLiteConstraintException exception)
    {
        ok = exception.getMessage().toLowerCase().contains("unique");
    }
    catch(Exception exception)
    {
        ok = false;
    }
    finally
    {
        m_db.endTransaction();
    }

    return ok;
}
```

```java
public boolean writeParticipantName(Cryptography cryptography,
                                    String name,
                                    int oid)
{
    if(cryptography == null ||
       m_db == null ||
       name == null ||
       name.trim().isEmpty())
        return false;

    m_db.beginTransactionNonExclusive();

    try
    {
        ContentValues values = new ContentValues();

        values.put
            ("name",
             Base64.encodeToString(cryptography.etm(name.trim().getBytes()),
                                   Base64.DEFAULT));
        m_db.update("siphash_ids", values, "oid = ?",
                    new String[] {String.valueOf(oid)});
        m_db.setTransactionSuccessful();
    }
    catch(Exception exception)
    {
        return false;
    }
    finally
    {
        m_db.endTransaction();
    }

    return true;
}

public boolean writeSipHashParticipant(Cryptography cryptography,
                                       String name,
                                       String sipHashId)
{
    if(cryptography == null || m_db == null)
        return false;

    ContentValues values = null;
    boolean ok = true;

    try
    {
        values = new ContentValues();
    }
    catch(Exception exception)
    {
        ok = false;
    }

    if(!ok)
        return ok;

    try
    {
        SparseArray<String> sparseArray = new SparseArray<> ();
        byte bytes[] = null;
```

```java
        name = name.trim();

        if(name.isEmpty())
            name = "unknown";

        sipHashId = Miscellaneous.prepareSipHashId(sipHashId);
        sparseArray.append(0, "name");
        sparseArray.append(1, "siphash_id");
        sparseArray.append(2, "siphash_id_digest");
        sparseArray.append(3, "stream");

        int size = sparseArray.size();

        for(int i = 0; i < size; i++)
        {
            switch(sparseArray.get(i))
            {
            case "name":
                bytes = cryptography.etm(name.getBytes());
                break;
            case "siphash_id":
                bytes = cryptography.etm
                    (sipHashId.trim().getBytes(StandardCharsets.UTF_8));
                break;
            case "siphash_id_digest":
                bytes = cryptography.hmac
                    (sipHashId.trim().getBytes(StandardCharsets.UTF_8));
                break;
            default:
                byte salt[] = Cryptography.sha512
                    (sipHashId.trim().getBytes(StandardCharsets.UTF_8));
                byte temporary[] = Cryptography.
                    pbkdf2(salt,
                            sipHashId.toCharArray(),
                            SIPHASH_STREAM_CREATION_ITERATION_COUNT,
                            160); // SHA-1

                if(temporary != null)
                    bytes = cryptography.etm
                        (Cryptography.
                         pbkdf2(salt,
                                Base64.encodeToString(temporary,
                                                      Base64.NO_WRAP).
                                toCharArray(),
                                1,
                                // Bits.
                                8 * (Cryptography.CIPHER_KEY_LENGTH +
                                    Cryptography.HASH_KEY_LENGTH)));

                break;
            }

            if(bytes == null)
            {
                sparseArray.clear();

                StringBuilder stringBuilder = new StringBuilder();

                stringBuilder.append
                    ("Database::writeSipHashParticipant(): error with ");
                stringBuilder.append(sparseArray.get(i));
                stringBuilder.append(" field.");
                writeLog(stringBuilder.toString());
```

```java
                    throw new Exception();
                }

                String str = Base64.encodeToString(bytes, Base64.DEFAULT);

                values.put(sparseArray.get(i), str);
            }

            sparseArray.clear();
        }
        catch(Exception exception)
        {
            ok = false;
        }

        m_db.beginTransactionNonExclusive();

        try
        {
            if(ok)
            {
                if(m_db.
                   update("siphash_ids",
                          values,
                          "siphash_id_digest = ?",
                          new String[] {Base64.
                                        encodeToString
                                        (cryptography.
                                         hmac(sipHashId.toUpperCase().trim().
                                              getBytes(StandardCharsets.UTF_8)),
                                         Base64.DEFAULT)}) <= 0)
                {
                    if(m_db.replace("siphash_ids", null, values) == -1)
                        ok = false;
                }

                m_db.setTransactionSuccessful();
            }
        }
        catch(Exception exception)
        {
            ok = false;
        }
        finally
        {
            m_db.endTransaction();
        }

        return ok;
    }

    public boolean writeSteamKeys(Cryptography cryptography,
                                  KeyPair keyPair,
                                  byte keyStream[],
                                  int oid)
    {
        return writeSteamKeys
            (cryptography,
             keyStream,
             keyPair.getPrivate().getEncoded(),
             keyPair.getPublic().getEncoded(),
             oid);
    }
```

```java
public boolean writeSteamKeys(Cryptography cryptography,
                              byte keyStream[],
                              byte privateKey[],
                              byte publicKey[],
                              int oid)
{
    if(cryptography == null || m_db == null)
        return false;

    m_db.beginTransactionNonExclusive();

    try
    {
        ContentValues values = new ContentValues();

        values.put
            ("ephemeral_private_key",
             cryptography.etmBase64String(privateKey));
        values.put
            ("ephemeral_public_key",
             cryptography.etmBase64String(publicKey));
        values.put("keystream", cryptography.etmBase64String(keyStream));
        m_db.update
            ("steam_files",
             values,
             "oid = ?",
             new String[] {String.valueOf(oid)});
        m_db.setTransactionSuccessful();
    }
    catch(Exception exception)
    {
        return false;
    }
    finally
    {
        m_db.endTransaction();
    }

    return true;
}

public byte[] fireStream(Cryptography cryptography, String name)
{
    if(cryptography == null || m_db == null)
        return null;

    Cursor cursor = null;
    byte bytes[] = null;

    try
    {
        cursor = m_db.rawQuery
            ("SELECT stream FROM fire WHERE name_digest = ?",
             new String[] {Base64.
                            encodeToString
                            (cryptography.
                            hmac(name.
                                getBytes(StandardCharsets.ISO_8859_1)),
                            Base64.DEFAULT)});

        if(cursor != null && cursor.moveToFirst())
            bytes = cryptography.mtd
```

```java
                        (Base64.decode(cursor.getString(0).getBytes(),
                                Base64.DEFAULT));
        }
        catch(Exception exception)
        {
            bytes = null;
        }
        finally
        {
            if(cursor != null)
                cursor.close();
        }

        return bytes;
    }

    public byte[] neighborRemoteCertificate(Cryptography cryptography,
                                            int oid)
    {
        if(cryptography == null || m_db == null)
            return null;

        Cursor cursor = null;
        byte bytes[] = null;

        try
        {
            cursor = m_db.rawQuery
                ("SELECT remote_certificate FROM neighbors WHERE oid = ?",
                 new String[] {String.valueOf(oid)});

            if(cursor != null && cursor.moveToFirst())
                bytes = cryptography.mtd
                    (Base64.decode(cursor.getString(0).getBytes(),
                                Base64.DEFAULT));
        }
        catch(Exception exception)
        {
            bytes = null;
        }
        finally
        {
            if(cursor != null)
                cursor.close();
        }

        return bytes;
    }

    public byte[] participantKeyStream(Cryptography cryptography,
                                       String sipHashId)
    {
        if(cryptography == null || m_db == null)
            return null;

        Cursor cursor = null;
        byte bytes[] = null;

        try
        {
            cursor = m_db.rawQuery
                ("SELECT keystream FROM participants " +
                 "WHERE siphash_id_digest = ?",
```

```java
                new String[] {Base64.
                          encodeToString
                          (cryptography.
                          hmac(sipHashId.toUpperCase().trim().
                              getBytes(StandardCharsets.UTF_8)),
                          Base64.DEFAULT)});

        if(cursor != null && cursor.moveToFirst())
            bytes = cryptography.mtd
                (Base64.decode(cursor.getString(0).getBytes(),
                          Base64.DEFAULT));
    }
    catch(Exception exception)
    {
        bytes = null;
    }
    finally
    {
        if(cursor != null)
            cursor.close();
    }

    return bytes;
}

public byte[] participantKeyStream(Cryptography cryptography,
                                   byte digest[])
{
    if(cryptography == null || digest == null || m_db == null)
        return null;

    Cursor cursor = null;
    byte bytes[] = null;

    try
    {
        cursor = m_db.rawQuery
            ("SELECT keystream FROM participants " +
             "WHERE encryption_public_key_digest = ?",
             new String[] {Base64.encodeToString(digest, Base64.DEFAULT)});

        if(cursor != null && cursor.moveToFirst())
            bytes = cryptography.mtd
                (Base64.decode(cursor.getString(0).getBytes(),
                          Base64.DEFAULT));
    }
    catch(Exception exception)
    {
        bytes = null;
    }
    finally
    {
        if(cursor != null)
            cursor.close();
    }

    return bytes;
}

public byte[] participantKeyStream(Cryptography cryptography,
                                   byte digest[],
                                   byte array[],
                                   byte bytes[])
```

```java
    {
        if(array == null ||
           bytes == null ||
           cryptography == null ||
           digest == null ||
           m_db == null)
            return null;

        Cursor cursor = null;
        byte keyStream[] = null;

        try
        {
            cursor = m_db.rawQuery
                ("SELECT keystream FROM participants_keys " +
                 "WHERE siphash_id_digest = " +
                 "(SELECT siphash_id_digest FROM participants WHERE " +
                 "encryption_public_key_digest = ?) ORDER BY timestamp DESC",
                 new String[] {Base64.encodeToString(digest, Base64.DEFAULT)});

            if(cursor != null && cursor.moveToFirst())
                while(!cursor.isAfterLast())
                {
                    keyStream = cryptography.mtd
                        (Base64.decode(cursor.getString(0).getBytes(),
                                       Base64.DEFAULT));

                    if(keyStream == null)
                        continue;

                    byte hmac[] = Cryptography.hmac
                        (Arrays.copyOfRange(bytes,
                                            0,
                                            bytes.length -
                                            2 * Cryptography.HASH_KEY_LENGTH),
                         Arrays.copyOfRange(keyStream,
                                            Cryptography.CIPHER_KEY_LENGTH,
                                            keyStream.length));

                    if(Cryptography.memcmp(array, hmac))
                        break;

                    cursor.moveToNext();
                }
        }
        catch(Exception exception)
        {
            keyStream = null;
        }
        finally
        {
            if(cursor != null)
                cursor.close();
        }

        return keyStream;
    }

    public byte[] steamKeyStream(Cryptography cryptography,
                                 byte fileIdentity[])
    {
        if(cryptography == null || fileIdentity == null || m_db == null)
            return null;
```

```java
        Cursor cursor = null;
        byte keyStream[] = null;

        try
        {
            cursor = m_db.rawQuery
                ("SELECT keystream FROM steam_files " +
                 "WHERE file_identity_digest = ?",
                 new String[] {Base64.encodeToString(cryptography.
                                                hmac(fileIdentity),
                                                Base64.DEFAULT)});

            if(cursor != null && cursor.moveToFirst())
                keyStream = cryptography.mtd
                    (Base64.decode(cursor.getString(0).getBytes(),
                                Base64.DEFAULT));
        }
        catch(Exception exception)
        {
            keyStream = null;
        }
        finally
        {
            if(cursor != null)
                cursor.close();
        }

        return keyStream;
    }

    public int participantOidFromSipHash(Cryptography cryptography,
                                         String sipHashId)
    {
        if(cryptography == null || m_db == null)
            return -1;

        Cursor cursor = null;
        int oid = -1;

        try
        {
            cursor = m_db.rawQuery
                ("SELECT oid FROM participants WHERE siphash_id_digest = ?",
                 new String[] {Base64.
                                encodeToString
                                (cryptography.
                                hmac(sipHashId.toUpperCase().trim().
                                    getBytes(StandardCharsets.UTF_8)),
                                Base64.DEFAULT)});

            if(cursor != null && cursor.moveToFirst())
                oid = cursor.getInt(0);
        }
        catch(Exception exception)
        {
            oid = -1;
        }
        finally
        {
            if(cursor != null)
                cursor.close();
        }
```

```java
    return oid;
}

public int participantsWithSessionKeys(int oid)
{
    if(m_db == null)
        return -1;

    Cursor cursor = null;
    int count = 0;

    try
    {
        StringBuilder stringBuilder = new StringBuilder();

        if(oid == -1)
        {
            stringBuilder.append("SELECT COUNT(*) FROM participants ");
            stringBuilder.append("WHERE LENGTH(keystream) >= ");
            stringBuilder.append
                (4 * (Math.ceil(Cryptography.CIPHER_HASH_KEYS_LENGTH +
                                Cryptography.CIPHER_IV_LENGTH) / 3.0));
        }
        else
        {
            stringBuilder.append("SELECT COUNT(*) FROM participants ");
            stringBuilder.append("WHERE LENGTH(keystream) >= ");
            stringBuilder.append
                (4 * (Math.ceil(Cryptography.CIPHER_HASH_KEYS_LENGTH +
                                Cryptography.CIPHER_IV_LENGTH) / 3.0));
            stringBuilder.append(" AND oid = ");
            stringBuilder.append(oid);
        }

        cursor = m_db.rawQuery(stringBuilder.toString(), null);

        if(cursor != null && cursor.moveToFirst())
            count = cursor.getInt(0);
    }
    catch(Exception exception)
    {
        count = -1;
    }
    finally
    {
        if(cursor != null)
            cursor.close();
    }

    return count;
}

public int steamOidFromFileIdentity(Cryptography cryptography,
                                    byte fileIdentity[])
{
    if(cryptography == null || fileIdentity == null || m_db == null)
        return -1;

    Cursor cursor = null;
    int oid = -1;

    try
```

```java
        {
            cursor = m_db.rawQuery
                ("SELECT someoid FROM steam_files WHERE " +
                 "file_identity_digest = ?",
                 new String[] {Base64.encodeToString(cryptography.
                                                 hmac(fileIdentity),
                                                 Base64.DEFAULT)});

            if(cursor != null && cursor.moveToFirst())
                oid = cursor.getInt(0);
        }
        catch(Exception exception)
        {
            oid = -1;
        }
        finally
        {
            if(cursor != null)
                cursor.close();
        }

        return oid;
    }

    public long countOfMessages(Cryptography cryptography, String sipHashId)
    {
        if(cryptography == null || m_db == null)
            return -1L;

        Cursor cursor = null;
        long count = 0L;

        try
        {
            StringBuilder stringBuilder = new StringBuilder();

            stringBuilder.append("SELECT COUNT(*) FROM participants_messages
");
            stringBuilder.append("WHERE siphash_id_digest = ?");
            cursor = m_db.rawQuery
                (stringBuilder.toString(),
                 new String[] {Base64.
                               encodeToString
                               (cryptography.
                               hmac(sipHashId.toUpperCase().trim().
                                   getBytes(StandardCharsets.UTF_8)),
                               Base64.DEFAULT)});

            if(cursor != null && cursor.moveToFirst())
                count = cursor.getLong(0);
        }
        catch(Exception exception)
        {
            count = -1L;
        }
        finally
        {
            if(cursor != null)
                cursor.close();
        }

        return count;
    }
```

```java
public long countOfSteams()
{
    if(m_db == null)
        return -1L;

    Cursor cursor = null;
    long count = 0L;

    try
    {
        cursor = m_db.rawQuery("SELECT COUNT(*) FROM steam_files", null);

        if(cursor != null && cursor.moveToFirst())
            count = cursor.getLong(0);
    }
    catch(Exception exception)
    {
        count = -1L;
    }
    finally
    {
        if(cursor != null)
            cursor.close();
    }

    return count;
}

public static synchronized Database getInstance()
{
    return s_instance; // Should never be null.
}

public static synchronized Database getInstance(Context context)
{
    if(s_instance == null)
        s_instance = new Database(context.getApplicationContext());

    return s_instance;
}

public void cleanDanglingOutboundQueued()
{
    if(m_db == null)
        return;

    Cursor cursor = null;

    m_db.beginTransactionNonExclusive();

    try
    {
        cursor = m_db.rawQuery
            ("DELETE FROM outbound_queue WHERE neighbor_oid " +
             "NOT IN (SELECT oid FROM neighbors)",
             null);
        m_db.setTransactionSuccessful();
    }
    catch(Exception exception)
    {
    }
    finally
```

```java
        {
            if(cursor != null)
                cursor.close();

            m_db.endTransaction();
        }
    }

    public void cleanDanglingParticipants()
    {
        if(m_db == null)
            return;

        Cursor cursor = null;

        m_db.beginTransactionNonExclusive();

        try
        {
            cursor = m_db.rawQuery
                ("DELETE FROM participants WHERE siphash_id_digest " +
                 "NOT IN (SELECT siphash_id_digest FROM siphash_ids)",
                 null);
            m_db.setTransactionSuccessful();
        }
        catch(Exception exception)
         {
         }
        finally
        {
            if(cursor != null)
                cursor.close();

            m_db.endTransaction();
        }
    }

    public void cleanDanglingSteams()
    {
        if(m_db == null)
            return;

        Cursor cursor = null;

        m_db.beginTransactionNonExclusive();

        try
        {
            cursor = m_db.rawQuery
                ("DELETE FROM steam_files WHERE status = 'deleted'", null);
            m_db.setTransactionSuccessful();
        }
        catch(Exception exception)
         {
         }
        finally
        {
            if(cursor != null)
                cursor.close();

            m_db.endTransaction();
        }
    }
```

```java
public void cleanNeighborStatistics(Cryptography cryptography)
{
    ArrayList<NeighborElement> arrayList = readNeighborOids(cryptography);

    if(arrayList == null || arrayList.isEmpty())
        return;

    for(NeighborElement neighborElement : arrayList)
        if(neighborElement != null)
            saveNeighborInformation(cryptography,
                                    "0",                // Bytes Read
                                    "0",                // Bytes Written
                                    "0",                // Queue Size
                                    "",                 // Error
                                    "",                 // IP Address
                                    "0",                // Port
                                    "",                 // Session Cipher
                                    "disconnected",     // Status
                                    "0",                // Uptime
                                    String.valueOf(neighborElement.m_oid));

    arrayList.clear();
}

public void clearTable(String table)
{
    if(m_db == null)
        return;

    m_db.beginTransactionNonExclusive();

    try
    {
        m_db.delete(table, null, null);
        m_db.setTransactionSuccessful();
    }
    catch(Exception exception)
    {
    }
    finally
    {
        m_db.endTransaction();
    }

    if(table.equals("participants_messages"))
        synchronized(m_readMemberChatCursorMutex)
        {
            if(m_readMemberChatCursor != null)
                m_readMemberChatCursor.close();

            m_readMemberChatCursor = null;
            m_readMemberChatSipHashId = "";
        }
}


public void clearSteamRates(Cryptography cryptography)
{
    if(cryptography == null || m_db == null)
        return;

    m_db.beginTransactionNonExclusive();
```

```java
        try
        {
            ContentValues values = new ContentValues();

            values.put
                ("transfer_rate",
                 cryptography.etmBase64String(Miscellaneous.RATE));
            m_db.update("steam_files", values, null, null);
            m_db.setTransactionSuccessful();
        }
        catch(Exception exception)
        {
        }
        finally
        {
            m_db.endTransaction();
        }
    }

    public void deleteParticipantMessage(Cryptography cryptography,
                                         String sipHashId,
                                         int oid)
    {
        if(cryptography == null || m_db == null)
            return;

        m_db.beginTransactionNonExclusive();

        try
        {
            if(m_db.delete("participants_messages",
                           "oid = ? AND siphash_id_digest = ?",
                           new String[] {String.valueOf(oid),
                                         Base64.
                                         encodeToString
                                         (cryptography.
                                          hmac(sipHashId.toUpperCase().trim().
                                               getBytes(StandardCharsets.
                                                        UTF_8)),
                                          Base64.DEFAULT)}) > 0)
                synchronized(m_readMemberChatCursorMutex)
                {
                    if(m_readMemberChatSipHashId.equals(sipHashId))
                    {
                        if(m_readMemberChatCursor != null)
                            m_readMemberChatCursor.close();

                        m_readMemberChatCursor = null;
                    }
                }

            m_db.setTransactionSuccessful();
        }
        catch(Exception exception)
        {
        }
        finally
        {
            m_db.endTransaction();
        }
    }

    public void deleteParticipantMessages(Cryptography cryptography,
```

```java
                                        String sipHashId)
{
    if(cryptography == null || m_db == null)
        return;

    m_db.beginTransactionNonExclusive();

    try
    {
        if(m_db.delete("participants_messages", "siphash_id_digest = ?",
                       new String[] {Base64.
                                     encodeToString
                                     (cryptography.
                                      hmac(sipHashId.toUpperCase().trim().
                                           getBytes(StandardCharsets.
                                                    UTF_8)),
                                      Base64.DEFAULT)}) > 0)
            synchronized(m_readMemberChatCursorMutex)
            {
                if(m_readMemberChatSipHashId.equals(sipHashId))
                {
                    if(m_readMemberChatCursor != null)
                        m_readMemberChatCursor.close();

                    m_readMemberChatCursor = null;
                }
            }

        m_db.setTransactionSuccessful();
    }
    catch(Exception exception)
    {
    }
    finally
    {
        m_db.endTransaction();
    }
}

public void enqueueOutboundMessage(Cryptography cryptography,
                                   String message,
                                   byte messageIdentity[],
                                   int oid)
{
    if(cryptography == null ||
       m_db == null ||
       message == null ||
       message.trim().isEmpty())
        return;

    m_db.beginTransactionNonExclusive();

    try
    {
        ContentValues values = new ContentValues();

        values.put
            ("message",
             Base64.encodeToString(cryptography.etm(message.getBytes()),
                                   Base64.DEFAULT));

        if(messageIdentity == null)
            values.put
```

```java
                    ("message_identity_digest",
                     Base64.
                     encodeToString(Cryptography.
                                   randomBytes(Cryptography.HASH_KEY_LENGTH),
                                   Base64.DEFAULT));
            else
                values.put
                    ("message_identity_digest",
                     Base64.encodeToString(cryptography.hmac(messageIdentity),
                                   Base64.DEFAULT));

            values.put("neighbor_oid", oid);
            m_db.insertOrThrow("outbound_queue", null, values);
            m_db.setTransactionSuccessful();
        }
        catch(Exception exception)
        {
        }
        finally
        {
            m_db.endTransaction();
        }
    }

    public void neighborControlStatus(Cryptography cryptography,
                                      String controlStatus,
                                      String oid)
    {
        if(cryptography == null || m_db == null)
            return;

        m_db.beginTransactionNonExclusive();

        try
        {
            ContentValues values = new ContentValues();

            values.put
                ("status_control",
                 Base64.encodeToString(cryptography.
                                   etm(controlStatus.trim().getBytes()),
                                   Base64.DEFAULT));
            m_db.update("neighbors", values, "oid = ?", new String[] {oid});
            m_db.setTransactionSuccessful();
        }
        catch(Exception exception)
        {
        }
        finally
        {
            m_db.endTransaction();
        }
    }

    public void neighborRecordCertificate(Cryptography cryptography,
                                          String oid,
                                          byte certificate[])
    {
        if(cryptography == null || m_db == null)
            return;

        m_db.beginTransactionNonExclusive();
```

```java
        try
        {
            ContentValues values = new ContentValues();

            if(certificate == null)
                values.put
                    ("remote_certificate",
                     Base64.encodeToString(cryptography.etm("".getBytes()),
                                    Base64.DEFAULT));
            else
                values.put
                    ("remote_certificate",
                     Base64.encodeToString(cryptography.etm(certificate),
                                    Base64.DEFAULT));

            m_db.update("neighbors", values, "oid = ?", new String[] {oid});
            m_db.setTransactionSuccessful();
        }
        catch(Exception exception)
        {
        }
        finally
        {
            m_db.endTransaction();
        }
    }

    @Override
    public void onConfigure(SQLiteDatabase db)
    {
        if(db == null)
            return;

        try
        {
            db.enableWriteAheadLogging();
        }
        catch(Exception exception)
        {
        }

        try
        {
            db.execSQL("VACUUM");
        }
        catch(Exception exception)
        {
        }

        try
        {
            db.execSQL("PRAGMA secure_delete = True", null);
        }
        catch(Exception exception)
        {
        }

        try
        {
            db.setForeignKeyConstraintsEnabled(true);
        }
        catch(Exception exception)
        {
```

```java
        }
    }

    @Override
    public void onCreate(SQLiteDatabase db)
    {
        if(db == null)
            return;

        String str = "";

        /*
        ** Order is critical.
        */

        /*
        ** Create the siphash_ids table.
        */

        str = "CREATE TABLE IF NOT EXISTS siphash_ids (" +
            "name TEXT NOT NULL, " +
            "siphash_id TEXT NOT NULL, " +
            "siphash_id_digest TEXT NOT NULL PRIMARY KEY, " +
            "stream TEXT NOT NULL)";

        try
        {
            db.execSQL(str);
        }
        catch(Exception exception)
        {
        }

        /*
        ** Create the congestion_control table.
        */

        str = "CREATE TABLE IF NOT EXISTS congestion_control (" +
            "digest TEXT NOT NULL PRIMARY KEY, " +
            "timestamp DATETIME DEFAULT CURRENT_TIMESTAMP)";

        try
        {
            db.execSQL(str);
        }
        catch(Exception exception)
        {
        }

        /*
        ** Create the fire table.
        */

        str = "CREATE TABLE IF NOT EXISTS fire (" +
            "name TEXT NOT NULL, " +
            "name_digest TEXT NOT NULL, " +
            "stream TEXT NOT NULL, " +
            "stream_digest TEXT NOT NULL PRIMARY KEY)";

        try
        {
            db.execSQL(str);
        }
```

```
        catch(Exception exception)
        {
        }

        /*
        ** Create the log table.
        */

        str = "CREATE TABLE IF NOT EXISTS log (" +
            "event TEXT NOT NULL, " +
            "timestamp DATETIME DEFAULT CURRENT_TIMESTAMP)";

        try
        {
            db.execSQL(str);
        }
        catch(Exception exception)
        {
        }

        /*
        ** Create the neighbors table.
        */

        str = "CREATE TABLE IF NOT EXISTS neighbors (" +
            "bytes_read TEXT NOT NULL, " +
            "bytes_written TEXT NOT NULL, " +
            "echo_queue_size TEXT NOT NULL, " +
            "ip_version TEXT NOT NULL, " +
            "last_error TEXT NOT NULL, " +
            "local_ip_address TEXT NOT NULL, " +
            "local_ip_address_digest TEXT NOT NULL, " +
            "local_port TEXT NOT NULL, " +
            "local_port_digest TEXT NOT NULL, " +
            "non_tls TEXT NOT NULL, " +
            "passthrough TEXT NOT NULL, " +
            "proxy_ip_address TEXT NOT NULL, " +
            "proxy_port TEXT NOT NULL, " +
            "proxy_type TEXT NOT NULL, " +
            "remote_certificate TEXT NOT NULL, " +
            "remote_ip_address TEXT NOT NULL, " +
            "remote_ip_address_digest TEXT NOT NULL, " +
            "remote_port TEXT NOT NULL, " +
            "remote_port_digest TEXT NOT NULL, " +
            "remote_scope_id TEXT NOT NULL, " +
            "session_cipher TEXT NOT NULL, " +
            "status TEXT NOT NULL, " +
            "status_control TEXT NOT NULL, " +
            "transport TEXT NOT NULL, " +
            "transport_digest TEXT NOT NULL, " +
            "uptime TEXT NOT NULL, " +
            "user_defined_digest TEXT NOT NULL, " +
            "PRIMARY KEY (remote_ip_address_digest, " +
            "remote_port_digest, " +
            "transport_digest))";

        try
        {
            db.execSQL(str);
        }
        catch(Exception exception)
        {
        }
```

```java
        /*
        ** Create the outbound_queue table.
        ** A foreign-key constraint on the oid of the neighbors
        ** table cannot be assigned.
        */

        str = "CREATE TABLE IF NOT EXISTS outbound_queue (" +
            "message TEXT NOT NULL, " +
            "message_identity_digest TEXT NOT NULL, " +
            "neighbor_oid INTEGER NOT NULL, " +
            "PRIMARY KEY (message, neighbor_oid))";

        try
        {
            db.execSQL(str);
        }
        catch(Exception exception)
        {
        }


        /*
        ** Create the participants table.
        */

        str = "CREATE TABLE IF NOT EXISTS participants (" +
            "encryption_public_key TEXT NOT NULL, " +
            "encryption_public_key_algorithm TEXT NOT NULL, " +
            "encryption_public_key_digest TEXT NOT NULL, " +
            "encryption_public_key_signed TEXT NOT NULL, " +
            "identity TEXT NOT NULL, " + // Not recorded.
            "keystream TEXT NOT NULL, " + /*
                                ** Authentication and encryption
                                ** keys.
                                */
            "last_status_timestamp TEXT NOT NULL, " +
            "options TEXT NOT NULL, " +
            "signature_public_key TEXT NOT NULL, " +
            "signature_public_key_digest TEXT NOT NULL, " +
            "signature_public_key_signed TEXT NOT NULL, " +
            "siphash_id TEXT NOT NULL, " +
            "siphash_id_digest TEXT NOT NULL, " +
            "special_value_a TEXT, " + /*
                                ** Telephone number, for example.
                                */
            "special_value_b TEXT, " +
            "special_value_c TEXT, " +
            "special_value_d TEXT, " +
            "special_value_e TEXT, " +
            "FOREIGN KEY (siphash_id_digest) REFERENCES " +
            "siphash_ids (siphash_id_digest) ON DELETE CASCADE, " +
            "PRIMARY KEY (siphash_id_digest))";

        try
        {
            db.execSQL(str);
        }
        catch(Exception exception)
        {
        }

        /*
        ** Create the participants_keys table. Note that the
```

```java
    ** keystream_digest should be unique for all participants.
    */

    str = "CREATE TABLE IF NOT EXISTS participants_keys (" +
        "keystream TEXT NOT NULL, " + /*
                                      ** Authentication and encryption
                                      ** keys.
                                      */
        "keystream_digest TEXT NOT NULL PRIMARY KEY, " +
        "siphash_id_digest TEXT NOT NULL, " +
        "timestamp DATETIME DEFAULT CURRENT_TIMESTAMP, " +
        "FOREIGN KEY (siphash_id_digest) REFERENCES " +
        "siphash_ids (siphash_id_digest) ON DELETE CASCADE)";

    try
    {
        db.execSQL(str);
    }
    catch(Exception exception)
    {
    }

    /*
    ** Create the participants_messages table.
    */

    str = "CREATE TABLE IF NOT EXISTS participants_messages (" +
        "attachment BLOB NOT NULL, " +
        "from_smokestack TEXT NOT NULL, " +
        "message TEXT NOT NULL, " +
        "message_digest TEXT NOT NULL, " +
        "message_identity_digest TEXT NOT NULL, " + // Random.
        "message_read TEXT NOT NULL, " +
        "message_sent TEXT NOT NULL, " +
        "siphash_id_digest TEXT NOT NULL, " +
        "timestamp INTEGER NOT NULL, " +
        "FOREIGN KEY (siphash_id_digest) REFERENCES " +
        "siphash_ids (siphash_id_digest) ON DELETE CASCADE, " +
        "PRIMARY KEY (message_digest, siphash_id_digest))";

    try
    {
        db.execSQL(str);
    }
    catch(Exception exception)
    {
    }

    /*
    ** Create the settings table.
    */

    str = "CREATE TABLE IF NOT EXISTS settings (" +
        "name TEXT NOT NULL, " +
        "name_digest TEXT NOT NULL PRIMARY KEY, " +
        "value TEXT NOT NULL)";

    try
    {
        db.execSQL(str);
    }
    catch(Exception exception)
    {
```

```java
        }

        /*
        ** Create the steam_files table.
        */

    str = "CREATE TABLE IF NOT EXISTS steam_files (" +
            "absolute_filename TEXT NOT NULL, " +
            "destination TEXT NOT NULL, " +
            "display_filename TEXT NOT NULL, " +
            "ephemeral_private_key TEXT NOT NULL, " +
            "ephemeral_public_key TEXT NOT NULL, " +
            "file_digest TEXT NOT NULL, " +
            "file_identity TEXT NOT NULL, " +
            "file_identity_digest TEXT NOT NULL, " +
            "file_size TEXT NOT NULL, " +
            "is_download TEXT NOT NULL, " +
            "keystream TEXT NOT NULL, " + /*
                                        ** Authentication and encryption
                                        ** keys.
                                        */
            "read_interval TEXT NOT NULL, " +
            "read_offset TEXT NOT NULL, " +
            "someoid INTEGER NOT NULL PRIMARY KEY AUTOINCREMENT, " +
            "status TEXT NOT NULL, " +
            "transfer_rate TEXT NOT NULL)";

    try
    {
        db.execSQL(str);
    }
    catch(Exception exception)
    {
    }
    }

    @Override
    public void onDowngrade(SQLiteDatabase db, int oldVersion, int newVersion)
    {
        onUpgrade(db, oldVersion, newVersion);
    }

    @Override
    public void onUpgrade(SQLiteDatabase db, int oldVersion, int newVersion)
    {
        onCreate(db);
    }

    public void pauseAllSteams()
    {
        if(m_db == null)
            return;

        m_db.beginTransactionNonExclusive();

        try
        {
            ContentValues values = new ContentValues();

            values.put("status", "paused");
            m_db.update
                ("steam_files",
                 values,
```

```java
                    "is_download <> ?",
                    new String[] {String.valueOf(SteamElement.DOWNLOAD)});
            m_db.setTransactionSuccessful();
        }
        catch(Exception exception)
        {
        }
        finally
        {
            m_db.endTransaction();
        }
    }

    public void purgeCongestion(int lifetime)
    {
        if(m_db == null)
            return;

        m_db.beginTransactionNonExclusive();

        try
        {
            /*
            ** The bound string value must be cast to an integer.
            */

            m_db.delete
                ("congestion_control",
                 "ABS(STRFTIME('%s', 'now') - STRFTIME('%s', timestamp)) > " +
                 "CAST(? AS INTEGER)",
                 new String[] {String.valueOf(lifetime)});
            m_db.setTransactionSuccessful();
        }
        catch(Exception exception)
        {
        }
        finally
        {
            m_db.endTransaction();
        }
    }

    public void purgeNeighborQueue(final String oid)
    {
        if(m_db == null)
            return;

        Executors.newSingleThreadScheduledExecutor().schedule(new Runnable()
        {
            @Override
            public void run()
            {
                try
                {
                    m_db.beginTransactionNonExclusive();

                    try
                    {
                        m_db.delete("outbound_queue",
                                    "neighbor_oid = ?",
                                    new String[] {oid});
                        m_db.setTransactionSuccessful();
                    }
```

```java
                    catch(Exception exception)
                    {
                    }
                    finally
                    {
                        m_db.endTransaction();
                    }
                }
                catch(Exception exception)
                {
                }
            }
        }, 0L, TimeUnit.MILLISECONDS);
    }

    public void purgeParticipantsKeyStreams(int lifetime)
    {
        if(m_db == null)
            return;

        m_db.beginTransactionNonExclusive();

        try
        {
            /*
            ** The bound string value must be cast to an integer.
            */

            m_db.delete
                ("participants_keys",
                 "ABS(STRFTIME('%s', 'now') - STRFTIME('%s', timestamp)) > " +
                 "CAST(? AS INTEGER)",
                 new String[] {String.valueOf(lifetime)});
            m_db.setTransactionSuccessful();
        }
        catch(Exception exception)
        {
        }
        finally
        {
            m_db.endTransaction();
        }
    }

    public void reset()
    {
        if(m_db == null)
            return;

        m_db.beginTransactionNonExclusive();

        try
        {
            String tables[] = new String[]
                {"congestion_control",
                 "fire",
                 "log",
                 "neighbors",
                 "outbound_queue",
                 "participants",
                 "participants_keys",
                 "participants_messages",
                 "settings",
```

```java
                "siphash_ids",
                "steam_files"};

            for(String string : tables)
                try
                {
                    m_db.delete(string, null, null);
                }
                catch(Exception exception)
                {
                }

            m_db.setTransactionSuccessful();
        }
        catch(Exception exception)
        {
        }
        finally
        {
            m_db.endTransaction();
        }

        synchronized(m_readMemberChatCursorMutex)
        {
            if(m_readMemberChatCursor != null)
                m_readMemberChatCursor.close();

            m_readMemberChatCursor = null;
            m_readMemberChatSipHashId = "";
        }
    }

    public void resetAndDrop()
    {
        reset();

        if(m_db == null)
            return;

        String strings[] = new String[]
            {"DROP TABLE IF EXISTS congestion_control",
             "DROP TABLE IF EXISTS fire",
             "DROP TABLE IF EXISTS log",
             "DROP TABLE IF EXISTS neighbors",
             "DROP TABLE IF EXISTS outbound_queue",
             "DROP TABLE IF EXISTS participants",
             "DROP TABLE IF EXISTS participants_keys",
             "DROP TABLE IF EXISTS participants_messages",
             "DROP TABLE IF EXISTS settings",
             "DROP TABLE IF EXISTS siphash_ids",
             "DROP TABLE IF EXISTS steam_files"};

        for(String string : strings)
            try
            {
                m_db.execSQL(string);
            }
            catch(Exception exception)
            {
            }

        onCreate(m_db);
    }
```

```java
public void rewindAllSteams()
{
    if(m_db == null)
        return;

    /*
    ** Ignore received Steams.
    */

    m_db.beginTransactionNonExclusive();

    try
    {
        ContentValues values = new ContentValues();

        values.put("status", "rewind");
        m_db.update
            ("steam_files",
             values,
             "is_download <> ?",
             new String[] {String.valueOf(SteamElement.DOWNLOAD)});
        m_db.setTransactionSuccessful();
    }
    catch(Exception exception)
    {
    }
    finally
    {
        m_db.endTransaction();
    }
}

public void rewindAndResumeAllSteams()
{
    if(m_db == null)
        return;

    /*
    ** Ignore received Steams.
    */

    m_db.beginTransactionNonExclusive();

    try
    {
        ContentValues values = new ContentValues();

        values.put("status", "rewind & resume");
        m_db.update
            ("steam_files",
             values,
             "is_download <> ?",
             new String[] {String.valueOf(SteamElement.DOWNLOAD)});
        m_db.setTransactionSuccessful();
    }
    catch(Exception exception)
    {
    }
    finally
    {
        m_db.endTransaction();
    }
```

```java
    }

    public void saveFireChannel(Cryptography cryptography,
                                String name,
                                byte encryptionKey[],
                                byte keyStream[])
    {
        if(cryptography == null ||
           encryptionKey == null ||
           keyStream == null ||
           m_db == null ||
           name == null ||
           name.isEmpty())
            return;

        m_db.beginTransactionNonExclusive();

        try
        {
            ContentValues values = new ContentValues();
            byte bytes[] = Miscellaneous.joinByteArrays
                (encryptionKey, keyStream);

            values.put
                ("name",
                 Base64.encodeToString(cryptography.
                                       etm(name.getBytes(StandardCharsets.
                                                         ISO_8859_1)),
                                       Base64.DEFAULT));
            values.put
                ("name_digest",
                 Base64.encodeToString(cryptography.
                                       hmac(name.getBytes(StandardCharsets.
                                                          ISO_8859_1)),
                                       Base64.DEFAULT));
            values.put
                ("stream",
                 Base64.encodeToString(cryptography.etm(bytes),
                                       Base64.DEFAULT));
            values.put
                ("stream_digest",
                 Base64.encodeToString(cryptography.hmac(bytes),
                                       Base64.DEFAULT));
            m_db.insertOrThrow("fire", null, values);
            m_db.setTransactionSuccessful();
        }
        catch(Exception exception)
        {
        }
        finally
        {
            m_db.endTransaction();
        }
    }

    public void saveNeighborInformation(Cryptography cryptography,
                                        String bytesRead,
                                        String bytesWritten,
                                        String echoQueueSize,
                                        String error,
                                        String ipAddress,
                                        String ipPort,
                                        String sessionCipher,
```

```java
                                String status,
                                String uptime,
                                String oid)
    {
        if(cryptography == null || m_db == null)
            return;

        m_db.beginTransactionNonExclusive();

        try
        {
            ContentValues values = new ContentValues();

            if(!status.equals("connected"))
            {
                bytesRead = "";
                bytesWritten = "";
                echoQueueSize = "0";
                error = error.trim(); // Do not clear the error.
                ipAddress = "";
                ipPort = "";
                sessionCipher = "";
                uptime = "";
            }

            values.put
                ("bytes_read",
                 Base64.encodeToString(cryptography.etm(bytesRead.getBytes()),
                                 Base64.DEFAULT));
            values.put
                ("bytes_written",
                 Base64.encodeToString(cryptography.etm(bytesWritten.
                                                 getBytes()),
                                 Base64.DEFAULT));
            values.put
                ("echo_queue_size",
                 Base64.encodeToString(cryptography.etm(echoQueueSize.
                                                 getBytes()),
                                 Base64.DEFAULT));
            values.put
                ("last_error",
                 Base64.encodeToString(cryptography.etm(error.getBytes()),
                                 Base64.DEFAULT));
            values.put
                ("local_ip_address",
                 Base64.encodeToString(cryptography.
                                 etm(ipAddress.trim().getBytes()),
                                 Base64.DEFAULT));
            values.put
                ("local_ip_address_digest",
                 Base64.encodeToString(cryptography.
                                 hmac(ipAddress.trim().getBytes()),
                                 Base64.DEFAULT));
            values.put
                ("local_port",
                 Base64.encodeToString(cryptography.
                                 etm(ipPort.trim().getBytes()),
                                 Base64.DEFAULT));
            values.put
                ("local_port_digest",
                 Base64.encodeToString(cryptography.
                                 hmac(ipPort.trim().getBytes()),
                                 Base64.DEFAULT));
```

```java
                values.put
                    ("session_cipher",
                     Base64.encodeToString(cryptography.etm(sessionCipher.
                                                  getBytes()),
                                  Base64.DEFAULT));
                values.put
                    ("status",
                     Base64.encodeToString(cryptography.
                                      etm(status.trim().getBytes()),
                                      Base64.DEFAULT));
                values.put
                    ("uptime",
                     Base64.encodeToString(cryptography.
                                      etm(uptime.trim().getBytes()),
                                      Base64.DEFAULT));
                m_db.update("neighbors", values, "oid = ?", new String[] {oid});
                m_db.setTransactionSuccessful();
            }
        catch(Exception exception)
            {
            }
        finally
            {
                m_db.endTransaction();
            }
    }

    public void updateParticipantLastTimestamp(Cryptography cryptography,
                                               String sipHashId)
    {
        if(cryptography == null || m_db == null)
            return;

        m_db.beginTransactionNonExclusive();

        try
        {
            ContentValues values = new ContentValues();

            values.put
                ("last_status_timestamp",
                 Base64.
                 encodeToString(cryptography.
                              etm(Miscellaneous.
                                  longToByteArray(System.
                                               currentTimeMillis())),
                              Base64.DEFAULT));
            m_db.update("participants", values, "siphash_id_digest = ?",
                    new String[] {Base64.
                                  encodeToString
                                  (cryptography.
                                   hmac(sipHashId.toUpperCase().trim().
                                       getBytes(StandardCharsets.UTF_8)),
                                   Base64.DEFAULT)});
            m_db.setTransactionSuccessful();
        }
        catch(Exception exception)
         {
         }
        finally
            {
                m_db.endTransaction();
            }
```

```java
    }

    public void updateParticipantLastTimestamp(Cryptography cryptography,
                                               byte digest[])
    {
        if(cryptography == null || digest == null || m_db == null)
            return;

        m_db.beginTransactionNonExclusive();

        try
        {
            ContentValues values = new ContentValues();

            values.put
                ("last_status_timestamp",
                 Base64.
                 encodeToString(cryptography.
                               etm(Miscellaneous.
                                   longToByteArray(System.
                                             currentTimeMillis())),
                               Base64.DEFAULT));
            m_db.update("participants",
                        values,
                        "encryption_public_key_digest = ?",
                        new String[] {Base64.encodeToString(digest,
                                              Base64.DEFAULT)});
            m_db.setTransactionSuccessful();
        }
        catch(Exception exception)
        {
        }
        finally
        {
            m_db.endTransaction();
        }
    }

    public void writeCallKeys(Cryptography cryptography,
                              String sipHashId,
                              byte keyStream[])
    {
        if(cryptography == null || keyStream == null || m_db == null)
            return;

        m_db.beginTransactionNonExclusive();

        try
        {
            ContentValues values = new ContentValues();

            values.put
                ("keystream",
                 Base64.encodeToString(cryptography.etm(keyStream),
                                 Base64.DEFAULT));
            values.put
                ("last_status_timestamp",
                 Base64.
                 encodeToString(cryptography.
                               etm(Miscellaneous.
                                   longToByteArray(System.
                                             currentTimeMillis())),
                               Base64.DEFAULT));
```

```java
                m_db.update("participants", values, "siphash_id_digest = ?",
                        new String[] {Base64.
                                      encodeToString
                                      (cryptography.
                                       hmac(sipHashId.toUpperCase().trim().
                                            getBytes(StandardCharsets.UTF_8)),
                                       Base64.DEFAULT)});
            values.clear();
            values.put("keystream",
                    Base64.encodeToString(cryptography.etm(keyStream),
                                          Base64.DEFAULT));
            values.put("keystream_digest",
                    Base64.encodeToString(cryptography.hmac(keyStream),
                                          Base64.DEFAULT));
            values.put
                ("siphash_id_digest",
                 Base64.encodeToString(cryptography.
                                       hmac(sipHashId.toUpperCase().trim().
                                            getBytes(StandardCharsets.UTF_8)),
                                       Base64.DEFAULT));
            m_db.insertOrThrow("participants_keys", null, values);
            m_db.setTransactionSuccessful();
        }
        catch(Exception exception)
        {
        }
        finally
        {
            m_db.endTransaction();
        }
    }

    public void writeLog(String event)
    {
        if(m_db == null)
            return;

        m_db.beginTransactionNonExclusive();

        try
        {
            ContentValues values = new ContentValues();

            values.put("event", event.trim());
            m_db.insert("log", null, values);
            m_db.setTransactionSuccessful();
        }
        catch(Exception exception)
        {
        }
        finally
        {
            m_db.endTransaction();
        }
    }

    public void writeParticipantOptions(Cryptography cryptography,
                                        String options,
                                        String sipHashId)
    {
        if(cryptography == null || m_db == null)
            return;

```

```java
        m_db.beginTransactionNonExclusive();

        try
        {
            ContentValues values = new ContentValues();

            values.put
                ("options",
                 Base64.encodeToString(cryptography.etm(options.getBytes()),
                                       Base64.DEFAULT));
            m_db.update("participants",
                        values,
                        "siphash_id_digest = ?",
                        new String[] {Base64.
                                      encodeToString
                                      (cryptography.
                                       hmac(sipHashId.toUpperCase().trim().
                                            getBytes(StandardCharsets.UTF_8)),
                                       Base64.DEFAULT)});
            m_db.setTransactionSuccessful();
        }
        catch(Exception exception)
         {
        }
        finally
        {
            m_db.endTransaction();
        }
    }

    public void writeSetting(Cryptography cryptography,
                             String name,
                             String value)
    {
        if(m_db == null)
            return;

        m_db.beginTransactionNonExclusive();

        try
        {
            String a = name.trim();
            String b = name.trim();
            String c = value; // Do not trim.

            if(cryptography != null)
            {
                byte bytes[] = null;

                bytes = cryptography.etm(a.getBytes());

                if(bytes != null)
                    a = Base64.encodeToString(bytes, Base64.DEFAULT);
                else
                    a = "";

                bytes = cryptography.hmac(b.getBytes());

                if(bytes != null)
                    b = Base64.encodeToString(bytes, Base64.DEFAULT);
                else
                    b = "";
```

```java
            bytes = cryptography.etm(c.getBytes());

            if(bytes != null)
                c = Base64.encodeToString(bytes, Base64.DEFAULT);
            else
                c = "";

            if(a.isEmpty() || b.isEmpty() || c.isEmpty())
                throw new Exception();
        }

        ContentValues values = new ContentValues();

        values.put("name", a);
        values.put("name_digest", b);
        values.put("value", c);
        m_db.replace("settings", null, values);
        m_db.setTransactionSuccessful();
    }
    catch(Exception exception)
    {
    }
    finally
    {
        m_db.endTransaction();
    }
}

public void writeSteam(final Cryptography cryptography,
                       final SteamElement steamElement)
{
    /*
    ** Record received and transmitted Steams.
    */

    if(cryptography == null ||
       m_db == null ||
       steamElement == null ||
       steamElement.m_displayFileName.trim().isEmpty() ||
       steamElement.m_fileName.trim().isEmpty())
        return;

    Executors.newSingleThreadScheduledExecutor().schedule(new Runnable()
    {
        @Override
        public void run()
        {
            try
            {
                m_db.beginTransactionNonExclusive();

                try
                {
                    ContentValues values = new ContentValues();

                    values.put
                        ("absolute_filename",
                         cryptography.
                         etmBase64String(steamElement.m_fileName));
                    values.put
                        ("destination",
                         cryptography.
                         etmBase64String(steamElement.m_destination.
```

```java
                        getBytes(StandardCharsets.UTF_8)));
        values.put
            ("display_filename",
             cryptography.
             etmBase64String(steamElement.m_displayFileName.
                        getBytes(StandardCharsets.UTF_8)));
        values.put
            ("ephemeral_private_key",
             cryptography.
             etmBase64String(steamElement.
                        m_ephemeralPrivateKey));
        values.put
            ("ephemeral_public_key",
             cryptography.
             etmBase64String(steamElement.
                        m_ephemeralPublicKey));

        if(steamElement.m_fileDigest == null)
        {
            String fileName = steamElement.m_fileName;

            if(fileName.lastIndexOf('.') > 0)
                fileName = fileName.substring
                    (0, fileName.lastIndexOf('.'));

            values.put
                ("file_digest",
                 cryptography.
                 etmBase64String(Cryptography.
                        sha256FileDigest(fileName)));
        }
        else
            values.put
                ("file_digest",
                 cryptography.
                 etmBase64String(steamElement.m_fileDigest));

        if(steamElement.m_fileIdentity == null)
        {
            byte bytes[] = Cryptography.randomBytes
                (Cryptography.STEAM_FILE_IDENTITY_LENGTH);

            values.put
                ("file_identity",
                 cryptography.etmBase64String(bytes));
            values.put
                ("file_identity_digest",
                 Base64.encodeToString(cryptography.hmac(bytes),
                        Base64.DEFAULT));
        }
        else
        {
            values.put
                ("file_identity",
                 cryptography.
                 etmBase64String(steamElement.m_fileIdentity));
            values.put
                ("file_identity_digest",
                 Base64.
                 encodeToString(cryptography.
                        hmac(steamElement.
                            m_fileIdentity),
                        Base64.DEFAULT));
```

```java
                    }

                    values.put
                        ("file_size",
                         cryptography.
                         etmBase64String(steamElement.m_fileSize));
                    values.put
                        ("is_download",
                         String.valueOf(steamElement.m_direction));
                    values.put
                        ("keystream",
                         cryptography.
                         etmBase64String(steamElement.m_keyStream));
                    values.put
                        ("read_interval",
                         cryptography.
                         etmBase64String(steamElement.m_readInterval));
                    values.put
                        ("read_offset",
                         cryptography.
                         etmBase64String(steamElement.m_readOffset));
                    values.put("status", steamElement.m_status);

                    if(steamElement.m_transferRate.isEmpty())
                        values.put
                            ("transfer_rate",
                             cryptography.
                             etmBase64String(Miscellaneous.RATE));
                    else
                        values.put
                            ("transfer_rate",
                             cryptography.
                             etmBase64String(steamElement.m_transferRate));

                    m_db.insertOrThrow("steam_files", null, values);
                    m_db.setTransactionSuccessful();
                    Miscellaneous.sendBroadcast
                        ("org.purple.smoke.steam_added");
                }
                catch(Exception exception)
                {
                }
                finally
                {
                    m_db.endTransaction();
                }
            }
        catch(Exception exception)
        {
        }
        }
    }, 0L, TimeUnit.MILLISECONDS);
    }


    public void writeSteamStatus(final Cryptography cryptography,
                                 final String status,
                                 final String transferRate,
                                 final int oid)
    {
        if(cryptography == null || m_db == null)
            return;

        m_db.beginTransactionNonExclusive();
```

```java
        try
        {
            ContentValues values = new ContentValues();

            if(!status.isEmpty())
                values.put("status", status);

            if(transferRate.isEmpty())
                values.put
                    ("transfer_rate",
                     cryptography.etmBase64String(Miscellaneous.RATE));
            else
                values.put
                    ("transfer_rate",
                     cryptography.etmBase64String(transferRate));

            m_db.update("steam_files",
                        values,
                        "oid = ?",
                        new String[] {String.valueOf(oid)});
            m_db.setTransactionSuccessful();
        }
        catch(Exception exception)
        {
        }
        finally
        {
            m_db.endTransaction();
        }
    }

    public void writeSteamStatus(final Cryptography cryptography,
                                 final String status,
                                 final String transferRate,
                                 final int oid,
                                 final long offset)
    {
        if(cryptography == null || m_db == null)
            return;

        m_db.beginTransactionNonExclusive();

        try
        {
            ContentValues values = new ContentValues();

            values.put("read_offset", cryptography.etmBase64String(offset));

            if(!status.isEmpty())
                values.put("status", status);

            if(transferRate.isEmpty())
                values.put
                    ("transfer_rate",
                     cryptography.etmBase64String(Miscellaneous.RATE));
            else
                values.put
                    ("transfer_rate",
                     cryptography.etmBase64String(transferRate));

            m_db.update("steam_files",
                        values,
```

```java
                              "oid = ?",
                              new String[] {String.valueOf(oid)});
            m_db.setTransactionSuccessful();
        }
        catch(Exception exception)
        {
        }
        finally
        {
            m_db.endTransaction();
        }
    }

    public void writeSteamStatus(final Cryptography cryptography,
                                 final int oid,
                                 final int readInterval)
    {
        if(cryptography == null || m_db == null)
            return;

        m_db.beginTransactionNonExclusive();

        try
        {
            ContentValues values = new ContentValues();

            values.put
                ("read_interval", cryptography.etmBase64String(readInterval));
            m_db.update("steam_files",
                        values,
                        "oid = ?",
                        new String[] {String.valueOf(oid)});
            m_db.setTransactionSuccessful();
        }
        catch(Exception exception)
        {
        }
        finally
        {
            m_db.endTransaction();
        }
    }

    public void writeSteamStatus(final String status, final int oid)
    {
        if(m_db == null)
            return;

        m_db.beginTransactionNonExclusive();

        try
        {
            ContentValues values = new ContentValues();

            if(status.isEmpty())
                values.put("status", "deleted");
            else
                values.put("status", status);

            m_db.update("steam_files",
                        values,
                        "oid = ?",
                        new String[] {String.valueOf(oid)});
```

```java
            m_db.setTransactionSuccessful();
            Miscellaneous.sendBroadcast("org.purple.smoke.steam_status");
        }
        catch(Exception exception)
        {
        }
        finally
        {
            m_db.endTransaction();
        }
    }
}
```

/* Fire.java –

https://github.com/textbrowser/smoke/blob/master/Smoke/app/src/main/java/org/p urple/smoke/Fire.java

```java
** Copyright (c) Alexis Megas.
** All rights reserved.
**
** Redistribution and use in source and binary forms, with or without
** modification, are permitted provided that the following conditions
** are met:
** 1. Redistributions of source code must retain the above copyright
**    notice, this list of conditions and the following disclaimer.
** 2. Redistributions in binary form must reproduce the above copyright
**    notice, this list of conditions and the following disclaimer in the
**    documentation and/or other materials provided with the distribution.
** 3. The name of the author may not be used to endorse or promote products
**    derived from Smoke without specific prior written permission.
**
** SMOKE IS PROVIDED BY THE AUTHOR ``AS IS'' AND ANY EXPRESS OR
** IMPLIED WARRANTIES, INCLUDING, BUT NOT LIMITED TO, THE IMPLIED WARRANTIES
** OF MERCHANTABILITY AND FITNESS FOR A PARTICULAR PURPOSE ARE DISCLAIMED.
** IN NO EVENT SHALL THE AUTHOR BE LIABLE FOR ANY DIRECT, INDIRECT,
** INCIDENTAL, SPECIAL, EXEMPLARY, OR CONSEQUENTIAL DAMAGES (INCLUDING, BUT
** NOT LIMITED TO, PROCUREMENT OF SUBSTITUTE GOODS OR SERVICES; LOSS OF USE,
** DATA, OR PROFITS; OR BUSINESS INTERRUPTION) HOWEVER CAUSED AND ON ANY
** THEORY OF LIABILITY, WHETHER IN CONTRACT, STRICT LIABILITY, OR TORT
** (INCLUDING NEGLIGENCE OR OTHERWISE) ARISING IN ANY WAY OUT OF THE USE OF
** SMOKE, EVEN IF ADVISED OF THE POSSIBILITY OF SUCH DAMAGE.
*/

package org.purple.smoke;

import android.content.BroadcastReceiver;
import android.content.Context;
import android.content.DialogInterface;
import android.content.Intent;
import android.content.IntentFilter;
import android.os.Bundle;
import android.support.v4.content.LocalBroadcastManager;
import android.support.v7.app.AppCompatActivity;
import android.text.InputFilter;
import android.text.InputType;
import android.text.Spanned;
import android.util.DisplayMetrics;
import android.view.Menu;
import android.view.MenuItem;
import android.view.View;
import android.view.ViewGroup;
```

```java
import android.view.WindowManager;
import android.widget.AdapterView;
import android.widget.AdapterView.OnItemSelectedListener;
import android.widget.ArrayAdapter;
import android.widget.Button;
import android.widget.CompoundButton;
import android.widget.LinearLayout.LayoutParams;
import android.widget.ProgressBar;
import android.widget.Spinner;
import android.widget.Switch;
import android.widget.TextView;
import java.nio.charset.Charset;
import java.nio.charset.CharsetEncoder;
import java.util.ArrayList;
import java.util.Hashtable;
import java.util.Map;

public class Fire extends AppCompatActivity
{
    private Database m_databaseHelper = null;

    private class FireBroadcastReceiver extends BroadcastReceiver
    {
        public FireBroadcastReceiver()
        {
        }

        @Override
        public void onReceive(Context context, Intent intent)
        {
            if(intent == null || intent.getAction() == null)
                return;

            switch(intent.getAction())
            {
            case "org.purple.smoke.chat_message":
                Miscellaneous.showNotification
                    (Fire.this, intent, findViewById(R.id.main_layout));
                break;
            case "org.purple.smoke.fire_message":
                FireChannel fireChannel = State.getInstance().fireChannel
                    (intent.getStringExtra("org.purple.smoke.channel"));

                if(fireChannel != null)
                {
                    String id = intent.getStringExtra("org.purple.smoke.id");
                    String name = intent.getStringExtra
                        ("org.purple.smoke.name");

                    if(intent.getStringExtra("org.purple.smoke.message_type").
                       equals(Messages.FIRE_CHAT_MESSAGE_TYPE))
                    {
                        String message = intent.getStringExtra
                            ("org.purple.smoke.message");

                        fireChannel.append(id, message, name);
                    }
                    else if(intent.
                            getStringExtra("org.purple.smoke.message_type").
                            equals(Messages.FIRE_STATUS_MESSAGE_TYPE))
                        fireChannel.status(id, name);
                }
```

```java
                    break;
                case "org.purple.smoke.neighbor_aborted":
                case "org.purple.smoke.neighbor_disconnected":
                case "org.purple.smoke.network_connected":
                case "org.purple.smoke.network_disconnected":
                    prepareFireChannelStatus();
                    break;
                case "org.purple.smoke.state_participants_populated":
                    invalidateOptionsMenu();
                    break;
                case "org.purple.smoke.time":
                    Miscellaneous.showNotification
                        (Fire.this, intent, findViewById(R.id.main_layout));
                    break;
                default:
                    break;
            }
        }
    }

    private FireBroadcastReceiver m_receiver = null;
    private boolean m_receiverRegistered = false;
    private final Hashtable<String, Integer> m_fireHash = new Hashtable<> ();
    private final static String s_id = Miscellaneous.byteArrayAsHexString
        (Cryptography.randomBytes(128));
    private final static CharsetEncoder s_latin1Encoder = Charset.
        forName("ISO-8859-1").newEncoder();
    private final static Cryptography s_cryptography =
        Cryptography.getInstance();
    private final static InputFilter s_Latin1InputFilter = new InputFilter()
    {
        public CharSequence filter(CharSequence source,
                                   int start,
                                   int end,
                                   Spanned dest,
                                   int dstart,
                                   int dend)
        {

            for(int i = start; i < end; i++)
                if(!s_latin1Encoder.canEncode(source.charAt(i)))
                    return source.subSequence(start, i);

            return null;
        }
    };

    private void deleteFire(String name, final Integer oid)
    {
        /*
        ** Prepare a response.
        */

        final DialogInterface.OnCancelListener listener =
            new DialogInterface.OnCancelListener()
            {
                public void onCancel(DialogInterface dialog)
                {
                    if(State.getInstance().
                        getString("dialog_accepted").equals("true"))
                        if(m_databaseHelper.
                            deleteEntry(String.valueOf(oid.intValue()), "fire"))
                            populateFires();
```

```java
                        }
                };

        Miscellaneous.showPromptDialog
                (Fire.this,
                 listener,
                 "Are you sure that you wish to " +
                 "delete the Fire channel " + name + "?");
    }

    private void joinFire(String name)
    {
        if(State.getInstance().containsFire(name))
            return;

        FireChannel fireChannel = null;
        ViewGroup viewGroup = (ViewGroup) findViewById(R.id.linear_layout);

        fireChannel = new FireChannel(s_id, name, Fire.this, viewGroup);
        State.getInstance().addFire(fireChannel);

        int count = viewGroup.getChildCount();
        int index = -1;

        for(int i = 0; i < count; i++)
        {
            String other = State.getInstance().nameOfFireFromView
                (viewGroup.getChildAt(i));

            if(name.compareTo(other) < 0 && name.length() > 0)
            {
                index = i;
                break;
            }
        }

        DisplayMetrics displayMetrics = new DisplayMetrics();

        getWindowManager().getDefaultDisplay().getMetrics(displayMetrics);

        int height = (int) (1.0 * displayMetrics.heightPixels);

        viewGroup.addView
            (fireChannel.view(),
             index,
             new LayoutParams(LayoutParams.WRAP_CONTENT, height));
        viewGroup.requestLayout();
    }

    private void populateFires()
    {
        ArrayList<FireElement> arrayList =
            m_databaseHelper.readFires(s_cryptography);
        Spinner spinner = (Spinner) findViewById(R.id.fires);

        m_fireHash.clear();
        spinner.setAdapter(null);

        if(arrayList == null || arrayList.isEmpty())
        {
            ArrayAdapter<String> arrayAdapter = new ArrayAdapter<>
                (Fire.this,
                 android.R.layout.simple_spinner_item,
```

```java
                        new String[] {"(Empty)"});

            spinner.setAdapter(arrayAdapter);
            return;
        }

    ArrayList<String> array = new ArrayList<>();

    for(FireElement fireElement : arrayList)
    {
        if(fireElement == null)
            continue;

        array.add(fireElement.m_name);
        m_fireHash.put(fireElement.m_name, fireElement.m_oid);
    }

    ArrayAdapter<?> arrayAdapter = null;

    if(!array.isEmpty())
        arrayAdapter = new ArrayAdapter<>
            (Fire.this, android.R.layout.simple_spinner_item, array);
    else
        arrayAdapter = new ArrayAdapter<>
            (Fire.this,
             android.R.layout.simple_spinner_item,
             new String[] {"(Empty)"});

    arrayList.clear();
    spinner.setAdapter(arrayAdapter);
}

private void prepareAutoFill()
{
    Spinner spinner = (Spinner) findViewById(R.id.auto_fill);
    String array[] = new String[]
    {
        "Please Select",
        "Spot-On Developer Channel"
    };

    ArrayAdapter<String> arrayAdapter = new ArrayAdapter<>
        (Fire.this, android.R.layout.simple_spinner_item, array);

    spinner.setAdapter(arrayAdapter);
    spinner.setOnItemSelectedListener(new OnItemSelectedListener()
    {
        @Override
        public void onItemSelected(AdapterView<?> parent,
                                   View view,
                                   int position,
                                   long id)
        {
            if(position == 1)
            {
                TextView textView1 = (TextView) findViewById(R.id.channel);
                TextView textView2 = (TextView) findViewById(R.id.digest);
                TextView textView3 = (TextView) findViewById(R.id.salt);

                textView1.setText("Spot-On_Developer_Channel_Key");
                textView2.setText("Spot-On_Developer_Channel_Hash_Key");
                textView3.setText("Spot-On_Developer_Channel_Salt");
            }
```

```java
                    parent.setSelection(0);
                }

                @Override
                public void onNothingSelected(AdapterView<?> parent)
                {
                }
            });
    }

    private void prepareFireChannelStatus()
    {
        Map<String, FireChannel> map = State.getInstance().fireChannels();

        if(map != null)
        {
            boolean connected = Kernel.getInstance().isConnected();

            for(Map.Entry<String, FireChannel> entry : map.entrySet())
                if(entry.getValue() != null)
                    entry.getValue().setConnectedStatus(connected);
        }

        try
        {
            getSupportActionBar().setSubtitle(Smoke.networkStatusString());
        }
        catch(Exception exception)
        {
        }
    }

    private void prepareListeners()
    {
        Button button1 = null;

        button1 = (Button) findViewById(R.id.add_channel);
        button1.setOnClickListener(new View.OnClickListener()
        {
            public void onClick(View view)
            {
                if(Fire.this.isFinishing())
                    return;

                TextView textView1 = (TextView) findViewById(R.id.channel);
                TextView textView2 = (TextView) findViewById(R.id.digest);
                TextView textView3 = (TextView) findViewById(R.id.salt);

                if(textView1.getText().toString().trim().isEmpty())
                {
                    Miscellaneous.showErrorDialog
                        (Fire.this, "Please complete the Channel field.");
                    textView1.requestFocus();
                }
                else if(textView2.getText().toString().trim().isEmpty())
                {
                    Miscellaneous.showErrorDialog
                        (Fire.this, "Please complete the Digest Key field.");
                    textView2.requestFocus();
                }
                else if(textView3.getText().toString().trim().isEmpty())
                {
```

```java
            Miscellaneous.showErrorDialog
                (Fire.this, "Please complete the Salt field.");
            textView3.requestFocus();
        }
        else
        {
            textView1 = (TextView) findViewById(R.id.channel);

            final String channel = textView1.getText().toString().
                trim();

            textView1 = (TextView) findViewById(R.id.salt);

            final String salt = textView1.getText().toString().trim();

            /*
            ** Display a progress bar.
            */

            final ProgressBar bar = (ProgressBar) findViewById
                (R.id.progress_bar);

            bar.setIndeterminate(true);
            bar.setVisibility(ProgressBar.VISIBLE);
            getWindow().setFlags
                (WindowManager.LayoutParams.FLAG_NOT_TOUCHABLE,
                 WindowManager.LayoutParams.FLAG_NOT_TOUCHABLE);
            Miscellaneous.enableChildren
                (findViewById(R.id.linear_layout), false);

            class SingleShot implements Runnable
            {
                private byte m_encryptionKey[] = null;
                private byte m_keyStream[] = null;

                SingleShot()
                {
                }

                @Override
                public void run()
                {
                    try
                    {
                        final TextView textView1 =
                            (TextView) findViewById(R.id.digest);

                        m_encryptionKey = s_cryptography.
                            generateFireEncryptionKey(channel, salt);
                        m_keyStream = s_cryptography.
                            generateFireDigestKeyStream
                            (textView1.getText().toString().trim());

                        Fire.this.runOnUiThread(new Runnable()
                        {
                            @Override
                            public void run()
                            {
                                bar.setVisibility
                                    (ProgressBar.INVISIBLE);
                                getWindow().clearFlags
                                    (WindowManager.LayoutParams.
                                     FLAG_NOT_TOUCHABLE);
```

```java
                                Miscellaneous.enableChildren
                                    (findViewById(R.id.linear_layout),
                                     true);

                                if(m_encryptionKey != null &&
                                   m_keyStream != null)
                                {
                                    m_databaseHelper.saveFireChannel
                                        (s_cryptography,
                                         channel,
                                         m_encryptionKey,
                                         m_keyStream);
                                    populateFires();
                                }
                            }
                        });
                    }
                    catch(Exception exception)
                    {
                    }
                }
            }

            Thread thread = new Thread(new SingleShot());

            thread.start();
        }
    }
});

button1 = (Button) findViewById(R.id.delete);
 button1.setOnClickListener(new View.OnClickListener()
{
    public void onClick(View view)
    {
        if(Fire.this.isFinishing())
            return;

        Spinner spinner = (Spinner) findViewById(R.id.fires);

        if(spinner.getAdapter() != null &&
           spinner.getAdapter().getCount() > 0)
            deleteFire
                (spinner.getSelectedItem().toString(),
                 m_fireHash.get(spinner.getSelectedItem().toString()));
    }
});

button1 = (Button) findViewById(R.id.join);
 button1.setOnClickListener(new View.OnClickListener()
{
    public void onClick(View view)
    {
        if(Fire.this.isFinishing())
            return;

        Spinner spinner = (Spinner) findViewById(R.id.fires);

        if(spinner.getAdapter() != null &&
           spinner.getAdapter().getCount() > 0)
            joinFire(spinner.getSelectedItem().toString());
    }
});
```

```java
        button1 = (Button) findViewById(R.id.reset_fields);
        button1.setOnClickListener(new View.OnClickListener()
        {
            public void onClick(View view)
            {
                if(Fire.this.isFinishing())
                    return;

                TextView textView1 = (TextView) findViewById(R.id.channel);

                textView1.requestFocus();
                textView1.setText("");
                textView1 = (TextView) findViewById(R.id.digest);
                textView1.setText("");
                textView1 = (TextView) findViewById(R.id.salt);
                textView1.setText("");
            }
        });

        button1 = (Button) findViewById(R.id.save_name);
        button1.setOnClickListener(new View.OnClickListener()
        {
            public void onClick(View view)
            {
                if(Fire.this.isFinishing())
                    return;

                TextView textView1 = (TextView) findViewById(R.id.name);

                m_databaseHelper.writeSetting
                    (s_cryptography,
                     "fire_user_name",
                     textView1.getText().toString().trim());
                textView1.setText(textView1.getText().toString().trim());

                Map<String, FireChannel> map = State.getInstance().
                    fireChannels();

                if(map != null)
                    for(Map.Entry<String, FireChannel> entry : map.entrySet())
                    {
                        if(entry.getValue() == null)
                            continue;

                        entry.getValue().setUserName
                            (textView1.getText().toString().trim());
                    }
            }
        });

        Switch switch1 = (Switch) findViewById(R.id.show_details);

        switch1.setOnCheckedChangeListener
            (new CompoundButton.OnCheckedChangeListener()
            {
                @Override
                public void onCheckedChanged
                    (CompoundButton buttonView, boolean isChecked)
                {
                    showFireDetails(isChecked);

                    if(isChecked)
```

```java
                        m_databaseHelper.writeSetting
                            (null, "fire_show_details", "true");
                    else
                        m_databaseHelper.writeSetting
                            (null, "fire_show_details", "false");
                }
            });
    }

    private void showChatActivity()
    {
        Intent intent = new Intent(Fire.this, Chat.class);

        startActivity(intent);
        finish();
    }

    private void showFireDetails(boolean isChecked)
    {
        TextView textView1 = (TextView) findViewById(R.id.channel);
        View linearLayout1 = findViewById(R.id.auto_fill_layout);
        View linearLayout2 = findViewById(R.id.fire_buttons_layout);
        View gridLayout1 = findViewById(R.id.grid_layout);

        gridLayout1.setVisibility(isChecked ? View.VISIBLE : View.GONE);
        linearLayout1.setVisibility(isChecked ? View.VISIBLE : View.GONE);
        linearLayout2.setVisibility(isChecked ? View.VISIBLE : View.GONE);
        textView1.requestFocus();
    }

    private void showMemberChatActivity()
    {
        Intent intent = new Intent(Fire.this, MemberChat.class);

        startActivity(intent);
        finish();
    }

    private void showSettingsActivity()
    {
        Intent intent = new Intent(Fire.this, Settings.class);

        startActivity(intent);
        finish();
    }

    private void showSmokescreenActivity()
    {
        Intent intent = new Intent(Fire.this, Smokescreen.class);

        startActivity(intent);
        finish();
    }

    private void showSteamActivity()
    {
        Intent intent = new Intent(Fire.this, Steam.class);

        startActivity(intent);
        finish();
    }

    @Override
```

```java
protected void onCreate(Bundle savedInstanceState)
{
    super.onCreate(savedInstanceState);
    m_databaseHelper = Database.getInstance(getApplicationContext());
    m_receiver = new FireBroadcastReceiver();
    setContentView(R.layout.activity_fire);

    try
    {
        getSupportActionBar().setSubtitle(Smoke.networkStatusString());
        getSupportActionBar().setTitle("Smoke | Fire");
    }
    catch(Exception exception)
    {
    }

    if(State.getInstance().isAuthenticated())
        populateFires();

    Switch switch1 = (Switch) findViewById(R.id.show_details);

    switch1.setChecked
        (m_databaseHelper.readSetting(null, "fire_show_details").
         equals("true"));
    prepareAutoFill();
    prepareListeners();
    showFireDetails
        (m_databaseHelper.readSetting(null, "fire_show_details").
         equals("true"));

    Map<String, FireChannel> map = State.getInstance().fireChannels();

    if(map != null)
    {
        DisplayMetrics displayMetrics = new DisplayMetrics();
        ViewGroup viewGroup = (ViewGroup) findViewById(R.id.linear_layout);

        getWindowManager().getDefaultDisplay().getMetrics(displayMetrics);

        int height = (int) (1.0 * displayMetrics.heightPixels);

        for(Map.Entry<String, FireChannel> entry : map.entrySet())
        {
            if(entry.getValue() == null)
                continue;

            ViewGroup parent = (ViewGroup) entry.getValue().view().
                getParent();

            parent.removeView(entry.getValue().view());
            viewGroup.addView
                (entry.getValue().view(),
                 new LayoutParams(LayoutParams.WRAP_CONTENT, height));
        }

        viewGroup.requestLayout();
    }

    TextView textView1 = (TextView) findViewById(R.id.channel);

    textView1.setFilters(new InputFilter[] {s_Latin1InputFilter});
    textView1.setInputType(InputType.TYPE_TEXT_FLAG_NO_SUGGESTIONS |
                           InputType.TYPE_TEXT_VARIATION_VISIBLE_PASSWORD);
```

```java
        textView1 = (TextView) findViewById(R.id.digest);
        textView1.setFilters(new InputFilter[] {s_Latin1InputFilter});
        textView1.setInputType(InputType.TYPE_TEXT_FLAG_NO_SUGGESTIONS |
                            InputType.TYPE_TEXT_VARIATION_VISIBLE_PASSWORD);
        textView1 = (TextView) findViewById(R.id.name);
        textView1.setText
            (m_databaseHelper.
             readSetting(s_cryptography, "fire_user_name").trim());
        textView1 = (TextView) findViewById(R.id.salt);
        textView1.setInputType(InputType.TYPE_TEXT_FLAG_NO_SUGGESTIONS |
                            InputType.TYPE_TEXT_VARIATION_VISIBLE_PASSWORD);
        textView1.setFilters(new InputFilter[] {s_Latin1InputFilter});
    }

    @Override
    protected void onPause()
    {
        super.onPause();

        if(m_receiverRegistered)
        {
            LocalBroadcastManager.getInstance(getApplicationContext()).
                unregisterReceiver(m_receiver);
            m_receiverRegistered = false;
        }
    }

    @Override
    protected void onResume()
    {
        super.onResume();
        prepareFireChannelStatus();

        if(!m_receiverRegistered)
        {
            IntentFilter intentFilter = new IntentFilter();

            intentFilter.addAction("org.purple.smoke.chat_message");
            intentFilter.addAction("org.purple.smoke.fire_message");
            intentFilter.addAction("org.purple.smoke.neighbor_aborted");
            intentFilter.addAction("org.purple.smoke.neighbor_disconnected");
            intentFilter.addAction("org.purple.smoke.network_connected");
            intentFilter.addAction("org.purple.smoke.network_disconnected");
            intentFilter.addAction
                ("org.purple.smoke.state_participants_populated");
            intentFilter.addAction("org.purple.smoke.time");
            LocalBroadcastManager.getInstance(getApplicationContext()).
                registerReceiver(m_receiver, intentFilter);
            m_receiverRegistered = true;
        }
    }

    @Override
    public boolean onCreateOptionsMenu(Menu menu)
    {
        getMenuInflater().inflate(R.menu.fire_menu, menu);
        return true;
    }

    @Override
    public boolean onOptionsItemSelected(MenuItem menuItem)
    {
        int groupId = menuItem.getGroupId();
```

```java
        int itemId = menuItem.getItemId();

        if(groupId == Menu.NONE)
        {
            switch(itemId)
            {
            case R.id.action_chat:
                m_databaseHelper.writeSetting(null, "lastActivity", "Chat");
                showChatActivity();
                return true;
            case R.id.action_exit:
                Smoke.exit(Fire.this);
                return true;
            case R.id.action_settings:
                m_databaseHelper.writeSetting(null, "lastActivity", "Settings");
                showSettingsActivity();
                return true;
            case R.id.action_smokescreen:
                showSmokescreenActivity();
                return true;
            case R.id.action_steam:
                m_databaseHelper.writeSetting(null, "lastActivity", "Steam");
                showSteamActivity();
                return true;
            default:
                break;
            }
        }
        else
        {
            String sipHashId = menuItem.getTitle().toString();
            int indexOf = sipHashId.indexOf("(");

            if(indexOf >= 0)
                sipHashId = sipHashId.substring(indexOf + 1).replace(")", "");

            sipHashId = Miscellaneous.prepareSipHashId(sipHashId);
            State.getInstance().setString
                ("member_chat_oid", String.valueOf(itemId));
            State.getInstance().setString
                ("member_chat_siphash_id", sipHashId);
            m_databaseHelper.writeSetting
                (null, "lastActivity", "MemberChat");
            m_databaseHelper.writeSetting
                (s_cryptography, "member_chat_oid", String.valueOf(itemId));
            m_databaseHelper.writeSetting
                (s_cryptography, "member_chat_siphash_id", sipHashId);
            showMemberChatActivity();
        }

        return super.onOptionsItemSelected(menuItem);
    }

    @Override
    public boolean onPrepareOptionsMenu(Menu menu)
    {
        boolean isAuthenticated = State.getInstance().isAuthenticated();

        if(!m_databaseHelper.accountPrepared())
            /*
            ** The database may have been modified or removed.
            */
```

```java
            isAuthenticated = true;

        menu.findItem(R.id.action_authenticate).setEnabled(!isAuthenticated);
        Miscellaneous.addMembersToMenu(menu, 6, 250);
        return true;
    }
}



/* FireChannel.java -

https://github.com/textbrowser/smoke/blob/master/Smoke/app/src/main/java/org/p
urple/smoke/FireChannel.java
** Copyright (c) Alexis Megas.
** All rights reserved.
**
** Redistribution and use in source and binary forms, with or without
** modification, are permitted provided that the following conditions
** are met:
** 1. Redistributions of source code must retain the above copyright
**    notice, this list of conditions and the following disclaimer.
** 2. Redistributions in binary form must reproduce the above copyright
**    notice, this list of conditions and the following disclaimer in the
**    documentation and/or other materials provided with the distribution.
** 3. The name of the author may not be used to endorse or promote products
**    derived from Smoke without specific prior written permission.
**
** SMOKE IS PROVIDED BY THE AUTHOR ``AS IS'' AND ANY EXPRESS OR
** IMPLIED WARRANTIES, INCLUDING, BUT NOT LIMITED TO, THE IMPLIED WARRANTIES
** OF MERCHANTABILITY AND FITNESS FOR A PARTICULAR PURPOSE ARE DISCLAIMED.
** IN NO EVENT SHALL THE AUTHOR BE LIABLE FOR ANY DIRECT, INDIRECT,
** INCIDENTAL, SPECIAL, EXEMPLARY, OR CONSEQUENTIAL DAMAGES (INCLUDING, BUT
** NOT LIMITED TO, PROCUREMENT OF SUBSTITUTE GOODS OR SERVICES; LOSS OF USE,
** DATA, OR PROFITS; OR BUSINESS INTERRUPTION) HOWEVER CAUSED AND ON ANY
** THEORY OF LIABILITY, WHETHER IN CONTRACT, STRICT LIABILITY, OR TORT
** (INCLUDING NEGLIGENCE OR OTHERWISE) ARISING IN ANY WAY OUT OF THE USE OF
** SMOKE, EVEN IF ADVISED OF THE POSSIBILITY OF SUCH DAMAGE.
*/

package org.purple.smoke;

import android.app.Activity;
import android.content.Context;
import android.graphics.Color;
import android.support.v4.widget.NestedScrollView;
import android.text.Spannable;
import android.text.SpannableStringBuilder;
import android.text.style.ForegroundColorSpan;
import android.text.style.StyleSpan;
import android.view.LayoutInflater;
import android.view.View;
import android.view.ViewGroup;
import android.widget.Button;
import android.widget.TableLayout;
import android.widget.TableRow;
import android.widget.TextView;
import java.text.SimpleDateFormat;
import java.util.ArrayList;
import java.util.Collections;
import java.util.Comparator;
import java.util.Date;
import java.util.Hashtable;
```

```java
import java.util.Locale;
import java.util.concurrent.Executors;
import java.util.concurrent.ScheduledExecutorService;
import java.util.concurrent.TimeUnit;

public class FireChannel extends View
{
    private final static Comparator<Participant>
        s_participantComparator = new Comparator<Participant> ()
        {
            @Override
            public int compare(Participant p1, Participant p2)
            {
                return p1.m_name.compareTo(p2.m_name);
            }
        };

    private static class Participant
    {
        public String m_id = Miscellaneous.byteArrayAsHexString
            (Cryptography.randomBytes(128));
        public String m_name = "unknown";
        public long m_timestamp = -1L;
    }

    private Context m_context = null;
    private LayoutInflater m_inflater = null;
    private ScheduledExecutorService m_statusScheduler = null;
    private String m_id = "";
    private String m_name = "";
    private View m_view = null;
    private ViewGroup m_parent = null;
    private final Hashtable<String, Participant> m_participants =
        new Hashtable<> ();
    private final SimpleDateFormat m_simpleDateFormat =
        new SimpleDateFormat("MM/dd/yyyy HH:mm:ss", Locale.getDefault());
    private final static long STATUS_INTERVAL = 30000L;

    private void createSchedulers()
    {
        if(m_statusScheduler == null)
        {
            m_statusScheduler = Executors.newSingleThreadScheduledExecutor();
            m_statusScheduler.scheduleAtFixedRate(new Runnable()
            {
                @Override
                public void run()
                {
                    try
                    {
                        if(Kernel.getInstance().isConnected())
                            Kernel.getInstance().enqueueFireStatus
                                (m_id, m_name);

                        ((Activity) m_context).runOnUiThread(new Runnable()
                        {
                            @Override
                            public void run()
                            {
                                if(m_view == null)
                                    return;

                                TableLayout tableLayout = (TableLayout)
```

```java
        m_view.findViewById(R.id.participants);

    for(int i = tableLayout.getChildCount() - 1;
        i >= 0; i--)
    {
        TableRow row = (TableRow) tableLayout.
            getChildAt(i);

        if(row == null)
            continue;

        TextView textView1 = (TextView) row.
            getChildAt(0);

        if(textView1 == null)
        {
            tableLayout.removeView(row);
            continue;
        }

        if(textView1.getId() == -1)
            continue;

        Participant participant = null;

        try
        {
            participant = m_participants.
                get(textView1.
                    getTag(R.id.participants).
                    toString());
        }
        catch(Exception exception)
        {
            participant = null;
        }

        if(participant == null ||
            Math.abs(System.currentTimeMillis() -
                    participant.m_timestamp) >=
            2L * STATUS_INTERVAL)
        {
            try
            {
                m_participants.remove
                    (textView1.
                     getTag(R.id.participants).
                     toString());
            }
            catch(Exception exception)
            {
            }

            tableLayout.removeView(row);

            StringBuilder stringBuilder =
                new StringBuilder();

            stringBuilder.append
                (textView1.getText().toString());
            stringBuilder.append(" has left ");
            stringBuilder.append(m_name);
            stringBuilder.append(".\n\n");
```

```java
                                    SpannableStringBuilder spannable =
                                        new SpannableStringBuilder
                                        (stringBuilder);

                                    spannable.setSpan
                                        (new StyleSpan(android.graphics.
                                                Typeface.ITALIC),
                                        0,
                                        spannable.length(),
                                        Spannable.
                                        SPAN_EXCLUSIVE_EXCLUSIVE);

                                    TextView textView2 = (TextView) m_view.
                                        findViewById(R.id.chat_messages);

                                    textView2.append("[");
                                    textView2.append
                                        (m_simpleDateFormat.
                                         format(new Date()));
                                    textView2.append("] ");
                                    textView2.append(spannable);
                                    scrollMessagesView();
                                }
                            }
                        }
                    });
                }
                catch(Exception exception)
                {
                }
            }
        }, 1500L, STATUS_INTERVAL, TimeUnit.MILLISECONDS);
    }
}

private void populateParticipants()
{
    if(m_view == null)
        return;

    final TableLayout tableLayout = (TableLayout)
        m_view.findViewById(R.id.participants);

    if(m_participants.isEmpty())
    {
        tableLayout.removeAllViews();
        return;
    }
    else
        tableLayout.removeAllViews();

    ArrayList<Participant> arrayList = new ArrayList<>
        (m_participants.values());
    int i = 0;

    Collections.sort(arrayList, s_participantComparator);

    for(Participant participant : arrayList)
    {
        if(participant == null)
            continue;
```

```java
        TextView textView = new TextView(m_context);

        textView.setTag(R.id.participants, participant.m_id);
        textView.setText(participant.m_name.trim());

        TableRow row = new TableRow(m_context);

        row.addView(textView);
        tableLayout.addView(row, i);
        i += 1;

        if(m_id.equals(participant.m_id))
        {
            textView.setBackgroundColor(Color.rgb(255, 183, 77));
            textView.setId(-1);
        }
        else
            textView.setId(0);
    }

    arrayList.clear();
}

private void prepareListeners()
{
    if(m_view == null)
        return;

    Button button1 = null;

    button1 = (Button) m_view.findViewById(R.id.clear_chat_messages);
    button1.setOnClickListener(new View.OnClickListener()
    {
        public void onClick(View view)
        {
            TextView textView1 = (TextView) m_view.findViewById
                (R.id.chat_messages);

            textView1.setText("");
        }
    });

    button1 = (Button) m_view.findViewById(R.id.close);
    button1.setOnClickListener(new View.OnClickListener()
    {
        public void onClick(View view)
        {
            Kernel.getInstance().extinguishFire(m_name);

            if(m_statusScheduler != null)
            {
                try
                {
                    m_statusScheduler.shutdown();
                }
                catch(Exception exception)
                {
                }

                try
                {
                    if(!m_statusScheduler.
                        awaitTermination(60L, TimeUnit.SECONDS))
```

```java
                    m_statusScheduler.shutdownNow();
                }
                catch(Exception exception)
                {
                }
                finally
                {
                    m_statusScheduler = null;
                }
            }

        ViewGroup parent = (ViewGroup) m_view.getParent();

        parent.removeView(m_view);
        State.getInstance().removeFireChannel(m_name);
        }
    });

    button1 = (Button) m_view.findViewById(R.id.send_chat_message);
     button1.setOnClickListener(new View.OnClickListener()
    {
        public void onClick(View view)
        {
            TextView textView1 = (TextView) m_view.findViewById
                (R.id.chat_message);

            if(textView1.getText().toString().trim().isEmpty())
                return;

            String str = textView1.getText().toString().trim();
            StringBuilder stringBuilder = new StringBuilder();
            TextView textView2 = (TextView) m_view.findViewById
                (R.id.chat_messages);

            textView2.append("[");
            textView2.append(m_simpleDateFormat.format(new Date()));
            textView2.append("] ");

            {
                SpannableStringBuilder spannable =
                    new SpannableStringBuilder("me");

                spannable.setSpan
                    (new StyleSpan(android.graphics.Typeface.BOLD),
                     0,
                     spannable.length(),
                     Spannable.SPAN_EXCLUSIVE_EXCLUSIVE);
                textView2.append(spannable);
            }

            stringBuilder.append(": ");
            stringBuilder.append(str);
            stringBuilder.append("\n\n");
            textView2.append(stringBuilder);
            textView1.setText("");
            Kernel.getInstance().enqueueFireMessage(str, m_id, m_name);
            scrollMessagesView();

            final TextView textView3 = (TextView) m_view.findViewById
                (R.id.chat_message);

            textView3.post(new Runnable()
            {
```

```java
                @Override
                public void run()
                {
                    textView3.requestFocus();
                }
            });
        }
    });
}

private void scrollMessagesView()
{
    if(m_view == null)
        return;

    final NestedScrollView nestedScrollView = (NestedScrollView)
        m_view.findViewById(R.id.chat_scrollview);

    nestedScrollView.post(new Runnable()
    {
        @Override
        public void run()
        {
            nestedScrollView.fullScroll(NestedScrollView.FOCUS_DOWN);
        }
    });

    final TextView textView1 = (TextView) m_view.findViewById
        (R.id.chat_message);

    textView1.post(new Runnable()
    {
        @Override
        public void run()
        {
            textView1.requestFocus();
        }
    });
}

public FireChannel(String id,
                   String name,
                   Context context,
                   ViewGroup parent)
{
    super(context);
    m_context = context;
    m_id = id;
    m_inflater = (LayoutInflater) m_context.getSystemService
        (Context.LAYOUT_INFLATER_SERVICE);
    m_name = name;
    m_parent = parent;
    createSchedulers();
}

public String name()
{
    return m_name;
}

public View view()
{
    if(m_view == null)
```

```java
        {
            m_view = m_inflater.inflate(R.layout.fire_channel, m_parent,
false);
            prepareListeners();

            Participant participant = new Participant();

            participant.m_id = m_id;
            participant.m_name = Database.getInstance().readSetting
                (Cryptography.getInstance(), "fire_user_name").trim();

            if(participant.m_name.isEmpty())
                participant.m_name = "unknown";

            m_participants.put(m_id, participant);
            populateParticipants();

            TextView textView1 = (TextView)
m_view.findViewById(R.id.fire_name);

            textView1.setText(m_name);

            if(!Kernel.getInstance().igniteFire(m_name))
            {
                Button button1 = (Button) m_view.findViewById
                    (R.id.clear_chat_messages);

                button1.setEnabled(false);
                button1 = (Button) m_view.findViewById(R.id.send_chat_message);
                button1.setEnabled(false);
                textView1 = (TextView) m_view.findViewById(R.id.chat_messages);

                StringBuilder stringBuilder = new StringBuilder();

                stringBuilder.append("[");
                stringBuilder.append(m_simpleDateFormat.format(new Date()));
                stringBuilder.append("] ");
                stringBuilder.append("The Fire channel ");
                stringBuilder.append(m_name);
                stringBuilder.append(" cannot be registered with the Kernel." +
                                     " Please close this channel.");
                stringBuilder.append("\n\n");

                SpannableStringBuilder spannable = new SpannableStringBuilder
                    (stringBuilder.toString());

                spannable.setSpan
                    (new ForegroundColorSpan(Color.rgb(213, 0, 0)),
                     0, stringBuilder.length(),
                     Spannable.SPAN_EXCLUSIVE_EXCLUSIVE);
                textView1.append(spannable);
            }

            textView1 = (TextView) m_view.findViewById(R.id.chat_message);
            textView1.requestFocus();
        }

        return m_view;
    }

    public void append(String id, String message, String name)
    {
        if(id == null ||
```

```java
            id.trim().isEmpty() ||
            m_view == null ||
            message == null ||
            message.trim().isEmpty() ||
            name == null ||
            name.trim().isEmpty())
             return;

        status(id, name);

        StringBuilder stringBuilder = new StringBuilder();
        TextView textView = (TextView) m_view.findViewById(R.id.chat_messages);

        textView.append("[");
        textView.append(m_simpleDateFormat.format(new Date()));
        textView.append("] ");

        SpannableStringBuilder spannable = new SpannableStringBuilder
            (name.trim());

        spannable.setSpan
            (new StyleSpan(android.graphics.Typeface.BOLD),
             0,
             spannable.length(),
             Spannable.SPAN_EXCLUSIVE_EXCLUSIVE);
        textView.append(spannable);
        stringBuilder.append(": ");
        stringBuilder.append(message);
        stringBuilder.append("\n\n");
        textView.append(stringBuilder);
        scrollMessagesView();
    }

    public void setConnectedStatus(boolean state)
    {
        Button button1 = (Button) m_view.findViewById(R.id.send_chat_message);

        button1.setEnabled(state);

        if(state)
            button1.setBackgroundResource(R.drawable.send);
        else
            button1.setBackgroundResource(R.drawable.warning);
    }

    public void setUserName(String name)
    {
        status(m_id, name);
    }

    public void status(String id, String name)
    {
        if(id == null ||
           id.trim().isEmpty() ||
           name == null ||
           name.trim().isEmpty())
             return;

        if(m_participants.containsKey(id))
        {
            Participant participant = m_participants.get(id);

            if(participant != null)
```

```java
    {
        if(!name.trim().equals(participant.m_name))
        {
            StringBuilder stringBuilder = new StringBuilder();
            TextView textView = (TextView) m_view.findViewById
                (R.id.chat_messages);

            stringBuilder.append(participant.m_name);
            stringBuilder.append(" is now known as ");
            stringBuilder.append(name.trim());
            stringBuilder.append(".\n\n");
            textView.append("[");
            textView.append(m_simpleDateFormat.format(new Date()));
            textView.append("] ");

            SpannableStringBuilder spannable =
                new SpannableStringBuilder(stringBuilder);

            spannable.setSpan
                (new StyleSpan(android.graphics.Typeface.ITALIC),
                 0,
                 spannable.length(),
                 Spannable.SPAN_EXCLUSIVE_EXCLUSIVE);
            textView.append(spannable);
            scrollMessagesView();
            participant.m_name = name.trim();
            participant.m_timestamp = System.currentTimeMillis();
            m_participants.put(id, participant);
            populateParticipants();
        }
        else
        {
            participant.m_name = name.trim();
            participant.m_timestamp = System.currentTimeMillis();
            m_participants.put(id, participant);
        }

        return;
    }
    else
        m_participants.remove(id);
}

StringBuilder stringBuilder = new StringBuilder();

stringBuilder.append(name.trim());
stringBuilder.append(" has joined ");
stringBuilder.append(m_name);
stringBuilder.append(".\n\n");

SpannableStringBuilder spannable = new SpannableStringBuilder
    (stringBuilder);

spannable.setSpan
    (new StyleSpan(android.graphics.Typeface.ITALIC),
     0,
     spannable.length(),
     Spannable.SPAN_EXCLUSIVE_EXCLUSIVE);

TextView textView = (TextView) m_view.findViewById(R.id.chat_messages);

textView.append("[");
textView.append(m_simpleDateFormat.format(new Date()));
```

```java
        textView.append("] ");
        textView.append(spannable);
        scrollMessagesView();

        Participant participant = new Participant();

        participant.m_id = id;
        participant.m_name = name.trim();
        participant.m_timestamp = System.currentTimeMillis();
        m_participants.put(id, participant);
        populateParticipants();
    }
}
```

/* FireElement.java –


```java
package org.purple.smoke;

public class FireElement
{
    public String m_name = "";
    public int m_oid = -1;

    public FireElement()
    {
    }
}
```

/* Juggernaut.java –

```
https://github.com/textbrowser/smoke/blob/master/Smoke/app/src/main/java/org/p
urple/smoke/Juggernaut.java
** Copyright (c) Alexis Megas.
** All rights reserved.
**
** Redistribution and use in source and binary forms, with or without
** modification, are permitted provided that the following conditions
** are met:
** 1. Redistributions of source code must retain the above copyright
**    notice, this list of conditions and the following disclaimer.
** 2. Redistributions in binary form must reproduce the above copyright
**    notice, this list of conditions and the following disclaimer in the
**    documentation and/or other materials provided with the distribution.
** 3. The name of the author may not be used to endorse or promote products
**    derived from Smoke without specific prior written permission.
**
** SMOKE IS PROVIDED BY THE AUTHOR ``AS IS'' AND ANY EXPRESS OR
** IMPLIED WARRANTIES, INCLUDING, BUT NOT LIMITED TO, THE IMPLIED WARRANTIES
** OF MERCHANTABILITY AND FITNESS FOR A PARTICULAR PURPOSE ARE DISCLAIMED.
** IN NO EVENT SHALL THE AUTHOR BE LIABLE FOR ANY DIRECT, INDIRECT,
** INCIDENTAL, SPECIAL, EXEMPLARY, OR CONSEQUENTIAL DAMAGES (INCLUDING, BUT
** NOT LIMITED TO, PROCUREMENT OF SUBSTITUTE GOODS OR SERVICES; LOSS OF USE,
** DATA, OR PROFITS; OR BUSINESS INTERRUPTION) HOWEVER CAUSED AND ON ANY
** THEORY OF LIABILITY, WHETHER IN CONTRACT, STRICT LIABILITY, OR TORT
** (INCLUDING NEGLIGENCE OR OTHERWISE) ARISING IN ANY WAY OUT OF THE USE OF
** SMOKE, EVEN IF ADVISED OF THE POSSIBILITY OF SUCH DAMAGE.
*/

package org.purple.smoke;

import android.util.Base64;
import android.util.Log;
import java.math.BigInteger;
import java.nio.charset.StandardCharsets;
import java.security.SecureRandom;
import org.bouncycastle.crypto.Digest;
import org.bouncycastle.crypto.agreement.jpake.JPAKEParticipant;
import org.bouncycastle.crypto.agreement.jpake.JPAKEPrimeOrderGroup;
import org.bouncycastle.crypto.agreement.jpake.JPAKEPrimeOrderGroups;
import org.bouncycastle.crypto.agreement.jpake.JPAKERound1Payload;
import org.bouncycastle.crypto.agreement.jpake.JPAKERound2Payload;
import org.bouncycastle.crypto.agreement.jpake.JPAKERound3Payload;
import org.bouncycastle.crypto.digests.SHA512Digest;

public class Juggernaut
{
    private BigInteger m_keyingMaterial = null;
    private JPAKEParticipant m_participant = null;
    private boolean m_isJuggerKnot = false;
    private final Digest m_digest = new SHA512Digest();
    private final SecureRandom m_random = new SecureRandom();
    private final static JPAKEPrimeOrderGroup s_group =
        JPAKEPrimeOrderGroups.NIST_3072;
    private final static int ITERATION_COUNT = 4096;
    private long m_lastEventTime = 0L;

    Juggernaut(String participantId, String secret, boolean isJuggerKnot)
    {
        m_isJuggerKnot = isJuggerKnot;
        m_lastEventTime = System.currentTimeMillis();
```

```java
        try
        {
            m_participant = new JPAKEParticipant
                (participantId,
                 secret.toCharArray(),
                 s_group,
                 m_digest,
                 m_random);
        }
        catch(Exception exception)
        {
            m_participant = null;
        }
    }

    private BigInteger keyingMaterial()
    {
        m_lastEventTime = System.currentTimeMillis();

        try
        {
            if(m_keyingMaterial == null)
                m_keyingMaterial = m_participant.calculateKeyingMaterial();
        }
        catch(Exception exception)
        {
            m_keyingMaterial = null;
        }

        return m_keyingMaterial;
    }

    private String payload1Stream()
    {
        try
        {
            JPAKERound1Payload payload = m_participant.
                createRound1PayloadToSend();
            StringBuffer stringBuffer = new StringBuffer();

            stringBuffer.append
                (Base64.encodeToString(payload.getGx1().toByteArray(),
                                       Base64.NO_WRAP));
            stringBuffer.append("\n");
            stringBuffer.append
                (Base64.encodeToString(payload.getGx2().toByteArray(),
                                       Base64.NO_WRAP));
            stringBuffer.append("\n");

            BigInteger array[] = payload.getKnowledgeProofForX1();

            stringBuffer.append
                (Base64.encodeToString(String.valueOf(array.length).getBytes(),
                                       Base64.NO_WRAP));
            stringBuffer.append("\n");

            for(BigInteger b : array)
            {
                stringBuffer.append
                    (Base64.encodeToString(b.toByteArray(), Base64.NO_WRAP));
                stringBuffer.append("\n");
            }
```

```java
        array = payload.getKnowledgeProofForX2();
        stringBuffer.append
            (Base64.encodeToString(String.valueOf(array.length).getBytes(),
                            Base64.NO_WRAP));
        stringBuffer.append("\n");

        for(BigInteger b : array)
        {
            stringBuffer.append
                (Base64.encodeToString(b.toByteArray(), Base64.NO_WRAP));
            stringBuffer.append("\n");
        }

        stringBuffer.append
            (Base64.encodeToString(payload.getParticipantId().getBytes(),
                            Base64.NO_WRAP));
        return stringBuffer.toString();
    }
    catch(Exception exception)
    {
    }

    return "";
}

private String payload2Stream()
{
    try
    {
        JPAKERound2Payload payload = m_participant.
            createRound2PayloadToSend();
        StringBuffer stringBuffer = new StringBuffer();

        stringBuffer.append
            (Base64.encodeToString(payload.getA().toByteArray(),
                            Base64.NO_WRAP));
        stringBuffer.append("\n");

        BigInteger array[] = payload.getKnowledgeProofForX2s();

        stringBuffer.append
            (Base64.encodeToString(String.valueOf(array.length).getBytes(),
                            Base64.NO_WRAP));
        stringBuffer.append("\n");

        for(BigInteger b : array)
        {
            stringBuffer.append
                (Base64.encodeToString(b.toByteArray(), Base64.NO_WRAP));
            stringBuffer.append("\n");
        }

        stringBuffer.append
            (Base64.encodeToString(payload.getParticipantId().getBytes(),
                            Base64.NO_WRAP));
        return stringBuffer.toString();
    }
    catch(Exception exception)
    {
    }

    return "";
}
```

```java
    private String payload3Stream(BigInteger keyingMaterial)
    {
        try
        {
            JPAKERound3Payload payload =
m_participant.createRound3PayloadToSend
                (keyingMaterial);
            StringBuffer stringBuffer = new StringBuffer();

            stringBuffer.append
                (Base64.encodeToString(payload.getMacTag().toByteArray(),
                                 Base64.NO_WRAP));
            stringBuffer.append("\n");
            stringBuffer.append
                (Base64.encodeToString(payload.getParticipantId().getBytes(),
                                 Base64.NO_WRAP));
            return stringBuffer.toString();
        }
        catch(Exception exception)
        {
        }

        return "";
    }

    private boolean validatePayload1(String strings[])
    {
        try
        {
            BigInteger gx1 = null;
            BigInteger gx2 = null;
            BigInteger kpx1[] = null;
            BigInteger kpx2[] = null;
            String participantId = "";
            byte bytes[] = null;

            /*
            ** strings[0]      - gx1
            ** strings[1]      - gx2
            ** strings[2]      - length of kpx1
            ** strings[3]      - kpx1[0]
            ** ...
            ** strings[n]      - length of kpx2
            ** strings[n + 1]  - kpx2[0]
            ** ...
            ** strings[o]      - participant identity
            */

            bytes = Base64.decode(strings[0], Base64.NO_WRAP);
            gx1 = new BigInteger(bytes);
            bytes = Base64.decode(strings[1], Base64.NO_WRAP);
            gx2 = new BigInteger(bytes);
            bytes = Base64.decode(strings[2], Base64.NO_WRAP);
            kpx1 = new BigInteger[Integer.parseInt(new String(bytes))];

            for(int i = 0; i < kpx1.length; i++)
            {
                bytes = Base64.decode(strings[i + 3], Base64.NO_WRAP);
                kpx1[i] = new BigInteger(bytes);
            }

            bytes = Base64.decode(strings[kpx1.length + 3], Base64.NO_WRAP);
```

```java
            kpx2 = new BigInteger[Integer.parseInt(new String(bytes))];

            for(int i = 0; i < kpx2.length; i++)
            {
                bytes = Base64.decode
                    (strings[i + kpx1.length + 4], Base64.NO_WRAP);
                kpx2[i] = new BigInteger(bytes);
            }

            participantId = new String
                (Base64.decode(strings[kpx1.length + kpx2.length + 4],
                               Base64.NO_WRAP), StandardCharsets.UTF_8);

            JPAKERound1Payload payload = new JPAKERound1Payload
                (participantId, gx1, gx2, kpx1, kpx2);

            m_participant.validateRound1PayloadReceived(payload);
        }
    catch(Exception exception)
        {
            return false;
        }

        return true;
    }

private boolean validatePayload2(String strings[])
    {
        try
        {
            BigInteger a = null;
            BigInteger kpx2s[] = null;
            String participantId = "";
            byte bytes[] = null;

            /*
            ** strings[0] - a
            ** strings[1] - length of kpx2s
            ** strings[2] - kpx2s[0]
            ** ...
            ** strings[n] - participant identity
            */

            bytes = Base64.decode(strings[0], Base64.NO_WRAP);
            a = new BigInteger(bytes);
            bytes = Base64.decode(strings[1], Base64.NO_WRAP);
            kpx2s = new BigInteger[Integer.parseInt(new String(bytes))];

            for(int i = 0; i < kpx2s.length; i++)
            {
                bytes = Base64.decode(strings[i + 2], Base64.NO_WRAP);
                kpx2s[i] = new BigInteger(bytes);
            }

            participantId = new String
                (Base64.decode(strings[kpx2s.length + 2], Base64.NO_WRAP),
                 StandardCharsets.UTF_8);

            JPAKERound2Payload payload = new JPAKERound2Payload
                (participantId, a, kpx2s);

            m_participant.validateRound2PayloadReceived(payload);
        }
```

```java
        catch(Exception exception)
        {
            return false;
        }

        return true;
    }

    private boolean validatePayload3(BigInteger keyingMaterial,
                                     String strings[])
    {
        try
        {
            BigInteger macTag = null;
            String participantId = "";
            byte bytes[] = null;

            /*
            ** strings[0] - mac tag
            ** strings[1] - participant identity
            */

            bytes = Base64.decode(strings[0], Base64.NO_WRAP);
            macTag = new BigInteger(bytes);
            bytes = Base64.decode(strings[1], Base64.NO_WRAP);
            participantId = new String(bytes, StandardCharsets.UTF_8);

            JPAKERound3Payload payload = new JPAKERound3Payload
                (participantId, macTag);

            m_participant.validateRound3PayloadReceived
                (payload, keyingMaterial);
        }
        catch(Exception exception)
        {
            return false;
        }

        return true;
    }

    public String next(String payload)
    {
        m_lastEventTime = System.currentTimeMillis();

        String string = "";

        switch(m_participant.getState())
        {
        case JPAKEParticipant.STATE_INITIALIZED:
            string = payload1Stream();
            break;
        case JPAKEParticipant.STATE_ROUND_1_CREATED:
            if(payload != null && validatePayload1(payload.split("\\n")))
                string = payload2Stream();

            break;
        case JPAKEParticipant.STATE_ROUND_2_CREATED:
            if(payload != null && validatePayload2(payload.split("\\n")))
                string = payload3Stream(keyingMaterial());

            break;
        case JPAKEParticipant.STATE_ROUND_3_CREATED:
```

```java
            if(payload != null)
                validatePayload3(keyingMaterial(), payload.split("\\n"));

            break;
        default:
            break;
        }

        return string;
    }

    public boolean isJuggerKnot()
    {
        return m_isJuggerKnot;
    }

    public byte[] deriveSessionCredentials()
    {
        if(m_isJuggerKnot)
            try
            {
                String string = Base64.encodeToString
                    (m_keyingMaterial.toByteArray(), Base64.NO_WRAP);
                byte bytes[] = Cryptography.pbkdf2
                    (Cryptography.
                     sha512(string.getBytes(StandardCharsets.UTF_8)),
                     string.toCharArray(),
                     ITERATION_COUNT,
                     160); // SHA-1

                if(bytes != null)
                    bytes = Cryptography.pbkdf2
                        (Cryptography.
                         sha512(string.getBytes(StandardCharsets.UTF_8)),
                         string.toCharArray(),
                         1,
                         Cryptography.CIPHER_HASH_KEYS_LENGTH * 8);

                return bytes;
            }
            catch(Exception exception)
            {
                return null;
            }
        else
            return null;
    }

    public int state()
    {
        return m_participant.getState();
    }

    public long lastEventTime()
    {
        return m_lastEventTime;
    }

    public static String stateToText(int state)
    {
        switch(state)
        {
        case JPAKEParticipant.STATE_INITIALIZED:
```

```java
            return "initialized";
        case JPAKEParticipant.STATE_KEY_CALCULATED:
            return "key calculated";
        case JPAKEParticipant.STATE_ROUND_1_CREATED:
            return "round 1 created";
        case JPAKEParticipant.STATE_ROUND_1_VALIDATED:
            return "round 1 validated";
        case JPAKEParticipant.STATE_ROUND_2_CREATED:
            return "round 2 created";
        case JPAKEParticipant.STATE_ROUND_2_VALIDATED:
            return "round 2 validated";
        case JPAKEParticipant.STATE_ROUND_3_CREATED:
            return "round 3 created";
        case JPAKEParticipant.STATE_ROUND_3_VALIDATED:
            return "round 3 validated";
        default:
            return "unknown";
        }
    }

public static void test1()
{
    Juggernaut juggernaut1 = new Juggernaut("a", "The Juggernaut!", false);
    Juggernaut juggernaut2 = new Juggernaut("b", "The Juggernaut!", false);
    String payload1 = juggernaut1.payload1Stream();
    String payload2 = juggernaut2.payload1Stream();
    boolean ok1 = false;
    boolean ok2 = false;

    /*
    ** Payload 1
    */

    ok1 = juggernaut1.validatePayload1(payload2.split("\\n"));
    Log.e("test1: Participant a validated payload1?", ok1 + "");
    ok2 = juggernaut2.validatePayload1(payload1.split("\\n"));
    Log.e("test1: Participant b validated payload1?", ok2 + "");

    /*
    ** Payload 2
    */

    payload1 = juggernaut1.payload2Stream();
    payload2 = juggernaut2.payload2Stream();
    ok1 = juggernaut1.validatePayload2(payload2.split("\\n"));
    Log.e("test1: Participant a validated payload2?", ok1 + "");
    ok2 = juggernaut2.validatePayload2(payload1.split("\\n"));
    Log.e("test1: Participant b validated payload2?", ok2 + "");

    /*
    ** Payload 3
    */

    payload1 = juggernaut1.payload3Stream(juggernaut1.keyingMaterial());
    payload2 = juggernaut2.payload3Stream(juggernaut2.keyingMaterial());
    ok1 = juggernaut1.validatePayload3
        (juggernaut1.keyingMaterial(), payload2.split("\\n"));
    Log.e("test1: Participant a validated payload3?", ok1 + "");
    ok2 = juggernaut2.validatePayload3
        (juggernaut2.keyingMaterial(), payload1.split("\\n"));
    Log.e("test1: Participant b validated payload3?", ok2 + "");
}
```

```java
public static void test2()
{
    Juggernaut juggernaut1 = new Juggernaut("a", "The Juggernaut!", false);
    Juggernaut juggernaut2 = new Juggernaut("b", "The Juggernaut.", false);
    String payload1 = juggernaut1.payload1Stream();
    String payload2 = juggernaut2.payload1Stream();
    boolean ok1 = false;
    boolean ok2 = false;

    /*
    ** Payload 1
    */

    ok1 = juggernaut1.validatePayload1(payload2.split("\\n"));
    Log.e("test2: Participant a validated payload1?", ok1 + "");
    ok2 = juggernaut2.validatePayload1(payload1.split("\\n"));
    Log.e("test2: Participant b validated payload1?", ok2 + "");

    /*
    ** Payload 2
    */

    payload1 = juggernaut1.payload2Stream();
    payload2 = juggernaut2.payload2Stream();
    ok1 = juggernaut1.validatePayload2(payload2.split("\\n"));
    Log.e("test2: Participant a validated payload2?", ok1 + "");
    ok2 = juggernaut2.validatePayload2(payload1.split("\\n"));
    Log.e("test2: Participant b validated payload2?", ok2 + "");

    /*
    ** Payload 3
    */

    payload1 = juggernaut1.payload3Stream(juggernaut1.keyingMaterial());
    payload2 = juggernaut2.payload3Stream(juggernaut2.keyingMaterial());
    ok1 = juggernaut1.validatePayload3
        (juggernaut1.keyingMaterial(), payload2.split("\\n"));
    Log.e("test2: Participant a validated payload3?", ok1 + "");
    ok2 = juggernaut2.validatePayload3
        (juggernaut2.keyingMaterial(), payload1.split("\\n"));
    Log.e("test2: Participant b validated payload3?", ok2 + "");
}

public static void test3()
{
    Juggernaut juggernaut1 = new Juggernaut("a", "The Juggernaut!", false);
    Juggernaut juggernaut2 = new Juggernaut("b", "The Juggernaut!", false);

    /*
    ** Participants initialize. Send payloads.
    */

    String payload1a = juggernaut1.next(null); // STATE_INITIALIZED
    String payload2a = juggernaut2.next(null); // STATE_INITIALIZED

    /*
    ** Validate state 1, create state 2. Send payloads.
    */

    String payload1b = juggernaut1.next
        (payload2a); // STATE_ROUND_2_CREATED
    String payload2b = juggernaut2.next
        (payload1a); // STATE_ROUND_2_CREATED
```

```java
	/*
	** Validate state 2, create keying material, create state 3.
	** Send payloads.
	*/

	String payload1c = juggernaut1.next
	    (payload2b); // STATE_ROUND_3_CREATED
	String payload2c = juggernaut2.next
	    (payload1b); // STATE_ROUND_3_CREATED

	/*
	** Validate state 3.
	*/

	juggernaut1.next(payload2c); // STATE_3_VALIDATED
	juggernaut2.next(payload1c); // STATE_3_VALIDATED
	Log.e(juggernaut1.state() + "", "test3: Participant a state?");
	Log.e(juggernaut2.state() + "", "test3: Participant b state?");
    }

}
```

/* Kernel.java –

```java
https://github.com/textbrowser/smoke/blob/master/Smoke/app/src/main/java/org/p
urple/smoke/Kernel.java
** Copyright (c) Alexis Megas.
** All rights reserved.
**
** Redistribution and use in source and binary forms, with or without
** modification, are permitted provided that the following conditions
** are met:
** 1. Redistributions of source code must retain the above copyright
**    notice, this list of conditions and the following disclaimer.
** 2. Redistributions in binary form must reproduce the above copyright
**    notice, this list of conditions and the following disclaimer in the
**    documentation and/or other materials provided with the distribution.
** 3. The name of the author may not be used to endorse or promote products
**    derived from Smoke without specific prior written permission.
**
** SMOKE IS PROVIDED BY THE AUTHOR ``AS IS'' AND ANY EXPRESS OR
** IMPLIED WARRANTIES, INCLUDING, BUT NOT LIMITED TO, THE IMPLIED WARRANTIES
** OF MERCHANTABILITY AND FITNESS FOR A PARTICULAR PURPOSE ARE DISCLAIMED.
** IN NO EVENT SHALL THE AUTHOR BE LIABLE FOR ANY DIRECT, INDIRECT,
** INCIDENTAL, SPECIAL, EXEMPLARY, OR CONSEQUENTIAL DAMAGES (INCLUDING, BUT
** NOT LIMITED TO, PROCUREMENT OF SUBSTITUTE GOODS OR SERVICES; LOSS OF USE,
** DATA, OR PROFITS; OR BUSINESS INTERRUPTION) HOWEVER CAUSED AND ON ANY
** THEORY OF LIABILITY, WHETHER IN CONTRACT, STRICT LIABILITY, OR TORT
** (INCLUDING NEGLIGENCE OR OTHERWISE) ARISING IN ANY WAY OUT OF THE USE OF
** SMOKE, EVEN IF ADVISED OF THE POSSIBILITY OF SUCH DAMAGE.
*/

package org.purple.smoke;

import android.content.BroadcastReceiver;
import android.content.Context;
import android.content.Intent;
import android.content.IntentFilter;
import android.net.ConnectivityManager;
import android.net.NetworkInfo;
import android.net.wifi.WifiManager.WifiLock;
```

```java
import android.net.wifi.WifiManager;
import android.os.PowerManager.WakeLock;
import android.os.PowerManager;
import android.support.v4.content.LocalBroadcastManager;
import android.util.Base64;
import android.util.SparseArray;
import java.net.InetAddress;
import java.nio.charset.StandardCharsets;
import java.security.PublicKey;
import java.sql.Timestamp;
import java.text.SimpleDateFormat;
import java.util.ArrayList;
import java.util.Arrays;
import java.util.Date;
import java.util.Hashtable;
import java.util.Iterator;
import java.util.Locale;
import java.util.TimeZone;
import java.util.TreeSet;
import java.util.concurrent.Executors;
import java.util.concurrent.ScheduledExecutorService;
import java.util.concurrent.TimeUnit;
import java.util.concurrent.atomic.AtomicBoolean;
import java.util.concurrent.atomic.AtomicLong;
import java.util.concurrent.locks.ReentrantReadWriteLock;
import org.bouncycastle.crypto.agreement.jpake.JPAKEParticipant;

public class Kernel
{
    private class KernelBroadcastReceiver extends BroadcastReceiver
    {
        public KernelBroadcastReceiver()
        {
        }

        @Override
        public void onReceive(Context context, Intent intent)
        {
            if(intent == null || intent.getAction() == null)
                return;

            switch(intent.getAction())
            {
            case "org.purple.smoke.steam_read_interval_change":
                int oid = -1;
                int readInterval = 4;

                try
                {
                    oid = intent.getIntExtra("org.purple.smoke.extra1", oid);
                    readInterval = intent.getIntExtra
                        ("org.purple.smoke.extra2", readInterval);
                }
                catch(Exception exception)
                {
                }

                if(oid != -1)
                {
                    /*
                    ** Discover the Steam reader and prepare its new read
                    ** interval.
                    */
```

```java
                    m_steamsMutex.readLock().lock();

                    try
                    {
                        int size = m_steams.size();

                        for(int i = 0; i < size; i++)
                        {
                            int j = m_steams.keyAt(i);

                            if(m_steams.get(j) != null &&
                               m_steams.get(j).getOid() == oid)
                            {
                                m_steams.get(j).setReadInterval(readInterval);
                                return;
                            }
                        }
                    }
                    catch(Exception exception)
                    {
                    }
                    finally
                    {
                        m_steamsMutex.readLock().unlock();
                    }
                }

            break;
        default:
            break;
        }
    }
}

private ArrayList<MessageElement> m_messagesToSend = null;
private AtomicLong m_chatTemporaryIdentityLastTick = null;
private AtomicLong m_shareSipHashIdIdentity = null;
private AtomicLong m_shareSipHashIdIdentityLastTick = null;
private Hashtable<String, Juggernaut> m_juggernauts = null;
private Hashtable<String, ParticipantCall> m_callQueue = null;
private Hashtable<String, byte[]> m_fireStreams = null;
private Object m_messagesToSendSchedulerMutex = new Object();
private ScheduledExecutorService m_callScheduler = null;
private ScheduledExecutorService m_messagesToSendScheduler = null;
private ScheduledExecutorService m_networkStatusScheduler = null;
private ScheduledExecutorService m_neighborsScheduler = null;
private ScheduledExecutorService m_publishKeysScheduler = null;
private ScheduledExecutorService m_purgeScheduler = null;
private ScheduledExecutorService m_requestMessagesScheduler = null;
private ScheduledExecutorService m_statusScheduler = null;
private ScheduledExecutorService m_steamScheduler = null;
private ScheduledExecutorService m_temporaryIdentityScheduler = null;
private SteamKeyExchange m_steamKeyExchange = null;
private Time m_time = null;
private WakeLock m_wakeLock = null;
private WifiLock m_wifiLock = null;
private byte m_chatMessageRetrievalIdentity[] = null;
private final KernelBroadcastReceiver m_receiver =
    new KernelBroadcastReceiver();
private final Object m_callSchedulerMutex = new Object();
private final ReentrantReadWriteLock m_callQueueMutex =
    new ReentrantReadWriteLock();
```

```java
    private final ReentrantReadWriteLock m_chatMessageRetrievalIdentityMutex =
        new ReentrantReadWriteLock();
    private final ReentrantReadWriteLock m_fireStreamsMutex =
        new ReentrantReadWriteLock();
    private final ReentrantReadWriteLock m_juggernautsMutex =
        new ReentrantReadWriteLock();
    private final ReentrantReadWriteLock m_messagesToSendMutex =
        new ReentrantReadWriteLock();
    private final ReentrantReadWriteLock m_neighborsMutex =
        new ReentrantReadWriteLock();
    private final ReentrantReadWriteLock m_steamsMutex =
        new ReentrantReadWriteLock();
    private final SparseArray<Neighbor> m_neighbors = new SparseArray<> ();
    private final SparseArray<SteamReader> m_steams = new SparseArray<> ();
    private final SteamWriter m_steamWriter = new SteamWriter();
    private final static Cryptography s_cryptography =
        Cryptography.getInstance();
    private final static Database s_databaseHelper = Database.getInstance();
    private final static SimpleDateFormat s_fireSimpleDateFormat =
        new SimpleDateFormat("MMddyyyyHHmmss", Locale.getDefault());
    private final static SipHash s_congestionSipHash = new SipHash
        (Cryptography.randomBytes(SipHash.KEY_LENGTH));
    private final static int CONGESTION_LIFETIME = 60; // 60 seconds.
    private final static int FIRE_TIME_DELTA = 30000; // 30 seconds.
    private final static int MCELIECE_OUTPUT_SIZES[] = {304,  // 48 bytes.
                                            320,  // 64 bytes.
                                            352,  // 96 bytes.
                                            491,  // 48 bytes.
                                            507,  // 64 bytes.
                                            539,  // 96 bytes.
                                            560,  // 48 bytes.
                                            576,  // 64 bytes.
                                            608}; // 96 bytes.
    private final static int PARTICIPANTS_KEYSTREAMS_LIFETIME =
        864000; // Seconds in ten days.
    private final static long CALL_INTERVAL = 250L; // 0.250 seconds.
    private final static long CALL_LIFETIME = 30000L; // 30 seconds.
    private final static long JUGGERNAUT_LIFETIME = 15000L; // 15 seconds.
    private final static long JUGGERNAUT_WINDOW = 10000L; // 10 seconds.
    private final static long MESSAGES_TO_SEND_INTERVAL =
        50L; // 50 milliseconds.
    private final static long NEIGHBORS_INTERVAL = 5000L; // 5 seconds.
    private final static long NETWORK_STATUS_INTERVAL = 1500L; // 1.5 seconds.
    private final static long PUBLISH_KEYS_INTERVAL = 45000L; // 45 seconds.
    private final static long PURGE_INTERVAL = 30000L; // 30 seconds.
    private final static long REQUEST_MESSAGES_INTERVAL = 60000L; // 60
seconds.
    private final static long SHARE_SIPHASH_ID_CONFIRMATION_WINDOW =
        15000L; // 15 seconds.
    private final static long STATUS_INTERVAL = 15000L; /*
                                            ** Should be less than
                                            ** Chat.STATUS_WINDOW.
                                            */
    private final static long STEAM_INTERVAL = 7500L; // 7.5 seconds.
    private final static long STEAM_SHARE_WINDOW = 15000L; // 15 seconds.
    private final static long TEMPORARY_IDENTITY_INTERVAL = 5000L; // 5
seconds.
    private final static long TEMPORARY_IDENTITY_LIFETIME =
        60000L; // 60 seconds.
    private static Kernel s_instance = null;
    public final static long JUGGERNAUT_DELAY = 7500L; // 7.5 seconds.

    private Kernel()
```

```java
    {
        m_callQueue = new Hashtable<> ();
        m_chatTemporaryIdentityLastTick = new AtomicLong
            (System.currentTimeMillis());
        m_fireStreams = new Hashtable<> ();
        m_juggernauts = new Hashtable<> ();
        m_messagesToSend = new ArrayList<> ();
        m_shareSipHashIdIdentity = new AtomicLong(0L);
        m_shareSipHashIdIdentityLastTick = new AtomicLong
            (System.currentTimeMillis());
        m_steamKeyExchange = new SteamKeyExchange();
        m_time = new Time();

        try
        {
            LocalBroadcastManager.getInstance(Smoke.getApplication()).
                unregisterReceiver(m_receiver);

            IntentFilter intentFilter = new IntentFilter();

            intentFilter.addAction
                ("org.purple.smoke.steam_read_interval_change");
            LocalBroadcastManager.getInstance(Smoke.getApplication()).
                registerReceiver(m_receiver, intentFilter);
        }
        catch(Exception exception)
        {
        }

        try
        {
            WifiManager wifiManager = (WifiManager)
                Smoke.getApplication().getApplicationContext().
                getSystemService(Context.WIFI_SERVICE);

            if(wifiManager != null)
                m_wifiLock = wifiManager.createWifiLock
                    (WifiManager.WIFI_MODE_FULL_HIGH_PERF, "SmokeWiFiLockTag");

            if(m_wifiLock != null)
            {
                m_wifiLock.setReferenceCounted(false);
                m_wifiLock.acquire();
            }
        }
        catch(Exception exception)
        {
        }

        prepareSchedulers();
        s_fireSimpleDateFormat.setTimeZone(TimeZone.getTimeZone("UTC"));
    }

    private void prepareNeighbors()
    {
        if(!State.getInstance().isAuthenticated())
            return;

        ArrayList<NeighborElement> neighbors = purgeDeletedNeighbors();

        if(neighbors == null)
            return;

```

```java
for(NeighborElement neighborElement : neighbors)
{
    if(neighborElement == null)
        continue;
    else
    {
        m_neighborsMutex.readLock().lock();

        try
        {
            if(m_neighbors.get(neighborElement.m_oid) != null)
                continue;
        }
        catch(Exception exception)
        {
        }
        finally
        {
            m_neighborsMutex.readLock().unlock();
        }

        if(neighborElement.m_statusControl.toLowerCase().
            equals("delete") ||
            neighborElement.m_statusControl.toLowerCase().
            equals("disconnect"))
        {
            if(neighborElement.m_statusControl.toLowerCase().
                equals("disconnect"))
                s_databaseHelper.saveNeighborInformation
                    (s_cryptography,
                     "0",              // Bytes Read
                     "0",              // Bytes Written
                     "0",              // Queue Size
                     "",               // Error
                     "",               // IP Address
                     "0",              // Port
                     "",               // Session Cipher
                     "disconnected",   // Status
                     "0",              // Uptime
                     String.valueOf(neighborElement.m_oid));

            continue;
        }
    }

    Neighbor neighbor = null;

    if(neighborElement.m_transport.equals("TCP"))
    {
        if(neighborElement.m_nonTls.equals("true"))
            neighbor = new TcpNeighbor
                (neighborElement.m_passthrough,
                 neighborElement.m_proxyIpAddress,
                 neighborElement.m_proxyPort,
                 neighborElement.m_proxyType,
                 neighborElement.m_remoteIpAddress,
                 neighborElement.m_remotePort,
                 neighborElement.m_remoteScopeId,
                 neighborElement.m_ipVersion,
                 neighborElement.m_oid);
        else
            neighbor = new TcpTlsNeighbor
                (neighborElement.m_passthrough,
```

```java
                        neighborElement.m_proxyIpAddress,
                        neighborElement.m_proxyPort,
                        neighborElement.m_proxyType,
                        neighborElement.m_remoteIpAddress,
                        neighborElement.m_remotePort,
                        neighborElement.m_remoteScopeId,
                        neighborElement.m_ipVersion,
                        neighborElement.m_oid);
            }
            else if(neighborElement.m_transport.equals("UDP"))
            {
                try
                {
                    InetAddress inetAddress = InetAddress.getByName
                        (neighborElement.m_remoteIpAddress);

                    if(inetAddress.isMulticastAddress())
                        neighbor = new UdpMulticastNeighbor
                            (neighborElement.m_passthrough,
                             neighborElement.m_remoteIpAddress,
                             neighborElement.m_remotePort,
                             neighborElement.m_remoteScopeId,
                             neighborElement.m_ipVersion,
                             neighborElement.m_oid);
                    else
                        neighbor = new UdpNeighbor
                            (neighborElement.m_passthrough,
                             neighborElement.m_remoteIpAddress,
                             neighborElement.m_remotePort,
                             neighborElement.m_remoteScopeId,
                             neighborElement.m_ipVersion,
                             neighborElement.m_oid);
                }
                catch(Exception exception)
                {
                }
            }

            if(neighbor == null)
                continue;

            m_neighborsMutex.writeLock().lock();

            try
            {
                m_neighbors.append(neighborElement.m_oid, neighbor);
            }
            catch(Exception exception)
            {
            }
            finally
            {
                m_neighborsMutex.writeLock().unlock();
            }
        }

        neighbors.clear();
    }

    private void prepareSchedulers()
    {
        if(m_callScheduler == null)
        {
```

```java
m_callScheduler = Executors.newSingleThreadScheduledExecutor();
m_callScheduler.scheduleAtFixedRate(new Runnable()
{
    @Override
    public void run()
    {
        try
        {
            boolean empty = false;

            m_callQueueMutex.readLock().lock();

            try
            {
                empty = m_callQueue.isEmpty();
            }
            catch(Exception exception)
            {
                empty = false;
            }
            finally
            {
                m_callQueueMutex.readLock().unlock();
            }

            if(empty)
                synchronized(m_callSchedulerMutex)
                {
                    try
                    {
                        m_callSchedulerMutex.wait();
                    }
                    catch(Exception exception)
                    {
                    }
                }

            ParticipantCall participantCall = null;
            String sipHashId = "";

            /*
            ** Allow the UI to respond to calling requests
            ** while the kernel attempts to generate
            ** ephemeral keys.
            */

            m_callQueueMutex.writeLock().lock();

            try
            {
                if(m_callQueue.isEmpty())
                    return;

                /*
                ** Remove expired calls.
                */

                Iterator<Hashtable.Entry<String, ParticipantCall> >
                    it = m_callQueue.entrySet().iterator();

                while(it.hasNext())
                {
                    Hashtable.Entry<String, ParticipantCall> entry =
```

```java
                    it.next();

                if(entry.getValue() == null)
                {
                    it.remove();
                    continue;
                }

                if((System.nanoTime() - entry.getValue().
                    m_startTime) / 1000000L > CALL_LIFETIME)
                    it.remove();
            }

            /*
            ** Discover a pending call.
            */

            int participantOid = -1;

            for(String string : m_callQueue.keySet())
            {
                if(m_callQueue.get(string).m_keyPair != null)
                    continue;

                participantOid = m_callQueue.get(string).
                    m_participantOid;
                sipHashId = string;
                break;
            }

            if(participantOid == -1)
                /*
                ** A new call does not exist.
                */

                return;

            participantCall = m_callQueue.get(sipHashId);
        }
    catch(Exception exception)
    {
    }
    finally
    {
        m_callQueueMutex.writeLock().unlock();
    }

    if(participantCall == null)
        return;
    else
        participantCall.preparePrivatePublicKey();

    m_callQueueMutex.writeLock().lock();

    try
    {
        /*
        ** The entry may have been removed.
        */

        if(m_callQueue.containsKey(sipHashId))
            m_callQueue.put(sipHashId, participantCall);
    }
```

```java
            catch(Exception exception)
            {
            }
            finally
            {
                m_callQueueMutex.writeLock().unlock();
            }

            if(isConnected())
            {
                byte publicKeyType = Cryptography.
                    MESSAGES_KEY_TYPES[0];

                if(participantCall.m_algorithm ==
                    ParticipantCall.Algorithms.RSA)
                    publicKeyType =
                        Cryptography.MESSAGES_KEY_TYPES[1];

                /*
                ** Place a call request to all neighbors.
                */

                byte bytes[] = Messages.callMessage
                    (s_cryptography,
                     participantCall.m_sipHashId,
                     participantCall.m_keyPair.getPublic().
                     getEncoded(),
                     publicKeyType,
                     Messages.CALL_HALF_AND_HALF_TAGS[0]);

                if(bytes != null)
                    scheduleSend
                        (Messages.bytesToMessageString(bytes));
            }
        }
        catch(Exception exception)
        {
        }
    }
}, 1500L, CALL_INTERVAL, TimeUnit.MILLISECONDS);
    }

    if(m_messagesToSendScheduler == null)
    {
        m_messagesToSendScheduler = Executors.
            newSingleThreadScheduledExecutor();
        m_messagesToSendScheduler.scheduleAtFixedRate(new Runnable()
        {
            @Override
            public void run()
            {
                try
                {
                    MessageElement messageElement = null;
                    boolean empty = false;

                    m_messagesToSendMutex.writeLock().lock();

                    try
                    {
                        if(!m_messagesToSend.isEmpty())
                        {
                            messageElement = m_messagesToSend.get
```

```java
                (m_messagesToSend.size() - 1);

            if(messageElement == null)
            {
                m_messagesToSend.remove
                    (m_messagesToSend.size() - 1);
                return;
            }

            long delay = messageElement.m_delay;

            if(delay > 0)
            {
                long delta = System.currentTimeMillis() -
                    messageElement.m_timestamp;

                if(delay > delta)
                    return;
                else
                    m_messagesToSend.remove
                        (m_messagesToSend.size() - 1);
            }
            else
                m_messagesToSend.remove
                    (m_messagesToSend.size() - 1);
        }
        else
            empty = true;
    }
    catch(Exception exception)
    {
    }
    finally
    {
        m_messagesToSendMutex.writeLock().unlock();
    }

    if(empty)
        synchronized(m_messagesToSendSchedulerMutex)
        {
            try
            {
                m_messagesToSendSchedulerMutex.wait();
            }
            catch(Exception exception)
            {
            }
        }

    if(messageElement == null)
        return;
    else
        messageElement.m_timestamp =
            System.currentTimeMillis();

    byte bytes[] = null;

    try
    {
        switch(messageElement.m_messageType)
        {
        case MessageElement.CHAT_MESSAGE_TYPE:
        case MessageElement.RESEND_CHAT_MESSAGE_TYPE:
```

```java
            if(messageElement.m_messageType ==
               MessageElement.RESEND_CHAT_MESSAGE_TYPE)
            {
                MemberChatElement memberChatElement =
                    s_databaseHelper.readMemberChat
                    (s_cryptography,
                     messageElement.m_id,
                     messageElement.m_position);

                if(memberChatElement != null)
                {
                    messageElement.m_attachment =
                        memberChatElement.m_attachment;
                    messageElement.m_keyStream =
                        s_databaseHelper.
                        participantKeyStream
                        (s_cryptography,
                         messageElement.m_id);
                    messageElement.m_message =
                        memberChatElement.m_message;
                }
            }

            bytes = Messages.chatMessage
                (s_cryptography,
                 messageElement.m_message,
                 messageElement.m_id,
                 messageElement.m_attachment,
                 Cryptography.
                 sha512(messageElement.m_id.
                        getBytes(StandardCharsets.UTF_8)),
                 messageElement.m_keyStream,
                 messageElement.m_messageIdentity,
                 State.getInstance().
                 chatSequence(messageElement.m_id),
                 messageElement.m_timestamp);
            s_databaseHelper.writeParticipantMessage
                (s_cryptography,
                 "local",
                 messageElement.m_message,
                 messageElement.m_id,
                 messageElement.m_attachment,
                 messageElement.m_messageIdentity,
                 messageElement.m_timestamp);

            Intent intent = new Intent
                ("org.purple.smoke.chat_local_message");

            intent.putExtra
                ("org.purple.smoke.message",
                 messageElement.m_message);
            intent.putExtra
                ("org.purple.smoke.sipHashId",
                 messageElement.m_id);
            Miscellaneous.sendBroadcast(intent);
            break;
        case MessageElement.FIRE_MESSAGE_TYPE:
            bytes = Messages.fireMessage
                (s_cryptography,
                 messageElement.m_id,
                 messageElement.m_message,
                 s_databaseHelper.
                 readSetting(s_cryptography,
```

```java
                                     "fire_user_name"),
                    messageElement.m_keyStream);
                break;
            case MessageElement.FIRE_STATUS_MESSAGE_TYPE:
                bytes = Messages.fireStatus
                    (s_cryptography,
                     messageElement.m_id,
                     s_databaseHelper.
                     readSetting(s_cryptography,
                                 "fire_user_name"),
                     messageElement.m_keyStream);
                break;
            case MessageElement.JUGGERNAUT_MESSAGE_TYPE:
                m_juggernautsMutex.readLock().lock();

                try
                {
                    Juggernaut juggernaut = m_juggernauts.
                        get(messageElement.m_id);

                    if(juggernaut.state() ==
                       JPAKEParticipant.STATE_INITIALIZED)
                        bytes = juggernaut.next(null).
                            getBytes();
                    else
                        bytes = null;
                }
                catch(Exception exception)
                {
                    bytes = null;
                }
                finally
                {
                    m_juggernautsMutex.readLock().unlock();
                }

                if(bytes != null)
                    bytes = Messages.juggernautMessage
                        (s_cryptography,
                         messageElement.m_id,
                         bytes,
                         messageElement.m_keyStream);

                if(bytes != null)
                {
                    s_databaseHelper.writeParticipantMessage
                        (s_cryptography,
                         "local-protocol",
                         "Juggernaut Protocol initiated.",
                         messageElement.m_id,
                         null,
                         null,
                         messageElement.m_timestamp);
                    Miscellaneous.sendBroadcast
                        ("org.purple.smoke." +
                         "notify_data_set_changed");
                }

                break;
            case MessageElement.RETRIEVE_MESSAGES_MESSAGE_TYPE:
                bytes = Messages.chatMessageRetrieval
                    (s_cryptography);
```

```java
                        if(!messageElement.m_id.isEmpty())
                        {
                            s_databaseHelper.writeParticipantMessage
                                (s_cryptography,
                                 "local-protocol",
                                 "Requesting messages from " +
                                 "SmokeStack(s).",
                                 messageElement.m_id,
                                 null,
                                 null,
                                 messageElement.m_timestamp);
                            Miscellaneous.sendBroadcast
                                ("org.purple.smoke." +
                                 "notify_data_set_changed");
                        }

                    break;
                case MessageElement.SHARE_SIPHASH_ID_MESSAGE_TYPE:
                    m_shareSipHashIdIdentity.set
                        (Miscellaneous.
                         byteArrayToLong
                         (Cryptography.
                          randomBytes(Cryptography.IDENTITY_SIZE)));
                    m_shareSipHashIdIdentityLastTick.set
                        (System.currentTimeMillis());

                    if(messageElement.m_id.equals("-1"))
                        bytes = Messages.shareSipHashIdMessage
                            (s_cryptography,
                             s_cryptography.sipHashId(),
                             m_shareSipHashIdIdentity.get());
                    else
                    {
                        String sipHashId = s_databaseHelper.
                            readSipHashIdString
                            (s_cryptography,
                             messageElement.m_id);

                        bytes = Messages.shareSipHashIdMessage
                            (s_cryptography,
                             sipHashId,
                             m_shareSipHashIdIdentity.get());
                    }

                    break;
                case MessageElement.
                    STEAM_KEY_EXCHANGE_MESSAGE_TYPE:
                    bytes = new byte[1];
                    break;
                default:
                    break;
                }
            }
        catch(Exception exception)
        {
            bytes = null;
        }

        try
        {
            if(bytes != null)
            {
                switch(messageElement.m_messageType)
```

```java
                            {
                            case MessageElement.CHAT_MESSAGE_TYPE:
                            case MessageElement.RESEND_CHAT_MESSAGE_TYPE:
                                enqueueMessage
                                    (Messages.
                                     bytesToMessageString(bytes),
                                     messageElement.m_messageIdentity);

                                if(messageElement.m_messageType !=
                                    MessageElement.
                                    RESEND_CHAT_MESSAGE_TYPE)
                                    State.getInstance().
                                        incrementChatSequence
                                        (messageElement.m_id);

                                break;
                            case MessageElement.FIRE_MESSAGE_TYPE:
                                enqueueMessage
                                    (Messages.
                                     bytesToMessageStringNonBase64(bytes),
                                     null);
                                break;
                            case MessageElement.FIRE_STATUS_MESSAGE_TYPE:
                                scheduleSend
                                    (Messages.
                                     bytesToMessageStringNonBase64
                                     (bytes));
                                break;
                            case MessageElement.JUGGERNAUT_MESSAGE_TYPE:
                                scheduleSend
                                    (Messages.
                                     bytesToMessageString(bytes));
                                break;
                            case MessageElement.
                                RETRIEVE_MESSAGES_MESSAGE_TYPE:
                                scheduleSend
                                    (Messages.
                                     identityMessage
                                     (messageRetrievalIdentity()));
                                scheduleSend
                                    (Messages.
                                     bytesToMessageString(bytes));
                                break;
                            case MessageElement.
                                SHARE_SIPHASH_ID_MESSAGE_TYPE:
                                enqueueMessage
                                    (Messages.
                                     bytesToMessageString(bytes),
                                     null);
                                break;
                            case MessageElement.
                                STEAM_KEY_EXCHANGE_MESSAGE_TYPE:
                                enqueueMessage
                                    (messageElement.m_message, null);
                                break;
                            default:
                                break;
                            }
                        }
                    }
                catch(Exception exception)
                    {
                    }
```

```java
                    switch(messageElement.m_messageType)
                    {
                    case MessageElement.CHAT_MESSAGE_TYPE:
                    case MessageElement.RESEND_CHAT_MESSAGE_TYPE:
                        if(s_cryptography.hasValidOzoneMacKey())
                        {
                            bytes = Messages.chatMessage
                                (s_cryptography,
                                 messageElement.m_message,
                                 messageElement.m_id,
                                 messageElement.m_attachment,
                                 null,
                                 messageElement.m_keyStream,
                                 messageElement.m_messageIdentity,
                                 State.getInstance().
                                 chatSequence(messageElement.m_id),
                                 messageElement.m_timestamp);

                            if(bytes != null)
                                enqueueMessage
                                    ("OZONE-" + Base64.
                                     encodeToString(bytes,
                                             Base64.NO_WRAP),
                                     null);
                        }

                        break;
                    default:
                        break;
                    }
                }
                catch(Exception exception)
                {
                }
            }
        }, 1500L, MESSAGES_TO_SEND_INTERVAL, TimeUnit.MILLISECONDS);
    }

    if(m_neighborsScheduler == null)
    {
        m_neighborsScheduler =
Executors.newSingleThreadScheduledExecutor();
        m_neighborsScheduler.scheduleAtFixedRate(new Runnable()
        {
            @Override
            public void run()
            {
                try
                {
                    prepareNeighbors();
                }
                catch(Exception exception)
                {
                }
            }
        }, 1500L, NEIGHBORS_INTERVAL, TimeUnit.MILLISECONDS);
    }

    if(m_networkStatusScheduler == null)
    {
        m_networkStatusScheduler = Executors.
            newSingleThreadScheduledExecutor();
```

```java
        m_networkStatusScheduler.scheduleAtFixedRate(new Runnable()
        {
            private AtomicBoolean m_connected = new AtomicBoolean(false);

            @Override
            public void run()
            {
                try
                {
                    boolean isConnected = isConnected();

                    if(isConnected != m_connected.get())
                    {
                        if(isConnected)
                            Miscellaneous.sendBroadcast
                                ("org.purple.smoke.network_connected");
                        else
                            Miscellaneous.sendBroadcast
                                ("org.purple.smoke.network_disconnected");

                        m_connected.set(isConnected);
                    }
                }
                catch(Exception exception)
                {
                }
            }
        }, 1500L, NETWORK_STATUS_INTERVAL, TimeUnit.MILLISECONDS);
    }

    if(m_publishKeysScheduler == null)
    {
        m_publishKeysScheduler = Executors.
            newSingleThreadScheduledExecutor();
        m_publishKeysScheduler.scheduleAtFixedRate(new Runnable()
        {
            private byte m_state = 0x00;

            @Override
            public void run()
            {
                try
                {
                    if(!isConnected())
                        return;

                    if(m_state == 0x00)
                    {
                        /*
                        ** EPKS!
                        */

                        m_state = 0x01;

                        ArrayList<SipHashIdElement> arrayList =
                            s_databaseHelper.readNonSharedSipHashIds
                            (s_cryptography);

                        if(arrayList != null)
                        {
                            for(SipHashIdElement sipHashIdElement :
                                    arrayList)
                            {
```

```
                            if(sipHashIdElement == null)
                                continue;

                            byte bytes[] = Messages.epksMessage
                                (s_cryptography,
                                 sipHashIdElement.m_sipHashId,
                                 sipHashIdElement.m_stream,
                                 Messages.CHAT_KEY_TYPE);

                            if(bytes != null)
                                enqueueMessage
                                    (Messages.
                                     bytesToMessageString(bytes),
                                     null);
                        }

                        arrayList.clear();
                    }
                }
                else
                {
                    /*
                    ** Request keys!
                    */

                    m_state = 0x00;

                    ArrayList<SipHashIdElement> arrayList =
                        s_databaseHelper.readNonSharedSipHashIds
                        (s_cryptography);

                    if(arrayList != null)
                    {
                        for(SipHashIdElement sipHashIdElement :
                                arrayList)
                        {
                            if(sipHashIdElement == null)
                                continue;

                            byte bytes[] = Messages.pkpRequestMessage
                                (s_cryptography,
                                 sipHashIdElement.m_sipHashId);

                            if(bytes != null)
                                enqueueMessage
                                    (Messages.
                                     bytesToMessageString(bytes),
                                     null);
                        }

                        arrayList.clear();
                    }
                }
            }
            catch(Exception exception)
            {
            }
        }
    }, 1500L, PUBLISH_KEYS_INTERVAL, TimeUnit.MILLISECONDS);
}

if(m_purgeScheduler == null)
{
```

```java
        m_purgeScheduler = Executors.newSingleThreadScheduledExecutor();
        m_purgeScheduler.scheduleAtFixedRate(new Runnable()
        {
            @Override
            public void run()
            {
                m_juggernautsMutex.writeLock().lock();

                try
                {
                }
                catch(Exception exception)
                {
                    Iterator<Hashtable.Entry<String, Juggernaut> >
                        it = m_juggernauts.entrySet().iterator();

                    while(it.hasNext())
                    {
                        Hashtable.Entry<String, Juggernaut> entry =
                            it.next();

                        if(entry.getValue() == null)
                        {
                            it.remove();
                            continue;
                        }

                        if((System.currentTimeMillis() -
                            entry.getValue().lastEventTime()) >
                            JUGGERNAUT_LIFETIME)
                            it.remove();
                    }
                }
                finally
                {
                    m_juggernautsMutex.writeLock().unlock();
                }

                try
                {
                    s_databaseHelper.purgeCongestion(CONGESTION_LIFETIME);
                    s_databaseHelper.purgeParticipantsKeyStreams
                        (PARTICIPANTS_KEYSTREAMS_LIFETIME);
                }
                catch(Exception exception)
                {
                }
            }
        }, 1500L, PURGE_INTERVAL, TimeUnit.MILLISECONDS);
    }

    if(m_requestMessagesScheduler == null)
    {
        m_requestMessagesScheduler = Executors.
            newSingleThreadScheduledExecutor();
        m_requestMessagesScheduler.scheduleAtFixedRate(new Runnable()
        {
            @Override
            public void run()
            {
                if(isConnected() && s_cryptography.ozoneMacKey() != null)
                    retrieveChatMessages("");
            }
```

```java
        }, 10000L, REQUEST_MESSAGES_INTERVAL, TimeUnit.MILLISECONDS);
    }

    if(m_statusScheduler == null)
    {
        m_statusScheduler = Executors.newSingleThreadScheduledExecutor();
        m_statusScheduler.scheduleAtFixedRate(new Runnable()
        {
            @Override
            public void run()
            {
                try
                {
                    if(!isConnected())
                        return;

                    ArrayList<ParticipantElement> arrayList =
                        s_databaseHelper.
                        readParticipants(s_cryptography, "");

                    if(arrayList == null || arrayList.isEmpty())
                        return;

                    for(ParticipantElement participantElement : arrayList)
                        if(participantElement != null)
                        {
                            byte bytes[] = Messages.chatStatus
                                (s_cryptography,
                                 participantElement.m_sipHashId,
                                 participantElement.m_keyStream);

                            if(bytes != null)
                                scheduleSend
                                    (Messages.bytesToMessageString(bytes));
                        }

                    arrayList.clear();
                }
                catch(Exception exception)
                {
                }
            }
        }, 1500L, STATUS_INTERVAL, TimeUnit.MILLISECONDS);
    }

    if(m_steamScheduler == null)
    {
        m_steamScheduler = Executors.newSingleThreadScheduledExecutor();
        m_steamScheduler.scheduleAtFixedRate(new Runnable()
        {
            @Override
            public void run()
            {
                try
                {
                    prepareSteams();
                }
                catch(Exception exception)
                {
                }
            }
        }, 1500L, STEAM_INTERVAL, TimeUnit.MILLISECONDS);
    }
```

```java
    if(m_temporaryIdentityScheduler == null)
    {
        m_temporaryIdentityScheduler = Executors.
            newSingleThreadScheduledExecutor();
        m_temporaryIdentityScheduler.scheduleAtFixedRate(new Runnable()
        {
            @Override
            public void run()
            {
                m_chatMessageRetrievalIdentityMutex.writeLock().lock();

                try
                {
                    if(System.currentTimeMillis() -
                        m_chatTemporaryIdentityLastTick.get() >
                        TEMPORARY_IDENTITY_LIFETIME)
                         m_chatMessageRetrievalIdentity = null;
                }
                catch(Exception exception)
                {
                }
                finally
                {
                    m_chatMessageRetrievalIdentityMutex.
                        writeLock().unlock();
                }

                if(System.currentTimeMillis() -
                    m_shareSipHashIdIdentityLastTick.get() >
                    TEMPORARY_IDENTITY_LIFETIME)
                    m_shareSipHashIdIdentity.set(0L);
            }
        }, 1500L, TEMPORARY_IDENTITY_INTERVAL, TimeUnit.MILLISECONDS);
    }
}

private void prepareSteams()
{
    if(!State.getInstance().isAuthenticated())
        return;

    ArrayList<SteamElement> steams = purgeDeletedSteams();

    if(steams == null)
        return;

    for(SteamElement steamElement : steams)
    {
        if(steamElement == null)
            continue;
        else
        {
            m_steamsMutex.readLock().lock();

            try
            {
                if(m_steams.get(steamElement.m_oid) != null)
                    continue;
            }
            catch(Exception exception)
            {
            }
```

```java
            finally
            {
                m_steamsMutex.readLock().unlock();
            }
        }

        SteamReader steam = null;

        if(steamElement.m_destination.equals(Steam.OTHER))
            steam = new SteamReaderSimple(steamElement.m_fileName,
                                    steamElement.m_oid,
                                    steamElement.m_readInterval,
                                    steamElement.m_readOffset);
        else
            steam = new SteamReaderFull(steamElement.m_destination,
                                    steamElement.m_fileName,
                                    steamElement.m_fileIdentity,
                                    steamElement.m_oid,
                                    steamElement.m_fileSize,
                                    steamElement.m_readOffset);

        if(steam == null)
            continue;

        m_steamsMutex.writeLock().lock();

        try
        {
            m_steams.append(steamElement.m_oid, steam);
        }
        catch(Exception exception)
        {
        }
        finally
        {
            m_steamsMutex.writeLock().unlock();
        }
    }

    steams.clear();
}

private void purgeNeighbors()
{
    /*
    ** Disconnect all existing sockets.
    */

    m_neighborsMutex.writeLock().lock();

    try
    {
        int size = m_neighbors.size();

        for(int i = 0; i < size; i++)
        {
            int j = m_neighbors.keyAt(i);

            if(m_neighbors.get(j) != null)
                m_neighbors.get(j).abort();
        }

        m_neighbors.clear();
```

```java
        }
        catch(Exception exception)
        {
        }
        finally
        {
            m_neighborsMutex.writeLock().unlock();
        }
    }

    private void purgeSteams()
    {
        m_steamsMutex.writeLock().lock();

        try
        {
            int size = m_steams.size();

            for(int i = 0; i < size; i++)
            {
                int j = m_steams.keyAt(i);

                if(m_steams.get(j) != null)
                    m_steams.get(j).delete();
            }

            m_steams.clear();
        }
        catch(Exception exception)
        {
        }
        finally
        {
            m_steamsMutex.writeLock().unlock();
        }
    }

    private void scheduleSend(String message)
    {
        if(message == null || message.trim().isEmpty())
            return;

        m_neighborsMutex.readLock().lock();

        try
        {
            int size = m_neighbors.size();

            for(int i = 0; i < size; i++)
            {
                int j = m_neighbors.keyAt(i);

                if(m_neighbors.get(j) != null)
                    if(!m_neighbors.get(j).passthrough())
                        m_neighbors.get(j).scheduleSend(message);
            }
        }
        catch(Exception exception)
        {
        }
        finally
        {
            m_neighborsMutex.readLock().unlock();
```

```java
        }
    }

    private void wakeMessagesToSendScheduler()
    {
        synchronized(m_messagesToSendSchedulerMutex)
        {
            m_messagesToSendSchedulerMutex.notify();
        }
    }

    public ArrayList<NeighborElement> purgeDeletedNeighbors()
    {
        ArrayList<NeighborElement> neighbors =
            s_databaseHelper.readNeighbors(s_cryptography);

        if(neighbors == null || neighbors.isEmpty())
        {
            purgeNeighbors();
            return neighbors;
        }

        m_neighborsMutex.writeLock().lock();

        try
        {
            /*
            ** Remove neighbor objects which do not exist in the database.
            ** Also removed will be neighbors having disconnected statuses.
            */

            for(int i = m_neighbors.size() - 1; i >= 0; i--)
            {
                boolean found = false;
                int oid = m_neighbors.keyAt(i);

                for(NeighborElement neighbor : neighbors)
                    if(neighbor != null && neighbor.m_oid == oid)
                    {
                        if(!neighbor.m_statusControl.toLowerCase().
                           equals("disconnect"))
                            found = true;

                        break;
                    }

                if(!found)
                {
                    if(m_neighbors.get(oid) != null)
                        m_neighbors.get(oid).abort();

                    m_neighbors.remove(oid);
                }
            }
        }
        catch(Exception exception)
        {
        }
        finally
        {
            m_neighborsMutex.writeLock().unlock();
        }
```

```java
        return neighbors;
    }

    public ArrayList<SteamElement> purgeDeletedSteams()
    {
        ArrayList<SteamElement> steams = s_databaseHelper.readSteams
            (s_cryptography, SteamElement.UPLOAD);

        if(steams == null || steams.isEmpty())
        {
            purgeSteams();
            return steams;
        }

        m_steamsMutex.writeLock().lock();

        try
        {
            /*
            ** Remove Steam objects which do not exist in the database.
            ** Also removed will be Steams having completed or deleted
            ** statuses.
            */

            for(int i = m_steams.size() - 1; i >= 0; i--)
            {
                boolean found = false;
                int oid = m_steams.keyAt(i);

                for(SteamElement steamElement : steams)
                    if(steamElement != null && steamElement.m_oid == oid)
                    {
                        String status = steamElement.m_status.toLowerCase();

                        if(!status.equals("completed") &&
                           !status.equals("deleted"))
                            found = true;

                        break;
                    }

                if(!found)
                {
                    if(m_steams.get(oid) != null)
                        m_steams.get(oid).delete();

                    m_steams.remove(oid);
                }
            }
        }
        catch(Exception exception)
        {
        }
        finally
        {
            m_steamsMutex.writeLock().unlock();
        }

        return steams;
    }

    public String connectedNeighborAddress()
    {
```

```java
        /*
        ** If a connected, non-passthrough neighbor is available, return its
        ** address. Otherwise, return the address of a connected, passthrough
        ** neighbor.
        */

        TreeSet<String> addresses = new TreeSet<String> ();

        m_neighborsMutex.readLock().lock();

        try
        {
            int size = m_neighbors.size();

            for(int i = 0; i < size; i++)
            {
                int j = m_neighbors.keyAt(i);

                if(m_neighbors.get(j) != null)
                    if(m_neighbors.get(j).connected())
                    {
                        if(m_neighbors.get(j).passthrough())
                            addresses.add
                                ("|" + m_neighbors.get(j).address() + "|");
                        else
                            addresses.add(m_neighbors.get(j).address());
                    }
            }
        }
        catch(Exception exception)
        {
        }
        finally
        {
            m_neighborsMutex.readLock().unlock();
        }

        if(addresses.isEmpty())
            return "";
        else
            return addresses.first().replace("|", "");
    }

    public String fireIdentities()
    {
        m_fireStreamsMutex.readLock().lock();

        try
        {
            if(!m_fireStreams.isEmpty())
            {
                StringBuilder stringBuilder = new StringBuilder();

                for(Hashtable.Entry<String, byte[]> entry :
                        m_fireStreams.entrySet())
                {
                    if(entry.getValue() == null)
                        continue;

                    stringBuilder.append
                        (Messages.
                         identityMessage
                         (Cryptography.
```

```java
                            sha512(Arrays.
                                copyOfRange(entry.getValue(),
                                        Cryptography.
                                        CIPHER_KEY_LENGTH +
                                        Cryptography.
                                        FIRE_HASH_KEY_LENGTH,
                                        entry.getValue().length))));
                }

                return stringBuilder.toString();
            }
        }
        catch(Exception exception)
        {
        }
        finally
        {
            m_fireStreamsMutex.readLock().unlock();
        }

        return "";
    }

    public boolean call(int participantOid,
                        ParticipantCall.Algorithms algorithm,
                        String sipHashId)
    {
        /*
        ** Calling messages are not placed in the outbound_queue
        ** as they are considered temporary.
        */

        m_callQueueMutex.writeLock().lock();

        try
        {
            if(m_callQueue.containsKey(sipHashId))
                return false;

            s_databaseHelper.writeParticipantMessage
                (s_cryptography,
                 "local-protocol",
                 "Preparing a call via " +
                 (algorithm == ParticipantCall.Algorithms.MCELIECE ?
                  "McEliece." : "RSA.") + " Please be patient.",
                 sipHashId,
                 null,
                 null,
                 System.currentTimeMillis());
            Miscellaneous.sendBroadcast
                ("org.purple.smoke.notify_data_set_changed");
            m_callQueue.put
                (sipHashId,
                 new ParticipantCall(algorithm, sipHashId, participantOid));
        }
        catch(Exception exception)
        {
        }
        finally
        {
            m_callQueueMutex.writeLock().unlock();
        }
```

```java
        synchronized(m_callSchedulerMutex)
        {
            m_callSchedulerMutex.notify();
        }

        return true;
    }

    public boolean enqueueMessage(String message, byte messageIdentity[])
    {
        if(message == null || message.trim().isEmpty())
            return false;

        ArrayList<NeighborElement> arrayList =
            s_databaseHelper.readNeighborOids(s_cryptography);

        if(arrayList == null || arrayList.isEmpty())
            return false;

        int size = arrayList.size();

        for(int i = 0; i < size; i++)
            if(arrayList.get(i) != null &&
                arrayList.get(i).m_passthrough.toLowerCase().equals("false") &&

arrayList.get(i).m_statusControl.toLowerCase().equals("connect"))
                s_databaseHelper.enqueueOutboundMessage
                    (s_cryptography,
                     message,
                     messageIdentity,
                     arrayList.get(i).m_oid);

        arrayList.clear();
        return true;
    }

    public boolean igniteFire(String name)
    {
        m_fireStreamsMutex.writeLock().lock();

        try
        {
            if(!m_fireStreams.containsKey(name))
            {
                byte bytes[] = s_databaseHelper.fireStream
                    (s_cryptography, name);

                if(bytes != null)
                {
                    m_fireStreams.put(name, bytes);
                    return true;
                }
            }
        }
        catch(Exception exception)
        {
        }
        finally
        {
            m_fireStreamsMutex.writeLock().unlock();
        }

        return false;
```

```java
    }

    public boolean isConnected()
    {
        if(!isNetworkConnected())
            return false;

        m_neighborsMutex.readLock().lock();

        try
        {
            int size = m_neighbors.size();

            for(int i = 0; i < size; i++)
            {
                int j = m_neighbors.keyAt(i);

                if(m_neighbors.get(j) != null)
                    if(m_neighbors.get(j).connected() &&
                        !m_neighbors.get(j).passthrough())
                        return true;
            }
        }
        catch(Exception exception)
        {
        }
        finally
        {
            m_neighborsMutex.readLock().unlock();
        }

        return false;
    }

    public boolean isNetworkConnected()
    {
        try
        {
            ConnectivityManager connectivityManager = (ConnectivityManager)
                Smoke.getApplication().getApplicationContext().
                getSystemService(Context.CONNECTIVITY_SERVICE);
            NetworkInfo networkInfo = connectivityManager.
                getActiveNetworkInfo();

            return networkInfo != null &&
                networkInfo.getType() == ConnectivityManager.TYPE_WIFI &&
                networkInfo.isConnected();
        }
        catch(Exception exception)
        {
        }

        return false;
    }

    public boolean wakeLocked()
    {
        if(m_wakeLock != null)
            return m_wakeLock.isHeld();

        return false;
    }
```

```java
public boolean wifiLocked()
{
    if(m_wifiLock != null)
        return m_wifiLock.isHeld();

    return false;
}

public byte[] messageRetrievalIdentity()
{
    m_chatMessageRetrievalIdentityMutex.writeLock().lock();

    try
    {
        if(m_chatMessageRetrievalIdentity == null)
        {
            m_chatMessageRetrievalIdentity =
                Cryptography.randomBytes(Cryptography.HASH_KEY_LENGTH);
            m_chatTemporaryIdentityLastTick.set(System.currentTimeMillis());
        }

        return m_chatMessageRetrievalIdentity;
    }
    catch(Exception exception)
    {
    }
    finally
    {
        m_chatMessageRetrievalIdentityMutex.writeLock().unlock();
    }

    return null;
}

public int availableNeighbors()
{
    m_neighborsMutex.readLock().lock();

    try
    {
        return m_neighbors.size();
    }
    catch(Exception exception)
    {
    }
    finally
    {
        m_neighborsMutex.readLock().unlock();
    }

    return 0;
}

public int nextSimpleSteamOid()
{
    /*
    ** Discover the oldest, incomplete Simple Steam.
    */

    m_steamsMutex.readLock().lock();

    try
    {
```

```java
            int size = m_steams.size();

            for(int i = 0; i < size; i++)
            {
                int j = m_steams.keyAt(i);

                if(m_steams.get(j) instanceof SteamReaderSimple &&
                   m_steams.get(j).completed() == false)
                    return m_steams.get(j).getOid();
            }
        }
        catch(Exception exception)
        {
        }
        finally
        {
            m_steamsMutex.readLock().unlock();
        }

        return -1;
    }

    public int ourMessage(String buffer)
    {
        /*
        ** 0 - Echo
        ** 1 - Fine (Do not Echo)
        ** 2 - Force Echo
        */

        if(buffer == null)
            return 1;

        try
        {
            long value = s_congestionSipHash.hmac
                (buffer.getBytes(), Cryptography.SIPHASH_OUTPUT_LENGTH / 2)[0];

            if(s_databaseHelper.containsCongestionDigest(value))
                return 1;
            else if(s_databaseHelper.writeCongestionDigest(value))
                return 1;

            /*
            ** Fire!
            */

            m_fireStreamsMutex.readLock().lock();

            try
            {
                if(!m_fireStreams.isEmpty())
                {
                    String strings[] = Messages.stripMessage(buffer).
                        split("\\n");

                    if(strings != null && strings.length >= 2)
                    {
                        byte ciphertext[] = Base64.decode
                            (strings[0], Base64.NO_WRAP);
                        byte hmac[] = Base64.decode
                            (strings[1], Base64.NO_WRAP);
```

```java
for(Hashtable.Entry<String, byte[]> entry :
        m_fireStreams.entrySet())
{
    if(entry.getValue() == null)
        continue;

    if(Cryptography.
        memcmp
        (Cryptography.
        hmacFire(ciphertext,
                Arrays.
                copyOfRange(entry.getValue(),
                        Cryptography.
                        CIPHER_KEY_LENGTH,
                        Cryptography.
                        CIPHER_KEY_LENGTH +
                        Cryptography.
                        FIRE_HASH_KEY_LENGTH)),
        hmac))
    {
        ciphertext = Cryptography.decryptFire
            (ciphertext,
             Arrays.copyOfRange(entry.getValue(),
                        0,
                        Cryptography.
                        CIPHER_KEY_LENGTH));

        if(ciphertext == null)
            return 1;

        ciphertext = Arrays.copyOfRange

            /*
            ** Remove the size information of the
            ** original data.
            */

            (ciphertext, 0, ciphertext.length - 4);
        strings = new String(ciphertext).split("\\n");

        if(!(strings.length == 4 ||
            strings.length == 5))
            return 1;

        strings[strings.length - 1] = new
            String(Base64.
                decode(strings[strings.length - 1],
                    Base64.NO_WRAP));

        Date date = s_fireSimpleDateFormat.parse
            (strings[strings.length - 1]);
        Timestamp timestamp = new Timestamp
            (date.getTime());

        if(Math.abs(System.currentTimeMillis() -
                timestamp.getTime()) >
            FIRE_TIME_DELTA)
            return 1;

        int length = strings.length - 1;

        for(int i = 0; i < length; i++)
            strings[i] = new String
```

```java
                                    (Base64.decode(strings[i],
                                               Base64.NO_WRAP),
                                    StandardCharsets.UTF_8);

                        value = s_congestionSipHash.hmac
                            (("fire" +
                              entry.getKey() +
                              strings[2] +
                              strings[3] +
                              timestamp).getBytes(),
                             Cryptography.SIPHASH_OUTPUT_LENGTH / 2)[0];

                        if(s_databaseHelper.
                           writeCongestionDigest(value))
                            return 1;

                        Intent intent = new Intent
                            ("org.purple.smoke.fire_message");

                        intent.putExtra
                            ("org.purple.smoke.channel",
                             entry.getKey());
                        intent.putExtra
                            ("org.purple.smoke.id", strings[2]);
                        intent.putExtra
                            ("org.purple.smoke.message_type",
                             strings[0]);
                        intent.putExtra
                            ("org.purple.smoke.name", strings[1]);

                        if(strings[0].
                           equals(Messages.FIRE_CHAT_MESSAGE_TYPE))
                            intent.putExtra
                                ("org.purple.smoke.message",
                                 strings[3]);

                        Miscellaneous.sendBroadcast(intent);
                        return 2; // Echo Fire!
                    }
                }
            }
        }
    }
    catch(Exception exception)
    {
    }
    finally
    {
        m_fireStreamsMutex.readLock().unlock();
    }

    byte bytes[] =
        Base64.decode(Messages.stripMessage(buffer), Base64.DEFAULT);

    if(bytes == null || bytes.length < 128)
        return 0;

    /*
    ** Ozone!
    */

    if(m_shareSipHashIdIdentity.get() != 0 &&
       s_cryptography.ozoneEncryptionKey() != null &&
```

```java
        s_cryptography.ozoneMacKey() != null)
    {
        byte data[] = Arrays.copyOfRange
            (bytes,
             0,
             bytes.length - 2 * Cryptography.HASH_KEY_LENGTH);
        byte hmac[] = Arrays.copyOfRange
            (bytes,
             bytes.length - 2 * Cryptography.HASH_KEY_LENGTH,
             bytes.length - Cryptography.HASH_KEY_LENGTH);

        if(Cryptography.
           memcmp(hmac,
                  Cryptography.hmac(data,
                                    s_cryptography.ozoneMacKey())))
        {
            byte ciphertext[] = Cryptography.decrypt
                (data, s_cryptography.ozoneEncryptionKey());

            if(ciphertext == null)
                return 1;

            long timestamp = Miscellaneous.byteArrayToLong
                (Arrays.copyOfRange(ciphertext, 1, 9));

            if(Math.abs(System.currentTimeMillis() - timestamp) >
               SHARE_SIPHASH_ID_CONFIRMATION_WINDOW)
                return 1;

            /*
            ** Did we share something?
            */

            long identity = Miscellaneous.byteArrayToLong
                (Arrays.
                 copyOfRange(ciphertext,
                             9 + Cryptography.SIPHASH_IDENTITY_LENGTH,
                             9 +
                             Cryptography.IDENTITY_SIZE +
                             Cryptography.SIPHASH_IDENTITY_LENGTH));

            if(identity != m_shareSipHashIdIdentity.get())
                return 1;

            m_shareSipHashIdIdentity.set(0L);

            Intent intent = new Intent
                ("org.purple.smoke.siphash_share_confirmation");
            String sipHashId = new String
                (Arrays.
                 copyOfRange(ciphertext,
                             9,
                             9 + Cryptography.SIPHASH_IDENTITY_LENGTH),
                 StandardCharsets.UTF_8);

            intent.putExtra("org.purple.smoke.sipHashId", sipHashId);
            Miscellaneous.sendBroadcast(intent);
            return 1;
        }
    }

    boolean ourMessageViaChatTemporaryIdentity = false; /*
                                        ** Did the
```

```java
                                                    ** message
                                                    ** arrive from
                                                    ** SmokeStack?
                                                    */
            byte data[] = Arrays.copyOfRange // Blocks #1, #2, etc.
                (bytes, 0, bytes.length - 2 * Cryptography.HASH_KEY_LENGTH);
            byte destination[] = Arrays.copyOfRange
                (bytes,
                 bytes.length - Cryptography.HASH_KEY_LENGTH,
                 bytes.length);
            byte hmac[] = Arrays.copyOfRange
                (bytes,
                 bytes.length - 2 * Cryptography.HASH_KEY_LENGTH,
                 bytes.length - Cryptography.HASH_KEY_LENGTH);
            byte sha512OfMessage[] = Cryptography.sha512
                (Arrays.
                 copyOfRange(bytes,
                            0,
                            bytes.length - Cryptography.HASH_KEY_LENGTH));

            m_chatMessageRetrievalIdentityMutex.readLock().lock();

            try
            {
                if(m_chatMessageRetrievalIdentity != null)
                    if(Cryptography.
                       memcmp(Cryptography.hmac(Arrays.
                                                copyOfRange(bytes,
                                                            0,
                                                            bytes.length -
                                                            Cryptography.
                                                            HASH_KEY_LENGTH),
                                                m_chatMessageRetrievalIdentity),
                              destination))
                    {
                        m_chatTemporaryIdentityLastTick.set
                            (System.currentTimeMillis());
                        ourMessageViaChatTemporaryIdentity = true;
                    }
            }
            catch(Exception exception)
            {
            }
            finally
            {
                m_chatMessageRetrievalIdentityMutex.readLock().unlock();
            }

            /*
            ** What's the destination?
            */

            if(!ourMessageViaChatTemporaryIdentity)
                if(!s_cryptography.
                   iAmTheDestination(Arrays.copyOfRange(bytes,
                                                        0,
                                                        bytes.length -
                                                        Cryptography.
                                                        HASH_KEY_LENGTH),
                                     destination))
                    return 0;

            if(s_cryptography.isValidSipHashMac(data, hmac))
```

```java
    {
        /*
        ** EPKS
        */

        data = s_cryptography.decryptWithSipHashKey(data);

        String sipHashId = s_databaseHelper.writeParticipant
            (s_cryptography, data);

        if(!sipHashId.isEmpty())
        {
            /*
            ** New participant.
            */

            State.getInstance().populateParticipants();
            Miscellaneous.sendBroadcast
                ("org.purple.smoke.populate_participants");

            /*
            ** Response-share.
            */

            byte salt[] = Cryptography.sha512
                (sipHashId.trim().getBytes(StandardCharsets.UTF_8));
            byte temporary[] = Cryptography.
                pbkdf2(salt,
                       sipHashId.toCharArray(),
                       Database.
                       SIPHASH_STREAM_CREATION_ITERATION_COUNT,
                       160); // SHA-1

            if(temporary != null)
                bytes = Cryptography.
                    pbkdf2(salt,
                           Base64.encodeToString(temporary,
                                                 Base64.NO_WRAP).
                           toCharArray(),
                           1,
                           // Bits.
                           8 * (Cryptography.CIPHER_KEY_LENGTH +
                                Cryptography.HASH_KEY_LENGTH));
            else
                bytes = null;

            if(bytes != null)
                bytes = Messages.epksMessage
                    (s_cryptography,
                     sipHashId,
                     bytes,
                     Messages.CHAT_KEY_TYPE);

            if(bytes != null)
                enqueueMessage
                    (Messages.bytesToMessageString(bytes), null);
        }

        return 1;
    }

    byte pki[] = null;
    int pki_output_size = 0;
```

```java
        if(s_cryptography.chatEncryptionPublicKeyAlgorithm().
           startsWith("McEliece"))
        {
            int e = 0;
            int s = 0;

            if(s_cryptography.chatEncryptionPublicKeyAlgorithm().
               startsWith("McEliece-Fujisaki"))
            {
                int t = s_cryptography.chatEncryptionPublicKeyT();

                if(t == 50)
                {
                    e = 3;
                    s = 0;
                }
                else
                {
                    e = 9;
                    s = 6;
                }
            }
            else
            {
                e = 6;
                s = 3;
            }

            for(int i = s; i < e; i++)
            {
                pki = s_cryptography.pkiDecrypt
                    (Arrays.copyOfRange(bytes,
                                        0,
                                        MCELIECE_OUTPUT_SIZES[i]));

                if(pki != null)
                {
                    pki_output_size = MCELIECE_OUTPUT_SIZES[i];
                    break;
                }
            }
        }
        else
        {
            pki = s_cryptography.pkiDecrypt
                (Arrays.
                 copyOfRange(bytes,
                             0,
                             Cryptography.PKI_ENCRYPTION_KEY_SIZES[0] / 8));
            pki_output_size = Cryptography.PKI_ENCRYPTION_KEY_SIZES[0] / 8;
        }

        if(pki == null)
            return 1;

        if(pki.length == Cryptography.HASH_KEY_LENGTH)
        {
            /*
            ** Chat
            ** Chat Status
            ** Juggernaut
            ** Message-Read Proof
```

```java
                */

            byte keyStream[] = s_databaseHelper.participantKeyStream
                (s_cryptography, pki);

            if(keyStream == null)
                return 1;

            byte hmacc[] = Cryptography.hmac
                (Arrays.copyOfRange(bytes,
                                    0,
                                    bytes.length -
                                    2 * Cryptography.HASH_KEY_LENGTH),
                  Arrays.copyOfRange(keyStream,
                                    Cryptography.CIPHER_KEY_LENGTH,
                                    keyStream.length));

            if(!Cryptography.memcmp(hmac, hmacc))
            {
                if(ourMessageViaChatTemporaryIdentity)
                {
                    keyStream = s_databaseHelper.participantKeyStream
                        (s_cryptography, pki, hmac, bytes);

                    if(keyStream == null)
                        return 1;
                }
                else
                    return 1;
            }

            byte ciphertext[] = Cryptography.decrypt
                (Arrays.
                 copyOfRange(bytes,
                            pki_output_size,
                            bytes.length -
                            2 * Cryptography.HASH_KEY_LENGTH),
                  Arrays.copyOfRange(keyStream,
                                    0,
                                    Cryptography.CIPHER_KEY_LENGTH));

            if(ciphertext == null)
                return 1;

            byte abyte[] = new byte[] {ciphertext[0]};

            if(abyte[0] == Messages.CHAT_STATUS_MESSAGE_TYPE[0])
            {
                String array[] = s_databaseHelper.nameSipHashIdFromDigest
                    (s_cryptography, pki);

                if(array == null || array.length != 2)
                    return 1;

                String sipHashId = array[1];

                if(s_databaseHelper.readParticipantOptions(s_cryptography,
                                                           sipHashId).
                   contains("optional_signatures = false"))
                {
                    long timestamp = Miscellaneous.byteArrayToLong
                        (Arrays.copyOfRange(ciphertext, 1, 9));
```

```java
                    if(Math.abs(System.currentTimeMillis() - timestamp) >
                      Chat.STATUS_WINDOW)
                        return 1;

                    PublicKey signatureKey = s_databaseHelper.
                        signatureKeyForDigest(s_cryptography, pki);

                    if(signatureKey == null)
                        return 1;

                    if(!Cryptography.
                      verifySignature
                      (signatureKey,
                       Arrays.copyOfRange(ciphertext,
                                          10,
                                          ciphertext.length),
                        Miscellaneous.
                        joinByteArrays(pki,
                                       Arrays.
                                       copyOfRange(ciphertext,
                                                   0,
                                                   10),
                                       s_cryptography.
                                       chatEncryptionPublicKeyDigest())))
                        return 1;
                }

            s_databaseHelper.updateParticipantLastTimestamp
                (s_cryptography, pki);
            return 1;
        }
        else if(abyte[0] == Messages.JUGGERNAUT_TYPE[0])
        {
            ciphertext = Arrays.copyOfRange
                (ciphertext, 1, ciphertext.length);

            String payload = "";
            String strings[] = new String(ciphertext).split("\\n");
            int ii = 0;

            for(String string : strings)
                switch(ii)
                {
                case 0:
                    long timestamp = Miscellaneous.byteArrayToLong
                        (Base64.
                         decode(string.getBytes(), Base64.NO_WRAP));

                    if(Math.abs(System.currentTimeMillis() -
                                timestamp) > JUGGERNAUT_WINDOW)
                        return 1;

                    ii += 1;
                    break;
                case 1:
                    payload = new String
                        (Base64.
                         decode(string.getBytes(), Base64.NO_WRAP));
                    ii += 1;
                    break;
                case 2:
                    PublicKey signatureKey = s_databaseHelper.
                        signatureKeyForDigest(s_cryptography, pki);
```

```java
                    if(signatureKey == null)
                        return 1;

                    byte publicKeySignature[] = Base64.decode
                        (string.getBytes(), Base64.NO_WRAP);

                    if(!Cryptography.verifySignature
                        (signatureKey,
                        publicKeySignature,
                        Miscellaneous.
                        joinByteArrays
                        (pki,
                         abyte,
                         strings[0].getBytes(),
                         "\n".getBytes(),
                         strings[1].getBytes(),
                         "\n".getBytes(),
                         s_cryptography.
                         chatEncryptionPublicKeyDigest())))
                        return 1;

                break;
            default:
                break;
            }

        String array[] = s_databaseHelper.
            nameSipHashIdFromDigest(s_cryptography, pki);

        if(array == null || array.length != 2)
            return 1;

        byte sessionCredentials[] = null;
        int state = -1;

        m_juggernautsMutex.writeLock().lock();

        try
        {
            if(!m_juggernauts.containsKey(array[1]))
                /*
                ** Misplaced Juggernaut!
                */

                return 1;

            Juggernaut juggernaut = m_juggernauts.get(array[1]);

            if(juggernaut == null)
            {
                m_juggernauts.remove(array[1]);
                return 1;
            }

            if(juggernaut.state() ==
               JPAKEParticipant.STATE_INITIALIZED)
            {
                bytes = juggernaut.next(null).getBytes();
                bytes = Messages.juggernautMessage
                    (s_cryptography,
                     array[1],
                     bytes,
```

```java
                        keyStream);
                    scheduleSend
                        (Messages.bytesToMessageString(bytes));
                }

            bytes = juggernaut.next(payload).getBytes();

            if(bytes != null)
            {
                bytes = Messages.juggernautMessage
                    (s_cryptography,
                     array[1],
                     bytes,
                     keyStream);
                scheduleSend
                    (Messages.bytesToMessageString(bytes));
            }

            if((state = juggernaut.state()) ==
               JPAKEParticipant.STATE_ROUND_3_VALIDATED)
            {
                sessionCredentials = juggernaut.
                    deriveSessionCredentials();
                m_juggernauts.remove(array[1]);
            }
        }
        catch(Exception exception)
        {
            bytes = null;
        }
        finally
        {
            m_juggernautsMutex.writeLock().unlock();
        }

        if(bytes != null)
        {
            s_databaseHelper.writeParticipantMessage
                (s_cryptography,
                 "local-protocol",
                 "Received a Juggernaut bundle. State of " +
                 state + " (" + Juggernaut.stateToText(state) +
                 "). Responded.",
                 array[1],
                 null,
                 null,
                 System.currentTimeMillis());
            Miscellaneous.sendBroadcast
                ("org.purple.smoke.notify_data_set_changed");
        }
        else
        {
            if(state == JPAKEParticipant.STATE_ROUND_3_VALIDATED)
            {
                if(sessionCredentials != null)
                {
                    int oid = s_databaseHelper.
                        participantOidFromSipHash
                        (s_cryptography, array[1]);

                    s_databaseHelper.setParticipantKeyStream
                        (s_cryptography, sessionCredentials, oid);
                }
```

```java
                    s_databaseHelper.writeParticipantMessage
                        (s_cryptography,
                         "local-protocol",
                         "The Juggernaut Protocol has been verified!",
                         array[1],
                         null,
                         null,
                         System.currentTimeMillis());
                }
                else
                    s_databaseHelper.writeParticipantMessage
                        (s_cryptography,
                         "local-protocol",
                         "Juggernaut Protocol failure (" +
                         Juggernaut.stateToText(state) + ")!",
                         array[1],
                         null,
                         null,
                         System.currentTimeMillis());

                Miscellaneous.sendBroadcast
                    ("org.purple.smoke.notify_data_set_changed");
            }

            return 1;
        }
        else if(abyte[0] == Messages.MESSAGE_READ_TYPE[0])
        {
            /*
            ** We do not have a timestamp!
            */

            PublicKey signatureKey = s_databaseHelper.
                signatureKeyForDigest(s_cryptography, pki);

            if(signatureKey == null)
                return 1;

            if(!Cryptography.
               verifySignature
               (signatureKey,
               Arrays.copyOfRange(ciphertext,
                            Cryptography.HASH_KEY_LENGTH + 1,
                            ciphertext.length),
               Miscellaneous.
               joinByteArrays(pki,
                            Arrays.
                            copyOfRange(ciphertext,
                                   0,
                                   Cryptography.
                                   HASH_KEY_LENGTH + 1),
                            s_cryptography.
                            chatEncryptionPublicKeyDigest())))
                return 1;

            String array[] = s_databaseHelper.nameSipHashIdFromDigest
                (s_cryptography, pki);

            if(array == null || array.length != 2)
                return 1;

            if(s_databaseHelper.
```

```java
                    writeMessageStatus
                    (s_cryptography,
                    array[1],
                    Arrays.copyOfRange(ciphertext,
                                       1,
                                       Cryptography.
                                       HASH_KEY_LENGTH + 1)))
                notifyOfDataSetChange("-1");

            return 1;
        }

        ciphertext = Arrays.copyOfRange
            (ciphertext, 1, ciphertext.length);

        String strings[] = new String(ciphertext).split("\\n");

        if(strings.length != Messages.CHAT_GROUP_TWO_ELEMENT_COUNT)
            return 1;

        String message = null;
        boolean updateTimeStamp = true;
        byte attachment[] = null;
        byte messageIdentity[] = null;
        byte publicKeySignature[] = null;
        int ii = 0;
        long sequence = 0;
        long timestamp = 0;

        for(String string : strings)
            switch(ii)
            {
            case 0:
                timestamp = Miscellaneous.byteArrayToLong
                    (Base64.decode(string.getBytes(), Base64.NO_WRAP));

                if(Math.abs(System.currentTimeMillis() - timestamp) >
                   Chat.CHAT_WINDOW)
                    updateTimeStamp = false;

                if(!updateTimeStamp)
                    /*
                    ** Ignore expired messages unless the messages
                    ** were discharged by SmokeStack per our
                    ** temporary identity.
                    */

                    if(!ourMessageViaChatTemporaryIdentity)
                        return 1;

                ii += 1;
                break;
            case 1:
                message = new String
                    (Base64.decode(string.getBytes(), Base64.NO_WRAP),
                     StandardCharsets.UTF_8).trim();
                ii += 1;
                break;
            case 2:
                sequence = Miscellaneous.byteArrayToLong
                    (Base64.decode(string.getBytes(), Base64.NO_WRAP));
                ii += 1;
                break;
```

```java
case 3:
    attachment = Miscellaneous.
        decompressed(Base64.decode(string.getBytes(),
                              Base64.NO_WRAP));
    ii += 1;
    break;
case 4:
    messageIdentity = Base64.decode
        (string.getBytes(), Base64.NO_WRAP);
    ii += 1;
    break;
case 5:
    String array[] = s_databaseHelper.
        nameSipHashIdFromDigest(s_cryptography, pki);

    if(array == null || array.length != 2)
        return 1;

    String sipHashId = array[1];

    if(s_databaseHelper.
       readParticipantOptions(s_cryptography,
                          sipHashId).
       contains("optional_signatures = false"))
    {
        PublicKey signatureKey = s_databaseHelper.
            signatureKeyForDigest(s_cryptography, pki);

        if(signatureKey == null)
            return 1;

        publicKeySignature = Base64.decode
            (string.getBytes(), Base64.NO_WRAP);

        if(!Cryptography.
           verifySignature
           (signatureKey,
           publicKeySignature,
           Miscellaneous.
           joinByteArrays
           (pki,
            abyte,
            strings[0].getBytes(),
            "\n".getBytes(),
            strings[1].getBytes(),
            "\n".getBytes(),
            strings[2].getBytes(),
            "\n".getBytes(),
            strings[3].getBytes(),
            "\n".getBytes(),
            strings[4].getBytes(),
            "\n".getBytes(),
            s_cryptography.
            chatEncryptionPublicKeyDigest())))
            return 1;
    }

    strings = array;
    break;
default:
    break;
}
```

```java
            if(message == null)
                return 1;

            if(updateTimeStamp)
                s_databaseHelper.updateParticipantLastTimestamp
                    (s_cryptography, strings[1]);

            value = s_congestionSipHash.hmac
                (("chat" + message + strings[1] + timestamp).getBytes(),
                 Cryptography.SIPHASH_OUTPUT_LENGTH)[0];

            if(s_databaseHelper.writeCongestionDigest(value))
                return 1;

            if(s_databaseHelper.
                writeParticipantMessage(s_cryptography,
                                        ourMessageViaChatTemporaryIdentity ?
                                        "true" : "false",
                                        message,
                                        strings[1],
                                        attachment,
                                        messageIdentity,
                                        timestamp) !=
                Database.ExceptionLevels.EXCEPTION_PERMISSIBLE)
            {
                Intent intent = new Intent
                    ("org.purple.smoke.chat_message");

                intent.putExtra("org.purple.smoke.message", message);
                intent.putExtra("org.purple.smoke.name", strings[0]);
                intent.putExtra
                    ("org.purple.smoke.purple",
                     ourMessageViaChatTemporaryIdentity);
                intent.putExtra("org.purple.smoke.sequence", sequence);
                intent.putExtra("org.purple.smoke.sipHashId", strings[1]);
                intent.putExtra("org.purple.smoke.timestamp", timestamp);
                Miscellaneous.sendBroadcast(intent);

                /*
                ** Prepare a read-proof message.
                */

                keyStream = s_databaseHelper.participantKeyStream
                    (s_cryptography, pki); // Current key stream.
                enqueueMessage
                    (Messages.
                     bytesToMessageString(Messages.
                                          messageRead(s_cryptography,
                                                      strings[1],
                                                      keyStream,
                                                      messageIdentity)),
                     null);

                if(ourMessageViaChatTemporaryIdentity)
                    enqueueMessage
                        (Messages.
                         bytesToMessageString(Messages.
                                              messageRead(s_cryptography,
                                                          sha512OfMessage)),
                         null);
            }

        return 1;
```

```java
                }
            else if(pki.length == Cryptography.CIPHER_HASH_KEYS_LENGTH)
            {
                /*
                ** Organic Half-And-Half
                ** Steam Key Exchange A
                ** Steam Key Exchange B
                */

                byte hmacc[] = Cryptography.hmac
                    (Arrays.copyOfRange(bytes,
                                        0,
                                        bytes.length -
                                        2 * Cryptography.HASH_KEY_LENGTH),
                     Arrays.copyOfRange(pki,
                                        Cryptography.CIPHER_KEY_LENGTH,
                                        pki.length));

                if(!Cryptography.memcmp(hmac, hmacc))
                    return 1;

                byte ciphertext[] = Cryptography.decrypt
                    (Arrays.
                     copyOfRange(bytes,
                                 pki_output_size,
                                 bytes.length -
                                 2 * Cryptography.HASH_KEY_LENGTH),
                     Arrays.copyOfRange(pki,
                                        0,
                                        Cryptography.CIPHER_KEY_LENGTH));

                if(ciphertext == null)
                    return 1;

                byte tag = ciphertext[0];

                if(!(tag == Messages.CALL_HALF_AND_HALF_TAGS[0] ||
                     tag == Messages.CALL_HALF_AND_HALF_TAGS[1] ||
                     tag == Messages.STEAM_KEY_EXCHANGE[0] ||
                     tag == Messages.STEAM_KEY_EXCHANGE[1]))
                    return 1;
                else if(tag == Messages.STEAM_KEY_EXCHANGE[0] ||
                        tag == Messages.STEAM_KEY_EXCHANGE[1])
                {
                    m_steamKeyExchange.append(ciphertext, pki);
                    return 1;
                }

                ciphertext = Arrays.copyOfRange
                    (ciphertext, 1, ciphertext.length);

                String strings[] = new String(ciphertext).split("\\n");

                if(strings.length != Messages.CALL_GROUP_TWO_ELEMENT_COUNT)
                    return 1;

                byte ephemeralPublicKey[] = null;
                byte ephemeralPublicKeyType[] = null;
                byte publicKeySignature[] = null;
                byte senderPublicEncryptionKeyDigest[] = null;
                int ii = 0;
                long timestamp = 0;
```

```java
for(String string : strings)
    switch(ii)
    {
    case 0:
        timestamp = Miscellaneous.byteArrayToLong
            (Base64.decode(string.getBytes(), Base64.NO_WRAP));

        if(Math.abs(System.currentTimeMillis() - timestamp) >
          CALL_LIFETIME)
            return 1;

        ii += 1;
        break;
    case 1:
        ephemeralPublicKey = Base64.decode
            (string.getBytes(), Base64.NO_WRAP);
        ii += 1;
        break;
    case 2:
        ephemeralPublicKeyType = Base64.decode
            (string.getBytes(), Base64.NO_WRAP);
        ii += 1;
        break;
    case 3:
        ii += 1;
        break;
    case 4:
        senderPublicEncryptionKeyDigest = Base64.
            decode(string.getBytes(), Base64.NO_WRAP);
        ii += 1;
        break;
    case 5:
        PublicKey signatureKey = s_databaseHelper.
            signatureKeyForDigest
            (s_cryptography, senderPublicEncryptionKeyDigest);

        if(signatureKey == null)
            return 1;

        publicKeySignature = Base64.decode
            (string.getBytes(), Base64.NO_WRAP);

        if(!Cryptography.
          verifySignature(signatureKey,
                          publicKeySignature,
                          Miscellaneous.
                          joinByteArrays
                          (pki,
                           new byte[] {tag},
                           strings[0].getBytes(),
                           "\n".getBytes(),
                           strings[1].getBytes(),
                           "\n".getBytes(),
                           strings[2].getBytes(),
                           "\n".getBytes(),
                           strings[3].getBytes(),
                           "\n".getBytes(),
                           strings[4].getBytes(),
                           "\n".getBytes(),
                           s_cryptography.
                           chatEncryptionPublicKeyDigest()))))
            return 1;
```

```
                    ii += 1;
                break;
            default:
                break;
            }

        String array[] = s_databaseHelper.nameSipHashIdFromDigest
            (s_cryptography, senderPublicEncryptionKeyDigest);

        if(array != null && array.length == 2)
        {
            PublicKey publicKey = null;
            byte keyStream[] = null;

            if(tag == Messages.CALL_HALF_AND_HALF_TAGS[0])
            {
                ParticipantCall participantCall = null;

                m_callQueueMutex.readLock().lock();

                try
                {
                    participantCall = m_callQueue.get(array[1]);
                }
                catch(Exception exception)
                {
                }
                finally
                {
                    m_callQueueMutex.readLock().unlock();
                }

                if(participantCall == null)
                {
                    switch(ephemeralPublicKeyType[0])
                    {
                    case (byte) 'M':
                        publicKey = Cryptography.publicKeyFromBytes
                            (ephemeralPublicKey);
                        break;
                    case (byte) 'R':
                        publicKey = Cryptography.publicRSAKeyFromBytes
                            (ephemeralPublicKey);
                        break;
                    default:
                        break;
                    }

                    if(publicKey == null)
                        return 1;

                    /*
                    ** Generate new AES-256 and SHA-512 keys.
                    */

                    keyStream = Miscellaneous.joinByteArrays
                        (Cryptography.aes256KeyBytes(),
                         Cryptography.sha512KeyBytes());
                }
                else
                {
                    /*
                    ** We're busy!
```

```java
                           */

                           m_callQueueMutex.writeLock().lock();

                           try
                           {
                               m_callQueue.remove(array[1]);
                           }
                           finally
                           {
                               m_callQueueMutex.writeLock().unlock();
                           }

                           Intent intent = new Intent
                               ("org.purple.smoke.busy_call");

                           intent.putExtra("org.purple.smoke.name", array[0]);
                           intent.putExtra
                               ("org.purple.smoke.sipHashId", array[1]);
                           Miscellaneous.sendBroadcast(intent);
                           return 1;
                       }
                   }
               else if(tag == Messages.CALL_HALF_AND_HALF_TAGS[1])
               {
                   ParticipantCall participantCall = null;

                   m_callQueueMutex.readLock().lock();

                   try
                   {
                       participantCall = m_callQueue.get(array[1]);
                   }
                   finally
                   {
                       m_callQueueMutex.readLock().unlock();
                   }

                   if(participantCall == null)
                       return 1;

                   m_callQueueMutex.writeLock().lock();

                   try
                   {
                       m_callQueue.remove(array[1]);
                   }
                   catch(Exception exception)
                   {
                   }
                   finally
                   {
                       m_callQueueMutex.writeLock().unlock();
                   }

                   keyStream = Cryptography.pkiDecrypt
                       (participantCall.m_keyPair.getPrivate(),
                        ephemeralPublicKey);

                   if(keyStream == null)
                       return 1;
               }
               else
```

```java
                return 1;

            s_databaseHelper.writeCallKeys
                (s_cryptography, array[1], keyStream);

            Intent intent = new Intent
                ("org.purple.smoke.half_and_half_call");

            if(tag == Messages.CALL_HALF_AND_HALF_TAGS[0])
            {
                intent.putExtra("org.purple.smoke.initial", true);
                s_databaseHelper.writeParticipantMessage
                    (s_cryptography,
                     "local-protocol",
                     "Received a half-and-half call. " +
                     "Dispatching a response. Please be patient.",
                     array[1],
                     null,
                     null,
                     System.currentTimeMillis());
            }
            else
            {
                intent.putExtra("org.purple.smoke.initial", false);
                s_databaseHelper.writeParticipantMessage
                    (s_cryptography,
                     "local-protocol",
                     "Received a half-and-half call-response.",
                     array[1],
                     null,
                     null,
                     System.currentTimeMillis());
            }

            intent.putExtra
                ("org.purple.smoke.keyType",
                 ephemeralPublicKeyType[0] ==
                 Cryptography.MESSAGES_KEY_TYPES[0] ? 'M' : 'R');
            intent.putExtra("org.purple.smoke.name", array[0]);
            intent.putExtra("org.purple.smoke.refresh", true);
            intent.putExtra("org.purple.smoke.sipHashId", array[1]);
            Miscellaneous.sendBroadcast(intent);
            Miscellaneous.sendBroadcast
                ("org.purple.smoke.notify_data_set_changed");

            if(tag == Messages.CALL_HALF_AND_HALF_TAGS[0])
            {
                /*
                ** Respond via all neighbors.
                */

                bytes = Messages.callMessage
                    (s_cryptography,
                     array[1],
                     Cryptography.pkiEncrypt(publicKey,
                                             "McEliece-Fujisaki",
                                             keyStream),
                     ephemeralPublicKeyType[0],
                     Messages.CALL_HALF_AND_HALF_TAGS[1]);

                if(bytes != null)
                    scheduleSend(Messages.bytesToMessageString(bytes));
            }
```

```java
                    /*
                    ** Refresh the Settings activity's Participants table.
                    */

                    Miscellaneous.sendBroadcast
                        ("org.purple.smoke.populate_participants");
                    State.getInstance().populateParticipants();
                    return 1;
                }
            }
        else if(pki.length == Cryptography.STEAM_FILE_IDENTITY_LENGTH)
        {
            /*
            ** Steam A
            ** Steam B
            */

            /*
            ** Discover the Steam having the presented identity.
            */

            byte keyStream[] = s_databaseHelper.steamKeyStream
                (s_cryptography, pki);

            if(keyStream == null)
                return 1;

            byte hmacc[] = Cryptography.hmac
                (Arrays.copyOfRange(bytes,
                                    0,
                                    bytes.length -
                                    2 * Cryptography.HASH_KEY_LENGTH),
                    Arrays.copyOfRange(keyStream,
                                    Cryptography.CIPHER_KEY_LENGTH,
                                    keyStream.length));

            if(!Cryptography.memcmp(hmac, hmacc))
                return 1;

            byte ciphertext[] = Cryptography.decrypt
                (Arrays.
                 copyOfRange(bytes,
                                pki_output_size,
                                bytes.length -
                                2 * Cryptography.HASH_KEY_LENGTH),
                    Arrays.copyOfRange(keyStream,
                                    0,
                                    Cryptography.CIPHER_KEY_LENGTH));

            if(ciphertext == null)
                return 1;

            long timestamp = Miscellaneous.byteArrayToLong
                (Arrays.copyOfRange(ciphertext, 1, 9));

            if(Math.abs(System.currentTimeMillis() - timestamp) >
                STEAM_SHARE_WINDOW)
                return 1;

            long offset = Miscellaneous.byteArrayToLong
                (Arrays.copyOfRange(ciphertext, 9, 17));
```

```
        if(offset < 0)
            return 1;

        byte abyte[] = new byte[] {ciphertext[0]};

        if(abyte[0] == Messages.STEAM_SHARE[0])
        {
            if(m_steamWriter.
               write(pki,
                     Arrays.copyOfRange(ciphertext,
                                        17,
                                        ciphertext.length),
                     offset))
            {
                String sipHashId = s_databaseHelper.steamSipHashId
                    (s_cryptography, pki);

                bytes = Messages.steamShare
                    (s_cryptography,
                     sipHashId,
                     pki,
                     keyStream,
                     null,
                     Messages.STEAM_SHARE[1],
                     offset);

                if(bytes != null)
                    sendSteam
                        (false,
                         Messages.bytesToMessageString(bytes).
                         getBytes());
            }
        }
        else if(abyte[0] == Messages.STEAM_SHARE[1])
        {
            m_steamsMutex.readLock().lock();

            try
            {
                int size = m_steams.size();

                for(int i = 0; i < size; i++)
                {
                    int j = m_steams.keyAt(i);

                    if(m_steams.get(j) instanceof SteamReaderFull)
                    {
                        SteamReaderFull steamReaderFull =
                            (SteamReaderFull) m_steams.get(j);

                        if(Arrays.
                           equals(pki, steamReaderFull.fileIdentity()))
                        {
                            steamReaderFull.setAcknowledgedOffset
                                (offset);
                            break;
                        }
                    }
                }
            }
            catch(Exception exception)
            {
            }
```

```java
                finally
                {
                    m_steamsMutex.readLock().unlock();
                }
            }
        }
    }
    catch(Exception exception)
    {
        return 0;
    }

    return 0;
}

public long callTimeRemaining(String sipHashId)
{
    m_callQueueMutex.readLock().lock();

    try
    {
        if(m_callQueue.containsKey(sipHashId))
            return Math.abs
                (CALL_LIFETIME / 1000L - (System.nanoTime() -
                                    m_callQueue.get(sipHashId).
                                    m_startTime) / 1000000000L);
    }
    catch(Exception exception)
    {
    }
    finally
    {
        m_callQueueMutex.readLock().unlock();
    }

    return 0L;
}

public static synchronized Kernel getInstance()
{
    if(s_instance == null)
        s_instance = new Kernel();

    return s_instance;
}

public static void writeCongestionDigest(String message)
{
    if(message != null)
        try
        {
            s_databaseHelper.writeCongestionDigest
                (s_congestionSipHash.
                    hmac(message.getBytes(),
                        Cryptography.SIPHASH_OUTPUT_LENGTH / 2)[0]);
        }
        catch(Exception exception)
        {
        }
}

public static void writeCongestionDigest(byte data[])
{
```

```java
    try
    {
        s_databaseHelper.writeCongestionDigest
            (s_congestionSipHash.
             hmac(data, Cryptography.SIPHASH_OUTPUT_LENGTH / 2)[0]);
    }
    catch(Exception exception)
    {
    }
}

public void clearMessagesToSend()
{
    m_messagesToSendMutex.writeLock().lock();

    try
    {
        m_messagesToSend.clear();
    }
    catch(Exception exception)
    {
    }
    finally
    {
        m_messagesToSendMutex.writeLock().unlock();
    }
}

public void clearNeighborQueues()
{
    m_neighborsMutex.readLock().lock();

    try
    {
        int size = m_neighbors.size();

        for(int i = 0; i < size; i++)
        {
            int j = m_neighbors.keyAt(i);

            if(m_neighbors.get(j) != null)
            {
                m_neighbors.get(j).clearEchoQueue();
                m_neighbors.get(j).clearQueue();
            }
        }
    }
    catch(Exception exception)
    {
    }
    finally
    {
        m_neighborsMutex.readLock().unlock();
    }
}

public void echo(String message, int oid)
{
    if(!State.getInstance().neighborsEcho() ||
       message == null ||
       message.trim().isEmpty())
        return;
```

```java
        m_neighborsMutex.readLock().lock();

        try
        {
            int size = m_neighbors.size();

            for(int i = 0; i < size; i++)
            {
                int j = m_neighbors.keyAt(i);

                if(m_neighbors.get(j) != null &&
                    m_neighbors.get(j).getOid() != oid &&
                    !m_neighbors.get(j).passthrough())
                     m_neighbors.get(j).scheduleEchoSend(message);
            }
        }
        catch(Exception exception)
        {
        }
        finally
        {
            m_neighborsMutex.readLock().unlock();
        }
    }

    public void echoForce(String message, int oid)
    {
        if(message == null || message.trim().isEmpty())
            return;

        m_neighborsMutex.readLock().lock();

        try
        {
            int size = m_neighbors.size();

            for(int i = 0; i < size; i++)
            {
                int j = m_neighbors.keyAt(i);

                if(m_neighbors.get(j) != null &&
                    m_neighbors.get(j).getOid() != oid &&
                    !m_neighbors.get(j).passthrough())
                     m_neighbors.get(j).scheduleEchoSend(message);
            }
        }
        catch(Exception exception)
        {
        }
        finally
        {
            m_neighborsMutex.readLock().unlock();
        }
    }

    public void enqueueChatMessage(String message,
                                   String sipHashId,
                                   byte imageBytes[],
                                   byte keyStream[])
    {
        m_messagesToSendMutex.writeLock().lock();

        try
```

```java
{
    MessageElement messageElement = new MessageElement();

    messageElement.m_attachment = imageBytes;
    messageElement.m_id = sipHashId;
    messageElement.m_keyStream = keyStream;
    messageElement.m_message = message;
    messageElement.m_messageIdentity = Cryptography.randomBytes
        (Cryptography.HASH_KEY_LENGTH);
    messageElement.m_messageType = MessageElement.CHAT_MESSAGE_TYPE;
    m_messagesToSend.add(messageElement);
    }
    catch(Exception exception)
    {
    }
    finally
    {
        m_messagesToSendMutex.writeLock().unlock();
    }

    wakeMessagesToSendScheduler();
}

public void enqueueFireMessage(String message, String id, String name)
{
    byte keyStream[] = null;

    m_fireStreamsMutex.readLock().lock();

    try
    {
        if(m_fireStreams.containsKey(name))
            keyStream = m_fireStreams.get(name);
    }
    catch(Exception exception)
    {
    }
    finally
    {
        m_fireStreamsMutex.readLock().unlock();
    }

    if(keyStream == null)
        return;

    m_messagesToSendMutex.writeLock().lock();

    try
    {
        MessageElement messageElement = new MessageElement();

        messageElement.m_id = id;
        messageElement.m_keyStream = keyStream;
        messageElement.m_message = message;
        messageElement.m_messageType = MessageElement.FIRE_MESSAGE_TYPE;
        m_messagesToSend.add(messageElement);
    }
    catch(Exception exception)
    {
    }
    finally
    {
        m_messagesToSendMutex.writeLock().unlock();
```

```java
        }

    wakeMessagesToSendScheduler();
    }

    public void enqueueFireStatus(String id, String name)
    {
        byte keyStream[] = null;

        m_fireStreamsMutex.readLock().lock();

        try
        {
            if(m_fireStreams.containsKey(name))
                keyStream = m_fireStreams.get(name);
        }
        catch(Exception exception)
        {
        }
        finally
        {
            m_fireStreamsMutex.readLock().unlock();
        }

        if(keyStream == null)
            return;

        m_messagesToSendMutex.writeLock().lock();

        try
        {
            MessageElement messageElement = new MessageElement();

            messageElement.m_id = id;
            messageElement.m_keyStream = keyStream;
            messageElement.m_messageType =
                MessageElement.FIRE_STATUS_MESSAGE_TYPE;
            m_messagesToSend.add(messageElement);
        }
        catch(Exception exception)
        {
        }
        finally
        {
            m_messagesToSendMutex.writeLock().unlock();
        }

        wakeMessagesToSendScheduler();
    }

    public void enqueueJuggernaut(String secret,
                                  String sipHashId,
                                  boolean isJuggerKnot,
                                  byte keyStream[])
    {
        m_juggernautsMutex.writeLock().lock();

        try
        {
            if(m_juggernauts.containsKey(sipHashId))
                m_juggernauts.remove(sipHashId);

            Juggernaut juggernaut = new Juggernaut
```

```java
            (sipHashId, secret, isJuggerKnot);

            m_juggernauts.put(sipHashId, juggernaut);
        }
        catch(Exception exception)
        {
        }
        finally
        {
            m_juggernautsMutex.writeLock().unlock();
        }

        m_messagesToSendMutex.writeLock().lock();

        try
        {
            MessageElement messageElement = new MessageElement();

            messageElement.m_delay = JUGGERNAUT_DELAY;
            messageElement.m_id = sipHashId;
            messageElement.m_keyStream = keyStream;
            messageElement.m_message = secret;
            messageElement.m_messageType =
                MessageElement.JUGGERNAUT_MESSAGE_TYPE;
            messageElement.m_timestamp = System.currentTimeMillis();
            m_messagesToSend.add(messageElement);
        }
        catch(Exception exception)
        {
        }
        finally
        {
            m_messagesToSendMutex.writeLock().unlock();
        }

        wakeMessagesToSendScheduler();
    }

    public void enqueueShareSipHashIdMessage(int oid)
    {
        m_messagesToSendMutex.writeLock().lock();

        try
        {
            MessageElement messageElement = new MessageElement();

            messageElement.m_id = String.valueOf(oid);
            messageElement.m_messageType = MessageElement.
                SHARE_SIPHASH_ID_MESSAGE_TYPE;
            m_messagesToSend.add(messageElement);
        }
        catch(Exception exception)
        {
        }
        finally
        {
            m_messagesToSendMutex.writeLock().unlock();
        }

        wakeMessagesToSendScheduler();
    }

    public void enqueueSteamKeyExchange(String message, String sipHashId)
```

```java
    {
        m_messagesToSendMutex.writeLock().lock();

        try
        {
            MessageElement messageElement = new MessageElement();

            messageElement.m_id = sipHashId;
            messageElement.m_message = message;
            messageElement.m_messageType =
                MessageElement.STEAM_KEY_EXCHANGE_MESSAGE_TYPE;
            m_messagesToSend.add(messageElement);
        }
        catch(Exception exception)
        {
        }
        finally
        {
            m_messagesToSendMutex.writeLock().unlock();
        }

        wakeMessagesToSendScheduler();
    }

    public void extinguishFire(String name)
    {
        m_fireStreamsMutex.writeLock().lock();

        try
        {
            m_fireStreams.remove(name);
        }
        catch(Exception exception)
        {
        }
        finally
        {
            m_fireStreamsMutex.writeLock().unlock();
        }
    }

    public void notifyOfDataSetChange(String oid)
    {
        /*
        ** The oid parameter represents the oid of the database entry.
        ** The value of oid may be -1 or some other meaningless value.
        */

        Miscellaneous.sendBroadcast
            ("org.purple.smoke.notify_data_set_changed", oid);
    }

    public void resendMessage(String sipHashId, int position)
    {
        m_messagesToSendMutex.writeLock().lock();

        try
        {
            MessageElement messageElement = new MessageElement();

            messageElement.m_id = sipHashId;
            messageElement.m_messageIdentity = Cryptography.randomBytes
                (Cryptography.HASH_KEY_LENGTH);
```

```java
            messageElement.m_messageType =
                MessageElement.RESEND_CHAT_MESSAGE_TYPE;
            messageElement.m_position = position;
            m_messagesToSend.add(messageElement);
        }
    catch(Exception exception)
        {
        }
    finally
        {
            m_messagesToSendMutex.writeLock().unlock();
        }

        wakeMessagesToSendScheduler();
    }

    public void retrieveChatMessages(String sipHashId)
    {
        m_messagesToSendMutex.writeLock().lock();

        try
        {
            MessageElement messageElement = new MessageElement();

            messageElement.m_id = sipHashId;
            messageElement.m_messageType =
                MessageElement.RETRIEVE_MESSAGES_MESSAGE_TYPE;
            m_messagesToSend.add(messageElement);
        }
    catch(Exception exception)
        {
        }
    finally
        {
            m_messagesToSendMutex.writeLock().unlock();
        }

        wakeMessagesToSendScheduler();
    }

    public int sendSteam(boolean simple, byte bytes[])
    {
        int sent = 0;

        if(bytes == null || bytes.length == 0)
            return sent;

        m_neighborsMutex.readLock().lock();

        try
        {
            int size = m_neighbors.size();

            for(int i = 0; i < size; i++)
            {
                int j = m_neighbors.keyAt(i);

                if(m_neighbors.get(j) != null && m_neighbors.get(j).connected())
                {
                    /*
                    ** Increase the offset by the minimum number of bytes.
                    */
```

```java
                    if(simple)
                    {
                        if(m_neighbors.get(j).passthrough())
                        {
                            int rc = m_neighbors.get(j).send(bytes);

                            sent = Math.max(0, Math.min(Integer.MAX_VALUE, rc));
                        }
                    }
                    else
                    {
                        if(!m_neighbors.get(j).passthrough())
                        {
                            int rc = m_neighbors.get(j).send(bytes);

                            sent = Math.max(0, Math.min(Integer.MAX_VALUE, rc));
                        }
                    }
                }
            }
        }
        catch(Exception exception)
        {
        }
        finally
        {
            m_neighborsMutex.readLock().unlock();
        }

        return sent;
    }

    public void setWakeLock(boolean state)
    {
        if(m_wakeLock == null)
            try
            {
                PowerManager powerManager = (PowerManager)
                    Smoke.getApplication().getApplicationContext().
                    getSystemService(Context.POWER_SERVICE);

                if(powerManager != null)
                    m_wakeLock = powerManager.newWakeLock
                        (PowerManager.PARTIAL_WAKE_LOCK,
                         "Smoke:SmokeWakeLockTag");

                if(m_wakeLock != null)
                    m_wakeLock.setReferenceCounted(false);
            }
            catch(Exception exception)
            {
            }

        try
        {
            if(m_wakeLock != null)
            {
                if(state)
                {
                    if(m_wakeLock.isHeld())
                        m_wakeLock.release();

                    m_wakeLock.acquire();
```

```java
            }
            else if(m_wakeLock.isHeld())
                m_wakeLock.release();
        }
    }
    catch(Exception exception)
    {
    }
  }
}
```

/* MemberChat.java –


```java
package org.purple.smoke;

import android.app.Dialog;
import android.content.BroadcastReceiver;
import android.content.ClipData;
import android.content.ClipboardManager;
import android.content.Context;
import android.content.DialogInterface;
import android.content.Intent;
import android.content.IntentFilter;
import android.graphics.Bitmap.Config;
import android.graphics.Bitmap;
import android.graphics.BitmapFactory;
import android.media.Ringtone;
import android.media.RingtoneManager;
import android.net.Uri;
import android.os.Bundle;
import android.os.Environment;
import android.support.v4.content.LocalBroadcastManager;
import android.support.v7.app.AppCompatActivity;
```

```java
import android.support.v7.widget.LinearLayoutManager;
import android.support.v7.widget.RecyclerView;
import android.support.v7.widget.Toolbar;
import android.text.SpannableStringBuilder;
import android.util.Base64;
import android.view.ContextMenu.ContextMenuInfo;
import android.view.ContextMenu;
import android.view.Menu;
import android.view.MenuItem;
import android.view.View;
import android.view.WindowManager;
import android.widget.Button;
import android.widget.ImageView;
import android.widget.ProgressBar;
import android.widget.TextView;
import java.io.ByteArrayInputStream;
import java.io.ByteArrayOutputStream;
import java.io.File;
import java.io.FileOutputStream;
import java.io.InputStream;
import java.nio.charset.StandardCharsets;
import java.util.ArrayList;
import java.util.Arrays;
import java.util.Hashtable;
import java.util.Iterator;
import java.util.concurrent.Executors;
import java.util.concurrent.ScheduledExecutorService;
import java.util.concurrent.TimeUnit;
import java.util.concurrent.locks.ReentrantReadWriteLock;

public class MemberChat extends AppCompatActivity
{
    private class MemberChatBroadcastReceiver extends BroadcastReceiver
    {
        public MemberChatBroadcastReceiver()
        {
        }

        @Override
        public void onReceive(Context context, Intent intent)
        {
            if(intent == null || intent.getAction() == null)
                return;

            switch(intent.getAction())
            {
            case "org.purple.smoke.chat_local_message":
            case "org.purple.smoke.chat_message":
                boolean local = intent.getAction().equals
                ("org.purple.smoke.chat_local_message");

                 if(intent.
                    getStringExtra("org.purple.smoke.sipHashId") != null &&
                    intent.getStringExtra("org.purple.smoke.sipHashId").
                    equals(m_sipHashId))
                {
                    try
                    {
                        m_adapter.notifyDataSetChanged(); /*
                                                          ** Items are inserted
                                                          ** into the database
                                                          ** haphazardly.
                                                          */
```

```java
                        m_adapter.notifyItemInserted
                            (m_adapter.getItemCount() - 1);
                }
                catch(Exception exception)
                {
                }

                if(!local)
                {
                    try
                    {
                        Ringtone ringtone = null;
                        Uri notification = RingtoneManager.getDefaultUri
                            (RingtoneManager.TYPE_NOTIFICATION);

                        ringtone = RingtoneManager.getRingtone
                            (getApplicationContext(), notification);
                        ringtone.play();
                    }
                    catch(Exception exception)
                    {
                    }
                }
            }
            else
                Miscellaneous.showNotification
                    (MemberChat.this,
                     intent,
                     findViewById(R.id.main_layout));

            break;
        case "org.purple.smoke.half_and_half_call":
        case "org.purple.smoke.neighbor_aborted":
        case "org.purple.smoke.neighbor_disconnected":
        case "org.purple.smoke.network_connected":
        case "org.purple.smoke.network_disconnected":
            prepareStatus();
            break;
        case "org.purple.smoke.state_participants_populated":
            invalidateOptionsMenu();
            break;
        case "org.purple.smoke.time":
            Miscellaneous.showNotification
                (MemberChat.this, intent, findViewById(R.id.main_layout));
            break;
        default:
            break;
        }
    }
}

private class RemoveSelectedMessages implements Runnable
{
    private Dialog m_dialog = null;
    private String m_sipHashId = null;

    private RemoveSelectedMessages(Dialog dialog, String sipHashId)
    {
        m_dialog = dialog;
        m_sipHashId = sipHashId;
    }

    @Override
```

```java
        public void run()
        {
            m_selectedMessagesMutex.writeLock().lock();

            try
            {
                Iterator<Hashtable.Entry<Integer, Boolean> >
                    it = m_selectedMessages.entrySet().iterator();

                while(it.hasNext())
                {
                    Hashtable.Entry<Integer, Boolean> entry = it.next();

                    if(entry.getKey() == null || entry.getValue() == null)
                    {
                        it.remove();
                        continue;
                    }

                    m_databaseHelper.deleteParticipantMessage
                        (s_cryptography, m_sipHashId, entry.getKey());
                    it.remove();
                }
            }
            catch(Exception exception)
            {
            }
            finally
            {
                m_selectedMessagesMutex.writeLock().unlock();
            }
        }
    }

    private static class SmokeLinearLayoutManager extends LinearLayoutManager
    {
        SmokeLinearLayoutManager(Context context)
        {
            super(context);
        }

        @Override
        public void onLayoutChildren(RecyclerView.Recycler recycler,
                                     RecyclerView.State state)
        {
            /*
            ** Android may terminate!
            */

            try
            {
                super.onLayoutChildren(recycler, state);
            }
            catch(Exception exception)
            {
            }
        }
    }

    private Hashtable<Integer, Boolean> m_selectedMessages = null;
    private MemberChatAdapter m_adapter = null;
    private MemberChatBroadcastReceiver m_receiver = null;
    private RecyclerView m_recyclerView = null;
```

```java
private ScheduledExecutorService m_statusScheduler = null;
private SmokeLinearLayoutManager m_layoutManager = null;
private String m_name = Cryptography.DEFAULT_SIPHASH_ID;
private String m_sipHashId = m_name;
private boolean m_messageSelectionStateEnabled = false;
private boolean m_receiverRegistered = false;
private byte m_attachment[] = null;
private final Database m_databaseHelper = Database.getInstance();
private final ReentrantReadWriteLock m_selectedMessagesMutex =
    new ReentrantReadWriteLock();
private final static Cryptography s_cryptography =
    Cryptography.getInstance();
private final static int SELECT_IMAGE_REQUEST = 0;
private int m_oid = -1;

public abstract static class ContextMenuEnumerator
{
    public final static int CALL_VIA_MCELIECE = 0;
    public final static int CALL_VIA_RSA = 1;
    public final static int COPY_TEXT = 2;
    public final static int CUSTOM_SESSION = 3;
    public final static int DELETE_ALL_MESSAGES = 4;
    public final static int DELETE_MESSAGE = 5;
    public final static int DELETE_SELECTED_MESSAGES = 6;
    public final static int JUGGERKNOT = 7;
    public final static int JUGGERNAUT = 8;
    public final static int OPTIONAL_SIGNATURES = 9;
    public final static int RESEND_MESSAGE = 10;
    public final static int RETRIEVE_MESSAGES = 11;
    public final static int SAVE_ATTACHMENT = 12;
    public final static int SELECTION_STATE = 13;
}


private boolean isParticipantPaired(ArrayList<ParticipantElement>
arrayList)
{
    if(arrayList == null)
        arrayList = m_databaseHelper.readParticipants
            (s_cryptography, m_sipHashId);

    ParticipantElement participantElement =
        arrayList == null || arrayList.isEmpty() ? null : arrayList.get(0);

    if(arrayList != null)
        arrayList.clear();

    return participantElement != null &&
        participantElement.m_keyStream != null &&
        participantElement.m_keyStream.length ==
        Cryptography.CIPHER_HASH_KEYS_LENGTH;
}

private int getBytesPerPixel(Config config)
{
    switch(config)
    {
    case ALPHA_8:
        return 1;
    case ARGB_4444:
        return 2;
    case ARGB_8888:
        return 4;
    case RGB_565:
```

```java
                return 2;
        default:
            break;
        }

        return 1;
    }

    private void prepareListeners()
    {
        Button button1 = (Button) findViewById(R.id.attachment);

        button1.setOnClickListener(new View.OnClickListener()
        {
            public void onClick(View view)
            {
                if(MemberChat.this.isFinishing())
                    return;

                showGalleryActivity();
            }
        });

        button1 = (Button) findViewById(R.id.remove_preview);
        button1.setOnClickListener(new View.OnClickListener()
        {
            public void onClick(View view)
            {
                if(MemberChat.this.isFinishing())
                    return;

                findViewById(R.id.preview_layout).setVisibility(View.GONE);
                m_attachment = null;
            }
        });

        button1 = (Button) findViewById(R.id.send_chat_message);
        button1.setOnClickListener(new View.OnClickListener()
        {
            public void onClick(View view)
            {
                if(MemberChat.this.isFinishing())
                    return;

                final TextView textView1 = (TextView) findViewById
                    (R.id.chat_message);

                if(m_attachment == null &&
                    textView1.getText().toString().trim().isEmpty())
                    return;

                String str = textView1.getText().toString().trim();
                int size = Chat.CHAT_MESSAGE_PREFERRED_SIZE *
                    (int) Math.ceil((1.0 * str.length()) /
                            (1.0 * Chat.CHAT_MESSAGE_PREFERRED_SIZE));

                if(size > str.length())
                {
                    char a[] = new char[size - str.length()];

                    Arrays.fill(a, ' ');
                    str += new String(a);
                }
```

```java
                else if(str.length() > 0)
                {
                    char a[] = new char[1024 + str.length() % 2];

                    Arrays.fill(a, ' ');
                    str += new String(a);
                }

                byte keyStream[] = m_databaseHelper.participantKeyStream
                    (s_cryptography, m_sipHashId);

                if(keyStream == null ||
                   keyStream.length != Cryptography.CIPHER_HASH_KEYS_LENGTH)
                    return;

                Kernel.getInstance().enqueueChatMessage
                    (str, m_sipHashId, m_attachment, keyStream);
                findViewById(R.id.preview_layout).setVisibility(View.GONE);
                m_attachment = null;
                textView1.post(new Runnable()
                {
                    @Override
                    public void run()
                    {
                        textView1.requestFocus();
                    }
                });
                textView1.setText("");
            }
        });

    button1 = (Button) findViewById(R.id.status);
     button1.setOnClickListener(new View.OnClickListener()
    {
        public void onClick(View view)
        {
            if(MemberChat.this.isFinishing())
                return;

            registerForContextMenu(findViewById(R.id.status));
            openContextMenu(findViewById(R.id.status));
        }
    });
    }

    private void prepareSchedulers()
    {
        if(m_statusScheduler == null)
        {
            m_statusScheduler = Executors.newSingleThreadScheduledExecutor();
            m_statusScheduler.scheduleAtFixedRate(new Runnable()
            {
                @Override
                public void run()
                {
                    try
                    {
                        ArrayList<ParticipantElement> arrayList =
                            m_databaseHelper.readParticipants
                            (s_cryptography, m_sipHashId);
                        final ParticipantElement participantElement =
                            arrayList == null || arrayList.isEmpty() ?
                            null : arrayList.get(0);
```

```java
                    final boolean isConnected = Kernel.getInstance().
                        isConnected();
                    final boolean isPaired = isParticipantPaired(arrayList);

                    try
                    {
                        MemberChat.this.runOnUiThread(new Runnable()
                        {
                            @Override
                            public void run()
                            {
                                Button button =
                                    (Button) findViewById(R.id.status);

                                if(!isPaired)
                                    button.setBackgroundResource
                                        (R.drawable.chat_faulty_session);
                                else if(Math.abs(System.
                                            currentTimeMillis() -
                                            participantElement.
                                            m_lastStatusTimestamp) >
                                    Chat.STATUS_WINDOW || !isConnected)
                                    button.setBackgroundResource
                                        (R.drawable.chat_status_offline);
                                else
                                    button.setBackgroundResource
                                        (R.drawable.chat_status_online);

                                if(!m_adapter.contextMenuShown())
                                    m_adapter.notifyDataSetChanged();
                            }
                        });
                    }
                    catch(Exception exception)
                    {
                    }

                    if(arrayList != null)
                        arrayList.clear();
                }
                catch(Exception exception)
                {
                }
            }
        }, 0L, Chat.CONNECTION_STATUS_INTERVAL, TimeUnit.MILLISECONDS);
    }
}

private void prepareStatus()
{
    try
    {
        ArrayList<ParticipantElement> arrayList =
            m_databaseHelper.readParticipants(s_cryptography, m_sipHashId);
        Button button = (Button) findViewById(R.id.send_chat_message);
        ParticipantElement participantElement =
            arrayList == null || arrayList.isEmpty() ?
            null : arrayList.get(0);
        boolean isPaired = isParticipantPaired(arrayList);
        int availableNeighbors = Kernel.getInstance().availableNeighbors();

        if(availableNeighbors > 0 && isPaired)
        {
```

```java
            button.setBackgroundResource(R.drawable.send);
            button.setEnabled(true);
        }
        else
        {
            button.setBackgroundResource(R.drawable.warning);
            button.setEnabled(false);
        }

        button = (Button) findViewById(R.id.status);

        if(!isPaired)
            button.setBackgroundResource(R.drawable.chat_faulty_session);
        else if(!Kernel.getInstance().isConnected() ||
                Math.abs(System.currentTimeMillis() -
                        participantElement.m_lastStatusTimestamp) >
                Chat.STATUS_WINDOW)
            button.setBackgroundResource(R.drawable.chat_status_offline);
        else
            button.setBackgroundResource(R.drawable.chat_status_online);

        if(arrayList != null)
            arrayList.clear();
    }
    catch(Exception exception)
    {
    }

    try
    {
        getSupportActionBar().setSubtitle(Smoke.networkStatusString());
    }
    catch(Exception exception)
    {
    }
}

private void releaseResources()
{
    if(m_statusScheduler != null)
    {
        try
        {
            m_statusScheduler.shutdown();
        }
        catch(Exception exception)
        {
        }

        try
        {
            if(!m_statusScheduler.awaitTermination(60L, TimeUnit.SECONDS))
                m_statusScheduler.shutdownNow();
        }
        catch(Exception exception)
        {
        }
        finally
        {
            m_statusScheduler = null;
        }
    }
}
```

```java
    private void saveState()
    {
        TextView textView1 = (TextView) findViewById(R.id.chat_message);

        State.getInstance().writeCharSequence
            ("member_chat.message", textView1.getText());
    }

    private void showChatActivity()
    {
        saveState();

        Intent intent = new Intent(MemberChat.this, Chat.class);

        startActivity(intent);
        finish();
    }

    private void showFireActivity()
    {
        saveState();

        Intent intent = new Intent(MemberChat.this, Fire.class);

        startActivity(intent);
        finish();
    }

    private void showGalleryActivity()
    {
        Intent intent = new Intent
            (Intent.ACTION_PICK,
             android.provider.MediaStore.Images.Media.EXTERNAL_CONTENT_URI);

        startActivityForResult(intent, SELECT_IMAGE_REQUEST);
    }

    private void showMemberChatActivity()
    {
        saveState();

        Intent intent = new Intent(MemberChat.this, MemberChat.class);

        startActivity(intent);
        finish();
    }

    private void showSettingsActivity()
    {
        saveState();

        Intent intent = new Intent(MemberChat.this, Settings.class);

        startActivity(intent);
        finish();
    }

    private void showSmokescreenActivity()
    {
        Intent intent = new Intent(MemberChat.this, Smokescreen.class);

        startActivity(intent);
```

```java
        finish();
    }

    private void showSteamActivity()
    {
        saveState();

        Intent intent = new Intent(MemberChat.this, Steam.class);

        startActivity(intent);
        finish();
    }

    @Override
    protected void onActivityResult(int requestCode,
                                    int resultCode,
                                    Intent data)
    {
        super.onActivityResult(requestCode, resultCode, data);

        try
        {
            if(data != null &&
                requestCode == SELECT_IMAGE_REQUEST &&
                resultCode == RESULT_OK)
            {
                final ProgressBar bar = (ProgressBar) findViewById
                    (R.id.progress_bar);

                bar.setIndeterminate(true);
                bar.setVisibility(ProgressBar.VISIBLE);
                findViewById(R.id.preview_layout).setVisibility(View.GONE);
                getWindow().setFlags
                    (WindowManager.LayoutParams.FLAG_NOT_TOUCHABLE,
                     WindowManager.LayoutParams.FLAG_NOT_TOUCHABLE);
                m_attachment = null;
                Miscellaneous.enableChildren
                    (findViewById(R.id.main_layout), false);

                class SingleShot implements Runnable
                {
                    private Uri m_uri = null;
                    private byte m_bytes[] = null;

                    SingleShot(Uri uri)
                    {
                        m_uri = uri;
                    }

                    @Override
                    public void run()
                    {
                        ByteArrayOutputStream byteArrayOutputStream = null;
                        InputStream inputStream = null;

                        try
                        {
                            Bitmap bitmap = null;
                            BitmapFactory.Options options = new
                                BitmapFactory.Options();

                            options.inSampleSize = 2;
                            inputStream = getContentResolver().
```

```java
                    openInputStream(m_uri);
                bitmap = BitmapFactory.decodeStream
                    (inputStream, null, options);

                if(bitmap != null)
                {
                    byteArrayOutputStream =
                        new ByteArrayOutputStream();
                    bitmap.compress
                        (Bitmap.CompressFormat.JPEG,
                         Miscellaneous.
                         imagePercentFromArrayLength
                         (bitmap.getByteCount() *
                          getBytesPerPixel(bitmap.getConfig())),
                         byteArrayOutputStream);
                    m_bytes = byteArrayOutputStream.toByteArray();
                }
                else
                    m_bytes = null;
            }
            catch(Exception exception)
            {
                m_bytes = null;
            }
            finally
            {
                try
                {
                    if(byteArrayOutputStream != null)
                        byteArrayOutputStream.close();
                }
                catch(Exception exception)
                {
                }

                try
                {
                    if(inputStream != null)
                        inputStream.close();
                }
                catch(Exception exception)
                {
                }
            }

            try
            {
                MemberChat.this.runOnUiThread(new Runnable()
                {
                    @Override
                    public void run()
                    {
                        try(ByteArrayInputStream
                            byteArrayOutputStream =
                            new ByteArrayInputStream(m_bytes))
                        {
                            BitmapFactory.Options options = new
                                BitmapFactory.Options();

                            options.inSampleSize = 2;

                            Bitmap bitmap =
                                BitmapFactory.decodeStream
```

```java
                                (byteArrayOutputStream,
                                 null,
                                 options);

                            if(bitmap != null)
                            {
                                ImageView imageView = (ImageView)
                                    findViewById(R.id.preview);

                                findViewById(R.id.preview_layout).
                                    setVisibility(View.VISIBLE);
                                imageView.setImageBitmap
                                    (Bitmap.
                                     createScaledBitmap
                                     (bitmap,
                                      bitmap.getWidth(),
                                      Math.min(200,
                                               bitmap.getHeight()),
                                      false));
                                m_attachment = m_bytes;
                            }
                            else
                                findViewById(R.id.preview_layout).
                                    setVisibility(View.GONE);
                        }
                        catch(Exception exception)
                        {
                        }

                        bar.setVisibility(ProgressBar.INVISIBLE);
                        getWindow().clearFlags
                            (WindowManager.LayoutParams.
                             FLAG_NOT_TOUCHABLE);
                        Miscellaneous.enableChildren
                            (findViewById(R.id.main_layout), true);
                    }
                });
            }
            catch(Exception exception)
            {
            }
        }
    }

    Thread thread = new Thread(new SingleShot(data.getData()));

    thread.start();
        }
    }
    catch(Exception exception)
    {
        m_attachment = null;
    }
    }

    @Override
    protected void onCreate(Bundle savedInstanceState)
    {
        super.onCreate(savedInstanceState);
        setContentView(R.layout.activity_member_chat);
        setSupportActionBar((Toolbar) findViewById(R.id.toolbar));
        m_layoutManager = new SmokeLinearLayoutManager(MemberChat.this);
        m_layoutManager.setOrientation(LinearLayoutManager.VERTICAL);
```

```java
        m_layoutManager.setReverseLayout(true);
        m_layoutManager.setStackFromEnd(true);
        m_name = m_sipHashId = State.getInstance().getString
            ("member_chat_siphash_id");

        try
        {
            m_oid = Integer.parseInt
                (State.getInstance().getString("member_chat_oid"));
        }
        catch(Exception exception)
        {
            m_oid = -1;
        }


        m_receiver = new MemberChatBroadcastReceiver();
        m_recyclerView = (RecyclerView) findViewById(R.id.recycler_view);
        m_recyclerView.setHasFixedSize(true);
        m_selectedMessages = new Hashtable<> ();

        if(m_sipHashId.isEmpty())
            m_name = m_sipHashId = Cryptography.DEFAULT_SIPHASH_ID;

        /*
        ** Prepare various widgets.
        */

        m_adapter = new MemberChatAdapter(this, m_sipHashId);
        m_adapter.registerAdapterDataObserver
            (new RecyclerView.AdapterDataObserver()
            {
                @Override
                public void onItemRangeInserted
                    (int positionStart, int itemCount)
                {
                    m_layoutManager.smoothScrollToPosition
                        (m_recyclerView, null, positionStart);
                }

                @Override
                public void onItemRangeRemoved
                    (int positionStart, int itemCount)
                {
                    m_layoutManager.smoothScrollToPosition
                        (m_recyclerView, null, positionStart - itemCount);
                }
            });
        m_name = m_databaseHelper.nameFromSipHashId
            (s_cryptography, m_sipHashId);

        if(m_name.isEmpty())
            m_name = m_sipHashId;

        m_recyclerView.setAdapter(m_adapter);
        m_recyclerView.setLayoutManager(m_layoutManager);

        String string =        Miscellaneous.prepareSipHashId(m_sipHashId);

        try
        {
            getSupportActionBar().setSubtitle(Smoke.networkStatusString());

            if(string.isEmpty())
```

```java
                getSupportActionBar().setTitle("Smoke | Member Chat");
            else
                getSupportActionBar().setTitle
                    ("Smoke | " + m_name + "@" + string);
        }
        catch(Exception exception)
        {
        }

        /*
        ** Prepare listeners.
        */

        prepareListeners();

        /*
        ** Restore states.
        */

        try
        {
            m_layoutManager.smoothScrollToPosition
                (m_recyclerView, null, m_adapter.getItemCount() - 1);

            TextView textView1 = (TextView) findViewById(R.id.chat_message);

            textView1.setText
                (State.getInstance().getCharSequence("member_chat.message"));
        }
        catch(Exception exception)
        {
        }
    }

    @Override
    protected void onPause()
    {
        super.onPause();

        if(m_receiverRegistered)
        {
            LocalBroadcastManager.getInstance(getApplicationContext()).
                unregisterReceiver(m_receiver);
            m_receiverRegistered = false;
        }

        releaseResources();
        saveState();
    }

    @Override
    protected void onResume()
    {
        super.onResume();

        if(!m_receiverRegistered)
        {
            IntentFilter intentFilter = new IntentFilter();

            intentFilter.addAction("org.purple.smoke.chat_local_message");
            intentFilter.addAction("org.purple.smoke.chat_message");
            intentFilter.addAction("org.purple.smoke.half_and_half_call");
            intentFilter.addAction("org.purple.smoke.neighbor_aborted");
```

```java
            intentFilter.addAction("org.purple.smoke.neighbor_disconnected");
            intentFilter.addAction("org.purple.smoke.network_connected");
            intentFilter.addAction("org.purple.smoke.network_disconnected");
            intentFilter.addAction
                ("org.purple.smoke.state_participants_populated");
            intentFilter.addAction("org.purple.smoke.time");
            LocalBroadcastManager.getInstance(getApplicationContext()).
                registerReceiver(m_receiver, intentFilter);
            m_receiverRegistered = true;
        }

        prepareSchedulers();
        prepareStatus();

        try
        {
            m_adapter.notifyDataSetChanged();
            m_layoutManager.smoothScrollToPosition
                (m_recyclerView, null, m_adapter.getItemCount() - 1);

            TextView textView1 = (TextView) findViewById(R.id.chat_message);

            textView1.setText
                (State.getInstance().getCharSequence("member_chat.message"));
        }
        catch(Exception exception)
        {
        }
    }

    public boolean isMessageSelected(int oid)
    {
        m_selectedMessagesMutex.readLock().lock();

        try
        {
            if(m_selectedMessages.containsKey(oid))
                return m_selectedMessages.get(oid);
            else
                return false;
        }
        finally
        {
            m_selectedMessagesMutex.readLock().unlock();
        }
    }

    @Override
    public boolean onContextItemSelected(MenuItem menuItem)
    {
        if(menuItem == null)
            return false;

        final int groupId = menuItem.getGroupId();
        final int itemId = menuItem.getItemId();

        /*
        ** Prepare a listener.
        */

        DialogInterface.OnCancelListener listener =
            new DialogInterface.OnCancelListener()
            {
```

```java
            public void onCancel(DialogInterface dialog)
            {
                switch(groupId)
                {
                case ContextMenuEnumerator.CUSTOM_SESSION:
                    try
                    {
                        String string = State.getInstance().
                            getString("member_chat_secret_input").trim();

                        if(!string.isEmpty())
                        {
                            byte bytes[] = Cryptography.pbkdf2
                                (Cryptography.
                                 sha512(string.getBytes(StandardCharsets.
                                                        UTF_8)),
                                 string.toCharArray(),
                                 Chat.CUSTOM_SESSION_ITERATION_COUNT,
                                 160); // SHA-1
                            int oid = m_databaseHelper.
                                participantOidFromSipHash
                                (s_cryptography, m_sipHashId);

                            if(bytes != null)
                                bytes = Cryptography.pbkdf2
                                    (Cryptography.
                                     sha512(string.
                                            getBytes(StandardCharsets.
                                                     UTF_8)),
                                     Base64.
                                     encodeToString(bytes, Base64.NO_WRAP).
                                     toCharArray(),
                                     1,
                                     Cryptography.CIPHER_HASH_KEYS_LENGTH *
                                     8);

                            m_databaseHelper.setParticipantKeyStream
                                (s_cryptography, bytes, oid);
                        }
                    }
                    catch(Exception exception)
                    {
                    }

                    State.getInstance().removeKey
                        ("member_chat_secret_input");
                    break;
                case ContextMenuEnumerator.DELETE_ALL_MESSAGES:
                    if(State.getInstance().getString("dialog_accepted").
                       equals("true"))
                    {
                        m_databaseHelper.deleteParticipantMessages
                            (s_cryptography, m_sipHashId);
                        m_selectedMessages.clear();
                        m_adapter.notifyDataSetChanged();
                    }

                    break;
                case ContextMenuEnumerator.DELETE_MESSAGE:
                    if(State.getInstance().getString("dialog_accepted").
                       equals("true"))
                    {
                        m_databaseHelper.deleteParticipantMessage
```

```java
                        (s_cryptography, m_sipHashId, itemId);
                m_selectedMessages.remove(itemId);
                m_adapter.notifyDataSetChanged();
            }

        break;
        case ContextMenuEnumerator.DELETE_SELECTED_MESSAGES:
            if(State.getInstance().getString("dialog_accepted").
                equals("true"))
            {
                Dialog d = null;

                try
                {
                    d = new Dialog(MemberChat.this);
                    Windows.showProgressDialog
                        (MemberChat.this,
                         d,
                         "Deleting selected message(s).");

                    Thread thread = new Thread
                        (new RemoveSelectedMessages(d,
                                                    m_sipHashId));

                    thread.start();
                    thread.join();
                }
                catch(Exception exception_1)
                {
                }
                finally
                {
                    try
                    {
                        if(d != null)
                            d.dismiss();
                    }
                    catch(Exception exception_2)
                    {
                    }
                }

                m_adapter.notifyDataSetChanged();
            }

        break;
        case ContextMenuEnumerator.JUGGERKNOT:
        case ContextMenuEnumerator.JUGGERNAUT:
            try
            {
                String string = State.getInstance().
                    getString("member_chat_secret_input").trim();

                if(!string.isEmpty())
                {
                    byte keyStream[] = m_databaseHelper.
                        participantKeyStream
                        (s_cryptography, m_sipHashId);

                    if(!(keyStream == null ||
                         keyStream.length !=
                         Cryptography.CIPHER_HASH_KEYS_LENGTH))
                        Kernel.getInstance().enqueueJuggernaut
```

```
                                    (string,
                                    m_sipHashId,
                                    groupId ==
                                    ContextMenuEnumerator.JUGGERKNOT,
                                    keyStream);
                    }
                }
                catch(Exception exception)
                {
                }

                State.getInstance().removeKey
                    ("member_chat_secret_input");
                break;
            default:
                break;
            }
        }
    };

    switch(groupId)
    {
    case ContextMenuEnumerator.CALL_VIA_MCELIECE:
        Kernel.getInstance().call
            (m_oid, ParticipantCall.Algorithms.MCELIECE, m_sipHashId);
        break;
    case ContextMenuEnumerator.CALL_VIA_RSA:
        Kernel.getInstance().
            call(m_oid, ParticipantCall.Algorithms.RSA, m_sipHashId);
        break;
    case ContextMenuEnumerator.COPY_TEXT:
        try
        {
            View view = m_layoutManager.findViewByPosition(itemId);

            if(view != null)
            {
                TextView textView = (TextView) view.findViewById
                    (R.id.text);

                if(textView != null)
                {
                    ClipboardManager clipboardManager = (ClipboardManager)
                        getSystemService(Context.CLIPBOARD_SERVICE);

                    if(clipboardManager != null)
                    {
                        ClipData clipData = null;
                        SpannableStringBuilder spannableStringBuilder =
                            new SpannableStringBuilder(textView.getText());

                        spannableStringBuilder.clearSpans();
                        clipData = ClipData.newPlainText
                            ("Smoke", spannableStringBuilder.toString());
                        clipboardManager.setPrimaryClip(clipData);
                    }
                }
            }
        }
        catch(Exception exception)
        {
        }
```

```java
            break;
        case ContextMenuEnumerator.CUSTOM_SESSION:
            Miscellaneous.showTextInputDialog
                (MemberChat.this,
                 listener,
                 "Please provide a secret.",
                 "",
                 "Secret");
            break;
        case ContextMenuEnumerator.DELETE_ALL_MESSAGES:
            Miscellaneous.showPromptDialog
                (MemberChat.this,
                 listener,
                 "Are you sure that you wish to delete all " +
                 "of the messages?");
            break;
        case ContextMenuEnumerator.DELETE_MESSAGE:
            Miscellaneous.showPromptDialog
                (MemberChat.this,
                 listener,
                 "Are you sure that you wish to delete the " +
                 "selected message?");
            break;
        case ContextMenuEnumerator.DELETE_SELECTED_MESSAGES:
            Miscellaneous.showPromptDialog
                (MemberChat.this,
                 listener,
                 "Are you sure that you wish to delete the " +
                 "selected message(s)?");
            break;
        case ContextMenuEnumerator.JUGGERKNOT:
        case ContextMenuEnumerator.JUGGERNAUT:
            if(groupId == ContextMenuEnumerator.JUGGERKNOT)
                Miscellaneous.showTextInputDialog
                    (MemberChat.this,
                     listener,
                     "Please provide a secret. The Juggernaut Protocol " +
                     "will be initiated shortly (" +
                     Kernel.JUGGERNAUT_DELAY / 1000.0 +
                     " seconds) after this dialog is confirmed. If the " +
                     "protocol completes correctly, new session credentials " +
                     "will be generated.",
                     "",
                     "Juggernaut Secret");
            else
                Miscellaneous.showTextInputDialog
                    (MemberChat.this,
                     listener,
                     "Please provide a secret. The Juggernaut Protocol " +
                     "will be initiated shortly (" +
                     Kernel.JUGGERNAUT_DELAY / 1000.0 +
                     " seconds) after this dialog is confirmed.",
                     "",
                     "Juggernaut Secret");

            break;
        case ContextMenuEnumerator.OPTIONAL_SIGNATURES:
            menuItem.setChecked(!menuItem.isChecked());

            String strings[] = null;
            StringBuilder stringBuilder = new StringBuilder
                (m_databaseHelper.
                 readParticipantOptions(s_cryptography, m_sipHashId));
```

```java
        strings = stringBuilder.toString().split(";");

        if(strings == null || strings.length == 0)
        {
            if(menuItem.isChecked())
                stringBuilder.append("optional_signatures = true");
            else
                stringBuilder.append("optional_signatures = false");
        }
        else
        {
            stringBuilder.delete(0, stringBuilder.length());

            int i = 0;
            int length = strings.length;

            for(String string : strings)
            {
                if(!(string.equals("optional_signatures = false") ||
                    string.equals("optional_signatures = true")))
                {
                    stringBuilder.append(string);

                    if(i != length - 1)
                        stringBuilder.append(";");
                }

                i += 1;
            }

            if(stringBuilder.length() > 0)
                stringBuilder.append(";");

            stringBuilder.append("optional_signatures = ");
            stringBuilder.append(menuItem.isChecked() ? "true" : "false");
        }

        m_databaseHelper.writeParticipantOptions
            (s_cryptography, stringBuilder.toString(), m_sipHashId);
        break;
    case ContextMenuEnumerator.RESEND_MESSAGE:
        Kernel.getInstance().resendMessage(m_sipHashId, itemId);
        break;
    case ContextMenuEnumerator.RETRIEVE_MESSAGES:
        Kernel.getInstance().retrieveChatMessages(m_sipHashId);
        break;
    case ContextMenuEnumerator.SAVE_ATTACHMENT:
        try
        {
            View view = m_layoutManager.findViewByPosition(itemId);

            if(view != null)
            {
                ImageView imageView = (ImageView) view.findViewById
                    (R.id.image);

                if(imageView != null)
                {
                    final ProgressBar bar = (ProgressBar) findViewById
                        (R.id.progress_bar);

                    bar.setIndeterminate(true);
```

```java
bar.setVisibility(ProgressBar.VISIBLE);
getWindow().setFlags
    (WindowManager.LayoutParams.FLAG_NOT_TOUCHABLE,
     WindowManager.LayoutParams.FLAG_NOT_TOUCHABLE);
Miscellaneous.enableChildren
    (findViewById(R.id.main_layout), false);

class SingleShot implements Runnable
{
    public SingleShot()
    {
    }

    @Override
    public void run()
    {
        ByteArrayInputStream byteArrayInputStream =
            null;
        ByteArrayOutputStream byteArrayOutputStream =
            null;

        try
        {
            BitmapFactory.Options options =
                new BitmapFactory.Options();

            options.inSampleSize = 2;

            MemberChatElement memberChatElement =
                m_databaseHelper.
                readMemberChat(s_cryptography,
                               m_sipHashId,
                               itemId);

            byteArrayInputStream =
                new ByteArrayInputStream
                (memberChatElement.m_attachment);

            /*
            ** Convert the bytes into a bitmap.
            */

            Bitmap bitmap = BitmapFactory.decodeStream
                (byteArrayInputStream, null, options);

            if(bitmap != null)
            {
                byteArrayOutputStream = new
                    ByteArrayOutputStream();
                bitmap.compress
                    (Bitmap.CompressFormat.JPEG,
                     100,
                     byteArrayOutputStream);

                File file = new File
                    (Environment.
                     getExternalStoragePublicDirectory
                     (Environment.DIRECTORY_DOWNLOADS),
                     "smoke-" +
                     System.currentTimeMillis() +
                     ".jpg");
                FileOutputStream fileOutputStream =
                    null;
```

```java
            try
            {
                if(!file.exists())
                    file.createNewFile();

                fileOutputStream =
                    new FileOutputStream(file);
                fileOutputStream.write
                    (byteArrayOutputStream.
                    toByteArray());
            }
            catch(Exception exception)
            {
            }
            finally
            {
                if(fileOutputStream != null)
                    fileOutputStream.close();
            }
        }
    }
    catch(Exception exception)
    {
    }
    finally
    {
        try
        {
            if(byteArrayInputStream != null)
                byteArrayInputStream.close();
        }
        catch(Exception exception)
        {
        }

        try
        {
            if(byteArrayOutputStream != null)
                byteArrayOutputStream.close();
        }
        catch(Exception exception)
        {
        }
    }

    try
    {
        MemberChat.this.runOnUiThread(new Runnable()
        {
            @Override
            public void run()
            {
                bar.setVisibility
                    (ProgressBar.INVISIBLE);
                getWindow().clearFlags
                    (WindowManager.LayoutParams.
                    FLAG_NOT_TOUCHABLE);
                Miscellaneous.enableChildren
                    (findViewById(R.id.main_layout),
                    true);
            }
        });
```

```java
                                    }
                            catch(Exception exception)
                                {
                                }
                        }
                    }

                    Thread thread = new Thread(new SingleShot());

                    thread.start();
                }
            }
        }
        catch(Exception exception)
        {
        }

        break;
    case ContextMenuEnumerator.SELECTION_STATE:
        m_messageSelectionStateEnabled = !m_messageSelectionStateEnabled;
        m_selectedMessages.clear();
        m_adapter.notifyDataSetChanged();
        break;
    default:
        break;
    }

    return true;
}

@Override
public boolean onCreateOptionsMenu(Menu menu)
{
    getMenuInflater().inflate(R.menu.member_chat_menu, menu);
    return true;
}

@Override
public boolean onOptionsItemSelected(MenuItem menuItem)
{
    int groupId = menuItem.getGroupId();
    int itemId = menuItem.getItemId();

    if(groupId == Menu.NONE)
        switch(itemId)
        {
        case R.id.action_chat:
            m_databaseHelper.writeSetting(null, "lastActivity", "Chat");
            showChatActivity();
            return true;
        case R.id.action_exit:
            Smoke.exit(MemberChat.this);
            return true;
        case R.id.action_fire:
            m_databaseHelper.writeSetting(null, "lastActivity", "Fire");
            showFireActivity();
            return true;
        case R.id.action_settings:
            m_databaseHelper.writeSetting(null, "lastActivity", "Settings");
            showSettingsActivity();
            return true;
        case R.id.action_smokescreen:
            showSmokescreenActivity();
```

```java
                return true;
            case R.id.action_steam:
                m_databaseHelper.writeSetting(null, "lastActivity", "Steam");
                showSteamActivity();
                return true;
            default:
                break;
            }
    else
        {
            String sipHashId = menuItem.getTitle().toString();
            int indexOf = sipHashId.indexOf("(");

            if(indexOf >= 0)
                sipHashId = sipHashId.substring(indexOf + 1).replace(")", "");

            sipHashId = Miscellaneous.prepareSipHashId(sipHashId);
            State.getInstance().setString
                ("member_chat_oid", String.valueOf(itemId));
            State.getInstance().setString
                ("member_chat_siphash_id", sipHashId);
            m_databaseHelper.writeSetting
                (null, "lastActivity", "MemberChat");
            m_databaseHelper.writeSetting
                (s_cryptography, "member_chat_oid", String.valueOf(itemId));
            m_databaseHelper.writeSetting
                (s_cryptography, "member_chat_siphash_id", sipHashId);
            showMemberChatActivity();
        }

        return super.onOptionsItemSelected(menuItem);
    }

    public boolean messageSelectionState()
    {
        return m_messageSelectionStateEnabled;
    }

    public int selectedMessagesCount()
    {
        return m_selectedMessages.size();
    }

    @Override
    public void onBackPressed()
    {
        Intent intent = new Intent();

        intent.putExtra("Result", "Done");
        setResult(RESULT_OK, intent);
        super.onBackPressed();
    }

    @Override
    public void onContextMenuClosed(Menu menu)
    {
        m_adapter.setContextMenuClosed();
        super.onContextMenuClosed(menu);
    }

    @Override
    public void onCreateContextMenu(ContextMenu menu,
                                    View view,
```

```java
                                ContextMenuInfo menuInfo)
    {
        if(menu == null || view == null)
            return;

        super.onCreateContextMenu(menu, view, menuInfo);

        ArrayList<ParticipantElement> arrayList =
            m_databaseHelper.readParticipants
            (s_cryptography, m_sipHashId);
        MenuItem menuItem = null;
        boolean isParticipantPaired = isParticipantPaired(null);
        boolean state = Kernel.getInstance().isConnected();

        menu.add(ContextMenuEnumerator.CALL_VIA_MCELIECE,
                -1,
                0,
                "Call via McEliece (Fujisaki)").setEnabled(state);
        menu.add(ContextMenuEnumerator.CALL_VIA_RSA,
                -1,
                0,
                "Call via RSA").setEnabled(state);
        menu.add(ContextMenuEnumerator.CUSTOM_SESSION,
                -1,
                0,
                "Custom Session");
        menu.add(ContextMenuEnumerator.JUGGERKNOT,
                -1,
                0,
                "JuggerKnot Credentials").
            setEnabled(isParticipantPaired && state);
        menu.add(ContextMenuEnumerator.JUGGERNAUT,
                -1,
                0,
                "Juggernaut").setEnabled(isParticipantPaired && state);
        menuItem = menu.add(ContextMenuEnumerator.OPTIONAL_SIGNATURES,
                    -1,
                    0,
                    "Optional Signatures");
        menuItem.setCheckable(true);
        menuItem.setChecked
            (m_databaseHelper.
             readParticipantOptions(s_cryptography, m_sipHashId).toString().
             contains("optional_signatures = true"));
        menu.add(ContextMenuEnumerator.RETRIEVE_MESSAGES,
                -1,
                0,
                "Retrieve Messages").setEnabled
            (!m_databaseHelper.readSetting(s_cryptography, "ozone_address").
             isEmpty() && state);
    }

    @Override
    public boolean onPrepareOptionsMenu(Menu menu)
    {
        boolean isAuthenticated = State.getInstance().isAuthenticated();

        if(!m_databaseHelper.accountPrepared())
            /*
            ** The database may have been modified or removed.
            */

            isAuthenticated = true;
```

```java
        menu.findItem(R.id.action_authenticate).setEnabled(!isAuthenticated);
        Miscellaneous.addMembersToMenu(menu, 7, 250);
        return true;
    }

    public void setMessageSelected(int oid, boolean isChecked)
    {
        if(isChecked)
            m_selectedMessages.put(oid, isChecked);
        else
            m_selectedMessages.remove(oid);
    }
}
```

/* MemberChatAdapter.java –

```
https://github.com/textbrowser/smoke/blob/master/Smoke/app/src/main/java/org/p
urple/smoke/MemberChatAdapter.java
** Copyright (c) Alexis Megas.
** All rights reserved.
**
** Redistribution and use in source and binary forms, with or without
** modification, are permitted provided that the following conditions
** are met:
** 1. Redistributions of source code must retain the above copyright
**    notice, this list of conditions and the following disclaimer.
** 2. Redistributions in binary form must reproduce the above copyright
**    notice, this list of conditions and the following disclaimer in the
**    documentation and/or other materials provided with the distribution.
** 3. The name of the author may not be used to endorse or promote products
**    derived from Smoke without specific prior written permission.
**
** SMOKE IS PROVIDED BY THE AUTHOR ``AS IS'' AND ANY EXPRESS OR
** IMPLIED WARRANTIES, INCLUDING, BUT NOT LIMITED TO, THE IMPLIED WARRANTIES
** OF MERCHANTABILITY AND FITNESS FOR A PARTICULAR PURPOSE ARE DISCLAIMED.
** IN NO EVENT SHALL THE AUTHOR BE LIABLE FOR ANY DIRECT, INDIRECT,
** INCIDENTAL, SPECIAL, EXEMPLARY, OR CONSEQUENTIAL DAMAGES (INCLUDING, BUT
** NOT LIMITED TO, PROCUREMENT OF SUBSTITUTE GOODS OR SERVICES; LOSS OF USE,
** DATA, OR PROFITS; OR BUSINESS INTERRUPTION) HOWEVER CAUSED AND ON ANY
** THEORY OF LIABILITY, WHETHER IN CONTRACT, STRICT LIABILITY, OR TORT
** (INCLUDING NEGLIGENCE OR OTHERWISE) ARISING IN ANY WAY OUT OF THE USE OF
** SMOKE, EVEN IF ADVISED OF THE POSSIBILITY OF SUCH DAMAGE.
*/

package org.purple.smoke;

import android.support.v7.widget.RecyclerView;
import android.view.ContextMenu;
import android.view.ContextMenu.ContextMenuInfo;
import android.view.MenuItem;
import android.view.View;
import android.view.View.OnCreateContextMenuListener;
import android.view.ViewGroup;

public class MemberChatAdapter extends RecyclerView.Adapter
                                    <MemberChatAdapter.ViewHolder>
{
    private MemberChat m_memberChat = null;
    private String m_sipHashId = "";
    private boolean m_contextMenuShown = false;
```

```java
private final static Cryptography s_cryptography =
    Cryptography.getInstance();
private final static Database s_database = Database.getInstance();

public class ViewHolder extends RecyclerView.ViewHolder
    implements OnCreateContextMenuListener
{
    ChatBubble m_chatBubble = null;
    String m_name = "";
    String m_sipHashId = "";
    boolean m_canResend = false;
    boolean m_hasAttachment = false;
    int m_position = -1;

     public ViewHolder(ChatBubble chatBubble, String sipHashId)
     {
         super(chatBubble.view());
         chatBubble.view().setOnCreateContextMenuListener(this);
         m_chatBubble = chatBubble;
         m_name = s_database.nameFromSipHashId(s_cryptography, sipHashId);
         m_sipHashId = sipHashId;
     }

    public void onCreateContextMenu(ContextMenu menu,
                                    View view,
                                    ContextMenuInfo menuInfo)
    {
        if(menu == null || view == null)
           return;

        m_contextMenuShown = true;

        /*
        ** Please update the first parameter if the context menu
        ** in MemberChat is modified!
        */

        MenuItem menuItem = null;

        menu.add(MemberChat.ContextMenuEnumerator.COPY_TEXT,
                 m_position,
                 0,
                 "Copy Text");
        menu.add(MemberChat.ContextMenuEnumerator.DELETE_ALL_MESSAGES,
                 -1,
                 1,
                 "Delete All Messages");
        menu.add(MemberChat.ContextMenuEnumerator.DELETE_MESSAGE,
                 view.getId(),
                 2,
                 "Delete Message").setEnabled(view.getId() != -1);
        menu.add(MemberChat.ContextMenuEnumerator.DELETE_SELECTED_MESSAGES,
                 -1,
                 3,
                 "Delete Selected Message(s)").setEnabled
             (m_memberChat.selectedMessagesCount() > 0);
        menu.add(MemberChat.ContextMenuEnumerator.RESEND_MESSAGE,
                 m_position,
                 4,
                 "Resend Message").setEnabled(m_canResend);
        menu.add
            (MemberChat.ContextMenuEnumerator.SAVE_ATTACHMENT,
             m_position,
```

```java
                    5,
                    "Save Attachment").setEnabled(m_hasAttachment);
                menuItem = menu.add
                    (MemberChat.ContextMenuEnumerator.SELECTION_STATE,
                     m_position,
                     6,
                     "Selection State").setCheckable(true);
                menuItem.setChecked(m_memberChat.messageSelectionState());
        }

        public void setData(MemberChatElement memberChatElement, int position)
        {
            if(m_chatBubble == null)
                return;
            else if(memberChatElement == null)
            {
                m_canResend = false;
                m_chatBubble.setError(true);
                m_chatBubble.setMessageSelectionStateEnabled(false);
                m_chatBubble.setName(ChatBubble.Locations.LEFT, "?");
                m_chatBubble.setText
                    (ChatBubble.Locations.LEFT,
                     "Smoke malfunction! The database entry is zero!\n");
                m_hasAttachment = false;
                m_position = position;
                return;
            }

            StringBuilder stringBuilder = new StringBuilder();
            boolean local = false;

            if(memberChatElement.m_fromSmokeStack.equals("local") ||
                memberChatElement.m_fromSmokeStack.equals("local-protocol"))
                local = true;

            stringBuilder.append(memberChatElement.m_message.trim());

            if(!memberChatElement.m_message.trim().isEmpty())
                stringBuilder.append("\n");

            m_canResend = memberChatElement.m_fromSmokeStack.equals("local");
            m_chatBubble.setDate(memberChatElement.m_timestamp);
            m_chatBubble.setFromeSmokeStack
                (memberChatElement.m_fromSmokeStack.equals("true"));
            m_chatBubble.setImageAttachment(memberChatElement.m_attachment);
            m_chatBubble.setLocal(local);
            m_chatBubble.setMessageSelected
                (m_memberChat.isMessageSelected(memberChatElement.m_oid));
            m_chatBubble.setMessageSelectionStateEnabled
                (m_memberChat.messageSelectionState());
            m_chatBubble.setOid(memberChatElement.m_oid);

            if(!local)
            {
                m_chatBubble.setName(ChatBubble.Locations.LEFT, m_name);
                m_chatBubble.setRead(ChatBubble.Locations.LEFT, false);
                m_chatBubble.setSent
                    (ChatBubble.Locations.LEFT,
                     memberChatElement.m_messageSent);
                m_chatBubble.setText
                    (ChatBubble.Locations.LEFT, stringBuilder.toString());
            }
            else
```

```java
            {
                m_chatBubble.setName(ChatBubble.Locations.RIGHT, "M");
                m_chatBubble.setRead
                    (ChatBubble.Locations.RIGHT,
                     memberChatElement.m_messageRead);
                m_chatBubble.setSent
                    (ChatBubble.Locations.RIGHT,
                     memberChatElement.m_messageSent);
                m_chatBubble.setText
                    (ChatBubble.Locations.RIGHT, stringBuilder.toString());
            }

            m_hasAttachment = memberChatElement.m_attachment != null &&
                memberChatElement.m_attachment.length > 0;
            m_position = position;
        }
    }

    public MemberChatAdapter(MemberChat memberChat, String sipHashId)
    {
        m_memberChat = memberChat;
        m_sipHashId = sipHashId;
    }

    @Override
    public MemberChatAdapter.ViewHolder onCreateViewHolder
        (ViewGroup parent, int viewType)
    {
        return new ViewHolder
            (new ChatBubble(parent.getContext(), m_memberChat, parent),
             m_sipHashId);
    }

    public boolean contextMenuShown()
    {
        return m_contextMenuShown;
    }

    @Override
    public int getItemCount()
    {
        return (int) s_database.countOfMessages(s_cryptography, m_sipHashId);
    }

    @Override
    public void onBindViewHolder(ViewHolder viewHolder, int position)
    {
        if(viewHolder == null)
            return;

        MemberChatElement memberChatElement = s_database.readMemberChat
            (s_cryptography, m_sipHashId, position);

        viewHolder.setData(memberChatElement, position);
    }

    public void setContextMenuClosed()
    {
        m_contextMenuShown = false;
    }
}
```

/* MemberChatElement.java –

```
https://github.com/textbrowser/smoke/blob/master/Smoke/app/src/main/java/org/p
urple/smoke/MemberChatElement.java
** Copyright (c) Alexis Megas.
** All rights reserved.
**
** Redistribution and use in source and binary forms, with or without
** modification, are permitted provided that the following conditions
** are met:
** 1. Redistributions of source code must retain the above copyright
**    notice, this list of conditions and the following disclaimer.
** 2. Redistributions in binary form must reproduce the above copyright
**    notice, this list of conditions and the following disclaimer in the
**    documentation and/or other materials provided with the distribution.
** 3. The name of the author may not be used to endorse or promote products
**    derived from Smoke without specific prior written permission.
**
** SMOKE IS PROVIDED BY THE AUTHOR ``AS IS'' AND ANY EXPRESS OR
** IMPLIED WARRANTIES, INCLUDING, BUT NOT LIMITED TO, THE IMPLIED WARRANTIES
** OF MERCHANTABILITY AND FITNESS FOR A PARTICULAR PURPOSE ARE DISCLAIMED.
** IN NO EVENT SHALL THE AUTHOR BE LIABLE FOR ANY DIRECT, INDIRECT,
** INCIDENTAL, SPECIAL, EXEMPLARY, OR CONSEQUENTIAL DAMAGES (INCLUDING, BUT
** NOT LIMITED TO, PROCUREMENT OF SUBSTITUTE GOODS OR SERVICES; LOSS OF USE,
** DATA, OR PROFITS; OR BUSINESS INTERRUPTION) HOWEVER CAUSED AND ON ANY
** THEORY OF LIABILITY, WHETHER IN CONTRACT, STRICT LIABILITY, OR TORT
** (INCLUDING NEGLIGENCE OR OTHERWISE) ARISING IN ANY WAY OUT OF THE USE OF
** SMOKE, EVEN IF ADVISED OF THE POSSIBILITY OF SUCH DAMAGE.
*/

package org.purple.smoke;

public class MemberChatElement
{
    public String m_fromSmokeStack = "";
    public String m_message = "";
    public boolean m_messageRead = false;
    public boolean m_messageSent = false;
    public byte m_attachment[] = null;
    public int m_oid = -1;
    public long m_timestamp = -1L;

    public MemberChatElement()
    {
    }
}
```

/* MessageElement.java –

```
https://github.com/textbrowser/smoke/blob/master/Smoke/app/src/main/java/org/p
urple/smoke/MessageElement.java
** Copyright (c) Alexis Megas.
** All rights reserved.
**
** Redistribution and use in source and binary forms, with or without
** modification, are permitted provided that the following conditions
** are met:
** 1. Redistributions of source code must retain the above copyright
**    notice, this list of conditions and the following disclaimer.
** 2. Redistributions in binary form must reproduce the above copyright
**    notice, this list of conditions and the following disclaimer in the
```

```java
**     documentation and/or other materials provided with the distribution.
** 3. The name of the author may not be used to endorse or promote products
**    derived from Smoke without specific prior written permission.
**
** SMOKE IS PROVIDED BY THE AUTHOR ``AS IS'' AND ANY EXPRESS OR
** IMPLIED WARRANTIES, INCLUDING, BUT NOT LIMITED TO, THE IMPLIED WARRANTIES
** OF MERCHANTABILITY AND FITNESS FOR A PARTICULAR PURPOSE ARE DISCLAIMED.
** IN NO EVENT SHALL THE AUTHOR BE LIABLE FOR ANY DIRECT, INDIRECT,
** INCIDENTAL, SPECIAL, EXEMPLARY, OR CONSEQUENTIAL DAMAGES (INCLUDING, BUT
** NOT LIMITED TO, PROCUREMENT OF SUBSTITUTE GOODS OR SERVICES; LOSS OF USE,
** DATA, OR PROFITS; OR BUSINESS INTERRUPTION) HOWEVER CAUSED AND ON ANY
** THEORY OF LIABILITY, WHETHER IN CONTRACT, STRICT LIABILITY, OR TORT
** (INCLUDING NEGLIGENCE OR OTHERWISE) ARISING IN ANY WAY OUT OF THE USE OF
** SMOKE, EVEN IF ADVISED OF THE POSSIBILITY OF SUCH DAMAGE.
*/

package org.purple.smoke;

public class MessageElement
{
    public String m_id = "";
    public String m_message = "";
    public String m_name = "";
    public boolean m_purple = false;
    public byte m_attachment[] = null;
    public byte m_keyStream[] = null;
    public byte m_messageIdentity[] = null;
    public final static int CHAT_MESSAGE_TYPE = 0;
    public final static int FIRE_MESSAGE_TYPE = 1;
    public final static int FIRE_STATUS_MESSAGE_TYPE = 2;
    public final static int JUGGERNAUT_MESSAGE_TYPE = 3;
    public final static int RESEND_CHAT_MESSAGE_TYPE = 4;
    public final static int RETRIEVE_MESSAGES_MESSAGE_TYPE = 5;
    public final static int SHARE_SIPHASH_ID_MESSAGE_TYPE = 6;
    public final static int STEAM_KEY_EXCHANGE_MESSAGE_TYPE = 7;
    public int m_messageType = -1;
    public int m_position = -1;
    public long m_delay = -1L;
    public long m_sequence = -1L;
    public long m_timestamp = -1L;

    public MessageElement()
    {
    }
}
```

/* Messages.java –

```java
** 3. The name of the author may not be used to endorse or promote products
**    derived from Smoke without specific prior written permission.
**
** SMOKE IS PROVIDED BY THE AUTHOR ``AS IS'' AND ANY EXPRESS OR
** IMPLIED WARRANTIES, INCLUDING, BUT NOT LIMITED TO, THE IMPLIED WARRANTIES
** OF MERCHANTABILITY AND FITNESS FOR A PARTICULAR PURPOSE ARE DISCLAIMED.
** IN NO EVENT SHALL THE AUTHOR BE LIABLE FOR ANY DIRECT, INDIRECT,
** INCIDENTAL, SPECIAL, EXEMPLARY, OR CONSEQUENTIAL DAMAGES (INCLUDING, BUT
** NOT LIMITED TO, PROCUREMENT OF SUBSTITUTE GOODS OR SERVICES; LOSS OF USE,
** DATA, OR PROFITS; OR BUSINESS INTERRUPTION) HOWEVER CAUSED AND ON ANY
** THEORY OF LIABILITY, WHETHER IN CONTRACT, STRICT LIABILITY, OR TORT
** (INCLUDING NEGLIGENCE OR OTHERWISE) ARISING IN ANY WAY OUT OF THE USE OF
** SMOKE, EVEN IF ADVISED OF THE POSSIBILITY OF SUCH DAMAGE.
*/

package org.purple.smoke;

import android.util.Base64;
import java.nio.charset.StandardCharsets;
import java.security.PublicKey;
import java.text.SimpleDateFormat;
import java.util.Arrays;
import java.util.Date;
import java.util.Locale;
import java.util.TimeZone;

public class Messages
{
    private final static SimpleDateFormat s_fireSimpleDateFormat = new
        SimpleDateFormat("MMddyyyyHHmmss", Locale.getDefault());
    public final static String EOM = "\r\n\r\n\r\n";
    public final static String AUTHENTICATE_MESSAGE_TYPE = "0097b";
    public final static String FIRE_CHAT_MESSAGE_TYPE = "0040b";
    public final static String FIRE_STATUS_MESSAGE_TYPE = "0040a";
    public final static String IDENTITY_MESSAGE_TYPE = "0095a";
    public final static byte CALL_HALF_AND_HALF_TAGS[] =
        new byte[] {0x00, 0x01};
    public final static byte CHAT_KEY_TYPE[] = new byte[] {0x00};
    public final static byte CHAT_MESSAGE_RETRIEVAL[] = new byte[] {0x00};
    public final static byte CHAT_MESSAGE_TYPE[] = new byte[] {0x00};
    public final static byte CHAT_STATUS_MESSAGE_TYPE[] = new byte[] {0x01};
    public final static byte JUGGERNAUT_TYPE[] = new byte[] {0x03};
    public final static byte MCELIECE_FUJISAKI_11_50 = 0x01;
    public final static byte MCELIECE_FUJISAKI_12_68 = 0x02;
    public final static byte MCELIECE_POINTCHEVAL = 0x03;
    public final static byte MESSAGE_READ_SMOKESTACK[] = new byte[] {0x04};
    public final static byte MESSAGE_READ_TYPE[] = new byte[] {0x02};
    public final static byte PKP_MESSAGE_REQUEST[] = new byte[] {0x01};
    public final static byte SHARE_SIPHASH_ID[] = new byte[] {0x02};
    public final static byte STEAM_KEY_EXCHANGE[] = new byte[] {0x04, 0x05};
    public final static byte STEAM_SHARE[] = new byte[] {0x06, 0x07};
    public final static int CALL_GROUP_TWO_ELEMENT_COUNT = 6; /*
                                                    ** The first
                                                    ** byte is not
                                                    ** considered.
                                                    */
    public final static int CHAT_GROUP_TWO_ELEMENT_COUNT = 6; /*
                                                    ** The first
                                                    ** byte is not
                                                    ** considered.
                                                    */
    public final static int EPKS_GROUP_ONE_ELEMENT_COUNT = 7;
    public final static int STEAM_KEY_EXCHANGE_GROUP_TWO_ELEMENT_COUNT =
```

```java
        9; // The first byte is not considered.

    public static String authenticateMessage(Cryptography cryptography,
                                             String string)
    {
        if(cryptography == null || string == null || string.length() == 0)
            return "";

        try
        {
            byte random[] = Cryptography.randomBytes
                (Cryptography.HASH_KEY_LENGTH);
            byte signature[] = null;

            signature = cryptography.signViaChatSignature
                (Miscellaneous.
                 joinByteArrays(random,
                            cryptography.chatSignaturePublicKeyDigest(),
                            string.getBytes()));

            if(signature == null)
                return "";

            StringBuilder results = new StringBuilder();

            results.append("POST HTTP/1.1\r\n");
            results.append
                ("Content-Type: application/x-www-form-urlencoded\r\n");
            results.append("Content-Length: %1\r\n");
            results.append("\r\n");
            results.append("type=");
            results.append(AUTHENTICATE_MESSAGE_TYPE);
            results.append("&content=%2\r\n\r\n\r\n");

            String base64 = Base64.encodeToString
                (Miscellaneous.
                 joinByteArrays(random,
                            cryptography.chatSignaturePublicKeyDigest(),
                            signature),
                 Base64.NO_WRAP);
            int indexOf = results.indexOf("%1");
            int length = base64.length() +
                ("type=" +
                 AUTHENTICATE_MESSAGE_TYPE +
                 "&content=\r\n\r\n\r\n").length();

            results = results.replace
                (indexOf, indexOf + 2, String.valueOf(length));
            indexOf = results.indexOf("%2");
            results = results.replace(indexOf, indexOf + 2, base64);
            return results.toString();
        }
        catch(Exception exception)
        {
        }

        return "";
    }

    public static String bytesToMessageString(byte bytes[])
    {
        if(bytes == null || bytes.length == 0)
            return "";
```

```java
    try
    {
        StringBuilder results = new StringBuilder();

        results.append("POST HTTP/1.1\r\n");
        results.append
            ("Content-Type: application/x-www-form-urlencoded\r\n");
        results.append("Content-Length: %1\r\n");
        results.append("\r\n");
        results.append("content=%2\r\n");
        results.append("\r\n\r\n");

        String base64 = Base64.encodeToString(bytes, Base64.NO_WRAP);
        int indexOf = results.indexOf("%1");
        int length = base64.length() + "content=\r\n\r\n\r\n".length();

        results = results.replace
            (indexOf, indexOf + 2, String.valueOf(length));
        indexOf = results.indexOf("%2");
        results = results.replace(indexOf, indexOf + 2, base64);
        return results.toString();
    }
    catch(Exception exception)
    {
    }

    return "";
}

public static String bytesToMessageStringNonBase64(byte bytes[])
{
    if(bytes == null || bytes.length == 0)
        return "";

    try
    {
        StringBuilder results = new StringBuilder();

        results.append("POST HTTP/1.1\r\n");
        results.append
            ("Content-Type: application/x-www-form-urlencoded\r\n");
        results.append("Content-Length: %1\r\n");
        results.append("\r\n");
        results.append("content=%2\r\n");
        results.append("\r\n\r\n");

        int indexOf = results.indexOf("%1");
        int length = bytes.length + "content=\r\n\r\n\r\n".length();

        results = results.replace
            (indexOf, indexOf + 2, String.valueOf(length));
        indexOf = results.indexOf("%2");
        results = results.replace
            (indexOf,
             indexOf + 2,
             new String(bytes, StandardCharsets.UTF_8));
        return results.toString();
    }
    catch(Exception exception)
    {
    }
```

```java
        return "";
    }

    public static String identityMessage(byte bytes[])
    {
        if(bytes == null || bytes.length == 0)
            return "";

        try
        {
            StringBuilder results = new StringBuilder();

            results.append("POST HTTP/1.1\r\n");
            results.append
                ("Content-Type: application/x-www-form-urlencoded\r\n");
            results.append("Content-Length: %1\r\n");
            results.append("\r\n");
            results.append("type=");
            results.append(IDENTITY_MESSAGE_TYPE);
            results.append("&content=%2;sha-512\r\n\r\n\r\n");

            String base64 = Base64.encodeToString(bytes, Base64.NO_WRAP);
            int indexOf = results.indexOf("%1");
            int length = base64.length() +
                ("type=" +
                 IDENTITY_MESSAGE_TYPE +
                 "&content=;sha-512\r\n\r\n\r\n").length();

            results = results.replace
                (indexOf, indexOf + 2, String.valueOf(length));
            indexOf = results.indexOf("%2");
            results = results.replace(indexOf, indexOf + 2, base64);
            return results.toString();
        }
        catch(Exception exception)
        {
        }

        return "";
    }

    public static String stripMessage(String message)
    {
        if(message == null)
            return "";

        /*
        ** Remove Smoke-specific leading and trailing data.
        */

        int indexOf = message.indexOf("content=");

        if(indexOf >= 0)
            message = message.substring(indexOf + 8);

        return message.trim();
    }

    public static byte[] callMessage(Cryptography cryptography,
                                     String sipHashId,
                                     byte keyStream[],
                                     byte publicKeyType,
                                     byte tag)
```

```java
{
    if(cryptography == null || keyStream == null || keyStream.length == 0)
        return null;

    try
    {
        /*
        ** [ Public Key Encryption ]
        */

        byte aesKey[] = Cryptography.aes256KeyBytes();

        if(aesKey == null)
            return null;

        byte shaKey[] = Cryptography.sha512KeyBytes();

        if(shaKey == null)
            return null;

        PublicKey publicKey = Database.getInstance().
            publicEncryptionKeyForSipHashId(cryptography, sipHashId);

        if(publicKey == null)
            return null;

        byte pki[] = Cryptography.pkiEncrypt
            (publicKey,
             Database.getInstance().
             publicKeyEncryptionAlgorithm(cryptography, sipHashId),
             Miscellaneous.joinByteArrays(aesKey, shaKey));

        if(pki == null)
            return null;

        StringBuilder stringBuilder = new StringBuilder();

        /*
        ** [ A Timestamp ]
        */

        stringBuilder.append
            (Base64.encodeToString(Miscellaneous.
                                   longToByteArray(System.
                                                   currentTimeMillis()),
                                   Base64.NO_WRAP));
        stringBuilder.append("\n");

        /*
        ** [ Ephemeral Public Key ]
        */

        stringBuilder.append
            (Base64.encodeToString(keyStream, Base64.NO_WRAP));
        stringBuilder.append("\n");

        /*
        ** [ Ephemeral Public Key Type ]
        */

        stringBuilder.append
            (Base64.encodeToString(new byte[] {publicKeyType},
                                   Base64.NO_WRAP));
```

```java
        stringBuilder.append("\n");


        /*
        ** [ Identity ]
        */

        stringBuilder.append
            (Base64.encodeToString(cryptography.identity(),
                                Base64.NO_WRAP));
        stringBuilder.append("\n");


        /*
        ** [ Encryption Public Key Digest ]
        */

        stringBuilder.append
            (Base64.encodeToString(cryptography.
                                chatEncryptionPublicKeyDigest(),
                                Base64.NO_WRAP));
        stringBuilder.append("\n");


        /*
        ** [ Public Key Signature ]
        */

        byte signature[] = cryptography.signViaChatSignature
            (Miscellaneous.
             joinByteArrays(aesKey,
                        shaKey,
                        new byte[] {tag},
                        stringBuilder.toString().getBytes(),
                        Cryptography.sha512(publicKey.getEncoded())));

        if(signature == null)
            return null;

        stringBuilder.append
            (Base64.encodeToString(signature, Base64.NO_WRAP));

        /*
        ** [ Ciphertext ]
        */

        byte ciphertext[] = Cryptography.encrypt
            (Miscellaneous.
             joinByteArrays(new byte[] {tag},
                        stringBuilder.toString().getBytes()),
             aesKey);

        if(ciphertext == null)
            return null;

        stringBuilder.delete(0, stringBuilder.length());

        /*
        ** [ HMAC ]
        */

        byte hmac[] = Cryptography.hmac
            (Miscellaneous.joinByteArrays(pki, ciphertext), shaKey);

        if(hmac == null)
            return null;
```

```java
        /*
        ** [ Destination ]
        */

        byte destination[] = Cryptography.hmac
            (Miscellaneous.joinByteArrays(pki, ciphertext, hmac),
             Cryptography.
             sha512(sipHashId.getBytes(StandardCharsets.UTF_8)));

        return Miscellaneous.joinByteArrays
            (pki, ciphertext, hmac, destination);
    }
    catch(Exception exception)
    {
    }

    return null;
}

public static byte[] chatMessage(Cryptography cryptography,
                                 String message,
                                 String sipHashId,
                                 byte attachment[],
                                 byte destinationKey[],
                                 byte keyStream[],
                                 byte messageIdentity[],
                                 long sequence,
                                 long timestamp)
{
    if(cryptography == null ||
       keyStream == null ||
       keyStream.length == 0 ||
       messageIdentity == null ||
       messageIdentity.length == 0)
        return null;

    /*
    ** keyStream
    ** [0 ... 31] - AES-256 Encryption Key
    ** [32 ... 95] - SHA-512 HMAC Key
    */

    try
    {
        PublicKey publicKey = Database.getInstance().
            publicEncryptionKeyForSipHashId(cryptography, sipHashId);

        if(publicKey == null)
            return null;

        /*
        ** [ PKI ]
        */

        byte pki[] = Cryptography.pkiEncrypt
            (publicKey,
             Database.getInstance().
             publicKeyEncryptionAlgorithm(cryptography, sipHashId),
             cryptography.chatEncryptionPublicKeyDigest());

        if(pki == null)
            return null;
```

```java
        StringBuilder stringBuilder = new StringBuilder();

        /*
        ** [ A Timestamp ]
        */

        stringBuilder.append
            (Base64.encodeToString(Miscellaneous.longToByteArray(timestamp),
                                Base64.NO_WRAP));
        stringBuilder.append("\n");

        /*
        ** [ Message ]
        */

        stringBuilder.append
            (Base64.encodeToString(message.getBytes(StandardCharsets.UTF_8),
                                Base64.NO_WRAP));
        stringBuilder.append("\n");

        /*
        ** [ Sequence ]
        */

        stringBuilder.append
            (Base64.encodeToString(Miscellaneous.
                                longToByteArray(sequence),
                                Base64.NO_WRAP));
        stringBuilder.append("\n");

        /*
        ** [ Attachment ]
        */

        if(attachment != null)
            stringBuilder.append
                (Base64.
                 encodeToString(Miscellaneous.compressed(attachment),
                        Base64.NO_WRAP));
        else
            stringBuilder.append
                (Base64.
                 encodeToString(Miscellaneous.compressed(new byte[1]),
                        Base64.NO_WRAP));

        stringBuilder.append("\n");

        /*
        ** [ Message Identity ]
        */

        stringBuilder.append
            (Base64.encodeToString(messageIdentity, Base64.NO_WRAP));
        stringBuilder.append("\n");

        /*
        ** [ Public Key Signature ]
        */

        byte signature[] = null;

        if(Database.getInstance().readParticipantOptions(cryptography,
```

```java
                                                    sipHashId).
    contains("optional_signatures = false"))
    signature = cryptography.signViaChatSignature
        (Miscellaneous.
          joinByteArrays(cryptography.
                           chatEncryptionPublicKeyDigest(),
                           CHAT_MESSAGE_TYPE,
                           stringBuilder.toString().getBytes(),
                           Cryptography.sha512(publicKey.
                                        getEncoded()))));
else
    signature = new byte[1];

if(signature == null)
    return null;

stringBuilder.append
    (Base64.encodeToString(signature, Base64.NO_WRAP));

/*
** [ Ciphertext ]
*/

byte ciphertext[] = Cryptography.encrypt
    (Miscellaneous.
      joinByteArrays(CHAT_MESSAGE_TYPE,
                    stringBuilder.toString().getBytes()),
      Arrays.copyOfRange(keyStream,
                        0,
                        Cryptography.CIPHER_KEY_LENGTH));

stringBuilder.delete(0, stringBuilder.length());

if(ciphertext == null)
    return null;

/*
** [ HMAC ]
*/

byte hmac[] = Cryptography.hmac
    (Miscellaneous.joinByteArrays(pki, ciphertext),
     Arrays.copyOfRange(keyStream,
                        Cryptography.CIPHER_KEY_LENGTH,
                        keyStream.length));

if(hmac == null)
    return null;

/*
** [ Destination ]
*/

if(destinationKey != null)
{
    byte destination[] = Cryptography.hmac
        (Miscellaneous.joinByteArrays(pki, ciphertext, hmac),
         destinationKey);

    return Miscellaneous.joinByteArrays
        (pki, ciphertext, hmac, destination);
}
else
```

```java
                return Miscellaneous.joinByteArrays
                    /*
                    ** The SipHash ID will be removed by the Neighbor object
                    ** before the message is created.
                    */

                    (pki,
                     ciphertext,
                     hmac,
                     sipHashId.getBytes(StandardCharsets.UTF_8)),
        }
        catch(Exception exception)
        {
        }

        return null;
    }

    public static byte[] chatMessageRetrieval(Cryptography cryptography)
    {
        if(cryptography == null)
            return null;

        /*
        ** keyStream
        ** [0 ... 31] - AES-256 Encryption Key
        ** [32 ... 95] - SHA-512 HMAC Key
        */

        try
        {
            byte bytes[] = Miscellaneous.joinByteArrays
                (
                 /*
                 ** [ A Byte ]
                 */

                 CHAT_MESSAGE_RETRIEVAL,

                 /*
                 ** [ A Timestamp ]
                 */

                 Miscellaneous.longToByteArray(System.currentTimeMillis()),

                 /*
                 ** [ Some Identity ]
                 */

                 Kernel.getInstance().messageRetrievalIdentity(),

                 /*
                 ** [ Encryption Public Key Digest ]
                 */

                 cryptography.chatEncryptionPublicKeyDigest());
            /*
            ** [ Public Key Signature ]
            */

            byte signature[] = cryptography.signViaChatSignature(bytes);
```

```java
        if(signature == null)
            return null;

        /*
        ** [ Ciphertext ]
        */

        byte ciphertext[] = Cryptography.encrypt
            (Miscellaneous.joinByteArrays(bytes, signature),
             cryptography.ozoneEncryptionKey());

        if(ciphertext == null)
            return null;

        /*
        ** [ HMAC ]
        */

        byte hmac[] = Cryptography.hmac
            (ciphertext, cryptography.ozoneMacKey());

        if(hmac == null)
            return null;

        return Miscellaneous.joinByteArrays(ciphertext, hmac);
    }
    catch(Exception exception)
    {
    }

    return null;
}

public static byte[] chatStatus(Cryptography cryptography,
                                String sipHashId,
                                byte keyStream[])
{
    if(cryptography == null || keyStream == null || keyStream.length == 0)
        return null;

    /*
    ** keyStream
    ** [0 ... 31] - AES-256 Encryption Key
    ** [32 ... 95] - SHA-512 HMAC Key
    */

    try
    {
        PublicKey publicKey = Database.getInstance().
            publicEncryptionKeyForSipHashId(cryptography, sipHashId);

        if(publicKey == null)
            return null;

        /*
        ** [ PKI ]
        */

        byte pki[] = Cryptography.pkiEncrypt
            (publicKey,
             Database.getInstance().
             publicKeyEncryptionAlgorithm(cryptography, sipHashId),
             cryptography.chatEncryptionPublicKeyDigest());
```

```java
        if(pki == null)
           return null;

        byte bytes[] = Miscellaneous.joinByteArrays
           (
            /*
            ** [ A Byte ]
            */

            CHAT_STATUS_MESSAGE_TYPE,

            /*
            ** [ A Timestamp ]
            */

            Miscellaneous.longToByteArray(System.currentTimeMillis()),

            /*
            ** [ Status ]
            */

            new byte[] {0x00});

        /*
        ** [ Public Key Signature ]
        */

        byte signature[] = null;

        if(Database.getInstance().readParticipantOptions(cryptography,
                                            sipHashId).
           contains("optional_signatures = false"))
           signature = cryptography.signViaChatSignature
               (Miscellaneous.
                 joinByteArrays(cryptography.
                               chatEncryptionPublicKeyDigest(),
                               bytes,
                               Cryptography.sha512(publicKey.
                                            getEncoded()))));
        else
           signature = new byte[1];

        if(signature == null)
           return null;

        /*
        ** [ Ciphertext ]
        */

        byte ciphertext[] = Cryptography.encrypt
           (Miscellaneous.joinByteArrays(bytes, signature),
            Arrays.copyOfRange(keyStream,
                               0,
                               Cryptography.CIPHER_KEY_LENGTH));

        if(ciphertext == null)
           return null;

        /*
        ** [ HMAC ]
        */
```

```java
        byte hmac[] = Cryptography.hmac
            (Miscellaneous.joinByteArrays(pki, ciphertext),
             Arrays.copyOfRange(keyStream,
                            Cryptography.CIPHER_KEY_LENGTH,
                            keyStream.length));

        if(hmac == null)
            return null;

        /*
        ** [ Destination ]
        */

        byte destination[] = Cryptography.hmac
            (Miscellaneous.joinByteArrays(pki, ciphertext, hmac),
             Cryptography.
             sha512(sipHashId.getBytes(StandardCharsets.UTF_8)));

        return Miscellaneous.joinByteArrays
            (pki, ciphertext, hmac, destination);
    }
    catch(Exception exception)
    {
    }

    return null;
}

public static byte[] epksMessage(Cryptography cryptography,
                                 String sipHashId,
                                 byte keyStream[],
                                 byte keyType[])
{
    if(cryptography == null ||
       keyStream == null ||
       keyStream.length == 0 ||
       keyType == null ||
       keyType.length == 0)
        return null;

    /*
    ** keyStream
    ** [0 ... 31] - AES-256 Encryption Key
    ** [32 ... 95] - SHA-512 HMAC Key
    */

    try
    {
        StringBuilder stringBuilder = new StringBuilder();

        /*
        ** [ A Timestamp ]
        */

        stringBuilder.append
            (Base64.encodeToString(Miscellaneous.
                                longToByteArray(System.
                                            currentTimeMillis()),
                                Base64.NO_WRAP));
        stringBuilder.append("\n");

        /*
        ** [ Key Type ]
```

```java
        */

        stringBuilder.append
            (Base64.encodeToString(keyType, Base64.NO_WRAP));
        stringBuilder.append("\n");

        /*
        ** [ Sender's Smoke Identity ]
        */

        stringBuilder.append
            (Base64.encodeToString(cryptography.sipHashId().
                                getBytes(StandardCharsets.UTF_8),
                                Base64.NO_WRAP));
        stringBuilder.append("\n");

        /*
        ** [ Encryption and Signature Public Keys ]
        */

        PublicKey encryptionKey = cryptography.chatEncryptionPublicKey();
        PublicKey signatureKey = cryptography.chatSignaturePublicKey();

        if(encryptionKey == null || signatureKey == null)
            return null;

        byte bytes[] = null;

        /*
        ** [ Encryption Public Key Signature ]
        */

        if(!encryptionKey.getAlgorithm().equals("McEliece-CCA2"))
        {
            bytes = cryptography.signViaChatEncryption
                (Miscellaneous.
                  joinByteArrays(cryptography.sipHashId().
                                getBytes(StandardCharsets.UTF_8),
                                encryptionKey.getEncoded(),
                                signatureKey.getEncoded()));

            if(bytes == null)
                return null;
        }
        else
        {
            bytes = new byte[1];

            if(cryptography.chatEncryptionPublicKeyAlgorithm().
                startsWith("McEliece-Fujisaki (11"))
                bytes[0] = MCELIECE_FUJISAKI_11_50;
            else if(cryptography.chatEncryptionPublicKeyAlgorithm().
                    startsWith("McEliece-Fujisaki (12"))
                bytes[0] = MCELIECE_FUJISAKI_12_68;
            else
                bytes[0] = MCELIECE_POINTCHEVAL;
        }

        stringBuilder.
            append(Base64.encodeToString(encryptionKey.getEncoded(),
                                Base64.NO_WRAP));
        stringBuilder.append("\n");
        stringBuilder.append(Base64.encodeToString(bytes, Base64.NO_WRAP));
```

```java
            stringBuilder.append("\n");

            /*
            ** [ Signature Public Key Signature ]
            */

            bytes = cryptography.signViaChatSignature
                (Miscellaneous.
                 joinByteArrays(cryptography.sipHashId().
                                getBytes(StandardCharsets.UTF_8),
                                encryptionKey.getEncoded(),
                                signatureKey.getEncoded()));

            if(bytes == null)
                return null;

            stringBuilder.
                append(Base64.encodeToString(signatureKey.getEncoded(),
                                             Base64.NO_WRAP));
            stringBuilder.append("\n");
            stringBuilder.append(Base64.encodeToString(bytes, Base64.NO_WRAP));

            byte ciphertext[] = Cryptography.encrypt
                (stringBuilder.toString().getBytes(),
                 Arrays.copyOfRange(keyStream,
                                    0,
                                    Cryptography.CIPHER_KEY_LENGTH));

            stringBuilder.delete(0, stringBuilder.length());

            if(ciphertext == null)
                return null;

            /*
            ** [ HMAC ]
            */

            byte hmac[] = Cryptography.hmac
                (ciphertext,
                 Arrays.copyOfRange(keyStream,
                                    Cryptography.CIPHER_KEY_LENGTH,
                                    keyStream.length));

            if(hmac == null)
                return null;

            /*
            ** [ Destination ]
            */

            byte destination[] = Cryptography.hmac
                (Miscellaneous.joinByteArrays(ciphertext, hmac),
                 Cryptography.
                 sha512(sipHashId.getBytes(StandardCharsets.UTF_8)));

            return Miscellaneous.joinByteArrays(ciphertext, hmac, destination);
        }
    catch(Exception exception)
        {
        }

    return null;
    }
```

```java
public static byte[] epksMessage(String encryptionAlgorithm,
                                 String sipHashId,
                                 byte encryptionPublicKey[],
                                 byte signaturePublicKey[],
                                 byte keyStream[],
                                 byte keyType[])
{
    if(encryptionPublicKey == null ||
       encryptionPublicKey.length == 0 ||
       keyStream == null ||
       keyStream.length == 0 ||
       keyType == null ||
       keyType.length == 0 ||
       signaturePublicKey == null ||
       signaturePublicKey.length == 0)
        return null;

    /*
    ** keyStream
    ** [0 ... 31] - AES-256 Encryption Key
    ** [32 ... 95] - SHA-512 HMAC Key
    */

    try
    {
        StringBuilder stringBuilder = new StringBuilder();

        /*
        ** [ A Timestamp ]
        */

        stringBuilder.append
            (Base64.encodeToString(Miscellaneous.
                                   longToByteArray(System.
                                                   currentTimeMillis()),
                                   Base64.NO_WRAP));
        stringBuilder.append("\n");

        /*
        ** [ Key Type ]
        */

        stringBuilder.append
            (Base64.encodeToString(keyType, Base64.NO_WRAP));
        stringBuilder.append("\n");

        /*
        ** [ Sender's Smoke Identity ]
        */

        stringBuilder.append
            (Base64.encodeToString(sipHashId.
                                   getBytes(StandardCharsets.UTF_8),
                                   Base64.NO_WRAP));
        stringBuilder.append("\n");

        byte bytes[] = new byte[1]; // Artificial signatures.

        if(encryptionAlgorithm.startsWith("McEliece-Fujisaki (11"))
            bytes[0] = MCELIECE_FUJISAKI_11_50;
        else if(encryptionAlgorithm.startsWith("McEliece-Fujisaki (12"))
            bytes[0] = MCELIECE_FUJISAKI_12_68;
```

```java
        else if(encryptionAlgorithm.startsWith("McEliece-Pointcheval"))
            bytes[0] = MCELIECE_POINTCHEVAL;
        else
            bytes[0] = 0;

        /*
        ** [ Encryption Public Key ]
        */

        stringBuilder.append
            (Base64.encodeToString(encryptionPublicKey, Base64.NO_WRAP));
        stringBuilder.append("\n");
        stringBuilder.append(Base64.encodeToString(bytes, Base64.NO_WRAP));
        stringBuilder.append("\n");

        /*
        ** [ Signature Public Key ]
        */

        bytes[0] = 0; // Artificial signatures.
        stringBuilder.append
            (Base64.encodeToString(signaturePublicKey, Base64.NO_WRAP));
        stringBuilder.append("\n");
        stringBuilder.append(Base64.encodeToString(bytes, Base64.NO_WRAP));

        byte ciphertext[] = Cryptography.encrypt
            (stringBuilder.toString().getBytes(),
             Arrays.copyOfRange(keyStream,
                                0,
                                Cryptography.CIPHER_KEY_LENGTH));

        stringBuilder.delete(0, stringBuilder.length());

        if(ciphertext == null)
            return null;

        /*
        ** [ HMAC ]
        */

        byte hmac[] = Cryptography.hmac
            (ciphertext,
             Arrays.copyOfRange(keyStream,
                                Cryptography.CIPHER_KEY_LENGTH,
                                keyStream.length));

        if(hmac == null)
            return null;

        /*
        ** [ Destination ]
        */

        byte destination[] = Cryptography.hmac
            (Miscellaneous.joinByteArrays(ciphertext, hmac),
             Cryptography.
             sha512(sipHashId.getBytes(StandardCharsets.UTF_8)));

        return Miscellaneous.joinByteArrays(ciphertext, hmac, destination);
    }
catch(Exception exception)
    {
    }
```

```java
        return null;
    }

    public static byte[] fireMessage(Cryptography cryptography,
                                     String id,
                                     String message,
                                     String name,
                                     byte keyStream[])
    {
        if(cryptography == null || keyStream == null || keyStream.length == 0)
            return null;

        /*
        ** keyStream
        ** [0 ... 31] - AES-256 Encryption Key
        ** [32 ... 79] - SHA-384 HMAC Key
        ** [80 ... N] - Destination SHA-512 HMAC Key
        */

        try
        {
            StringBuilder stringBuilder = new StringBuilder();

            stringBuilder.append
                (Base64.
                 encodeToString(FIRE_CHAT_MESSAGE_TYPE.
                                getBytes(StandardCharsets.ISO_8859_1),
                                Base64.NO_WRAP));
            stringBuilder.append("\n");

            if(name.trim().isEmpty())
                stringBuilder.append
                    (Base64.encodeToString("unknown".
                                           getBytes(StandardCharsets.UTF_8),
                                           Base64.NO_WRAP));
            else
                stringBuilder.append
                    (Base64.encodeToString(name.trim().
                                           getBytes(StandardCharsets.UTF_8),
                                           Base64.NO_WRAP));

            stringBuilder.append("\n");
            stringBuilder.append
                (Base64.encodeToString(id.getBytes(StandardCharsets.ISO_8859_1),
                                       Base64.NO_WRAP));
            stringBuilder.append("\n");
            stringBuilder.append
                (Base64.encodeToString(message.getBytes(StandardCharsets.UTF_8),
                                       Base64.NO_WRAP));
            stringBuilder.append("\n");

            TimeZone utc = TimeZone.getTimeZone("UTC");

            s_fireSimpleDateFormat.setTimeZone(utc);
            stringBuilder.append
                (Base64.
                 encodeToString(s_fireSimpleDateFormat.
                                format(new Date(System.currentTimeMillis())).
                                getBytes(StandardCharsets.ISO_8859_1),
                                Base64.NO_WRAP));

            byte ciphertext[] = Cryptography.encryptFire
```

```java
                        (stringBuilder.toString().getBytes(StandardCharsets.ISO_8859_1),
                         Arrays.copyOfRange(keyStream,
                                            0,
                                            Cryptography.CIPHER_KEY_LENGTH));

            if(ciphertext == null)
                return null;

            /*
            ** [ HMAC ]
            */

            byte hmac[] = Cryptography.hmacFire
                (ciphertext,
                 Arrays.copyOfRange(keyStream,
                                    Cryptography.CIPHER_KEY_LENGTH,
                                    Cryptography.CIPHER_KEY_LENGTH +
                                    Cryptography.FIRE_HASH_KEY_LENGTH));

            if(hmac == null)
                return null;

            /*
            ** [ Destination ]
            */

            byte destination[] = Cryptography.hmac
                (Miscellaneous.joinByteArrays(ciphertext, hmac),
                 Cryptography.sha512(Arrays.copyOfRange(keyStream,
                                                        Cryptography.
                                                        CIPHER_KEY_LENGTH +
                                                        Cryptography.
                                                        FIRE_HASH_KEY_LENGTH,
                                                        keyStream.length)));

            stringBuilder.delete(0, stringBuilder.length());
            stringBuilder.append
                (Base64.encodeToString(ciphertext, Base64.NO_WRAP));
            stringBuilder.append("\n");
            stringBuilder.append
                (Base64.encodeToString(hmac, Base64.NO_WRAP));
            stringBuilder.append("\n");
            stringBuilder.append
                (Base64.encodeToString(destination, Base64.NO_WRAP));
            return stringBuilder.toString().getBytes
                (StandardCharsets.ISO_8859_1);
        }
        catch(Exception exception)
        {
        }

        return null;
    }

    public static byte[] fireStatus(Cryptography cryptography,
                                    String id,
                                    String name,
                                    byte keyStream[])
    {
        if(cryptography == null || keyStream == null || keyStream.length == 0)
            return null;

        /*
```

```
** keyStream
** [0 ... 31] - AES-256 Encryption Key
** [32 ... 79] - SHA-384 HMAC Key
** [80 ... N] - Destination SHA-512 HMAC Key
*/

try
{
    StringBuilder stringBuilder = new StringBuilder();

    stringBuilder.append
        (Base64.
          encodeToString(FIRE_STATUS_MESSAGE_TYPE.
                          getBytes(StandardCharsets.ISO_8859_1),
                          Base64.NO_WRAP));
    stringBuilder.append("\n");

    if(name.trim().isEmpty())
        stringBuilder.append
            (Base64.encodeToString("unknown".
                                    getBytes(StandardCharsets.UTF_8),
                                    Base64.NO_WRAP));
    else
        stringBuilder.append
            (Base64.encodeToString(name.trim().
                                    getBytes(StandardCharsets.UTF_8),
                                    Base64.NO_WRAP));

    stringBuilder.append("\n");
    stringBuilder.append
        (Base64.encodeToString(id.getBytes(StandardCharsets.ISO_8859_1),
                            Base64.NO_WRAP));
    stringBuilder.append("\n");

    TimeZone utc = TimeZone.getTimeZone("UTC");

    s_fireSimpleDateFormat.setTimeZone(utc);
    stringBuilder.append
        (Base64.
          encodeToString(s_fireSimpleDateFormat.
                          format(new Date(System.currentTimeMillis())).
                          getBytes(StandardCharsets.ISO_8859_1),
                          Base64.NO_WRAP));

    byte ciphertext[] = Cryptography.encryptFire
        (stringBuilder.toString().getBytes(StandardCharsets.ISO_8859_1),
         Arrays.copyOfRange(keyStream,
                            0,
                            Cryptography.CIPHER_KEY_LENGTH));

    if(ciphertext == null)
        return null;

    /*
    ** [ HMAC ]
    */

    byte hmac[] = Cryptography.hmacFire
        (ciphertext,
         Arrays.copyOfRange(keyStream,
                            Cryptography.CIPHER_KEY_LENGTH,
                            Cryptography.CIPHER_KEY_LENGTH +
                            Cryptography.FIRE_HASH_KEY_LENGTH));
```

```java
        if(hmac == null)
           return null;

        /*
        ** [ Destination ]
        */

        byte destination[] = Cryptography.hmac
           (Miscellaneous.joinByteArrays(ciphertext, hmac),
            Cryptography.sha512(Arrays.copyOfRange(keyStream,
                                      Cryptography.
                                      CIPHER_KEY_LENGTH +
                                      Cryptography.
                                      FIRE_HASH_KEY_LENGTH,
                                      keyStream.length)));

        stringBuilder.delete(0, stringBuilder.length());
        stringBuilder.append
           (Base64.encodeToString(ciphertext, Base64.NO_WRAP));
        stringBuilder.append("\n");
        stringBuilder.append
           (Base64.encodeToString(hmac, Base64.NO_WRAP));
        stringBuilder.append("\n");
        stringBuilder.append
           (Base64.encodeToString(destination, Base64.NO_WRAP));
        return stringBuilder.toString().
           getBytes(StandardCharsets.ISO_8859_1);
    }
    catch(Exception exception)
    {
    }

    return null;
}

public static byte[] juggernautMessage(Cryptography cryptography,
                                 String sipHashId,
                                 byte bytes[],
                                 byte keyStream[])
{
    if(bytes == null ||
       bytes.length == 0 ||
       cryptography == null ||
       keyStream == null ||
       keyStream.length == 0)
        return null;

    /*
    ** keyStream
    ** [0 ... 31] - AES-256 Encryption Key
    ** [32 ... 95] - SHA-512 HMAC Key
    */

    try
    {
        PublicKey publicKey = Database.getInstance().
           publicEncryptionKeyForSipHashId(cryptography, sipHashId);

        if(publicKey == null)
           return null;

        /*
```

```java
        ** [ PKI ]
        */

        byte pki[] = Cryptography.pkiEncrypt
            (publicKey,
             Database.getInstance().
             publicKeyEncryptionAlgorithm(cryptography, sipHashId),
             cryptography.chatEncryptionPublicKeyDigest());

        if(pki == null)
            return null;

        StringBuilder stringBuilder = new StringBuilder();

        /*
        ** [ A Timestamp ]
        */

        stringBuilder.append
            (Base64.
             encodeToString(Miscellaneous.
                        longToByteArray(System.currentTimeMillis()),
                        Base64.NO_WRAP));
        stringBuilder.append("\n");

        /*
        ** [ Payload ]
        */

        stringBuilder.append(Base64.encodeToString(bytes, Base64.NO_WRAP));
        stringBuilder.append("\n");

        /*
        ** [ Public Key Signature ]
        */

        byte signature[] = cryptography.signViaChatSignature
            (Miscellaneous.
             joinByteArrays(cryptography.
                        chatEncryptionPublicKeyDigest(),
                        JUGGERNAUT_TYPE,
                        stringBuilder.toString().getBytes(),
                        Cryptography.sha512(publicKey.getEncoded())));

        if(signature == null)
            return null;

        stringBuilder.append
            (Base64.encodeToString(signature, Base64.NO_WRAP));

        /*
        ** [ Ciphertext ]
        */

        byte ciphertext[] = Cryptography.encrypt
            (Miscellaneous.
             joinByteArrays(JUGGERNAUT_TYPE,
                        stringBuilder.toString().getBytes()),
             Arrays.copyOfRange(keyStream,
                            0,
                            Cryptography.CIPHER_KEY_LENGTH));

        stringBuilder.delete(0, stringBuilder.length());
```

```java
            if(ciphertext == null)
                return null;

            /*
            ** [ HMAC ]
            */

            byte hmac[] = Cryptography.hmac
                (Miscellaneous.joinByteArrays(pki, ciphertext),
                 Arrays.copyOfRange(keyStream,
                                    Cryptography.CIPHER_KEY_LENGTH,
                                    keyStream.length));

            if(hmac == null)
                return null;

            /*
            ** [ Destination ]
            */

            byte destination[] = Cryptography.hmac
                (Miscellaneous.joinByteArrays(pki, ciphertext, hmac),
                 Cryptography.
                 sha512(sipHashId.getBytes(StandardCharsets.UTF_8)));

            return Miscellaneous.joinByteArrays
                (pki, ciphertext, hmac, destination);
        }
    catch(Exception exception)
        {
        }

    return null;
    }

public static byte[] messageRead(Cryptography cryptography,
                                 String sipHashId,
                                 byte keyStream[],
                                 byte messageIdentity[])
    {
    if(cryptography == null ||
       keyStream == null ||
       keyStream.length == 0 ||
       messageIdentity == null ||
       messageIdentity.length == 0)
        return null;

    /*
    ** keyStream
    ** [0 ... 31] - AES-256 Encryption Key
    ** [32 ... 95] - SHA-512 HMAC Key
    */

    try
        {
            PublicKey publicKey = Database.getInstance().
                publicEncryptionKeyForSipHashId(cryptography, sipHashId);

            if(publicKey == null)
                return null;

            /*
```

```java
        ** [ PKI ]
        */

        byte pki[] = Cryptography.pkiEncrypt
            (publicKey,
             Database.getInstance().
             publicKeyEncryptionAlgorithm(cryptography, sipHashId),
             cryptography.chatEncryptionPublicKeyDigest());

        if(pki == null)
            return null;

        byte bytes[] = Miscellaneous.joinByteArrays
            (
             /*
             ** [ A Byte ]
             */

             MESSAGE_READ_TYPE,

             /*
             ** [ Message Identity ]
             */

             messageIdentity);

        /*
        ** [ Public Key Signature ]
        */

        byte signature[] = cryptography.signViaChatSignature
            (Miscellaneous.
             joinByteArrays(cryptography.
                            chatEncryptionPublicKeyDigest(),
                            bytes,
                            Cryptography.sha512(publicKey.getEncoded())));

        if(signature == null)
            return null;

        /*
        ** [ Ciphertext ]
        */

        byte ciphertext[] = Cryptography.encrypt
            (Miscellaneous.joinByteArrays(bytes, signature),
             Arrays.copyOfRange(keyStream,
                                0,
                                Cryptography.CIPHER_KEY_LENGTH));

        if(ciphertext == null)
            return null;

        /*
        ** [ HMAC ]
        */

        byte hmac[] = Cryptography.hmac
            (Miscellaneous.joinByteArrays(pki, ciphertext),
             Arrays.copyOfRange(keyStream,
                                Cryptography.CIPHER_KEY_LENGTH,
                                keyStream.length));
```

```java
        if(hmac == null)
            return null;

        /*
        ** [ Destination ]
        */

        byte destination[] = Cryptography.hmac
            (Miscellaneous.joinByteArrays(pki, ciphertext, hmac),
             Cryptography.
             sha512(sipHashId.getBytes(StandardCharsets.UTF_8)));

        return Miscellaneous.joinByteArrays
            (pki, ciphertext, hmac, destination);
    }
    catch(Exception exception)
    {
    }

    return null;
    }

    public static byte[] messageRead(Cryptography cryptography,
                                     byte messageIdentity[])
    {
        if(cryptography == null ||
           messageIdentity == null ||
           messageIdentity.length == 0)
            return null;

        /*
        ** keyStream
        ** [0 ... 31] - AES-256 Encryption Key
        ** [32 ... 95] - SHA-512 HMAC Key
        */

        try
        {
            byte bytes[] = Miscellaneous.joinByteArrays
                (
                 /*
                 ** [ A Byte ]
                 */

                 MESSAGE_READ_SMOKESTACK,

                 /*
                 ** [ A Timestamp ]
                 */

                 Miscellaneous.longToByteArray(System.currentTimeMillis()),

                 /*
                 ** [ Message Identity ]
                 */

                 messageIdentity,

                 /*
                 ** [ Encryption Public Key Digest ]
                 */

                 cryptography.chatEncryptionPublicKeyDigest());
```

```java
        /*
        ** [ Public Key Signature ]
        */

        byte signature[] = cryptography.signViaChatSignature(bytes);

        if(signature == null)
           return null;

        /*
        ** [ Ciphertext ]
        */

        byte ciphertext[] = Cryptography.encrypt
           (Miscellaneous.joinByteArrays(bytes, signature),
            cryptography.ozoneEncryptionKey());

        if(ciphertext == null)
           return null;

        /*
        ** [ HMAC ]
        */

        byte hmac[] = Cryptography.hmac
           (ciphertext, cryptography.ozoneMacKey());

        if(hmac == null)
           return null;

        return Miscellaneous.joinByteArrays(ciphertext, hmac);
    }
    catch(Exception exception)
    {
    }

    return null;
}

public static byte[] pkpRequestMessage(Cryptography cryptography,
                                       String requestedSipHashId)
{
    if(cryptography == null)
        return null;

    try
    {
        byte bytes[] = Miscellaneous.joinByteArrays
            (
             /*
             ** [ A Byte ]
             */

             PKP_MESSAGE_REQUEST,

             /*
             ** [ A Timestamp ]
             */

             Miscellaneous.longToByteArray(System.currentTimeMillis()),

             /*
```

```java
                ** [ Destination SipHash Identity ]
                */

                cryptography.sipHashId().getBytes(StandardCharsets.UTF_8),

                /*
                ** [ Requested SipHash Identity ]
                */

                requestedSipHashId.getBytes(StandardCharsets.UTF_8));

            /*
            ** [ Ciphertext ]
            */

            byte ciphertext[] = Cryptography.encrypt
                (bytes, cryptography.ozoneEncryptionKey());

            if(ciphertext == null)
                return null;

            /*
            ** [ HMAC ]
            */

            byte hmac[] = Cryptography.hmac
                (ciphertext, cryptography.ozoneMacKey());

            if(hmac == null)
                return null;

            return Miscellaneous.joinByteArrays(ciphertext, hmac);
        }
        catch(Exception exception)
        {
        }

        return null;
    }

    public static byte[] shareSipHashIdMessage(Cryptography cryptography,
                                               String sipHashId,
                                               long identity)
    {
        if(cryptography == null)
            return null;

        try
        {
            byte bytes[] = Miscellaneous.joinByteArrays
                (
                 /*
                 ** [ A Byte ]
                 */

                 SHARE_SIPHASH_ID,

                 /*
                 ** [ A Timestamp ]
                 */

                 Miscellaneous.longToByteArray(System.currentTimeMillis()),
```

```java
                /*
                ** [ SipHash Identity ]
                */

                sipHashId.getBytes(StandardCharsets.UTF_8),

                /*
                ** [ Temporary Identity ]
                */

                Miscellaneous.longToByteArray(identity));

            /*
            ** [ Ciphertext ]
            */

            byte ciphertext[] = Cryptography.encrypt
                (bytes, cryptography.ozoneEncryptionKey());

            if(ciphertext == null)
                return null;

            /*
            ** [ HMAC ]
            */

            byte hmac[] = Cryptography.hmac
                (ciphertext, cryptography.ozoneMacKey());

            if(hmac == null)
                return null;

            return Miscellaneous.joinByteArrays(ciphertext, hmac);
        }
        catch(Exception exception)
        {
        }

        return null;
    }

    public static byte[] steamCall(Cryptography cryptography,
                                   String fileName,
                                   String sipHashId,
                                   byte fileDigest[],
                                   byte fileIdentity[],
                                   byte keyStream[],
                                   byte publicKeyType,
                                   byte tag,
                                   long fileSize)
    {
        if(cryptography == null ||
           fileDigest == null ||
           fileDigest.length == 0 ||
           fileIdentity == null ||
           fileIdentity.length == 0 ||
           fileName.isEmpty() ||
           keyStream == null ||
           keyStream.length == 0)
            return null;

        try
        {
```

```java
/*
** [ Public Key Encryption ]
*/

byte aesKey[] = Cryptography.aes256KeyBytes();

if(aesKey == null)
    return null;

byte shaKey[] = Cryptography.sha512KeyBytes();

if(shaKey == null)
    return null;

PublicKey publicKey = Database.getInstance().
    publicEncryptionKeyForSipHashId(cryptography, sipHashId);

if(publicKey == null)
    return null;

byte pki[] = Cryptography.pkiEncrypt
    (publicKey,
     Database.getInstance().
     publicKeyEncryptionAlgorithm(cryptography, sipHashId),
     Miscellaneous.joinByteArrays(aesKey, shaKey));

if(pki == null)
    return null;

StringBuilder stringBuilder = new StringBuilder();

/*
** [ A Timestamp ]
*/

stringBuilder.append
    (Base64.encodeToString(Miscellaneous.
                           longToByteArray(System.
                                           currentTimeMillis()),
                           Base64.NO_WRAP));
stringBuilder.append("\n");

/*
** [ Ephemeral Public Key ]
*/

stringBuilder.append
    (Base64.encodeToString(keyStream, Base64.NO_WRAP));
stringBuilder.append("\n");

/*
** [ Ephemeral Public Key Type ]
*/

stringBuilder.append
    (Base64.encodeToString(new byte[] {publicKeyType},
                           Base64.NO_WRAP));
stringBuilder.append("\n");

/*
** [ File Digest ]
*/
```

```java
        stringBuilder.append
            (Base64.encodeToString(fileDigest, Base64.NO_WRAP));
        stringBuilder.append("\n");

        /*
        ** [ File Identity ]
        */

        stringBuilder.append
            (Base64.encodeToString(fileIdentity, Base64.NO_WRAP));
        stringBuilder.append("\n");

        /*
        ** [ File Name ]
        */

        stringBuilder.append
            (Base64.
             encodeToString(fileName.getBytes(StandardCharsets.UTF_8),
                            Base64.NO_WRAP));
        stringBuilder.append("\n");

        /*
        ** [ File Size ]
        */

        stringBuilder.append
            (Base64.
             encodeToString(Miscellaneous.longToByteArray(fileSize),
                            Base64.NO_WRAP));
        stringBuilder.append("\n");

        /*
        ** [ Encryption Public Key Digest ]
        */

        stringBuilder.append
            (Base64.encodeToString(cryptography.
                                   chatEncryptionPublicKeyDigest(),
                                   Base64.NO_WRAP));
        stringBuilder.append("\n");

        /*
        ** [ Public Key Signature ]
        */

        byte signature[] = cryptography.signViaChatSignature
            (Miscellaneous.
             joinByteArrays(aesKey,
                            shaKey,
                            new byte[] {tag},
                            stringBuilder.toString().getBytes(),
                            Cryptography.sha512(publicKey.getEncoded())));

        if(signature == null)
            return null;

        stringBuilder.append
            (Base64.encodeToString(signature, Base64.NO_WRAP));

        /*
        ** [ Ciphertext ]
        */
```

```java
        byte ciphertext[] = Cryptography.encrypt
            (Miscellaneous.
             joinByteArrays(new byte[] {tag},
                            stringBuilder.toString().getBytes()),
             aesKey);

        if(ciphertext == null)
            return null;

        stringBuilder.delete(0, stringBuilder.length());

        /*
        ** [ HMAC ]
        */

        byte hmac[] = Cryptography.hmac
            (Miscellaneous.joinByteArrays(pki, ciphertext), shaKey);

        if(hmac == null)
            return null;

        /*
        ** [ Destination ]
        */

        byte destination[] = Cryptography.hmac
            (Miscellaneous.joinByteArrays(pki, ciphertext, hmac),
             Cryptography.
             sha512(sipHashId.getBytes(StandardCharsets.UTF_8)));

        return Miscellaneous.joinByteArrays
            (pki, ciphertext, hmac, destination);
    }
    catch(Exception exception)
    {
    }

    return null;
}

public static byte[] steamShare(Cryptography cryptography,
                                String sipHashId,
                                byte fileIdentity[],
                                byte keyStream[],
                                byte packet[],
                                byte tag,
                                long fileOffset)
{
    if(cryptography == null ||
       fileIdentity == null ||
       fileIdentity.length == 0 ||
       keyStream == null ||
       keyStream.length == 0)
        return null;

    /*
    ** keyStream
    ** [0 ... 31] - AES-256 Encryption Key
    ** [32 ... 95] - SHA-512 HMAC Key
    */

    try
```

```java
{
    /*
    ** [ Public Key Encryption ]
    */

    PublicKey publicKey = Database.getInstance().
        publicEncryptionKeyForSipHashId(cryptography, sipHashId);

    if(publicKey == null)
        return null;

    byte pki[] = Cryptography.pkiEncrypt
        (publicKey,
         Database.getInstance().
         publicKeyEncryptionAlgorithm(cryptography, sipHashId),
         fileIdentity);

    if(pki == null)
        return null;

    byte bytes[] = Miscellaneous.joinByteArrays
        (
         /*
         ** [ A Tag ]
         */

         new byte[] {tag},

         /*
         ** [ A Timestamp ]
         */

         Miscellaneous.longToByteArray(System.currentTimeMillis()),

         /*
         ** [ File Offset ]
         */

         Miscellaneous.longToByteArray(fileOffset),

         /*
         ** [ File Packet ]
         */

         packet != null ? packet : null);

    /*
    ** [ Ciphertext ]
    */

    byte ciphertext[] = Cryptography.encrypt
        (bytes,
         Arrays.copyOfRange(keyStream,
                            0,
                            Cryptography.CIPHER_KEY_LENGTH));

    if(ciphertext == null)
        return null;

    /*
    ** [ HMAC ]
    */
```

```java
            byte hmac[] = Cryptography.hmac
                (Miscellaneous.joinByteArrays(pki, ciphertext),
                 Arrays.copyOfRange(keyStream,
                                    Cryptography.CIPHER_KEY_LENGTH,
                                    keyStream.length));

            if(hmac == null)
                return null;

            /*
            ** [ Destination ]
            */

            byte destination[] = Cryptography.hmac
                (Miscellaneous.joinByteArrays(pki, ciphertext, hmac),
                 Cryptography.
                 sha512(sipHashId.getBytes(StandardCharsets.UTF_8)));

            return Miscellaneous.joinByteArrays
                (pki, ciphertext, hmac, destination);
        }
        catch(Exception exception)
        {
        }

        return null;
    }
}
```

/* Miscellaneous.java –


```java
package org.purple.smoke;
```

```java
import android.app.Activity;
import android.app.AlertDialog;
import android.content.Context;
import android.content.DialogInterface;
import android.content.Intent;
import android.content.res.AssetFileDescriptor;
import android.graphics.Color;
import android.media.Ringtone;
import android.media.RingtoneManager;
import android.net.Uri;
import android.os.Build;
import android.os.Handler;
import android.support.v4.content.LocalBroadcastManager;
import android.text.InputType;
import android.util.Base64;
import android.view.Gravity;
import android.view.Menu;
import android.view.SubMenu;
import android.view.View;
import android.view.ViewGroup;
import android.widget.Button;
import android.widget.CheckBox;
import android.widget.CompoundButton;
import android.widget.EditText;
import android.widget.PopupWindow;
import android.widget.TextView;
import java.io.ByteArrayInputStream;
import java.io.ByteArrayOutputStream;
import java.io.OutputStream;
import java.lang.ref.WeakReference;
import java.nio.ByteBuffer;
import java.nio.charset.StandardCharsets;
import java.text.DecimalFormat;
import java.util.ArrayList;
import java.util.zip.GZIPInputStream;
import java.util.zip.GZIPOutputStream;

public abstract class Miscellaneous
{
    public static final String RATE = "0.00 B / s";
    public static final int INTEGER_BYTES = 4;
    public static final int LONG_BYTES = 8;
    public static final long LONG_LONG_BYTES = 8L;

    public static String byteArrayAsHexString(byte bytes[])
    {
        if(bytes == null || bytes.length == 0)
            return "";

        try
        {
            StringBuilder stringBuilder = new StringBuilder();

            for(byte b : bytes)
                stringBuilder.append(String.format("%02x", b));

            return stringBuilder.toString();
        }
        catch(Exception exception)
        {
            return "";
        }
    }
```

```java
    public static String byteArrayAsHexStringDelimited(byte bytes[],
                                                        char delimiter,
                                                        int offset)
    {
        if(bytes == null || bytes.length == 0 || offset < 0)
            return "";

        String string = byteArrayAsHexString(bytes);

        try
        {
            StringBuilder stringBuilder = new StringBuilder();
            int length = string.length();

            for(int i = 0; i < length; i += offset)
            {
                if(i < length - offset)
                    stringBuilder.append(string, i, i + offset);
                else
                    stringBuilder.append(string.substring(i));

                stringBuilder.append(delimiter);
            }

            if(stringBuilder.length() > 0 &&
                stringBuilder.charAt(stringBuilder.length() - 1) == delimiter)
                return stringBuilder.substring(0, stringBuilder.length() - 1);
            else
                return stringBuilder.toString();
        }
        catch(Exception exception)
        {
            return "";
        }
    }

    public static String delimitString(String string,
                                        char delimiter,
                                        int offset)
    {
        if(offset < 0)
            return "";

        try
        {
            StringBuilder stringBuilder = new StringBuilder();
            int length = string.length();

            for(int i = 0; i < length; i += offset)
            {
                if(i < length - offset)
                    stringBuilder.append(string, i, i + offset);
                else
                    stringBuilder.append(string.substring(i));

                stringBuilder.append(delimiter);
            }

            if(stringBuilder.length() > 0 &&
                stringBuilder.charAt(stringBuilder.length() - 1) == delimiter)
                return stringBuilder.substring(0, stringBuilder.length() - 1);
            else
```

```java
                return stringBuilder.toString();
        }
        catch(Exception exception)
        {
            return "";
        }
    }

    public static String formattedDigitalInformation(String bytes)
    {
        try
        {
            DecimalFormat decimalFormat = new DecimalFormat("0.00");
            StringBuilder stringBuilder = new StringBuilder();
            long v = Integer.decode(bytes).longValue();

            if(v < 1024L)
            {
                stringBuilder.append(decimalFormat.format(v));
                stringBuilder.append(" B");
            }
            else if(v < 1048576L)
            {
                stringBuilder.append(decimalFormat.format(v / (1024.0)));
                stringBuilder.append(" KiB");
            }
            else if(v < 1073741824L)
            {
                stringBuilder.append
                    (decimalFormat.format(v / (1048576.0)));
                stringBuilder.append(" MiB");
            }
            else
            {
                stringBuilder.append
                    (decimalFormat.format(v / (1073741824.0)));
                stringBuilder.append(" GiB");
            }

            return stringBuilder.toString();
        }
        catch(Exception exception)
        {
            return "";
        }
    }

    public static String niceBoolean(boolean state)
    {
        if(state)
            return "True";
        else
            return "False";
    }

    public static String pemFormat(byte bytes[])
    {
        if(bytes == null || bytes.length == 0)
            return "";

        try
        {
            String string = Base64.encodeToString(bytes, Base64.NO_WRAP);
```

```java
            StringBuilder stringBuilder = new StringBuilder();
            int length = string.length();

            stringBuilder.append("-----BEGIN CERTIFICATE-----\n");

            for(int i = 0; i < length; i += 64)
                if(i < length - 64)
                {
                    stringBuilder.append(string, i, i + 64);
                    stringBuilder.append("\n");
                }
                else
                {
                    stringBuilder.append(string.substring(i));
                    stringBuilder.append("\n");
                    break;
                }

            stringBuilder.append("-----END CERTIFICATE-----\n");
            return stringBuilder.toString();
        }
    catch(Exception exception)
        {
            return "";
        }
    }

    public static String prepareSipHashId(String string)
    {
        if(string == null)
            return "";
        else
            return delimitString
                (string.replace("-", "").toUpperCase().trim(), '-', 4);
    }

    public static String sipHashIdFromData(byte bytes[])
    {
        SipHash sipHash = new SipHash();

        return byteArrayAsHexStringDelimited
            (longArrayToByteArray(sipHash.
                            hmac(bytes,
                                    Cryptography.keyForSipHash(bytes),
                                    Cryptography.SIPHASH_OUTPUT_LENGTH)),
            '-', 4).toUpperCase();
    }

    public static String sipHashIdFromDestination(String string)
    {
        int index1 = string.indexOf('(');
        int index2 = string.indexOf(')');

        if(index1 < index2 && index1 > 0 && index2 > 0)
            return string.substring(index1 + 1, index2).trim();

        return "";
    }

    public static SubMenu addMembersToMenu(Menu menu, int count, int position)
    {
        if(menu == null)
            return null;
```

```java
    ArrayList<ParticipantElement> arrayList = State.getInstance().
        participants();

    /*
    ** Do not clear arrayList!
    */

    if(arrayList != null && arrayList.size() > 0)
    {
        SubMenu subMenu = null;

        if(count == menu.size())
            subMenu = menu.addSubMenu
                (Menu.NONE,
                 Menu.NONE,
                 position,
                 "Chat Messaging Window");
        else
            subMenu = menu.getItem(menu.size() - 1).getSubMenu();

        if(subMenu == null)
            return subMenu;

        subMenu.clear();

        for(ParticipantElement participantElement : arrayList)
        {
            if(participantElement == null)
                continue;

            subMenu.add
                (1,
                 participantElement.m_oid,
                 0,
                 participantElement.m_name +
                 " (" +
                 prepareSipHashId(participantElement.m_sipHashId) +
                 ")");
        }

        return subMenu;
    }

    return null;
}

public static byte[] compressed(byte bytes[])
{
    if(bytes == null)
        return null;

    try
    {
        ByteArrayOutputStream byteArrayOutputStream =
            new ByteArrayOutputStream(bytes.length);

        try
        {
            try(GZIPOutputStream gzipOutputStream =
                new GZIPOutputStream(byteArrayOutputStream))
            {
                gzipOutputStream.write(bytes);
```

```java
                }

                return byteArrayOutputStream.toByteArray();
            }
        catch(Exception exception)
        {
        }
        finally
        {
            try
            {
                byteArrayOutputStream.close();
            }
            catch(Exception exception)
            {
            }
        }
    }
    catch(Exception exception)
    {
    }

    return null;
}

public static byte[] decompressed(byte bytes[])
{
    if(bytes == null)
        return null;

    try
    {
        ByteArrayInputStream byteArrayInputStream = null;
        ByteArrayOutputStream byteArrayOutputStream = null;

        try
        {
            byteArrayInputStream = new ByteArrayInputStream(bytes);
            byteArrayOutputStream = new ByteArrayOutputStream();

            try(GZIPInputStream gzipInputStream =
                new GZIPInputStream(byteArrayInputStream))
            {
                byte buffer[] = new byte[4096];
                int rc = 0;

                while((rc = gzipInputStream.read(buffer)) > 0)
                    byteArrayOutputStream.write(buffer, 0, rc);
            }

            return byteArrayOutputStream.toByteArray();
        }
        catch(Exception exception)
        {
        }
        finally
        {
            try
            {
                if(byteArrayInputStream != null)
                    byteArrayInputStream.close();
            }
            catch(Exception exception)
```

```java
                {
                }

                try
                {
                    if(byteArrayOutputStream != null)
                        byteArrayOutputStream.close();
                }
                catch(Exception exception)
                {
                }
            }
        }
        catch(Exception exception)
        {
        }

        return null;
    }

    public static byte[] intToByteArray(int value)
    {
        try
        {
            return ByteBuffer.allocate(INTEGER_BYTES).putInt(value).array();
        }
        catch(Exception exception)
        {
            return null;
        }
    }

    public static byte[] joinByteArrays(byte[] ... data)
    {
        if(data == null)
            return null;

        try
        {
            int length = 0;

            for(byte b[] : data)
                if(b != null && b.length > 0)
                    length += b.length;

            if(length == 0)
                return null;

            byte bytes[] = new byte[length];
            int i = 0;

            for(byte b[] : data)
                if(b != null && b.length > 0)
                {
                    System.arraycopy(b, 0, bytes, i, b.length);
                    i += b.length;
                }

            return bytes; // data[0] + data[1] + ... + data[n - 1]
        }
        catch(Exception exception)
        {
            return null;
```

```java
        }
    }

    public static byte[] longArrayToByteArray(long value[])
    {
        try
        {
            ByteBuffer byteBuffer = ByteBuffer.allocate
                (LONG_BYTES * value.length);

            for(long l : value)
                byteBuffer.putLong(l);

            return byteBuffer.array();
        }
        catch(Exception exception)
        {
            return null;
        }
    }

    public static byte[] longToByteArray(long value)
    {
        try
        {
            return ByteBuffer.allocate(LONG_BYTES).putLong(value).array();
        }
        catch(Exception exception)
        {
            return null;
        }
    }

    public static int countOf(StringBuilder stringBuilder, char character)
    {
        if(stringBuilder == null || stringBuilder.length() == 0)
            return 0;

        int count = 0;
        int length = stringBuilder.length();

        for(int i = 0; i < length; i++)
            if(character == stringBuilder.charAt(i))
                count += 1;

        return count;
    }

    public static int imagePercentFromArrayLength(int length)
    {
        final int upper = 8 * 1024 * 1024;

        if(length <= upper)
            return 100;
        else
            return (int) ((100.0 * ((double) upper)) / ((double) length));
    }

    public static long byteArrayToLong(byte bytes[])
    {
        if(bytes == null || bytes.length != LONG_BYTES)
            return 0L;
```

```java
        try
        {
            ByteBuffer byteBuffer = ByteBuffer.allocate(LONG_BYTES);

            byteBuffer.put(bytes);
            byteBuffer.flip();
            return byteBuffer.getLong();
        }
        catch(Exception exception)
        {
            return 0L;
        }
    }

    public static long fileSize(String fileName)
    {
        AssetFileDescriptor assetFileDescriptor = null;

        try
        {
            Uri uri = Uri.parse(fileName);

            assetFileDescriptor = Smoke.getApplication().getContentResolver().
                openAssetFileDescriptor(uri, "r");
            return assetFileDescriptor.getParcelFileDescriptor().getStatSize();
        }
        catch(Exception exception)
        {
        }
        finally
        {
            try
            {
                if(assetFileDescriptor != null)
                    assetFileDescriptor.close();
            }
            catch(Exception exception)
            {
            }
        }

        return 0L;
    }

    public static void enableChildren(View view, boolean state)
    {
        if(Build.VERSION.SDK_INT > Build.VERSION_CODES.N)
            /*
            ** Otherwise, children will force their scrollable parents
            ** to scroll after said children are enabled. Android 9
            ** garbage.
            */

            return;

        if(view == null)
            return;
        else if(!(view instanceof ViewGroup))
        {
            view.setEnabled(state);
            return;
        }
```

```java
        ViewGroup viewGroup = (ViewGroup) view;
        int count = viewGroup.getChildCount();

        for(int i = 0; i < count; i++)
        {
            View child = viewGroup.getChildAt(i);

            enableChildren(child, state);
        }
    }

    public static void sendBroadcast(Intent intent)
    {
        if(intent == null)
            return;

        try
        {
            LocalBroadcastManager localBroadcastManager =
                LocalBroadcastManager.getInstance(Smoke.getApplication());

            localBroadcastManager.sendBroadcast(intent);
        }
        catch(Exception exception)
        {
        }
    }

    public static void sendBroadcast(String action)
    {
        try
        {
            Intent intent = new Intent(action);
            LocalBroadcastManager localBroadcastManager =
                LocalBroadcastManager.getInstance(Smoke.getApplication());

            localBroadcastManager.sendBroadcast(intent);
        }
        catch(Exception exception)
        {
        }
    }

    public static void sendBroadcast(String action, String extra1)
    {
        try
        {
            Intent intent = new Intent(action);
            LocalBroadcastManager localBroadcastManager =
                LocalBroadcastManager.getInstance(Smoke.getApplication());

            intent.putExtra("org.purple.smoke.extra1", extra1);
            localBroadcastManager.sendBroadcast(intent);
        }
        catch(Exception exception)
        {
        }
    }

    public static void sendBroadcast(String action, int extra1, int extra2)
    {
        try
        {
```

```
        Intent intent = new Intent(action);
        LocalBroadcastManager localBroadcastManager =
            LocalBroadcastManager.getInstance(Smoke.getApplication());

        intent.putExtra("org.purple.smoke.extra1", extra1);
        intent.putExtra("org.purple.smoke.extra2", extra2);
        localBroadcastManager.sendBroadcast(intent);
    }
    catch(Exception exception)
    {
    }
}

public static void showErrorDialog(Context context, String error)
{
    if(context == null ||
       !(context instanceof Activity) ||
       ((Activity) context).isFinishing())
        return;

    AlertDialog alertDialog = new AlertDialog.Builder(context).create();

    alertDialog.setButton
        (AlertDialog.BUTTON_NEUTRAL, "Dismiss",
         new DialogInterface.OnClickListener()
         {
             public void onClick(DialogInterface dialog, int which)
             {
                 dialog.dismiss();
             }
         });
    alertDialog.setMessage(error);
    alertDialog.setTitle("Error");
    alertDialog.show();
}

public static void showNotification(Context context,
                                    Intent intent,
                                    View view)
{
    if(context == null ||
       !(context instanceof Activity) ||
       intent == null ||
       intent.getAction() == null ||
       view == null)
        return;

    String message = "";
    String sipHashId = "";

    switch(intent.getAction())
    {
    case "org.purple.smoke.chat_message":
        if(((Activity) context).isFinishing())
            return;

        message = intent.getStringExtra("org.purple.smoke.message");

        if(message == null)
            return;

        String name = intent.getStringExtra("org.purple.smoke.name");
```

```java
        if(name == null)
            return;
        else
            name = name.trim();

        sipHashId = intent.getStringExtra("org.purple.smoke.sipHashId");

        if(sipHashId == null)
            return;
        else
            sipHashId = sipHashId.toUpperCase();

        if(name.isEmpty())
            name = "unknown";

        boolean purple = intent.getBooleanExtra
            ("org.purple.smoke.purple", false);
        long sequence = intent.getLongExtra
            ("org.purple.smoke.sequence", 1L);
        long timestamp = intent.getLongExtra
            ("org.purple.smoke.timestamp", 0L);

        State.getInstance().logChatMessage
            (message, name, sipHashId, purple, sequence, timestamp);
        message = message.trim();

        if(name.length() > 15)
        {
            name = name.substring(0, 15);

            if(!name.endsWith("..."))
            {
                if(name.endsWith(".."))
                    name += ".";
                else if(name.endsWith("."))
                    name += "..";
                else
                    name += "...";
            }
        }

        if(message.length() > 15)
        {
            message = message.substring(0, 15);

            if(!message.endsWith("..."))
            {
                if(message.endsWith(".."))
                    message += ".";
                else if(message.endsWith("."))
                    message += "..";
                else
                    message += "...";
            }
        }

        if(message.isEmpty())
            message = "A message from " + name + " has arrived.";
        else
            message = "A message (" + message + ") from " + name +
                " has arrived.";

        break;
```

```java
case "org.purple.smoke.siphash_share_confirmation":
    sipHashId = intent.getStringExtra("org.purple.smoke.sipHashId");

    if(sipHashId == null)
        return;
    else
        sipHashId = sipHashId.toUpperCase();

    if(Cryptography.SIPHASH_IDENTITY_LENGTH == sipHashId.length())
        message = "A SmokeStack has received the Smoke Identity " +
            sipHashId + ".";
    else
        message = "A SmokeStack has received the Smoke Identity.";

    break;
case "org.purple.smoke.time":
    String string = intent.getStringExtra("org.purple.smoke.extra1");

    if(string == null)
        return;
    else
        message = string;

    break;
default:
    break;
}

if(message.isEmpty())
    return;

TextView textView1 = new TextView(context);
final WeakReference<PopupWindow> popupWindow =
    new WeakReference<> (new PopupWindow(context));

textView1.setBackgroundColor(Color.rgb(255, 236, 179));
textView1.setText(message);

float density = context.getResources().getDisplayMetrics().density;

textView1.setPaddingRelative
    ((int) (10 * density),
     (int) (10 * density),
     (int) (10 * density),
     (int) (10 * density));
textView1.setTextSize(16);
popupWindow.get().setContentView(textView1);
popupWindow.get().setOutsideTouchable(true);

if(Build.VERSION.SDK_INT < Build.VERSION_CODES.M)
{
    popupWindow.get().setHeight(300);
    popupWindow.get().setWidth(450);
}

popupWindow.get().showAtLocation
    (view, Gravity.START | Gravity.TOP, 75, 75);

try
{
    Ringtone ringtone = null;
    Uri notification = RingtoneManager.getDefaultUri
        (RingtoneManager.TYPE_NOTIFICATION);
```

```java
        ringtone = RingtoneManager.getRingtone(context, notification);
        ringtone.play();
    }
    catch(Exception exception)
    {
    }

    Handler handler = new Handler();

    handler.postDelayed(new Runnable()
    {
        @Override
        public void run()
        {
            if(popupWindow.get() != null)
                popupWindow.get().dismiss();
        }
    }, 10000L); // 10 seconds.
}


public static void showPromptDialog
    (Context context,
     DialogInterface.OnCancelListener cancelListener,
     String prompt)
{
    if(context == null ||
       !(context instanceof Activity) ||
       ((Activity) context).isFinishing())
        return;

    AlertDialog alertDialog = new AlertDialog.Builder(context).create();
    CheckBox checkBox1 = new CheckBox(context);

    State.getInstance().removeKey("dialog_accepted");
    alertDialog.setButton
        (AlertDialog.BUTTON_NEGATIVE, "No",
         new DialogInterface.OnClickListener()
         {
            public void onClick(DialogInterface dialog, int which)
            {
                State.getInstance().removeKey("dialog_accepted");
                dialog.dismiss();
            }
         });
    alertDialog.setButton
        (AlertDialog.BUTTON_POSITIVE, "Yes",
         new DialogInterface.OnClickListener()
         {
            public void onClick(DialogInterface dialog, int which)
            {
                State.getInstance().setString("dialog_accepted", "true");
                dialog.cancel();
            }
         });
    alertDialog.setMessage(prompt);
    alertDialog.setOnCancelListener(cancelListener); /*
                                        ** We cannot wait
                                        ** for a response.
                                        */
    alertDialog.setTitle("Confirmation");
    alertDialog.setView(checkBox1);
    alertDialog.show();
```

```java
        final Button button1 = alertDialog.getButton
            (AlertDialog.BUTTON_POSITIVE);

        button1.setEnabled(false);
        checkBox1.setOnCheckedChangeListener
            (new CompoundButton.OnCheckedChangeListener()
            {
                @Override
                public void onCheckedChanged
                    (CompoundButton buttonView, boolean isChecked)
                {
                    button1.setEnabled(isChecked);
                }
            });
        checkBox1.setText("Confirm");
    }

    public static void showTextInputDialog
        (Context context,
         DialogInterface.OnCancelListener cancelListener,
         String prompt,
         String text,
         String title)
    {
        if(context == null ||
           !(context instanceof Activity) ||
           ((Activity) context).isFinishing())
            return;

        AlertDialog alertDialog = new AlertDialog.Builder(context).create();
        final EditText editText = new EditText(context);
        final boolean contextIsChat = context instanceof Chat;
        final boolean contextIsMemberChat = context instanceof MemberChat;
        final boolean contextIsSettings = context instanceof Settings;

        alertDialog.setButton
            (AlertDialog.BUTTON_NEGATIVE, "Cancel",
             new DialogInterface.OnClickListener()
            {
                public void onClick(DialogInterface dialog, int which)
                {
                    if(contextIsChat)
                        State.getInstance().removeKey("chat_secret_input");
                    else if(contextIsMemberChat)
                        State.getInstance().removeKey
                            ("member_chat_secret_input");
                    else if(contextIsSettings)
                        State.getInstance().removeKey
                            ("settings_participant_name_input");

                    dialog.dismiss();
                }
            });
        alertDialog.setButton
            (AlertDialog.BUTTON_POSITIVE, "Accept",
             new DialogInterface.OnClickListener()
            {
                public void onClick(DialogInterface dialog, int which)
                {
                    if(contextIsChat)
                    {
                        String string = editText.getText().toString();
```

```java
                    if(string.length() <= Cryptography.HASH_KEY_LENGTH)
                        string = Base64.encodeToString
                            (Cryptography.
                                sha512(string.
                                    getBytes(StandardCharsets.UTF_8)),
                                Base64.NO_WRAP);

                    State.getInstance().setString
                        ("chat_secret_input", string);
                }
                else if(contextIsMemberChat)
                {
                    String string = editText.getText().toString();

                    if(string.length() <= Cryptography.HASH_KEY_LENGTH)
                        string = Base64.encodeToString
                            (Cryptography.
                                sha512(string.
                                    getBytes(StandardCharsets.UTF_8)),
                                Base64.NO_WRAP);

                    State.getInstance().setString
                        ("member_chat_secret_input", string);
                }
                else if(contextIsSettings)
                    State.getInstance().setString
                        ("settings_participant_name_input",
                         editText.getText().toString());

                dialog.cancel();
            }
        });
    alertDialog.setMessage(prompt);
    alertDialog.setOnCancelListener(cancelListener); /*
                                        ** We cannot wait
                                        ** for a response.
                                        */
    alertDialog.setTitle(title);
    editText.setInputType(InputType.TYPE_CLASS_TEXT);
    editText.setText(text);
    alertDialog.setView(editText);
    alertDialog.show();
    }
}
```

/* Neighbor.java –

```java
** 3. The name of the author may not be used to endorse or promote products
**    derived from Smoke without specific prior written permission.
**
** SMOKE IS PROVIDED BY THE AUTHOR ``AS IS'' AND ANY EXPRESS OR
** IMPLIED WARRANTIES, INCLUDING, BUT NOT LIMITED TO, THE IMPLIED WARRANTIES
** OF MERCHANTABILITY AND FITNESS FOR A PARTICULAR PURPOSE ARE DISCLAIMED.
** IN NO EVENT SHALL THE AUTHOR BE LIABLE FOR ANY DIRECT, INDIRECT,
** INCIDENTAL, SPECIAL, EXEMPLARY, OR CONSEQUENTIAL DAMAGES (INCLUDING, BUT
** NOT LIMITED TO, PROCUREMENT OF SUBSTITUTE GOODS OR SERVICES; LOSS OF USE,
** DATA, OR PROFITS; OR BUSINESS INTERRUPTION) HOWEVER CAUSED AND ON ANY
** THEORY OF LIABILITY, WHETHER IN CONTRACT, STRICT LIABILITY, OR TORT
** (INCLUDING NEGLIGENCE OR OTHERWISE) ARISING IN ANY WAY OUT OF THE USE OF
** SMOKE, EVEN IF ADVISED OF THE POSSIBILITY OF SUCH DAMAGE.
*/

package org.purple.smoke;

import android.content.Context;
import android.net.ConnectivityManager;
import android.net.NetworkInfo;
import android.util.Base64;
import java.nio.charset.StandardCharsets;
import java.util.ArrayList;
import java.util.Arrays;
import java.util.UUID;
import java.util.concurrent.Executors;
import java.util.concurrent.ScheduledExecutorService;
import java.util.concurrent.TimeUnit;
import java.util.concurrent.atomic.AtomicBoolean;
import java.util.concurrent.atomic.AtomicInteger;
import java.util.concurrent.atomic.AtomicLong;

public abstract class Neighbor
{
    private ArrayList<String> m_echoQueue = null;
    private ArrayList<String> m_queue = null;
    private AtomicBoolean m_capabilitiesSent = null;
    private UUID m_uuid = null;
    private final Object m_echoQueueMutex = new Object();
    private final Object m_queueMutex = new Object();
    private final ScheduledExecutorService m_parsingScheduler =
        Executors.newSingleThreadScheduledExecutor();
    private final ScheduledExecutorService m_scheduler =
        Executors.newSingleThreadScheduledExecutor();
    private final ScheduledExecutorService m_sendOutboundScheduler =
        Executors.newSingleThreadScheduledExecutor();
    private final static int LANE_WIDTH = 8 * 1024 * 1024; // 8 MiB.
    private final static long DATA_LIFETIME = 15000L; // 15 seconds.
    private final static long PARSING_INTERVAL = 100L; // 100 milliseconds.
    private final static long SEND_OUTBOUND_TIMER_INTERVAL =
        200L; // 200 milliseconds.
    private final static long SILENCE = 90000L; // 90 seconds.
    private final static long TIMER_INTERVAL = 3500L; // 3.5 seconds.
    protected AtomicBoolean m_aborted = null;
    protected AtomicBoolean m_passthrough = null;
    protected AtomicInteger m_oid = null;
    protected AtomicLong m_bytesRead = null;
    protected AtomicLong m_bytesWritten = null;
    protected AtomicLong m_lastParsed = null;
    protected AtomicLong m_lastTimeRead = null;
    protected AtomicLong m_startTime = null;
    protected Cryptography m_cryptography = null;
    protected Database m_databaseHelper = null;
```

```java
    protected String m_ipAddress = "";
    protected String m_ipPort = "";
    protected String m_version = "";
    protected final Object m_errorMutex = new Object();
    protected final Object m_mutex = new Object();
    protected final Object m_parsingSchedulerMutex = new Object();
    protected final ScheduledExecutorService m_readSocketScheduler =
        Executors.newSingleThreadScheduledExecutor();
    protected final StringBuffer m_stringBuffer = new StringBuffer();
    protected final StringBuilder m_error = new StringBuilder();
    protected final static int BYTES_PER_READ = 1024 * 1024; // 1 MiB.
    protected final static int MAXIMUM_BYTES = LANE_WIDTH;
    protected final static int SO_RCVBUF = 65536;
    protected final static int SO_SNDBUF = 65536;
    protected final static int SO_TIMEOUT = 0; // 0 seconds, block.
    protected final static long READ_SOCKET_INTERVAL =
        100L; // 100 milliseconds.
    protected final static long WAIT_TIMEOUT = 10000L; // 10 seconds.
    public final static int MAXIMUM_QUEUED_ECHO_PACKETS = 256;

    private void saveStatistics()
    {
        String echoQueueSize = "";
        String error = "";
        String localIp = getLocalIp();
        String localPort = String.valueOf(getLocalPort());
        String sessionCiper = getSessionCipher();
        String status = "connecting";
        boolean connected = connected();
        long uptime = System.nanoTime() - m_startTime.get();

        synchronized(m_echoQueueMutex)
        {
            echoQueueSize = String.valueOf(m_echoQueue.size());
        }

        synchronized(m_errorMutex)
        {
            error = m_error.toString();
        }

        if(connected)
            status = "connected";
        else
            status = "disconnected";

        m_databaseHelper.saveNeighborInformation
            (m_cryptography,
             String.valueOf(m_bytesRead.get()),
             String.valueOf(m_bytesWritten.get()),
             echoQueueSize,
             error,
             localIp,
             localPort,
             sessionCiper,
             status,
             String.valueOf(uptime),
             String.valueOf(m_oid.get()));
    }

    private void terminateOnSilence()
    {
        if(m_passthrough.get())
```

```java
            return;

        if((System.nanoTime() - m_lastTimeRead.get()) / 1000000L > SILENCE)
            disconnect();
    }

    protected Neighbor(String passthrough,
                       String ipAddress,
                       String ipPort,
                       String scopeId,
                       String transport,
                       String version,
                       int oid)
    {
        m_aborted = new AtomicBoolean(false);
        m_bytesRead = new AtomicLong(0L);
        m_bytesWritten = new AtomicLong(0L);
        m_capabilitiesSent = new AtomicBoolean(false);
        m_cryptography = Cryptography.getInstance();
        m_databaseHelper = Database.getInstance();
        m_echoQueue = new ArrayList<> ();
        m_ipAddress = ipAddress;
        m_ipPort = ipPort;
        m_lastParsed = new AtomicLong(System.currentTimeMillis());
        m_lastTimeRead = new AtomicLong(System.nanoTime());
        m_oid = new AtomicInteger(oid);
        m_passthrough = new AtomicBoolean(passthrough.equals("true"));
        m_queue = new ArrayList<> ();
        m_startTime = new AtomicLong(System.nanoTime());
        m_uuid = UUID.randomUUID();
        m_version = version;

        /*
        ** Start the schedules.
        */

        m_parsingScheduler.scheduleAtFixedRate(new Runnable()
        {
            @Override
            public void run()
            {
                try
                {
                    if(!connected() && !m_aborted.get())
                        synchronized(m_mutex)
                        {
                            try
                            {
                                m_mutex.wait(WAIT_TIMEOUT);
                            }
                            catch(Exception exception)
                            {
                            }
                        }

                    if(!connected() || m_aborted.get())
                        return;

                    /*
                    ** Await new data.
                    */

                    synchronized(m_parsingSchedulerMutex)
```

```
{
    try
    {
        m_parsingSchedulerMutex.wait(WAIT_TIMEOUT);
    }
    catch(Exception exception)
    {
    }
}

if(m_passthrough.get())
{
    echo(m_stringBuffer.toString());
    m_lastParsed.set(System.currentTimeMillis());
    m_stringBuffer.delete(0, m_stringBuffer.length());
}
else
{
    /*
    ** Detect our end-of-message delimiter.
    */

    int indexOf = -1;

    while((indexOf = m_stringBuffer.
                     indexOf(Messages.EOM)) >= 0)
    {
        if(m_aborted.get())
            break;

        m_lastParsed.set(System.currentTimeMillis());

        String buffer = m_stringBuffer.
            substring(0, indexOf + Messages.EOM.length());

        m_stringBuffer.delete(0, buffer.length());

        if(buffer.contains("type=0097a&content="))
        {
            scheduleSend
                (Messages.
                 authenticateMessage(m_cryptography,
                                     Messages.
                                     stripMessage(buffer)));
            continue;
        }

        switch(Kernel.getInstance().ourMessage(buffer))
        {
        case 0:
            echo(buffer);
            break;
        case 2:
            echoForce(buffer);
            break;
        default:
            break;
        }
    }
}

if(System.currentTimeMillis() - m_lastParsed.get() >
   DATA_LIFETIME ||
```

```java
                                   m_stringBuffer.length() > MAXIMUM_BYTES)
                                m_stringBuffer.delete(0, m_stringBuffer.length());

                            m_stringBuffer.trimToSize();
                        }
                        catch(Exception exception)
                        {
                        }
                    }
                }, 0L, PARSING_INTERVAL, TimeUnit.MILLISECONDS);
        m_scheduler.scheduleAtFixedRate(new Runnable()
        {
            @Override
            public void run()
            {
                try
                {
                    String statusControl = m_databaseHelper.
                        readNeighborStatusControl(m_cryptography, m_oid.get());

                    switch(statusControl)
                    {
                    case "connect":
                        connect();
                        break;
                    case "disconnect":
                        disconnect();
                        setError("");
                        break;
                    default:
                        /*
                        ** Abort!
                        */

                        disconnect();
                        return;
                    }

                    saveStatistics();
                    terminateOnSilence();
                }
                catch(Exception exception)
                {
                }
            }
        }, 0L, TIMER_INTERVAL, TimeUnit.MILLISECONDS);
        m_sendOutboundScheduler.scheduleAtFixedRate(new Runnable()
        {
            private long m_accumulatedTime = System.nanoTime();

            @Override
            public void run()
            {
                try
                {
                    if(!connected() && !m_aborted.get())
                        synchronized(m_mutex)
                        {
                            try
                            {
                                m_mutex.wait(WAIT_TIMEOUT);
                            }
                            catch(Exception exception)
```

```java
                {
                }
            }

        if(!connected() || m_aborted.get())
            return;

        if(System.nanoTime() - m_accumulatedTime >= 15000000000L)
        {
            /*
            ** Send every 15 seconds.
            */

            m_accumulatedTime = System.nanoTime();

            if(!m_passthrough.get())
            {
                if(!m_capabilitiesSent.get())
                    m_capabilitiesSent.set
                        (send(getCapabilities()) > 0);

                send(getIdentities());
            }
        }

        /*
        ** Retrieve a database message.
        */

        String array[] = m_databaseHelper.readOutboundMessage
            (m_oid.get());

        /*
        ** array[0]: Message
        ** array[1]: Message Identity Digest
        ** array[2]: OID
        */

        /*
        ** If the message is sent successfully, remove it
        ** from the database.
        */

        if(array != null && array.length == 3)
        {
            byte bytes[] = m_cryptography.mtd
                (Base64.decode(array[0], Base64.DEFAULT));

            if(bytes != null)
                array[0] = new String(bytes);
            else
                array[0] = "";

            if(array[0].startsWith("OZONE-"))
            {
                bytes = Base64.decode
                    (array[0].substring(6), Base64.NO_WRAP);

                if(bytes != null)
                {
                    byte timestamp[] = Miscellaneous.longToByteArray
                        (TimeUnit.MILLISECONDS.
                        toMinutes(System.currentTimeMillis()));
```

```java
                        bytes = Miscellaneous.joinByteArrays
                            /*
                            ** Remove the embedded SipHash.
                            */

                                (Arrays.
                                 copyOfRange(bytes,
                                             0,
                                             bytes.length -
                                             Cryptography.
                                             SIPHASH_IDENTITY_LENGTH),
                                    Cryptography.
                                    hmac(Miscellaneous.
                                        joinByteArrays(bytes, timestamp),
                                        m cryptography.ozoneMacKey()));
                    }
                else
                    array[0] = "";

                if(bytes != null)
                    array[0] = Messages.bytesToMessageString(bytes);
                else
                    array[0] = "";
            }

        if(array[0].isEmpty())
            m_databaseHelper.deleteEntry
                (array[2], "outbound_queue");
        else if(send(array[0]) > 0)
        {
            m_databaseHelper.deleteEntry
                (array[2], "outbound_queue");

            if(m_databaseHelper.
                writeMessageStatus(m_cryptography, array[1]))
                Kernel.getInstance().notifyOfDataSetChange
                    (array[2]);
        }
    }

    /*
    ** Echo packets.
    */

    synchronized(m_echoQueueMutex)
    {
        if(!m_echoQueue.isEmpty())
            /*
            ** Results of send() are ignored.
            */

            send(m_echoQueue.remove(m_echoQueue.size() - 1));
    }

    /*
    ** Transfer real-time packets.
    */

    synchronized(m_queueMutex)
    {
        if(!m_queue.isEmpty())
            /*
```

```java
                        ** Results of send() are ignored.
                        */

                        send(m_queue.remove(m_queue.size() - 1));
                    }
                }
            catch(Exception exception)
                {
                }
            }
        }, 0L, SEND_OUTBOUND_TIMER_INTERVAL, TimeUnit.MILLISECONDS);
    }

    protected String getCapabilities()
    {
        if(m_passthrough.get())
            return "";

        try
        {
            StringBuilder message = new StringBuilder();

            message.append(m_uuid.toString());
            message.append("\n");
            message.append(String.valueOf(LANE_WIDTH));
            message.append("\n");
            message.append("full"); // Echo Mode

            StringBuilder results = new StringBuilder();

            results.append("POST HTTP/1.1\r\n");
            results.append
                ("Content-Type: application/x-www-form-urlencoded\r\n");
            results.append("Content-Length: %1\r\n");
            results.append("\r\n");
            results.append("type=0014&content=%2\r\n");
            results.append("\r\n\r\n");

            String base64 = Base64.encodeToString
                (message.toString().getBytes(), Base64.DEFAULT);
            int indexOf = results.indexOf("%1");
            int length = base64.length() +
                "type=0014&content=\r\n\r\n\r\n".length();

            results = results.replace
                (indexOf, indexOf + 2, String.valueOf(length));
            indexOf = results.indexOf("%2");
            results = results.replace(indexOf, indexOf + 2, base64);
            return results.toString();
        }
        catch(Exception exception)
        {
            return "";
        }
    }

    protected String getIdentities()
    {
        if(m_passthrough.get())
            return "";

        try
        {
```

```java
        StringBuilder stringBuilder = new StringBuilder();

        stringBuilder.append(Kernel.getInstance().fireIdentities());
        stringBuilder.append
            (Messages.
             identityMessage(Cryptography.
                        sha512(m_cryptography.sipHashId().
                             getBytes(StandardCharsets.UTF_8))));
        return stringBuilder.toString();
    }
    catch(Exception exception)
    {
        return "";
    }
}

protected String getSessionCipher()
{
    return "";
}

protected abstract String getLocalIp();
protected abstract boolean connected();
protected abstract int getLocalPort();
protected abstract int send(String message);
protected abstract int send(byte bytes[]);
protected abstract void connect();

protected boolean isNetworkConnected()
{
    try
    {
        ConnectivityManager connectivityManager = (ConnectivityManager)
            Smoke.getApplication().getApplicationContext().
            getSystemService(Context.CONNECTIVITY_SERVICE);
        NetworkInfo networkInfo = connectivityManager.
            getActiveNetworkInfo();

        return networkInfo != null && networkInfo.isConnected();
    }
    catch(Exception exception)
    {
    }

    return false;
}

protected void abort()
{
    m_aborted.set(true);

    synchronized(m_mutex)
    {
        m_mutex.notifyAll();
    }

    synchronized(m_parsingScheduler)
    {
        try
        {
            m_parsingScheduler.shutdown();
        }
        catch(Exception exception)
```

```
        {
        }
    }

    synchronized(m_parsingSchedulerMutex)
    {
        m_parsingSchedulerMutex.notify();
    }

    synchronized(m_parsingScheduler)
    {
        try
        {
            if(!m_parsingScheduler.awaitTermination(60L, TimeUnit.SECONDS))
                m_parsingScheduler.shutdownNow();
        }
        catch(Exception exception)
        {
        }
    }

    synchronized(m_scheduler)
    {
        try
        {
            m_scheduler.shutdown();
        }
        catch(Exception exception)
        {
        }

        try
        {
            if(!m_scheduler.awaitTermination(60L, TimeUnit.SECONDS))
                m_scheduler.shutdownNow();
        }
        catch(Exception exception)
        {
        }
    }

    synchronized(m_sendOutboundScheduler)
    {
        try
        {
            m_sendOutboundScheduler.shutdown();
        }
        catch(Exception exception)
        {
        }

        try
        {
            if(!m_sendOutboundScheduler.
                awaitTermination(60L, TimeUnit.SECONDS))
                m_sendOutboundScheduler.shutdownNow();
        }
        catch(Exception exception)
        {
        }
    }

    Miscellaneous.sendBroadcast
```

```java
        ("org.purple.smoke.neighbor_aborted", address());
   }

   protected void disconnect()
   {
      m_capabilitiesSent.set(false);

      synchronized(m_echoQueueMutex)
      {
         m_echoQueue.clear();
      }

      synchronized(m_mutex)
      {
         m_mutex.notifyAll();
      }

      synchronized(m_parsingSchedulerMutex)
      {
         m_parsingSchedulerMutex.notify();
      }

      synchronized(m_queueMutex)
      {
         m_queue.clear();
      }

      m_stringBuffer.delete(0, m_stringBuffer.length());
      m_stringBuffer.trimToSize();
      Miscellaneous.sendBroadcast
         ("org.purple.smoke.neighbor_disconnected", address());
   }

   protected void echo(String message)
   {
      Kernel.getInstance().echo(message, m_oid.get());
   }

   protected void echoForce(String message)
   {
      Kernel.getInstance().echoForce(message, m_oid.get());
   }

   protected void setError(String error)
   {
      synchronized(m_errorMutex)
      {
         m_error.delete(0, m_error.length());
         m_error.trimToSize();
         m_error.append(error);
      }
   }

   public boolean passthrough()
   {
      return m_passthrough.get();
   }

   public int getOid()
   {
      return m_oid.get();
   }
```

```java
    public synchronized String address()
    {
        return m_ipAddress + ":" + m_ipPort;
    }

    public void clearEchoQueue()
    {
        synchronized(m_echoQueueMutex)
        {
            m_echoQueue.clear();
        }
    }

    public void clearQueue()
    {
        synchronized(m_queueMutex)
        {
            m_queue.clear();
        }
    }

    public void scheduleEchoSend(String message)
    {
        if(!connected() ||
           m_passthrough.get() ||
           message == null ||
           message.trim().isEmpty())
            return;

        synchronized(m_echoQueueMutex)
        {
            if(m_echoQueue.size() < MAXIMUM_QUEUED_ECHO_PACKETS)
                m_echoQueue.add(message);
        }
    }

    public void scheduleSend(String message)
    {
        if(!connected() ||
           m_passthrough.get() ||
           message == null ||
           message.trim().isEmpty())
            return;

        synchronized(m_queueMutex)
        {
            m_queue.add(message);
        }
    }
}
```

```java
/* NeighborElement.java –

https://github.com/textbrowser/smoke/blob/master/Smoke/app/src/main/java/org/p
urple/smoke/NeighborElement.java
** Copyright (c) Alexis Megas.
** All rights reserved.
**
** Redistribution and use in source and binary forms, with or without
** modification, are permitted provided that the following conditions
** are met:
** 1. Redistributions of source code must retain the above copyright
**    notice, this list of conditions and the following disclaimer.
** 2. Redistributions in binary form must reproduce the above copyright
**    notice, this list of conditions and the following disclaimer in the
**    documentation and/or other materials provided with the distribution.
** 3. The name of the author may not be used to endorse or promote products
**    derived from Smoke without specific prior written permission.
**
** SMOKE IS PROVIDED BY THE AUTHOR ``AS IS'' AND ANY EXPRESS OR
** IMPLIED WARRANTIES, INCLUDING, BUT NOT LIMITED TO, THE IMPLIED WARRANTIES
** OF MERCHANTABILITY AND FITNESS FOR A PARTICULAR PURPOSE ARE DISCLAIMED.
** IN NO EVENT SHALL THE AUTHOR BE LIABLE FOR ANY DIRECT, INDIRECT,
** INCIDENTAL, SPECIAL, EXEMPLARY, OR CONSEQUENTIAL DAMAGES (INCLUDING, BUT
** NOT LIMITED TO, PROCUREMENT OF SUBSTITUTE GOODS OR SERVICES; LOSS OF USE,
** DATA, OR PROFITS; OR BUSINESS INTERRUPTION) HOWEVER CAUSED AND ON ANY
** THEORY OF LIABILITY, WHETHER IN CONTRACT, STRICT LIABILITY, OR TORT
** (INCLUDING NEGLIGENCE OR OTHERWISE) ARISING IN ANY WAY OUT OF THE USE OF
** SMOKE, EVEN IF ADVISED OF THE POSSIBILITY OF SUCH DAMAGE.
*/

package org.purple.smoke;

public class NeighborElement
{
    public String m_bytesRead = "";
    public String m_bytesWritten = "";
    public String m_echoQueueSize = "";
    public String m_error = "";
    public String m_ipVersion = "";
    public String m_localIpAddress = "";
    public String m_localPort = "";
    public String m_nonTls = "";
    public String m_passthrough = "";
    public String m_proxyIpAddress = "";
    public String m_proxyPort = "";
    public String m_proxyType = "";
    public String m_remoteIpAddress = "";
    public String m_remotePort = "";
    public String m_remoteScopeId = "";
    public String m_sessionCipher = "";
    public String m_status = "";
    public String m_statusControl = "";
    public String m_transport = "";
    public String m_uptime = "";
    public byte m_remoteCertificate[] = null;
    public int m_oid = -1;
    public long m_outboundQueued = 0L;

    public NeighborElement()
    {
    }
}
```

```java
/* ParticipantCall.java –
https://github.com/textbrowser/smoke/blob/master/Smoke/app/src/main/java/org/p
urple/smoke/ParticipantCall.java
** Copyright (c) Alexis Megas.
** All rights reserved.
**
** Redistribution and use in source and binary forms, with or without
** modification, are permitted provided that the following conditions
** are met:
** 1. Redistributions of source code must retain the above copyright
**    notice, this list of conditions and the following disclaimer.
** 2. Redistributions in binary form must reproduce the above copyright
**    notice, this list of conditions and the following disclaimer in the
**    documentation and/or other materials provided with the distribution.
** 3. The name of the author may not be used to endorse or promote products
**    derived from Smoke without specific prior written permission.
**
** SMOKE IS PROVIDED BY THE AUTHOR ``AS IS'' AND ANY EXPRESS OR
** IMPLIED WARRANTIES, INCLUDING, BUT NOT LIMITED TO, THE IMPLIED WARRANTIES
** OF MERCHANTABILITY AND FITNESS FOR A PARTICULAR PURPOSE ARE DISCLAIMED.
** IN NO EVENT SHALL THE AUTHOR BE LIABLE FOR ANY DIRECT, INDIRECT,
** INCIDENTAL, SPECIAL, EXEMPLARY, OR CONSEQUENTIAL DAMAGES (INCLUDING, BUT
** NOT LIMITED TO, PROCUREMENT OF SUBSTITUTE GOODS OR SERVICES; LOSS OF USE,
** DATA, OR PROFITS; OR BUSINESS INTERRUPTION) HOWEVER CAUSED AND ON ANY
** THEORY OF LIABILITY, WHETHER IN CONTRACT, STRICT LIABILITY, OR TORT
** (INCLUDING NEGLIGENCE OR OTHERWISE) ARISING IN ANY WAY OUT OF THE USE OF
** SMOKE, EVEN IF ADVISED OF THE POSSIBILITY OF SUCH DAMAGE.
*/

package org.purple.smoke;

import java.security.KeyPair;

public class ParticipantCall
{
    public Algorithms m_algorithm = Algorithms.RSA;
    public KeyPair m_keyPair = null;
    public String m_sipHashId = "";
    public int m_participantOid = -1;
    public long m_startTime = -1L; // Calls expire.
    public enum Algorithms {MCELIECE, RSA}

    public ParticipantCall(Algorithms algorithm,
                           String sipHashId,
                           int participantOid)
    {
        m_algorithm = algorithm;
        m_participantOid = participantOid;
        m_sipHashId = sipHashId;
        m_startTime = System.nanoTime();
    }

    public void preparePrivatePublicKey()
    {
        try
        {
            switch(m_algorithm)
            {
            case MCELIECE:
                m_keyPair = Cryptography.generatePrivatePublicKeyPair
                    (Cryptography.PARTICIPANT_CALL_MCELIECE_KEY_SIZE, 0, 0);
                break;
```

```java
                case RSA:
                    m_keyPair = Cryptography.generatePrivatePublicKeyPair
                        ("RSA", Cryptography.PARTICIPANT_CALL_RSA_KEY_SIZE, 0);
                    break;
                default:
                    break;
                }
            }
        catch(Exception exception)
        {
            m_keyPair = null;
        }
    }
}
```

/* ParticipantElement.java –

```java
https://github.com/textbrowser/smoke/blob/master/Smoke/app/src/main/java/org/p
urple/smoke/ParticipantElement.java
** Copyright (c) Alexis Megas.
** All rights reserved.
**
** Redistribution and use in source and binary forms, with or without
** modification, are permitted provided that the following conditions
** are met:
** 1. Redistributions of source code must retain the above copyright
**    notice, this list of conditions and the following disclaimer.
** 2. Redistributions in binary form must reproduce the above copyright
**    notice, this list of conditions and the following disclaimer in the
**    documentation and/or other materials provided with the distribution.
** 3. The name of the author may not be used to endorse or promote products
**    derived from Smoke without specific prior written permission.
**
** SMOKE IS PROVIDED BY THE AUTHOR ``AS IS'' AND ANY EXPRESS OR
** IMPLIED WARRANTIES, INCLUDING, BUT NOT LIMITED TO, THE IMPLIED WARRANTIES
** OF MERCHANTABILITY AND FITNESS FOR A PARTICULAR PURPOSE ARE DISCLAIMED.
** IN NO EVENT SHALL THE AUTHOR BE LIABLE FOR ANY DIRECT, INDIRECT,
** INCIDENTAL, SPECIAL, EXEMPLARY, OR CONSEQUENTIAL DAMAGES (INCLUDING, BUT
** NOT LIMITED TO, PROCUREMENT OF SUBSTITUTE GOODS OR SERVICES; LOSS OF USE,
** DATA, OR PROFITS; OR BUSINESS INTERRUPTION) HOWEVER CAUSED AND ON ANY
** THEORY OF LIABILITY, WHETHER IN CONTRACT, STRICT LIABILITY, OR TORT
** (INCLUDING NEGLIGENCE OR OTHERWISE) ARISING IN ANY WAY OUT OF THE USE OF
** SMOKE, EVEN IF ADVISED OF THE POSSIBILITY OF SUCH DAMAGE.
*/

package org.purple.smoke;

public class ParticipantElement
{
    public String m_name = "";
    public String m_sipHashId = "";
    public byte m_keyStream[] = null;
    public int m_oid = -1;
    public long m_lastStatusTimestamp = -1L;

    public ParticipantElement()
    {
    }
}
```

/* Settings.java –

```
https://github.com/textbrowser/smoke/blob/master/Smoke/app/src/main/java/org/p
urple/smoke/Settings.java
** Copyright (c) Alexis Megas.
** All rights reserved.
**
** Redistribution and use in source and binary forms, with or without
** modification, are permitted provided that the following conditions
** are met:
** 1. Redistributions of source code must retain the above copyright
**    notice, this list of conditions and the following disclaimer.
** 2. Redistributions in binary form must reproduce the above copyright
**    notice, this list of conditions and the following disclaimer in the
**    documentation and/or other materials provided with the distribution.
** 3. The name of the author may not be used to endorse or promote products
**    derived from Smoke without specific prior written permission.
**
** SMOKE IS PROVIDED BY THE AUTHOR ``AS IS'' AND ANY EXPRESS OR
** IMPLIED WARRANTIES, INCLUDING, BUT NOT LIMITED TO, THE IMPLIED WARRANTIES
** OF MERCHANTABILITY AND FITNESS FOR A PARTICULAR PURPOSE ARE DISCLAIMED.
** IN NO EVENT SHALL THE AUTHOR BE LIABLE FOR ANY DIRECT, INDIRECT,
** INCIDENTAL, SPECIAL, EXEMPLARY, OR CONSEQUENTIAL DAMAGES (INCLUDING, BUT
** NOT LIMITED TO, PROCUREMENT OF SUBSTITUTE GOODS OR SERVICES; LOSS OF USE,
** DATA, OR PROFITS; OR BUSINESS INTERRUPTION) HOWEVER CAUSED AND ON ANY
** THEORY OF LIABILITY, WHETHER IN CONTRACT, STRICT LIABILITY, OR TORT
** (INCLUDING NEGLIGENCE OR OTHERWISE) ARISING IN ANY WAY OUT OF THE USE OF
** SMOKE, EVEN IF ADVISED OF THE POSSIBILITY OF SUCH DAMAGE.
*/

package org.purple.smoke;

import android.Manifest;
import android.content.BroadcastReceiver;
import android.content.Context;
import android.content.DialogInterface;
import android.content.Intent;
import android.content.IntentFilter;
import android.graphics.Color;
import android.os.Build;
import android.os.Bundle;
import android.support.v4.app.ActivityCompat;
import android.support.v4.content.LocalBroadcastManager;
import android.support.v7.app.AppCompatActivity;
import android.text.Editable;
import android.text.InputFilter;
import android.text.InputType;
import android.text.Spannable;
import android.text.SpannableStringBuilder;
import android.text.Spanned;
import android.text.TextWatcher;
import android.text.style.ForegroundColorSpan;
import android.util.Base64;
import android.view.ContextMenu.ContextMenuInfo;
import android.view.ContextMenu;
import android.view.Gravity;
import android.view.Menu;
import android.view.MenuItem;
import android.view.View;
import android.view.ViewGroup;
import android.view.WindowManager;
import android.widget.AdapterView.OnItemSelectedListener;
import android.widget.AdapterView;
```

```java
import android.widget.ArrayAdapter;
import android.widget.Button;
import android.widget.CheckBox;
import android.widget.CompoundButton;
import android.widget.LinearLayout.LayoutParams;
import android.widget.PopupWindow;
import android.widget.ProgressBar;
import android.widget.RadioButton;
import android.widget.RadioGroup;
import android.widget.Spinner;
import android.widget.TableLayout;
import android.widget.TableRow;
import android.widget.TextView;
import java.nio.charset.StandardCharsets;
import java.security.KeyPair;
import java.util.ArrayList;
import java.util.Arrays;
import java.util.Locale;
import java.util.concurrent.Executors;
import java.util.concurrent.ScheduledExecutorService;
import java.util.concurrent.TimeUnit;
import javax.crypto.SecretKey;

public class Settings extends AppCompatActivity
{
    private abstract static class ContextMenuEnumerator
    {
        public final static int DELETE = 0;
        public final static int DELETE_FIASCO_KEYS = 1;
        public final static int DELETE_PUBLIC_KEYS = 2;
        public final static int NEW_NAME = 3;
        public final static int REQUEST_KEYS_VIA_OZONE = 4;
        public final static int SHARE_KEYS_OF = 5;
        public final static int SHARE_SMOKE_ID_OF = 6;
        public final static int VIEW_DETAILS = 7;
    }

    private class PopulateNeighbors implements Runnable
    {
        private ArrayList<NeighborElement> m_arrayList = null;

        public PopulateNeighbors(ArrayList<NeighborElement> arrayList)
        {
            m_arrayList = arrayList;
        }

        @Override
        public void run()
        {
            populateNeighbors(m_arrayList);

            if(m_arrayList != null)
                m_arrayList.clear();
        }
    }

    private class SettingsBroadcastReceiver extends BroadcastReceiver
    {
        public SettingsBroadcastReceiver()
        {
        }

        @Override
```

```java
    public void onReceive(Context context, Intent intent)
    {
        if(intent == null || intent.getAction() == null)
            return;

        switch(intent.getAction())
        {
        case "org.purple.smoke.chat_message":
            Miscellaneous.showNotification
                (Settings.this, intent, findViewById(R.id.main_layout));
            break;
        case "org.purple.smoke.neighbor_aborted":
        case "org.purple.smoke.neighbor_disconnected":
            networkStatusChanged();
            break;
        case "org.purple.smoke.network_connected":
            networkStatusChanged();
            break;
        case "org.purple.smoke.network_disconnected":
            networkStatusChanged();
            break;
        case "org.purple.smoke.populate_participants":
            populateParticipants();
            break;
        case "org.purple.smoke.siphash_share_confirmation":
            Miscellaneous.showNotification
                (Settings.this, intent, findViewById(R.id.main_layout));
            break;
        case "org.purple.smoke.time":
            Miscellaneous.showNotification
                (Settings.this, intent, findViewById(R.id.main_layout));
            break;
        default:
            break;
        }
    }
}

private Database m_databaseHelper = null;
private ScheduledExecutorService m_scheduler = null;
private SettingsBroadcastReceiver m_receiver = null;
private boolean m_receiverRegistered = false;
private final static Cryptography s_cryptography =
    Cryptography.getInstance();
private final static InputFilter s_portFilter = new InputFilter()
{
    public CharSequence filter(CharSequence source,
                               int start,
                               int end,
                               Spanned dest,
                               int dstart,
                               int dend)
    {
        try
        {
            int port = Integer.parseInt
                (dest.toString() + source.toString());

            if(port >= 0 && port <= 65535)
                return null;
        }
        catch(Exception exception)
        {
```

```java
                    }

            return "";
        }
    };
    private final static InputFilter s_sipHashInputFilter = new InputFilter()
    {
        public CharSequence filter(CharSequence source,
                                   int start,
                                   int end,
                                   Spanned dest,
                                   int dstart,
                                   int dend)
        {
            for(int i = start; i < end; i++)
                /*
                ** Allow hexadecimal characters only and some delimiters.
                */

                if(!((source.charAt(i) == ' ' || source.charAt(i) == '-') ||
                     (source.charAt(i) >= '0' && source.charAt(i) <= '9') ||
                     (source.charAt(i) >= '@' && source.charAt(i) <= 'F') ||
                     (source.charAt(i) >= 'a' && source.charAt(i) <= 'f')))
                    return source.subSequence(start, i);

            return null;
        }
    };
    private final static int OZONE_STREAM_CREATION_ITERATION_COUNT = 4096;
    private final static int TEXTVIEW_WIDTH = 500;
    private final static long TIMER_INTERVAL = 2500L; // 2.5 seconds.

    private boolean generateOzone(String string)
    {
        boolean ok = true;
        byte bytes[] = null;
        byte salt[] = null;

        try
        {
            if(!string.trim().isEmpty())
            {
                salt = Cryptography.sha512
                    (string.trim().getBytes(StandardCharsets.UTF_8));

                if(salt != null)
                    bytes = Cryptography.pbkdf2
                        (salt,
                         string.trim().toCharArray(),
                         OZONE_STREAM_CREATION_ITERATION_COUNT,
                         160); // SHA-1
                else
                    ok = false;

                if(bytes != null)
                    bytes = Cryptography.
                        pbkdf2(salt,
                               Base64.encodeToString(bytes, Base64.NO_WRAP).
                               toCharArray(),
                               1,
                               8 * (Cryptography.CIPHER_KEY_LENGTH +
                                    Cryptography.HASH_KEY_LENGTH)); // Bits.
                else
```

```java
                    ok = false;
            }

            if(bytes != null || string.trim().isEmpty())
            {
                m_databaseHelper.writeSetting
                    (s_cryptography, "ozone_address", string.trim());

                if(string.trim().isEmpty())
                {
                    m_databaseHelper.writeSetting
                        (s_cryptography,
                         "ozone_address_stream",
                         "");
                    ok = true;
                    s_cryptography.setOzoneEncryptionKey(null);
                    s_cryptography.setOzoneMacKey(null);
                }
                else if(bytes != null &&
                        bytes.length == Cryptography.CIPHER_HASH_KEYS_LENGTH)
                {
                    m_databaseHelper.writeSetting
                        (s_cryptography,
                         "ozone_address_stream",
                         Base64.encodeToString(bytes, Base64.DEFAULT));
                    s_cryptography.setOzoneEncryptionKey
                        (Arrays.copyOfRange(bytes,
                                            0,
                                            Cryptography.
                                            CIPHER_KEY_LENGTH));
                    s_cryptography.setOzoneMacKey
                        (Arrays.copyOfRange(bytes,
                                            Cryptography.CIPHER_KEY_LENGTH,
                                            bytes.length));
                }
            }
        }
        catch(Exception exception)
        {
            ok = false;
        }

        return ok;
    }

    private void addNeighbor()
    {
        CheckBox checkBox1 = (CheckBox) findViewById(R.id.automatic_refresh);
        CheckBox checkBox2 = (CheckBox) findViewById(R.id.initialize_ozone);
        CheckBox checkBox3 = (CheckBox) findViewById(R.id.non_tls);
        CheckBox checkBox4 = (CheckBox) findViewById(R.id.passthrough);
        RadioGroup radioGroup1 = (RadioGroup) findViewById
            (R.id.neighbors_ipv_radio_group);
        Spinner spinner1 = (Spinner) findViewById(R.id.neighbors_transport);
        Spinner spinner2 = (Spinner) findViewById(R.id.proxy_type);
        String ipVersion = "";
        TextView proxyIpAddress = (TextView) findViewById
            (R.id.proxy_ip_address);
        TextView proxyPort = (TextView) findViewById(R.id.proxy_port);
        TextView textView1 = (TextView)
findViewById(R.id.neighbors_ip_address);
        TextView textView2 = (TextView) findViewById(R.id.neighbors_port);
        TextView textView3 = (TextView) findViewById(R.id.neighbors_scope_id);
```

```java
        if(radioGroup1.getCheckedRadioButtonId() == R.id.neighbors_ipv4)
            ipVersion = "IPv4";
        else
            ipVersion = "IPv6";

        if(textView1.getText().toString().trim().isEmpty())
            Miscellaneous.showErrorDialog
                (Settings.this, "Please complete the IP Address field.");
        else if(!m_databaseHelper.
                writeNeighbor(s_cryptography,
                              checkBox3.isChecked() ? "true" : "false",
                              checkBox4.isChecked() ? "true" : "false",
                              proxyIpAddress.getText().toString(),
                              proxyPort.getText().toString(),
                              spinner2.getSelectedItem().toString(),
                              textView1.getText().toString(),
                              textView2.getText().toString(),
                              textView3.getText().toString(),
                              spinner1.getSelectedItem().toString(),
                              ipVersion))
            Miscellaneous.showErrorDialog
                (Settings.this,
                 "An error occurred while saving the neighbor information.");
        else
        {
            if(!checkBox1.isChecked())
                populateNeighbors(null);

            if(checkBox2.isChecked())
            {
                String string = textView1.getText().toString() + ":" +
                    textView2.getText().toString() + ":" +
                    spinner1.getSelectedItem();

                if(generateOzone(string))
                {
                    textView1 = (TextView) findViewById(R.id.ozone);
                    textView1.setText(string);
                }
            }
        }
    }

    private void addParticipant()
    {
        if(Settings.this.isFinishing())
            return;

        CheckBox checkBox1 = (CheckBox) findViewById(R.id.as_alias);
        String string = "";
        TextView textView1 = (TextView) findViewById
            (R.id.participant_siphash_id);
        TextView textView2 = (TextView) findViewById(R.id.siphash_identity);

        if(checkBox1.isChecked())
        {
            string = textView1.getText().toString().trim();

            if(string.length() < 8)
            {
                Miscellaneous.showErrorDialog
                    (Settings.this,
```

```java
                        "A Smoke Alias must include at least eight characters.");
                return;
            }
        else if(m_databaseHelper.
                readSetting(s_cryptography, "alias").equals(string))
            {
            Miscellaneous.showErrorDialog
                (Settings.this, "Please do not assign your Smoke Alias.");
            return;
            }

        string = Cryptography.sipHashIdFromString(string);

        if(string.isEmpty())
            {
            Miscellaneous.showErrorDialog
                (Settings.this, "A transformation failure occurred!");
            return;
            }
    }
else
    {
        StringBuilder stringBuilder = new StringBuilder();

        stringBuilder.append
            (Miscellaneous.
             prepareSipHashId(textView1.getText().toString().
                            replace(" ", "").
                            replace("-", "").
                            replace(":", "").
                            replace("@", "").trim()));
        string = stringBuilder.toString().trim();

        if(string.length() != Cryptography.SIPHASH_IDENTITY_LENGTH)
            {
            Miscellaneous.showErrorDialog
                (Settings.this,
                 "A Smoke ID must be of the form " +
                 "HHHH-HHHH-HHHH-HHHH-HHHH-HHHH-HHHH-HHHH.");
            return;
            }
        else if(textView2.getText().toString().equals(string))
            {
            Miscellaneous.showErrorDialog
                (Settings.this, "Please do not assign your Smoke ID.");
            return;
            }
    }

final ProgressBar bar = (ProgressBar) findViewById
    (R.id.add_participants_progress_bar);

bar.setIndeterminate(true);
bar.setVisibility(ProgressBar.VISIBLE);
getWindow().setFlags
    (WindowManager.LayoutParams.FLAG_NOT_TOUCHABLE,
     WindowManager.LayoutParams.FLAG_NOT_TOUCHABLE);
Miscellaneous.enableChildren
    (findViewById(R.id.linear_layout), false);

class SingleShot implements Runnable
    {
        private String m_name = "";
```

```java
        private String m_sipHashId = "";
        private boolean m_error = false;

        SingleShot(String name, String sipHashId)
        {
            m_name = name;
            m_sipHashId = sipHashId;
        }

        @Override
        public void run()
        {
            if(!m_databaseHelper.writeSipHashParticipant(s_cryptography,
                                                         m_name,
                                                         m_sipHashId))
                m_error = true;

            Settings.this.runOnUiThread(new Runnable()
            {
                @Override
                public void run()
                {
                    bar.setVisibility(ProgressBar.INVISIBLE);
                    getWindow().clearFlags
                        (WindowManager.LayoutParams.FLAG_NOT_TOUCHABLE);
                    Miscellaneous.enableChildren
                        (findViewById(R.id.linear_layout), true);
                    disablePKIButtons();

                    if(m_error)
                        Miscellaneous.showErrorDialog
                            (Settings.this,
                             "An error occurred while attempting " +
                             "to save the specified Smoke Alias / ID.");
                    else
                        populateParticipants();
                }
            });
        }
    }

    Thread thread = new Thread
        (new SingleShot(((TextView) findViewById(R.id.participant_name)).
                    getText().toString(), string));

    thread.start();
    }

    private void deleteNeighbor(String ipAndPort, int id)
    {
        final int oid = id;

        /*
        ** Prepare a response.
        */

        final DialogInterface.OnCancelListener listener =
            new DialogInterface.OnCancelListener()
            {
                public void onCancel(DialogInterface dialog)
                {
                    if(State.getInstance().getString("dialog_accepted").
                        equals("true"))
```

```java
                    if(m_databaseHelper.
                        deleteEntry(String.valueOf(oid), "neighbors"))
                    {
                        /*
                        ** Prepare the kernel's neighbors container
                        ** if a neighbor was deleted as the OID
                        ** field may represent a recycled value.
                        */

                        Kernel.getInstance().purgeDeletedNeighbors();

                        TableLayout tableLayout = (TableLayout)
                            findViewById(R.id.neighbors);
                        TableRow row = (TableRow) findViewById(oid);

                        if(row != null)
                            tableLayout.removeView(row);
                    }
                }
            };

        Miscellaneous.showPromptDialog
            (Settings.this,
             listener,
             "Are you sure that you wish to " +
             "delete the neighbor " + ipAndPort + "?");
    }

    private void disablePKIButtons()
    {
        Button button1 = (Button) findViewById(R.id.generate_pki);
        CheckBox checkBox1 = (CheckBox) findViewById(R.id.overwrite);

        button1.setEnabled(checkBox1.isChecked());
        button1 = (Button) findViewById(R.id.set_password);
        button1.setEnabled(checkBox1.isChecked());
    }

    private void enableWidgets(boolean state)
    {
        Button button1 = null;

        button1 = (Button) findViewById(R.id.add_neighbor);
        button1.setEnabled(state);
        button1 = (Button) findViewById(R.id.add_participant);
        button1.setEnabled(state);
        button1 = (Button) findViewById(R.id.epks);
        button1.setEnabled(state);
        button1 = (Button) findViewById(R.id.refresh_neighbors);
        button1.setEnabled(state);
        button1 = (Button) findViewById(R.id.refresh_participants);
        button1.setEnabled(state);
        button1 = (Button) findViewById(R.id.reset_neighbor_fields);
        button1.setEnabled(state);
        button1 = (Button) findViewById(R.id.reset_participants_fields);
        button1.setEnabled(state);
        button1 = (Button) findViewById(R.id.save_ozone);
        button1.setEnabled(state);
        button1 = (Button) findViewById(R.id.share_via_ozone);
        button1.setEnabled(state);

        CheckBox checkBox1 = null;
```

```java
            checkBox1 = (CheckBox) findViewById(R.id.overwrite);
            checkBox1.setChecked(!state);
            checkBox1.setEnabled(state);
            button1 = (Button) findViewById(R.id.generate_pki);
            button1.setEnabled(!state);
            button1 = (Button) findViewById(R.id.set_password);
            button1.setEnabled(!state);

            RadioButton radioButton1 = null;

            radioButton1 = (RadioButton) findViewById(R.id.neighbors_ipv4);
            radioButton1.setEnabled(state);
            radioButton1 = (RadioButton) findViewById(R.id.neighbors_ipv6);
            radioButton1.setEnabled(state);

            Spinner spinner1 = null;

            spinner1 = (Spinner) findViewById(R.id.neighbors_transport);
            spinner1.setEnabled(state);
            spinner1 = (Spinner) findViewById(R.id.proxy_type);
            spinner1.setEnabled(state);

            TextView textView1 = null;

            textView1 = (TextView) findViewById(R.id.neighbors_ip_address);
            textView1.setEnabled(state);
            textView1 = (TextView) findViewById(R.id.neighbors_port);
            textView1.setEnabled(state);
            textView1 = (TextView) findViewById(R.id.neighbors_scope_id);
            textView1.setEnabled(state);
            textView1 = (TextView) findViewById(R.id.ozone);
            textView1.setEnabled(state);
            textView1 = (TextView) findViewById(R.id.participant_name);
            textView1.setEnabled(state);
            textView1 = (TextView) findViewById(R.id.participant_siphash_id);
            textView1.setEnabled(state);
            textView1 = (TextView) findViewById(R.id.proxy_ip_address);
            textView1.setEnabled(state);
            textView1 = (TextView) findViewById(R.id.proxy_port);
            textView1.setEnabled(state);
    }

    private void epks(final String sipHashId)
    {
        if(Settings.this.isFinishing())
            return;

        final ProgressBar bar = (ProgressBar) findViewById
            (R.id.share_keys_progress_bar);

        bar.setIndeterminate(true);
        bar.setVisibility(ProgressBar.VISIBLE);
        getWindow().setFlags
            (WindowManager.LayoutParams.FLAG_NOT_TOUCHABLE,
             WindowManager.LayoutParams.FLAG_NOT_TOUCHABLE);
        Miscellaneous.enableChildren
            (findViewById(R.id.linear_layout), false);

        class SingleShot implements Runnable
        {
            private String m_error = "";

            SingleShot()
```

```java
        {
        }

        @Override
        public void run()
        {
            ArrayList<SipHashIdElement> arrayList =
                m_databaseHelper.readSipHashIds(sipHashId, s_cryptography);

            if(arrayList == null)
                arrayList = new ArrayList<> ();

            {
                /*
                ** Self-sending.
                */

                SipHashIdElement sipHashIdElement = new SipHashIdElement();

                sipHashIdElement.m_sipHashId = s_cryptography.sipHashId();
                sipHashIdElement.m_stream = Miscellaneous.joinByteArrays
                    (s_cryptography.sipHashEncryptionKey(),
                     s_cryptography.sipHashMacKey());
                arrayList.add(sipHashIdElement);
            }

            for(SipHashIdElement sipHashIdElement : arrayList)
            {
                if(sipHashIdElement == null)
                {
                    m_error = "zero element";
                    break;
                }

                byte bytes[] = Messages.epksMessage
                    (s_cryptography,
                     sipHashIdElement.m_sipHashId,
                     sipHashIdElement.m_stream,
                     Messages.CHAT_KEY_TYPE);

                if(bytes == null)
                {
                    m_error = "epksMessage() failure";
                    break;
                }

                if(!Kernel.getInstance().
                    enqueueMessage(Messages.bytesToMessageString(bytes),
                                   null))
                {
                    m_error = "enqueueMessage() failure";
                    break;
                }
            }

            if(sipHashId.isEmpty())
                Settings.this.runOnUiThread(new Runnable()
                {
                    @Override
                    public void run()
                    {
                        bar.setVisibility(ProgressBar.INVISIBLE);
                        getWindow().clearFlags
```

```java
                              (WindowManager.LayoutParams.
                               FLAG_NOT_TOUCHABLE);
                         Miscellaneous.enableChildren
                            (findViewById(R.id.linear_layout), true);
                         disablePKIButtons();

                         if(!m_error.isEmpty())
                            Miscellaneous.showErrorDialog
                              (Settings.this,
                               "An error (" + m_error +
                               ") occurred while " +
                               "preparing to transfer public key " +
                               "material. " +
                               "Please verify that participant Smoke " +
                               "Identities have been defined.");
                    }
                });

            arrayList.clear();
        }
    }

    Thread thread = new Thread(new SingleShot());

    thread.start();
}

private void networkStatusChanged()
{
    try
    {
        getSupportActionBar().setSubtitle(Smoke.networkStatusString());
    }
    catch(Exception exception)
    {
    }
}

private void populateFancyKeyData()
{
    StringBuilder stringBuilder = null;
    TextView textView1 = null;

    textView1 = (TextView) findViewById(R.id.chat_encryption_key_data);

    if(s_cryptography.chatEncryptionKeyPair() == null ||
       s_cryptography.chatEncryptionKeyPair().getPublic() == null)
        textView1.setVisibility(View.GONE);
    else
    {
        stringBuilder = new StringBuilder();
        stringBuilder.append("Chat Encryption Key\n");
        stringBuilder.append
            (Cryptography.
             fancyKeyInformationOutput(s_cryptography.
                                       chatEncryptionKeyPair(),
                                       s_cryptography.
                                       chatEncryptionPublicKeyAlgorithm()));
        textView1.setText(stringBuilder);
        textView1.setVisibility(View.VISIBLE);
    }

    textView1 = (TextView) findViewById(R.id.chat_signature_key_data);
```

```java
        if(s_cryptography.chatSignatureKeyPair() == null ||
           s_cryptography.chatSignatureKeyPair().getPublic() == null)
            textView1.setVisibility(View.GONE);
        else
        {
            if(stringBuilder == null)
                stringBuilder = new StringBuilder();
            else
                stringBuilder.delete(0, stringBuilder.length());

            stringBuilder.append("Chat Signature Key\n");
            stringBuilder.append
                (Cryptography.
                 fancyKeyInformationOutput(s_cryptography.
                                           chatSignatureKeyPair(), ""));
            textView1.setText(stringBuilder);
            textView1.setVisibility(View.VISIBLE);
        }

        textView1 = (TextView) findViewById(R.id.siphash_identity);

        if(stringBuilder == null)
            textView1.setVisibility(View.GONE);
        else
        {
            stringBuilder.delete(0, stringBuilder.length());
            stringBuilder.append
                (Miscellaneous.prepareSipHashId(s_cryptography.sipHashId()));
            textView1.setText(stringBuilder);
            textView1.setTextIsSelectable(true);
            textView1.setVisibility(View.VISIBLE);
        }
    }

    private void populateNeighbors(ArrayList<NeighborElement> arrayList)
    {
        if(arrayList == null)
            arrayList = m_databaseHelper.readNeighbors(s_cryptography);

        final TableLayout tableLayout = (TableLayout)
            findViewById(R.id.neighbors);

        if(arrayList == null || arrayList.isEmpty())
        {
            tableLayout.removeAllViews();
            return;
        }

        StringBuilder stringBuilder = new StringBuilder();
        int i = 0;

        /*
        ** Remove table entries which do not exist in smoke.db.
        */

        for(i = tableLayout.getChildCount() - 1; i >= 0; i--)
        {
            TableRow row = (TableRow) tableLayout.getChildAt(i);

            if(row == null)
                continue;
```

```java
            TextView textView1 = (TextView) row.getChildAt(1);

            if(textView1 == null)
            {
                tableLayout.removeView(row);
                continue;
            }

            boolean found = false;

            for(NeighborElement neighborElement : arrayList)
            {
                stringBuilder.delete(0, stringBuilder.length());
                stringBuilder.append(neighborElement.m_remoteIpAddress);

                if(neighborElement.m_ipVersion.equals("IPv6"))
                    if(!neighborElement.m_remoteScopeId.isEmpty())
                    {
                        stringBuilder.append("-");
                        stringBuilder.append(neighborElement.m_remoteScopeId);
                    }

                stringBuilder.append(":");
                stringBuilder.append(neighborElement.m_remotePort);
                stringBuilder.append(":");
                stringBuilder.append(neighborElement.m_transport);

                if(textView1.getText().toString().
                    contains(stringBuilder.toString()))
                {
                    found = true;
                    break;
                }
            }

            if(!found)
                tableLayout.removeView(row);
        }

    CheckBox checkBox1 = (CheckBox) findViewById(R.id.neighbor_details);

    i = 0;

    for(NeighborElement neighborElement : arrayList)
    {
        if(neighborElement == null)
            continue;

        Spinner spinner = null;
        TableRow row = null;
        TextView textView1 = null;
        int count = tableLayout.getChildCount();

        for(int j = 0; j < count; j++)
        {
            TableRow r = (TableRow) tableLayout.getChildAt(j);

            if(r == null)
                continue;

            TextView t = (TextView) r.getChildAt(1);

            if(t == null)
```

```java
                    continue;

                stringBuilder.delete(0, stringBuilder.length());
                stringBuilder.append(neighborElement.m_remoteIpAddress);

                if(neighborElement.m_ipVersion.equals("IPv6"))
                    if(!neighborElement.m_remoteScopeId.isEmpty())
                    {
                        stringBuilder.append("-");
                        stringBuilder.append(neighborElement.m_remoteScopeId);
                    }

                stringBuilder.append(":");
                stringBuilder.append(neighborElement.m_remotePort);
                stringBuilder.append(":");
                stringBuilder.append(neighborElement.m_transport);

                if(t.getText().toString().contains(stringBuilder.toString()))
                {
                    textView1 = t;
                    break;
                }
            }

            if(textView1 == null)
            {
                TableRow.LayoutParams layoutParams = new
                    TableRow.LayoutParams(TableRow.LayoutParams.WRAP_CONTENT);

                row = new TableRow(Settings.this);
                row.setId(neighborElement.m_oid);
                row.setLayoutParams(layoutParams);
                spinner = new Spinner(Settings.this);

                ArrayAdapter<String> arrayAdapter = null;
                String array[] = null;
                final String ipAndPort = neighborElement.
                    m_remoteIpAddress + ":" + neighborElement.m_remotePort;

                if(neighborElement.m_transport.equals("TCP"))
                    array = new String[]
                    {
                        "Action",
                        "Connect",
                        "Delete",
                        "Disconnect",
                        "Purge Queue",
                        "Reset SSL/TLS Credentials"
                    };
                else
                    array = new String[]
                    {
                        "Action",
                        "Connect",
                        "Delete",
                        "Disconnect",
                        "Purge Queue"
                    };

                arrayAdapter = new ArrayAdapter<>
                    (Settings.this,
                     android.R.layout.simple_spinner_item,
                     array);
```

```java
            spinner.setAdapter(arrayAdapter);
            spinner.setId(neighborElement.m_oid);
            spinner.setOnItemSelectedListener
                (new OnItemSelectedListener()
                {
                    @Override
                    public void onItemSelected(AdapterView<?> parent,
                                               View view,
                                               int position,
                                               long id)
                    {
                        switch(position)
                        {
                        case 1: // Connect.
                            m_databaseHelper.neighborControlStatus
                                (s_cryptography,
                                 "connect",
                                 String.valueOf(parent.getId()));
                            break;
                        case 2: // Delete.
                            deleteNeighbor(ipAndPort, parent.getId());
                            break;
                        case 3: // Disconnect.
                            m_databaseHelper.neighborControlStatus
                                (s_cryptography,
                                 "disconnect",
                                 String.valueOf(parent.getId()));
                            break;
                        case 4: // Purge queue.
                            m_databaseHelper.purgeNeighborQueue
                                (String.valueOf(parent.getId()));
                            break;
                        case 5: // Reset SSL/TLS credentials.
                            m_databaseHelper.neighborRecordCertificate
                                (s_cryptography,
                                 String.valueOf(parent.getId()),
                                 null);
                            m_databaseHelper.neighborControlStatus
                                (s_cryptography,
                                 "disconnect",
                                 String.valueOf(parent.getId()));
                            break;
                        default:
                            break;
                        }

                        parent.setSelection(0);
                    }

                    @Override
                    public void onNothingSelected(AdapterView<?> parent)
                    {
                    }
                });

        textView1 = new TextView(Settings.this);
    }

    switch(neighborElement.m_status)
    {
     case "connected":
        textView1.setTextColor(Color.rgb(27, 94, 32)); // Dark Green
        break;
```

```java
            case "connecting":
                textView1.setTextColor(Color.rgb(255, 111, 0)); // Dark Orange
                break;
            default:
                textView1.setTextColor(Color.rgb(183, 28, 28)); // Dark Red
                break;
        }

        stringBuilder.delete(0, stringBuilder.length());
        stringBuilder.append("Control: ");

        try
        {
            stringBuilder.append
                (neighborElement.m_statusControl.substring(0, 1).
                 toUpperCase());
            stringBuilder.append
                (neighborElement.m_statusControl.substring(1));
        }
        catch(Exception exception)
        {
            stringBuilder.append("Disconnect");
        }

        stringBuilder.append("\n");
        stringBuilder.append("Status: ");

        try
        {
            stringBuilder.append
                (neighborElement.m_status.substring(0, 1).toUpperCase());
            stringBuilder.append(neighborElement.m_status.substring(1));
        }
        catch(Exception exception)
        {
            stringBuilder.append("Disconnected");
        }

        stringBuilder.append("\n");

        if(!neighborElement.m_error.isEmpty())
        {
            stringBuilder.append("Error: ");
            stringBuilder.append(neighborElement.m_error);
            stringBuilder.append("\n");
        }

        stringBuilder.append(neighborElement.m_remoteIpAddress);

        if(neighborElement.m_ipVersion.equals("IPv6"))
            if(!neighborElement.m_remoteScopeId.isEmpty())
            {
                stringBuilder.append("-");
                stringBuilder.append(neighborElement.m_remoteScopeId);
            }

        stringBuilder.append(":");
        stringBuilder.append(neighborElement.m_remotePort);
        stringBuilder.append(":");
        stringBuilder.append(neighborElement.m_transport);

        if(!neighborElement.m_localIpAddress.isEmpty() &&
           !neighborElement.m_localPort.isEmpty())
```

```java
    {
        stringBuilder.append("\n");
        stringBuilder.append(neighborElement.m_localIpAddress);
        stringBuilder.append(":");
        stringBuilder.append(neighborElement.m_localPort);
    }

    stringBuilder.append("\nPassthrough: ");
    stringBuilder.append(neighborElement.m_passthrough);
    stringBuilder.append("\nProxy: ");

    if(!neighborElement.m_proxyIpAddress.isEmpty() &&
       !neighborElement.m_proxyPort.isEmpty())
    {
        stringBuilder.append(neighborElement.m_proxyIpAddress);
        stringBuilder.append(":");
        stringBuilder.append(neighborElement.m_proxyPort);
        stringBuilder.append(":");
        stringBuilder.append(neighborElement.m_proxyType);
    }

    if(checkBox1.isChecked())
    {
        if(neighborElement.m_remoteCertificate != null &&
           neighborElement.m_remoteCertificate.length > 0)
        {
            stringBuilder.append("\n");
            stringBuilder.append
                ("Remote Certificate's Fingerprint: ");
            stringBuilder.append
                (Cryptography.
                 fingerPrint(Miscellaneous.
                            pemFormat(neighborElement.
                                     m_remoteCertificate).
                            getBytes()));
        }

        if(!neighborElement.m_sessionCipher.isEmpty())
        {
            stringBuilder.append("\n");
            stringBuilder.append("Session Cipher: ");
            stringBuilder.append(neighborElement.m_sessionCipher);
        }
    }

    stringBuilder.append("\n");
    stringBuilder.append("Temp. Queued: ");
    stringBuilder.append(neighborElement.m_echoQueueSize);
    stringBuilder.append(" / ");
    stringBuilder.append(Neighbor.MAXIMUM_QUEUED_ECHO_PACKETS);
    stringBuilder.append("\n");
    stringBuilder.append("In: ");
    stringBuilder.append
        (Miscellaneous.
         formattedDigitalInformation(neighborElement.m_bytesRead));
    stringBuilder.append("\n");
    stringBuilder.append("Out: ");
    stringBuilder.append
        (Miscellaneous.
         formattedDigitalInformation(neighborElement.m_bytesWritten));
    stringBuilder.append("\n");
    stringBuilder.append("Outbound Queued: ");
    stringBuilder.append(neighborElement.m_outboundQueued);
```

```java
        stringBuilder.append("\n");
        stringBuilder.append("Uptime: ");

        try
        {
            long uptime = Long.parseLong(neighborElement.m_uptime);

            stringBuilder.append
                (String.
                 format(Locale.getDefault(),
                        "%d:%02d",
                        TimeUnit.NANOSECONDS.toMinutes(uptime),
                        TimeUnit.NANOSECONDS.toSeconds(uptime) -
                        TimeUnit.MINUTES.
                        toSeconds(TimeUnit.NANOSECONDS.
                                  toMinutes(uptime))));
        }
        catch(Exception exception)
        {
            stringBuilder.append("0:00");
        }

        stringBuilder.append(" Min.\n");
        textView1.setGravity(Gravity.CENTER_VERTICAL);
        textView1.setLayoutParams
            (new TableRow.LayoutParams(0, LayoutParams.WRAP_CONTENT, 1));
        textView1.setText(stringBuilder);
        textView1.setWidth(TEXTVIEW_WIDTH);

        if(row != null)
        {
            row.addView(spinner);
            row.addView(textView1);
            tableLayout.addView(row, i);
        }

        i += 1;
    }

    arrayList.clear();
}

private void populateOzone()
{
    TextView textView1 = (TextView) findViewById(R.id.ozone);

    textView1.setText
        (m_databaseHelper.readSetting(s_cryptography, "ozone_address"));
}

private void populateParticipants()
{
    ArrayList<SipHashIdElement> arrayList =
        m_databaseHelper.readSipHashIds("", s_cryptography);
    TableLayout tableLayout = (TableLayout) findViewById
        (R.id.participants);

    invalidateOptionsMenu();
    tableLayout.removeAllViews();

    if(arrayList == null || arrayList.isEmpty())
        return;
```

```java
            int i = 0;

            for(SipHashIdElement sipHashIdElement : arrayList)
            {
                if(sipHashIdElement == null)
                    continue;

                String sipHashId = Miscellaneous.prepareSipHashId
                    (sipHashIdElement.m_sipHashId);
                TableRow.LayoutParams layoutParams = new
                    TableRow.LayoutParams(TableRow.LayoutParams.WRAP_CONTENT);
                TableRow row = new TableRow(Settings.this);

                row.setLayoutParams(layoutParams);

                for(int j = 0; j < 3; j++)
                {
                    TextView textView1 = new TextView(Settings.this);

                    textView1.setId(sipHashIdElement.m_oid);

                    switch(j)
                    {
                    case 0:
                        textView1.setGravity(Gravity.CENTER_VERTICAL);
                        textView1.setLayoutParams
                            (new TableRow.LayoutParams(0,
                                                 LayoutParams.MATCH_PARENT,
                                                 1));
                        textView1.setTag
                            (R.id.participants, sipHashIdElement.m_name);
                        textView1.setText(sipHashIdElement.m_name);
                        break;
                    case 1:
                        if(sipHashIdElement.m_epksCompleted &&
                            sipHashIdElement.m_keysSigned)
                               textView1.setCompoundDrawablesWithIntrinsicBounds
                                 (R.drawable.keys_signed, 0, 0, 0);
                          else if(sipHashIdElement.m_epksCompleted)
                               textView1.setCompoundDrawablesWithIntrinsicBounds
                                 (R.drawable.keys_not_signed, 0, 0, 0);
                          else
                               textView1.setCompoundDrawablesWithIntrinsicBounds
                                 (R.drawable.warning, 0, 0, 0);

                        textView1.setCompoundDrawablePadding(5);
                        textView1.setGravity(Gravity.CENTER_VERTICAL);
                        textView1.setLayoutParams
                            (new TableRow.LayoutParams(0,
                                                 LayoutParams.WRAP_CONTENT,
                                                 1));
                        textView1.setTag(R.id.participants, sipHashId);
                        textView1.setText(sipHashId);
                        break;
                    case 2:
                        textView1.setGravity(Gravity.CENTER);
                        textView1.setLayoutParams
                            (new TableRow.LayoutParams(0,
                                                 LayoutParams.MATCH_PARENT,
                                                 1));
                        textView1.setTag(R.id.participants, sipHashId);
                        textView1.setText
                            (String.valueOf(sipHashIdElement.m_fiascoKeys));
```

```java
                    break;
                default:
                    break;
                }

                textView1.setTag
                    (R.id.refresh_participants,
                     sipHashIdElement.m_epksCompleted);
                registerForContextMenu(textView1);
                row.addView(textView1);
            }

            tableLayout.addView(row, i);
            i += 1;
        }

        arrayList.clear();
    }

    private void prepareCredentials()
    {
        if(Settings.this.isFinishing())
            return;

        final Spinner spinner1 = (Spinner) findViewById(R.id.iteration_count);
        final Spinner spinner2 = (Spinner) findViewById
            (R.id.key_derivation_function);
        final Spinner spinner3 = (Spinner) findViewById
            (R.id.pki_encryption_algorithm);
        final Spinner spinner4 = (Spinner) findViewById
            (R.id.pki_signature_algorithm);
        final TextView textView1 = (TextView) findViewById
            (R.id.password1);
        final TextView textView2 = (TextView) findViewById
            (R.id.password2);
        int iterationCount = 1000;
        int keyDerivationFunction = 1; // PBKDF2

        try
        {
            iterationCount = Integer.parseInt
                (spinner1.getSelectedItem().toString());
        }
        catch(Exception exception)
        {
            iterationCount = 1000;
        }

        try
        {
            switch(spinner2.getSelectedItem().toString())
            {
            case "Argon2id":
                keyDerivationFunction = 0;
                break;
            default:
                keyDerivationFunction = 1;
                break;
            }
        }
        catch(Exception exception)
        {
            keyDerivationFunction = 1; // PBKDF2
```

```java
        }

    final ProgressBar bar = (ProgressBar) findViewById
        (R.id.generate_progress_bar);

    bar.setIndeterminate(true);
    bar.setVisibility(ProgressBar.VISIBLE);
    getWindow().setFlags
        (WindowManager.LayoutParams.FLAG_NOT_TOUCHABLE,
         WindowManager.LayoutParams.FLAG_NOT_TOUCHABLE);
    Miscellaneous.enableChildren
        (findViewById(R.id.linear_layout), false);

    class SingleShot implements Runnable
    {
        private String m_encryptionAlgorithm = "";
        private String m_error = "";
        private String m_password = "";
        private String m_signatureAlgorithm = "";
        private int m_iterationCount = 1000;
        private int m_keyDerivationFunction = 1; // PBKDF2

        SingleShot(String encryptionAlgorithm,
                   String password,
                   String signatureAlgorithm,
                   int iterationCount,
                   int keyDerivationFunction)
        {
            m_encryptionAlgorithm = encryptionAlgorithm;
            m_iterationCount = iterationCount;
            m_keyDerivationFunction = keyDerivationFunction;
            m_password = password;
            m_signatureAlgorithm = signatureAlgorithm;

            if(m_signatureAlgorithm.equals("ECDSA"))
                m_signatureAlgorithm = "EC";
        }

        @Override
        public void run()
        {
            KeyPair chatEncryptionKeyPair = null;
            KeyPair chatSignatureKeyPair = null;
            SecretKey encryptionKey = null;
            SecretKey macKey = null;
            byte encryptionSalt[] = null;
            byte macSalt[] = null;

            encryptionSalt = Cryptography.randomBytes
                (Cryptography.CIPHER_KEY_LENGTH);
            macSalt = Cryptography.randomBytes
                (Cryptography.HASH_KEY_LENGTH);
            m_databaseHelper.reset();

            try
            {
                int index = 0;

                if(m_encryptionAlgorithm.contains("12, 68"))
                    index = 1;

                chatEncryptionKeyPair = Cryptography.
                    generatePrivatePublicKeyPair
```

```
               (m_encryptionAlgorithm,
                Cryptography.PKI_ENCRYPTION_KEY_SIZES[0],
                index);

        if(chatEncryptionKeyPair == null)
        {
           m_error = "encryption-key " +
               "generatePrivatePublicKeyPair() failure";
           s_cryptography.reset();
           return;
        }

        if(m_signatureAlgorithm.equals("EC"))
           chatSignatureKeyPair = Cryptography.
               generatePrivatePublicKeyPair
               ("EC", Cryptography.PKI_SIGNATURE_KEY_SIZES[0], 0);
        else
           chatSignatureKeyPair = Cryptography.
               generatePrivatePublicKeyPair
               (m_signatureAlgorithm,
                Cryptography.PKI_SIGNATURE_KEY_SIZES[1],
                0);

        if(chatSignatureKeyPair == null)
        {
           m_error = "signature-key " +
               "generatePrivatePublicKeyPair() failure";
           s_cryptography.reset();
           return;
        }

        encryptionKey = Cryptography.
           generateEncryptionKey
           (encryptionSalt,
            m_password.toCharArray(),
            m_iterationCount,
            m_keyDerivationFunction);

        if(encryptionSalt == null)
        {
           m_error = "generateEncryptionKey() failure";
           s_cryptography.reset();
           return;
        }

        macKey = Cryptography.generateMacKey
           (macSalt,
            m_password.toCharArray(),
            m_iterationCount,
            m_keyDerivationFunction);

        if(macKey == null)
        {
           m_error = "generateMacKey() failure";
           s_cryptography.reset();
           return;
        }

        /*
        ** Prepare the Cryptography object's data.
        */

        s_cryptography.setChatEncryptionPublicKeyAlgorithm
```

```java
            (m_encryptionAlgorithm);
        s_cryptography.setChatEncryptionPublicKeyPair
            (chatEncryptionKeyPair);
        s_cryptography.setChatSignaturePublicKeyPair
            (chatSignatureKeyPair);
        s_cryptography.setEncryptionKey
            (encryptionKey);
        s_cryptography.setMacKey(macKey);

        /*
        ** Record the data.
        */

        m_databaseHelper.writeSetting
            (null,
             "encryptionSalt",
             Base64.encodeToString(encryptionSalt,
                                   Base64.DEFAULT));
        m_databaseHelper.writeSetting
            (null,
             "iterationCount",
             String.valueOf(m_iterationCount));
        m_databaseHelper.writeSetting
            (null,
             "keyDerivationFunction",
             String.valueOf(m_keyDerivationFunction));
        m_databaseHelper.writeSetting
            (null,
             "macSalt",
             Base64.encodeToString(macSalt,
                                   Base64.DEFAULT));
        m_databaseHelper.writeSetting
            (s_cryptography,
             "pki_chat_encryption_algorithm",
             m_encryptionAlgorithm);
        m_databaseHelper.writeSetting
            (s_cryptography,
             "pki_chat_encryption_private_key",
             Base64.
             encodeToString(chatEncryptionKeyPair.
                            getPrivate().
                            getEncoded(),
                            Base64.DEFAULT));
        m_databaseHelper.writeSetting
            (s_cryptography,
             "pki_chat_encryption_public_key",
             Base64.
             encodeToString(chatEncryptionKeyPair.
                            getPublic().
                            getEncoded(),
                            Base64.DEFAULT));
        m_databaseHelper.writeSetting
            (s_cryptography,
             "pki_chat_signature_algorithm",
             m_signatureAlgorithm);
        m_databaseHelper.writeSetting
            (s_cryptography,
             "pki_chat_signature_private_key",
             Base64.encodeToString(chatSignatureKeyPair.
                            getPrivate().
                            getEncoded(),
                            Base64.DEFAULT));
        m_databaseHelper.writeSetting
```

```
                    (s_cryptography,
                     "pki_chat_signature_public_key",
                     Base64.encodeToString(chatSignatureKeyPair.
                                    getPublic().
                                    getEncoded(),
                                    Base64.DEFAULT));

            boolean e1 = s_cryptography.prepareSipHashIds(null);
            boolean e2 = s_cryptography.prepareSipHashKeys();
            byte saltedPassword[] = Cryptography.
                sha512(m_password.getBytes(),
                        encryptionSalt,
                        macSalt);

            if(e1 && e2 && saltedPassword != null)
                m_databaseHelper.writeSetting
                    (null,
                     "saltedPassword",
                     Base64.encodeToString(saltedPassword,
                                    Base64.DEFAULT));
            else
            {
                if(!e1)
                    m_error = "prepareSipHashIds() failure";
                else if(!e2)
                    m_error = "prepareSipHashKeys() failure";

                s_cryptography.reset();
            }
        }
        catch(Exception exception)
        {
            m_error = exception.getMessage().toLowerCase().trim();
            s_cryptography.reset();
        }

        Settings.this.runOnUiThread(new Runnable()
        {
            @Override
            public void run()
            {
                bar.setVisibility(ProgressBar.INVISIBLE);
                getWindow().clearFlags
                    (WindowManager.LayoutParams.
                     FLAG_NOT_TOUCHABLE);
                Miscellaneous.enableChildren
                    (findViewById(R.id.linear_layout), true);
                disablePKIButtons();

                if(!m_error.isEmpty())
                    Miscellaneous.showErrorDialog
                        (Settings.this,
                         "An error (" + m_error +
                         ") occurred while " +
                         "generating the confidential " +
                         "data.");
                else
                {
                    Kernel.getInstance().setWakeLock(true);
                    Settings.this.enableWidgets(true);
                    Settings.this.showWidgets();
                    State.getInstance().setAuthenticated(true);
                    spinner3.setSelection(3); // RSA
```

```java
                        spinner4.setSelection(1); // RSA
                        textView1.requestFocus();
                        textView1.setText("");
                        textView2.setText("");
                        m_databaseHelper.writeNeighbor
                            (s_cryptography,
                             "false",
                             "false",
                             "",
                             "",
                             "HTTP",
                             BuildConfig.SMOKE_IPV4_HOST,
                             BuildConfig.SMOKE_IPV4_PORT,
                             "",
                             "TCP",
                             "IPv4");
                        populateFancyKeyData();
                        populateOzone();
                        populateParticipants();
                        startKernel();

                        if(m_databaseHelper.
                            readSetting(null, "automatic_neighbors_refresh").
                            equals("true"))
                            startTimers();
                    }
                }
            });

            m_password = "";
        }
    }

    Thread thread = new Thread
        (new SingleShot(spinner3.getSelectedItem().toString(),
                        textView1.getText().toString(),
                        spinner4.getSelectedItem().toString(),
                        iterationCount,
                        keyDerivationFunction));

    thread.start();
}

private void prepareForegroundService()
{
    if(m_databaseHelper.
        readSetting(null, "foreground_service").equals("false"))
        SmokeService.stopForegroundTask(getApplicationContext());
    else
        SmokeService.startForegroundTask(getApplicationContext());
}

private void prepareListeners()
{
    Button button1 = null;
    Spinner spinner1 = (Spinner) findViewById(R.id.neighbors_transport);
    TextView textView1 = (TextView) findViewById(R.id.participant_name);

    button1 = (Button) findViewById(R.id.add_neighbor);
    button1.setOnClickListener(new View.OnClickListener()
    {
        public void onClick(View view)
        {
```

```java
                if(Settings.this.isFinishing())
                    return;

                addNeighbor();
            }
        });

        button1 = (Button) findViewById(R.id.add_participant);
        button1.setOnClickListener(new View.OnClickListener()
        {
            public void onClick(View view)
            {
                if(Settings.this.isFinishing())
                    return;

                addParticipant();
            }
        });

        button1 = (Button) findViewById(R.id.clear_log);
        button1.setOnClickListener(new View.OnClickListener()
        {
            public void onClick(View view)
            {
                if(Settings.this.isFinishing())
                    return;

                m_databaseHelper.clearTable("log");
            }
        });

        button1 = (Button) findViewById(R.id.epks);
        button1.setOnClickListener(new View.OnClickListener()
        {
            public void onClick(View view)
            {
                if(Settings.this.isFinishing())
                    return;

                epks("");
            }
        });

        button1 = (Button) findViewById(R.id.generate_pki);
        button1.setOnClickListener(new View.OnClickListener()
        {
            public void onClick(View view)
            {
                if(Settings.this.isFinishing())
                    return;

                preparePKI();
            }
        });

        button1 = (Button) findViewById(R.id.ozone_help);
        button1.setOnClickListener(new View.OnClickListener()
        {
            public void onClick(View view)
            {
                if(Settings.this.isFinishing())
                    return;
```

```java
            PopupWindow popupWindow = new PopupWindow(Settings.this);
            TextView textView1 = new TextView(Settings.this);
            float density = getApplicationContext().getResources().
                getDisplayMetrics().density;

            textView1.setBackgroundColor(Color.rgb(232, 234, 246));
            textView1.setPaddingRelative
                ((int) (10 * density),
                 (int) (10 * density),
                 (int) (10 * density),
                 (int) (10 * density));
            textView1.setText
                ("An Ozone Address defines a virtual location, " +
                 "a separate device where messages are to be stored for " +
                 "later retrieval. A virtual post office. " +
                 "Please remember to share your Ozone Address with your " +
                 "friends as well as at least one SmokeStack.");
            textView1.setTextSize(16);
            popupWindow.setContentView(textView1);
            popupWindow.setOutsideTouchable(true);

            if(Build.VERSION.SDK_INT < Build.VERSION_CODES.M)
            {
                popupWindow.setHeight(450);
                popupWindow.setWidth(700);
            }

            popupWindow.showAsDropDown(view);
        }
    });

    button1 = (Button) findViewById(R.id.refresh_neighbors);
    button1.setOnClickListener(new View.OnClickListener()
    {
        public void onClick(View view)
        {
            if(Settings.this.isFinishing())
                return;

            populateNeighbors(null);
        }
    });

    button1 = (Button) findViewById(R.id.refresh_participants);
    button1.setOnClickListener(new View.OnClickListener()
    {
        public void onClick(View view)
        {
            if(Settings.this.isFinishing())
                return;

            populateParticipants();
        }
    });

    final DialogInterface.OnCancelListener listener1 =
        new DialogInterface.OnCancelListener()
        {
            public void onCancel(DialogInterface dialog)
            {
                if(State.getInstance().getString("dialog_accepted").
                   equals("true"))
                {
```

```java
                    State.getInstance().reset();
                    m_databaseHelper.resetAndDrop();
                    s_cryptography.reset();

                    Intent intent = getIntent();

                    startActivity(intent);
                    finish();
                }
            }
        };

    button1 = (Button) findViewById(R.id.reset);
     button1.setOnClickListener(new View.OnClickListener()
    {
        public void onClick(View view)
        {
            Miscellaneous.showPromptDialog(Settings.this,
                                  listener1,
                                  "Are you sure that you " +
                                  "wish to reset Smoke? All " +
                                  "of the data will be removed.");
        }
    });

    button1 = (Button) findViewById(R.id.reset_neighbor_fields);
     button1.setOnClickListener(new View.OnClickListener()
    {
        public void onClick(View view)
        {
            if(Settings.this.isFinishing())
                return;

            CheckBox checkBox1 = (CheckBox) findViewById
                (R.id.initialize_ozone);
            CheckBox checkBox2 = (CheckBox) findViewById(R.id.non_tls);
            CheckBox checkBox3 = (CheckBox) findViewById(R.id.passthrough);
            RadioButton radioButton1 = (RadioButton) findViewById
                (R.id.neighbors_ipv4);
            Spinner spinner1 = (Spinner) findViewById
                (R.id.neighbors_transport);
            Spinner spinner2 = (Spinner) findViewById
                (R.id.proxy_type);
            TextView proxyIpAddress = (TextView) findViewById
                (R.id.proxy_ip_address);
            TextView proxyPort = (TextView) findViewById
                (R.id.proxy_port);
            TextView textView1 = (TextView) findViewById
                (R.id.neighbors_ip_address);
            TextView textView2 = (TextView) findViewById
                (R.id.neighbors_port);
            TextView textView3 = (TextView) findViewById
                (R.id.neighbors_scope_id);

            checkBox1.setChecked(false);
            checkBox2.setChecked(false);
            checkBox3.setChecked(false);
            proxyIpAddress.setText("");
            proxyPort.setText("");
            radioButton1.setChecked(true);
            spinner1.setSelection(0);
            spinner2.setSelection(0);
            textView1.setText("");
```

```java
                textView2.setText("4710");
                textView3.setText("");
                textView1.requestFocus();
            }
        });

        button1 = (Button) findViewById(R.id.reset_participants_fields);
        button1.setOnClickListener(new View.OnClickListener()
        {
            public void onClick(View view)
            {
                if(Settings.this.isFinishing())
                    return;

                CheckBox checkBox1 = (CheckBox) findViewById(R.id.as_alias);
                TextView textView1 = (TextView) findViewById
                    (R.id.participant_name);
                TextView textView2 = (TextView) findViewById
                    (R.id.participant_siphash_id);

                checkBox1.setChecked(true);
                textView1.setText("");
                textView2.setText("");
                textView1.requestFocus();
            }
        });

        final DialogInterface.OnCancelListener listener2 =
            new DialogInterface.OnCancelListener()
            {
                public void onCancel(DialogInterface dialog)
                {
                    if(State.getInstance().getString("dialog_accepted").
                       equals("true"))
                    {
                        TextView textView1 = (TextView) findViewById
                            (R.id.ozone);

                        textView1.setText("");
                        m_databaseHelper.reset();
                        populateFancyKeyData();
                        populateNeighbors(null);
                        populateParticipants();
                        prepareCredentials();
                    }
                }
            };

        button1 = (Button) findViewById(R.id.save_alias);
        button1.setOnClickListener(new View.OnClickListener()
        {
            public void onClick(View view)
            {
                if(Settings.this.isFinishing())
                    return;

                String alias = ((TextView) findViewById(R.id.alias)).
                    getText().toString().trim();

                if(!alias.isEmpty() && alias.length() < 8)
                    Miscellaneous.showErrorDialog
                        (Settings.this,
                         "A Smoke Alias must include at " +
```

```java
                    "least eight characters. ");
                else if(alias.isEmpty())
                {
                    m_databaseHelper.writeSetting(s_cryptography, "alias", "");
                    s_cryptography.prepareSipHashIds(null);
                    s_cryptography.prepareSipHashKeys();
                }
                else
                {
                    if(m_databaseHelper.
                       readSetting(s_cryptography, "fire_user_name").trim().
                       isEmpty())
                       m_databaseHelper.writeSetting
                            (s_cryptography, "fire_user_name", alias);

                    m_databaseHelper.writeSetting
                        (s_cryptography, "alias", alias);
                    s_cryptography.prepareSipHashIds(alias);
                    s_cryptography.prepareSipHashKeys();
                }

                StringBuilder stringBuilder = new StringBuilder();
                TextView textView1 = (TextView) findViewById
                    (R.id.siphash_identity);

                stringBuilder.append
                    (Miscellaneous.
                     prepareSipHashId(s_cryptography.sipHashId()));
                textView1.setText(stringBuilder);
                textView1.setTextIsSelectable(true);
                textView1.setVisibility(View.VISIBLE);
            }
        });

    button1 = (Button) findViewById(R.id.save_ozone);
    button1.setOnClickListener(new View.OnClickListener()
    {
        public void onClick(View view)
        {
            if(Settings.this.isFinishing())
                return;

            TextView textView1 = (TextView) findViewById(R.id.ozone);

            if(!generateOzone(textView1.getText().toString()))
            {
                Miscellaneous.showErrorDialog
                    (Settings.this,
                     "An error occurred while processing the Ozone data.");
                textView1.requestFocus();
            }
        }
    });

    button1 = (Button) findViewById(R.id.set_password);
    button1.setOnClickListener(new View.OnClickListener()
    {
        public void onClick(View view)
        {
            if(Settings.this.isFinishing())
                return;

            Spinner spinner1 = null;
```

```java
        TextView textView1 = (TextView) findViewById(R.id.password1);
        TextView textView2 = (TextView) findViewById(R.id.password2);

        textView1.setSelectAllOnFocus(true);
        textView2.setSelectAllOnFocus(true);

        if(textView1.getText().length() < 1 ||
           !textView1.getText().toString().
            equals(textView2.getText().toString()))
        {
            String error = "";

            if(textView1.getText().length() < 1)
                error = "Each password must contain " +
                    "at least one character.";
            else
                error = "The provided passwords are not identical.";

            Miscellaneous.showErrorDialog(Settings.this, error);
            textView1.requestFocus();
            return;
        }

        int iterationCount = 1000;
        int iterationCountLimit = 7500;

        try
        {
            spinner1 = (Spinner) findViewById(R.id.iteration_count);
            iterationCount = Integer.parseInt
                (spinner1.getSelectedItem().toString());
        }
        catch(Exception exception)
        {
            iterationCount = 1000;
        }

        spinner1 = (Spinner) findViewById(R.id.key_derivation_function);

        if(spinner1.getSelectedItem().toString().equals("Argon2id"))
            iterationCountLimit = 10;
        else
            iterationCountLimit = 7500;

        if(iterationCount > iterationCountLimit)
            Miscellaneous.showPromptDialog
                (Settings.this,
                 listener2,
                 "You have selected an elevated iteration count. " +
                 "If you proceed, the initialization process may " +
                 "require a significant amount of time to complete. " +
                 "Continue?");
        else
            prepareCredentials();
    }
});

button1 = (Button) findViewById(R.id.share_via_ozone);
button1.setOnClickListener(new View.OnClickListener()
{
    public void onClick(View view)
    {
        if(Settings.this.isFinishing())
```

```java
                return;

            shareSipHashId(-1);
        }
    });

    button1 = (Button) findViewById(R.id.siphash_help);
    button1.setOnClickListener(new View.OnClickListener()
    {
        public void onClick(View view)
        {
            if(Settings.this.isFinishing())
                return;

            PopupWindow popupWindow = new PopupWindow(Settings.this);
            TextView textView1 = new TextView(Settings.this);
            float density = getApplicationContext().getResources().
                getDisplayMetrics().density;

            textView1.setBackgroundColor(Color.rgb(232, 234, 246));
            textView1.setPaddingRelative
                ((int) (10 * density),
                 (int) (10 * density),
                 (int) (10 * density),
                 (int) (10 * density));

            if(((CheckBox) findViewById(R.id.as_alias)).isChecked())
                textView1.setText
                    ("A Smoke Alias is an arrangement of digits and " +
                     "letters assigned to a specific subscriber " +
                     "(public key pair). " +
                     "The tokens allow participants to exchange public " +
                     "key pairs via the Echo Public Key Sharing (EPKS) " +
                     "protocol. " +
                     "An example Smoke Alias is account@e-mail.org.");
            else
                textView1.setText
                    ("A Smoke ID is an arrangement of hexadecimal " +
                     "characters assigned to a specific subscriber " +
                     "(public key pair). " +
                     "The tokens allow participants to exchange public " +
                     "key pairs via the Echo Public Key Sharing (EPKS) " +
                     "protocol.");

            textView1.setTextSize(16);
            popupWindow.setContentView(textView1);
            popupWindow.setOutsideTouchable(true);

            if(Build.VERSION.SDK_INT < Build.VERSION_CODES.M)
            {
                popupWindow.setHeight(450);
                popupWindow.setWidth(700);
            }

            popupWindow.showAsDropDown(view);
        }
    });


    CheckBox checkBox1 = null;

    checkBox1 = (CheckBox) findViewById(R.id.as_alias);
    checkBox1.setOnCheckedChangeListener
        (new CompoundButton.OnCheckedChangeListener()
```

```java
        {
            @Override
            public void onCheckedChanged
                (CompoundButton buttonView, boolean isChecked)
            {
                TextView textView1 = (TextView) findViewById(R.id.at_sign);
                TextView textView2 = (TextView) findViewById
                    (R.id.participant_name);
                TextView textView3 = (TextView) findViewById
                    (R.id.participant_siphash_id);

                if(isChecked)
                {
                    textView1.setText("|");
                    textView3.setFilters(new InputFilter[] {});
                    textView3.setHint("Smoke Alias");
                    textView3.setText(textView2.getText());
                }
                else
                {
                    textView1.setText("@");
                    textView3.setFilters
                        (new InputFilter[] {new InputFilter.AllCaps(),
                                            s_sipHashInputFilter});
                    textView3.setHint("Smoke ID");
                    textView3.setText("");
                }
            }
        });

    checkBox1 = (CheckBox) findViewById(R.id.automatic_refresh);
    checkBox1.setOnCheckedChangeListener
        (new CompoundButton.OnCheckedChangeListener()
        {
            @Override
            public void onCheckedChanged
                (CompoundButton buttonView, boolean isChecked)
            {
                if(isChecked)
                {
                    m_databaseHelper.writeSetting
                        (null, "automatic_neighbors_refresh", "true");
                    startTimers();
                }
                else
                {
                    m_databaseHelper.writeSetting
                        (null, "automatic_neighbors_refresh", "false");
                    stopTimers();
                }
            }
        });

    checkBox1 = (CheckBox) findViewById(R.id.echo);
    checkBox1.setOnCheckedChangeListener
        (new CompoundButton.OnCheckedChangeListener()
        {
            @Override
            public void onCheckedChanged
                (CompoundButton buttonView, boolean isChecked)
            {
                if(isChecked)
                {
```

```java
                m_databaseHelper.writeSetting
                    (null, "neighbors_echo", "true");
                State.getInstance().setNeighborsEcho(true);
            }
            else
            {
                m_databaseHelper.writeSetting
                    (null, "neighbors_echo", "false");
                Kernel.getInstance().clearNeighborQueues();
                State.getInstance().setNeighborsEcho(false);
            }
        }
    });

    checkBox1 = (CheckBox) findViewById(R.id.foreground_service);
    checkBox1.setOnCheckedChangeListener
        (new CompoundButton.OnCheckedChangeListener()
        {
            @Override
            public void onCheckedChanged
                (CompoundButton buttonView, boolean isChecked)
            {
                if(isChecked)
                {
                    SmokeService.startForegroundTask
                        (getApplicationContext());
                    m_databaseHelper.writeSetting
                        (null, "foreground_service", "true");
                }
                else
                {
                    SmokeService.stopForegroundTask
                        (getApplicationContext());
                    m_databaseHelper.writeSetting
                        (null, "foreground_service", "false");
                }
            }
        });

    checkBox1 = (CheckBox) findViewById(R.id.neighbor_details);
    checkBox1.setOnCheckedChangeListener
        (new CompoundButton.OnCheckedChangeListener()
        {
            @Override
            public void onCheckedChanged
                (CompoundButton buttonView, boolean isChecked)
            {
                if(isChecked)
                    m_databaseHelper.writeSetting
                        (null, "neighbors_details", "true");
                else
                    m_databaseHelper.writeSetting
                        (null, "neighbors_details", "false");

                CheckBox checkBox1 = (CheckBox) findViewById
                    (R.id.automatic_refresh);

                if(!checkBox1.isChecked())
                    populateNeighbors(null);
            }
        });

    checkBox1 = (CheckBox) findViewById(R.id.overwrite);
```

```java
checkBox1.setOnCheckedChangeListener
    (new CompoundButton.OnCheckedChangeListener()
    {
        @Override
        public void onCheckedChanged
            (CompoundButton buttonView, boolean isChecked)
        {
            Button button1 = null;

            button1 = (Button) findViewById(R.id.generate_pki);
            button1.setEnabled(isChecked);
            button1 = (Button) findViewById(R.id.set_password);
            button1.setEnabled(isChecked);
        }
    });

checkBox1 = (CheckBox) findViewById(R.id.query_time_server);
checkBox1.setOnCheckedChangeListener
    (new CompoundButton.OnCheckedChangeListener()
    {
        @Override
        public void onCheckedChanged
            (CompoundButton buttonView, boolean isChecked)
        {
            State.getInstance().setQueryTimerServer(isChecked);
            m_databaseHelper.writeSetting
                (null,
                 "query_time_server",
                 isChecked ? "true" : "false");
        }
    });

checkBox1 = (CheckBox) findViewById(R.id.sleepless);
checkBox1.setOnCheckedChangeListener
    (new CompoundButton.OnCheckedChangeListener()
    {
        @Override
        public void onCheckedChanged
            (CompoundButton buttonView, boolean isChecked)
        {
            Kernel.getInstance().setWakeLock(isChecked);
            m_databaseHelper.writeSetting
                (null, "always_awake", isChecked ? "true" : "false");

            TextView textView1 = (TextView) findViewById(R.id.about);
            textView1.setText(About.s_about);
            textView1.append("\n");
            textView1.append
                ("WakeLock Locked: " +
                 Miscellaneous.niceBoolean(Kernel.getInstance().
                                            wakeLocked()));
            textView1.append("\n");
            textView1.append
                ("WiFiLock Locked: " +
                 Miscellaneous.niceBoolean(Kernel.getInstance().
                                            wifiLocked()));
        }
    });

spinner1.setOnItemSelectedListener
    (new OnItemSelectedListener()
    {
        @Override
```

```java
            public void onItemSelected(AdapterView<?> parent,
                                  View view,
                                  int position,
                                  long id)
        {
            CheckBox nonTls = (CheckBox) findViewById(R.id.non_tls);
            Spinner proxyType = (Spinner)
                findViewById(R.id.proxy_type);
            TextView proxyIpAddress =
                (TextView) findViewById(R.id.proxy_ip_address);
            TextView proxyPort = (TextView) findViewById
                (R.id.proxy_port);

            if(position == 0)
            {
                /*
                ** Events may occur prematurely.
                */

                boolean isAuthenticated = State.getInstance().
                    isAuthenticated();

                nonTls.setEnabled(isAuthenticated);
                proxyIpAddress.setEnabled(isAuthenticated);
                proxyPort.setEnabled(isAuthenticated);
                proxyType.setEnabled(isAuthenticated);
            }
            else
            {
                nonTls.setChecked(false);
                nonTls.setEnabled(false);
                proxyIpAddress.setEnabled(false);
                proxyIpAddress.setText("");
                proxyPort.setEnabled(false);
                proxyPort.setText("");
                proxyType.setEnabled(false);
            }
        }

        @Override
        public void onNothingSelected(AdapterView<?> parent)
        {
        }
    });

textView1.addTextChangedListener
    (new TextWatcher()
    {
        @Override
        public void afterTextChanged(Editable s)
        {
            if(s != null)
            {
                CheckBox checkBox1 = (CheckBox) findViewById
                    (R.id.as_alias);

                if(checkBox1.isChecked())
                {
                    TextView textView1 = (TextView)
                        findViewById(R.id.participant_siphash_id);

                    textView1.setText(s);
                }
```

```java
                    }
                }

                @Override
                public void beforeTextChanged(CharSequence s,
                                              int start,
                                              int count,
                                              int after)
                {
                }

                @Override
                public void onTextChanged(CharSequence s,
                                          int start,
                                          int before,
                                          int count)
                {
                }
            });
    }

    private void preparePKI()
    {
        if(Settings.this.isFinishing())
            return;

        final ProgressBar bar = (ProgressBar) findViewById
            (R.id.generate_progress_bar);
        final Spinner spinner1 = (Spinner) findViewById
            (R.id.pki_encryption_algorithm);
        final Spinner spinner2 = (Spinner) findViewById
            (R.id.pki_signature_algorithm);

        bar.setIndeterminate(true);
        bar.setVisibility(ProgressBar.VISIBLE);
        getWindow().setFlags
            (WindowManager.LayoutParams.FLAG_NOT_TOUCHABLE,
             WindowManager.LayoutParams.FLAG_NOT_TOUCHABLE);
        Miscellaneous.enableChildren
            (findViewById(R.id.linear_layout), false);

        class SingleShot implements Runnable
        {
            private String m_encryptionAlgorithm = "";
            private String m_error = "";
            private String m_signatureAlgorithm = "";

            SingleShot(String encryptionAlgorithm, String signatureAlgorithm)
            {
                m_encryptionAlgorithm = encryptionAlgorithm;
                m_signatureAlgorithm = signatureAlgorithm;

                if(m_signatureAlgorithm.equals("ECDSA"))
                    m_signatureAlgorithm = "EC";
            }

            @Override
            public void run()
            {
                KeyPair chatEncryptionKeyPair = null;
                KeyPair chatSignatureKeyPair = null;

                try
```

```java
                {
            int index = 0;

            if(m_encryptionAlgorithm.contains("12, 68"))
                index = 1;

            chatEncryptionKeyPair = Cryptography.
                generatePrivatePublicKeyPair
                (m_encryptionAlgorithm,
                 Cryptography.PKI_ENCRYPTION_KEY_SIZES[0],
                 index);

            if(chatEncryptionKeyPair == null)
            {
                m_error = "encryption-key " +
                    "generatePrivatePublicKeyPair() failure";
                s_cryptography.resetPKI();
                return;
            }

            if(m_signatureAlgorithm.equals("EC"))
                chatSignatureKeyPair = Cryptography.
                    generatePrivatePublicKeyPair
                    ("EC", Cryptography.PKI_SIGNATURE_KEY_SIZES[0], 0);
            else
                chatSignatureKeyPair = Cryptography.
                    generatePrivatePublicKeyPair
                    (m_signatureAlgorithm,
                     Cryptography.PKI_SIGNATURE_KEY_SIZES[1],
                     0);

            if(chatSignatureKeyPair == null)
            {
                m_error = "signature-key " +
                    "generatePrivatePublicKeyPair() failure";
                s_cryptography.resetPKI();
                return;
            }

            /*
            ** Prepare the Cryptography object's data.
            */

            s_cryptography.setChatEncryptionPublicKeyPair
                (chatEncryptionKeyPair);
            s_cryptography.setChatEncryptionPublicKeyAlgorithm
                (m_encryptionAlgorithm);
            s_cryptography.setChatSignaturePublicKeyPair
                (chatSignatureKeyPair);

            /*
            ** Record the data.
            */

            m_databaseHelper.writeSetting
                (s_cryptography,
                 "pki_chat_encryption_algorithm",
                 m_encryptionAlgorithm);
            m_databaseHelper.writeSetting
                (s_cryptography,
                 "pki_chat_encryption_private_key",
                 Base64.
                 encodeToString(chatEncryptionKeyPair.
```

```
                              getPrivate().
                              getEncoded(),
                              Base64.DEFAULT));
            m_databaseHelper.writeSetting
                (s_cryptography,
                 "pki_chat_encryption_public_key",
                 Base64.
                 encodeToString(chatEncryptionKeyPair.
                              getPublic().
                              getEncoded(),
                              Base64.DEFAULT));
            m_databaseHelper.writeSetting
                (s_cryptography,
                 "pki_chat_signature_algorithm",
                 m_signatureAlgorithm);
            m_databaseHelper.writeSetting
                (s_cryptography,
                 "pki_chat_signature_private_key",
                 Base64.encodeToString(chatSignatureKeyPair.
                              getPrivate().
                              getEncoded(),
                              Base64.DEFAULT));
            m_databaseHelper.writeSetting
                (s_cryptography,
                 "pki_chat_signature_public_key",
                 Base64.encodeToString(chatSignatureKeyPair.
                              getPublic().
                              getEncoded(),
                              Base64.DEFAULT));

            boolean e1 = s_cryptography.prepareSipHashIds
                (m_databaseHelper.readSetting(s_cryptography, "alias"));
            boolean e2 = s_cryptography.prepareSipHashKeys();

            if(!e1 || !e2)
            {
                if(!e1)
                    m_error = "prepareSipHashIds() failure";
                else if(!e2)
                    m_error = "prepareSipHashKeys() failure";

                s_cryptography.resetPKI();
            }
        }
        catch(Exception exception)
        {
            m_error = exception.getMessage().toLowerCase().trim();
            s_cryptography.resetPKI();
        }

        Settings.this.runOnUiThread(new Runnable()
        {
            @Override
            public void run()
            {
                bar.setVisibility(ProgressBar.INVISIBLE);
                getWindow().clearFlags
                    (WindowManager.LayoutParams.
                     FLAG_NOT_TOUCHABLE);
                Miscellaneous.enableChildren
                    (findViewById(R.id.linear_layout), true);
                disablePKIButtons();
```

```java
                    if(!m_error.isEmpty())
                        Miscellaneous.showErrorDialog
                            (Settings.this,
                             "An error (" + m_error +
                             ") occurred while " +
                             "generating the PKI " +
                             "data.");
                    else
                    {
                        Settings.this.enableWidgets(true);
                        Settings.this.showWidgets();
                        spinner1.setSelection(3); // RSA
                        spinner2.setSelection(1); // RSA
                        populateFancyKeyData();
                        populateOzone();
                    }
                }
            });
        }
    }

    Thread thread = new Thread
        (new SingleShot(spinner1.getSelectedItem().toString(),
                        spinner2.getSelectedItem().toString()));

    thread.start();
}

private void releaseResources()
{
    if(m_scheduler != null)
    {
        try
        {
            m_scheduler.shutdown();
        }
        catch(Exception exception)
        {
        }

        try
        {
            if(!m_scheduler.awaitTermination(60L, TimeUnit.SECONDS))
                m_scheduler.shutdownNow();
        }
        catch(Exception exception)
        {
        }
        finally
        {
            m_scheduler = null;
        }
    }
}

private void requestKeysOf(final String oid)
{
    if(Settings.this.isFinishing())
        return;

    final ProgressBar bar = (ProgressBar) findViewById
        (R.id.share_keys_progress_bar);
```

```java
        bar.setIndeterminate(true);
        bar.setVisibility(ProgressBar.VISIBLE);
        getWindow().setFlags
            (WindowManager.LayoutParams.FLAG_NOT_TOUCHABLE,
             WindowManager.LayoutParams.FLAG_NOT_TOUCHABLE);
        Miscellaneous.enableChildren
            (findViewById(R.id.linear_layout), false);

        class SingleShot implements Runnable
        {
            private String m_error = "";

            SingleShot()
            {
            }

            @Override
            public void run()
            {
                String sipHashId = m_databaseHelper.readSipHashIdString
                    (s_cryptography, oid);

                if(sipHashId.isEmpty())
                    m_error = "readSipHashIdString() failure";
                else
                {
                    byte bytes[] = Messages.pkpRequestMessage
                        (s_cryptography, sipHashId);

                    if(bytes == null)
                        m_error = "pkpRequestMessage() failure";
                    else if(!Kernel.getInstance().
                            enqueueMessage(Messages.
                                       bytesToMessageString(bytes),
                                       null))
                        m_error = "enqueueMessage() failure";
                }

                Settings.this.runOnUiThread(new Runnable()
                {
                    @Override
                    public void run()
                    {
                        bar.setVisibility(ProgressBar.INVISIBLE);
                        getWindow().clearFlags
                            (WindowManager.LayoutParams.
                             FLAG_NOT_TOUCHABLE);
                        Miscellaneous.enableChildren
                            (findViewById(R.id.linear_layout), true);
                        disablePKIButtons();

                        if(!m_error.isEmpty())
                            Miscellaneous.showErrorDialog
                                (Settings.this,
                                 "An error (" + m_error + ") occurred while " +
                                 "preparing a request of public key material.");
                    }
                });
            }
        }

        Thread thread = new Thread(new SingleShot());
```

```java
        thread.start();
    }

    private void shareKeysOf(final String oid)
    {
        if(Settings.this.isFinishing())
            return;

        final ProgressBar bar = (ProgressBar) findViewById
            (R.id.share_keys_progress_bar);

        bar.setIndeterminate(true);
        bar.setVisibility(ProgressBar.VISIBLE);
        getWindow().setFlags
            (WindowManager.LayoutParams.FLAG_NOT_TOUCHABLE,
             WindowManager.LayoutParams.FLAG_NOT_TOUCHABLE);
        Miscellaneous.enableChildren
            (findViewById(R.id.linear_layout), false);

        class SingleShot implements Runnable
        {
            private String m_error = "";

            SingleShot()
            {
            }

            @Override
            public void run()
            {
                SipHashIdElement sipHashIdElement =
                    m_databaseHelper.readSipHashId(s_cryptography, oid);

                if(sipHashIdElement == null)
                    m_error = "readSipHashId() failure";
                else
                {
                    byte bytes[] = Messages.epksMessage
                        (sipHashIdElement.m_encryptionAlgorithm,
                         sipHashIdElement.m_sipHashId,
                         sipHashIdElement.m_encryptionPublicKey,
                         sipHashIdElement.m_signaturePublicKey,
                         sipHashIdElement.m_stream,
                         Messages.CHAT_KEY_TYPE);

                    if(bytes == null)
                        m_error = "epksMessage() failure";
                    else if(!Kernel.getInstance().
                            enqueueMessage(Messages.
                                           bytesToMessageString(bytes),
                                           null))
                        m_error = "enqueueMessage() failure";
                }

                Settings.this.runOnUiThread(new Runnable()
                {
                    @Override
                    public void run()
                    {
                        bar.setVisibility(ProgressBar.INVISIBLE);
                        getWindow().clearFlags
                            (WindowManager.LayoutParams.
                             FLAG_NOT_TOUCHABLE);
```

```java
                    Miscellaneous.enableChildren
                        (findViewById(R.id.linear_layout), true);
                    disablePKIButtons();

                    if(!m_error.isEmpty())
                        Miscellaneous.showErrorDialog
                            (Settings.this,
                             "An error (" + m_error + ") occurred while " +
                             "preparing to transfer public key material.");
                }
            });
        }
    }

    Thread thread = new Thread(new SingleShot());

    thread.start();
    }

    private void shareSipHashId(int oid)
    {
        if(Settings.this.isFinishing())
            return;
        else if(!s_cryptography.hasValidOzoneKeys())
        {
            Miscellaneous.showErrorDialog
                (Settings.this, "Please prepare Ozone credentials.");
            return;
        }

        Kernel.getInstance().enqueueShareSipHashIdMessage(oid);
    }

    private void showAuthenticateActivity()
    {
        Intent intent = new Intent(Settings.this, Authenticate.class);

        startActivity(intent);
        finish();
    }

    private void showChatActivity()
    {
        Intent intent = new Intent(Settings.this, Chat.class);

        startActivity(intent);
        finish();
    }

    private void showDetailsOfParticipant(String oid)
    {
        if(Settings.this.isFinishing())
            return;

        final ProgressBar bar = (ProgressBar) findViewById
            (R.id.share_keys_progress_bar);

        bar.setIndeterminate(true);
        bar.setVisibility(ProgressBar.VISIBLE);
        getWindow().setFlags
            (WindowManager.LayoutParams.FLAG_NOT_TOUCHABLE,
             WindowManager.LayoutParams.FLAG_NOT_TOUCHABLE);
        Miscellaneous.enableChildren
```

```java
        (findViewById(R.id.linear_layout), false);

    class SingleShot implements Runnable
    {
        private String m_name = "";
        private String m_oid = "";
        private String m_sipHashId = "";
        private String m_string1 = "";
        private String m_string2 = "";
        private String m_strings[] = null;

        SingleShot(String oid)
        {
            m_oid = oid;
        }

        @Override
        public void run()
        {
            /*
            ** Retrieve everything that requires the SipHash.
            */

            SipHashIdElement sipHashIdElement = m_databaseHelper.
                readSipHashId(s_cryptography, m_oid);

            m_sipHashId = sipHashIdElement == null ?
                "" : sipHashIdElement.m_sipHashId;

            String chatEncryptionPublicKeyAlgorithm =
                sipHashIdElement == null ?
                "" : sipHashIdElement.m_encryptionAlgorithm;

            m_name = sipHashIdElement == null ?
                "" : sipHashIdElement.m_name;
            m_string1 = Cryptography.fancyKeyInformationOutput
                (m_databaseHelper.
                 publicEncryptionKeyForSipHashId(s_cryptography,
                                                 m_sipHashId),
                 chatEncryptionPublicKeyAlgorithm).trim();
            m_string2 = Cryptography.fancyKeyInformationOutput
                (m_databaseHelper.
                 publicSignatureKeyForSipHashId(s_cryptography,
                                                m_sipHashId),
                 "").trim();
            m_strings = m_databaseHelper.
                keysSigned(s_cryptography, m_sipHashId);

            if(m_name.isEmpty())
                m_name = m_sipHashId;

            if(m_strings == null)
                m_strings = new String[] {"false", "false"};

            Settings.this.runOnUiThread(new Runnable()
            {
                @Override
                public void run()
                {
                    bar.setVisibility(ProgressBar.INVISIBLE);
                    getWindow().clearFlags
                        (WindowManager.LayoutParams.FLAG_NOT_TOUCHABLE);
                    Miscellaneous.enableChildren
```

```java
                        (findViewById(R.id.linear_layout), true);
            disablePKIButtons();

            PopupWindow popupWindow = new PopupWindow
                (Settings.this);
            StringBuilder stringBuilder = new StringBuilder();
            TextView textView1 = new TextView(Settings.this);
            float density = getApplicationContext().getResources().
                getDisplayMetrics().density;

            if(m_string1.isEmpty() || m_string2.isEmpty())
            {
                if(m_sipHashId.isEmpty())
                {
                    stringBuilder.append
                        ("Unable to gather details ");
                    stringBuilder.append
                        ("for the selected participant.");
                }
                else
                {
                    stringBuilder.append
                        ("Unable to gather details for ");
                    stringBuilder.append(m_name);
                    stringBuilder.append(" (");
                    stringBuilder.append(m_sipHashId);
                    stringBuilder.append(").");
                }

                textView1.setText(stringBuilder.toString());
            }
            else
            {
                stringBuilder.append(m_name);
                stringBuilder.append(" (");
                stringBuilder.append(m_sipHashId);
                stringBuilder.append(")\n");
                stringBuilder.append("\nChat Encryption Key (");
                textView1.append(stringBuilder.toString());

                SpannableStringBuilder spannable =
                    new SpannableStringBuilder
                    (m_strings[0].equals("true") ?
                     "Signature Verified" :
                     "Signature Not Verified");

                if(m_strings[0].equals("true"))
                    spannable.setSpan
                        (new ForegroundColorSpan(Color.
                                            rgb(46, 125, 50)),
                        0, spannable.length(),
                        Spannable.SPAN_EXCLUSIVE_EXCLUSIVE);
                else
                    spannable.setSpan
                        (new ForegroundColorSpan(Color.
                                            rgb(198, 40, 40)),
                        0, spannable.length(),
                        Spannable.SPAN_EXCLUSIVE_EXCLUSIVE);

                textView1.append(spannable);
                stringBuilder.delete(0, stringBuilder.length());
                stringBuilder.append(")\n");
                stringBuilder.append(m_string1);
```

```java
                        stringBuilder.append("\nChat Signature Key (");
                        textView1.append(stringBuilder);
                        spannable = new SpannableStringBuilder
                            (m_strings[1].equals("true") ?
                             "Signature Verified" :
                             "Signature Not Verified");

                        if(m_strings[1].equals("true"))
                            spannable.setSpan
                                (new ForegroundColorSpan(Color.
                                                    rgb(46, 125, 50)),
                                 0, spannable.length(),
                                 Spannable.SPAN_EXCLUSIVE_EXCLUSIVE);
                        else
                            spannable.setSpan
                                (new ForegroundColorSpan(Color.
                                                    rgb(198, 40, 40)),
                                 0, spannable.length(),
                                 Spannable.SPAN_EXCLUSIVE_EXCLUSIVE);

                        textView1.append(spannable);
                        stringBuilder.delete(0, stringBuilder.length());
                        stringBuilder.append(")\n");
                        stringBuilder.append(m_string2);
                        textView1.append(stringBuilder.toString());
                    }

                    textView1.setBackgroundColor(Color.rgb(255, 255, 255));
                    textView1.setPaddingRelative
                        ((int) (10 * density),
                         (int) (10 * density),
                         (int) (10 * density),
                         (int) (10 * density));
                    textView1.setTextSize(16);
                    popupWindow.setContentView(textView1);
                    popupWindow.setOutsideTouchable(true);

                    if(Build.VERSION.SDK_INT < Build.VERSION_CODES.M)
                    {
                        popupWindow.setHeight(450);
                        popupWindow.setWidth(700);
                    }

                    popupWindow.showAsDropDown
                        (findViewById(R.id.participants));
                }
            });
        }
    }

    Thread thread = new Thread(new SingleShot(oid));

    thread.start();
}

private void showFireActivity()
{
    Intent intent = new Intent(Settings.this, Fire.class);

    startActivity(intent);
    finish();
}
```

```java
    private void showMemberChatActivity()
    {
        Intent intent = new Intent(Settings.this, MemberChat.class);

        startActivity(intent);
        finish();
    }

    private void showSmokescreenActivity()
    {
        Intent intent = new Intent(Settings.this, Smokescreen.class);

        startActivity(intent);
        finish();
    }

    private void showSteamActivity()
    {
        Intent intent = new Intent(Settings.this, Steam.class);

        startActivity(intent);
        finish();
    }

    private void showWidgets()
    {
        ViewGroup viewGroup = (ViewGroup) findViewById(R.id.linear_layout);
        int count = viewGroup.getChildCount();

        for(int i = 0; i < count; i++)
        {
            View child = viewGroup.getChildAt(i);

            if(child != findViewById(R.id.neighbors_scope_id))
                child.setVisibility(View.VISIBLE);
        }

        findViewById(R.id.generate_pki).setVisibility(View.VISIBLE);
        findViewById(R.id.overwrite).setVisibility(View.VISIBLE);
    }

    private void startKernel()
    {
        Kernel.getInstance();
    }

    private void startTimers()
    {
        if(m_scheduler == null)
        {
            m_scheduler = Executors.newSingleThreadScheduledExecutor();
            m_scheduler.scheduleAtFixedRate(new Runnable()
            {
                @Override
                public void run()
                {
                    try
                    {
                        ArrayList<NeighborElement> arrayList =
                            m_databaseHelper.readNeighbors(s_cryptography);

                        Settings.this.runOnUiThread
                            (new PopulateNeighbors(arrayList));
```

```java
                        m_databaseHelper.cleanDanglingOutboundQueued();
                        m_databaseHelper.cleanDanglingParticipants();
                    }
                    catch(Exception exception)
                    {
                    }
                }
            }, 1500L, TIMER_INTERVAL, TimeUnit.MILLISECONDS);
        }
    }

    private void stopTimers()
    {
        if(m_scheduler != null)
        {
            try
            {
                m_scheduler.shutdown();
            }
            catch(Exception exception)
            {
            }

            try
            {
                if(!m_scheduler.awaitTermination(60L, TimeUnit.SECONDS))
                    m_scheduler.shutdownNow();
            }
            catch(Exception exception)
            {
            }
            finally
            {
                m_scheduler = null;
            }
        }
    }

    @Override
    protected void onCreate(Bundle savedInstanceState)
    {
        super.onCreate(savedInstanceState);
        m_databaseHelper = Database.getInstance(getApplicationContext());
        m_receiver = new SettingsBroadcastReceiver();
        prepareForegroundService();
        setContentView(R.layout.activity_settings);

        try
        {
            getSupportActionBar().setSubtitle(Smoke.networkStatusString());
            getSupportActionBar().setTitle("Smoke | Settings");
        }
        catch(Exception exception)
        {
        }

        prepareListeners();

        boolean isAuthenticated = State.getInstance().isAuthenticated();
        Button button1 = (Button) findViewById(R.id.add_neighbor);

        button1.setEnabled(isAuthenticated);
        button1 = (Button) findViewById(R.id.add_participant);
```

```java
button1.setEnabled(isAuthenticated);
button1 = (Button) findViewById(R.id.epks);
button1.setCompoundDrawablesWithIntrinsicBounds
    (R.drawable.share, 0, 0, 0);
button1.setEnabled(isAuthenticated);
button1 = (Button) findViewById(R.id.ozone_help);
button1.setCompoundDrawablesWithIntrinsicBounds
    (R.drawable.help, 0, 0, 0);
 button1 = (Button) findViewById(R.id.refresh_neighbors);
 button1.setEnabled(isAuthenticated);
button1 = (Button) findViewById(R.id.refresh_participants);
button1.setEnabled(isAuthenticated);
button1 = (Button) findViewById(R.id.reset_neighbor_fields);
button1.setEnabled(isAuthenticated);
button1 = (Button) findViewById(R.id.reset_participants_fields);
button1.setEnabled(isAuthenticated);
button1 = (Button) findViewById(R.id.save_ozone);
button1.setEnabled(isAuthenticated);
button1 = (Button) findViewById(R.id.share_via_ozone);
button1.setCompoundDrawablesWithIntrinsicBounds
    (R.drawable.share, 0, 0, 0);
button1.setEnabled(isAuthenticated);
button1 = (Button) findViewById(R.id.siphash_help);
button1.setCompoundDrawablesWithIntrinsicBounds
    (R.drawable.help, 0, 0, 0);

CheckBox checkBox1 = null;

checkBox1 = (CheckBox) findViewById(R.id.as_alias);
checkBox1.setChecked(true);
checkBox1 = (CheckBox) findViewById(R.id.automatic_refresh);

if(m_databaseHelper.
   readSetting(null, "automatic_neighbors_refresh").isEmpty())
{
    checkBox1.setChecked(true);
    m_databaseHelper.writeSetting
        (null, "automatic_neighbors_refresh", "true");
}
else if(m_databaseHelper.
        readSetting(null, "automatic_neighbors_refresh").equals("true"))
    checkBox1.setChecked(true);
else
    checkBox1.setChecked(false);

if(checkBox1.isChecked())
    startTimers();

checkBox1 = (CheckBox) findViewById(R.id.echo);

if(m_databaseHelper.readSetting(null, "neighbors_echo").equals("true"))
    checkBox1.setChecked(true);
else
    checkBox1.setChecked(false);

checkBox1 = (CheckBox) findViewById(R.id.foreground_service);

if(m_databaseHelper.
   readSetting(null, "foreground_service").equals("false"))
    checkBox1.setChecked(false);
else
    checkBox1.setChecked(true);
```

```java
checkBox1 = (CheckBox) findViewById(R.id.neighbor_details);

if(m_databaseHelper.readSetting(null, "neighbors_details").
   equals("true"))
     checkBox1.setChecked(true);
else
     checkBox1.setChecked(false);

checkBox1 = (CheckBox) findViewById(R.id.query_time_server);

if(m_databaseHelper.readSetting(null, "query_time_server").
   equals("true"))
     checkBox1.setChecked(true);
else
     checkBox1.setChecked(false);

State.getInstance().setQueryTimerServer(checkBox1.isChecked());
checkBox1 = (CheckBox) findViewById(R.id.sleepless);

if(m_databaseHelper.readSetting(null, "always_awake").isEmpty())
{
    checkBox1.setChecked(true);
    m_databaseHelper.writeSetting(null, "always_awake", "true");
}
else if(m_databaseHelper.readSetting(null, "always_awake").
        equals("true"))
    checkBox1.setChecked(true);
else
    checkBox1.setChecked(false);

 RadioButton radioButton1 = (RadioButton) findViewById
    (R.id.neighbors_ipv4);

 radioButton1.setEnabled(isAuthenticated);
 radioButton1 = (RadioButton) findViewById(R.id.neighbors_ipv6);
 radioButton1.setEnabled(isAuthenticated);

Spinner spinner1 = (Spinner) findViewById(R.id.proxy_type);
 String array[] = new String[]
 {
     "HTTP", "SOCKS"
 };

spinner1.setEnabled(isAuthenticated);

ArrayAdapter<String> arrayAdapter = new ArrayAdapter<>
     (Settings.this, android.R.layout.simple_spinner_item, array);

 spinner1.setAdapter(arrayAdapter);
 spinner1 = (Spinner) findViewById(R.id.neighbors_transport);
 array = new String[]
 {
     "TCP", "UDP"
 };
 spinner1.setEnabled(isAuthenticated);
 arrayAdapter = new ArrayAdapter<>
     (Settings.this, android.R.layout.simple_spinner_item, array);
 spinner1.setAdapter(arrayAdapter);
array = new String[]
 {
     "5", "10", "15", "25", "50", // Argon2id
     "1000", "2500", "5000", "7500", "10000", "12500",
     "15000", "17500", "20000", "25000", "30000", "35000",
```

```java
    "40000", "45000", "50000", "55000", "60000", "65000",
    "70000", "100000"
};
arrayAdapter = new ArrayAdapter<>
    (Settings.this, android.R.layout.simple_spinner_item, array);

int index1 = arrayAdapter.getPosition
    (m_databaseHelper.readSetting(null, "iterationCount"));

spinner1 = (Spinner) findViewById(R.id.iteration_count);
spinner1.setAdapter(arrayAdapter);
array = new String[] {"Argon2id", "PBKDF2"};
arrayAdapter = new ArrayAdapter<>
    (Settings.this, android.R.layout.simple_spinner_item, array);

int index2 = 1; // PBKDF2

try
{
    index2 = Integer.parseInt
        (m_databaseHelper.readSetting(null, "keyDerivationFunction"));
}
catch(Exception exception)
{
}

spinner1 = (Spinner) findViewById(R.id.key_derivation_function);
spinner1.setAdapter(arrayAdapter);
array = new String[]
{
    "McEliece-Fujisaki (11, 50)",    // 0
    "McEliece-Fujisaki (12, 68)",    // 1
    "McEliece-Pointcheval (11, 50)", // 2
    "RSA"                            // 3
};
arrayAdapter = new ArrayAdapter<>
    (Settings.this, android.R.layout.simple_spinner_item, array);
spinner1 = (Spinner) findViewById(R.id.pki_encryption_algorithm);
spinner1.setAdapter(arrayAdapter);
array = new String[]
{
    "ECDSA", "RSA"
};
arrayAdapter = new ArrayAdapter<>
    (Settings.this, android.R.layout.simple_spinner_item, array);
spinner1 = (Spinner) findViewById(R.id.pki_signature_algorithm);
spinner1.setAdapter(arrayAdapter);

RadioGroup radioGroup1 = (RadioGroup) findViewById
    (R.id.neighbors_ipv_radio_group);

radioGroup1.setOnCheckedChangeListener
    (new RadioGroup.OnCheckedChangeListener()
{
    public void onCheckedChanged(RadioGroup group,
                                 int checkedId)
    {
        TextView textView1 = (TextView) findViewById
            (R.id.neighbors_scope_id);

        if(checkedId == R.id.neighbors_ipv4)
        {
            textView1.setEnabled(false);
```

```java
            textView1.setText("");
            textView1 = (TextView) findViewById(R.id.neighbors_port);
            textView1.setNextFocusDownId(R.id.proxy_ip_address);
        }
      else
        {
            textView1.setEnabled(true);
            textView1 = (TextView) findViewById(R.id.neighbors_port);
            textView1.setNextFocusDownId(R.id.neighbors_scope_id);
        }
    }
});

/*
** Enable widgets.
*/

checkBox1 = (CheckBox) findViewById(R.id.overwrite);
checkBox1.setChecked(false);
checkBox1.setEnabled(isAuthenticated);
button1 = (Button) findViewById(R.id.generate_pki);

if(isAuthenticated)
    button1.setEnabled(false);

button1 = (Button) findViewById(R.id.set_password);

if(isAuthenticated)
    button1.setEnabled(false);

TextView textView1 = null;

textView1 = (TextView) findViewById(R.id.about);
textView1.setText(About.s_about);
textView1.append("\n");
textView1.append
    ("WakeLock Locked: " +
     Miscellaneous.niceBoolean(Kernel.getInstance().wakeLocked()));
textView1.append("\n");
textView1.append
    ("WiFiLock Locked: " +
     Miscellaneous.niceBoolean(Kernel.getInstance().wifiLocked()));
textView1 = (TextView) findViewById(R.id.neighbors_scope_id);
 textView1.setEnabled(false);
 textView1 = (TextView) findViewById(R.id.neighbors_port);
 textView1.setEnabled(isAuthenticated);
textView1.setFilters(new InputFilter[] {s_portFilter});
 textView1.setText("4710");
 textView1 = (TextView) findViewById(R.id.neighbors_ip_address);

if(isAuthenticated)
    textView1.requestFocus();

textView1.setEnabled(isAuthenticated);
textView1 = (TextView) findViewById(R.id.ozone);
textView1.setEnabled(isAuthenticated);
textView1 = (TextView) findViewById(R.id.participant_name);
textView1.setEnabled(isAuthenticated);
textView1 = (TextView) findViewById(R.id.participant_siphash_id);
textView1.setEnabled(isAuthenticated);
textView1 = (TextView) findViewById(R.id.password1);

if(!isAuthenticated)
```

```java
        textView1.requestFocus();

    textView1.setText("");
    textView1 = (TextView) findViewById(R.id.password2);
    textView1.setText("");
    textView1 = (TextView) findViewById(R.id.proxy_ip_address);
    textView1.setEnabled(isAuthenticated);
    textView1 = (TextView) findViewById(R.id.proxy_port);
    textView1.setEnabled(isAuthenticated);
    textView1.setFilters(new InputFilter[] {s_portFilter});

    /*
    ** Restore some settings.
    */

    spinner1 = (Spinner) findViewById(R.id.iteration_count);

    if(index1 >= 0)
        spinner1.setSelection(index1);
    else
        spinner1.setSelection(0);

    spinner1 = (Spinner) findViewById(R.id.key_derivation_function);

    if(index2 >= 0)
        spinner1.setSelection(index2);
    else
        spinner1.setSelection(1); // PBKDF2

    spinner1 = (Spinner) findViewById(R.id.pki_encryption_algorithm);
    spinner1.setSelection(3); // RSA
    spinner1 = (Spinner) findViewById(R.id.pki_signature_algorithm);

    if(spinner1.getAdapter().getCount() > 1)
        spinner1.setSelection(1); // RSA

    populateFancyKeyData();

    if(isAuthenticated)
    {
        checkBox1 = (CheckBox) findViewById(R.id.automatic_refresh);
        textView1 = (TextView) findViewById(R.id.alias);
        textView1.setText
            (m_databaseHelper.readSetting(s_cryptography, "alias"));
        textView1 = (TextView) findViewById(R.id.ozone);
        textView1.setText
            (m_databaseHelper.readSetting(s_cryptography, "ozone_address"));
        populateParticipants();
        startKernel();

        if(!checkBox1.isChecked())
            populateNeighbors(null);
    }
    else
    {
        ViewGroup viewGroup = (ViewGroup) findViewById(R.id.linear_layout);
        int count = viewGroup.getChildCount();

        for(int i = 0; i < count; i++)
        {
            View child = viewGroup.getChildAt(i);

            if(!(child == findViewById(R.id.password1) ||
```

```java
                    child == findViewById(R.id.password2) ||
                    child == findViewById(R.id.password_separator) ||
                    child == findViewById(R.id.pki_layout) ||
                    child == findViewById(R.id.set_password_linear_layout)))
                child.setVisibility(View.GONE);
        }

            findViewById(R.id.generate_pki).setVisibility(View.GONE);
            findViewById(R.id.overwrite).setVisibility(View.GONE);
        }

        Kernel.getInstance().setWakeLock
            (m_databaseHelper.readSetting(null,
"always_awake").equals("true"));

        /*
        ** Show the Authenticate activity if an account is present.
        */

        if(!State.getInstance().isAuthenticated())
        {
            if(m_databaseHelper.accountPrepared())
                showAuthenticateActivity();
        }

        if(!m_databaseHelper.accountPrepared())
        {
            ActivityCompat.requestPermissions(this, new String[]
            {
                Manifest.permission.READ_EXTERNAL_STORAGE
            }, 1);
            ActivityCompat.requestPermissions(this, new String[]
            {
                Manifest.permission.WRITE_EXTERNAL_STORAGE
            }, 1);
        }
    }

    @Override
    protected void onDestroy()
    {
        stopTimers();
        super.onDestroy();
    }

    @Override
    protected void onPause()
    {
        super.onPause();

        if(m_receiverRegistered)
        {
            LocalBroadcastManager.getInstance(getApplicationContext()).
                unregisterReceiver(m_receiver);
            m_receiverRegistered = false;
        }

        releaseResources();
    }

    @Override
    protected void onRestoreInstanceState(Bundle savedInstanceState)
    {
```

```java
        /*
        ** Empty.
        */
    }

    @Override
    protected void onResume()
    {
        super.onResume();
        networkStatusChanged();

        if(!m_receiverRegistered)
        {
            IntentFilter intentFilter = new IntentFilter();

            intentFilter.addAction("org.purple.smoke.chat_message");
            intentFilter.addAction("org.purple.smoke.neighbor_aborted");
            intentFilter.addAction("org.purple.smoke.neighbor_disconnected");
            intentFilter.addAction("org.purple.smoke.network_connected");
            intentFilter.addAction("org.purple.smoke.network_disconnected");
            intentFilter.addAction("org.purple.smoke.populate_participants");
            intentFilter.addAction
                ("org.purple.smoke.siphash_share_confirmation");
            intentFilter.addAction("org.purple.smoke.time");
            LocalBroadcastManager.getInstance(getApplicationContext()).
                registerReceiver(m_receiver, intentFilter);
            m_receiverRegistered = true;
        }

        if(State.getInstance().isLocked())
        {
            showSmokescreenActivity();
            return;
        }

        /*
        ** Resume the last activity, if necessary.
        */

        String str = m_databaseHelper.readSetting(null, "lastActivity");

        switch(str)
        {
        case "Chat":
            showChatActivity();
            break;
        case "Fire":
            showFireActivity();
            break;
        case "MemberChat":
            showMemberChatActivity();
            break;
        case "Steam":
            showSteamActivity();
            break;
        default:
            if(m_databaseHelper.
                readSetting(null, "automatic_neighbors_refresh").equals("true"))
                startTimers();

            break;
        }
    }
```

```java
    @Override
    public boolean onContextItemSelected(MenuItem menuItem)
    {
        if(menuItem == null)
            return false;

        final int groupId = menuItem.getGroupId();
        final int itemId = menuItem.getItemId();


        /*
        ** Prepare a listener.
        */

        final DialogInterface.OnCancelListener listener =
            new DialogInterface.OnCancelListener()
            {
                public void onCancel(DialogInterface dialog)
                {
                    String string = "";

                    switch(groupId)
                    {
                    case ContextMenuEnumerator.DELETE:
                        switch(itemId)
                        {
                        default:
                            if(State.getInstance().
                                getString("dialog_accepted").equals("true"))
                                if(m_databaseHelper.
                                    deleteEntry(String.valueOf(itemId),
                                            "siphash_ids"))
                                {
                                    State.getInstance().populateParticipants();
                                    State.getInstance().
                                        removeChatCheckBoxOid(itemId);
                                    State.getInstance().setString
                                        ("member_chat_oid", "");
                                    State.getInstance().setString
                                        ("member_chat_siphash_id", "");
                                    m_databaseHelper.writeSetting
                                        (s_cryptography,
                                         "member_chat_oid", "");
                                    m_databaseHelper.writeSetting
                                        (s_cryptography,
                                         "member_chat_siphash_id", "");
                                    populateParticipants();
                                }

                            break;
                        }

                        break;
                    case ContextMenuEnumerator.DELETE_FIASCO_KEYS:
                        if(State.getInstance().
                            getString("dialog_accepted").equals("true"))
                            if(m_databaseHelper.
                                deleteFiascoKeys(String.valueOf(itemId)))
                                populateParticipants();

                        break;
                    case ContextMenuEnumerator.DELETE_PUBLIC_KEYS:
                        if(State.getInstance().
```

```
                    getString("dialog_accepted").equals("true"))
                      if(m_databaseHelper.
                          deletePublicKeys(String.valueOf(itemId)))
                          populateParticipants();

                  break;
                case ContextMenuEnumerator.NEW_NAME:
                    string = State.getInstance().
                        getString("settings_participant_name_input");

                    if(m_databaseHelper.
                        writeParticipantName(s_cryptography,
                                             string,
                                             itemId))
                    {
                        State.getInstance().populateParticipants();
                        populateParticipants();
                    }

                    State.getInstance().removeKey
                        ("settings_participant_name_input");
                    break;
                default:
                    break;
                }
            }
        };

    /*
    ** Regular expression?
    */

    switch(groupId)
    {
    case ContextMenuEnumerator.DELETE:
        Miscellaneous.showPromptDialog
            (Settings.this,
             listener,
             "Are you sure that you " +
             "wish to delete the participant " +
             menuItem.getTitle().toString().replace("Delete (", "").
             replace(")", "") + "?");
        break;
    case ContextMenuEnumerator.DELETE_FIASCO_KEYS:
        Miscellaneous.showPromptDialog
            (Settings.this,
             listener,
             "Are you sure that you " +
             "wish to delete the Fiasco keys of " +
             menuItem.getTitle().toString().
             replace("Delete Fiasco Keys (", "").replace(")", "") + "?");
        break;
    case ContextMenuEnumerator.DELETE_PUBLIC_KEYS:
        Miscellaneous.showPromptDialog
            (Settings.this,
             listener,
             "Are you sure that you " +
             "wish to delete the public keys of " +
             menuItem.getTitle().toString().
             replace("Delete Public Keys (", "").replace(")", "") + "?");
        break;
    case ContextMenuEnumerator.NEW_NAME:
        String string = menuItem.getTitle().toString().
```

```java
                    replace("New Name (", "").replace(")", "");

                Miscellaneous.showTextInputDialog
                    (Settings.this,
                     listener,
                     "Please provide a new name for " + string + ".",
                     string,
                     "Name");
                break;
            case ContextMenuEnumerator.REQUEST_KEYS_VIA_OZONE:
                requestKeysOf(String.valueOf(itemId));
                break;
            case ContextMenuEnumerator.SHARE_KEYS_OF:
                shareKeysOf(String.valueOf(itemId));
                break;
            case ContextMenuEnumerator.SHARE_SMOKE_ID_OF:
                shareSipHashId(itemId);
                break;
            case ContextMenuEnumerator.VIEW_DETAILS:
                showDetailsOfParticipant(String.valueOf(itemId));
                break;
            default:
                break;
        }

        return true;
    }

    @Override
    public boolean onCreateOptionsMenu(Menu menu)
    {
        getMenuInflater().inflate(R.menu.settings_menu, menu);
        return true;
    }

    @Override
    public boolean onOptionsItemSelected(MenuItem menuItem)
    {
        int groupId = menuItem.getGroupId();
        int itemId = menuItem.getItemId();

        if(groupId == Menu.NONE)
        {
            switch(itemId)
            {
            case R.id.action_chat:
                m_databaseHelper.writeSetting(null, "lastActivity", "Chat");
                showChatActivity();
                return true;
            case R.id.action_exit:
                Smoke.exit(Settings.this);
                return true;
            case R.id.action_fire:
                m_databaseHelper.writeSetting(null, "lastActivity", "Fire");
                showFireActivity();
                return true;
            case R.id.action_smokescreen:
                showSmokescreenActivity();
                return true;
            case R.id.action_steam:
                m_databaseHelper.writeSetting(null, "lastActivity", "Steam");
                showSteamActivity();
                return true;
```

```java
                default:
                    break;
            }
        }
        else
        {
            String sipHashId = menuItem.getTitle().toString();
            int indexOf = sipHashId.indexOf("(");

            if(indexOf >= 0)
                sipHashId = sipHashId.substring(indexOf + 1).replace(")", "");

            sipHashId = Miscellaneous.prepareSipHashId(sipHashId);
            State.getInstance().setString
                ("member_chat_oid", String.valueOf(itemId));
            State.getInstance().setString
                ("member_chat_siphash_id", sipHashId);
            m_databaseHelper.writeSetting
                (null, "lastActivity", "MemberChat");
            m_databaseHelper.writeSetting
                (s_cryptography, "member_chat_oid", String.valueOf(itemId));
            m_databaseHelper.writeSetting
                (s_cryptography, "member_chat_siphash_id", sipHashId);
            showMemberChatActivity();
        }

        return super.onOptionsItemSelected(menuItem);
    }


    @Override
    public boolean onPrepareOptionsMenu(Menu menu)
    {
        boolean isAuthenticated = State.getInstance().isAuthenticated();

        if(!m_databaseHelper.accountPrepared())
            /*
            ** The database may have been modified or removed.
            */

            isAuthenticated = true;

        menu.findItem(R.id.action_authenticate).setEnabled(!isAuthenticated);
        menu.findItem(R.id.action_chat).setEnabled
            (State.getInstance().isAuthenticated());
        menu.findItem(R.id.action_fire).setEnabled
            (State.getInstance().isAuthenticated());
        menu.findItem(R.id.action_smokescreen).setEnabled
            (State.getInstance().isAuthenticated());
        menu.findItem(R.id.action_steam).setEnabled
            (State.getInstance().isAuthenticated());
        Miscellaneous.addMembersToMenu(menu, 6, 250);
        return true;
    }


    @Override
    public void onCreateContextMenu(ContextMenu menu,
                                    View view,
                                    ContextMenuInfo menuInfo)
    {
        if(menu == null || view == null)
            return;

        Object tag1 = view.getTag(R.id.participants);
```

```java
        Object tag2 = view.getTag(R.id.refresh_participants);

        if(tag1 != null && tag2 != null)
        {
            super.onCreateContextMenu(menu, view, menuInfo);
            menu.add(ContextMenuEnumerator.DELETE,
                    view.getId(),
                    0,
                    "Delete (" + tag1 + ")");
            menu.add(ContextMenuEnumerator.DELETE_FIASCO_KEYS,
                    view.getId(),
                    0,
                    "Delete Fiasco Keys (" + tag1 + ")");
            menu.add(ContextMenuEnumerator.DELETE_PUBLIC_KEYS,
                    view.getId(),
                    0,
                    "Delete Public Keys (" + tag1 + ")");
            menu.add(ContextMenuEnumerator.NEW_NAME,
                    view.getId(),
                    0,
                    "New Name (" + tag1 + ")");

            boolean validOzone = s_cryptography.hasValidOzoneKeys();

            menu.add
                (ContextMenuEnumerator.REQUEST_KEYS_VIA_OZONE,
                 view.getId(),
                 0,
                 "Request Keys via Ozone (" + tag1 + ")").
                setEnabled(validOzone);
            menu.add(ContextMenuEnumerator.SHARE_KEYS_OF,
                    view.getId(),
                    0,
                    "Share Keys Of (" + tag1 + ")").
                setEnabled((boolean) tag2);
            menu.add(ContextMenuEnumerator.SHARE_SMOKE_ID_OF,
                    view.getId(),
                    0,
                    "Share Smoke ID Of (" + tag1 + ")").
                setEnabled(validOzone);
            menu.add(ContextMenuEnumerator.VIEW_DETAILS,
                    view.getId(),
                    0,
                    "View Details (" + tag1 + ")");
        }
    }
}
```

```java
/* SipHash.java –
https://github.com/textbrowser/smoke/blob/master/Smoke/app/src/main/java/org/p
urple/smoke/SipHash.java
** Copyright (c) Alexis Megas.
** All rights reserved.
**
** Redistribution and use in source and binary forms, with or without
** modification, are permitted provided that the following conditions
** are met:
** 1. Redistributions of source code must retain the above copyright
**    notice, this list of conditions and the following disclaimer.
** 2. Redistributions in binary form must reproduce the above copyright
**    notice, this list of conditions and the following disclaimer in the
**    documentation and/or other materials provided with the distribution.
** 3. The name of the author may not be used to endorse or promote products
**    derived from Smoke without specific prior written permission.
**
** SMOKE IS PROVIDED BY THE AUTHOR ``AS IS'' AND ANY EXPRESS OR
** IMPLIED WARRANTIES, INCLUDING, BUT NOT LIMITED TO, THE IMPLIED WARRANTIES
** OF MERCHANTABILITY AND FITNESS FOR A PARTICULAR PURPOSE ARE DISCLAIMED.
** IN NO EVENT SHALL THE AUTHOR BE LIABLE FOR ANY DIRECT, INDIRECT,
** INCIDENTAL, SPECIAL, EXEMPLARY, OR CONSEQUENTIAL DAMAGES (INCLUDING, BUT
** NOT LIMITED TO, PROCUREMENT OF SUBSTITUTE GOODS OR SERVICES; LOSS OF USE,
** DATA, OR PROFITS; OR BUSINESS INTERRUPTION) HOWEVER CAUSED AND ON ANY
** THEORY OF LIABILITY, WHETHER IN CONTRACT, STRICT LIABILITY, OR TORT
** (INCLUDING NEGLIGENCE OR OTHERWISE) ARISING IN ANY WAY OUT OF THE USE OF
** SMOKE, EVEN IF ADVISED OF THE POSSIBILITY OF SUCH DAMAGE.
*/

/*
** Implementation of https://131002.net/siphash.
*/

package org.purple.smoke;

public class SipHash
{
    private final static int C_ROUNDS[] = {2, 4};
    private final static int D_ROUNDS[] = {4, 8};
    private final static long C0 = 0x736f6d6570736575L;
    private final static long C1 = 0x646f72616e646f6dL;
    private final static long C2 = 0x6c7967656e657261L;
    private final static long C3 = 0x7465646279746573L;
    private byte m_key[] = null;
    private int m_c_rounds_index = 1;
    private int m_d_rounds_index = 1;
    private long m_v0 = 0L;
    private long m_v1 = 0L;
    private long m_v2 = 0L;
    private long m_v3 = 0L;
    public final static int KEY_LENGTH = 16; // Bytes.

    private long byteArrayToLong(byte bytes[], int offset)
    {
        if(bytes == null || (bytes.length - offset) < Miscellaneous.LONG_BYTES)
            return 0L;

        long value = 0L;

        value |= (((long) bytes[0 + offset]) & 0xffL) <<
            (Miscellaneous.LONG_LONG_BYTES * 0L);
        value |= (((long) bytes[1 + offset]) & 0xffL) <<
```

```java
                    (Miscellaneous.LONG_LONG_BYTES * 1L);
        value |= (((long) bytes[2 + offset]) & 0xffL) <<
                    (Miscellaneous.LONG_LONG_BYTES * 2L);
        value |= (((long) bytes[3 + offset]) & 0xffL) <<
                    (Miscellaneous.LONG_LONG_BYTES * 3L);
        value |= (((long) bytes[4 + offset]) & 0xffL) <<
                    (Miscellaneous.LONG_LONG_BYTES * 4L);
        value |= (((long) bytes[5 + offset]) & 0xffL) <<
                    (Miscellaneous.LONG_LONG_BYTES * 5L);
        value |= (((long) bytes[6 + offset]) & 0xffL) <<
                    (Miscellaneous.LONG_LONG_BYTES * 6L);
        value |= (((long) bytes[7 + offset]) & 0xffL) <<
                    (Miscellaneous.LONG_LONG_BYTES * 7L);
        return value;
    }

    private long rotl(long x, long b)
    {
        return (x << b) | (x >>> (64L - b));
    }

    private void round()
    {
        m_v0 += m_v1;
        m_v1 = rotl(m_v1, 13L);
        m_v1 ^= m_v0;
        m_v0 = rotl(m_v0, 32L);
        m_v2 += m_v3;
        m_v3 = rotl(m_v3, 16L);
        m_v3 ^= m_v2;
        m_v2 += m_v1;
        m_v1 = rotl(m_v1, 17L);
        m_v1 ^= m_v2;
        m_v2 = rotl(m_v2, 32L);
        m_v0 += m_v3;
        m_v3 = rotl(m_v3, 21L);
        m_v3 ^= m_v0;
    }

    public SipHash()
    {
    }

    public SipHash(byte key[])
    {
        if(key == null || key.length != KEY_LENGTH)
            return;

        m_key = key;
    }

    public SipHash(byte key[], int c_rounds_index, int d_rounds_index)
    {
        if(key == null || key.length != KEY_LENGTH)
            return;

        if(c_rounds_index >= 0 && c_rounds_index < C_ROUNDS.length)
            m_c_rounds_index = c_rounds_index;

        if(d_rounds_index >= 0 && d_rounds_index < D_ROUNDS.length)
            m_d_rounds_index = d_rounds_index;

        m_key = key;
```

```java
    }

    public long[] hmac(byte data[], int outputLength)
    {
        return hmac(data, m_key, outputLength);
    }

    @SuppressWarnings("fallthrough")
    public synchronized long[] hmac(byte data[], byte key[], int outputLength)
    {
        if(data == null || key == null || key.length != KEY_LENGTH)
            return new long[] {0L, 0L};

        /*
        ** Initialization
        */

        long k0 = byteArrayToLong(key, 0);
        long k1 = byteArrayToLong(key, Miscellaneous.LONG_BYTES);

        m_v0 = k0 ^ C0;
        m_v1 = k1 ^ C1;
        m_v2 = k0 ^ C2;
        m_v3 = k1 ^ C3;

        if(outputLength == 16)
            m_v1 ^= 0xeeL;

        /*
        ** Compression
        */

        int length1 = data.length / 8;
        int length2 = C_ROUNDS[m_c_rounds_index];

        for(int i = 0; i < length1; i++)
        {
            long m = byteArrayToLong(data, 8 * i);

            m_v3 ^= m;

            switch(length2)
            {
            case 2:
                round();
                round();
                break;
            case 4:
                round();
                round();
                round();
                round();
                break;
            default:
                break;
            }

            m_v0 ^= m;
            m = 0L;
        }

        int offset = (data.length / 8) * 8;
        long b = ((long) data.length) << 56L;
```

```java
        switch(data.length % 8)
        {
        case 7:
            b |= ((long) data[offset + 6]) << 48L;
        case 6:
            b |= ((long) data[offset + 5]) << 40L;
        case 5:
            b |= ((long) data[offset + 4]) << 32L;
        case 4:
            b |= ((long) data[offset + 3]) << 24L;
        case 3:
            b |= ((long) data[offset + 2]) << 16L;
        case 2:
            b |= ((long) data[offset + 1]) << 8L;
        case 1:
            b |= ((long) data[offset]);
            break;
        case 0:
            break;
        default:
            break;
        }

        m_v3 ^= b;

        switch(C_ROUNDS[m_c_rounds_index])
        {
        case 2:
            round();
            round();
            break;
        case 4:
            round();
            round();
            round();
            round();
            break;
        default:
            break;
        }

        m_v0 ^= b;

        /*
        ** Finalization
        */

        if(outputLength == 16)
            m_v2 ^= 0xeeL;
        else
            m_v2 ^= 0xffL;

        switch(D_ROUNDS[m_d_rounds_index])
        {
        case 4:
            round();
            round();
            round();
            round();
            break;
        case 8:
            round();
```

```java
            round();
            round();
            round();
            round();
            round();
            round();
            round();
            break;
        default:
            break;
        }

        long output[] = new long[] {m_v0 ^ m_v1 ^ m_v2 ^ m_v3, 0};

        if(outputLength == 8)
        {
            k0 = k1 = m_v0 = m_v1 = m_v2 = m_v3 = 0L;
            return output;
        }

        m_v1 ^= 0xddL;

        switch(D_ROUNDS[m_d_rounds_index])
        {
        case 4:
            round();
            round();
            round();
            round();
            break;
        case 8:
            round();
            round();
            round();
            round();
            round();
            round();
            round();
            round();
            break;
        default:
            break;
        }

    output[1] = m_v0 ^ m_v1 ^ m_v2 ^ m_v3;
    k0 = k1 = m_v0 = m_v1 = m_v2 = m_v3 = 0L;
    return output;
    }

    public static boolean test1()
    {
        /*
        ** Please read the Test Values section of
        ** https://131002.net/siphash/siphash.pdf.
        */

        SipHash s = new SipHash
            (new byte[] {(byte) 0x00, (byte) 0x01, (byte) 0x02, (byte) 0x03,
                         (byte) 0x04, (byte) 0x05, (byte) 0x06, (byte) 0x07,
                         (byte) 0x08, (byte) 0x09, (byte) 0x0a, (byte) 0x0b,
                         (byte) 0x0c, (byte) 0x0d, (byte) 0x0e, (byte) 0x0f},
            0, 0);
        long result = Miscellaneous.byteArrayToLong
```

```java
                (new byte[] {(byte) 0xa1, (byte) 0x29, (byte) 0xca, (byte) 0x61,
                             (byte) 0x49, (byte) 0xbe, (byte) 0x45, (byte) 0xe5});
            long value[] = s.hmac
                (new byte[] {(byte) 0x00, (byte) 0x01, (byte) 0x02, (byte) 0x03,
                             (byte) 0x04, (byte) 0x05, (byte) 0x06, (byte) 0x07,
                             (byte) 0x08, (byte) 0x09, (byte) 0x0a, (byte) 0x0b,
                             (byte) 0x0c, (byte) 0x0d, (byte) 0x0e},
                 Cryptography.SIPHASH_OUTPUT_LENGTH / 2);

            return result == value[0];
        }
    }
```

/* SipHashIdElement.java

https://github.com/textbrowser/smoke/blob/master/Smoke/app/src/main/java/org/p
urple/smoke/SipHashIdElement.java

```java
** Copyright (c) Alexis Megas.
** All rights reserved.
**
** Redistribution and use in source and binary forms, with or without
** modification, are permitted provided that the following conditions
** are met:
** 1. Redistributions of source code must retain the above copyright
**    notice, this list of conditions and the following disclaimer.
** 2. Redistributions in binary form must reproduce the above copyright
**    notice, this list of conditions and the following disclaimer in the
**    documentation and/or other materials provided with the distribution.
** 3. The name of the author may not be used to endorse or promote products
**    derived from Smoke without specific prior written permission.
**
** SMOKE IS PROVIDED BY THE AUTHOR ``AS IS'' AND ANY EXPRESS OR
** IMPLIED WARRANTIES, INCLUDING, BUT NOT LIMITED TO, THE IMPLIED WARRANTIES
** OF MERCHANTABILITY AND FITNESS FOR A PARTICULAR PURPOSE ARE DISCLAIMED.
** IN NO EVENT SHALL THE AUTHOR BE LIABLE FOR ANY DIRECT, INDIRECT,
** INCIDENTAL, SPECIAL, EXEMPLARY, OR CONSEQUENTIAL DAMAGES (INCLUDING, BUT
** NOT LIMITED TO, PROCUREMENT OF SUBSTITUTE GOODS OR SERVICES; LOSS OF USE,
** DATA, OR PROFITS; OR BUSINESS INTERRUPTION) HOWEVER CAUSED AND ON ANY
** THEORY OF LIABILITY, WHETHER IN CONTRACT, STRICT LIABILITY, OR TORT
** (INCLUDING NEGLIGENCE OR OTHERWISE) ARISING IN ANY WAY OUT OF THE USE OF
** SMOKE, EVEN IF ADVISED OF THE POSSIBILITY OF SUCH DAMAGE.
*/

package org.purple.smoke;

public class SipHashIdElement
{
    public String m_encryptionAlgorithm = "";
    public String m_name = "";
    public String m_sipHashId = "";
    public boolean m_epksCompleted = false;
    public boolean m_keysSigned = false;
    public byte m_encryptionPublicKey[] = null;
    public byte m_signaturePublicKey[] = null;
    public byte m_stream[] = null;
    public int m_fiascoKeys = 0;
    public int m_oid = -1;

    public SipHashIdElement()
    {
    }
}
```

```java
/* Smoke.java -

https://github.com/textbrowser/smoke/blob/master/Smoke/app/src/main/java/org/p
urple/smoke/Smoke.java
** Copyright (c) Alexis Megas.
** All rights reserved.
**
** Redistribution and use in source and binary forms, with or without
** modification, are permitted provided that the following conditions
** are met:
** 1. Redistributions of source code must retain the above copyright
**    notice, this list of conditions and the following disclaimer.
** 2. Redistributions in binary form must reproduce the above copyright
**    notice, this list of conditions and the following disclaimer in the
**    documentation and/or other materials provided with the distribution.
** 3. The name of the author may not be used to endorse or promote products
**    derived from Smoke without specific prior written permission.
**
** SMOKE IS PROVIDED BY THE AUTHOR ``AS IS'' AND ANY EXPRESS OR
** IMPLIED WARRANTIES, INCLUDING, BUT NOT LIMITED TO, THE IMPLIED WARRANTIES
** OF MERCHANTABILITY AND FITNESS FOR A PARTICULAR PURPOSE ARE DISCLAIMED.
** IN NO EVENT SHALL THE AUTHOR BE LIABLE FOR ANY DIRECT, INDIRECT,
** INCIDENTAL, SPECIAL, EXEMPLARY, OR CONSEQUENTIAL DAMAGES (INCLUDING, BUT
** NOT LIMITED TO, PROCUREMENT OF SUBSTITUTE GOODS OR SERVICES; LOSS OF USE,
** DATA, OR PROFITS; OR BUSINESS INTERRUPTION) HOWEVER CAUSED AND ON ANY
** THEORY OF LIABILITY, WHETHER IN CONTRACT, STRICT LIABILITY, OR TORT
** (INCLUDING NEGLIGENCE OR OTHERWISE) ARISING IN ANY WAY OUT OF THE USE OF
** SMOKE, EVEN IF ADVISED OF THE POSSIBILITY OF SUCH DAMAGE.
*/

package org.purple.smoke;

import android.app.Activity;
import android.app.Application;
import android.content.Context;
import android.content.DialogInterface;

public class Smoke extends Application
{
    private static Smoke s_instance = null;

    public static String networkStatusString()
    {
        String address = Kernel.getInstance().connectedNeighborAddress();

        if(address.isEmpty())
            return "Disconnected";
        else
            return "Connected (" + address + ")";
    }

    public static synchronized Smoke getApplication()
    {
        /*
        ** An unpleasant and necessary solution.
        */

        return s_instance;
    }

    public static synchronized void exit(final Context context)
    {
        if(context != null)
```

```java
        {
            final DialogInterface.OnCancelListener listener =
                new DialogInterface.OnCancelListener()
            {
                public void onCancel(DialogInterface dialog)
                {
                    if(State.getInstance().getString("dialog_accepted").
                       equals("true"))
                    {
                        Cryptography.getInstance().exit();
                        SmokeService.stopForegroundTask(getApplication());

                        if(context instanceof Activity)
                            ((Activity) context).finishAndRemoveTask();

                        android.os.Process.killProcess
                            (android.os.Process.myPid());
                    }
                }
            };

            Miscellaneous.showPromptDialog
                (context, listener, "Terminate Smoke?");
        }
    }

    @Override
    public void onCreate()
    {
        super.onCreate();
        About.about();
        s_instance = this;
    }

    @Override
    public void onLowMemory()
    {
        super.onLowMemory();

        try
        {
            Kernel.getInstance().clearMessagesToSend();
        }
        catch(Exception exception)
        {
        }

        try
        {
            Kernel.getInstance().clearNeighborQueues();
        }
        catch(Exception exception)
        {
        }
    }
}
```

/* Smokescreen.java –

```
https://github.com/textbrowser/smoke/blob/master/Smoke/app/src/main/java/org/p
urple/smoke/Smokescreen.java
** Copyright (c) Alexis Megas.
** All rights reserved.
**
** Redistribution and use in source and binary forms, with or without
** modification, are permitted provided that the following conditions
** are met:
** 1. Redistributions of source code must retain the above copyright
**    notice, this list of conditions and the following disclaimer.
** 2. Redistributions in binary form must reproduce the above copyright
**    notice, this list of conditions and the following disclaimer in the
**    documentation and/or other materials provided with the distribution.
** 3. The name of the author may not be used to endorse or promote products
**    derived from Smoke without specific prior written permission.
**
** SMOKE IS PROVIDED BY THE AUTHOR ``AS IS'' AND ANY EXPRESS OR
** IMPLIED WARRANTIES, INCLUDING, BUT NOT LIMITED TO, THE IMPLIED WARRANTIES
** OF MERCHANTABILITY AND FITNESS FOR A PARTICULAR PURPOSE ARE DISCLAIMED.
** IN NO EVENT SHALL THE AUTHOR BE LIABLE FOR ANY DIRECT, INDIRECT,
** INCIDENTAL, SPECIAL, EXEMPLARY, OR CONSEQUENTIAL DAMAGES (INCLUDING, BUT
** NOT LIMITED TO, PROCUREMENT OF SUBSTITUTE GOODS OR SERVICES; LOSS OF USE,
** DATA, OR PROFITS; OR BUSINESS INTERRUPTION) HOWEVER CAUSED AND ON ANY
** THEORY OF LIABILITY, WHETHER IN CONTRACT, STRICT LIABILITY, OR TORT
** (INCLUDING NEGLIGENCE OR OTHERWISE) ARISING IN ANY WAY OUT OF THE USE OF
** SMOKE, EVEN IF ADVISED OF THE POSSIBILITY OF SUCH DAMAGE.
*/

package org.purple.smoke;

import android.content.Intent;
import android.os.Bundle;
import android.support.v7.app.AppCompatActivity;
import android.util.Base64;
import android.view.Menu;
import android.view.MenuItem;
import android.view.SubMenu;
import android.view.View;
import android.widget.Button;
import android.widget.TextView;
import java.util.ArrayList;

public class Smokescreen extends AppCompatActivity
{
    private Button m_lock = null;
    private Button m_unlock = null;
    private Database m_databaseHelper = null;
    private TextView m_label = null;
    private TextView m_password = null;
    private final static Cryptography s_cryptography =
        Cryptography.getInstance();

    private void authenticate()
    {
        if(Smokescreen.this.isFinishing())
            return;

        byte encryptionSalt[] = Base64.decode
            (m_databaseHelper.readSetting(null, "encryptionSalt").getBytes(),
             Base64.DEFAULT);
```

```java
        m_password.setSelectAllOnFocus(true);

    if(encryptionSalt == null)
    {
        m_password.setText("");
        m_password.requestFocus();
        return;
    }

    byte macSalt[] = Base64.decode
        (m_databaseHelper.readSetting(null, "macSalt").getBytes(),
         Base64.DEFAULT);

    if(macSalt == null)
    {
        m_password.setText("");
        m_password.requestFocus();
        return;
    }

    byte saltedPassword[] = Cryptography.sha512
        (m_password.getText().toString().getBytes(),
         encryptionSalt,
         macSalt);

    if(saltedPassword == null)
    {
        m_password.setText("");
        m_password.requestFocus();
        return;
    }

    if(!Cryptography.memcmp(m_databaseHelper.
                            readSetting(null, "saltedPassword").getBytes(),
                            Base64.encode(saltedPassword, Base64.DEFAULT)))
    {
        m_password.setText("");
        m_password.requestFocus();
        return;
    }

    State.getInstance().setLocked(false);
    m_password.setText("");
}

private void prepareListeners()
{
    if(m_lock != null)
        m_lock.setOnClickListener(new View.OnClickListener()
        {
            public void onClick(View view)
            {
                if(Smokescreen.this.isFinishing())
                    return;

                State.getInstance().setLocked(true);
                prepareWidgets();
            }
        });

    if(m_unlock != null)
        m_unlock.setOnClickListener(new View.OnClickListener()
        {
```

```java
            public void onClick(View view)
            {
                if(Smokescreen.this.isFinishing())
                    return;

                authenticate();
                prepareWidgets();
            }
        });
    }

    private void prepareWidgets()
    {
        boolean isLocked = State.getInstance().isLocked();

        m_label.setText
            (isLocked ?
             "Smoke is locked. To unlock, please provide the correct " +
             "password and click the below button." :
             "Smoke is unlocked. To lock, please click the below button.");
        m_lock.setVisibility(isLocked ? View.GONE : View.VISIBLE);
        m_password.setVisibility(isLocked ? View.VISIBLE : View.GONE);

        if(isLocked)
            m_password.post(new Runnable()
            {
                @Override
                public void run()
                {
                    m_password.requestFocus();
                }
            });

        m_unlock.setVisibility(isLocked ? View.VISIBLE : View.GONE);
    }

    private void showChatActivity()
    {
        Intent intent = new Intent(Smokescreen.this, Chat.class);

        startActivity(intent);
        finish();
    }

    private void showFireActivity()
    {
        Intent intent = new Intent(Smokescreen.this, Fire.class);

        startActivity(intent);
        finish();
    }

    private void showMemberChatActivity()
    {
        Intent intent = new Intent(Smokescreen.this, MemberChat.class);

        startActivity(intent);
        finish();
    }

    private void showSettingsActivity()
    {
        Intent intent = new Intent(Smokescreen.this, Settings.class);
```

```java
        startActivity(intent);
        finish();
    }

    private void showSteamActivity()
    {
        Intent intent = new Intent(Smokescreen.this, Steam.class);

        startActivity(intent);
        finish();
    }

    @Override
    protected void onCreate(Bundle savedInstanceState)
    {
        super.onCreate(savedInstanceState);
        m_databaseHelper = Database.getInstance(getApplicationContext());
         setContentView(R.layout.activity_smokescreen);

        try
        {
            getSupportActionBar().setTitle("Smoke | Smokescreen");
        }
        catch(Exception exception)
        {
        }

        m_label = (TextView) findViewById(R.id.label);
        m_lock = (Button) findViewById(R.id.lock);
        m_password = (TextView) findViewById(R.id.password);
        m_unlock = (Button) findViewById(R.id.authenticate);
        prepareListeners();
        prepareWidgets();
    }

    @Override
    public boolean onCreateOptionsMenu(Menu menu)
    {
        return true;
    }

    @Override
    public boolean onOptionsItemSelected(MenuItem menuItem)
    {
        int groupId = menuItem.getGroupId();
        int itemId = menuItem.getItemId();

        if(groupId == Menu.NONE)
            switch(itemId)
            {
            case R.id.action_chat:
                m_databaseHelper.writeSetting(null, "lastActivity", "Chat");
                showChatActivity();
                return true;
            case R.id.action_exit:
                Smoke.exit(Smokescreen.this);
                return true;
            case R.id.action_fire:
                m_databaseHelper.writeSetting(null, "lastActivity", "Fire");
                showFireActivity();
                return true;
            case R.id.action_settings:
```

```java
                m_databaseHelper.writeSetting(null, "lastActivity", "Settings");
                showSettingsActivity();
                return true;
            case R.id.action_steam:
                m_databaseHelper.writeSetting(null, "lastActivity", "Steam");
                showSteamActivity();
                return true;
            default:
                break;
            }
        else
        {
            String sipHashId = menuItem.getTitle().toString();
            int indexOf = sipHashId.indexOf("(");

            if(indexOf >= 0)
                sipHashId = sipHashId.substring(indexOf + 1).replace(")", "");

            sipHashId = Miscellaneous.prepareSipHashId(sipHashId);
            State.getInstance().setString
                ("member_chat_oid", String.valueOf(itemId));
            State.getInstance().setString
                ("member_chat_siphash_id", sipHashId);
            m_databaseHelper.writeSetting
                (null, "lastActivity", "MemberChat");
            m_databaseHelper.writeSetting
                (s_cryptography, "member_chat_oid", String.valueOf(itemId));
            m_databaseHelper.writeSetting
                (s_cryptography, "member_chat_siphash_id", sipHashId);
            showMemberChatActivity();
        }


        return super.onOptionsItemSelected(menuItem);
    }


    @Override
    public boolean onPrepareOptionsMenu(Menu menu)
    {
        menu.clear();
        getMenuInflater().inflate(R.menu.smokescreen_menu, menu);

        boolean isLocked = State.getInstance().isLocked();

        if(isLocked)
        {
            menu.findItem(R.id.action_authenticate).setEnabled(false);
            menu.findItem(R.id.action_chat).setEnabled(false);
            menu.findItem(R.id.action_fire).setEnabled(false);
            menu.findItem(R.id.action_settings).setEnabled(false);
            menu.findItem(R.id.action_steam).setEnabled(false);
        }
        else
        {
            boolean isAuthenticated = State.getInstance().isAuthenticated();

            if(!m_databaseHelper.accountPrepared())
                /*
                ** The database may have been modified or removed.
                */

                isAuthenticated = true;

            menu.findItem(R.id.action_authenticate).setEnabled
```

```java
                    (!isAuthenticated);
            menu.findItem(R.id.action_chat).setEnabled(isAuthenticated);
            menu.findItem(R.id.action_fire).setEnabled(isAuthenticated);
            menu.findItem(R.id.action_settings).setEnabled(isAuthenticated);
            menu.findItem(R.id.action_steam).setEnabled(isAuthenticated);
            Miscellaneous.addMembersToMenu(menu, 6, 250);
        }

        return true;
    }
}
```

/* SmokeService.java –

```java
https://github.com/textbrowser/smoke/blob/master/Smoke/app/src/main/java/org/p
urple/smoke/SmokeService.java
** Copyright (c) Alexis Megas.
** All rights reserved.
**
** Redistribution and use in source and binary forms, with or without
** modification, are permitted provided that the following conditions
** are met:
** 1. Redistributions of source code must retain the above copyright
**    notice, this list of conditions and the following disclaimer.
** 2. Redistributions in binary form must reproduce the above copyright
**    notice, this list of conditions and the following disclaimer in the
**    documentation and/or other materials provided with the distribution.
** 3. The name of the author may not be used to endorse or promote products
**    derived from Smoke without specific prior written permission.
**
** SMOKE IS PROVIDED BY THE AUTHOR ``AS IS'' AND ANY EXPRESS OR
** IMPLIED WARRANTIES, INCLUDING, BUT NOT LIMITED TO, THE IMPLIED WARRANTIES
** OF MERCHANTABILITY AND FITNESS FOR A PARTICULAR PURPOSE ARE DISCLAIMED.
** IN NO EVENT SHALL THE AUTHOR BE LIABLE FOR ANY DIRECT, INDIRECT,
** INCIDENTAL, SPECIAL, EXEMPLARY, OR CONSEQUENTIAL DAMAGES (INCLUDING, BUT
** NOT LIMITED TO, PROCUREMENT OF SUBSTITUTE GOODS OR SERVICES; LOSS OF USE,
** DATA, OR PROFITS; OR BUSINESS INTERRUPTION) HOWEVER CAUSED AND ON ANY
** THEORY OF LIABILITY, WHETHER IN CONTRACT, STRICT LIABILITY, OR TORT
** (INCLUDING NEGLIGENCE OR OTHERWISE) ARISING IN ANY WAY OUT OF THE USE OF
** SMOKE, EVEN IF ADVISED OF THE POSSIBILITY OF SUCH DAMAGE.
*/

package org.purple.smoke;

import android.app.Notification;
import android.app.PendingIntent;
import android.app.Service;
import android.content.Context;
import android.content.Intent;
import android.os.IBinder;

public class SmokeService extends Service
{
    private boolean m_isRunning = false;
    private final static int NOTIFICATION_ID = 1936551787;

    private void start()
    {
        if(m_isRunning)
            return;
        else
```

```java
            m_isRunning = true;

        Intent notificationIntent = new Intent(this, Settings.class);
        Notification notification = null;
        PendingIntent pendingIntent = PendingIntent.getActivity
            (this, 0, notificationIntent, 0);

        notification = new Notification.Builder(this).
            setContentIntent(pendingIntent).
            setContentText("Smoke Activity").
            setContentTitle("Smoke Activity").
            setSmallIcon(R.drawable.smoke).
            setTicker("Smoke Activity").
            build();
        startForeground(NOTIFICATION_ID, notification);
    }

    private void stop()
    {
        m_isRunning = false;
        stopForeground(true);
        stopSelf();
    }

    @Override
    public IBinder onBind(Intent intent)
    {
        return null;
    }

    @Override
    public int onStartCommand(Intent intent, int flags, int startId)
    {
        if(intent != null && intent.getAction() != null)
            switch(intent.getAction())
            {
            case "start":
                start();
                break;
            case "stop":
                stop();
                break;
            default:
                break;
            }

        return START_STICKY;
    }

    public static void startForegroundTask(Context context)
    {
        if(context == null)
            return;

        Intent intent = new Intent(context, SmokeService.class);

        intent.setAction("start");
        context.startService(intent);
    }

    public static void stopForegroundTask(Context context)
    {
        if(context == null)
```

```java
        return;

    Intent intent = new Intent(context, SmokeService.class);

    intent.setAction("stop");
    context.startService(intent);
    }

    @Override
    public void onCreate()
    {
        super.onCreate();
        start();
    }

    @Override
    public void onDestroy()
    {
        m_isRunning = false;
        super.onDestroy();
    }
}




/* State.java –

https://github.com/textbrowser/smoke/blob/master/Smoke/app/src/main/java/org/p
urple/smoke/State.java
** Copyright (c) Alexis Megas.
** All rights reserved.
**
** Redistribution and use in source and binary forms, with or without
** modification, are permitted provided that the following conditions
** are met:
** 1. Redistributions of source code must retain the above copyright
**    notice, this list of conditions and the following disclaimer.
** 2. Redistributions in binary form must reproduce the above copyright
**    notice, this list of conditions and the following disclaimer in the
**    documentation and/or other materials provided with the distribution.
** 3. The name of the author may not be used to endorse or promote products
**    derived from Smoke without specific prior written permission.
**
** SMOKE IS PROVIDED BY THE AUTHOR ``AS IS'' AND ANY EXPRESS OR
** IMPLIED WARRANTIES, INCLUDING, BUT NOT LIMITED TO, THE IMPLIED WARRANTIES
** OF MERCHANTABILITY AND FITNESS FOR A PARTICULAR PURPOSE ARE DISCLAIMED.
** IN NO EVENT SHALL THE AUTHOR BE LIABLE FOR ANY DIRECT, INDIRECT,
** INCIDENTAL, SPECIAL, EXEMPLARY, OR CONSEQUENTIAL DAMAGES (INCLUDING, BUT
** NOT LIMITED TO, PROCUREMENT OF SUBSTITUTE GOODS OR SERVICES; LOSS OF USE,
** DATA, OR PROFITS; OR BUSINESS INTERRUPTION) HOWEVER CAUSED AND ON ANY
** THEORY OF LIABILITY, WHETHER IN CONTRACT, STRICT LIABILITY, OR TORT
** (INCLUDING NEGLIGENCE OR OTHERWISE) ARISING IN ANY WAY OUT OF THE USE OF
** SMOKE, EVEN IF ADVISED OF THE POSSIBILITY OF SUCH DAMAGE.
*/

package org.purple.smoke;

import android.content.Intent;
import android.os.Bundle;
import android.support.v4.content.LocalBroadcastManager;
import android.view.View;
import java.util.ArrayList;
import java.util.Map;
```

```java
import java.util.TreeMap;
import java.util.concurrent.Executors;
import java.util.concurrent.ScheduledExecutorService;
import java.util.concurrent.TimeUnit;
import java.util.concurrent.atomic.AtomicBoolean;
import java.util.concurrent.locks.ReentrantReadWriteLock;

public class State
{
    private ArrayList<MessageElement> m_chatMessages = null;
    private ArrayList<ParticipantElement> m_participants = null;
    private AtomicBoolean m_queryTimerServer = null;
    private Bundle m_bundle = null;
    private Map<String, FireChannel> m_fireChannels = null;
    private Map<Integer, Boolean> m_steamDetailsStates = null;
    private ScheduledExecutorService m_participantsScheduler = null;
    private final ReentrantReadWriteLock m_bundleMutex = new
        ReentrantReadWriteLock();
    private final ReentrantReadWriteLock m_participantsMutex = new
        ReentrantReadWriteLock();
    private static State s_instance = null;

    private State()
    {
        m_bundle = new Bundle();
        m_queryTimerServer = new AtomicBoolean(false);
        m_steamDetailsStates = new TreeMap<> ();
        setAuthenticated(false);
    }

    public ArrayList<ParticipantElement> participants()
    {
        m_participantsMutex.readLock().lock();

        try
        {
            return m_participants;
        }
        finally
        {
            m_participantsMutex.readLock().unlock();
        }
    }

    public CharSequence getCharSequence(String key)
    {
        m_bundleMutex.readLock().lock();

        try
        {
            return m_bundle.getCharSequence(key, "");
        }
        catch(Exception exception)
        {
        }
        finally
        {
            m_bundleMutex.readLock().unlock();
        }

        return "";
    }
```

```java
public FireChannel fireChannel(String name)
{
    if(name == null)
        return null;

    if(m_fireChannels != null && m_fireChannels.containsKey(name))
        return m_fireChannels.get(name);

    return null;
}

public Map<String, FireChannel> fireChannels()
{
    return m_fireChannels;
}

public String getString(String key)
{
    m_bundleMutex.readLock().lock();

    try
    {
        return m_bundle.getString(key, "");
    }
    catch(Exception exception)
    {
    }
    finally
    {
        m_bundleMutex.readLock().unlock();
    }

    return "";
}

public String nameOfFireFromView(View view)
{
    if(m_fireChannels == null || view == null)
        return "";

    for(Map.Entry<String, FireChannel> entry : m_fireChannels.entrySet())
        if(entry.getValue() != null)
            if(entry.getValue().view() == view)
                return entry.getValue().name();

    return "";
}

public boolean chatCheckBoxIsSelected(int oid)
{
    m_bundleMutex.readLock().lock();

    try
    {
        return m_bundle.getChar
            ("chat_checkbox_" + String.valueOf(oid), '0') == '1';
    }
    catch(Exception exception)
    {
    }
    finally
    {
        m_bundleMutex.readLock().unlock();
```

```java
        }

        return false;
    }

    public boolean containsFire(String name)
    {
        return m_fireChannels != null && m_fireChannels.containsKey(name);
    }

    public boolean isAuthenticated()
    {
        m_bundleMutex.readLock().lock();

        try
        {
            return m_bundle.getChar("is_authenticated", '0') == '1';
        }
        catch(Exception exception)
        {
        }
        finally
        {
            m_bundleMutex.readLock().unlock();
        }

        return false;
    }

    public boolean isLocked()
    {
        m_bundleMutex.readLock().lock();

        try
        {
            return m_bundle.getChar("is_locked", '0') == '1';
        }
        catch(Exception exception)
        {
        }
        finally
        {
            m_bundleMutex.readLock().unlock();
        }

        return false;
    }

    public boolean neighborsEcho()
    {
        m_bundleMutex.readLock().lock();

        try
        {
            return m_bundle.getChar("neighbors_echo", '0') == '1';
        }
        catch(Exception exception)
        {
        }
        finally
        {
            m_bundleMutex.readLock().unlock();
        }
```

```java
        return false;
    }

    public boolean queryTimerServer()
    {
        return m_queryTimerServer.get();
    }

    public char getChar(String key)
    {
        m_bundleMutex.readLock().lock();

        try
        {
            return m_bundle.getChar(key, '0');
        }
        catch(Exception exception)
        {
        }
        finally
        {
            m_bundleMutex.readLock().unlock();
        }

        return '0';
    }

    public int chatCheckedParticipants()
    {
        m_bundleMutex.readLock().lock();

        try
        {
            return m_bundle.getInt("chat_checkbox_counter", 0);
        }
        catch(Exception exception)
        {
        }
        finally
        {
            m_bundleMutex.readLock().unlock();
        }

        return 0;
    }

    public long chatSequence(String sipHashId)
    {
        m_bundleMutex.readLock().lock();

        try
        {
            return m_bundle.getLong("chat_sequence" + sipHashId, 1L);
        }
        catch(Exception exception)
        {
        }
        finally
        {
            m_bundleMutex.readLock().unlock();
        }
```

```java
        return 0L;
    }

    public static synchronized State getInstance()
    {
        if(s_instance == null)
            s_instance = new State();

        return s_instance;
    }

    public synchronized ArrayList<MessageElement> chatLog()
    {
        return m_chatMessages;
    }

    public synchronized boolean steamDetailsState(int oid)
    {
        if(m_steamDetailsStates.containsKey(oid))
            return m_steamDetailsStates.get(oid);
        else
            return false;
    }

    public synchronized void clearChatLog()
    {
        if(m_chatMessages != null)
            m_chatMessages.clear();

        m_chatMessages = null;
    }

    public synchronized void clearSteamDetailsStates()
    {
        m_steamDetailsStates.clear();
    }

    public synchronized void logChatMessage(String message,
                                            String name,
                                            String sipHashId,
                                            boolean purple,
                                            long sequence,
                                            long timestamp)
    {
        if(message == null || name == null || sipHashId == null)
            return;

        if(m_chatMessages == null)
            m_chatMessages = new ArrayList<> ();

        MessageElement messageElement = new MessageElement();

        messageElement.m_id = sipHashId;
        messageElement.m_message = message;
        messageElement.m_name = name;
        messageElement.m_purple = purple;
        messageElement.m_sequence = sequence;
        messageElement.m_timestamp = timestamp;
        m_chatMessages.add(messageElement);
    }

    public synchronized void removeSteamDetailsState(int oid)
    {
```

```java
        m_steamDetailsStates.remove(oid);
    }

    public synchronized void setSteamDetailsState(boolean state, int oid)
    {
        m_steamDetailsStates.put(oid, state);
    }

    public void addFire(FireChannel fireChannel)
    {
        if(fireChannel == null)
            return;

        if(m_fireChannels == null)
            m_fireChannels = new TreeMap<> ();
        else if(m_fireChannels.containsKey(fireChannel.name()))
            return;

        m_fireChannels.put(fireChannel.name(), fireChannel);
    }

    public void incrementChatSequence(String sipHashId)
    {
        long sequence = chatSequence(sipHashId);

        m_bundleMutex.writeLock().lock();

        try
        {
            m_bundle.putLong("chat_sequence" + sipHashId, sequence + 1L);
        }
        catch(Exception exception)
        {
        }
        finally
        {
            m_bundleMutex.writeLock().unlock();
        }
    }

    public void populateParticipants()
    {
        m_participantsMutex.writeLock().lock();

        try
        {
            if(m_participants == null)
                m_participants = new ArrayList<> ();
            else
                m_participants.clear();
        }
        catch(Exception exception)
        {
        }
        finally
        {
            m_participantsMutex.writeLock().unlock();
        }

        if(m_participantsScheduler == null)
            m_participantsScheduler = Executors.
                newSingleThreadScheduledExecutor();
        else
```

```java
        {
            try
            {
                m_participantsScheduler.shutdownNow();
            }
            catch(Exception exception)
            {
            }

            m_participantsScheduler = Executors.
                newSingleThreadScheduledExecutor();
        }

        m_participantsScheduler.schedule(new Runnable()
        {
            @Override
            public void run()
            {
                try
                {
                    m_participantsMutex.writeLock().lock();

                    try
                    {
                        m_participants = Database.getInstance().
                            readParticipants(Cryptography.getInstance(), "");

                        Intent intent = new Intent
                            ("org.purple.smoke.state_participants_populated");
                        LocalBroadcastManager localBroadcastManager =
                            LocalBroadcastManager.
                            getInstance(Smoke.getApplication());

                        localBroadcastManager.sendBroadcast(intent);
                    }
                    catch(Exception exception)
                    {
                    }
                    finally
                    {
                        m_participantsMutex.writeLock().unlock();
                    }
                }
                catch(Exception exception)
                {
                }
            }
        }, 0L, TimeUnit.MILLISECONDS);
    }

    public void removeChatCheckBoxOid(int oid)
    {
        m_bundleMutex.writeLock().lock();

        try
        {
            m_bundle.remove("chat_checkbox_" + String.valueOf(oid));
        }
        catch(Exception exception)
        {
        }
        finally
        {
```

```java
                m_bundleMutex.writeLock().unlock();
        }
    }

    public void removeFireChannel(String name)
    {
        if(m_fireChannels == null)
            return;

        m_fireChannels.remove(name);
    }

    public void removeKey(String key)
    {
        m_bundleMutex.writeLock().lock();

        try
        {
            m_bundle.remove(key);
        }
        catch(Exception exception)
        {
        }
        finally
        {
            m_bundleMutex.writeLock().unlock();
        }
    }

    public void reset()
    {
        clearChatLog();
        clearSteamDetailsStates();
        m_bundleMutex.writeLock().lock();

        try
        {
            m_bundle.clear();
        }
        finally
        {
            m_bundleMutex.writeLock().unlock();
        }

        if(m_fireChannels != null)
            m_fireChannels.clear();

        m_participantsMutex.writeLock().lock();

        try
        {
            if(m_participants != null)
                m_participants.clear();
        }
        finally
        {
            m_participantsMutex.writeLock().unlock();
        }
    }

    public void setAuthenticated(boolean state)
    {
        m_bundleMutex.writeLock().lock();
```

```java
        try
        {
            m_bundle.putChar("is_authenticated", state ? '1' : '0');
        }
        catch(Exception exception)
        {
        }
        finally
        {
            m_bundleMutex.writeLock().unlock();
        }
    }

    public void setChatCheckBoxSelected(int oid, boolean checked)
    {
        boolean contains = false;

        m_bundleMutex.readLock().lock();

        try
        {
            contains = m_bundle.containsKey
                ("chat_checkbox_" + String.valueOf(oid));
        }
        catch(Exception exception)
        {
        }
        finally
        {
            m_bundleMutex.readLock().unlock();
        }

        if(checked)
        {
            m_bundleMutex.writeLock().lock();

            try
            {
                m_bundle.putChar("chat_checkbox_" + String.valueOf(oid), '1');

                if(!contains)
                    m_bundle.putInt
                        ("chat_checkbox_counter",
                         chatCheckedParticipants() + 1);
            }
            catch(Exception exception)
            {
            }
            finally
            {
                m_bundleMutex.writeLock().unlock();
            }
        }
        else
        {
            m_bundleMutex.writeLock().lock();

            try
            {
                m_bundle.remove("chat_checkbox_" + String.valueOf(oid));
            }
            catch(Exception exception)
```

```java
            {
            }
            finally
            {
                m_bundleMutex.writeLock().unlock();
            }

            if(contains)
            {
                int counter = chatCheckedParticipants(); // Read lock.

                if(counter > 0)
                    counter -= 1;

                m_bundleMutex.writeLock().lock();

                try
                {
                    m_bundle.putInt("chat_checkbox_counter", counter);
                }
                catch(Exception exception)
                {
                }
                finally
                {
                    m_bundleMutex.writeLock().unlock();
                }
            }
        }
    }

    public void setLocked(boolean state)
    {
        m_bundleMutex.writeLock().lock();

        try
        {
            m_bundle.putChar("is_locked", state ? '1' : '0');
        }
        catch(Exception exception)
        {
        }
        finally
        {
            m_bundleMutex.writeLock().unlock();
        }
    }

    public void setNeighborsEcho(boolean state)
    {
        m_bundleMutex.writeLock().lock();

        try
        {
            m_bundle.putChar("neighbors_echo", state ? '1' : '0');
        }
        catch(Exception exception)
        {
        }
        finally
        {
            m_bundleMutex.writeLock().unlock();
        }
```

```java
    }

    public void setQueryTimerServer(boolean state)
    {
        m_queryTimerServer.set(state);
    }

    public void setString(String key, String value)
    {
        m_bundleMutex.writeLock().lock();

        try
        {
            m_bundle.putString(key, value);
        }
        catch(Exception exception)
        {
        }
        finally
        {
            m_bundleMutex.writeLock().unlock();
        }
    }

    public void writeChar(String key, char character)
    {
        m_bundleMutex.writeLock().lock();

        try
        {
            m_bundle.putChar(key, character);
        }
        finally
        {
            m_bundleMutex.writeLock().unlock();
        }
    }

    public void writeCharSequence(String key, CharSequence text)
    {
        m_bundleMutex.writeLock().lock();

        try
        {
            m_bundle.putCharSequence(key, text);
        }
        finally
        {
            m_bundleMutex.writeLock().unlock();
        }
    }
}
```

```java
/* Steam.java -
https://github.com/textbrowser/smoke/blob/master/Smoke/app/src/main/java/org/p
urple/smoke/Steam.java
** Copyright (c) Alexis Megas.
** All rights reserved.
**
** Redistribution and use in source and binary forms, with or without
** modification, are permitted provided that the following conditions
** are met:
** 1. Redistributions of source code must retain the above copyright
**    notice, this list of conditions and the following disclaimer.
** 2. Redistributions in binary form must reproduce the above copyright
**    notice, this list of conditions and the following disclaimer in the
**    documentation and/or other materials provided with the distribution.
** 3. The name of the author may not be used to endorse or promote products
**    derived from Smoke without specific prior written permission.
**
** SMOKE IS PROVIDED BY THE AUTHOR ``AS IS'' AND ANY EXPRESS OR
** IMPLIED WARRANTIES, INCLUDING, BUT NOT LIMITED TO, THE IMPLIED WARRANTIES
** OF MERCHANTABILITY AND FITNESS FOR A PARTICULAR PURPOSE ARE DISCLAIMED.
** IN NO EVENT SHALL THE AUTHOR BE LIABLE FOR ANY DIRECT, INDIRECT,
** INCIDENTAL, SPECIAL, EXEMPLARY, OR CONSEQUENTIAL DAMAGES (INCLUDING, BUT
** NOT LIMITED TO, PROCUREMENT OF SUBSTITUTE GOODS OR SERVICES; LOSS OF USE,
** DATA, OR PROFITS; OR BUSINESS INTERRUPTION) HOWEVER CAUSED AND ON ANY
** THEORY OF LIABILITY, WHETHER IN CONTRACT, STRICT LIABILITY, OR TORT
** (INCLUDING NEGLIGENCE OR OTHERWISE) ARISING IN ANY WAY OUT OF THE USE OF
** SMOKE, EVEN IF ADVISED OF THE POSSIBILITY OF SUCH DAMAGE.
*/

package org.purple.smoke;

import android.content.BroadcastReceiver;
import android.content.Context;
import android.content.DialogInterface;
import android.content.Intent;
import android.content.IntentFilter;
import android.database.Cursor;
import android.os.Bundle;
import android.os.Environment;
import android.provider.DocumentsContract;
import android.provider.OpenableColumns;
import android.support.v4.content.LocalBroadcastManager;
import android.support.v7.app.AppCompatActivity;
import android.support.v7.widget.LinearLayoutManager;
import android.support.v7.widget.RecyclerView;
import android.text.style.StyleSpan;
import android.view.Menu;
import android.view.MenuItem;
import android.view.View;
import android.widget.ArrayAdapter;
import android.widget.Button;
import android.widget.Spinner;
import android.widget.TextView;
import java.io.File;
import java.util.ArrayList;
import java.util.concurrent.Executors;
import java.util.concurrent.ScheduledExecutorService;
import java.util.concurrent.TimeUnit;

public class Steam extends AppCompatActivity
{
    private class SteamBroadcastReceiver extends BroadcastReceiver
```

```java
{
    public SteamBroadcastReceiver()
    {
    }

    @Override
    public void onReceive(Context context, Intent intent)
    {
        if(intent == null || intent.getAction() == null)
            return;

        switch(intent.getAction())
        {
        case "org.purple.smoke.chat_message":
            Miscellaneous.showNotification
                (Steam.this, intent, findViewById(R.id.main_layout));
            break;
        case "org.purple.smoke.network_connected":
            networkStatusChanged();
            break;
        case "org.purple.smoke.network_disconnected":
            networkStatusChanged();
            break;
        case "org.purple.smoke.state_participants_populated":
            invalidateOptionsMenu();
            break;
        case "org.purple.smoke.steam_added":
        case "org.purple.smoke.steam_status":
            m_adapter.notifyDataSetChanged();
            break;
        case "org.purple.smoke.time":
            Miscellaneous.showNotification
                (Steam.this, intent, findViewById(R.id.main_layout));
            break;
        default:
            break;
        }
    }
}

private static class SteamLinearLayoutManager extends LinearLayoutManager
{
    SteamLinearLayoutManager(Context context)
    {
        super(context);
    }

    @Override
    public void onLayoutChildren(RecyclerView.Recycler recycler,
                                 RecyclerView.State state)
    {
        /*
        ** Android may terminate!
        */

        try
        {
            super.onLayoutChildren(recycler, state);
        }
        catch(Exception exception)
        {
        }
    }
```

```java
        }

    private Button m_attachmentButton = null;
    private Button m_sendButton = null;
    private Database m_databaseHelper = null;
    private RecyclerView m_recyclerView = null;
    private RecyclerView.Adapter<?> m_adapter = null;
    private ScheduledExecutorService m_statusScheduler = null;
    private Spinner m_participantsSpinner = null;
    private SteamBroadcastReceiver m_receiver = null;
    private SteamLinearLayoutManager m_layoutManager = null;
    private String m_absoluteFileName = "";
    private TextView m_displayFileName = null;
    private TextView m_downloads = null;
    private boolean m_receiverRegistered = false;
    private final static Cryptography s_cryptography =
        Cryptography.getInstance();
    private final static int SELECT_FILE_REQUEST = 0;
    private final static long STATUS_INTERVAL = 1500L; // 1.5 seconds.
    public final static String OTHER = "Other (Non-Smoke)";

    public abstract static class ContextMenuEnumerator
    {
        public final static int DELETE_ALL_STEAMS = 0;
        public final static int DELETE_STEAM = 1;
        public final static int PAUSE_ALL_STEAMS = 2;
        public final static int REWIND_ALL_STEAMS = 3;
        public final static int REWIND_AND_RESUME_ALL_STEAMS = 4;
        public final static int REWIND_STEAM = 5;
    }

    private void networkStatusChanged()
    {
        try
        {
            getSupportActionBar().setSubtitle(Smoke.networkStatusString());
        }
        catch(Exception exception)
        {
        }
    }

    private void populateParticipants()
    {
        if(m_participantsSpinner == null)
            return;

        ArrayList<ParticipantElement> arrayList = State.getInstance().
            participants();

        if(arrayList == null || arrayList.isEmpty())
        {
            ArrayAdapter<String> arrayAdapter = new ArrayAdapter<>
                (Steam.this,
                 android.R.layout.simple_spinner_item,
                 new String[] {OTHER});

            m_participantsSpinner.setAdapter(arrayAdapter);
            return;
        }

        m_participantsSpinner.setAdapter(null);
```

```java
        ArrayList<String> list = new ArrayList<> ();

        list.add(OTHER);

        for(ParticipantElement participant : arrayList)
            if(participant != null)
                list.add
                    (participant.m_name + " (" + participant.m_sipHashId + ")");

        ArrayAdapter<String> arrayAdapter = new ArrayAdapter<>
            (Steam.this, android.R.layout.simple_spinner_item, list);

        m_participantsSpinner.setAdapter(arrayAdapter);
    }


    private void prepareListeners()
    {
        if(m_attachmentButton != null)
            m_attachmentButton.setOnClickListener(new View.OnClickListener()
            {
                public void onClick(View view)
                {
                    if(Steam.this.isFinishing())
                        return;

                    showFileActivity();
                }
            });

        if(m_sendButton != null)
            m_sendButton.setOnClickListener(new View.OnClickListener()
            {
                public void onClick(View view)
                {
                    if(Steam.this.isFinishing())
                        return;

                    saveSteam();
                }
            });
    }

    private void prepareSchedulers()
    {
        if(m_statusScheduler == null)
        {
            m_statusScheduler = Executors.newSingleThreadScheduledExecutor();
            m_statusScheduler.scheduleAtFixedRate(new Runnable()
            {
                @Override
                public void run()
                {
                    try
                    {
                        Steam.this.runOnUiThread(new Runnable()
                        {
                            @Override
                            public void run()
                            {
                                m_adapter.notifyDataSetChanged();
                            }
                        });
                    }
```

```java
                    catch(Exception exception)
                    {
                    }
                }
            }, 0L, STATUS_INTERVAL, TimeUnit.MILLISECONDS);
        }
    }

    private void prepareWidgets()
    {
        if(m_adapter == null && m_recyclerView != null)
        {
            m_adapter = new SteamAdapter(this);
            m_adapter.registerAdapterDataObserver
                (new RecyclerView.AdapterDataObserver()
            {
                @Override
                public void onItemRangeInserted
                    (int positionStart, int itemCount)
                {
                    m_layoutManager.smoothScrollToPosition
                        (m_recyclerView, null, positionStart);
                }

                @Override
                public void onItemRangeRemoved
                    (int positionStart, int itemCount)
                {
                    m_layoutManager.smoothScrollToPosition
                        (m_recyclerView, null, positionStart - itemCount);
                }
            });
            m_recyclerView.setAdapter(m_adapter);
            m_recyclerView.setLayoutManager(m_layoutManager);
        }
    }

    private void releaseResources()
    {
        if(m_statusScheduler != null)
        {
            try
            {
                m_statusScheduler.shutdown();
            }
            catch(Exception exception)
            {
            }

            try
            {
                if(!m_statusScheduler.awaitTermination(60L, TimeUnit.SECONDS))
                    m_statusScheduler.shutdownNow();
            }
            catch(Exception exception)
            {
            }
            finally
            {
                m_statusScheduler = null;
            }
        }
    }
```

```java
private void saveSteam()
{
    SteamElement steamElement = null;
    String displayFileName = m_displayFileName.getText().toString();

    steamElement = new SteamElement(displayFileName, m_absoluteFileName);
    steamElement.m_destination =
        m_participantsSpinner.getSelectedItem().toString();
    m_absoluteFileName = "";
    m_databaseHelper.writeSteam(s_cryptography, steamElement);
    m_displayFileName.setText("");
    m_participantsSpinner.setSelection(0); // Other (Non-Smoke)
}

private void showChatActivity()
{
    Intent intent = new Intent(Steam.this, Chat.class);

    startActivity(intent);
    finish();
}

private void showFileActivity()
{
    Intent intent = new Intent(Intent.ACTION_OPEN_DOCUMENT);

    intent.setType("*/*");
    startActivityForResult(intent, SELECT_FILE_REQUEST);
}

private void showFireActivity()
{
    Intent intent = new Intent(Steam.this, Fire.class);

    startActivity(intent);
    finish();
}

private void showMemberChatActivity()
{
    Intent intent = new Intent(Steam.this, MemberChat.class);

    startActivity(intent);
    finish();
}

private void showSettingsActivity()
{
    Intent intent = new Intent(Steam.this, Settings.class);

    startActivity(intent);
    finish();
}

private void showSmokescreenActivity()
{
    Intent intent = new Intent(Steam.this, Smokescreen.class);

    startActivity(intent);
    finish();
}
```

```java
@Override
protected void onActivityResult(int requestCode,
                                int resultCode,
                                Intent data)
{
    super.onActivityResult(requestCode, resultCode, data);

    try
    {
        if(data != null &&
           requestCode == SELECT_FILE_REQUEST &&
           resultCode == RESULT_OK)
        {
            Cursor cursor = null;
            String type = getContentResolver().getType(data.getData());

            if(type.lastIndexOf('/') > 0)
                type = type.substring(type.lastIndexOf('/') + 1);

            m_absoluteFileName = data.getData().toString() + "." + type;

            try
            {
                cursor = getContentResolver().query
                    (data.getData(), null, null, null, null);

                if(cursor != null && cursor.moveToFirst())
                {
                    String string = cursor.getString
                        (cursor.
                         getColumnIndex(OpenableColumns.DISPLAY_NAME));

                    if(string.isEmpty())
                        m_displayFileName.setText("." + type);
                    else
                        m_displayFileName.setText(string);
                }
            }
            catch(Exception exception)
            {
                /*
                ** Special failure.
                */

                m_displayFileName.setText("." + type);
            }
            finally
            {
                if(cursor != null)
                    cursor.close();
            }
        }
    }
    catch(Exception exception)
    {
    }
}

@Override
protected void onCreate(Bundle savedInstanceState)
{
    super.onCreate(savedInstanceState);
    m_databaseHelper = Database.getInstance(getApplicationContext());
```

```java
        m_databaseHelper.clearSteamRates(s_cryptography);
        m_receiver = new SteamBroadcastReceiver();
         setContentView(R.layout.activity_steam);
        m_layoutManager = new SteamLinearLayoutManager(Steam.this);
        m_layoutManager.setOrientation(LinearLayoutManager.VERTICAL);

        try
        {
            getSupportActionBar().setSubtitle(Smoke.networkStatusString());
            getSupportActionBar().setTitle("Smoke | Steam");
        }
        catch(Exception exception)
        {
        }

        m_attachmentButton = (Button) findViewById(R.id.attachment);
        m_displayFileName = (TextView) findViewById(R.id.filename);
        m_downloads = (TextView) findViewById(R.id.downloads);
        m_downloads.setText
            ("Downloads Directory: " +
             Environment.
             getExternalStoragePublicDirectory(Environment.
                                   DIRECTORY_DOWNLOADS).
             toString());
        m_participantsSpinner = (Spinner) findViewById(R.id.participants);
        m_recyclerView = (RecyclerView) findViewById(R.id.recycler_view);
        m_recyclerView.setHasFixedSize(true);
        m_sendButton = (Button) findViewById(R.id.send);
        populateParticipants();
        prepareListeners();
        prepareWidgets();

        /*
        ** Restore states.
        */

        try
        {
            m_layoutManager.smoothScrollToPosition(m_recyclerView, null, 0);
        }
        catch(Exception exception)
        {
        }
    }

    @Override
    protected void onPause()
    {
        super.onPause();

        if(m_receiverRegistered)
        {
            LocalBroadcastManager.getInstance(getApplicationContext()).
                unregisterReceiver(m_receiver);
            m_receiverRegistered = false;
        }

        releaseResources();
    }

    @Override
    protected void onResume()
    {
```

```java
        super.onResume();
        networkStatusChanged();

        if(!m_receiverRegistered)
        {
            IntentFilter intentFilter = new IntentFilter();

            intentFilter.addAction("org.purple.smoke.chat_message");
            intentFilter.addAction("org.purple.smoke.network_connected");
            intentFilter.addAction("org.purple.smoke.network_disconnected");
            intentFilter.addAction
                ("org.purple.smoke.state_participants_populated");
            intentFilter.addAction("org.purple.smoke.steam_added");
            intentFilter.addAction("org.purple.smoke.steam_status");
            intentFilter.addAction("org.purple.smoke.time");
            LocalBroadcastManager.getInstance(getApplicationContext()).
                registerReceiver(m_receiver, intentFilter);
            m_receiverRegistered = true;
        }

        try
        {
            m_adapter.notifyDataSetChanged();
            m_layoutManager.smoothScrollToPosition(m_recyclerView, null, 0);
        }
        catch(Exception exception)
        {
        }

        prepareSchedulers();
    }

    @Override
    public boolean onContextItemSelected(MenuItem menuItem)
    {
        if(menuItem == null)
            return false;

        final int groupId = menuItem.getGroupId();
        final int itemId = menuItem.getItemId();

        /*
        ** Prepare a listener.
        */

        DialogInterface.OnCancelListener listener =
            new DialogInterface.OnCancelListener()
            {
                public void onCancel(DialogInterface dialog)
                {
                    switch(groupId)
                    {
                    case ContextMenuEnumerator.DELETE_ALL_STEAMS:
                        if(State.getInstance().
                            getString("dialog_accepted").equals("true"))
                          try
                          {
                              State.getInstance().clearSteamDetailsStates();
                              m_databaseHelper.clearTable("steam_files");
                              m_adapter.notifyDataSetChanged();
                          }
                          catch(Exception exception)
                          {
```

```java
                            }

                break;
            case ContextMenuEnumerator.DELETE_STEAM:
                if(State.getInstance().
                    getString("dialog_accepted").equals("true"))
                  try
                  {
                      if(m_databaseHelper.
                          deleteEntry(String.valueOf(itemId),
                                "steam_files"))
                      {
                          State.getInstance().removeSteamDetailsState
                              (itemId);
                          m_adapter.notifyDataSetChanged();
                      }
                  }
                  catch(Exception exception)
                  {
                  }

                break;
            default:
                break;
            }
        }
    };

    switch(groupId)
    {
    case ContextMenuEnumerator.DELETE_ALL_STEAMS:
        Miscellaneous.showPromptDialog
            (Steam.this,
             listener,
             "Are you sure that you wish to delete all of the Steams?");
        break;
    case ContextMenuEnumerator.DELETE_STEAM:
        Miscellaneous.showPromptDialog
            (Steam.this,
             listener,
             "Are you sure that you wish to delete the selected Steam?");
        break;
    case ContextMenuEnumerator.PAUSE_ALL_STEAMS:
        m_databaseHelper.pauseAllSteams();
        m_adapter.notifyDataSetChanged();
        break;
    case ContextMenuEnumerator.REWIND_ALL_STEAMS:
        m_databaseHelper.rewindAllSteams();
        m_adapter.notifyDataSetChanged();
        break;
    case ContextMenuEnumerator.REWIND_AND_RESUME_ALL_STEAMS:
        m_databaseHelper.rewindAndResumeAllSteams();
        m_adapter.notifyDataSetChanged();
        break;
    case ContextMenuEnumerator.REWIND_STEAM:
        m_databaseHelper.writeSteamStatus
            (s_cryptography, "rewind", Miscellaneous.RATE, itemId, 0);
        m_adapter.notifyDataSetChanged();
        break;
    default:
        break;
    }
```

```java
        return true;
    }

    @Override
    public boolean onCreateOptionsMenu(Menu menu)
    {
        getMenuInflater().inflate(R.menu.steam_menu, menu);
        return true;
    }

    @Override
    public boolean onOptionsItemSelected(MenuItem menuItem)
    {
        int groupId = menuItem.getGroupId();
        int itemId = menuItem.getItemId();

        if(groupId == Menu.NONE)
        {
            switch(itemId)
            {
            case R.id.action_chat:
                m_databaseHelper.writeSetting(null, "lastActivity", "Chat");
                showChatActivity();
                return true;
            case R.id.action_exit:
                Smoke.exit(Steam.this);
                return true;
            case R.id.action_fire:
                m_databaseHelper.writeSetting(null, "lastActivity", "Fire");
                showFireActivity();
                return true;
            case R.id.action_settings:
                m_databaseHelper.writeSetting(null, "lastActivity", "Settings");
                showSettingsActivity();
                return true;
            case R.id.action_smokescreen:
                showSmokescreenActivity();
                return true;
            default:
                break;
            }
        }
        else
        {
            String sipHashId = menuItem.getTitle().toString();
            int indexOf = sipHashId.indexOf("(");

            if(indexOf >= 0)
                sipHashId = sipHashId.substring(indexOf + 1).replace(")", "");

            sipHashId = Miscellaneous.prepareSipHashId(sipHashId);
            State.getInstance().setString
                ("member_chat_oid", String.valueOf(itemId));
            State.getInstance().setString
                ("member_chat_siphash_id", sipHashId);
            m_databaseHelper.writeSetting
                (null, "lastActivity", "MemberChat");
            m_databaseHelper.writeSetting
                (s_cryptography, "member_chat_oid", String.valueOf(itemId));
            m_databaseHelper.writeSetting
                (s_cryptography, "member_chat_siphash_id", sipHashId);
            showMemberChatActivity();
        }
```

```java
        return super.onOptionsItemSelected(menuItem);
    }

    @Override
    public boolean onPrepareOptionsMenu(Menu menu)
    {
        boolean isAuthenticated = State.getInstance().isAuthenticated();

        if(!m_databaseHelper.accountPrepared())
            /*
            ** The database may have been modified or removed.
            */

            isAuthenticated = true;

        menu.findItem(R.id.action_authenticate).setEnabled(!isAuthenticated);
        Miscellaneous.addMembersToMenu(menu, 6, 250);
        return true;
    }

    @Override
    public void onBackPressed()
    {
        Intent intent = new Intent();

        intent.putExtra("Result", "Done");
        setResult(RESULT_OK, intent);
        super.onBackPressed();
    }

    public void showContextMenu(View view)
    {
        if(view != null)
        {
            registerForContextMenu(view);
            openContextMenu(view);
        }
    }
}



/* SteamAdapter.java –
```

```java
** OF MERCHANTABILITY AND FITNESS FOR A PARTICULAR PURPOSE ARE DISCLAIMED.
** IN NO EVENT SHALL THE AUTHOR BE LIABLE FOR ANY DIRECT, INDIRECT,
** INCIDENTAL, SPECIAL, EXEMPLARY, OR CONSEQUENTIAL DAMAGES (INCLUDING, BUT
** NOT LIMITED TO, PROCUREMENT OF SUBSTITUTE GOODS OR SERVICES; LOSS OF USE,
** DATA, OR PROFITS; OR BUSINESS INTERRUPTION) HOWEVER CAUSED AND ON ANY
** THEORY OF LIABILITY, WHETHER IN CONTRACT, STRICT LIABILITY, OR TORT
** (INCLUDING NEGLIGENCE OR OTHERWISE) ARISING IN ANY WAY OUT OF THE USE OF
** SMOKE, EVEN IF ADVISED OF THE POSSIBILITY OF SUCH DAMAGE.
*/

package org.purple.smoke;

import android.support.v7.widget.RecyclerView;
import android.view.ContextMenu;
import android.view.ContextMenu.ContextMenuInfo;
import android.view.MenuItem;
import android.view.View;
import android.view.View.OnCreateContextMenuListener;
import android.view.ViewGroup;

public class SteamAdapter extends
RecyclerView.Adapter<SteamAdapter.ViewHolder>
{
    private Steam m_steam = null;
    private final static Cryptography s_cryptography =
        Cryptography.getInstance();
    private final static Database s_database = Database.getInstance();

    public static class ViewHolder extends RecyclerView.ViewHolder
        implements OnCreateContextMenuListener
    {
        SteamBubble m_steamBubble = null;
        int m_position = -1;

        public ViewHolder(SteamBubble steamBubble)
        {
            super(steamBubble.view());
            steamBubble.view().setOnCreateContextMenuListener(this);
            m_steamBubble = steamBubble;
        }

        public void onCreateContextMenu(ContextMenu menu,
                                        View view,
                                        ContextMenuInfo menuInfo)
        {
            if(menu == null || view == null)
                return;

            /*
            ** Please update the first parameter if the context menu
            ** in Steam is modified!
            */

            MenuItem menuItem = null;

            menu.add(Steam.ContextMenuEnumerator.DELETE_ALL_STEAMS,
                     -1,
                     0,
                     "Delete All Steams");
            menu.add(Steam.ContextMenuEnumerator.DELETE_STEAM,
                     view.getId(),
                     1,
                     "Delete Steam").setEnabled(view.getId() != -1);
```

```java
            menu.add(Steam.ContextMenuEnumerator.PAUSE_ALL_STEAMS,
                    -1,
                    3,
                    "Pause All Steams");
            menu.add(Steam.ContextMenuEnumerator.REWIND_AND_RESUME_ALL_STEAMS,
                    -1,
                    3,
                    "Rewind & Resume All Steams");
            menu.add(Steam.ContextMenuEnumerator.REWIND_ALL_STEAMS,
                    -1,
                    4,
                    "Rewind All Steams");

            SteamElement steamElement = s_database.readSteam
                (s_cryptography, -1, view.getId() - 1);

            menu.add(Steam.ContextMenuEnumerator.REWIND_STEAM,
                    view.getId(),
                    5,
                    "Rewind Steam").setEnabled(view.getId() != -1).
                setEnabled
                (steamElement == null ?
                 true : steamElement.m_direction == SteamElement.UPLOAD);
        }

    public void setData(SteamElement steamElement, int count, int position)
        {
            if(m_steamBubble == null)
                return;
            else if(steamElement == null)
            {
                m_position = position;
                return;
            }

            m_position = position;
            m_steamBubble.setData(steamElement, count, position);
        }
    }

    public SteamAdapter(Steam steam)
    {
        m_steam = steam;
    }

    @Override
    public SteamAdapter.ViewHolder onCreateViewHolder
        (ViewGroup parent, int viewType)
    {
        return new ViewHolder
            (new SteamBubble(parent.getContext(), m_steam, parent));
    }

    @Override
    public int getItemCount()
    {
        return (int) s_database.countOfSteams();
    }

    @Override
    public void onBindViewHolder(ViewHolder viewHolder, int position)
    {
        if(viewHolder == null)
```

```java
            return;

        SteamElement steamElement = s_database.readSteam
            (s_cryptography, Math.max(0, position), -1);

        viewHolder.setData(steamElement, getItemCount(), position);
    }
}
```

/* SteamBubble.java –

https://github.com/textbrowser/smoke/blob/master/Smoke/app/src/main/java/org/p
urple/smoke/SteamBubble.java

```java
** Copyright (c) Alexis Megas.
** All rights reserved.
**
** Redistribution and use in source and binary forms, with or without
** modification, are permitted provided that the following conditions
** are met:
** 1. Redistributions of source code must retain the above copyright
**    notice, this list of conditions and the following disclaimer.
** 2. Redistributions in binary form must reproduce the above copyright
**    notice, this list of conditions and the following disclaimer in the
**    documentation and/or other materials provided with the distribution.
** 3. The name of the author may not be used to endorse or promote products
**    derived from Smoke without specific prior written permission.
**
** SMOKE IS PROVIDED BY THE AUTHOR ``AS IS'' AND ANY EXPRESS OR
** IMPLIED WARRANTIES, INCLUDING, BUT NOT LIMITED TO, THE IMPLIED WARRANTIES
** OF MERCHANTABILITY AND FITNESS FOR A PARTICULAR PURPOSE ARE DISCLAIMED.
** IN NO EVENT SHALL THE AUTHOR BE LIABLE FOR ANY DIRECT, INDIRECT,
** INCIDENTAL, SPECIAL, EXEMPLARY, OR CONSEQUENTIAL DAMAGES (INCLUDING, BUT
** NOT LIMITED TO, PROCUREMENT OF SUBSTITUTE GOODS OR SERVICES; LOSS OF USE,
** DATA, OR PROFITS; OR BUSINESS INTERRUPTION) HOWEVER CAUSED AND ON ANY
** THEORY OF LIABILITY, WHETHER IN CONTRACT, STRICT LIABILITY, OR TORT
** (INCLUDING NEGLIGENCE OR OTHERWISE) ARISING IN ANY WAY OUT OF THE USE OF
** SMOKE, EVEN IF ADVISED OF THE POSSIBILITY OF SUCH DAMAGE.
*/

package org.purple.smoke;

import android.content.Context;
import android.view.LayoutInflater;
import android.view.View;
import android.view.ViewGroup;
import android.widget.Button;
import android.widget.CompoundButton;
import android.widget.ImageButton;
import android.widget.LinearLayout;
import android.widget.ProgressBar;
import android.widget.SeekBar.OnSeekBarChangeListener;
import android.widget.SeekBar;
import android.widget.Switch;
import android.widget.TextView;
import java.text.DecimalFormat;
import java.text.NumberFormat;

public class SteamBubble extends View
{
    private Button m_control = null;
    private Context m_context = null;
```

```java
private ImageButton m_menuButton = null;
private LinearLayout m_layoutA = null;
private LinearLayout m_layoutB = null;
private ProgressBar m_progress = null;
private SeekBar m_readInterval = null;
private Steam m_steam = null;
private String m_controlString = "";
private Switch m_details = null;
private TextView m_destination = null;
private TextView m_digest = null;
private TextView m_eta = null;
private TextView m_fileIdentity = null;
private TextView m_fileName = null;
private TextView m_fileSize = null;
private TextView m_keyStreamDigest = null;
private TextView m_readIntervalLabel = null;
private TextView m_sent = null;
private TextView m_status = null;
private TextView m_transferRate = null;
private View m_direction = null;
private View m_keyExchangeStatus = null;
private View m_separator = null;
private View m_view = null;
private final static Cryptography s_cryptography =
    Cryptography.getInstance();
private final static Database s_databaseHelper = Database.getInstance();
private final static DecimalFormat s_decimalFormat =
    new DecimalFormat("0.00");
private final static NumberFormat s_numberFormat =
    NumberFormat.getInstance();
private int m_oid = -1;

private String formatSize(long size)
{
    return Miscellaneous.formattedDigitalInformation(String.valueOf(size));
}

private String niceBytes(long size)
{
    return s_numberFormat.format(size);
}

private String prettyEta(String transferRate,
                         long fileSize,
                         long readOffset)
{
    if(fileSize == readOffset)
        return "ETA: completed";

    try
    {
        double rate = Double.parseDouble
            (transferRate.substring(0, transferRate.indexOf(' ')));

        if(transferRate.contains("GiB"))
            rate *= 1073741824.0;
        else if(transferRate.contains("KiB"))
            rate *= 1024.0;
        else if(transferRate.contains("MiB"))
            rate *= 1048576.0;

        if(rate > 0.0)
            return "ETA: " +
```

```java
                    s_decimalFormat.format((((fileSize - readOffset) / rate) /
                                    60.0) +
                    " minutes";
        }
    catch(Exception exception)
        {
        }

    return "ETA: stalled";
    }

    public SteamBubble(Context context, Steam steam, ViewGroup viewGroup)
    {
        super(context);
        m_context = context;
        m_steam = steam;

        LayoutInflater inflater = (LayoutInflater) m_context.getSystemService
            (Context.LAYOUT_INFLATER_SERVICE);

        m_view = inflater.inflate(R.layout.steam_bubble, viewGroup, false);
        m_control = (Button) m_view.findViewById(R.id.control);
        m_control.setOnClickListener(new View.OnClickListener()
        {
            public void onClick(View view)
            {
                switch(m_controlString)
                {
                case "pause":
                    m_eta.setText("ETA: stalled");
                    s_databaseHelper.writeSteamStatus
                        (s_cryptography, "paused", Miscellaneous.RATE, m_oid);
                    Miscellaneous.sendBroadcast
                        ("org.purple.smoke.steam_status");
                    break;
                case "resume":
                    s_databaseHelper.writeSteamStatus("transferring", m_oid);
                    Miscellaneous.sendBroadcast
                        ("org.purple.smoke.steam_status");
                    break;
                case "rewind":
                    s_databaseHelper.writeSteamStatus
                        (s_cryptography,
                         "rewind",
                         Miscellaneous.RATE,
                         m_oid,
                         0);
                    Miscellaneous.sendBroadcast
                        ("org.purple.smoke.steam_status");
                    break;
                default:
                    break;
                }
            }
        });
        m_destination = (TextView) m_view.findViewById(R.id.destination);
        m_details = (Switch) m_view.findViewById(R.id.details);
        m_details.setOnCheckedChangeListener
            (new CompoundButton.OnCheckedChangeListener()
            {
                @Override
                public void onCheckedChanged
                    (CompoundButton buttonView, boolean isChecked)
```

```java
                {
                    State.getInstance().setSteamDetailsState(isChecked, m_oid);

                    if(isChecked)
                    {
                        m_layoutA.setVisibility(LinearLayout.VISIBLE);
                        m_layoutB.setVisibility(LinearLayout.VISIBLE);
                    }
                    else
                    {
                        m_layoutA.setVisibility(LinearLayout.GONE);
                        m_layoutB.setVisibility(LinearLayout.GONE);
                    }
                }
            });
        m_digest = (TextView) m_view.findViewById(R.id.digest);
        m_direction = m_view.findViewById(R.id.direction);
        m_eta = (TextView) m_view.findViewById(R.id.eta);
        m_fileIdentity = (TextView) m_view.findViewById(R.id.file_identity);
        m_fileName = (TextView) m_view.findViewById(R.id.filename);
        m_fileSize = (TextView) m_view.findViewById(R.id.file_size);
        m_keyExchangeStatus = m_view.findViewById(R.id.key_exchange_status);
        m_keyStreamDigest = (TextView)
            m_view.findViewById(R.id.keystream_digest);
        m_layoutA = (LinearLayout) m_view.findViewById(R.id.layout_a);
        m_layoutA.setVisibility(LinearLayout.GONE);
        m_layoutB = (LinearLayout) m_view.findViewById(R.id.layout_b);
        m_layoutB.setVisibility(LinearLayout.GONE);
        m_menuButton = (ImageButton) m_view.findViewById(R.id.menu);
        m_menuButton.setOnClickListener(new View.OnClickListener()
        {
            public void onClick(View view)
            {
                m_steam.showContextMenu(view);
            }
        });
        m_progress = (ProgressBar) m_view.findViewById(R.id.progress_bar);
        m_readInterval = (SeekBar) m_view.findViewById(R.id.read_interval);
        m_readInterval.setOnSeekBarChangeListener(new OnSeekBarChangeListener()
        {
            @Override
            public void onProgressChanged(SeekBar seekBar,
                                          int progress,
                                          boolean fromUser)
            {
                switch(progress)
                {
                case 0:
                case 1:
                case 2:
                case 3:
                case 4:
                    String text = "4 reads / s";
                    int readInterval = 4;

                    switch(progress)
                    {
                    case 1:
                        readInterval = 10;
                        text = "10 reads / s";
                        break;
                    case 2:
                        readInterval = 20;
```

```java
                    text = "20 reads / s";
                    break;
                case 3:
                    readInterval = 50;
                    text = "50 reads / s";
                    break;
                case 4:
                    readInterval = 100;
                    text = "100 reads / s";
                    break;
                }

                m_readIntervalLabel.setText(text);

                if(fromUser)
                {
                    s_databaseHelper.writeSteamStatus
                        (s_cryptography, m_oid, readInterval);
                    Miscellaneous.sendBroadcast
                        ("org.purple.smoke.steam_read_interval_change",
                         m_oid,
                         readInterval);
                }

                break;
            default:
                break;
            }
        }

        @Override
        public void onStartTrackingTouch(SeekBar seekBar)
        {
        }

        @Override
        public void onStopTrackingTouch(SeekBar seekBar)
        {
        }
    });
    m_readIntervalLabel = (TextView) m_view.findViewById
        (R.id.read_interval_label);
    m_readIntervalLabel.setText("4 reads / s");
    m_sent = (TextView) m_view.findViewById(R.id.sent);
    m_separator = m_view.findViewById(R.id.separator);
    m_status = (TextView) m_view.findViewById(R.id.status);
    m_transferRate = (TextView) m_view.findViewById(R.id.transfer_rate);
    m_view.setId(-1);
    s_numberFormat.setGroupingUsed(true);
}

public View view()
{
    return m_view;
}

public void setData(SteamElement steamElement, int count, int position)
{
    if(steamElement == null)
        return;

    m_oid = steamElement.m_oid;
```

```java
        switch(steamElement.m_status)
        {
        case "completed":
            if(steamElement.m_direction == SteamElement.DOWNLOAD)
            {
                m_control.setText("Pause");
                m_controlString = "";
            }
            else
            {
                m_control.setText("Rewind");
                m_controlString = "rewind";
            }

            m_progress.setVisibility(View.GONE);
            break;
        case "paused":
            m_control.setText("Resume");
            m_controlString = "resume";
            m_progress.setVisibility(View.GONE);
            break;
        case "receiving":
            m_progress.setVisibility(View.VISIBLE);
            break;
        case "transferring":
            m_control.setText("Pause");
            m_controlString = "pause";
            m_progress.setVisibility(View.VISIBLE);
            break;
        default:
            break;
        }

        if(steamElement.m_destination.equals(Steam.OTHER))
        {
            /*
            ** Simple Steams.
            */

            int oid = Kernel.getInstance().nextSimpleSteamOid();

            m_control.setEnabled(m_oid == oid || oid == -1);
            m_control.setVisibility(View.VISIBLE);
            m_destination.setText("Destination: " +
steamElement.m_destination);
            m_direction.setBackgroundResource(R.drawable.upload);
            m_keyExchangeStatus.setVisibility(View.GONE);
            m_keyStreamDigest.setVisibility(View.GONE);
            m_readInterval.setVisibility(View.VISIBLE);
            m_readIntervalLabel.setVisibility(View.VISIBLE);
            m_sent.setText("Sent: " + formatSize(steamElement.m_readOffset));
        }
        else if(steamElement.m_direction == SteamElement.DOWNLOAD)
        {
            m_control.setVisibility(View.GONE);
            m_destination.setText("Origin: " + steamElement.m_destination);
            m_direction.setBackgroundResource(R.drawable.download);
            m_keyExchangeStatus.setBackgroundResource
                (steamElement.m_keyStream != null &&
                 steamElement.m_keyStream.length ==
                 Cryptography.CIPHER_HASH_KEYS_LENGTH ?
                 R.drawable.lock : R.drawable.unlock);
            m_keyExchangeStatus.setVisibility(View.VISIBLE);
```

```java
            m_keyStreamDigest.setVisibility(View.VISIBLE);
            m_readInterval.setVisibility(View.GONE);
            m_readIntervalLabel.setVisibility(View.GONE);
            m_sent.setText
                ("Received: " +
                 formatSize(steamElement.m_readOffset) +
                 " (" +
                 niceBytes(steamElement.m_readOffset) +
                 ")");
        }
    else
    {
        /*
        ** Full Steams.
        */

        m_control.setEnabled
            (steamElement.m_keyStream != null &&
             steamElement.m_keyStream.length ==
             Cryptography.CIPHER_HASH_KEYS_LENGTH);
        m_control.setVisibility(View.VISIBLE);
        m_destination.setText("Destination: " +
steamElement.m_destination);
            m_direction.setBackgroundResource(R.drawable.upload);
            m_keyExchangeStatus.setBackgroundResource
                (steamElement.m_keyStream != null &&
                 steamElement.m_keyStream.length ==
                 Cryptography.CIPHER_HASH_KEYS_LENGTH ?
                 R.drawable.lock : R.drawable.unlock);
            m_keyExchangeStatus.setVisibility(View.VISIBLE);
            m_keyStreamDigest.setVisibility(View.VISIBLE);
            m_readInterval.setVisibility(View.GONE);
            m_sent.setText("Sent: " + formatSize(steamElement.m_readOffset));
        }

    m_details.setChecked(State.getInstance().steamDetailsState(m_oid));
    m_digest.setText
        ("SHA-256: " +
         Miscellaneous.byteArrayAsHexString(steamElement.m_fileDigest));
    m_eta.setText(prettyEta(steamElement.m_transferRate,
                           steamElement.m_fileSize,
                           steamElement.m_readOffset));
    m_fileIdentity.setText
        ("File Identity: " +
         Miscellaneous.byteArrayAsHexString(steamElement.m_fileIdentity));
    m_fileName.setText("File: " + steamElement.m_displayFileName);
    m_fileSize.setText
        ("Size: " +
         formatSize(steamElement.m_fileSize) +
         " (" +
         niceBytes(steamElement.m_fileSize) +
         ")");

    if(steamElement.m_keyStream == null ||
       steamElement.m_keyStream.length !=
       Cryptography.CIPHER_HASH_KEYS_LENGTH)
        m_keyStreamDigest.setText("Key Stream SHA-256: N/A");
    else
        m_keyStreamDigest.setText
            ("Key Stream SHA-256: " +
             Miscellaneous.
             byteArrayAsHexString(Cryptography.
                                  sha256(steamElement.m_keyStream)));
```

```java
        m_progress.setMax((int) steamElement.m_fileSize);
        m_progress.setProgress((int) steamElement.m_readOffset);

        switch((int) steamElement.m_readInterval)
        {
        case 4:
            m_readInterval.setProgress(0);
            break;
        case 10:
            m_readInterval.setProgress(1);
            break;
        case 20:
            m_readInterval.setProgress(2);
            break;
        case 50:
            m_readInterval.setProgress(3);
            break;
        case 100:
            m_readInterval.setProgress(4);
            break;
        default:
            break;
        }

        m_separator.setVisibility
            (count - 1 == position ? View.GONE : View.VISIBLE);
        m_status.setText("Status: " + steamElement.m_status);

        if(steamElement.m_direction == SteamElement.DOWNLOAD)
            m_transferRate.setText
                ("Receive Rate: " + steamElement.m_transferRate);
        else
            m_transferRate.setText
                ("Transfer Rate: " + steamElement.m_transferRate);

        m_view.setId(m_oid);
    }
}
```

/* SteamElement.java –

```java
** IN NO EVENT SHALL THE AUTHOR BE LIABLE FOR ANY DIRECT, INDIRECT,
** INCIDENTAL, SPECIAL, EXEMPLARY, OR CONSEQUENTIAL DAMAGES (INCLUDING, BUT
** NOT LIMITED TO, PROCUREMENT OF SUBSTITUTE GOODS OR SERVICES; LOSS OF USE,
** DATA, OR PROFITS; OR BUSINESS INTERRUPTION) HOWEVER CAUSED AND ON ANY
** THEORY OF LIABILITY, WHETHER IN CONTRACT, STRICT LIABILITY, OR TORT
** (INCLUDING NEGLIGENCE OR OTHERWISE) ARISING IN ANY WAY OUT OF THE USE OF
** SMOKE, EVEN IF ADVISED OF THE POSSIBILITY OF SUCH DAMAGE.
*/

package org.purple.smoke;

public class SteamElement
{
    public String m_destination = "";
    public String m_displayFileName = "";
    public String m_fileName = "";
    public String m_status = "paused";
    public String m_transferRate = "";
    public byte m_ephemeralPrivateKey[] = null;
    public byte m_ephemeralPublicKey[] = null;
    public byte m_fileDigest[] = null;
    public byte m_fileIdentity[] = null;
    public byte m_keyStream[] = null;
    public int m_oid = -1;
    public int m_someOid = -1;
    public long m_fileSize = 0L;
    public long m_readInterval = 4L; // 4 reads / s
    public long m_readOffset = 0L;
    public short m_direction = DOWNLOAD;
    public final static short DOWNLOAD = 0;
    public final static short UPLOAD = 1;

    public SteamElement()
    {
    }

    public SteamElement(String displayFileName, String fileName)
    {
        m_direction = UPLOAD;
        m_displayFileName = displayFileName;
        m_fileName = fileName;

        if(fileName.lastIndexOf('.') > 0)
            fileName = fileName.substring(0, fileName.lastIndexOf('.'));

        m_fileSize = Miscellaneous.fileSize(fileName);
    }
}
```

/* SteamKeyExchange.java –


```java
package org.purple.smoke;

import android.util.Base64;
import java.nio.charset.StandardCharsets;
import java.security.KeyPair;
import java.security.PrivateKey;
import java.security.PublicKey;
import java.util.ArrayList;
import java.util.Arrays;
import java.util.concurrent.Executors;
import java.util.concurrent.ScheduledExecutorService;
import java.util.concurrent.TimeUnit;
import java.util.concurrent.atomic.AtomicInteger;
import java.util.concurrent.locks.ReentrantReadWriteLock;

public class SteamKeyExchange
{
    private class Pair
    {
        public byte m_ciphertext[] = null;
        public byte m_pki[] = null;

        public Pair(byte ciphertext[], byte pki[])
        {
            m_ciphertext = ciphertext;
            m_pki = pki;
        }
    }

    private ArrayList<Pair> m_pairs = null;
    private AtomicInteger m_lastReadSteamOid = null;
    private ScheduledExecutorService m_parseScheduler = null;
    private ScheduledExecutorService m_readScheduler = null;
```

```java
private final Object m_parseSchedulerMutex = new Object();
private final ReentrantReadWriteLock m_pairsMutex =
    new ReentrantReadWriteLock();
private final static Cryptography s_cryptography =
    Cryptography.getInstance();
private final static Database s_databaseHelper = Database.getInstance();
private final static long KEY_EXCHANGE_LIFETIME = 30000L;
private final static long PARSE_INTERVAL = 50L;
private final static long READ_INTERVAL = 1500L;
private final static long WAIT_TIMEOUT = 10000L; // 10 seconds.

private void shareB(SteamElement steamElement)
{
    /*
    ** Enqueue information if the network is not available.
    */

    if(steamElement == null)
        return;

    PublicKey publicKey = Cryptography.publicKeyFromBytes
        (steamElement.m_ephemeralPublicKey);

    if(publicKey == null)
        return;

    String sipHashId = Miscellaneous.sipHashIdFromDestination
        (steamElement.m_destination);
    byte bytes[] = null;

    bytes = Messages.steamCall
        (s_cryptography,
         steamElement.m_displayFileName,
         sipHashId,
         steamElement.m_fileDigest,
         steamElement.m_fileIdentity,
         Cryptography.pkiEncrypt(publicKey, "", steamElement.m_keyStream),
         Cryptography.MESSAGES_KEY_TYPES[1], // RSA, ignored.
         Messages.STEAM_KEY_EXCHANGE[1],
         steamElement.m_fileSize);

    if(bytes != null)
        Kernel.getInstance().enqueueSteamKeyExchange
            (Messages.bytesToMessageString(bytes), sipHashId);
}

private void steamAorB(byte ciphertext[], byte pki[])
{
    if(ciphertext == null ||
       ciphertext.length == 0 ||
       pki == null ||
       pki.length == 0)
        return;

    byte tag = ciphertext[0];

    ciphertext = Arrays.copyOfRange(ciphertext, 1, ciphertext.length);

    String strings[] = new String(ciphertext).split("\\n");

    if(strings.length !=
       Messages.STEAM_KEY_EXCHANGE_GROUP_TWO_ELEMENT_COUNT)
        return;
```

```java
        String displayFileName = "";
        String fileExtension = "";
        byte ephemeralPublicKey[] = null;
        byte ephemeralPublicKeyType[] = null;
        byte fileDigest[] = null;
        byte fileIdentity[] = null;
        byte publicKeySignature[] = null;
        byte senderPublicEncryptionKeyDigest[] = null;
        int ii = 0;
        long fileSize = 0;

        for(String string : strings)
            switch(ii)
            {
            case 0:
                long timestamp = Miscellaneous.byteArrayToLong
                    (Base64.decode(string.getBytes(), Base64.NO_WRAP));

                if(Math.abs(System.currentTimeMillis() - timestamp) >
                   KEY_EXCHANGE_LIFETIME)
                    return;

                ii += 1;
                break;
            case 1:
                ephemeralPublicKey = Base64.decode
                    (string.getBytes(), Base64.NO_WRAP);
                ii += 1;
                break;
            case 2:
                ephemeralPublicKeyType = Base64.decode
                    (string.getBytes(), Base64.NO_WRAP);
                ii += 1;
                break;
            case 3:
                fileDigest = Base64.decode(string.getBytes(), Base64.NO_WRAP);
                ii += 1;
                break;
            case 4:
                fileIdentity = Base64.decode(string.getBytes(), Base64.NO_WRAP);

                /*
                ** Is the Steam already registered?
                ** If so, return the generated private key pair.
                */

                if(tag == Messages.STEAM_KEY_EXCHANGE[0]) // A
                {
                    int oid = s_databaseHelper.steamOidFromFileIdentity
                        (s_cryptography, fileIdentity);

                    if(oid > -1)
                    {
                        SteamElement steamElement = s_databaseHelper.readSteam
                            (s_cryptography, -1, oid - 1);

                        if(steamElement != null)
                        {
                            shareB(steamElement);
                            return;
                        }
                    }
```

```java
            }

        ii += 1;
        break;
case 5:
    displayFileName = new String
        (Base64.decode(string.getBytes(), Base64.NO_WRAP),
         StandardCharsets.UTF_8);

    if(displayFileName.indexOf('.') == 0)
        fileExtension = displayFileName.substring
            (displayFileName.indexOf('.'));

    ii += 1;
    break;
case 6:
    fileSize = Miscellaneous.byteArrayToLong
        (Base64.decode(string.getBytes(), Base64.NO_WRAP));

    if(fileSize < 0)
        return;

    ii += 1;
    break;
case 7:
    senderPublicEncryptionKeyDigest = Base64.decode
        (string.getBytes(), Base64.NO_WRAP);
    ii += 1;
    break;
case 8:
    PublicKey signatureKey = s_databaseHelper.signatureKeyForDigest
        (s_cryptography, senderPublicEncryptionKeyDigest);

    if(signatureKey == null)
        return;

    publicKeySignature = Base64.decode
        (string.getBytes(), Base64.NO_WRAP);

    if(!Cryptography.
        verifySignature(signatureKey,
                        publicKeySignature,
                        Miscellaneous.
                        joinByteArrays
                        (pki,
                         new byte[] {tag},
                         strings[0].getBytes(), // Timestamp
                         "\n".getBytes(),
                         strings[1].getBytes(), /*
                                                ** Ephemeral
                                                ** Public Key
                                                */
                         "\n".getBytes(),
                         strings[2].getBytes(), /*
                                                ** Ephemeral
                                                ** Public Key Type
                                                */
                         "\n".getBytes(),
                         strings[3].getBytes(), // File Digest
                         "\n".getBytes(),
                         strings[4].getBytes(), // File Identity
                         "\n".getBytes(),
                         strings[5].getBytes(), // File Name
```

```java
                            "\n".getBytes(),
                            strings[6].getBytes(), // File Size
                            "\n".getBytes(),
                            strings[7].getBytes(), /*
                                            ** Sender's Public
                                            ** Encryption Key
                                            ** Digest
                                            */
                            "\n".getBytes(),
                            s_cryptography.
                            chatEncryptionPublicKeyDigest())))
            return;

        ii += 1;
        break;
    default:
        break;
    }

    if(tag == Messages.STEAM_KEY_EXCHANGE[0])
    {
        /*
        ** Record the new Steam.
        */

        SteamElement steamElement = new SteamElement();
        String array[] = s_databaseHelper.nameSipHashIdFromDigest
            (s_cryptography, senderPublicEncryptionKeyDigest);

        if(array[1].isEmpty())
            steamElement.m_destination = array[0];
        else
            steamElement.m_destination = array[0] + " (" + array[1] + ")";

        if(displayFileName.indexOf('.') == 0)
            steamElement.m_displayFileName = "Smoke_Steam_" +
                Miscellaneous.byteArrayAsHexString(fileIdentity) +
                fileExtension;
        else
            steamElement.m_displayFileName =
                "Smoke_Steam_" + displayFileName;

        steamElement.m_ephemeralPublicKey = ephemeralPublicKey;
        steamElement.m_fileDigest = fileDigest;
        steamElement.m_fileIdentity = fileIdentity;
        steamElement.m_fileName = steamElement.m_displayFileName;
        steamElement.m_fileSize = fileSize;
        steamElement.m_keyStream = Miscellaneous.joinByteArrays
            (Cryptography.aes256KeyBytes(), Cryptography.sha512KeyBytes());
        steamElement.m_readInterval = 0L;
        steamElement.m_status = "created private-key pair";
        s_databaseHelper.writeSteam(s_cryptography, steamElement);

        /*
        ** Transfer the new credentials.
        */

        shareB(steamElement);
    }
    else
    {
        SteamElement steamElement = null;
        int oid = s_databaseHelper.steamOidFromFileIdentity
```

```java
                    (s_cryptography, fileIdentity);

            steamElement = s_databaseHelper.readSteam
                (s_cryptography, -1, oid - 1);

            if(steamElement == null)
                return;

            PrivateKey privateKey = Cryptography.privateKeyFromBytes
                (steamElement.m_ephemeralPrivateKey);

            if(privateKey == null)
                /*
                ** Something is strange!
                */

                return;

            byte bytes[] = Cryptography.pkiDecrypt
                (privateKey, ephemeralPublicKey);

            if(bytes == null)
                return;

            /*
            ** Erase the ephemeral keys.
            */

            s_databaseHelper.writeSteamKeys
                (s_cryptography, bytes, null, null, oid);
            s_databaseHelper.writeSteamStatus
                (s_cryptography, "received private-key pair", "", oid);
        }
    }

    public SteamKeyExchange()
    {
        m_lastReadSteamOid = new AtomicInteger(-1);
        m_pairs = new ArrayList<> ();
        m_parseScheduler = Executors.newSingleThreadScheduledExecutor();
        m_parseScheduler.scheduleAtFixedRate(new Runnable()
        {
            @Override
            public void run()
            {
                try
                {
                    Pair pair = null;

                    m_pairsMutex.writeLock().lock();

                    try
                    {
                        if(!m_pairs.isEmpty())
                            pair = m_pairs.remove(m_pairs.size() - 1);
                    }
                    catch(Exception exception)
                    {
                    }
                    finally
                    {
                        m_pairsMutex.writeLock().unlock();
                    }
```

```java
                    if(pair == null)
                        synchronized(m_parseSchedulerMutex)
                        {
                            try
                            {
                                m_parseSchedulerMutex.wait(WAIT_TIMEOUT);
                            }
                            catch(Exception exception)
                            {
                            }
                        }

                    if(pair != null)
                        if(pair.m_ciphertext[0] ==
Messages.STEAM_KEY_EXCHANGE[0] ||
                           pair.m_ciphertext[0] ==
Messages.STEAM_KEY_EXCHANGE[1])
                            steamAorB(pair.m_ciphertext, pair.m_pki);
                }
                catch(Exception exception)
                {
                }
            }
        }, 1500L, PARSE_INTERVAL, TimeUnit.MILLISECONDS);
        m_readScheduler = Executors.newSingleThreadScheduledExecutor();
        m_readScheduler.scheduleAtFixedRate(new Runnable()
        {
            @Override
            public void run()
            {
                try
                {
                    if(!State.getInstance().isAuthenticated())
                        return;

                    /*
                    ** Discover Steam instances which have not established
                    ** key pairs.
                    */

                    SteamElement steamElement = s_databaseHelper.readSteam
                        (s_cryptography, -1, m_lastReadSteamOid.get());

                    if(steamElement == null ||
                       steamElement.m_destination.equals(Steam.OTHER) ||
                       steamElement.m_direction == SteamElement.DOWNLOAD ||
                       steamElement.m_fileSize == 0)
                    {
                        if(steamElement != null)
                            m_lastReadSteamOid.set(steamElement.m_someOid);
                        else
                            m_lastReadSteamOid.set(-1);

                        return;
                    }

                    if(steamElement.m_keyStream != null &&
                       steamElement.m_keyStream.length == Cryptography.
                       CIPHER_HASH_KEYS_LENGTH)
                    {
                        /*
                        ** Keys were exchanged.
```

```
            */

            m_lastReadSteamOid.set(steamElement.m_someOid);
            return;
        }

        KeyPair keyPair = null;

        if(steamElement.m_ephemeralPrivateKey == null ||
           steamElement.m_ephemeralPrivateKey.length == 0 ||
           steamElement.m_ephemeralPublicKey == null ||
           steamElement.m_ephemeralPublicKey.length == 0)
        {
            /*
            ** Create an RSA key pair.
            */

            keyPair = Cryptography.generatePrivatePublicKeyPair
                ("RSA",
                 Cryptography.STEAM_KEY_EXCHANGE_RSA_KEY_SIZE,
                 0);

            if(keyPair == null)
                return;

            /*
            ** Record the key pair.
            */

            if(!s_databaseHelper.
               writeSteamKeys(s_cryptography,
                              keyPair,
                              null,
                              steamElement.m_someOid))
                return;
        }
        else if(Kernel.getInstance().isNetworkConnected())
            /*
            ** Do not enqueue key information if the network
            ** is not available.
            */

            keyPair = Cryptography.generatePrivatePublicKeyPair
                ("RSA",
                 steamElement.m_ephemeralPrivateKey,
                 steamElement.m_ephemeralPublicKey);

        /*
        ** Do not enqueue key information if the network is not
        ** available.
        */

        if(Kernel.getInstance().isNetworkConnected() &&
           keyPair != null)
        {
            /*
            ** Share the key pair.
            */

            String sipHashId = Miscellaneous.
                sipHashIdFromDestination
                (steamElement.m_destination);
            byte bytes[] = null;
```

```java
                    bytes = Messages.steamCall
                        (s_cryptography,
                         steamElement.m_displayFileName,
                         sipHashId,
                         steamElement.m_fileDigest,
                         steamElement.m_fileIdentity,
                         keyPair.getPublic().getEncoded(),
                         Cryptography.MESSAGES_KEY_TYPES[1],
                         Messages.STEAM_KEY_EXCHANGE[0],
                         steamElement.m_fileSize);

                    if(bytes != null)
                        Kernel.getInstance().enqueueSteamKeyExchange
                            (Messages.bytesToMessageString(bytes),
                             sipHashId);
                    }

                    /*
                    ** Next element!
                    */

                    m_lastReadSteamOid.set(steamElement.m_someOid);
                }
                catch(Exception exception)
                {
                }
            }
        }, 1500L, READ_INTERVAL, TimeUnit.MILLISECONDS);
    }

    public void append(byte ciphertext[], byte pki[])
    {
        if(ciphertext == null ||
           ciphertext.length == 0 ||
           pki == null ||
           pki.length == 0)
            return;

        try
        {
            m_pairsMutex.writeLock().lock();

            try
            {
                m_pairs.add(new Pair(ciphertext, pki));
            }
            catch(Exception exception)
            {
            }
            finally
            {
                m_pairsMutex.writeLock().unlock();
            }

            synchronized(m_parseSchedulerMutex)
            {
                m_parseSchedulerMutex.notify();
            }
        }
        catch(Exception exception)
        {
        }
```

```java
    }
}



/* SteamReader.java –
```



```java
package org.purple.smoke;

import android.content.res.AssetFileDescriptor;
import android.net.Uri;
import java.io.FileInputStream;
import java.util.concurrent.Executors;
import java.util.concurrent.ScheduledExecutorService;
import java.util.concurrent.TimeUnit;
import java.util.concurrent.atomic.AtomicBoolean;
import java.util.concurrent.atomic.AtomicLong;

public abstract class SteamReader
{
    protected AssetFileDescriptor m_assetFileDescriptor = null;
    protected AtomicBoolean m_canceled = null;
    protected AtomicBoolean m_completed = null;
    protected AtomicLong m_rate = null;
    protected AtomicLong m_readOffset = null;
    protected AtomicLong m_time0 = null;
    protected FileInputStream m_fileInputStream = null;
    protected Object m_fileInputStreamMutex = new Object();
    protected ScheduledExecutorService m_reader = null;
    protected final static Cryptography s_cryptography =
        Cryptography.getInstance();
    protected final static Database s_databaseHelper = Database.getInstance();
    protected int m_oid = -1;

    protected String prettyRate()
```

```java
    {
        return Miscellaneous.formattedDigitalInformation
            (String.valueOf(m_rate.get())) + " / s";
    }

    protected void cancelReader()
    {
        if(m_reader != null)
        {
            try
            {
                m_reader.shutdown();
            }
            catch(Exception exception)
            {
            }

            try
            {
                if(!m_reader.awaitTermination(60L, TimeUnit.SECONDS))
                    m_reader.shutdownNow();
            }
            catch(Exception exception)
            {
            }
            finally
            {
                m_reader = null;
            }
        }
    }

    public SteamReader(String fileName, int oid, long readOffset)
    {
        try
        {
            if(fileName.lastIndexOf('.') > 0)
                fileName = fileName.substring(0, fileName.lastIndexOf('.'));

            Uri uri = Uri.parse(fileName);

            m_assetFileDescriptor = Smoke.getApplication().
                getContentResolver().openAssetFileDescriptor(uri, "r");
            m_fileInputStream = m_assetFileDescriptor.createInputStream();
            m_fileInputStream.getChannel().position(readOffset);
        }
        catch(Exception exception1)
        {
            try
            {
                if(m_assetFileDescriptor != null)
                    m_assetFileDescriptor.close();
            }
            catch(Exception exception2)
            {
            }
            finally
            {
                m_assetFileDescriptor = null;
                m_fileInputStream = null;
            }
        }
```

```java
        m_canceled = new AtomicBoolean(false);
        m_completed = new AtomicBoolean(false);
        m_oid = oid;
        m_rate = new AtomicLong(0L);
        m_readOffset = new AtomicLong(readOffset);
        m_time0 = new AtomicLong(System.currentTimeMillis());
    }

    public abstract void setReadInterval(int readInterval);

    public boolean completed()
    {
        return m_completed.get();
    }

    public int getOid()
    {
        return m_oid;
    }

    public void delete()
    {
        try
        {
            if(m_assetFileDescriptor != null)
                m_assetFileDescriptor.close();
        }
        catch(Exception exception)
        {
        }
        finally
        {
            m_assetFileDescriptor = null;
        }

        m_canceled.set(true);
        m_completed.set(false);
        m_rate.set(0L);
        m_readOffset.set(0L);
        cancelReader();
    }
}
```

/* SteamReaderFull.java –

```java
** SMOKE IS PROVIDED BY THE AUTHOR ``AS IS'' AND ANY EXPRESS OR
** IMPLIED WARRANTIES, INCLUDING, BUT NOT LIMITED TO, THE IMPLIED WARRANTIES
** OF MERCHANTABILITY AND FITNESS FOR A PARTICULAR PURPOSE ARE DISCLAIMED.
** IN NO EVENT SHALL THE AUTHOR BE LIABLE FOR ANY DIRECT, INDIRECT,
** INCIDENTAL, SPECIAL, EXEMPLARY, OR CONSEQUENTIAL DAMAGES (INCLUDING, BUT
** NOT LIMITED TO, PROCUREMENT OF SUBSTITUTE GOODS OR SERVICES; LOSS OF USE,
** DATA, OR PROFITS; OR BUSINESS INTERRUPTION) HOWEVER CAUSED AND ON ANY
** THEORY OF LIABILITY, WHETHER IN CONTRACT, STRICT LIABILITY, OR TORT
** (INCLUDING NEGLIGENCE OR OTHERWISE) ARISING IN ANY WAY OUT OF THE USE OF
** SMOKE, EVEN IF ADVISED OF THE POSSIBILITY OF SUCH DAMAGE.
*/

package org.purple.smoke;

import java.util.Arrays;
import java.util.concurrent.Executors;
import java.util.concurrent.ScheduledExecutorService;
import java.util.concurrent.TimeUnit;
import java.util.concurrent.atomic.AtomicBoolean;
import java.util.concurrent.atomic.AtomicInteger;
import java.util.concurrent.atomic.AtomicLong;

public class SteamReaderFull extends SteamReader
{
    private AtomicBoolean m_read = null; // Perform another read.
    private AtomicInteger m_stalled = null;
    private AtomicLong m_fileSize = null;
    private AtomicLong m_lastResponse = null;
    private AtomicLong m_previousOffset = null;
    private AtomicLong m_rc = null;
    private Object m_waitMutex = new Object();
    private String m_sipHashId = "";
    private byte m_fileIdentity[] = null;
    private final static int PACKET_SIZE = 32768;
    private final static long READ_INTERVAL = 250L; // 250 milliseconds.
    private final static long RESPONSE_WINDOW = 7500L; // 7.5 seconds.

    private void computeRate()
    {
        long seconds = Math.abs
            (System.currentTimeMillis() / 1000L - m_time0.get());

        if(seconds >= 1L)
        {
            long rate = m_rate.get();

            m_rate.set
                ((long) ((double) (m_readOffset.get() -
                            m_previousOffset.get()) / (double) seconds));

            if(m_rate.get() > 0L)
                m_stalled.set(0);
            else if(m_stalled.getAndIncrement() <= 5)
                m_rate.set(rate);

            m_previousOffset.set(m_readOffset.get());
            m_time0.set(System.currentTimeMillis() / 1000L);
        }
    }

    private void prepareReader()
    {
        if(m_reader == null)
```

```java
        {
    m_reader = Executors.newSingleThreadScheduledExecutor();
    m_reader.scheduleAtFixedRate(new Runnable()
    {
        private byte m_keyStream[] = null;

        @Override
        public void run()
        {
            try
            {
                switch(s_databaseHelper.
                        steamStatus(m_oid).toLowerCase().trim())
                {
                case "":
                    /*
                    ** Deleted.
                    */

                    return;
                case "completed":
                    m_completed.set(true);
                    return;
                case "deleted":
                    return;
                case "paused":
                    s_databaseHelper.writeSteamStatus
                        (s_cryptography, "", Miscellaneous.RATE, m_oid);
                    return;
                case "received private-key pair":
                    s_databaseHelper.writeSteamStatus
                        (s_cryptography, "transferring", "", m_oid, 0);
                    break;
                case "rewind":
                    rewind();
                    s_databaseHelper.writeSteamStatus
                        (s_cryptography, "paused", "", m_oid, 0);
                    return;
                case "rewind & resume":
                    rewind();
                    s_databaseHelper.writeSteamStatus
                        (s_cryptography, "transferring", "", m_oid, 0);
                    break;
                default:
                    if(m_fileSize.get() == m_readOffset.get())
                    {
                        m_completed.set(true);
                        s_databaseHelper.writeSteamStatus
                            (s_cryptography,
                             "completed",
                             "",
                             m_oid,
                             m_readOffset.get());
                    }

                    break;
                }

                computeRate();
                saveReadOffset();

                if(m_canceled.get() || m_completed.get())
                    return;
```

```java
        synchronized(m_fileInputStreamMutex)
        {
            if(m_fileInputStream == null)
                return;
        }

        synchronized(m_waitMutex)
        {
            m_waitMutex.wait(RESPONSE_WINDOW);
        }

        if(!m_read.get())
        {
            if(System.currentTimeMillis() -
                m_lastResponse.get() <= RESPONSE_WINDOW ||
                m_canceled.get() ||
                m_completed.get())
                /*
                ** Completed or missing response.
                */

                return;
            else
                m_lastResponse.set(System.currentTimeMillis());
        }

        if(m_keyStream == null)
        {
            m_keyStream = s_databaseHelper.readSteam
                (s_cryptography, -1, m_oid - 1).m_keyStream;

            if(m_keyStream == null)
                return;
        }

        byte bytes[] = new byte[PACKET_SIZE];
        int offset = 0;

        synchronized(m_fileInputStreamMutex)
        {
            m_fileInputStream.getChannel().position
                (m_readOffset.get());
            offset = m_fileInputStream.read(bytes);
        }

        if(offset == -1)
        {
            /*
            ** A response is required, do not set m_completed.
            */

            m_read.set(false);
            return;
        }
        else
            m_rc.set((long) offset);

        m_read.set(false);

        /*
        ** Send a Steam packet.
        */
```

```java
                        bytes = Messages.steamShare
                            (s_cryptography,
                             m_sipHashId,
                             m_fileIdentity,
                             m_keyStream,
                             Arrays.copyOfRange(bytes, 0, offset),
                             Messages.STEAM_SHARE[0],
                             m_readOffset.get());

                        if(bytes != null)
                            Kernel.getInstance().
                                sendSteam(false,
                                          Messages.bytesToMessageString(bytes).
                                          getBytes());
                    }
                    catch(Exception exception)
                    {
                    }
                }
            }, 1500L, READ_INTERVAL, TimeUnit.MILLISECONDS);
        }
    }

    private void rewind()
    {
        m_completed.set(false);

        try
        {
            synchronized(m_fileInputStreamMutex)
            {
                if(m_fileInputStream != null)
                    m_fileInputStream.getChannel().position(0);
            }
        }
        catch(Exception exception)
        {
        }

        m_lastResponse.set(0L);
        m_previousOffset.set(0L);
        m_rc.set(0L);
        m_read.set(true);
        m_readOffset.set(0L);
        saveReadOffset();

        synchronized(m_waitMutex)
        {
            m_waitMutex.notify();
        }
    }

    private void saveReadOffset()
    {
        s_databaseHelper.writeSteamStatus
            (s_cryptography, "", prettyRate(), m_oid, m_readOffset.get());
    }

    public SteamReaderFull(String destination,
                           String fileName,
                           byte fileIdentity[],
                           int oid,
```

```java
                              long fileSize,
                              long readOffset)
    {
        super(fileName, oid, readOffset);
        m_fileIdentity = fileIdentity;
        m_fileSize = new AtomicLong(fileSize);
        m_lastResponse = new AtomicLong(System.currentTimeMillis());
        m_previousOffset = new AtomicLong(readOffset);
        m_rc = new AtomicLong(0L);
        m_read = new AtomicBoolean(true);
        m_sipHashId = Miscellaneous.sipHashIdFromDestination(destination);
        m_stalled = new AtomicInteger(0);
        prepareReader();
    }

    public byte[] fileIdentity()
    {
        return m_fileIdentity;
    }

    public void delete()
    {
        super.delete();
        m_lastResponse.set(0L);
        m_previousOffset.set(0L);
        m_rc.set(0L);
        m_read.set(false);

        synchronized(m_waitMutex)
        {
            m_waitMutex.notify();
        }
    }

    public void setAcknowledgedOffset(long readOffset)
    {
        boolean read = false;

        if(m_readOffset.get() == readOffset)
        {
            m_lastResponse.set(System.currentTimeMillis());
            m_readOffset.addAndGet(m_rc.get());
            read = true;
            saveReadOffset();
        }

        if(m_fileSize.get() == m_readOffset.get())
        {
            m_completed.set(true);
            read = false;
            s_databaseHelper.writeSteamStatus
                (s_cryptography, "completed", "", m_oid, m_readOffset.get());
        }

        m_read.set(read);

        synchronized(m_waitMutex)
        {
            m_waitMutex.notify();
        }
    }

    public void setReadInterval(int readInterval)
```

```java
        {
        }
}




/* SteamReaderSimple.java –
https://github.com/textbrowser/smoke/blob/master/Smoke/app/src/main/java/org/p
urple/smoke/SteamReaderSimple.java
** Copyright (c) Alexis Megas.
** All rights reserved.
**
** Redistribution and use in source and binary forms, with or without
** modification, are permitted provided that the following conditions
** are met:
** 1. Redistributions of source code must retain the above copyright
**    notice, this list of conditions and the following disclaimer.
** 2. Redistributions in binary form must reproduce the above copyright
**    notice, this list of conditions and the following disclaimer in the
**    documentation and/or other materials provided with the distribution.
** 3. The name of the author may not be used to endorse or promote products
**    derived from Smoke without specific prior written permission.
**
** SMOKE IS PROVIDED BY THE AUTHOR ``AS IS'' AND ANY EXPRESS OR
** IMPLIED WARRANTIES, INCLUDING, BUT NOT LIMITED TO, THE IMPLIED WARRANTIES
** OF MERCHANTABILITY AND FITNESS FOR A PARTICULAR PURPOSE ARE DISCLAIMED.
** IN NO EVENT SHALL THE AUTHOR BE LIABLE FOR ANY DIRECT, INDIRECT,
** INCIDENTAL, SPECIAL, EXEMPLARY, OR CONSEQUENTIAL DAMAGES (INCLUDING, BUT
** NOT LIMITED TO, PROCUREMENT OF SUBSTITUTE GOODS OR SERVICES; LOSS OF USE,
** DATA, OR PROFITS; OR BUSINESS INTERRUPTION) HOWEVER CAUSED AND ON ANY
** THEORY OF LIABILITY, WHETHER IN CONTRACT, STRICT LIABILITY, OR TORT
** (INCLUDING NEGLIGENCE OR OTHERWISE) ARISING IN ANY WAY OUT OF THE USE OF
** SMOKE, EVEN IF ADVISED OF THE POSSIBILITY OF SUCH DAMAGE.
*/

package org.purple.smoke;

import java.util.Arrays;
import java.util.concurrent.Executors;
import java.util.concurrent.ScheduledExecutorService;
import java.util.concurrent.TimeUnit;
import java.util.concurrent.atomic.AtomicLong;

public class SteamReaderSimple extends SteamReader
{
    /*
    ** Anywhere transfers.
    */

    private AtomicLong m_lastBytesSent = null;
    private AtomicLong m_readInterval = null;
    private final static int PACKET_SIZE = 8192;

    private void computeRate(long bytesSent)
    {
        long seconds = Math.abs
            (System.currentTimeMillis() - m_time0.get()) / 1000L;

        m_lastBytesSent.getAndAdd(bytesSent);

        if(seconds >= 1L)
        {
```

```java
        m_rate.set
            ((long) ((double) (m_lastBytesSent.get()) / (double) seconds));
        m_lastBytesSent.set(0L);
        m_time0.set(System.currentTimeMillis());
    }
}

private void prepareReader()
{
    if(m_reader == null)
    {
        m_reader = Executors.newSingleThreadScheduledExecutor();
        m_reader.scheduleAtFixedRate(new Runnable()
        {
            @Override
            public void run()
            {
                try
                {
                    switch(s_databaseHelper.
                            steamStatus(m_oid).toLowerCase().trim())
                    {
                    case "":
                        /*
                        ** Deleted.
                        */

                        return;
                    case "completed":
                        m_completed.set(true);
                        return;
                    case "deleted":
                        return;
                    case "paused":
                        s_databaseHelper.writeSteamStatus
                            (s_cryptography, "", Miscellaneous.RATE, m_oid);
                        return;
                    case "rewind":
                        rewind();
                        s_databaseHelper.writeSteamStatus
                            (s_cryptography, "paused", "", m_oid, 0);
                        return;
                    case "rewind & resume":
                        rewind();
                        s_databaseHelper.writeSteamStatus
                            (s_cryptography, "transferring", "", m_oid, 0);
                        break;
                    default:
                        break;
                    }

                    if(Kernel.getInstance().nextSimpleSteamOid() != m_oid ||
                        m_canceled.get())
                        return;

                    synchronized(m_fileInputStreamMutex)
                    {
                        if(m_fileInputStream == null)
                            return;

                        m_fileInputStream.getChannel().position
                            (m_readOffset.get());
                    }
```

```java
                    byte bytes[] = new byte[PACKET_SIZE];
                    int offset = -1;

                    synchronized(m_fileInputStreamMutex)
                    {
                        offset = m_fileInputStream.read(bytes);
                    }

                    if(offset == -1)
                    {
                        /*
                        ** Completed!
                        */

                        m_completed.set(true);
                        s_databaseHelper.writeSteamStatus
                            (s_cryptography,
                             "completed",
                             "",
                             m_oid,
                             m_readOffset.get());
                        return;
                    }

                    /*
                    ** Send raw bytes.
                    */

                    int sent = Kernel.getInstance().sendSteam
                        (true, Arrays.copyOfRange(bytes, 0, offset));

                    computeRate(sent);
                    m_readOffset.addAndGet((long) sent);
                    s_databaseHelper.writeSteamStatus
                        (s_cryptography,
                         "",
                         prettyRate(),
                         m_oid,
                         m_readOffset.get());
                }
                catch(Exception exception)
                {
                }
                finally
                {
                }
            }
        }, 1500L, m_readInterval.get(), TimeUnit.MILLISECONDS);
    }
}

private void rewind()
{
    m_completed.set(false);

    try
    {
        synchronized(m_fileInputStreamMutex)
        {
            if(m_fileInputStream != null)
                m_fileInputStream.getChannel().position(0);
        }
```

```java
            }
        catch(Exception exception)
            {
            }

        m_lastBytesSent.set(0L);
        m_readOffset.set(0L);
        }

    public SteamReaderSimple(String fileName,
                             int oid,
                             long readInterval,
                             long readOffset)
        {
        super(fileName, oid, readOffset);
        m_lastBytesSent = new AtomicLong(0L);
        m_readInterval = new AtomicLong(1000L / Math.max(4L, readInterval));
        prepareReader();
        }

    public void delete()
        {
        super.delete();
        m_lastBytesSent.set(0L);
        m_time0.set(0L);
        }

    public void setReadInterval(int interval)
        {
        if(1000L / (long) interval == m_readInterval.get())
            return;

        switch(interval)
            {
            case 4:
            case 10:
            case 20:
            case 50:
            case 100:
                m_readInterval.set(1000L / (long) interval);
                break;
            default:
                m_readInterval.set(250L);
                break;
            }

        m_canceled.set(true);
        cancelReader();
        m_canceled.set(false);
        prepareReader();
        }
    }
```

/* SteamWriter.java –


```java
package org.purple.smoke;

import android.os.Environment;
import java.io.File;
import java.io.RandomAccessFile;
import java.util.Hashtable;
import java.util.Iterator;
import java.util.concurrent.Executors;
import java.util.concurrent.ScheduledExecutorService;
import java.util.concurrent.TimeUnit;
import java.util.concurrent.locks.ReentrantReadWriteLock;

public class SteamWriter
{
    private class FileInformation
    {
        public byte m_fileIdentity[] = null;
        public int m_oid = -1;
        public long m_lastStatusTimestamp = 0L;
        public long m_offset = 0L;
        public long m_previousOffset = 0L;
        public long m_rate = 0L;
        public long m_time0 = 0L;
        public short m_stalled = 0;

        public FileInformation(byte fileIdentity[], int oid, long offset)
        {
            m_fileIdentity = fileIdentity;
            m_lastStatusTimestamp = System.currentTimeMillis();
            m_offset = offset;
            m_oid = oid;
            m_time0 = System.currentTimeMillis();
        }
```

```java
        public String prettyRate()
        {
            return Miscellaneous.formattedDigitalInformation
                (String.valueOf(m_rate)) + " / s";
        }

        public void computeRate()
        {
            long seconds = Math.abs
                (System.currentTimeMillis() / 1000L - m_time0);

            if(seconds >= 1L)
            {
                long rate = m_rate;

                m_rate = (long) ((double) (m_offset - m_previousOffset) /
                                (double) seconds);

                if(m_rate > 0L)
                    m_stalled = 0;
                else if(m_stalled++ <= 5)
                    m_rate = rate;

                m_previousOffset = m_offset;
                m_time0 = System.currentTimeMillis() / 1000L;
            }
        }
    }

    private Hashtable<Integer, FileInformation> m_files;
    private ScheduledExecutorService m_scheduler = null;
    private final Object m_schedulerMutex = new Object();
    private final ReentrantReadWriteLock m_filesMutex =
        new ReentrantReadWriteLock();
    private final static Cryptography s_cryptography =
        Cryptography.getInstance();
    private final static Database s_databaseHelper = Database.getInstance();
    private final static long FILE_INFORMATION_LIFETIME = 15000L; // 15
Seconds
    private final static long SCHEDULER_INTERVAL = 1500L;

    private void removeFileInformation(int oid)
    {
        m_filesMutex.writeLock().lock();

        try
        {
            m_files.remove(oid);
        }
        catch(Exception exception)
        {
        }
        finally
        {
            m_filesMutex.writeLock().unlock();
        }
    }

    public SteamWriter()
    {
        m_files = new Hashtable<> ();
        m_scheduler = Executors.newSingleThreadScheduledExecutor();
```

```java
    m_scheduler.scheduleAtFixedRate(new Runnable()
    {
        @Override
        public void run()
        {
            try
            {
                boolean empty = false;

                m_filesMutex.readLock().lock();

                try
                {
                    empty = m_files.isEmpty();
                }
                catch(Exception exception)
                {
                }
                finally
                {
                    m_filesMutex.readLock().unlock();
                }

                if(empty)
                    synchronized(m_schedulerMutex)
                    {
                        try
                        {
                            m_schedulerMutex.wait(SCHEDULER_INTERVAL);
                        }
                        catch(Exception exception)
                        {
                        }
                    }

                m_filesMutex.writeLock().lock();

                try
                {
                    Iterator<Hashtable.Entry<Integer, FileInformation> >
                        it = m_files.entrySet().iterator();

                    while(it.hasNext())
                    {
                        Hashtable.Entry<Integer, FileInformation> entry =
                            it.next();

                        if(entry.getValue() == null)
                         {
                             it.remove();
                             continue;
                         }

                        int oid = s_databaseHelper.steamOidFromFileIdentity
                            (s_cryptography,
                             entry.getValue().m_fileIdentity);

                        if(Math.
                            abs(System.currentTimeMillis() -
                                entry.getValue().m_lastStatusTimestamp) >
                            FILE_INFORMATION_LIFETIME ||
                            oid == -1)
                        {
```

```java
                            it.remove();
                            continue;
                          }

                        entry.getValue().computeRate();
                        s_databaseHelper.writeSteamStatus
                            (s_cryptography,
                             "receiving",
                             entry.getValue().prettyRate(),
                             entry.getValue().m_oid,
                             entry.getValue().m_offset);
                      }
                  }
                catch(Exception exception)
                {
                }
                finally
                {
                    m_filesMutex.writeLock().unlock();
                }
            }
        catch(Exception exception)
        {
        }
      }
    }, 1500L, SCHEDULER_INTERVAL, TimeUnit.MILLISECONDS);
}

public boolean write(byte fileIdentity[], byte packet[], long offset)
{
    if(fileIdentity == null ||
       fileIdentity.length == 0 ||
       offset < 0 ||
       packet == null ||
       packet.length == 0)
        return false;

    int oid = s_databaseHelper.steamOidFromFileIdentity
        (s_cryptography, fileIdentity);

    if(oid == -1)
        return false;

    SteamElement steamElement = s_databaseHelper.readSteam
        (s_cryptography, -1, oid - 1);

    if(steamElement == null)
        return false;

    RandomAccessFile randomAccessFile = null;

    try
    {
        File file = new File
            (Environment.
             getExternalStoragePublicDirectory(Environment.
                                               DIRECTORY_DOWNLOADS),
             steamElement.m_fileName);

        if(!file.exists())
            file.createNewFile();

        randomAccessFile = new RandomAccessFile(file, "rwd");
```

```java
        randomAccessFile.seek(offset);
        randomAccessFile.write(packet);

    if(offset == 0)
        /*
        ** Erase the ephemeral key.
        */

        s_databaseHelper.writeEphemeralSteamKeys
            (s_cryptography, null, null, oid);

    if(offset + packet.length == steamElement.m_fileSize)
    {
        removeFileInformation(oid);
        s_databaseHelper.writeSteamStatus
            (s_cryptography,
             "completed",
             "",
             oid,
             offset + packet.length);
        return true;
    }

    m_filesMutex.writeLock().lock();

    try
    {
        FileInformation fileInformation = m_files.get(oid);

        if(fileInformation == null)
            fileInformation = new FileInformation
                (fileIdentity, oid, offset + packet.length);
        else
        {
            fileInformation.m_lastStatusTimestamp =
                System.currentTimeMillis();
            fileInformation.m_offset = offset + packet.length;
        }

        m_files.put(oid, fileInformation);
    }
    catch(Exception exception)
    {
    }
    finally
    {
        m_filesMutex.writeLock().unlock();
    }

    synchronized(m_schedulerMutex)
    {
        m_schedulerMutex.notify();
    }
    }
catch(Exception exception)
{
    return false;
}
finally
{
    try
    {
        if(randomAccessFile != null)
```

```java
                    randomAccessFile.close();
            }
         catch(Exception exception)
            {
            }
      }

      return true;
   }
}
```

/* TcpNeighbor.java –


```java
package org.purple.smoke;

import java.net.InetSocketAddress;
import java.net.Proxy;
import java.net.Socket;
import java.util.concurrent.TimeUnit;

public class TcpNeighbor extends Neighbor
{
    private InetSocketAddress m_proxyInetSocketAddress = null;
    private Socket m_socket = null;
    private String m_proxyIpAddress = "";
    private String m_proxyType = "";
    private final static int CONNECTION_TIMEOUT = 10000; // 10 seconds.
    private int m_proxyPort = -1;

    protected String getLocalIp()
    {
        try
        {
```

```java
            if(m_socket != null && m_socket.getLocalAddress() != null)
                return m_socket.getLocalAddress().getHostAddress();
        }
        catch(Exception exception)
        {
        }

        if(m_version.equals("IPv4"))
            return "0.0.0.0";
        else
            return "::";
    }

    protected String getSessionCipher()
    {
        return "";
    }

    protected boolean connected()
    {
        try
        {
            return isNetworkConnected() &&
                m_socket != null &&
                !m_socket.isClosed();
        }
        catch(Exception exception)
        {
        }

        return false;
    }

    protected int getLocalPort()
    {
        try
        {
            if(m_socket != null && !m_socket.isClosed())
                return m_socket.getLocalPort();
        }
        catch(Exception exception)
        {
        }

        return 0;
    }

    protected int send(String message)
    {
        if(!connected() || message == null || message.length() == 0)
            return 0;
        else
            return send(message.getBytes());
    }

    protected int send(byte bytes[])
    {
        int sent = 0;

        if(bytes == null || bytes.length == 0 || !connected())
            return sent;

        try
```

```java
        {
            if(m_socket == null || m_socket.getOutputStream() == null)
                return sent;
            else
                m_socket.getOutputStream().write(bytes);

            Kernel.writeCongestionDigest(bytes);
            m_bytesWritten.getAndAdd(bytes.length);
            sent += bytes.length;
        }
        catch(Exception exception)
        {
            setError("A socket error occurred on send().");
            disconnect();
        }

        return sent;
    }

    protected void abort()
    {
        disconnect();
        super.abort();

        synchronized(m_readSocketScheduler)
        {
            try
            {
                m_readSocketScheduler.shutdown();
            }
            catch(Exception exception)
            {
            }

            try
            {
                if(!m_readSocketScheduler.
                    awaitTermination(60, TimeUnit.SECONDS))
                    m_readSocketScheduler.shutdownNow();
            }
            catch(Exception exception)
            {
            }
        }
    }

    protected void connect()
    {
        if(connected())
            return;
        else if(!isNetworkConnected())
        {
            setError("A network is not available.");
            return;
        }

        try
        {
            m_bytesRead.set(0L);
            m_bytesWritten.set(0L);
            m_lastParsed.set(System.currentTimeMillis());
            m_lastTimeRead.set(System.nanoTime());
```

```java
            InetSocketAddress inetSocketAddress = new InetSocketAddress
                (m_ipAddress, Integer.parseInt(m_ipPort));

            if(m_proxyInetSocketAddress == null)
            {
                m_socket = new Socket();
                m_socket.setReceiveBufferSize(SO_RCVBUF);
                m_socket.setSendBufferSize(SO_RCVBUF);
                m_socket.connect(inetSocketAddress, CONNECTION_TIMEOUT);
            }
            else
            {
                Socket socket = null;

                if(m_proxyType.equals("HTTP"))
                    m_socket = new Socket
                        (new Proxy(Proxy.Type.HTTP, m_proxyInetSocketAddress));
                else
                    m_socket = new Socket
                        (new Proxy(Proxy.Type.SOCKS, m_proxyInetSocketAddress));

                m_socket.setReceiveBufferSize(SO_RCVBUF);
                m_socket.setSendBufferSize(SO_SNDBUF);
                m_socket.connect(inetSocketAddress, CONNECTION_TIMEOUT);
            }

            m_socket.setSoTimeout(CONNECTION_TIMEOUT);
            m_socket.setTcpNoDelay(true);
            m_startTime.set(System.nanoTime());
            setError("");

            if(!m_passthrough.get())
                Kernel.getInstance().retrieveChatMessages
                    (m_cryptography.sipHashId());

            synchronized(m_mutex)
            {
                m_mutex.notifyAll();
            }
        }
    catch(Exception exception)
        {
            setError("An error (" +
                    exception.getMessage() +
                    ") occurred while attempting a connection (" +
                    System.nanoTime() + ").");
            disconnect();
        }
    }

    protected void disconnect()
    {
        super.disconnect();

        try
        {
            if(m_socket != null)
                m_socket.close();
        }
    catch(Exception exception)
        {
        }
    finally
```

```java
    {
        m_bytesRead.set(0L);
        m_bytesWritten.set(0L);
        m_lastParsed.set(0L);
        m_socket = null;
        m_startTime.set(System.nanoTime());
    }
}

public TcpNeighbor(String passthrough,
                   String proxyIpAddress,
                   String proxyPort,
                   String proxyType,
                   String ipAddress,
                   String ipPort,
                   String scopeId,
                   String version,
                   int oid)
{
    super(passthrough, ipAddress, ipPort, scopeId, "TCP", version, oid);
    m_proxyIpAddress = proxyIpAddress;

    try
    {
        m_proxyPort = Integer.parseInt(proxyPort);
    }
    catch(Exception exception)
    {
        m_proxyPort = -1;
    }

    m_proxyType = proxyType;

    if(!m_proxyIpAddress.isEmpty() &&
       m_proxyPort != -1 &&
       !m_proxyType.isEmpty())
        try
        {
            m_proxyInetSocketAddress = new InetSocketAddress
                (m_proxyIpAddress, m_proxyPort);
        }
        catch(Exception exception)
        {
            m_proxyInetSocketAddress = null;
        }

    m_readSocketScheduler.scheduleAtFixedRate(new Runnable()
    {
        private boolean m_error = false;

        @Override
        public void run()
        {
            try
            {
                if(!connected() && !m_aborted.get())
                    synchronized(m_mutex)
                    {
                        try
                        {
                            m_mutex.wait(WAIT_TIMEOUT);
                        }
                        catch(Exception exception)
```

```java
                {
                }
            }

        if(!connected())
            return;
        else if(m_error)
        {
            if(connected())
                m_error = false;
            else
                return;
        }
        else if(m_socket == null ||
                m_socket.getInputStream() == null)
            return;

        byte bytes[] = new byte[BYTES_PER_READ];
        int i = 0;

        try
        {
            i = m_socket.getInputStream().read(bytes);
        }
        catch(java.net.SocketTimeoutException exception)
        {
            i = 0;
        }
        catch(Exception exception)
        {
            m_error = true;
        }

        long bytesRead = (long) i;

        if(bytesRead < 0L || m_error)
        {
            m_error = true;
            setError("A socket read() error occurred.");
            disconnect();
            return;
        }
        else if(bytesRead == 0L)
            return;

        m_bytesRead.getAndAdd(bytesRead);
        m_lastTimeRead.set(System.nanoTime());

        if(m_stringBuffer.length() < MAXIMUM_BYTES)
            m_stringBuffer.append
                (new String(bytes, 0, (int) bytesRead));

        synchronized(m_parsingSchedulerMutex)
        {
            m_parsingSchedulerMutex.notify();
        }
    }
    catch(java.net.SocketException exception)
    {
        m_error = true;
        setError("A socket error occurred while reading data.");
        disconnect();
    }
```

```java
            catch(Exception exception)
            {
            }
          }
        }, 0L, READ_SOCKET_INTERVAL, TimeUnit.MILLISECONDS);
    }
}
```

/* TcpTlsNeighbor.java –

```
https://github.com/textbrowser/smoke/blob/master/Smoke/app/src/main/java/org/p
urple/smoke/TcpTlsNeighbor.java
** Copyright (c) Alexis Megas.
** All rights reserved.
**
** Redistribution and use in source and binary forms, with or without
** modification, are permitted provided that the following conditions
** are met:
** 1. Redistributions of source code must retain the above copyright
**    notice, this list of conditions and the following disclaimer.
** 2. Redistributions in binary form must reproduce the above copyright
**    notice, this list of conditions and the following disclaimer in the
**    documentation and/or other materials provided with the distribution.
** 3. The name of the author may not be used to endorse or promote products
**    derived from Smoke without specific prior written permission.
**
** SMOKE IS PROVIDED BY THE AUTHOR ``AS IS'' AND ANY EXPRESS OR
** IMPLIED WARRANTIES, INCLUDING, BUT NOT LIMITED TO, THE IMPLIED WARRANTIES
** OF MERCHANTABILITY AND FITNESS FOR A PARTICULAR PURPOSE ARE DISCLAIMED.
** IN NO EVENT SHALL THE AUTHOR BE LIABLE FOR ANY DIRECT, INDIRECT,
** INCIDENTAL, SPECIAL, EXEMPLARY, OR CONSEQUENTIAL DAMAGES (INCLUDING, BUT
** NOT LIMITED TO, PROCUREMENT OF SUBSTITUTE GOODS OR SERVICES; LOSS OF USE,
** DATA, OR PROFITS; OR BUSINESS INTERRUPTION) HOWEVER CAUSED AND ON ANY
** THEORY OF LIABILITY, WHETHER IN CONTRACT, STRICT LIABILITY, OR TORT
** (INCLUDING NEGLIGENCE OR OTHERWISE) ARISING IN ANY WAY OUT OF THE USE OF
** SMOKE, EVEN IF ADVISED OF THE POSSIBILITY OF SUCH DAMAGE.
*/
```

```java
package org.purple.smoke;

import android.os.Build;
import java.net.InetSocketAddress;
import java.net.Proxy;
import java.net.Socket;
import java.security.SecureRandom;
import java.security.cert.X509Certificate;
import java.util.concurrent.TimeUnit;
import java.util.concurrent.atomic.AtomicBoolean;
import javax.net.ssl.HandshakeCompletedEvent;
import javax.net.ssl.HandshakeCompletedListener;
import javax.net.ssl.SSLContext;
import javax.net.ssl.SSLSocket;
import javax.net.ssl.TrustManager;
import javax.net.ssl.X509TrustManager;

public class TcpTlsNeighbor extends Neighbor
{
    private AtomicBoolean m_handshakeCompleted = null;
    private AtomicBoolean m_isValidCertificate = null;
    private InetSocketAddress m_proxyInetSocketAddress = null;
    private SSLSocket m_socket = null;
```

```java
    private String m_protocols[] = null;
    private String m_proxyIpAddress = "";
    private String m_proxyType = "";
    private TrustManager m_trustManagers[] = null;
    private final static int CONNECTION_TIMEOUT = 10000; // 10 seconds.
    private final static int HANDSHAKE_TIMEOUT = 10000; // 10 seconds.
    private int m_proxyPort = -1;

    protected String getLocalIp()
    {
        try
        {
            if(m_socket != null && m_socket.getLocalAddress() != null)
                return m_socket.getLocalAddress().getHostAddress();
        }
        catch(Exception exception)
        {
        }

        if(m_version.equals("IPv4"))
            return "0.0.0.0";
        else
            return "::";
    }

    protected String getSessionCipher()
    {
        try
        {
            if(m_socket != null &&
                m_socket.getSession() != null &&
                m_socket.getSession().isValid())
                 return m_socket.getSession().getCipherSuite();
        }
        catch(Exception exception)
        {
        }

        return "";
    }

    protected boolean connected()
    {
        try
        {
            return isNetworkConnected() &&
                m_handshakeCompleted.get() &&
                m_isValidCertificate.get() &&
                m_socket != null &&
                !m_socket.isClosed();
        }
        catch(Exception exception)
        {
        }

        return false;
    }

    protected int getLocalPort()
    {
        try
        {
            if(m_socket != null && !m_socket.isClosed())
```

```java
            return m_socket.getLocalPort();
    }
    catch(Exception exception)
    {
    }

    return 0;
}

protected int send(String message)
{
    if(!connected() || message == null || message.length() == 0)
        return 0;
    else
        return send(message.getBytes());
}

protected int send(byte bytes[])
{
    if(bytes == null || bytes.length == 0 || !connected())
        return 0;

    int sent = 0;

    try
    {
        if(m_socket == null || m_socket.getOutputStream() == null)
            return sent;
        else
            m_socket.getOutputStream().write(bytes);

        Kernel.writeCongestionDigest(bytes);
        m_bytesWritten.getAndAdd(bytes.length);
        sent += bytes.length;
    }
    catch(Exception exception)
    {
        setError("A socket error occurred on send().");
        disconnect();
    }

    return sent;
}

protected void abort()
{
    disconnect();
    super.abort();
    m_handshakeCompleted.set(false);
    m_isValidCertificate.set(false);

    synchronized(m_readSocketScheduler)
    {
        try
        {
            m_readSocketScheduler.shutdown();
        }
        catch(Exception exception)
        {
        }

        try
        {
```

```java
            if(!m_readSocketScheduler.
                awaitTermination(60, TimeUnit.SECONDS))
                m_readSocketScheduler.shutdownNow();
        }
        catch(Exception exception)
        {
        }
    }
}

protected void connect()
{
    if(connected())
        return;
    else if(!isNetworkConnected())
    {
        setError("A network is not available.");
        return;
    }

    try
    {
        m_bytesRead.set(0L);
        m_bytesWritten.set(0L);
        m_handshakeCompleted.set(false);
        m_lastParsed.set(System.currentTimeMillis());
        m_lastTimeRead.set(System.nanoTime());

        InetSocketAddress inetSocketAddress = new InetSocketAddress
            (m_ipAddress, Integer.parseInt(m_ipPort));
        SSLContext sslContext = null;

        if(Build.VERSION.SDK_INT >= Build.VERSION_CODES.LOLLIPOP)
            sslContext = SSLContext.getInstance("TLS");
        else
            sslContext = SSLContext.getInstance("SSL");

        sslContext.init(null, m_trustManagers, new SecureRandom());

        if(m_proxyInetSocketAddress == null)
        {
            m_socket = (SSLSocket) sslContext.getSocketFactory().
                createSocket();
            m_socket.setReceiveBufferSize(SO_RCVBUF);
            m_socket.setSendBufferSize(SO_SNDBUF);
            m_socket.connect(inetSocketAddress, CONNECTION_TIMEOUT);
        }
        else
        {
            Socket socket = null;

            if(m_proxyType.equals("HTTP"))
                socket = new Socket
                    (new Proxy(Proxy.Type.HTTP, m_proxyInetSocketAddress));
            else
                socket = new Socket
                    (new Proxy(Proxy.Type.SOCKS, m_proxyInetSocketAddress));

            socket.setReceiveBufferSize(SO_RCVBUF);
            socket.setSendBufferSize(SO_SNDBUF);
            socket.connect(inetSocketAddress, CONNECTION_TIMEOUT);
            m_socket = (SSLSocket) sslContext.getSocketFactory().
                createSocket(socket, m_proxyIpAddress, m_proxyPort, true);
```

```java
            }

            m_socket.addHandshakeCompletedListener
                (new HandshakeCompletedListener()
                {
                    @Override
                    public void handshakeCompleted
                        (HandshakeCompletedEvent event)
                    {
                        m_handshakeCompleted.set(true);
                        scheduleSend(getCapabilities());
                        scheduleSend(getIdentities());
                        Kernel.getInstance().retrieveChatMessages
                            (m_cryptography.sipHashId());

                        synchronized(m_mutex)
                        {
                            m_mutex.notifyAll();
                        }
                    }
                });
            m_socket.setEnabledProtocols(m_protocols);
            m_socket.setSoTimeout(HANDSHAKE_TIMEOUT); // SSL/TLS process.
            m_socket.setTcpNoDelay(true);
            m_startTime.set(System.nanoTime());
            setError("");

            synchronized(m_mutex)
            {
                m_mutex.notifyAll();
            }
        }
        catch(Exception exception)
        {
            setError("An error (" +
                     exception.getMessage() +
                     ") occurred while attempting a connection (" +
                     System.nanoTime() + ").");
            disconnect();
        }
    }

    protected void disconnect()
    {
        super.disconnect();

        try
        {
            if(m_socket != null)
                m_socket.close();
        }
        catch(Exception exception)
        {
        }
        finally
        {
            m_bytesRead.set(0L);
            m_bytesWritten.set(0L);
            m_handshakeCompleted.set(false);
            m_isValidCertificate.set(false);
            m_lastParsed.set(0L);
            m_socket = null;
            m_startTime.set(System.nanoTime());
```

```java
        }
    }

    public TcpTlsNeighbor(String passthrough,
                          String proxyIpAddress,
                          String proxyPort,
                          String proxyType,
                          String ipAddress,
                          String ipPort,
                          String scopeId,
                          String version,
                          int oid)
    {
        super(passthrough, ipAddress, ipPort, scopeId, "TCP", version, oid);
        m_handshakeCompleted = new AtomicBoolean(false);
        m_isValidCertificate = new AtomicBoolean(false);

        if(Build.VERSION.RELEASE.startsWith("10"))
            m_protocols = Cryptography.TLS_NEW;
        else if(Build.VERSION.SDK_INT >= Build.VERSION_CODES.LOLLIPOP)
            m_protocols = Cryptography.TLS_V1_V12;
        else
            m_protocols = Cryptography.TLS_LEGACY_V12;

        m_proxyIpAddress = proxyIpAddress;

        try
        {
            m_proxyPort = Integer.parseInt(proxyPort);
        }
        catch(Exception exception)
        {
            m_proxyPort = -1;
        }

        m_proxyType = proxyType;

        if(!m_proxyIpAddress.isEmpty() &&
           m_proxyPort != -1 &&
           !m_proxyType.isEmpty())
            try
            {
                m_proxyInetSocketAddress = new InetSocketAddress
                    (m_proxyIpAddress, m_proxyPort);
            }
            catch(Exception exception)
            {
                m_proxyInetSocketAddress = null;
            }

        m_readSocketScheduler.scheduleAtFixedRate(new Runnable()
        {
            private boolean m_error = false;

            @Override
            public void run()
            {
                try
                {
                    if(!connected() && !m_aborted.get())
                        synchronized(m_mutex)
                        {
                            try
```

```java
                    {
                        m_mutex.wait(WAIT_TIMEOUT);
                    }
                catch(Exception exception)
                    {
                    }
                }

            if(!connected())
                return;
            else if(m_error)
            {
                if(connected())
                    m_error = false;
                else
                    return;
            }
            else if(m_socket == null ||
                    m_socket.getInputStream() == null)
                return;
            else if(m_socket.getSoTimeout() == HANDSHAKE_TIMEOUT)
                /*
                ** Reset SO_TIMEOUT from HANDSHAKE_TIMEOUT.
                */

                m_socket.setSoTimeout(SO_TIMEOUT);

            byte bytes[] = new byte[BYTES_PER_READ];
            int i = 0;

            try
            {
                i = m_socket.getInputStream().read(bytes);
            }
            catch(java.net.SocketTimeoutException exception)
            {
                i = 0;
            }
            catch(Exception exception)
            {
                m_error = true;
            }

            long bytesRead = (long) i;

            if(bytesRead < 0L || m_error)
            {
                m_error = true;
                setError("A socket read() error occurred.");
                disconnect();
                return;
            }
            else if(bytesRead == 0L)
                return;

            m_bytesRead.getAndAdd(bytesRead);
            m_lastTimeRead.set(System.nanoTime());

            if(m_stringBuffer.length() < MAXIMUM_BYTES)
                m_stringBuffer.append
                    (new String(bytes, 0, (int) bytesRead));

            synchronized(m_parsingSchedulerMutex)
```

```
                    {
                        m_parsingSchedulerMutex.notify();
                    }
                }
            catch(java.net.SocketException exception)
            {
                m_error = true;
                setError("A socket error occurred while reading data.");
                disconnect();
            }
            catch(Exception exception)
            {
            }
        }
    }, 0, READ_SOCKET_INTERVAL, TimeUnit.MILLISECONDS);
    m_trustManagers = new TrustManager[]
    {
        new X509TrustManager()
        {
            public X509Certificate[] getAcceptedIssuers()
            {
                return new X509Certificate[0];
            }

            public void checkClientTrusted
                (X509Certificate chain[], String authType)
            {
            }

            public void checkServerTrusted
                (X509Certificate chain[], String authType)
            {
                if(authType == null || authType.length() == 0)
                    m_isValidCertificate.set(false);
                else if(chain == null || chain.length == 0)
                    m_isValidCertificate.set(false);
                else
                {
                    try
                    {
                        chain[0].checkValidity();

                        byte bytes[] = m_databaseHelper.
                            neighborRemoteCertificate
                            (m_cryptography, m_oid.get());

                        if(bytes == null || bytes.length == 0)
                        {
                            m_databaseHelper.neighborRecordCertificate
                                (m_cryptography,
                                 String.valueOf(m_oid.get()),
                                 chain[0].getEncoded());
                            m_isValidCertificate.set(true);
                        }
                        else if(!Cryptography.memcmp(bytes,
                                                chain[0].getEncoded()))
                        {
                            m_databaseHelper.neighborControlStatus
                                (m_cryptography,
                                 "disconnect",
                                 String.valueOf(m_oid.get()));
                            m_isValidCertificate.set(false);
                            setError("The stored server's " +
```

```java
                                "certificate does not match the " +
                                "certificate that was provided by " +
                                "the server.");
                    }
                    else
                        m_isValidCertificate.set(true);
                }
                catch(Exception exception)
                {

                    m_databaseHelper.neighborControlStatus
                        (m_cryptography,
                         "disconnect",
                         String.valueOf(m_oid.get()));
                    m_isValidCertificate.set(false);
                    setError("A certificate error (" +
                             exception.getMessage() +
                             ") occurred.");
                }
            }

            if(!m_isValidCertificate.get())
                synchronized(m_errorMutex)
                {
                    if(m_error.length() == 0)
                        m_error.append
                            ("A generic certificate error occurred.");
                }
        }
    };
    }
}
```

/* Time.java –

```java
** SMOKE, EVEN IF ADVISED OF THE POSSIBILITY OF SUCH DAMAGE.
*/

package org.purple.smoke;

import java.io.BufferedReader;
import java.io.InputStreamReader;
import java.net.HttpURLConnection;
import java.net.URL;
import java.util.concurrent.Executors;
import java.util.concurrent.ScheduledExecutorService;
import java.util.concurrent.TimeUnit;

public class Time
{
    private ScheduledExecutorService m_scheduler = null;
    private final static long DELTA = 5L;
    private final static long QUERY_INTERVAL = 30L;

    public Time()
    {
        m_scheduler = Executors.newSingleThreadScheduledExecutor();
        m_scheduler.scheduleAtFixedRate(new Runnable()
        {
            @Override
            public void run()
            {
                if(!Kernel.getInstance().isNetworkConnected() ||
                   !State.getInstance().isAuthenticated() ||
                   !State.getInstance().queryTimerServer())
                    return;

                BufferedReader bufferedReader = null;
                HttpURLConnection httpURLConnection = null;

                try
                {
                    String string = "";
                    URL url = new URL
                        ("https://worldtimeapi.org/api/timezone/Etc/UTC.txt");

                    httpURLConnection = (HttpURLConnection)
                        url.openConnection();
                    httpURLConnection.setRequestMethod("GET");
                    bufferedReader = new BufferedReader
                        (new InputStreamReader(httpURLConnection.
                                               getInputStream()));

                    while((string = bufferedReader.readLine()) != null)
                        if(string.startsWith("unixtime: "))
                        {
                            long current = System.currentTimeMillis() / 1000L;

                            if(Math.abs(current -
                                    Long.parseLong(string.substring(10))) >
                               DELTA)
                                Miscellaneous.sendBroadcast
                                    ("org.purple.smoke.time",
                                     "Please correct the device's time as " +
                                     "it is incorrect by at least " +
                                     DELTA +
                                     " seconds. Local Unix Time: " +
                                     current +
```

```java
                                    ". Source Unix Time: " +
                                    string +
                                    ".");

                        break;
                    }

                httpURLConnection.disconnect();
            }
            catch(Exception exception)
            {
            }
            finally
            {
                try
                {
                    if(bufferedReader != null)
                        bufferedReader.close();
                }
                catch(Exception exception)
                {
                }

                try
                {
                    if(httpURLConnection != null)
                        httpURLConnection.disconnect();
                }
                catch(Exception exception)
                {
                }
            }
        }
    }, 1L, QUERY_INTERVAL, TimeUnit.SECONDS);
    }
}
```

/* UdpMulticastNeighbor.java –

```
https://github.com/textbrowser/smoke/blob/master/Smoke/app/src/main/java/org/p
urple/smoke/UdpMulticastNeighbor.java
** Copyright (c) Alexis Megas.
** All rights reserved.
**
** Redistribution and use in source and binary forms, with or without
** modification, are permitted provided that the following conditions
** are met:
** 1. Redistributions of source code must retain the above copyright
**    notice, this list of conditions and the following disclaimer.
** 2. Redistributions in binary form must reproduce the above copyright
**    notice, this list of conditions and the following disclaimer in the
**    documentation and/or other materials provided with the distribution.
** 3. The name of the author may not be used to endorse or promote products
**    derived from Smoke without specific prior written permission.
**
** SMOKE IS PROVIDED BY THE AUTHOR ``AS IS'' AND ANY EXPRESS OR
** IMPLIED WARRANTIES, INCLUDING, BUT NOT LIMITED TO, THE IMPLIED WARRANTIES
** OF MERCHANTABILITY AND FITNESS FOR A PARTICULAR PURPOSE ARE DISCLAIMED.
** IN NO EVENT SHALL THE AUTHOR BE LIABLE FOR ANY DIRECT, INDIRECT,
** INCIDENTAL, SPECIAL, EXEMPLARY, OR CONSEQUENTIAL DAMAGES (INCLUDING, BUT
** NOT LIMITED TO, PROCUREMENT OF SUBSTITUTE GOODS OR SERVICES; LOSS OF USE,
```

```java
** DATA, OR PROFITS; OR BUSINESS INTERRUPTION) HOWEVER CAUSED AND ON ANY
** THEORY OF LIABILITY, WHETHER IN CONTRACT, STRICT LIABILITY, OR TORT
** (INCLUDING NEGLIGENCE OR OTHERWISE) ARISING IN ANY WAY OUT OF THE USE OF
** SMOKE, EVEN IF ADVISED OF THE POSSIBILITY OF SUCH DAMAGE.
*/

package org.purple.smoke;

import java.io.ByteArrayInputStream;
import java.io.ByteArrayOutputStream;
import java.net.DatagramPacket;
import java.net.InetAddress;
import java.net.MulticastSocket;
import java.util.concurrent.TimeUnit;

public class UdpMulticastNeighbor extends Neighbor
{
    private MulticastSocket m_socket = null;
    private final static int TTL = 255;

    protected String getLocalIp()
    {
        return m_ipAddress;
    }

    protected boolean connected()
    {
        try
        {
            return isNetworkConnected() &&
                m_socket != null &&
                !m_socket.isClosed();
        }
        catch(Exception exception)
        {
            return false;
        }
    }

    protected int getLocalPort()
    {
        try
        {
            if(m_socket != null && !m_socket.isClosed())
                return m_socket.getLocalPort();
        }
        catch(Exception exception)
        {
        }

        return 0;
    }

    protected int send(String message)
    {
        if(!connected() || message == null || message.length() == 0)
            return 0;
        else
            return send(message.getBytes());
    }

    protected int send(byte bytes[])
    {
```

```java
        int sent = 0;

        if(bytes == null || bytes.length == 0 || !connected())
            return sent;

        try
        {
            if(m_socket == null)
                return sent;

            ByteArrayInputStream byteArrayInputStream = new
                ByteArrayInputStream(bytes);

            while(byteArrayInputStream.available() > 0)
            {
                if(m_aborted.get())
                    break;

                byte b[] = new byte
                    [Math.min(576, byteArrayInputStream.available())];

                byteArrayInputStream.read(b);
                m_socket.send
                    (new DatagramPacket(b,
                                        b.length,
                                        InetAddress.getByName(m_ipAddress),
                                        Integer.parseInt(m_ipPort)));
                sent += b.length;
            }

            Kernel.writeCongestionDigest(bytes);
            m_bytesWritten.getAndAdd(sent);
            setError("");
        }
        catch(Exception exception)
        {
            setError("A socket error occurred on send().");
            disconnect();
        }

        return sent;
    }

    protected void abort()
    {
        disconnect();
        super.abort();

        synchronized(m_readSocketScheduler)
        {
            try
            {
                m_readSocketScheduler.shutdown();
            }
            catch(Exception exception)
            {
            }

            try
            {
                if(!m_readSocketScheduler.
                    awaitTermination(60L, TimeUnit.SECONDS))
                    m_readSocketScheduler.shutdownNow();
```

```java
                }
            catch(Exception exception)
                {
                }
        }
    }

    protected void connect()
    {
        if(connected())
            return;
        else if(!isNetworkConnected())
        {
            setError("A network is not available.");
            return;
        }

        try
        {
            m_bytesRead.set(0L);
            m_bytesWritten.set(0L);
            m_lastParsed.set(System.currentTimeMillis());
            m_lastTimeRead.set(System.nanoTime());
            m_socket = new MulticastSocket(Integer.parseInt(m_ipPort));
            m_socket.joinGroup(InetAddress.getByName(m_ipAddress));
            m_socket.setLoopbackMode(true);
            m_socket.setSoTimeout(SO_TIMEOUT);
            m_socket.setTimeToLive(TTL);
            m_startTime.set(System.nanoTime());
            setError("");

            synchronized(m_mutex)
            {
                m_mutex.notifyAll();
            }
        }
        catch(Exception exception)
        {
            setError("An error occurred while attempting a connection.");
            disconnect();
        }
    }

    protected void disconnect()
    {
        super.disconnect();

        try
        {
            if(m_socket != null)
            {
                m_socket.leaveGroup(InetAddress.getByName(m_ipAddress));
                m_socket.close();
            }
        }
        catch(Exception exception)
        {
        }
        finally
        {
            m_bytesRead.set(0L);
            m_bytesWritten.set(0L);
            m_lastParsed.set(0L);
```

```java
            m_socket = null;
            m_startTime.set(System.nanoTime());
        }
    }

    public UdpMulticastNeighbor(String passthrough,
                                String ipAddress,
                                String ipPort,
                                String scopeId,
                                String version,
                                int oid)
    {
        super(passthrough, ipAddress, ipPort, scopeId, "UDP", version, oid);
        m_readSocketScheduler.scheduleAtFixedRate(new Runnable()
        {
            private boolean m_error = false;

            @Override
            public void run()
            {
                ByteArrayOutputStream byteArrayOutputStream = null;

                try
                {
                    if(!connected() && !m_aborted.get())
                        synchronized(m_mutex)
                        {
                            try
                            {
                                m_mutex.wait(WAIT_TIMEOUT);
                            }
                            catch(Exception exception)
                            {
                            }
                        }

                    if(!connected())
                        return;
                    else if(m_error)
                    {
                        if(connected())
                            m_error = false;
                        else
                            return;
                    }
                    else if(m_socket == null)
                        return;

                    DatagramPacket datagramPacket = null;
                    byte bytes[] = new byte[BYTES_PER_READ];

                    datagramPacket = new DatagramPacket(bytes, bytes.length);

                    try
                    {
                        m_socket.receive(datagramPacket);
                    }
                    catch(Exception exception)
                    {
                        m_error = true;
                        setError("A socket receive() error occurred.");
                        disconnect();
                        return;
```

```java
                }

                if(datagramPacket.getLength() > 0)
                {
                    byteArrayOutputStream = new ByteArrayOutputStream();
                    byteArrayOutputStream.write
                        (datagramPacket.getData(),
                         0,
                         datagramPacket.getLength());
                }

                int bytesRead = datagramPacket.getLength();

                if(bytesRead < 0)
                {
                    m_error = true;
                    setError("A socket receive() error occurred.");
                    disconnect();
                    return;
                }
                else if(bytesRead == 0)
                    return;

                m_bytesRead.getAndAdd(bytesRead);
                m_lastTimeRead.set(System.nanoTime());

                if(byteArrayOutputStream != null &&
                   m_stringBuffer.length() < MAXIMUM_BYTES)
                   m_stringBuffer.append
                        (new String(byteArrayOutputStream.toByteArray()));

                synchronized(m_parsingSchedulerMutex)
                {
                    m_parsingSchedulerMutex.notify();
                }
            }
            catch(Exception exception)
            {
            }
            finally
            {
                try
                {
                    if(byteArrayOutputStream != null)
                        byteArrayOutputStream.close();
                }
                catch(Exception exception)
                {
                }
            }
        }
    }, 0L, READ_SOCKET_INTERVAL, TimeUnit.MILLISECONDS);
    }
}
```

/* UdpNeighbor.java –


```java
package org.purple.smoke;

import java.io.ByteArrayInputStream;
import java.io.ByteArrayOutputStream;
import java.net.DatagramPacket;
import java.net.DatagramSocket;
import java.net.InetAddress;
import java.util.concurrent.TimeUnit;

public class UdpNeighbor extends Neighbor
{
    private DatagramSocket m_socket = null;

    protected String getLocalIp()
    {
        try
        {
            if(m_socket != null && m_socket.getLocalAddress() != null)
                return m_socket.getLocalAddress().getHostAddress();
        }
        catch(Exception exception)
        {
        }

        if(m_version.equals("IPv4"))
            return "0.0.0.0";
        else
            return "::";
    }

    protected boolean connected()
    {
        try
```

```java
        {
            return isNetworkConnected() &&
                m_socket != null &&
                !m_socket.isClosed();
        }
        catch(Exception exception)
        {
            return false;
        }
    }

    protected int getLocalPort()
    {
        try
        {
            if(m_socket != null && !m_socket.isClosed())
                return m_socket.getLocalPort();
        }
        catch(Exception exception)
        {
        }

        return 0;
    }

    protected int send(String message)
    {
        if(!connected() || message == null || message.length() == 0)
            return 0;
        else
            return send(message.getBytes());
    }

    protected int send(byte bytes[])
    {
        int sent = 0;

        if(bytes == null || bytes.length == 0 || !connected())
            return sent;

        try
        {
            if(m_socket == null)
                return sent;

            ByteArrayInputStream byteArrayInputStream = new
                ByteArrayInputStream(bytes);

            while(byteArrayInputStream.available() > 0)
            {
                if(m_aborted.get())
                    break;

                byte b[] = new byte
                    [Math.min(576, byteArrayInputStream.available())];

                byteArrayInputStream.read(b);
                m_socket.send
                    (new DatagramPacket(b,
                                        b.length,
                                        InetAddress.getByName(m_ipAddress),
                                        Integer.parseInt(m_ipPort)));
                sent += b.length;
```

```java
            }

            Kernel.writeCongestionDigest(bytes);
            m_bytesWritten.getAndAdd(sent);
            setError("");
        }
        catch(Exception exception)
        {
            setError("A socket error occurred on send().");
            disconnect();
        }

        return sent;
    }

    protected void abort()
    {
        disconnect();
        super.abort();

        synchronized(m_readSocketScheduler)
        {
            try
            {
                m_readSocketScheduler.shutdown();
            }
            catch(Exception exception)
            {
            }

            try
            {
                if(!m_readSocketScheduler.
                    awaitTermination(60L, TimeUnit.SECONDS))
                     m_readSocketScheduler.shutdownNow();
            }
            catch(Exception exception)
            {
            }
        }
    }

    protected void connect()
    {
        if(connected())
            return;
        else if(!isNetworkConnected())
        {
            setError("A network is not available.");
            return;
        }

        try
        {
            m_bytesRead.set(0L);
            m_bytesWritten.set(0L);
            m_lastParsed.set(System.currentTimeMillis());
            m_lastTimeRead.set(System.nanoTime());
            m_socket = new DatagramSocket();
            m_socket.connect(InetAddress.getByName(m_ipAddress),
                        Integer.parseInt(m_ipPort));
            m_socket.setSoTimeout(SO_TIMEOUT);
            m_startTime.set(System.nanoTime());
```

```java
        setError("");

        synchronized(m_mutex)
        {
            m_mutex.notifyAll();
        }
    }
    catch(Exception exception)
    {
        setError("An error occurred while attempting a connection.");
        disconnect();
    }
}

protected void disconnect()
{
    super.disconnect();

    try
    {
        if(m_socket != null)
            m_socket.close();
    }
    catch(Exception exception)
    {
    }
    finally
    {
        m_bytesRead.set(0L);
        m_bytesWritten.set(0L);
        m_lastTimeRead.set(0L);
        m_socket = null;
        m_startTime.set(System.nanoTime());
    }
}

public UdpNeighbor(String passthrough,
                   String ipAddress,
                   String ipPort,
                   String scopeId,
                   String version,
                   int oid)
{
    super(passthrough, ipAddress, ipPort, scopeId, "UDP", version, oid);
    m_readSocketScheduler.scheduleAtFixedRate(new Runnable()
    {
        private boolean m_error = false;

        @Override
        public void run()
        {
            ByteArrayOutputStream byteArrayOutputStream = null;

            try
            {
                if(!connected() && !m_aborted.get())
                    synchronized(m_mutex)
                    {
                        try
                        {
                            m_mutex.wait(WAIT_TIMEOUT);
                        }
                        catch(Exception exception)
```

```java
            {
            }
        }

        if(!connected())
            return;
        else if(m_error)
        {
            if(connected())
                m_error = false;
            else
                return;
        }
        else if(m_socket == null)
            return;

        DatagramPacket datagramPacket = null;
        byte bytes[] = new byte[BYTES_PER_READ];

        datagramPacket = new DatagramPacket(bytes, bytes.length);

        try
        {
            m_socket.receive(datagramPacket);
        }
        catch(Exception exception)
        {
            m_error = true;
            setError("A socket receive() error occurred.");
            disconnect();
            return;
        }

        if(datagramPacket.getLength() > 0)
        {
            byteArrayOutputStream = new ByteArrayOutputStream();
            byteArrayOutputStream.write
                (datagramPacket.getData(),
                 0,
                 datagramPacket.getLength());
        }

        int bytesRead = datagramPacket.getLength();

        if(bytesRead < 0)
        {
            m_error = true;
            setError("A socket receive() error occurred.");
            disconnect();
            return;
        }
        else if(bytesRead == 0)
            return;

        m_bytesRead.getAndAdd(bytesRead);
        m_lastTimeRead.set(System.nanoTime());

        if(byteArrayOutputStream != null &&
           m_stringBuffer.length() < MAXIMUM_BYTES)
           m_stringBuffer.append
               (new String(byteArrayOutputStream.toByteArray()));

        synchronized(m_parsingSchedulerMutex)
```

```java
                    {
                        m_parsingSchedulerMutex.notify();
                    }
                }
            catch(Exception exception)
            {
            }
            finally
            {
                try
                {
                    if(byteArrayOutputStream != null)
                        byteArrayOutputStream.close();
                }
                catch(Exception exception)
                {
                }
            }
        }
    }, 0L, READ_SOCKET_INTERVAL, TimeUnit.MILLISECONDS);
    }
}
```

/* Windows.java –


```java
package org.purple.smoke;

import android.app.Activity;
import android.app.Dialog;
import android.content.Context;
import android.view.LayoutInflater;
import android.view.View;
import android.widget.TextView;
```

```java
public abstract class Windows
{
    public static void showProgressDialog(Context context,
                                          Dialog dialog,
                                          String text)
    {
        if(context == null ||
           !(context instanceof Activity) ||
           dialog == null ||
           text == null ||
           text.trim().isEmpty())
            return;

        try
        {
            if(((Activity) context).isFinishing())
                return;

            LayoutInflater inflater = (LayoutInflater) context.getSystemService
                (Context.LAYOUT_INFLATER_SERVICE);
            View view = inflater.inflate(R.layout.progress, null);

            ((TextView) view.findViewById(R.id.text)).setText(text);
            dialog.setCancelable(false);
            dialog.setContentView(view);
            dialog.show();
        }
        catch(Exception exception_1)
        {
            try
            {
                dialog.dismiss();
            }
            catch(Exception exception_2)
            {
            }
        }
    }
}
```

bubble_error.xml


```xml
<?xml version="1.0" encoding="utf-8"?>
<shape xmlns:android="http://schemas.android.com/apk/res/android" >
  <corners android:radius="5dp" />
  <padding
      android:left="1dp"
      android:right="1dp"
      android:top="1dp" />
  <solid android:color="#e57373" />
  <stroke
      android:width="1px"
      android:color="#ffab00" />
</shape>
```

bubble_left_text.xml


```xml
<?xml version="1.0" encoding="utf-8"?>
<shape xmlns:android="http://schemas.android.com/apk/res/android" >
  <corners android:radius="5dp" />
  <padding
      android:left="1dp"
      android:right="1dp"
      android:top="1dp" />
  <solid android:color="#448aff" />
  <stroke
      android:width="1px"
      android:color="#2962ff" />
</shape>
```

bubble_name.xml


```xml
<?xml version="1.0" encoding="utf-8"?>
<shape xmlns:android="http://schemas.android.com/apk/res/android"
android:shape="oval" >
  <stroke
      android:width="2px"
      android:color="#757575" />
</shape>
```

bubble_ozone_text.xml


```xml
<?xml version="1.0" encoding="utf-8"?>
<shape xmlns:android="http://schemas.android.com/apk/res/android" >
  <corners android:radius="5dp" />
  <padding
      android:left="1dp"
      android:right="1dp"
      android:top="1dp" />
```

```xml
    <solid android:color="#757575" />
    <stroke
        android:width="1px"
        android:color="#212121" />
</shape>
```

bubble_right_text.xml

**https://github.com/textbrowser/smoke/blob/master/Smoke/app/src/main/res/drawab
le/bubble_right_text.xml**

```xml
<?xml version="1.0" encoding="utf-8"?>
<shape xmlns:android="http://schemas.android.com/apk/res/android" >
  <corners android:radius="5dp" />
  <padding
      android:left="1dp"
      android:right="1dp"
      android:top="1dp" />
  <solid android:color="#ffe57f" />
  <stroke
      android:width="1px"
      android:color="#ffab00" />
</shape>
```

sectiongradient.xml

**https://github.com/textbrowser/smoke/blob/master/Smoke/app/src/main/res/drawab
le/sectiongradient.xml**

```xml
<?xml version="1.0" encoding="UTF-8"?>
<shape xmlns:android="http://schemas.android.com/apk/res/android"
android:shape="rectangle">
  <gradient
      android:angle="0"
      android:centerColor="#81d4fa"
      android:endColor="#b3e5fc"
      android:startColor="#4fc3f7"/>
</shape>
```

```
15.11.2020  23:01                807 chat_faulty_session.png
15.11.2020  23:01              1.041 chat_status_offline.png
15.11.2020  23:01              1.134 chat_status_online.png
15.11.2020  23:01                508 download.png
15.11.2020  23:01                873 file.png
15.11.2020  23:01                607 file_select.png
15.11.2020  23:01                736 file_send.png
15.11.2020  23:01              1.100 help.png
15.11.2020  23:01                832 keys_not_signed.png
15.11.2020  23:01                933 keys_signed.png
15.11.2020  23:01              1.345 lock.png
15.11.2020  23:01                400 menu.png
15.11.2020  23:01                870 message_read.png
15.11.2020  23:01                847 message_sent.png
15.11.2020  23:01              1.142 minus.png
15.11.2020  23:01                284 sectiongradient.xml
15.11.2020  23:01              1.096 send.png
15.11.2020  23:01              1.141 send_disabled.png
15.11.2020  23:01                960 share.png
15.11.2020  23:01            546.059 smoke.png
15.11.2020  23:01              1.345 smokescreen_lock.png
```

```
1  15.11.2020  23:01            1.329 smokescreen_unlock.png
2  15.11.2020  23:01            1.329 unlock.png
3  15.11.2020  23:01              521 upload.png
4  15.11.2020  23:01            1.032 verified.png
5  15.11.2020  23:01              937 warning.png
6
7
8
9
```

activity_authenticate.xml

https://github.com/textbrowser/smoke/blob/master/Smoke/app/src/main/res/layout
/activity_authenticate.xml

```xml
<?xml version="1.0" encoding="utf-8"?>
<android.support.design.widget.CoordinatorLayout
xmlns:android="http://schemas.android.com/apk/res/android"
    android:layout_width="match_parent"
    android:layout_height="match_parent"
    android:layout_marginStart="10dp"
    android:layout_marginEnd="10dp">

    <android.support.design.widget.AppBarLayout
        android:layout_width="match_parent"
        android:layout_height="wrap_content">

        <android.support.v7.widget.Toolbar
            android:id="@+id/toolbar"
            android:layout_width="match_parent"
            android:layout_height="0dp"
            android:background="?attr/colorPrimary"
            android:theme="?attr/actionBarTheme" />

    </android.support.design.widget.AppBarLayout>

    <RelativeLayout
        android:id="@+id/relative_layout"
        android:layout_width="match_parent"
        android:layout_height="match_parent">

        <Button
            android:id="@+id/authenticate"
            android:layout_width="wrap_content"
            android:layout_height="wrap_content"
            android:layout_below="@+id/password"
            android:layout_alignParentStart="true"
            android:text="@string/authenticate_authenticate"
            android:textAllCaps="false" />

        <Button
            android:id="@+id/reset"
            style="@style/Widget.AppCompat.Button.Colored"
            android:layout_width="wrap_content"
            android:layout_height="wrap_content"
            android:layout_alignBottom="@+id/authenticate"
```

```
android:layout_toEndOf="@+id/authenticate"
android:text="@string/reset_smoke"
android:textAllCaps="false" />

    <EditText
        android:id="@+id/password"
        android:layout_width="wrap_content"
        android:layout_height="wrap_content"
        android:layout_alignParentStart="true"
        android:layout_alignParentEnd="true"
        android:ems="10"
        android:hint="@string/authenticate_password"
        android:inputType="textPassword"
        android:selectAllOnFocus="true" />

    <ProgressBar
        android:id="@+id/progress_bar"

style="@android:style/Widget.DeviceDefault.Light.ProgressBar.Large"
        android:layout_width="wrap_content"
        android:layout_height="wrap_content"
        android:layout_centerHorizontal="true"
        android:layout_centerVertical="true"
        android:visibility="invisible" />

    </RelativeLayout>

</android.support.design.widget.CoordinatorLayout>
```

activity_chat.xml

https://github.com/textbrowser/smoke/blob/master/Smoke/app/src/main/res/layout/activity_chat.xml

```xml
<?xml version="1.0" encoding="utf-8"?>
<android.support.design.widget.CoordinatorLayout
xmlns:android="http://schemas.android.com/apk/res/android"
    xmlns:app="http://schemas.android.com/apk/res-auto"
    xmlns:tools="http://schemas.android.com/tools"
    android:layout_width="match_parent"
    android:layout_height="match_parent"
    android:fitsSystemWindows="true"
    tools:context="org.purple.smoke.Chat">

    <android.support.design.widget.AppBarLayout
        android:layout_width="match_parent"
        android:layout_height="wrap_content"
        android:theme="@style/AppTheme.AppBarOverlay">

        <android.support.v7.widget.Toolbar
            android:id="@+id/toolbar"
            android:layout_width="match_parent"
            android:layout_height="?attr/actionBarSize"
            android:background="?attr/colorPrimary"
            app:popupTheme="@style/AppTheme.PopupOverlay" />

    </android.support.design.widget.AppBarLayout>

    <include layout="@layout/content_chat" />

</android.support.design.widget.CoordinatorLayout>
```

activity_fire.xml


```xml
<?xml version="1.0" encoding="utf-8"?>
<android.support.design.widget.CoordinatorLayout
xmlns:android="http://schemas.android.com/apk/res/android"
    xmlns:tools="http://schemas.android.com/tools"
    android:id="@+id/main_layout"
    android:layout_width="match_parent"
    android:layout_height="match_parent"
    android:fadeScrollbars="false">

    <android.support.design.widget.AppBarLayout
        android:layout_width="match_parent"
        android:layout_height="wrap_content">

        <android.support.v7.widget.Toolbar
            android:id="@+id/toolbar"
            android:layout_width="match_parent"
            android:layout_height="0dp"
            android:background="?attr/colorPrimary"
            android:minHeight="?attr/actionBarSize"
            android:theme="?attr/actionBarTheme" />

    </android.support.design.widget.AppBarLayout>

    <RelativeLayout
        android:layout_width="match_parent"
        android:layout_height="match_parent"
        android:layout_marginStart="10dp"
        android:layout_marginEnd="10dp"
        android:fadeScrollbars="false"
        tools:context="org.purple.smoke.Settings">

        <ScrollView
            android:layout_width="match_parent"
            android:layout_height="match_parent"
            android:fadeScrollbars="false">

            <LinearLayout
                android:id="@+id/linear_layout"
                android:layout_width="match_parent"
                android:layout_height="wrap_content"
                android:orientation="vertical">

                <TextView
                    android:layout_width="match_parent"
                    android:layout_height="0dp"
                    android:layout_marginEnd="5dp"
                    android:layout_weight="1"
                    android:background="@drawable/sectiongradient"
                    android:paddingStart="5dp"
                    android:paddingEnd="5dp"
                    android:text="@string/details"
                    android:textColor="@android:color/white"
                    android:textSize="18sp"
                    android:textStyle="normal|bold" />

                <LinearLayout
                    android:layout_width="match_parent"
                    android:layout_height="match_parent"
                    android:layout_marginEnd="5dp"
```

```xml
            android:orientation="horizontal">

            <EditText
                android:id="@+id/name"
                android:layout_width="0dp"
                android:layout_height="wrap_content"
                android:layout_weight="1"
                android:ems="10"
                android:hint="@string/your_name"
                android:inputType="textPersonName" />

            <Button
                android:id="@+id/save_name"
                style="@style/Widget.AppCompat.Button"
                android:layout_width="wrap_content"
                android:layout_height="wrap_content"
                android:text="@string/save"
                android:textAllCaps="false" />

        </LinearLayout>

        <LinearLayout
            android:layout_width="match_parent"
            android:layout_height="match_parent"
            android:layout_marginEnd="5dp"
            android:orientation="horizontal">

            <TextView
                android:layout_width="match_parent"
                android:layout_height="wrap_content"
                android:layout_weight="1"
                android:background="@drawable/sectiongradient"
                android:paddingStart="5dp"
                android:paddingEnd="5dp"
                android:text="@string/fire"
                android:textColor="@android:color/white"
                android:textSize="18sp"
                android:textStyle="normal|bold" />

            <Switch
                android:id="@+id/show_details"
                android:layout_width="100dp"
                android:layout_height="match_parent"
                android:layout_gravity="center"
                android:layout_weight="1"
                android:checked="true" />

        </LinearLayout>

        <LinearLayout
            android:id="@+id/auto_fill_layout"
            android:layout_width="match_parent"
            android:layout_height="match_parent"
            android:layout_marginEnd="5dp"
            android:orientation="horizontal">

            <Spinner
                android:id="@+id/auto_fill"
                android:layout_width="0dp"
                android:layout_height="match_parent"
                android:layout_weight="1" />

            <TextView
```

```xml
                android:layout_width="wrap_content"
                android:layout_height="wrap_content"
                android:text="@string/auto_fill" />
        </LinearLayout>

        <GridLayout
            android:id="@+id/grid_layout"
            android:layout_width="match_parent"
            android:layout_height="match_parent"
            android:layout_marginEnd="5dp"
            android:columnCount="1">

            <EditText
                android:id="@+id/channel"
                android:layout_width="match_parent"
                android:layout_height="wrap_content"
                android:ems="10"
                android:hint="@string/channel"
                android:inputType="textPersonName" />

            <EditText
                android:id="@+id/digest"
                android:layout_width="match_parent"
                android:layout_height="wrap_content"
                android:ems="10"
                android:hint="@string/digest_key"
                android:inputType="textPersonName" />

            <EditText
                android:id="@+id/salt"
                android:layout_width="match_parent"
                android:layout_height="wrap_content"
                android:ems="10"
                android:hint="@string/salt"
                android:inputType="textPersonName" />
        </GridLayout>

        <LinearLayout
            android:id="@+id/fire_buttons_layout"
            android:layout_width="match_parent"
            android:layout_height="match_parent"
            android:layout_marginEnd="5dp"
            android:orientation="horizontal">

            <Button
                android:id="@+id/add_channel"
                style="@style/Widget.AppCompat.Button"
                android:layout_width="wrap_content"
                android:layout_height="wrap_content"
                android:text="@string/add"
                android:textAllCaps="false" />

            <Button
                android:id="@+id/reset_fields"
                style="@style/Widget.AppCompat.Button"
                android:layout_width="wrap_content"
                android:layout_height="wrap_content"
                android:text="@string/reset_fields"
                android:textAllCaps="false" />

            <ProgressBar
                android:id="@+id/progress_bar"
```

```xml
            style="@android:style/Widget.DeviceDefault.ProgressBar"
                            android:layout_width="wrap_content"
                            android:layout_height="wrap_content"
                            android:visibility="invisible" />

                </LinearLayout>

                <TextView
                    android:layout_width="match_parent"
                    android:layout_height="wrap_content"
                    android:layout_marginEnd="5dp"
                    android:background="@drawable/sectiongradient"
                    android:paddingStart="5dp"
                    android:paddingEnd="5dp"
                    android:text="@string/fire_channels"
                    android:textColor="@android:color/white"
                    android:textSize="18sp"
                    android:textStyle="normal|bold" />

                <LinearLayout
                    android:layout_width="wrap_content"
                    android:layout_height="match_parent"
                    android:layout_marginEnd="5dp"
                    android:orientation="horizontal">

                    <Spinner
                        android:id="@+id/fires"
                        android:layout_width="0dp"
                        android:layout_height="match_parent"
                        android:layout_weight="1" />

                    <Button
                        android:id="@+id/delete"
                        style="@style/Widget.AppCompat.Button.Colored"
                        android:layout_width="wrap_content"
                        android:layout_height="wrap_content"
                        android:text="@string/delete"
                        android:textAllCaps="false" />

                    <Button
                        android:id="@+id/join"
                        style="@style/Widget.AppCompat.Button"
                        android:layout_width="wrap_content"
                        android:layout_height="wrap_content"
                        android:text="@string/join"
                        android:textAllCaps="false" />

                </LinearLayout>

            </LinearLayout>

        </ScrollView>
    </RelativeLayout>

</android.support.design.widget.CoordinatorLayout>
```

activity_member_chat.xml

https://github.com/textbrowser/smoke/blob/master/Smoke/app/src/main/res/layout/activity_member_chat.xml

```xml
<?xml version="1.0" encoding="utf-8"?>
<android.support.design.widget.CoordinatorLayout
xmlns:android="http://schemas.android.com/apk/res/android"
    xmlns:app="http://schemas.android.com/apk/res-auto"
    xmlns:tools="http://schemas.android.com/tools"
    android:layout_width="match_parent"
    android:layout_height="match_parent"
    android:fitsSystemWindows="true"
    tools:context="org.purple.smoke.MemberChat">

    <android.support.design.widget.AppBarLayout
        android:layout_width="match_parent"
        android:layout_height="wrap_content"
        android:theme="@style/AppTheme.AppBarOverlay">

        <android.support.v7.widget.Toolbar
            android:id="@+id/toolbar"
            android:layout_width="match_parent"
            android:layout_height="?attr/actionBarSize"
            android:background="?attr/colorPrimary"
            app:popupTheme="@style/AppTheme.PopupOverlay" />

    </android.support.design.widget.AppBarLayout>

    <include layout="@layout/content_member_chat" />

</android.support.design.widget.CoordinatorLayout>
```

activity_settings.xml

https://github.com/textbrowser/smoke/blob/master/Smoke/app/src/main/res/layout/activity_settings.xml

```xml
<?xml version="1.0" encoding="utf-8"?>
<android.support.design.widget.CoordinatorLayout
xmlns:android="http://schemas.android.com/apk/res/android"
    xmlns:tools="http://schemas.android.com/tools"
    android:id="@+id/main_layout"
    android:layout_width="match_parent"
    android:layout_height="match_parent"
    android:fadeScrollbars="false">

    <android.support.design.widget.AppBarLayout
        android:layout_width="match_parent"
        android:layout_height="wrap_content">

        <android.support.v7.widget.Toolbar
            android:id="@+id/toolbar"
            android:layout_width="match_parent"
            android:layout_height="0dp"
            android:background="?attr/colorPrimary"
            android:minHeight="?attr/actionBarSize"
            android:theme="?attr/actionBarTheme" />

    </android.support.design.widget.AppBarLayout>

    <RelativeLayout
        android:layout_width="match_parent"
```

```xml
        android:layout_height="match_parent"
        android:layout_marginStart="10dp"
        android:layout_marginEnd="10dp"
        android:background="@android:color/transparent"
        android:fadeScrollbars="false"
        tools:context="org.purple.smoke.Settings">

    <ScrollView
        android:layout_width="match_parent"
        android:layout_height="match_parent"
        android:background="@android:color/transparent"
        android:fadeScrollbars="false">

        <LinearLayout
            android:id="@+id/linear_layout"
            android:layout_width="match_parent"
            android:layout_height="wrap_content"
            android:orientation="vertical">

            <TextView
                android:layout_width="match_parent"
                android:layout_height="wrap_content"
                android:layout_marginEnd="5dp"
                android:background="@drawable/sectiongradient"
                android:paddingStart="5dp"
                android:paddingEnd="5dp"
                android:text="@string/about"
                android:textColor="@android:color/white"
                android:textSize="18sp"
                android:textStyle="normal|bold" />

            <TextView
                android:id="@+id/about"
                android:layout_width="match_parent"
                android:layout_height="wrap_content"
                android:layout_marginEnd="5dp"
                android:textIsSelectable="true" />

            <CheckBox
                android:id="@+id/foreground_service"
                android:layout_width="wrap_content"
                android:layout_height="wrap_content"
                android:checked="true"
                android:text="@string/foreground_service" />

            <CheckBox
                android:id="@+id/sleepless"
                android:layout_width="wrap_content"
                android:layout_height="wrap_content"
                android:checked="true"
                android:text="@string/prefer_active_cpu" />

            <CheckBox
                android:id="@+id/query_time_server"
                android:layout_width="wrap_content"
                android:layout_height="wrap_content"
                android:text="@string/query_time_server" />

            <Button
                android:id="@+id/clear_log"
                android:layout_width="wrap_content"
                android:layout_height="wrap_content"
                android:text="@string/clear_log"
```

```xml
            android:textAllCaps="false" />

        <TextView
            android:layout_width="match_parent"
            android:layout_height="wrap_content"
            android:layout_marginEnd="5dp"
            android:background="@drawable/sectiongradient"
            android:paddingStart="5dp"
            android:paddingEnd="5dp"
            android:text="@string/neighbor_servers"
            android:textColor="@android:color/white"
            android:textSize="18sp"
            android:textStyle="normal|bold" />

        <LinearLayout
            android:layout_width="match_parent"
            android:layout_height="match_parent"
            android:layout_marginEnd="5dp"
            android:orientation="horizontal">

            <TextView
                android:layout_width="0dp"
                android:layout_height="wrap_content"
                android:layout_weight="0.31"
                android:text="@string/control" />

            <TextView
                android:layout_width="0dp"
                android:layout_height="wrap_content"
                android:layout_weight="0.31"
                android:text="@string/remote" />
        </LinearLayout>

        <android.support.v4.widget.NestedScrollView
            android:layout_width="match_parent"
            android:layout_height="250dp"
            android:layout_marginEnd="5dp"
            android:background="#00ffffff"
            android:fadeScrollbars="false"
            android:scrollbars="vertical">

            <TableLayout
                android:id="@+id/neighbors"
                android:layout_width="match_parent"
                android:layout_height="match_parent"
                android:scrollbars="horizontal|vertical">

            </TableLayout>
        </android.support.v4.widget.NestedScrollView>

        <LinearLayout
            android:layout_width="match_parent"
            android:layout_height="match_parent"
            android:layout_marginEnd="5dp"
            android:orientation="horizontal"
            android:weightSum="1">

            <CheckBox
                android:id="@+id/automatic_refresh"
                android:layout_width="wrap_content"
                android:layout_height="match_parent"
                android:checked="true"
                android:text="@string/automatic_refresh" />
```

```xml
        <CheckBox
            android:id="@+id/neighbor_details"
            android:layout_width="wrap_content"
            android:layout_height="match_parent"
            android:text="@string/details" />

    </LinearLayout>

    <CheckBox
        android:id="@+id/echo"
        android:layout_width="wrap_content"
        android:layout_height="match_parent"
        android:text="@string/echo" />

    <LinearLayout
        android:layout_width="match_parent"
        android:layout_height="match_parent"
        android:layout_marginEnd="5dp"
        android:orientation="horizontal">

        <Button
            android:id="@+id/refresh_neighbors"
            style="@style/Widget.AppCompat.Button"
            android:layout_width="wrap_content"
            android:layout_height="wrap_content"
            android:text="@string/refresh_neighbors"
            android:textAllCaps="false" />
    </LinearLayout>

    <EditText
        android:id="@+id/neighbors_ip_address"
        android:layout_width="match_parent"
        android:layout_height="wrap_content"
        android:layout_marginEnd="5dp"
        android:ems="10"
        android:hint="@string/ip_address"
        android:inputType="textPersonName"
        android:nextFocusDown="@+id/neighbors_port" />

    <LinearLayout
        android:layout_width="match_parent"
        android:layout_height="match_parent"
        android:layout_marginEnd="5dp"
        android:orientation="horizontal">

        <EditText
            android:id="@+id/neighbors_port"
            android:layout_width="0dp"
            android:layout_height="wrap_content"
            android:layout_weight="1"
            android:ems="10"
            android:hint="@string/port"
            android:inputType="number"
            android:nextFocusDown="@+id/proxy_ip_address" />

        <EditText
            android:id="@+id/neighbors_scope_id"
            android:layout_width="0dp"
            android:layout_height="wrap_content"
            android:layout_weight="1"
            android:ems="10"
            android:hint="@string/scope_id"
```

```xml
                android:inputType="textPersonName"
                android:nextFocusDown="@+id/proxy_ip_address" />

        </LinearLayout>

        <RadioGroup
            android:id="@+id/neighbors_ipv_radio_group"
            android:layout_width="match_parent"
            android:layout_height="0dp"
            android:layout_marginEnd="5dp"
            android:layout_weight="1"
            android:checkedButton="@+id/neighbors_ipv4"
            android:orientation="horizontal">

            <RadioButton
                android:id="@+id/neighbors_ipv4"
                android:layout_width="match_parent"
                android:layout_height="wrap_content"
                android:layout_weight="1"
                android:checked="true"
                android:text="@string/ipv4" />

            <RadioButton
                android:id="@+id/neighbors_ipv6"
                android:layout_width="match_parent"
                android:layout_height="wrap_content"
                android:layout_weight="1"
                android:text="@string/ipv6" />

            <Spinner
                android:id="@+id/neighbors_transport"
                android:layout_width="match_parent"
                android:layout_height="wrap_content"
                android:layout_weight="1" />

        </RadioGroup>

        <CheckBox
            android:id="@+id/initialize_ozone"
            android:layout_width="match_parent"
            android:layout_height="wrap_content"
            android:text="@string/initialize_ozone" />

        <CheckBox
            android:id="@+id/non_tls"
            android:layout_width="match_parent"
            android:layout_height="wrap_content"
            android:text="@string/non_tls" />

        <CheckBox
            android:id="@+id/passthrough"
            android:layout_width="match_parent"
            android:layout_height="wrap_content"
            android:text="@string/passthrough" />

        <EditText
            android:id="@+id/proxy_ip_address"
            android:layout_width="match_parent"
            android:layout_height="wrap_content"
            android:layout_marginEnd="5dp"
            android:ems="10"
            android:hint="@string/proxy_ip_address"
            android:inputType="textPersonName"
```

```xml
            android:nextFocusDown="@+id/proxy_port" />

        <LinearLayout
            android:layout_width="match_parent"
            android:layout_height="match_parent"
            android:layout_marginEnd="5dp"
            android:orientation="horizontal">

            <EditText
                android:id="@+id/proxy_port"
                android:layout_width="0dp"
                android:layout_height="wrap_content"
                android:layout_weight="1"
                android:ems="10"
                android:hint="@string/proxy_port"
                android:inputType="number"
                android:nextFocusDown="@+id/ozone" />

            <Spinner
                android:id="@+id/proxy_type"
                android:layout_width="0dp"
                android:layout_height="wrap_content"
                android:layout_weight="1" />
        </LinearLayout>

        <LinearLayout
            android:layout_width="match_parent"
            android:layout_height="match_parent"
            android:layout_marginEnd="5dp"
            android:orientation="horizontal">

            <Button
                android:id="@+id/add_neighbor"
                style="@style/Widget.AppCompat.Button"
                android:layout_width="wrap_content"
                android:layout_height="wrap_content"
                android:text="@string/add"
                android:textAllCaps="false" />

            <Button
                android:id="@+id/reset_neighbor_fields"
                style="@style/Widget.AppCompat.Button"
                android:layout_width="wrap_content"
                android:layout_height="wrap_content"
                android:text="@string/reset_fields"
                android:textAllCaps="false" />

        </LinearLayout>

        <TextView
            android:layout_width="match_parent"
            android:layout_height="wrap_content"
            android:layout_marginEnd="5dp"
            android:layout_weight="0.08"
            android:background="@drawable/sectiongradient"
            android:paddingStart="5dp"
            android:paddingEnd="5dp"
            android:text="@string/ozone"
            android:textColor="@android:color/white"
            android:textSize="18sp"
            android:textStyle="normal|bold" />

        <LinearLayout
```

```
android:layout_width="match_parent"
android:layout_height="match_parent"
android:layout_marginEnd="5dp"
android:orientation="horizontal">

<Button
    android:id="@+id/ozone_help"
    android:layout_width="32dp"
    android:layout_height="wrap_content"
    android:layout_weight="0"
    android:background="@android:color/transparent" />

<EditText
    android:id="@+id/ozone"
    android:layout_width="0dp"
    android:layout_height="wrap_content"
    android:layout_weight="1"
    android:ems="10"
    android:hint="@string/address"
    android:inputType="textPersonName" />

</LinearLayout>

<LinearLayout
    android:layout_width="match_parent"
    android:layout_height="match_parent"
    android:layout_marginEnd="5dp"
    android:orientation="horizontal">

<Button
    android:id="@+id/save_ozone"
    style="@style/Widget.AppCompat.Button"
    android:layout_width="wrap_content"
    android:layout_height="wrap_content"
    android:text="@string/save"
    android:textAllCaps="false" />

<Button
    android:id="@+id/share_via_ozone"
    style="@style/Widget.AppCompat.Button"
    android:layout_width="wrap_content"
    android:layout_height="wrap_content"
    android:text="@string/share_smoke_id"
    android:textAllCaps="false" />
</LinearLayout>

<TextView
    android:layout_width="match_parent"
    android:layout_height="wrap_content"
    android:layout_marginEnd="5dp"
    android:background="@drawable/sectiongradient"
    android:paddingStart="5dp"
    android:paddingEnd="5dp"
    android:text="@string/participants"
    android:textColor="@android:color/white"
    android:textSize="18sp"
    android:textStyle="normal|bold" />

<LinearLayout
    android:layout_width="match_parent"
    android:layout_height="match_parent"
    android:layout_marginEnd="5dp"
    android:orientation="horizontal">
```

```xml
        <TextView
            android:layout_width="0dp"
            android:layout_height="wrap_content"
            android:layout_weight="0.13"
            android:text="@string/name" />

        <TextView
            android:layout_width="0dp"
            android:layout_height="wrap_content"
            android:layout_weight="0.13"
            android:text="@string/smokeid" />

        <TextView
            android:layout_width="0dp"
            android:layout_height="wrap_content"
            android:layout_marginEnd="5dp"
            android:layout_weight="0.13"
            android:text="@string/fiasco_keys" />

    </LinearLayout>

    <android.support.v4.widget.NestedScrollView
        android:layout_width="match_parent"
        android:layout_height="250dp"
        android:layout_marginEnd="5dp"
        android:fadeScrollbars="false"
        android:scrollbars="vertical">

        <TableLayout
            android:id="@+id/participants"
            android:layout_width="match_parent"
            android:layout_height="wrap_content"
            android:layout_marginEnd="5dp">

        </TableLayout>
    </android.support.v4.widget.NestedScrollView>

    <LinearLayout
        android:layout_width="match_parent"
        android:layout_height="match_parent"
        android:layout_marginEnd="5dp"
        android:orientation="horizontal">

        <Button
            android:id="@+id/refresh_participants"
            style="@style/Widget.AppCompat.Button"
            android:layout_width="wrap_content"
            android:layout_height="wrap_content"
            android:text="@string/refresh_participants"
            android:textAllCaps="false" />

        <Button
            android:id="@+id/epks"
            style="@style/Widget.AppCompat.Button"
            android:layout_width="wrap_content"
            android:layout_height="wrap_content"
            android:text="@string/share_keys"
            android:textAllCaps="false" />

        <ProgressBar
            android:id="@+id/share_keys_progress_bar"
```

```xml
                style="@android:style/Widget.DeviceDefault.ProgressBar"
                        android:layout_width="wrap_content"
                        android:layout_height="wrap_content"
                        android:visibility="invisible" />


                </LinearLayout>

                <LinearLayout
                    android:layout_width="match_parent"
                    android:layout_height="match_parent"
                    android:layout_marginEnd="5dp"
                    android:orientation="horizontal">

                    <EditText
                        android:id="@+id/participant_name"
                        android:layout_width="0dp"
                        android:layout_height="wrap_content"
                        android:layout_weight="1"
                        android:ems="10"
                        android:hint="@string/name"
                        android:inputType="textPersonName"
                        android:nextFocusDown="@+id/participant_siphash_id" />

                    <TextView
                        android:id="@+id/at_sign"
                        android:layout_width="20dp"
                        android:layout_height="wrap_content"
                        android:text="@string/at"
                        android:textAlignment="center"
                        android:textSize="18sp"
                        android:textStyle="bold" />

                    <EditText
                        android:id="@+id/participant_siphash_id"
                        android:layout_width="0dp"
                        android:layout_height="wrap_content"
                        android:layout_weight="1"
                        android:ems="10"
                        android:hint="@string/smokeid"
                        android:inputType="textPersonName" />

                    <Button
                        android:id="@+id/siphash_help"
                        android:layout_width="32dp"
                        android:layout_height="wrap_content"
                        android:layout_weight="0"
                        android:background="@android:color/transparent" />

                </LinearLayout>

                <CheckBox
                    android:id="@+id/as_alias"
                    android:layout_width="match_parent"
                    android:layout_height="wrap_content"
                    android:layout_marginEnd="5dp"
                    android:text="@string/smoke_alias" />

                <LinearLayout
                    android:layout_width="match_parent"
                    android:layout_height="match_parent"
                    android:layout_marginEnd="5dp"
                    android:orientation="horizontal">
```

```xml
            <Button
                android:id="@+id/add_participant"
                style="@style/Widget.AppCompat.Button"
                android:layout_width="wrap_content"
                android:layout_height="wrap_content"
                android:text="@string/add"
                android:textAllCaps="false" />

            <Button
                android:id="@+id/reset_participants_fields"
                style="@style/Widget.AppCompat.Button"
                android:layout_width="wrap_content"
                android:layout_height="wrap_content"
                android:text="@string/reset_fields"
                android:textAllCaps="false" />

            <ProgressBar
                android:id="@+id/add_participants_progress_bar"

style="@android:style/Widget.DeviceDefault.ProgressBar"
                android:layout_width="wrap_content"
                android:layout_height="wrap_content"
                android:visibility="invisible" />
        </LinearLayout>

        <TextView
            android:id="@+id/password_separator"
            android:layout_width="match_parent"
            android:layout_height="wrap_content"
            android:layout_marginEnd="5dp"
            android:background="@drawable/sectiongradient"
            android:paddingStart="5dp"
            android:paddingEnd="5dp"
            android:text="@string/password"
            android:textColor="@android:color/white"
            android:textSize="18sp"
            android:textStyle="normal|bold" />

        <GridLayout
            android:id="@+id/pki_layout"
            android:layout_width="match_parent"
            android:layout_height="match_parent"
            android:layout_marginEnd="5dp"
            android:columnCount="2"
            android:rowCount="3">

            <TextView
                android:layout_width="wrap_content"
                android:layout_height="wrap_content"
                android:text="@string/iteration_count"
                android:textSize="14sp" />

            <Spinner
                android:id="@+id/iteration_count"
                android:layout_width="200dp"
                android:layout_height="wrap_content" />

            <TextView
                android:id="@+id/textView"
                android:layout_width="wrap_content"
                android:layout_height="wrap_content"
                android:text="@string/key_derivation_function" />
```

```xml
        <Spinner
            android:id="@+id/key_derivation_function"
            android:layout_width="200dp"
            android:layout_height="wrap_content" />

        <TextView
            android:layout_width="wrap_content"
            android:layout_height="wrap_content"
            android:text="@string/encryption" />

        <Spinner
            android:id="@+id/pki_encryption_algorithm"
            android:layout_width="200dp"
            android:layout_height="wrap_content" />

        <TextView
            android:layout_width="wrap_content"
            android:layout_height="wrap_content"
            android:text="@string/signature" />

        <Spinner
            android:id="@+id/pki_signature_algorithm"
            android:layout_width="200dp"
            android:layout_height="wrap_content" />
    </GridLayout>

    <EditText
        android:id="@+id/password1"
        android:layout_width="match_parent"
        android:layout_height="wrap_content"
        android:layout_marginEnd="5dp"
        android:ems="10"
        android:hint="@string/password"
        android:inputType="textPassword" />

    <EditText
        android:id="@+id/password2"
        android:layout_width="match_parent"
        android:layout_height="wrap_content"
        android:layout_marginEnd="5dp"
        android:ems="10"
        android:hint="@string/password_confirmation"
        android:inputType="textPassword" />

    <LinearLayout
        android:id="@+id/set_password_linear_layout"
        android:layout_width="match_parent"
        android:layout_height="match_parent"
        android:layout_marginEnd="5dp"
        android:orientation="horizontal">

        <CheckBox
            android:id="@+id/overwrite"
            android:layout_width="wrap_content"
            android:layout_height="wrap_content" />

        <Button
            android:id="@+id/set_password"
            style="@style/Widget.AppCompat.Button"
            android:layout_width="wrap_content"
            android:layout_height="wrap_content"
            android:text="@string/generate"
```

```xml
                            android:textAllCaps="false" />

                        <Button
                            android:id="@+id/generate_pki"
                            style="@style/Widget.AppCompat.Button"
                            android:layout_width="wrap_content"
                            android:layout_height="wrap_content"
                            android:text="@string/generate_pk"
                            android:textAllCaps="false" />

                        <ProgressBar
                            android:id="@+id/generate_progress_bar"

style="@android:style/Widget.DeviceDefault.ProgressBar"
                            android:layout_width="wrap_content"
                            android:layout_height="wrap_content"
                            android:visibility="invisible" />
                    </LinearLayout>

                    <TextView
                        android:layout_width="match_parent"
                        android:layout_height="wrap_content"
                        android:layout_marginEnd="5dp"
                        android:background="@drawable/sectiongradient"
                        android:paddingStart="5dp"
                        android:paddingEnd="5dp"
                        android:text="@string/public_data"
                        android:textColor="@android:color/white"
                        android:textSize="18sp"
                        android:textStyle="normal|bold" />

                    <LinearLayout
                        android:layout_width="match_parent"
                        android:layout_height="match_parent"
                        android:layout_marginEnd="5dp"
                        android:orientation="horizontal">

                        <EditText
                            android:id="@+id/alias"
                            android:layout_width="0dp"
                            android:layout_height="wrap_content"
                            android:layout_weight="1"
                            android:ems="10"
                            android:hint="@string/smoke_alias"
                            android:inputType="textPersonName" />

                        <Button
                            android:id="@+id/save_alias"
                            android:layout_width="wrap_content"
                            android:layout_height="wrap_content"
                            android:text="@string/save"
                            android:textAllCaps="false" />
                    </LinearLayout>

                    <TextView
                        android:id="@+id/chat_encryption_key_data"
                        android:layout_width="match_parent"
                        android:layout_height="wrap_content"
                        android:layout_marginEnd="5dp"
                        android:text="@string/chat_encryption_key_data" />

                    <TextView
                        android:id="@+id/chat_signature_key_data"
```

```xml
            android:layout_width="match_parent"
            android:layout_height="wrap_content"
            android:layout_marginEnd="5dp"
            android:text="@string/chat_signature_key_data" />

        <TextView
            android:layout_width="match_parent"
            android:layout_height="wrap_content"
            android:layout_marginEnd="5dp"
            android:text="@string/smoke_chat_id"
            android:textSize="16sp"
            android:textStyle="bold" />

        <TextView
            android:id="@+id/siphash_identity"
            android:layout_width="wrap_content"
            android:layout_height="wrap_content"
            android:layout_marginEnd="5dp"
            android:text="@string/smokeid"
            android:textSize="16sp"
            android:textStyle="bold" />

        <LinearLayout
            android:layout_width="match_parent"
            android:layout_height="match_parent"
            android:layout_marginEnd="5dp"
            android:orientation="horizontal">

            <Button
                android:id="@+id/reset"
                style="@style/Widget.AppCompat.Button.Colored"
                android:layout_width="wrap_content"
                android:layout_height="wrap_content"
                android:text="@string/reset_smoke"
                android:textAllCaps="false" />

        </LinearLayout>

    </LinearLayout>
    </ScrollView>
  </RelativeLayout>

</android.support.design.widget.CoordinatorLayout>
```

activity_smokescreen.xml

https://github.com/textbrowser/smoke/blob/master/Smoke/app/src/main/res/layout/activity_smokescreen.xml

```xml
<?xml version="1.0" encoding="utf-8"?>
<android.support.design.widget.CoordinatorLayout
xmlns:android="http://schemas.android.com/apk/res/android"
    android:layout_width="match_parent"
    android:layout_height="match_parent"
    android:layout_marginStart="10dp"
    android:layout_marginEnd="10dp">

    <android.support.design.widget.AppBarLayout
        android:layout_width="match_parent"
        android:layout_height="wrap_content">

        <android.support.v7.widget.Toolbar
            android:id="@+id/toolbar"
            android:layout_width="match_parent"
            android:layout_height="0dp"
            android:background="?attr/colorPrimary"
            android:theme="?attr/actionBarTheme" />

    </android.support.design.widget.AppBarLayout>

    <RelativeLayout
        android:id="@+id/relative_layout"
        android:layout_width="match_parent"
        android:layout_height="match_parent">

        <Button
            android:id="@+id/authenticate"
            android:layout_width="64dp"
            android:layout_height="64dp"
            android:layout_below="@id/password"
            android:layout_alignParentStart="false"
            android:layout_centerInParent="true"
            android:background="@drawable/smokescreen_unlock"
            android:textAllCaps="false" />

        <EditText
            android:id="@+id/password"
            android:layout_width="wrap_content"
            android:layout_height="wrap_content"
            android:layout_alignParentStart="false"
            android:layout_alignParentEnd="false"
            android:layout_centerInParent="true"
            android:layout_centerVertical="true"
            android:ems="10"
            android:hint="@string/authenticate_password"
            android:inputType="textPassword"
            android:selectAllOnFocus="true" />

        <TextView
            android:id="@+id/label"
            android:layout_width="wrap_content"
            android:layout_height="wrap_content"
            android:layout_centerInParent="false"
            android:layout_centerHorizontal="true" />

        <Button
            android:id="@+id/lock"
            android:layout_width="64dp"
```

```
            android:layout_height="64dp"
            android:layout_alignParentStart="false"
            android:layout_centerInParent="true"
            android:background="@drawable/smokescreen_lock"
            android:textAllCaps="false" />

    </RelativeLayout>

</android.support.design.widget.CoordinatorLayout>
```

activity_steam.xml


```
<?xml version="1.0" encoding="utf-8"?>
<android.support.design.widget.CoordinatorLayout
xmlns:android="http://schemas.android.com/apk/res/android"
    xmlns:app="http://schemas.android.com/apk/res-auto"
    xmlns:tools="http://schemas.android.com/tools"
    android:layout_width="match_parent"
    android:layout_height="match_parent"
    android:fitsSystemWindows="true"
    tools:context="org.purple.smoke.Steam">

    <include layout="@layout/content_steam" />

</android.support.design.widget.CoordinatorLayout>
```

chat_bubble.xml


```
<RelativeLayout xmlns:android="http://schemas.android.com/apk/res/android"
    xmlns:app="http://schemas.android.com/apk/res-auto"
    xmlns:tools="http://schemas.android.com/tools"
    android:layout_width="match_parent"
    android:layout_height="wrap_content"
    android:layout_marginBottom="5dp"
    android:layout_marginTop="5dp">

    <LinearLayout
        android:layout_width="match_parent"
        android:layout_height="match_parent"
        android:orientation="vertical">

        <CheckBox
            android:id="@+id/selected"
            android:layout_width="35dp"
            android:layout_height="35dp"
            android:layout_marginStart="5dp" />

        <TextView
            android:id="@+id/name_left"
            android:layout_width="35dp"
            android:layout_height="35dp"
            android:layout_marginStart="5dp"
            android:background="@drawable/bubble_name"
            android:gravity="center"
            android:textSize="20sp" />
```

```xml
    </LinearLayout>

    <TextView
        android:id="@+id/name_right"
        android:layout_width="35dp"
        android:layout_height="35dp"
        android:layout_alignParentEnd="true"
        android:layout_marginEnd="5dp"
        android:background="@drawable/bubble_name"
        android:gravity="center"
        android:textSize="20sp" />

    <LinearLayout
        android:id="@+id/linear_layout"
        android:layout_width="225dp"
        android:layout_height="match_parent"
        android:layout_marginEnd="5dp"
        android:layout_marginStart="45dp"
        android:layout_toStartOf="@+id/name_right"
        android:orientation="vertical">

        <ImageView
            android:id="@+id/image"
            android:layout_width="215dp"
            android:layout_height="wrap_content"
            android:layout_gravity="center_horizontal"
            android:layout_weight="1"
            android:adjustViewBounds="true"
            android:contentDescription="@string/attachment"
            android:paddingLeft="5dp"
            android:paddingRight="5dp"
            android:paddingTop="5dp"
            android:scaleType="fitXY"
            android:visibility="invisible" />

        <RelativeLayout
            android:layout_width="match_parent"
            android:layout_height="match_parent"
            android:layout_weight="1">

            <TextView
                android:id="@+id/text"
                android:layout_width="match_parent"
                android:layout_height="match_parent"
                />

            <ImageView
                android:id="@+id/message_status"
                android:layout_width="32dp"
                android:layout_height="32dp"
                android:layout_alignParentEnd="true"
                android:layout_alignParentBottom="true"
                android:contentDescription="@string/message_status"
                app:srcCompat="@drawable/message_sent" />

        </RelativeLayout>

    </LinearLayout>

</RelativeLayout>
```

content_chat.xml


```xml
<?xml version="1.0" encoding="utf-8"?>
<RelativeLayout xmlns:android="http://schemas.android.com/apk/res/android"
    xmlns:app="http://schemas.android.com/apk/res-auto"
    xmlns:tools="http://schemas.android.com/tools"
    android:layout_width="match_parent"
    android:layout_height="match_parent"
    android:layout_marginStart="10dp"
    android:layout_marginEnd="10dp"
    app:layout_behavior="@string/appbar_scrolling_view_behavior"
    tools:context="org.purple.smoke.Chat"
    tools:showIn="@layout/activity_chat">

    <Button
        android:id="@+id/clear_chat_messages"
        style="@style/Widget.AppCompat.Button.Colored"
        android:layout_width="wrap_content"
        android:layout_height="wrap_content"
        android:layout_alignParentTop="true"
        android:layout_alignParentEnd="true"
        android:text="@string/clear"
        android:textAllCaps="false" />

    <Button
        android:id="@+id/call"
        style="@style/Widget.AppCompat.Button"
        android:layout_width="wrap_content"
        android:layout_height="wrap_content"
        android:layout_toStartOf="@+id/clear_chat_messages"
        android:text="@string/call"
        android:textAllCaps="false" />

    <LinearLayout
        android:id="@+id/message_layout"
        android:layout_width="match_parent"
        android:layout_height="wrap_content"
        android:layout_alignParentBottom="true"
        android:orientation="horizontal">

        <EditText
            android:id="@+id/chat_message"
            android:layout_width="wrap_content"
            android:layout_height="wrap_content"
            android:layout_marginEnd="10dp"
            android:layout_weight="1"
            android:ems="10"
            android:hint="@string/please_type_a_message"
            android:inputType="textPersonName" />

        <Button
            android:id="@+id/send_chat_message"
            android:layout_width="32dp"
            android:layout_height="32dp"
            android:layout_weight="0"
            android:background="@drawable/send"
            android:textAllCaps="false" />

    </LinearLayout>

    <ScrollView
```

```xml
        android:id="@+id/chat_scrollview"
        android:layout_width="match_parent"
        android:layout_height="match_parent"
        android:layout_above="@id/message_layout"
        android:layout_toStartOf="@+id/call"
        android:fadeScrollbars="false">

        <TextView
            android:id="@+id/chat_messages"
            android:layout_width="match_parent"
            android:layout_height="wrap_content"
            android:layout_marginTop="5dp"
            android:layout_marginEnd="5dp"
            android:textIsSelectable="true" />
    </ScrollView>

    <View
        android:id="@+id/divider"
        android:layout_width="match_parent"
        android:layout_height="1dp"
        android:layout_above="@id/message_layout"
        android:background="?android:attr/listDivider" />

    <android.support.v4.widget.NestedScrollView
        android:layout_width="match_parent"
        android:layout_height="match_parent"
        android:layout_above="@id/message_layout"
        android:layout_below="@+id/clear_chat_messages"
        android:layout_toEndOf="@+id/chat_scrollview"
        android:fadeScrollbars="false"
        android:scrollbars="vertical">

        <TableLayout
            android:id="@+id/participants"
            android:layout_width="match_parent"
            android:layout_height="wrap_content"
            android:layout_marginEnd="5dp">

        </TableLayout>
    </android.support.v4.widget.NestedScrollView>

</RelativeLayout>
```

content_member_chat.xml

https://github.com/textbrowser/smoke/blob/master/Smoke/app/src/main/res/layout
/content_member_chat.xml
```xml
<?xml version="1.0" encoding="utf-8"?>
<RelativeLayout xmlns:android="http://schemas.android.com/apk/res/android"
    xmlns:app="http://schemas.android.com/apk/res-auto"
    xmlns:tools="http://schemas.android.com/tools"
    android:id="@+id/main_layout"
    android:layout_width="match_parent"
    android:layout_height="match_parent"
    android:layout_marginStart="10dp"
    android:layout_marginEnd="10dp"
    android:paddingStart="5dp"
    android:paddingEnd="5dp"
    app:layout_behavior="@string/appbar_scrolling_view_behavior"
    tools:context="org.purple.smoke.MemberChat"
    tools:showIn="@layout/activity_member_chat">
```

```
<FrameLayout
    android:layout_width="match_parent"
    android:layout_height="match_parent"
    android:layout_above="@+id/divider">

    <android.support.v7.widget.RecyclerView
        android:id="@+id/recycler_view"
        android:layout_width="match_parent"
        android:layout_height="match_parent"
        android:scrollbars="vertical"
        android:visibility="visible">

    </android.support.v7.widget.RecyclerView>

    <RelativeLayout
        android:id="@+id/preview_layout"
        android:layout_width="match_parent"
        android:layout_height="match_parent"
        android:layout_marginStart="5dp"
        android:layout_marginBottom="5dp"
        android:visibility="gone">

        <Button
            android:id="@+id/remove_preview"
            android:layout_width="32dp"
            android:layout_height="32dp"
            android:layout_alignParentStart="true"
            android:layout_alignParentBottom="true"
            android:layout_gravity="center_vertical"
            android:layout_marginStart="139dp"
            android:layout_marginBottom="139dp"
            android:background="@drawable/minus"
            android:visibility="visible" />

        <ImageView
            android:id="@+id/preview"
            android:layout_width="150dp"
            android:layout_height="150dp"
            android:layout_alignParentStart="true"
            android:layout_alignParentBottom="true"
            android:layout_gravity="bottom"
            android:layout_marginStart="5dp"
            android:adjustViewBounds="true"
            android:background="@android:color/transparent"
            android:contentDescription="@string/preview"
            android:scaleType="fitXY"
            android:visibility="visible" />
    </RelativeLayout>

</FrameLayout>

<LinearLayout
    android:id="@+id/linear_layout"
    android:layout_width="match_parent"
    android:layout_height="wrap_content"
    android:layout_alignParentStart="true"
    android:layout_alignParentBottom="true"
    android:orientation="horizontal">

    <Button
        android:id="@+id/attachment"
        android:layout_width="32dp"
```

```xml
        android:layout_height="32dp"
        android:layout_gravity="center_vertical"
        android:layout_marginEnd="10dp"
        android:layout_weight="0"
        android:background="@drawable/file" />

    <EditText
        android:id="@+id/chat_message"
        android:layout_width="wrap_content"
        android:layout_height="wrap_content"
        android:layout_marginEnd="10dp"
        android:layout_weight="1"
        android:ems="10"
        android:hint="@string/please_type_a_message"
        android:inputType="textPersonName" />

    <Button
        android:id="@+id/status"
        android:layout_width="32dp"
        android:layout_height="32dp"
        android:layout_marginEnd="10dp"
        android:layout_weight="0"
        android:background="@drawable/chat_status_offline" />

    <Button
        android:id="@+id/send_chat_message"
        android:layout_width="32dp"
        android:layout_height="32dp"
        android:layout_weight="0"
        android:background="@drawable/send" />

</LinearLayout>

<ProgressBar
    android:id="@+id/progress_bar"
    style="@android:style/Widget.DeviceDefault.Light.ProgressBar.Large"
    android:layout_width="wrap_content"
    android:layout_height="wrap_content"
    android:layout_centerInParent="true"
    android:visibility="invisible" />

<View
    android:id="@+id/divider"
    android:layout_width="match_parent"
    android:layout_height="1dp"
    android:layout_above="@+id/linear_layout"
    android:background="?android:attr/listDivider" />

</RelativeLayout>
```

content_steam.xml

https://github.com/textbrowser/smoke/blob/master/Smoke/app/src/main/res/layout/content_steam.xml

```xml
<?xml version="1.0" encoding="utf-8"?>
<RelativeLayout xmlns:android="http://schemas.android.com/apk/res/android"
    xmlns:app="http://schemas.android.com/apk/res-auto"
    xmlns:tools="http://schemas.android.com/tools"
    android:id="@+id/main_layout"
    android:layout_width="match_parent"
    android:layout_height="match_parent"
```

```xml
        android:layout_marginStart="10dp"
        android:layout_marginEnd="10dp"
        android:paddingStart="5dp"
        android:paddingEnd="5dp"
        app:layout_behavior="@string/appbar_scrolling_view_behavior"
        tools:context="org.purple.smoke.Steam"
        tools:showIn="@layout/activity_steam">

    <TextView
        android:id="@+id/downloads"
        android:layout_width="wrap_content"
        android:layout_height="wrap_content"
        android:textSize="18sp" />

    <View
        android:id="@+id/divider"
        android:layout_width="match_parent"
        android:layout_height="1dp"
        android:layout_below="@id/downloads"
        android:background="?android:attr/listDivider" />

    <FrameLayout
        android:layout_width="match_parent"
        android:layout_height="match_parent"
        android:layout_above="@+id/linear_layout"
        android:layout_below="@id/divider">

        <android.support.v7.widget.RecyclerView
            android:id="@+id/recycler_view"
            android:layout_width="match_parent"
            android:layout_height="match_parent"
            android:scrollbars="vertical"
            android:visibility="visible">

        </android.support.v7.widget.RecyclerView>
    </FrameLayout>

    <LinearLayout
        android:id="@+id/linear_layout"
        android:layout_width="match_parent"
        android:layout_height="wrap_content"
        android:layout_alignParentStart="true"
        android:layout_alignParentBottom="true"
        android:orientation="horizontal">

        <Button
            android:id="@+id/attachment"
            android:layout_width="32dp"
            android:layout_height="32dp"
            android:layout_gravity="center_vertical"
            android:layout_weight="0"
            android:background="@drawable/file_select" />

        <EditText
            android:id="@+id/filename"
            android:layout_width="wrap_content"
            android:layout_height="wrap_content"
            android:layout_weight="1"
            android:ems="10"
            android:enabled="false"
            android:hint="@string/please_select"
            android:inputType="textPersonName" />
```

```xml
        <Spinner
            android:id="@+id/participants"
            android:layout_width="wrap_content"
            android:layout_height="wrap_content"
            android:layout_gravity="center_vertical"
            android:layout_weight="1" />

        <Button
            android:id="@+id/send"
            android:layout_width="32dp"
            android:layout_height="32dp"
            android:layout_gravity="center_vertical"
            android:layout_weight="0"
            android:background="@drawable/file_send" />
    </LinearLayout>

</RelativeLayout>
```

fire_channel.xml

https://github.com/textbrowser/smoke/blob/master/Smoke/app/src/main/res/layout/fire_channel.xml

```xml
<RelativeLayout xmlns:android="http://schemas.android.com/apk/res/android"
    android:layout_width="match_parent"
    android:layout_height="wrap_content"
    android:paddingEnd="5dp">

  <Button
      android:id="@+id/clear_chat_messages"
      style="@style/Widget.AppCompat.Button.Colored"
      android:layout_width="wrap_content"
      android:layout_height="wrap_content"
      android:layout_below="@+id/fire_name"
      android:layout_alignParentTop="false"
      android:layout_alignParentBottom="false"
      android:layout_toStartOf="@+id/close"
      android:text="@string/clear"
      android:textAllCaps="false" />

  <Button
      android:id="@+id/close"
      style="@style/Widget.AppCompat.Button.Colored"
      android:layout_width="wrap_content"
      android:layout_height="wrap_content"
      android:layout_below="@+id/fire_name"
      android:layout_alignParentEnd="true"
      android:text="@string/close"
      android:textAllCaps="false" />

  <LinearLayout
      android:id="@+id/message_layout"
      android:layout_width="match_parent"
      android:layout_height="wrap_content"
      android:layout_alignParentBottom="true"
      android:orientation="horizontal">

    <EditText
        android:id="@+id/chat_message"
        android:layout_width="wrap_content"
        android:layout_height="wrap_content"
        android:layout_marginEnd="10dp"
```

```xml
            android:layout_weight="1"
            android:ems="10"
            android:hint="@string/please_type_a_message"
            android:inputType="textPersonName" />

    <Button
            android:id="@+id/send_chat_message"
            android:layout_width="32dp"
            android:layout_height="32dp"
            android:layout_weight="0"
            android:background="@drawable/send" />

</LinearLayout>

<TextView
        android:id="@+id/fire_name"
        android:layout_width="match_parent"
        android:layout_height="wrap_content"
        android:layout_alignParentStart="true"
        android:layout_alignParentTop="true"
        android:layout_alignParentEnd="true"
        android:background="@drawable/sectiongradient"
        android:gravity="center_vertical"
        android:paddingStart="5dp"
        android:paddingEnd="5dp"
        android:textColor="@android:color/white"
        android:textSize="18sp"
        android:textStyle="normal|bold" />

<View
        android:id="@+id/divider"
        android:layout_width="match_parent"
        android:layout_height="1dp"
        android:layout_below="@+id/chat_scrollview"
        android:layout_alignParentStart="true"
        android:background="?android:attr/listDivider" />

<android.support.v4.widget.NestedScrollView
        android:id="@+id/chat_scrollview"
        android:layout_width="match_parent"
        android:layout_height="match_parent"
        android:layout_above="@id/message_layout"
        android:layout_below="@+id/fire_name"
        android:layout_toStartOf="@+id/clear_chat_messages"
        android:fadeScrollbars="false"
        android:fillViewport="true"
        android:scrollbars="vertical">

    <TextView
            android:id="@+id/chat_messages"
            android:layout_width="match_parent"
            android:layout_height="wrap_content"
            android:layout_marginStart="5dp"
            android:layout_marginEnd="5dp"
            android:paddingStart="5dp"
            android:paddingEnd="5dp"
            android:textIsSelectable="true" />

</android.support.v4.widget.NestedScrollView>

<android.support.v4.widget.NestedScrollView
        android:layout_width="match_parent"
        android:layout_height="match_parent"
```

```xml
        android:layout_above="@id/message_layout"
        android:layout_below="@+id/close"
        android:layout_toEndOf="@+id/chat_scrollview"
        android:fadeScrollbars="false"
        android:scrollbars="vertical">

    <TableLayout
        android:id="@+id/participants"
        android:layout_width="match_parent"
        android:layout_height="wrap_content"
        android:layout_marginStart="5dp"
        android:layout_marginEnd="5dp">

    </TableLayout>
  </android.support.v4.widget.NestedScrollView>

</RelativeLayout>
```


progress.xml

https://github.com/textbrowser/smoke/blob/master/Smoke/app/src/main/res/layout/progress.xml

```xml
<android.support.constraint.ConstraintLayout
xmlns:android="http://schemas.android.com/apk/res/android"
    xmlns:app="http://schemas.android.com/apk/res-auto"
    xmlns:tools="http://schemas.android.com/tools"
    android:layout_width="match_parent"
    android:layout_height="wrap_content"
    android:layout_marginBottom="5dp">

    <LinearLayout
        android:layout_width="wrap_content"
        android:layout_height="match_parent"
        android:layout_marginBottom="15dp"
        android:layout_marginEnd="15dp"
        android:layout_marginStart="15dp"
        android:layout_marginTop="15dp"
        android:orientation="vertical"
        app:layout_constraintBottom_toBottomOf="parent"
        app:layout_constraintEnd_toEndOf="parent"
        app:layout_constraintStart_toStartOf="parent"
        app:layout_constraintTop_toTopOf="parent">

        <TextView
            android:id="@+id/text"
            android:layout_width="wrap_content"
            android:layout_height="wrap_content"
            android:textSize="18sp" />

        <ProgressBar
            android:id="@+id/progress_bar"
            style="?android:attr/progressBarStyleHorizontal"
            android:layout_width="match_parent"
            android:layout_height="wrap_content"
            android:indeterminate="true" />

    </LinearLayout>

</android.support.constraint.ConstraintLayout>
```

steam_bubble.xml

https://github.com/textbrowser/smoke/blob/master/Smoke/app/src/main/res/layout/steam_bubble.xml

```xml
<RelativeLayout xmlns:android="http://schemas.android.com/apk/res/android"
    xmlns:app="http://schemas.android.com/apk/res-auto"
    xmlns:tools="http://schemas.android.com/tools"
    android:layout_width="match_parent"
    android:layout_height="wrap_content"
    android:layout_marginTop="5dp"
    android:layout_marginEnd="5dp"
    android:layout_marginBottom="5dp"
    android:background="@android:color/transparent">

    <LinearLayout
        android:layout_width="match_parent"
        android:layout_height="match_parent"
        android:background="@android:color/transparent"
        android:orientation="vertical">

        <TextView
            android:id="@+id/filename"
            android:layout_width="match_parent"
            android:layout_height="wrap_content" />

        <TextView
            android:id="@+id/destination"
            android:layout_width="match_parent"
            android:layout_height="wrap_content" />

        <TextView
            android:id="@+id/status"
            android:layout_width="match_parent"
            android:layout_height="wrap_content" />

        <LinearLayout
            android:layout_width="match_parent"
            android:layout_height="wrap_content"
            android:orientation="horizontal">

            <Switch
                android:id="@+id/details"
                android:layout_width="wrap_content"
                android:layout_height="wrap_content"
                android:gravity="center"
                android:text="@string/details" />

            <ProgressBar
                android:id="@+id/progress_bar"
                style="?android:attr/progressBarStyleHorizontal"
                android:layout_width="0dp"
                android:layout_height="wrap_content"
                android:layout_gravity="center"
                android:layout_weight="1"
                android:indeterminate="false" />

        </LinearLayout>

        <LinearLayout
            android:id="@+id/layout_a"
            android:layout_width="match_parent"
            android:layout_height="wrap_content"
            android:orientation="horizontal">
```

```xml
<LinearLayout
    android:layout_width="wrap_content"
    android:layout_height="wrap_content"
    android:layout_gravity="center_vertical"
    android:orientation="vertical">

    <ImageButton
        android:id="@+id/menu"
        android:layout_width="32dp"
        android:layout_height="32dp"
        android:layout_gravity="center_vertical"
        android:background="@drawable/menu" />

    <View
        android:id="@+id/direction"
        android:layout_width="32dp"
        android:layout_height="32dp"
        android:layout_gravity="center_vertical"
        android:background="@drawable/upload" />

    <View
        android:id="@+id/key_exchange_status"
        android:layout_width="32dp"
        android:layout_height="32dp"
        android:layout_gravity="center_vertical"
        android:background="@drawable/unlock" />
</LinearLayout>

<LinearLayout
    android:layout_width="match_parent"
    android:layout_height="wrap_content"
    android:orientation="vertical">

    <TextView
        android:id="@+id/eta"
        android:layout_width="match_parent"
        android:layout_height="wrap_content"
        android:layout_gravity="clip_vertical" />

    <TextView
        android:id="@+id/file_identity"
        android:layout_width="match_parent"
        android:layout_height="wrap_content" />

    <TextView
        android:id="@+id/digest"
        android:layout_width="match_parent"
        android:layout_height="wrap_content" />

    <TextView
        android:id="@+id/file_size"
        android:layout_width="match_parent"
        android:layout_height="wrap_content"
        android:layout_gravity="center_vertical" />

    <TextView
        android:id="@+id/keystream_digest"
        android:layout_width="match_parent"
        android:layout_height="wrap_content" />

    <TextView
        android:id="@+id/sent"
```

```xml
                android:layout_width="match_parent"
                android:layout_height="wrap_content"
                android:layout_gravity="center_vertical" />

            <TextView
                android:id="@+id/transfer_rate"
                android:layout_width="match_parent"
                android:layout_height="wrap_content"
                android:layout_gravity="center_vertical" />
        </LinearLayout>

    </LinearLayout>

    <LinearLayout
        android:id="@+id/layout_b"
        android:layout_width="match_parent"
        android:layout_height="wrap_content"
        android:orientation="horizontal">

        <Button
            android:id="@+id/control"
            style="@style/Widget.AppCompat.Button"
            android:layout_width="wrap_content"
            android:layout_height="wrap_content"
            android:text="@string/pause"
            android:textAllCaps="false" />

        <SeekBar
            android:id="@+id/read_interval"
            style="@style/Widget.AppCompat.SeekBar.Discrete"
            android:layout_width="200dp"
            android:layout_height="wrap_content"
            android:layout_gravity="center"
            android:max="4"
            android:progress="0" />

        <TextView
            android:id="@+id/read_interval_label"
            android:layout_width="wrap_content"
            android:layout_height="wrap_content"
            android:layout_gravity="center" />

    </LinearLayout>

    <View
        android:id="@+id/separator"
        android:layout_width="match_parent"
        android:layout_height="1dp"
        android:background="?android:attr/listDivider" />

    </LinearLayout>
</RelativeLayout>
```

authenticate_menu.xml

https://github.com/textbrowser/smoke/blob/master/Smoke/app/src/main/res/menu/authenticate_menu.xml

```xml
<menu xmlns:android="http://schemas.android.com/apk/res/android">
    <item
        android:id="@+id/action_chat"
        android:orderInCategory="100"
```

```xml
                android:title="@string/chat" />
    <item
            android:id="@+id/action_exit"
            android:orderInCategory="200"
            android:title="@string/exit" />
    <item
            android:id="@+id/action_fire"
            android:orderInCategory="300"
            android:title="@string/fire" />
    <item
            android:id="@+id/action_settings"
            android:orderInCategory="400"
            android:title="@string/action_settings" />
    <item
            android:id="@+id/action_smokescreen"
            android:orderInCategory="500"
            android:title="@string/smokescreen" />
    <item
            android:id="@+id/action_steam"
            android:orderInCategory="600"
            android:title="@string/steam" />
</menu>
```

chat_menu.xml

https://github.com/textbrowser/smoke/blob/master/Smoke/app/src/main/res/menu/chat_menu.xml

```xml
<menu xmlns:android="http://schemas.android.com/apk/res/android"
    xmlns:app="http://schemas.android.com/apk/res-auto"
    xmlns:tools="http://schemas.android.com/tools"
    tools:context="org.purple.smoke.Chat">
    <item android:title="@string/authenticate"
            android:id="@+id/action_authenticate"
            android:orderInCategory="100" />
    <item
            android:id="@+id/action_exit"
            android:orderInCategory="200"
            android:title="@string/exit" />
    <item
            android:id="@+id/action_fire"
            android:orderInCategory="300"
            android:title="@string/fire" />
    <item
            android:id="@+id/action_settings"
            android:orderInCategory="400"
            android:title="@string/action_settings" />
    <item
            android:id="@+id/action_smokescreen"
            android:orderInCategory="500"
            android:title="@string/smokescreen" />
    <item
            android:id="@+id/action_steam"
            android:orderInCategory="600"
            android:title="@string/steam" />
</menu>
```

fire_menu.xml


```xml
<menu xmlns:android="http://schemas.android.com/apk/res/android">
    <item
        android:id="@+id/action_authenticate"
        android:title="@string/authenticate"
        android:orderInCategory="100" />
    <item
        android:id="@+id/action_chat"
        android:orderInCategory="200"
        android:title="@string/chat" />
    <item
        android:id="@+id/action_exit"
        android:orderInCategory="300"
        android:title="@string/exit" />
    <item
        android:id="@+id/action_settings"
        android:orderInCategory="400"
        android:title="@string/action_settings" />
    <item
        android:id="@+id/action_smokescreen"
        android:orderInCategory="500"
        android:title="@string/smokescreen" />
    <item
        android:id="@+id/action_steam"
        android:orderInCategory="600"
        android:title="@string/steam" />
</menu>
```

member_chat_menu.xml


```xml
<menu xmlns:android="http://schemas.android.com/apk/res/android"
    xmlns:app="http://schemas.android.com/apk/res-auto"
    xmlns:tools="http://schemas.android.com/tools"
    tools:context="org.purple.smoke.MemberChat">
    <item
        android:id="@+id/action_authenticate"
        android:orderInCategory="100"
        android:title="@string/authenticate" />
    <item
        android:id="@+id/action_chat"
        android:orderInCategory="200"
        android:title="@string/chat" />
    <item
        android:id="@+id/action_exit"
        android:orderInCategory="300"
        android:title="@string/exit" />
    <item
        android:id="@+id/action_fire"
        android:orderInCategory="400"
        android:title="@string/fire" />
    <item
        android:id="@+id/action_settings"
        android:orderInCategory="500"
        android:title="@string/action_settings" />
    <item
        android:id="@+id/action_smokescreen"
```

```
        android:orderInCategory="600"
        android:title="@string/smokescreen" />
    <item
        android:id="@+id/action_steam"
        android:orderInCategory="700"
        android:title="@string/steam" />
</menu>
```

settings_menu.xml

https://github.com/textbrowser/smoke/blob/master/Smoke/app/src/main/res/menu/settings_menu.xml

```
<menu xmlns:android="http://schemas.android.com/apk/res/android">
    <item android:title="@string/authenticate"
        android:id="@+id/action_authenticate"
        android:orderInCategory="100" />
    <item
        android:id="@+id/action_chat"
        android:orderInCategory="200"
        android:title="@string/chat" />
    <item
        android:id="@+id/action_exit"
        android:orderInCategory="300"
        android:title="@string/exit" />
    <item
        android:id="@+id/action_fire"
        android:orderInCategory="400"
        android:title="@string/fire" />
    <item
        android:id="@+id/action_smokescreen"
        android:orderInCategory="500"
        android:title="@string/smokescreen" />
    <item
        android:id="@+id/action_steam"
        android:orderInCategory="600"
        android:title="@string/steam" />
</menu>
```

smokescreen_menu.xml

https://github.com/textbrowser/smoke/blob/master/Smoke/app/src/main/res/menu/smokescreen_menu.xml

```
<menu xmlns:android="http://schemas.android.com/apk/res/android">
    <item
        android:id="@+id/action_authenticate"
        android:orderInCategory="100"
        android:title="@string/authenticate" />
    <item
        android:id="@+id/action_chat"
        android:orderInCategory="200"
        android:title="@string/chat" />
    <item
        android:id="@+id/action_exit"
        android:orderInCategory="300"
        android:title="@string/exit" />
    <item
        android:id="@+id/action_fire"
        android:orderInCategory="400"
        android:title="@string/fire" />
```

```xml
    <item
        android:id="@+id/action_settings"
        android:orderInCategory="500"
        android:title="@string/action_settings" />
    <item
        android:id="@+id/action_steam"
        android:orderInCategory="600"
        android:title="@string/steam" />
</menu>
```

steam_menu.xml


```xml
<menu xmlns:android="http://schemas.android.com/apk/res/android">
    <item android:title="@string/authenticate"
        android:id="@+id/action_authenticate"
        android:orderInCategory="100" />
    <item
        android:id="@+id/action_chat"
        android:orderInCategory="200"
        android:title="@string/chat" />
    <item
        android:id="@+id/action_exit"
        android:orderInCategory="300"
        android:title="@string/exit" />
    <item
        android:id="@+id/action_fire"
        android:orderInCategory="400"
        android:title="@string/fire" />
    <item
        android:id="@+id/action_settings"
        android:orderInCategory="500"
        android:title="@string/action_settings" />
    <item
        android:id="@+id/action_smokescreen"
        android:orderInCategory="600"
        android:title="@string/smokescreen" />
</menu>
```

attrs_fire_channel.xml


```xml
<resources>
    <declare-styleable name="fire_channel">
    </declare-styleable>
</resources>
```

colors.xml


```xml
<?xml version="1.0" encoding="utf-8"?>
<resources>
  <color name="colorAccent">#FF4081</color>
  <color name="colorGray">#2B292E</color>
```

```xml
    <color name="colorPrimaryDark">#303F9F</color>
</resources>
```

dimens.xml

https://github.com/textbrowser/smoke/blob/master/Smoke/app/src/main/res/values/dimens.xml

```xml
<resources>
    <!-- Default screen margins, per the Android Design guidelines. -->
</resources>
```

strings.xml

https://github.com/textbrowser/smoke/blob/master/Smoke/app/src/main/res/values/strings.xml

```xml
<resources>
    <string name="about">About</string>
    <string name="action_settings">Settings</string>
    <string name="add">Add</string>
    <string name="address">Address</string>
    <string name="app_name">Smoke</string>
    <string name="at">\@</string>
    <string name="attachment">Attachment</string>
    <string name="authenticate">Authenticate</string>
    <string name="authenticate_authenticate">Authenticate</string>
    <string name="authenticate_password">Password</string>
    <string name="auto_fill">Auto Fill</string>
    <string name="automatic_refresh">Automatic Refresh</string>
    <string name="call">Call</string>
    <string name="channel">Channel</string>
    <string name="chat">Chat</string>
    <string name="chat_encryption_key_data">Chat Encryption Key Data</string>
    <string name="chat_signature_key_data">Chat Signature Key Data</string>
    <string name="clear">Clear</string>
    <string name="clear_log">Clear Log</string>
    <string name="close">Close</string>
    <string name="control">Control</string>
    <string name="delete">Delete</string>
    <string name="details">Details</string>
    <string name="digest_key">Digest Key</string>
    <string name="echo">Echo</string>
    <string name="encryption">Encryption</string>
    <string name="fiasco_keys">Fiasco Keys</string>
    <string name="fire">Fire</string>
    <string name="fire_channels">Fire Channels</string>
    <string name="foreground_service">Foreground Service</string>
    <string name="generate">Generate</string>
    <string name="generate_pk">Generate PK</string>
    <string name="initialize_ozone">Initialize Ozone</string>
    <string name="ip_address">IP Address</string>
    <string name="ipv4">IPv4</string>
    <string name="ipv6">IPv6</string>
    <string name="iteration_count">Iteration Count</string>
    <string name="join">Join</string>
    <string name="message">Message...</string>
    <string name="message_status">Message Status</string>
    <string name="name">Name</string>
    <string name="neighbor_servers">Neighbor Servers</string>
    <string name="ozone">Ozone</string>
```

```xml
    <string name="participants">Participants</string>
    <string name="password">Password</string>
    <string name="password_confirmation">Password Confirmation</string>
    <string name="please_type_a_message">Please type a message…</string>
    <string name="port">Port</string>
    <string name="prefer_active_cpu">Prefer Active CPU</string>
    <string name="preview">Preview</string>
    <string name="proxy_ip_address">Proxy IP Address</string>
    <string name="proxy_port">Proxy Port</string>
    <string name="public_data">Public Data</string>
    <string name="refresh_neighbors">Refresh</string>
    <string name="refresh_participants">Refresh</string>
    <string name="remote">Remote</string>
    <string name="reset_fields">Reset Fields</string>
    <string name="reset_smoke">Reset Smoke</string>
    <string name="salt">Salt</string>
    <string name="save">Save</string>
    <string name="scope_id">Scope ID</string>
    <string name="send">Send</string>
    <string name="share_keys">Share Keys</string>
    <string name="share_smoke_id">Share Smoke ID</string>
    <string name="signature">Signature</string>
    <string name="smoke_alias">Smoke Alias</string>
    <string name="smoke_chat_id">Smoke Chat ID</string>
    <string name="smokeid">Smoke ID</string>
    <string name="your_name">Your Name</string>
    <string name="exit">Exit</string>
    <string name="steam">Steam</string>
    <string name="key_derivation_function">Key Derivation Function</string>
    <string name="non_tls">Non-TLS</string>
    <string name="passthrough">Passthrough</string>
    <string name="pause">Pause</string>
    <string name="smokescreen">Smokescreen</string>
    <string name="please_select">Please Select</string>
    <string name="query_time_server">Query Time Server</string>
</resources>
```

styles.xml

https://github.com/textbrowser/smoke/blob/master/Smoke/app/src/main/res/values/styles.xml

```xml
<resources>
    <!-- Base application theme. -->
    <style name="AppTheme" parent="Theme.AppCompat.Light.DarkActionBar">
        <!-- Customize your theme here. -->
        <item name="colorPrimary">@color/colorGray</item>
        <item name="colorPrimaryDark">@color/colorPrimaryDark</item>
        <item name="colorAccent">@color/colorAccent</item>
    </style>

    <style name="AppTheme.NoActionBar">
        <item name="windowActionBar">false</item>
        <item name="windowNoTitle">true</item>
    </style>

    <style name="AppTheme.AppBarOverlay"
parent="ThemeOverlay.AppCompat.Dark.ActionBar" />
    <style name="AppTheme.PopupOverlay" parent="ThemeOverlay.AppCompat.Light"
/>
</resources>
```

```
Directory of C:\smoke-2020.11.15\Smoke\gradle\wrapper

15.11.2020   23:01    <DIR>              .
15.11.2020   23:01    <DIR>              ..
15.11.2020   23:01               53.636 gradle-wrapper.jar
15.11.2020   23:01                  230 gradle-wrapper.properties
               2 File(s),          53.866 Bytes
```

gradle-wrapper.properties

https://github.com/textbrowser/smoke/blob/master/Smoke/gradle/wrapper/gradle-wrapper.properties

```
#Wed Oct 21 15:53:18 EDT 2020
distributionBase=GRADLE_USER_HOME
distributionPath=wrapper/dists
zipStoreBase=GRADLE_USER_HOME
zipStorePath=wrapper/dists
distributionUrl=https\://services.gradle.org/distributions/gradle-6.5-bin.zip
```

References:

Ackermann, Evelyn & Klein, Michael (2020): Caesura in Cryptography: My first Workshop about Encryption - An Introduction with Teaching and Learning Material for School, University and Leisure, 2020, PDF-E-Book ISBN 978-3752676921.

Nomenclatura (2019): Encyclopedia of modern Cryptography and Internet Security: From AutoCrypt and Exponential Encryption to Zero-Knowledge-Proof Keys, ISBN: 978-3748191513 & ISBN: 978-3746066684.

Smoke (2017): Documentation of the Android Messenger Application Smoke, URL: https://github.com/textbrowser/smoke/raw/master/Documentation/Smoke.pdf, 2017.

SmokeStack (2017): Server Software for Echo Messaging, URL: https://github.com/textbrowser/smokestack.

Spot-On Suite: Handbook and User Manual as practical software guide, ISBN: 978-3749435067.